The World
in the
Twentieth Century

Sixth Edition

The World in the Twentieth Century

From Empires to Nations

DANIEL R. BROWER

University of California–Davis

PEARSON

Prentice
Hall

Upper Saddle River, New Jersey 07458

Library of Congress Cataloging-in-Publication Data

Brower, Daniel R.
   The world in the twentieth century: from empires to nations/Daniel R. Brower—6th ed.
      p. cm.
   Includes bibliographical references and index.
   ISBN 0-13-193042-7
   1. History, Modern—20th century.   2. Revolutions—History—20th century.   3.
Nationalism—History—20th century.   I.   Title.

D421.B725 2006
909.82—dc22   2005042953

VP/Editorial Director: Charlyce Jones Owen
Executive Editor: Charles Cavaliere
Editorial Assistant: Shannon Corliss
Marketing Manager: Heather Shelstad
Marketing Assistant: Cherron Gardner
Production Liaison: Marianne Peters-Riordan
Manufacturing Buyer: Benjamin Smith
Cover Art Director: Jayne Conte
Cover Design: Bruce Kenselaar

Cover Photos: Library of Congress
Director, Image Resource Center: Melinda Reo
Manager, Rights and Permissions: Zina Arabia
Manager, Visual Research: Beth Brenzel
Manager, Cover Visual Research
   & Permissions: Karen Sanatar
Image Permission Coordinator: Cynthia Vincenti
Composition/Full-Service Project Management: Preparé Inc.

Printed in Canada

Credits and acknowledgments borrowed from other sources and reproduced, with permission, in this textbook
appear on appropriate page within text.

Pearson Education LTD.
Pearson Education Singapore, Pte. Ltd
Pearson Education, Canada, Ltd
Pearson Education–Japan
Pearson Education Australia PTY, Limited

Pearson Education North Asia Ltd
Pearson Educación de Mexico, S.A. de C.V.
Pearson Education Malaysia, Pte. Ltd
Pearson Education, Upper Saddle River, New Jersey

ISBN 0-13-193042-7

Brief Contents

Contents

x   *Contents*

MAPS

BOXES

Preface

Priding ourselves on shaping history, we function day to day as slaves of the events that inexorably unroll themselves before our eyes, and fear possesses us and hatred follows in its train.

—Jawaharlal Nehru, 1949

The moment in August 1947 when the British Empire liberated its Indian colony was a time of triumph and celebration for Nehru, who was India's first prime minister. There, as in other colonies that achieved independence in the postwar years, nationalist leaders hoped that liberation would open an era of freedom and progress for the former subject peoples. But Nehru discovered that the transition of power brought human tragedy as well as triumph. He gave voice to that disillusionment two years later, recalling the anguish, helplessness, and despair that he experienced in the first months of independence. Nehru's confession is a timely warning not to exaggerate the achievements or minimize the destruction brought by the postimperial age. It remains as relevant to the history told in this sixth edition of my textbook as it did when the first edition appeared more than fifteen years ago.

When the modern empires collapsed, peoples and their leaders had to undertake extraordinary measures to create new political structures and to forge new bonds of trust to hold together their nation-states. Forging a national community has proven a complex, often painful task. These daunting efforts suggest the great scope of renewal that has been attempted in our postcolonial age. They include as well a dark side to this transformation, for hostility and fear among peoples have at times produced bitter conflict in the following decades. This ethnic and social unrest has undermined new governments and created political chaos within these states.

Nehru had imagined a far happier time for his newly liberated country. These shattered dreams are as much a part of the history of the world in the twentieth century as the achievements that countries such as India actually did experience. Knowledge of these events can help us to reach a balanced, sober understanding of human relations in our complex world.

Destruction and creation are inseparable parts of this history. The bitterness and suffering generated by the struggle of ideals and interests have made the world an uneasy, violent place. Perhaps the most appropriate—certainly the most optimistic—image of the century's history is provided by the Greek myth of the phoenix, the bird reborn from the ashes of its own destruction. To discern essential signs of the emerging new era represents the most challenging historical task of any survey of turbulent periods of change, particularly one so close to us.

IMPORTANT TOPICS

The fall of modern empires and the emergence of a world consisting of states claiming to be nations is the major theme of this textbook. The process has generated powerful new political ideals and created problems of human relations unknown to previous generations. It has thrust some peoples into unexpected prominence as a result of the violent history of this period. The textbook's chronological coverage extends from the late nineteenth century, when new Western empires and old Asian empires dominated vast areas of the world and ruled most of its peoples. It reaches forward to the early twenty-first century, when the collapse of the Soviet Union and the end of the Cold War appeared to herald a new era of peaceful relations among the world's nation-states. In this period, the power in the hands of a few states, especially the United States, gave them opportunities to shape the course of global relations. At the same time, that power and prosperity attracted enemies, some of whom took the path of terrorism to attack these states. Violence remains an integral part of the story told here.

The world-historical perspective adopted in this text is especially meaningful to make clear the increasing interaction among states and peoples provoked by falling empires, world wars, and the multiplication of nation-states throughout the world. The principal questions I seek to answer follow directly

from this premise: What have been the most significant trends shaping this interaction? How can we explain the emergence of these global trends? What has been their impact on peoples throughout the world? This brief survey cannot possibly explore in detail all the dimensions of this interaction; of necessity, it is very selective. To draw the reader's attention to important issues, each chapter contains a "Highlight" essay that addresses a key issue and a "Spotlight" essay offering a biographical sketch of an individual whose life encapsulates an essential trend in contemporary world history. Throughout the text, three subjects have guided the selection of the major trends and events to be addressed: the international history of states, the role of ideology in shaping political movements and reshaping cultural and social values; and the evolution of world economic relations.

All three emphasize related aspects of global interaction. International history examines the essential factors that have shaped the foreign policies of governments and the relations among states. These include, first, the political ideals and national interests of states; second, the economic and political influence of states in global affairs; and, third, the balance of power among countries. These three factors taken together explain in large measure the evolution of global conflict and cooperation from great confrontations of the world wars to the Cold War conflict between superpowers following the Second World War, and finally to wars and peacekeeping after the end of the Cold War. International history offers crucial insight into the global forces that shaped the world as we know it.

The potent force of political ideology emerges from deeply felt convictions of right and wrong, justice and injustice, giving rise to powerful mass movements and guiding the policies of governments. The importance of these aspirations in our time is such that some scholars have suggested calling the twentieth century the "age of ideology." Liberalism was the dominant political faith among Western countries in the early century, and it appeared in the late century to have won greater support around the world than ever before. During most of the century, Marxism provided ideologically the broad guidelines for state policy-making and cultural controls in the socialist countries of the communist bloc and in the Third World. Nationalism, of Western origin but without any single intellectual source or text, places the emergence of national communities and the formation of the nation-state at the center of human endeavor. It is undoubtedly the single strongest political bond among peoples in the world today. In the late twentieth century, influential political movements claiming to defend the Muslim religious community, often by violent means, drew their strength from their ideological nature. In studying these ideologies we can appreciate better the motives of important political leaders and the manner in which social discontent has been articulated and expressed in political movements.

Finally, economic history stresses the significance of productive resources, of new technology, and of ownership of these means of production. These factors have determined the profound differences separating developed and developing nations and the shifting dispersion across the globe of wealth and poverty. Vital natural resources, such as petroleum, have become so essential to the well-being of the global economy that countries possessing these resources have acquired vast wealth and have attracted the attention, both helpful and destructive, of foreign powers.

These three realms of inquiry—international relations, ideology, and economic history—are guides to interpreting the global forces of change. They suggest where and how powerful new historical trends have emerged. In simplest terms, they illuminate the process by which human power in various forms has, for good or ill, reshaped the twentieth-century world.

SIXTH EDITION FEATURES

The story told in this sixth edition follows the broad, topical guidelines of earlier editions but is enlarged and revised to address issues and events brought to prominence in recent years. The most notable change is the addition of two chapters. The first focuses on the First World War and its revolutionary aftermath; a new "Spotlight" essay on the life of John Reed suggests the attraction exerted by both Russian and Mexican revolutions on one radical American, while a new "Highlight" section explores the profound political impact of war on modern societies. The other new chapter is devoted to the revolutionary conflicts that erupted in East Asia in the years following the end of the Second World War. Both chapters incorporate subjects present in the fifth edition, but are given sharper focus than before. Their presence permits other chapters in Parts I and II in their turn to incorporate thematic materials in a more coherent manner than in the fifth edition. In particular, Chapter 7 is now devoted to the Cold War in the Western world through the crises of the 1960s, while Chapter 13 traces the decline of the Soviet empire to the end of the Cold War, the collapse of the Soviet Union, and the painful efforts to construct a new Russia.

Contemporary international conflicts call for more attention than previously to post–Cold War international relations. Considerable new material deals with the troubled history of the Middle East. Chapter 12 includes a "Highlight" section devoted to the impact of the Islamic religion on the evolution of nation-states in that region; a new "Spotlight" essay in Chapter 14 analyzes the extraordinary biography of Osama bin Laden, whose life encapsulates key features of radical Islamist terrorism that has so brutally marked global affairs in recent years. In a broader perspective, the growing importance of petroleum in modern international relations and politics is the subject of the new "Highlight" section of Chapter 3. And added to the "local wars" discussed in the closing chapter of the fifth edition are the recent wars initiated by the United States in Afghanistan and Iraq, both of which raise problems of war and peace crucial to an understanding of world history as it unfolds in the early years of this new century. These and other revisions tell a more comprehensive tale than was possible in the previous edition and make the sixth edition of *The World in the Twentieth Century* an up-to-date historical text.

INTERPRETIVE HISTORY

The story told here adheres to the simple principle that history is a tale of the past revealed over the passage of time. Its emphasis on international, political, and economic trends focuses that tale on the formative influences that have made the world as we know it today. Its frequent use of historical quotations and images of these trends, in the form of quotes from political leaders and observers, or reproductions of political posters and photographs, is inspired by the belief that the proper subject matter of history is the lived experience of the past. The meaning and purpose that participants attributed to those events are as much a part of our history as the events themselves. The tale retold here is one that they first wrote. We may praise or condemn what they did, but first we need to understand what they sought to do.

The judgments that we bring to a past as close as the twentieth century are inescapably influenced by our immediate perception of the world around us. To those who might object that such interpretations commit the sin of "presentism," that is, of distorting the past to make it fit the needs of the present, I would respond that history as we teach and write it is necessarily a dialogue between the present and the past. The essential requirement for historical understanding is to allow the voices from the past to answer in their own terms the questions and concerns that we judge to be historically meaningful.

The thematic focus of this text is in large measure drawn from my experience as lecturer and textbook author in the field of modern world history. This undertaking has occupied me during nearly three decades of teaching this subject and innumerable discussions with colleagues who have proven generous with their time and indulgent of my endeavor. The sober understanding of the past that we acquire with the passing of time is a privilege largely denied this text, whose last chapters touch on events that occurred only yesterday on a historical scale. Students in my twentieth-century world history course at the University of California-Davis have lived through the many stages of this work. The yearly renewal of this student audience has constantly challenged my conclusions and incited me to rethink the meaning of events for those who are creating the history of the twenty-first century. The comments solicited by the publisher from readers have proved of appreciable help in preparing my revisions to the text. This sixth edition is dedicated to my daughters, Caroline and Valerie; may they and their children, as their parents did with them, travel "down the rivers of windfall light."

Daniel R. Brower
Berkeley, California

The World
in the
Twentieth Century

Part I: The Age of Empires

Empires in Flux

THE WORLD IN THE EARLY

TWENTIETH CENTURY

- Western Colonial Empires
- Ancient Empires
- Western Liberalism and Nationalism

Highlight: The New Imperialism

Spotlight: The Empress Dowager of China

The twentieth century was a time of extraordinary upheaval and violence. Wars and revolutions disrupted the lives of millions of people in lands throughout the world. These conflicts also inspired grandiose projects and lofty expectations for a better life for future generations. Destruction and creation are inseparable themes of this history.

At the beginning of the century, empires ruled most of the world's population. The tradition of empire-building was as old as human civilizations. It had begun 5,000 years ago with the first warrior-states in the Middle East and continued into modern times. The simplest definition of *empire* is a state whose peoples are gathered together by a conquering army and that is ruled from a central territory by these conquerors. The mightiest of these conquerors had come from the Eurasian heartland. Nomadic tribes of northern Asia, organized in powerful cavalry forces, periodically invaded China, India, the Middle East, and Europe in search of wealth and power. Their armies left in their wake great swaths of destruction and bloodshed. Once the conquerors had settled in their new lands, they usually adapted their ways to the religious practices and imperial institutions of previous rulers. Arabic and Turkish-speaking tribes, united around their new Muslim religion, had in the Middle Ages conquered an enormous territory stretching from the Mediterranean to

India. Their empires were for centuries brilliant centers of civilization, commercial enterprise, and wealth.

By the end of the twentieth century, nation-states had supplanted empires throughout the world. With hindsight, it is clear that this momentous transformation was well under way by the time the First World War began in 1914. Some imperial states had begun the century on the verge of collapse. The Ottoman and Chinese empires had glorious histories behind them. They had once been centers of civilization and mighty warrior-states. By the end of the nineteenth century, both were powerless to prevent new empires from seizing their borderlands. The Spanish Empire, once an enormous collection of colonies extending over much of the Americas and into the eastern Pacific Ocean, had already lost most of its territory in revolutions and wars. Internal political opposition and social unrest were growing in all these states. With inadequate economic resources and feeble political leaders, these ancient empires were doomed soon to disappear.

The Allied victors in the First World War were themselves empire-builders, and they continued to defend their imperial holdings in the name of civilization and their own well-being. But that war seriously weakened the economies of Great Britain and France, greatest of the Western empires. The depression of the 1930s, then the Second World War, undermined their ability to hold their colonial lands. They abandoned their colonies, at times willingly, at other times only after colonial revolts. The leaders of the Soviet Union, even while defending anti-imperialist movements elsewhere, governed the last of the Western empires in ruling over a multi-national population. Its collapse in 1991 marked the final chapter in the story of the end of empires.

The story of the rise of nation-states was well under way by the beginning of the twentieth century. The Western empires of the nineteenth century wielded enormous power over the subject peoples in their colonies. Yet in their homelands, most of these states recognized the right, usually in some constitutional form, of their own people to participate in a national political community. These states also incorporated in some constitutional form the fundamental laws guaranteeing their citizens full civil liberties. Although empires on the outside, they were nation-states from within. These very principles of freedom and national sovereignty gave colonial peoples the justification for liberation from imperial rule. Western colonial empires were fated to endure only for a brief moment.

The wars that speeded their collapse were strongly influenced by nationalism. In the decades before the First World War, nationalist antagonism worsened the diplomatic rivalries among European states. These conflicts grew more acute in the early years of the twentieth century. The belligerence of Western governments and the deadly armaments produced by the industrial economy ultimately undermined the very existence of their empires.

WESTERN COLONIAL EMPIRES

The new imperialism of the nineteenth century built upon the experience of earlier European empires. European conquerors had come last of all to the task of empire-building in the sixteenth and seventeenth centuries. Making the oceans their path to conquest, they created trading centers along the coasts of Africa and Asia. A few daring explorers and determined Christian missionaries ventured far beyond the coast.

In the Western Hemisphere, European conquerors had extended their empires far into the interior regions. They brought to the native peoples their own civilization and their own infectious diseases. Spanish forces destroyed the empires of the Aztecs and the Incas in their search for gold and silver. Their own empire left a deep, painful mark on their conquered peoples. Spanish officials, the Spanish language, and Catholic missionary settlements were the tangible signs that a distant, alien empire had taken control. Native Americans suffered particularly in the French and British settler colonies of North America. Their lands were taken for farming; they were forced further and further into the interior. The expansion of Western peoples transformed, in places, the very landscape of imperial territories.

Nineteenth-century Western empires shared important characteristics unique to the age of new imperialism. Each was home to a relatively advanced economy that incorporated the technological skills and productive factories of the Industrial Revolution. With industrial resources, empire-builders had the capability to send their armies and officials across vast oceans and great deserts in pursuit of new conquests. In ways never before possible, the most distant areas of the globe were open to imperial exploration, conquest, and economic exploitation. For this reason, these empires could establish vast colonial territories. A few were "settler colonies" open to mass settlement by migrants from Europe, but in most colonies Westerners were there only to govern and extract what economic benefits were accessible.

Within the Western states, nationalists supported empires in the name of national glory and a civilizing mission. In national exhibitions, school books, and in many other ways the promoters of empires portrayed colonial rule as a part of the great epic story of the progress of humanity. The new colonies, distant from but tightly bound to the homeland, were by the end of the nineteenth century so numerous that we frequently refer to these states as colonial or overseas empires.

Western Empires and Industrialism

The economic foundations of the new empires lay in the West's Industrial Revolution. This profound transformation in the means of production, distribution of goods, and ownership of productive property had begun in Europe late in the eighteenth century. By the early twentieth century, it had spread to the outer edges of the Western world and to Japan. It brought to industrialized countries an extraordinary surplus of wealth, concentrated in the hands of successful capitalists, and increasingly controlled by financial and industrial corporations. With that wealth came the power to influence governments. Growing tax revenues fueled imperial expansion and military rearmament. The tools for constructing colonial empires depended on this industrial, technological base.

The Industrial Revolution needed new skills in the areas of engineering, risk taking, and factory labor. By the late nineteenth century, scientists had begun to play an important role in making new discoveries, such as electricity, that were applicable and profitable to industrialists. In the industrial age, knowledge was an indispensable tool of economic activity. Inventors and engineers were key in bringing these wonders into the domain of everyday usage. Thomas Edison was a self-taught American inventor and businessman who proved a genius at bringing electricity out of the theoretical, scientific realm into everyday life. Electric lighting transformed public spaces and living conditions among those segments of the population with the means to afford the new products. Engineers worked at making the internal combustion engine efficient enough and sufficiently easy to manufacture to permit the mass production of automobiles. Engineering skills brought chemical products, derived from coal and petroleum, into the realm of industrial production and the everyday life of consumers. These important new developments were transforming economic activity in the Western world so dramatically that Europe appeared to have begun a second Industrial Revolution.

These products held out the lure of profits to investors with the financial means and grasp of business skills necessary for the production and sale of new products. They worked within an economic system called a "market economy" or "capitalist economy." Its foundation was private ownership of production and distribution of goods and services. Individuals or corporations held in their hands responsibility for economic prosperity or depression. Their success or failure depended on profits or losses from their business, in competition with other business owners also seeking the most productive (hence, least expensive) means of operation. They enjoyed the protection of property and contract laws, the backing of governments sympathetic to the work of capitalists, unrestricted access to labor, and increasingly the ability to find international markets. Successful entrepreneurs built up fortunes, as did corporations whose managers were responsible for bringing yearly profits to stockholders. The system was open to newcomers, provided they had the funds, the skills, and the daring.

The economic freedom of choice that it required was at once its greatest strength and its greatest weakness. Nineteenth-century capitalism opened the way for greater economic initiative than had been possible in feudal times. But it operated without regard to the needs of those lacking the social and economic means to protect their well-being. By the late nineteenth century, cycles of prosperity and depression set the course of European and international economic development. When hard times came, they hit most severely the laboring population. Social welfare was not a part of the capitalist system. Workers' grievances became the source of mass movements of protest and the inspiration for the socialist alternative to capitalism. Karl Marx, the great prophet of socialist revolution, concluded his *Manifesto* with the ominous appeal:

"Workers of the world, unite! You have nothing to lose but your chains."

The growth of the industrial economy relied on labor in the factories and fields. An abundant and cheap supply of factory workers, drawn from rural areas, from artisan trades destroyed by cheap industrial products, and from the rapidly growing population of Europe, helped keep costs to manufacturers low and prevented workers from making effective demands for improved labor conditions. Workers in factories had to acquire increasingly complex skills or remain among the most poorly paid. With those skills, their power to deal with factory owners did increase, sometimes by conflict through labor stoppages and organized strikes. From the countryside came food to feed the growing urban populations. With the development of international commercial links, food supplies were found far beyond the industrial centers, even beyond the oceans. By the early twentieth century, living conditions for the urban population of the industrializing countries were gradually improving. Yet inequalities of wealth remained enormous. Defenders of the capitalist system claimed that those who prospered had proven their superior capabilities. The argument was another version of the harsh theory of Social Darwinism.

The inequalities of power and wealth that separated the industrialized Western countries and their colonial peoples in distant continents were as great as those within European societies. The major difference in economic terms was the increasing importance of non-Western lands as the source of natural resources needed for Western industry. The lure of finding great deposits of valuable commodities had drawn explorers and investors to lands outside Europe throughout the nineteenth century. Some of them took a direct hand in promoting imperial expansion by their governments. Cecil Rhodes combined ambitious moneymaking schemes in the diamond fields of South Africa with grandiose projects of British empire-building in east Africa; "coloring the map red" for Great Britain was his way of describing his goal for the continent. But most capitalists played only a secondary role in empire-building. Their activities became important once the imperial might of their country was well established.

The industrial economy was not responsible for the new imperialism, but it did produce economic links that were international in scope. International corporations found mass markets abroad for consumer goods such as soap (Lever Corporation) and sewing machines (Singer Corporation), and Western banks extended loans across borders within the West and to distant parts of the world. Though still independent, the Ottoman Empire was so deeply in debt to the West that European states established their own financial claims on part of the Ottoman tax revenues.

The search for valuable raw material led other corporations to invest in areas far from their own country. Great canal and railroad construction projects bound the world closer together by sea and land than ever before; the Suez Canal (opened in 1869) speeded European access to Asia, while the Panama Canal (completed in 1914) broke the barrier between Atlantic and Pacific oceans. Central America first became economically important to the United States when United Fruit Corporation set out to exploit its lands for crops to be sold to the American consumer. By the early twentieth century, the growing demand for petroleum products in the West had stimulated the search for oil deposits around the world. The oil-rich area around the Caspian Sea city of Baku, on the edge of the Russian Empire, attracted the wealthy Swedish family of the Nobel brothers. They even devised special barges and freight cars to transport the oil to the European market, where its quality and

low price made it competitive with petroleum from the United States sold by Standard Oil Corporation. Other investors went as far as the Dutch colony of the East Indies. There, under the protection of the government of the Netherlands, the Royal Dutch-Shell corporation began in the 1890s to exploit another of the world's major oil fields.

The British government for its part took a direct hand in backing another oil corporation, British Petroleum, which had discovered and developed the rich oil fields in southwestern Persia (Iran). Persia remained in the early twentieth century a sovereign, ancient empire, but Great Britain (and the Russian Empire) made sure its government did nothing to harm their interests. Chief among these was unimpeded access to its oil fields. Western imperial expansion brought with it the exploitation of those global resources of importance (and profit) to Western industry.

The New Colonial Empires

Both France and Great Britain had in earlier centuries seized overseas territories, partly for purposes of trade, partly for settlement. The turmoil of the French Revolution led to the loss of most of the lands once held by the French monarchy. Expansion began again in the nineteenth century, until the new French Empire was second largest in the world. The greatest was the British Empire, which had kept some territory from the previous era and added much more colonial land in the nineteenth century.

The renewal of French imperial annexations came sporadically throughout the century. This was partly the result of ambitious political leaders seeking the glory of foreign conquest. Their ambition led to France's first new colonial conquest. Across the Mediterranean Sea lay North Africa, whose local princes owed allegiance to the Ottoman sultan. It was a tempting target for the French government, unpopular at home and looking for a cause to stir up patriotic support. In a brief war in 1830, its troops defeated the forces of the local princes in that part of North Africa that the French named Algeria. Later in the century, France used the form of indirect rule called "protectorate" to force the local rulers of Tunisia and Morocco to accept French domination. These Muslim peoples, largely Arabic speaking, passed from the nominal rule of the Ottoman Empire to become subjects of the French Empire.

This empire expanded as a result also of the commitment by the French government to protect French Catholic missionaries and French traders operating in Asian and African lands. Their presence periodically stirred up local protest. National pride and lurid tales of suffering produced by the French popular press incited the government to send French imperial forces to settle these disputes. When they were successful, the result usually was annexation of that region by the empire.

The French had for centuries moved in small numbers through lands in Southeast Asia. There the Chinese Empire exercised a distant and increasingly feeble dominion. When disorders in the 1860s seemed to threaten French lives, French military forces moved into these lands. By the 1890s, the territory that they had seized from the local princes and Chinese forces included a large segment of Southeast Asia. The French baptized their colony Indochina. Their pattern of colonial rule, repeated in other colonies as well, included direct administrative and military rule over the peoples of these lands. Catholic missionaries continued to seek and find converts. Colonial officials encouraged assimilation into French culture by establishing a French school system and recruiting native volunteers for French military forces.

Africa became, later in the century, the continent of choice for French expansion. The process was begun in the 1870s by European explorers, moving up the great rivers of west Africa into the interior. After signing treaties (by persuasion or by force) with tribal leaders, they claimed enormous areas of central and west Africa for the French Empire. Without any clear knowledge of either the land or the peoples, the French government accepted these treaties to prevent other European states from taking the territories for themselves. This "scramble for Africa" was driven forward by political ambitions and nationalist passions, pitting the French against the other European imperial states.

Millions of African peoples fell under French rule. New borders divided them (at least on maps) from neighboring tribes whose lands belonged to another imperial power. Their new language of state became French, though only a few translators possessed the power to communicate between them and their French colonial officials. Their tribal chiefs became the lowest rung of imperial rule. When they rebelled against their new rulers, they faced troops sent from other parts of the empire with modern weapons and prepared to destroy whole villages to "teach the natives a lesson." Imperial rule disrupted African society in profound and permanent ways.

In those same years, the small country of Belgium extended its rule into the Congo basin. In the 1870s, the Belgian king had initiated the European "scramble for Africa" by financing exploration of the region, then by using the explorers' discoveries to claim the territory as the Congo Free State. It was the largest colony in all Africa. Afterward, his officials found in their lands rich mineral resources (especially diamonds and copper), which they began to exploit with the aid of

Partition of Africa, 1800–1914. (From Craig, Albert M.; Graham, William A.; Kagan, Donald M.; Ozment, Steven; Turner, Frank M.; *Heritage of World Civilization, Volume II: Since 1500*, 4th Edition, © 1997. Reprinted by permission of Pearson Education, Inc., Upper Saddle River, NJ)

forced labor. This economic benefit made the colony a valuable possession. The Belgian king was pleased, but not some missionaries and humanitarian visitors who denounced the brutality of his officials and traders. Their public campaign against his colonial rule became a human rights cause in Europe. The king had to pass control of the colony to his government. The international scandal faded, but the image of the Belgian Congo remained, in part thanks to Joseph Conrad's novel *Heart of Darkness*, as the worst example of the abuses committed by European imperialism.

The British Empire expanded through Asia and Africa in much the same sporadic, disorderly way as the French. By the early nineteenth century, British traders and manufacturers had built a vast trading network and had made Great Britain the emporium of the West. They played an important role in pushing the empire forward. The glory of conquest drove the empire onward as well. Ambitious colonial officers stationed in the British coastal trading centers on the Indian subcontinent began in the late eighteenth century to extend their control into the interior. By the 1850s, even the northern plains of India had come under British rule. Control came at a price to the empire. In 1857, resentment at British rule provoked a massive revolt that included Indian troops trained by the British as well as Indian princes who had originally promised loyalty to British rule. British repression of the rebels took several years and brought brutal punishments.

For the next ninety years, India was a "crown colony." It was the greatest of British possessions, the colony one British statesman called "the jewel in the crown" of his queen. British administrators governed directly in some places and through Indian princes (those who had remained loyal to the empire during the revolt) in others. They set about creating a colony where British law and British education would attract an elite among the native population ready to collaborate in ruling that vast land. They expanded the Indian army, creating regiments made up of Indian soldiers and British officers. Originally intended to maintain order in that subcontinent, the Indian army later helped to defend the empire in the First World War. In 1875, the British government proclaimed their queen, Victoria, to be the empress of India.

To ensure that naval forces could easily reach India and China, British naval authorities built coaling stations along the African, Arabian, and Asian coasts. One important consequence of this policy was the British decision in the 1870s to take control of the International Suez Company. Sale to the British of his controlling block of company shares seemed to the *khedive* (prince) of Egypt a simple way to pay his debts. The consequences proved momentous. Great Britain had a vital interest in protecting its influence in Egypt, for through this territory the Suez Canal provided direct maritime access between the Mediterranean Sea and the Indian Ocean. The British government soon afterward decided that Egypt itself had to come under imperial control. In 1882, it moved troops into Egypt, still a province of the Ottoman Empire. It became a British protectorate, where British officers and administrators indirectly exercised political authority in the name of the powerless Egyptian ruler. The British Empire had become a major power in the Middle East.

In the rush for lands in sub-Saharan Africa, the British laid plans for territorial annexation to link southern Africa with Egypt in one great north-south band of territory "from the Cape [of Good Hope] to Cairo." That was the vision of Cecil Rhodes, the most dynamic British promoter of an African empire. His efforts obtained by treaty and conquest lands

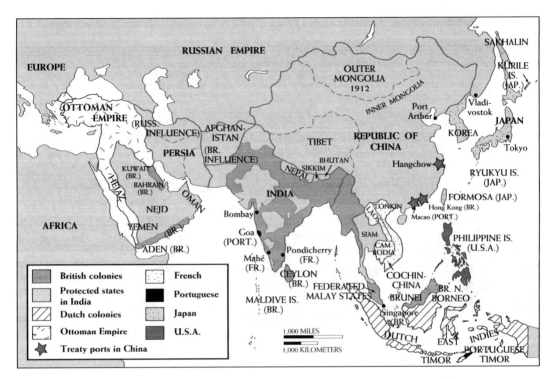

Empires in Asia, 1914

in east Africa including Kenya and a territory baptized in his honor Rhodesia. His greatest obstacle was the powerful Zulu kingdom. In 1870, its warriors inflicted a major defeat on a small British force that had invaded their land. A year later the British returned with more troops to defeat the Zulu. Their land became spoils of war for the empire. But "Cape to Cairo" did not become entirely British. The German Empire stepped in to claim in central Africa the kingdoms of Burundi and Rwanda, governed by Tutsi tribes, and the territory that they called German East Africa (later Tanganyika/Tanzania).

The most determined resistance to Rhodes's plans came from the Dutch settlers (called Boers, or Afrikaners) in southern Africa. They had long before settled on the coast, then had founded small inland republics in the 1830s to be free from British rule (and from laws protecting African peoples whose lands they had seized). Moving north from the Cape to the high plains, they established their farms and practiced their faith in an area between Britain's Cape Colony, at the southern tip of Africa, and Rhodesia. They found in their creed religious justification to treat the Africans as inferiors and to expel the tribes from their land. But they could not so easily get rid of Europeans in search of gold and diamonds when in the late nineteenth century these precious minerals were discovered in their territory. The Boers were determined to keep control of

White Settlers in South Africa: Boer Farmer on Way to Town (*Courtesy of the South African Consulate/Hoover Institution Archives*)

their "new Zion," the bastion of their Protestant church and community. British imperialists like Cecil Rhodes insisted that this land be incorporated in the British Empire and exploited by British capitalists. The two plans were irreconcilable.

As a result, Great Britain became involved in a major colonial war in sub-Saharan Africa. British administrators and officers in South Africa handled the dispute with the Boers with such arrogance and used their superior military force so provocatively that in 1899 the Boers proclaimed war on the British Empire. The military odds were hopelessly against them. They fought with the determination of religious zealots and the skill of guerrilla soldiers. The conflict did not end until 1902, when the Boer forces finally surrendered. By then even the British government was aware of the destructive folly of that expansionist war.

Soon after, Great Britain set up the Union of South Africa as a self-governing country (similar to Canada and Australia) within the British Empire. They left the Boers free to run their own internal affairs in their territories and to participate in the leadership of the federal Union as well. The Africans themselves played no part in the conflict. They, as well as their land, remained the spoils of empire.

Russia, Japan, and War for Empire

On the eastern borderlands of Europe, the Russian Empire combined traits of an ancient empire and of the new overseas empires of Western states. Its autocratic political system, headed by an absolute monarch with the titles of tsar and emperor, was in many ways as ineffective and brutal as that of the Ottoman Empire. Its subject peoples included in its western territories a large Polish population. Twice in the nineteenth century the Poles rebelled against Russian rule in the hope of creating their own nation-state. Each time the Russian Empire used its troops to defeat their rebellion. Maps of Europe omitted any mention of Poland. National rights of non-Russian peoples had no place in the authoritarian state of the Russian tsar-emperors. Its domination of these peoples earned it the grim title of "the prison of peoples."

Like the European empires, Russia set out in the mid-nineteenth century to seize colonial lands in Asia. Its Cossack soldiers and settlers had long before occupied the northern reaches of Asia inhabited mainly by hunter-gatherer tribes. The empire's enormous Siberian territories possessed abundant natural resources, and its peoples were too few and too weak to resist the Russian advance. Beginning in the 1860s, Russian leaders saw new opportunities for expansion into Turkestan, which consisted of oasis lands in Inner Asia ruled by weak Muslim princes. By the 1880s, the borders of the empire reached to Persia, Afghanistan, and China. The British Empire strongly protested the nearby presence of this greedy "Russian bear" but without success. The Russian government built railway lines to bind these distant areas to the imperial center. The most important of these was the Trans-Siberian railroad, which crossed all of Siberia to reach in 1900 the Pacific Ocean north of China and Korea.

The Japanese Empire disputed with Russia control of these East Asian lands. Until the mid-nineteenth century it had remained an isolated island empire. Its rulers, like the Chinese emperor, faced the threat of domination by expansionist Western empires. Western diplomats, backed by naval forces, had in the early 1860s obliged the Japanese government to accept their merchants on the same unequal terms as those imposed in China.

Confronted with the likelihood that their state, like China, would become a semicolonial area under the control of Western imperial powers, in 1868 a group of young Japanese reformers seized control of their government. They were nobles from the warrior class ("samurai") but were convinced that the old feudal system had to be abandoned. They were convinced that their rebellion was the only means to protect the honor and glory of the empire and their emperor, worshiped as a divine person in the state religion called Shintoism. This so-called Meiji Restoration ("Meiji," meaning "The Great," was the name taken afterward by the emperor) drew upon the patriotic pride and anti-foreign fervor of the Japanese people. It was a daring effort to make Japan powerful enough to become a great empire in its own right in East Asia. The reformers summed up their goal in the slogan "rich country, strong military." Their project relied on traditional Japanese institutions to attempt a remarkably daring strategy of "revolution from above."

Though they claimed to have restored their emperor to power, the new leaders, in fact, ruled in his name. Consciously borrowing Western technology and institutions, they succeeded by the 1890s in laying the foundations of an industrial economy, in forming a well-equipped army and navy, and in forcing Western states to renounce the unequal treaties. To obtain the cooperation of the population, they created the structure of a constitutional, representative government. Its powers were restricted by recognition of the authority of the emperor and his court, and by the informal powers of the leaders of the armed forces. Democracy was a means to mobilize the population, not an end in itself. The "imperial way" united the emperor and the reformed state in an ideology of emperor worship and imperialist expansion.

The reforms were so effective that the government was able to put in motion its plans for colonial conquest. Its goal was to seize neighboring areas on the Asian continent in advance of the Western empires. In 1894–1895, Japan waged a quick, successful war against China to force the Chinese government to cede territory and trade concessions in northern China. Their expansion brought protests from the Western empires, whose leaders could not grasp the sudden rise of this "oriental" empire in modern garb.

The Russian Empire was Japan's major imperial rival. Tempted by the riches of the northern Chinese province of Manchuria, the Russian and Japanese governments each hoped to exploit its economic resources and to enlarge their own sphere of influence at the expense of the feeble Chinese state. The Russian emperor refused to take seriously warnings from the Japanese not to continue expansion into the region. His disdainful attitude toward the "yellow" race blinded him to the reality of Japanese military might. Japan appeared to him an insignificant, inferior player in the global imperial game.

Fearing that Russia was on the verge of seizing all Manchuria, Japanese military forces launched a surprise naval attack on the Russian Pacific fleet in early 1904. Their army then crossed to the mainland to drive the Russian armed forces from north China. By 1905, the Japanese had defeated the Russian navy and had forced the Russian army to retreat far into northern Manchuria. A peace treaty that year recognized the Japanese victory. Although Manchuria remained nominally a part of China, the Japanese army established a sphere of influence in the southern area of the province. Japanese industrialists and workers moved into Manchuria to tap its mineral wealth. Soon after the war, Korea became a province of the Japanese Empire.

Japan had emerged as a powerful empire in East Asia. It rivaled Western countries in self-confidence, international might, and expansionist ambitions. Its conquest of Chinese territory stirred a movement of Chinese nationalist protest, directed as much against the feeble Chinese emperor as against the Japanese. Though it was too weak to concern the Japanese yet, Chinese resistance heralded trouble in the future for foreign intruders in China. In the early twentieth century, the new empires were beginning to confront political resistance and protest among their colonial peoples. Conflict among the new empires and national movements of protest among colonial peoples were signs that the age of empires would not endure for long.

An Empire for the United States

The expansion of the United States during the nineteenth century was continental in scope. It was a process at times brutal and aggressive. Its settlers and army had expelled Native Americans from vast fertile lands, placing them in small territorial "reservations" under government surveillance. In midcentury, U.S. forces had waged a brief war against Mexico, taking as the spoils of victory an enormous area stretching from Texas to California. By then U.S. borders extended as far west as the Pacific Ocean. In these terms, the United States was a continental empire.

Soon it obtained its own small overseas empire. Like the European states, it possessed both the economic resources and aggressive nationalists needed for empire-building. Its industrial economy was more productive than any other Western country. It had only a small army and navy, but its weapons of war were as deadly as any other modern military. At the end of the century, its political leaders proclaimed openly their ambition to begin overseas imperial expansion. Theodore Roosevelt, the most forceful of these nationalists, argued that a "really great nation" like the United States had the obligation to use its naval and diplomatic might in international affairs to expand U.S. power and influence. His nationalist ardor in defense of foreign expansion helped push the United States into the ranks of Western empires. The United States, through military conquest and economic expansion, acquired its colonial territory largely in Latin America.

Almost the entirety of this region consisted by then of independent states. A century earlier, the Spanish and Portugese settlers there had successfully rebelled against their European rulers. These political rebels held in their hands the leadership of the new states. They already dominated their societies, for they owned large agricultural estates and mines. Production from these sources was the major source of economic well-being of their countries. The peasant masses, including the Native American peoples, lived in poverty. The Catholic Church stood squarely behind this conservative social elite, recruiting its clergy from their midst and preaching obedience and loyalty to the faithful. The new countries of Latin America were sovereign nation-states in name only.

These states were comparatively weak and impoverished compared to their Yankee neighbor. American investors and bankers bought mines and built railroads and factories there. Latin American countries' reliance on foreign sales of raw materials and agricultural produce, whose prices fluctuated wildly from one year to the next, left them heavily dependent on the international market. Their governments frequently had to borrow from foreign (usually British) banks to meet the basic needs of state. When they failed to pay these debts, the British government was pre-

pared to send naval vessels to their shores to force them to pay. A disillusioned nationalist explained this dilemma by stating that "Latin America is a beggar sitting on top of a mountain of gold." The states there had the appearance, not the substance, of independence.

The process leading to a U.S. empire began on the island of Cuba. It still belonged to the Spanish Empire, whose remaining possessions included a few islands in the Caribbean, and the Philippine archipelago in the Pacific. In the mid-1890s, Cuban nationalists rebelled against Spanish rule. They appealed to the American government for help in winning independence. American nationalist leaders, backed by a newspaper campaign attacking Spanish brutality, took the lead in supporting the Cuban revolutionaries. Newspaper articles attracted readers with stories of Spanish atrocities and with appeals for American intervention on the side of the Cuban nationalists.

In this aggressive atmosphere, an explosion (probably accidental) on the American battleship *Maine*, docked in the harbor of Havana, Cuba, was sufficient pretext for a U.S. declaration of war on Spain. The 1898 war ended quickly after U.S. naval forces near the Philippines defeated the Spanish fleet; at the same time, the U.S. army seized Cuba. The peace treaty signed at the end of that year left these Spanish colonies under U.S. control.

The war for Cuban independence opened the way for U.S. expansion and territorial annexation. The U.S. government claimed (without real evidence) that another European empire would seize the Philippines if its forces left the archipelago. Filipino nationalists had fought alongside American troops against the Spanish army in the expectation of creating an independent nation-state. When the U.S. troops did not leave, they turned their arms against the United States Filipino forces were weak and poorly led, for the peoples of the archipelago were deeply divided by ethnic and religious differences. This colonial war lasted four years, but in the end, victory went to the conquerors.

Theodore Roosevelt was the most outspoken and eloquent defender of expansionism. He gloried in the newly achieved economic might of his country and argued that the country's national interest and prestige required that it retain control over the newly freed Spanish colonies. He welcomed what Kipling had called, in a poem written on the occasion of the U.S. conquest of the Philippines, "the white man's burden." Like other empire-builders of that era, the U.S. government took its victory as proof that the United States had an imperial mission. The Philippines became a U.S. colony.

Cuba became a part of the U.S. empire, not by annexation, but by becoming a protectorate. The peace treaty ending the war with Spain allowed Cuban revolutionaries to form their own nation-state. But the U.S. government insisted that the new Cuban leadership grant U.S. authorities the right to intervene in the island's affairs "to protect life, liberty, and individual property." In doing so, the Cubans allowed their giant neighbor to the north to intervene in their country's political affairs. By annexation and by treaty, the United States had created its own small empire.

It quickly became the dominant power in the Caribbean region. After Theodore Roosevelt became president in 1901, he actively encouraged the construction of a canal across the Panamanian isthmus. It was a matter of national interests. The fledgling U.S. navy would, he knew, make good use of the canal to patrol the shores of Latin American countries. U.S. business interests realized as well that U.S. merchant vessels would be able to travel quickly between the Pacific and Atlantic oceans. After negotiations with Colombia collapsed, Roosevelt helped Panamanian rebels create their own small state. They immediately agreed to cede territory for the construction of the canal, which finally opened in 1914. The Canal Zone, a U.S. possession, was a base for naval and marine forces.

Roosevelt made known to the European powers that the Caribbean was a U.S. sphere of influence, that is, a region in which his government was dominant. The small states there had to accept U.S. supervision of their foreign and domestic policy. This policy of intervention remained in place for the next quarter century. If Caribbean and Central American governments failed to pay foreign debts, financial advisers from the north took charge of their treasury. If they could not repress disorders or revolts, gunboats with marines from the Canal Zone arrived to take charge for a time. In 1911, when civil war threatened Nicaragua, marines assumed the role of police and remained there for twenty years. Roosevelt justified this "gunboat diplomacy" by proclaiming it to be in the spirit of Western empire-building and sanctioned by the moral obligations of "civilized nations." Latin American nationalists disagreed completely, but their countries lay too near the "Yankee giant" to escape U.S. domination.

● HIGHLIGHT: The New Imperialism ●

The entire world became the domain of the Western empires. It was also the territory of the *globetrotter*, a new term for travelers to distant lands. Readers of the popular novel *Around the World in Eighty Days*, written in 1873 by the French novelist Jules Verne, imagined themselves transported across oceans and continents by boat, train, and horseback alongside the English hero of the story. Phineas Fogg's mad race to circle the globe within eighty days or lose a reckless bet was made easier by the services of a new travel agency, Thomas Cook & Co. His chances were made better, too, because of the technological marvels of the Industrial Revolution. These included rail lines from Europe to Asia and across North America and steamship lines across the Atlantic and Pacific oceans. Translations of the book appeared in all Western languages, as well as in Japanese. The novel's success was a good indication that an international reading public was prepared to believe that time and distance no longer stood in the way of the ambitious traveler.

For similar reasons, time and distance were also no obstacle to expansionist empires. Clues to the new imperialism emerge within Verne's novel. It hints at an array of technological innovations that accompanied and made possible the triumph of the new empires. These tools of empire included new medicine, new arms, and new means of transportation.

The Industrial Revolution made travel far more rapid and reliable than before, thanks largely to the steam engine. Steamships moved rapidly across the seas, passed through mammoth canals to get from one ocean to the next, and sailed up rivers where no large ships had ever dared go. A French engineer, Ferdinand de Lesseps, put his technical and organizational skills to work building the Suez Canal, completed in 1869. It quickly became the crucial transportation link between Europe and Asia. On land, steam locomotives pulled trains through territories where mountains and rivers had once formed virtually impenetrable barriers. Steam engines powered new naval ships that could operate far from their own shores and were capable of carrying imperial forces to new conquests. Messages moved from these lands to the homeland with telegraphic speed, as telegraph wires spread out across continents and under oceans. In 1897, Queen Victoria of Great Britain received a unique gift as part of the celebration of her seventy-fifth birthday: the first telegram sent from London through her Asian colonies and around the world back to London.

Imperial military forces possessed new weapons with a firepower unknown to previous ages. Powerful naval cannons sent shells over several miles; breech loading rifles could be reloaded and fired with a speed unmatched by the old muskets. Most devastating of all, a single, rapid-firing "machine gun" could stop large attacking forces with a hail of bullets. All of these weapons were the products of technological innovation and precision manufacturing possible only with the Industrial Revolution. Imperial fighting forces were often made up of soldiers recruited from colonial populations, trained to use the new arms, and led by officers from the homeland. Though small in numbers, they conquered and held vast territories in Africa and Asia because of their skills in using these instruments of war.

Finally, the chances that travelers, traders, missionaries, and soldiers moving through distant continents could survive deadly diseases were better than ever before thanks to an array of medical discoveries of the late nineteenth century. The most important of these resulted from the so-called "bacteriological revolution." With the help of new equipment such as highly sophisticated microscopes, French and German scientists revealed that bacteria caused many infectious diseases. Before these discoveries revealed the causes of infection, remedies had come, if any were available, through trial and error. Death rates in especially infected areas had remained high, since the very nature of the diseases was unknown. The single most devastating illness that afflicted peoples in sub-Saharan Africa was malaria. By the end of the century, its bacteriological nature and its process of transmission were known; effective cures followed. These medical treatments greatly eased the difficulties of colonial rule for the new empires.

Western medical knowledge and facilities for treatment of these diseases became accessible to the local populations much more slowly. Public health services had only a small place in colonial concerns. Christian missionaries proved often the most effective emissaries of Western medicine. The Scotsman David Livingstone carried basic medicines on his travels through British East Africa. Later, Albert Schweitzer set up an entire clinic in the jungle of French West Africa. These missionaries hoped to spread the word of the Christian religion while ministering to the health of converts and non-Christians among colonial peoples.

Western empires shared an unusual imperial ideology. The yearning to travel, which Jules Verne used as the theme of his novel, was based on more than the desire for adventure. The urge to study and to understand distant lands and peoples accompanied Western moves to construct colonial empires. Explorers traveled to the most remote, inaccessible regions to fill in the remaining blank spots on maps of the world. Both Inner Asia and Africa, the two least-explored areas of the inhabited continents, were thoroughly mapped by the end of the century. Westerners' curiosity extended to the peoples of these lands. The very imperfect science of ethnography attempted to classify societies in terms of habits and customs of the peoples themselves. The impetus for this vast project derived, in part, from the new belief that all humanity shared a common historical evolution. Westerners, of course, had gone furthest on this road. Backward peoples still had a great distance to travel.

This potentially generous objective was accompanied by a profound sense of superiority among the colonizers, including the mapmakers and ethnographers. They came to these lands with the conviction that their industrial civilization was the supreme achievement of humanity. It followed that the West was superior to peoples not privileged to be a part of this civilization. "Primitive" tribes might hope to learn and adapt to the new way of life; until then, they occupied an inferior position in the hierarchy of humanity. Ancient cultures such as China and India had behind them a rich history worthy of study; still, they appeared to have fallen into a state of decay. The claim to conquer and rule colonial lands rested in part on the assumption that backward societies had no claim on an independent existence.

Leaders of colonial empires committed their states to raise their colonial peoples from backwardness to civilization. They shared with most citizens of their nations the belief that material and spiritual progress should be shared, at some point, with these peoples. How progress was defined, and how swiftly it should come, was to be the responsibility of imperial leaders and colonial officials. Western empires abolished slavery everywhere their rule extended. They introduced, or talked of introducing, laws to protect commerce and to encourage the spread of a free market (useful, too, in the sale of the homeland's mass-produced goods)—self-interest was never far from the concerns of empire-builders.

The writer Rudyard Kipling, born in India, became very popular with his tales and poems of empire. He used his writing to urge Westerners to take seriously their responsibility toward colonial peoples. He wrote his most famous imperial message in an 1899 poem, "The White Man's Burden." Its call to serve the needs of "your new-caught sullen peoples" was specifically addressed to the United States, which had just acquired its own small empire. Neither he nor his readers thought to ask these peoples if they wished to be taken in hand.

The desire to aid colonial peoples was interpreted in a somewhat different way by active members of the Protestant and Catholic churches. Missionaries such as David Livingstone wrote extensively to urge his European readers "to help their fellow-men in Africa" by sharing their "social and religious blessings." By the early twentieth century, these missionaries had converted millions in Asia and Africa. By doing so, though, they created divisions within native communities, provoking disorder and dissent among peoples previously united in their customs and faith. Conversion opened the way for the new Christians to enter more easily within colonial society. The Nigerian novelist Chinua Achebe entitled his anti-colonial novel *Things Fall Apart* to highlight the devastating impact of the arrival of the Christian missionaries and British colonial officials among African peoples. He was writing from personal experience, for his own father had renounced ancestral traditions to join a Protestant church. Its schools gave him a Western education and the fluency in English so complete that he made it his chosen literary language.

In the late nineteenth century, nationalist passions led political leaders to claim that their own states had to stake claim to more and more territory to prevent rival empires from getting ahead in a competition for land. Success would establish the superiority of their nation; failure, on the contrary, was the mark of decay. The popular theory of Social Darwinism asserted that nations, like animals, competed in a struggle of the "survival of the fittest." Imperialist leaders and their followers feared to be ranked among the unfit.

This attitude drove the Russian Empire far into East Asia. There it encountered another empire equally determined to expand into the same region. The leaders of the Japanese Empire, reformed on a Western model in the previous decades, made sure that their claim to the disputed areas was successful by defeating the Russians in a short war early in the twentieth century. For the first time, Western governments discovered that a non-Western state could put to its own use their tools of empire.

Christianity in Africa:
Rural Church,
Northern Rhodesia
(Zambia), approx.
1925 (*Hoover
Institution Archives*)

ANCIENT EMPIRES

The ancient empires of Africa and Asia differed in many ways from the Western empires of the nineteenth and twentieth centuries. They were governed by emperors whose authority was absolute, limited only by time-honored traditions, and whose power depended on officials and military chosen largely from the conquerors and recruited according to ancient practices. Nationalism was to them an alien concept, as was democracy and industrialization. They ruled over peoples of widely differing customs, languages, and religions. These subject peoples were often allowed to retain their customs and cultures, but they were denied access to power and wealth unless they adopted the language and religion of their rulers. A small ruling elite enjoyed great wealth and power, relying largely on traditional practices to maintain their rule. In times of disorder, their claim to govern rested ultimately on the might of their armies, equipped with arms sufficient to repress revolts but no match for modern Western armies.

Such imperial regimes had, at times, taken a hand in encouraging commerce and manufacturing. They did so for the sake of the tax revenues generated by this economic activity. Enterprise and investment did not interest them, for these activities appeared menial. The Industrial Revolution had no chance to thrive in these hostile surroundings.

Land trade and communication across Asia and Europe and over the seas had brought new manufactured products and agricultural crops to distant lands long before the modern age. In the Middle Ages, silk reached the West from China along routes protected by Asian nomadic empires; these routes also carried the bubonic plague to Europe. Spanish travelers of the sixteenth and seventeenth centuries transported new plants, such as potatoes and corn, from the Americas to Asia and Europe; they also spread deadly diseases to the New World. In these and other ways the ancient empires profoundly influenced human history. By the early twentieth century, the few remaining ancient empires were surviving on past glories and at the pleasure of the new empires of Europe and Japan.

The Fall of the Chinese Empire

In the seventeenth century, warrior tribes from the northeast, the Manchu, had seized control of the Chinese Empire. They founded a new imperial dynasty, the Qing (also written "Ching"). They were proud of their warrior culture and disdainful of the Chinese people. But, like other conquerors before them, the Qing rulers adopted the Chinese system of rule. Mastery of a complex corpus of writings on morality and government remained the essential requirement for entry into the empire's administration. Written more than 2,000 years earlier by the philosopher Confucius, these writings suited well the needs of the new dynasty. His philosophy emphasized the

overriding need for social harmony and order. At the heart of this system were the Three Bonds of obedience—subject to ruler, son to father, and wife to husband. State and family were all part of the same system, in which moral obligations, not rights, were the essential guide to behavior.

Unique traditions and religious practices had evolved around this state-sponsored set of ethical principles. Ancestor worship was widespread, within a set of religious practices known as Taoism. Among eminent families, women remained in seclusion. The mark of their attractiveness (and suitability for arranged marriages) was foot-binding, achieved by gradually breaking a young girl's foot bones to reduce by one-half the size of her feet. The practice gradually spread to the lower classes. Only the peasant women escaped, for their work in the fields required that they be fit to walk. Foot-binding satisfied Chinese men's taste in female beauty; it also revealed the implacable force of the Confucian bonds of obedience.

The coherence of the Confucian imperial system of rule was the secret to its survival for 2,000 years. New dynasties found that it met their needs to maintain order and guaranteed them an effective, loyal set of administrators to carry out their orders over that vast, populous empire. The Qing followed this tradition. For two centuries, China enjoyed peace and economic well-being. Its economic productivity in the eighteenth century was equal to any other region in the world.

The Qing's powers began to decline in the next century. A civil war, known as the Taiping Rebellion, lasted for two decades in mid-century, devastating large parts of the country until the Qing army defeated the rebels. The dynasty had survived thanks to its ability to call upon the time-proven methods of warfare and rule. It was the wrong message to have learned, though, when the Qing faced new foreign enemies.

The new threat to China came from across the seas. With the backing of their governments, Western traders had begun arriving in their sailing ships in increasing numbers in the eighteenth century. Chinese luxury goods, such as silk and porcelain, were much in demand in the West. But traders had a harder time finding goods that interested the Chinese. Opium did sell very well, and British merchants had ready access to abundant supplies in India. The Chinese authorities attempted to restrict foreign access to their market and to block the sale of opium. British traders appealed to their government to defend open access to Chinese markets. Their appeal was successful.

To end this dispute over trade, Great Britain waged two brief wars against China in the mid-nineteenth century. Its victories brought more spoils of war. The island of Hong Kong, on the southern coast of China, became a part of the British Empire. British citizens (as well as other Westerners) obtained the right to live in a few Chinese port cities in their own settlements, under their own laws. A small section of Shanghai became a flourishing miniature Western city, with Western-style houses and broad streets where its own police force kept public order. It was also a refuge for political enemies of the dynasty. And the opium trade flourished.

At the end of the century, the Chinese Empire fought and lost another brief war. The victor this time was the Japanese Empire. The Japanese government had decided to create its own overseas empire in East Asia. Its first target was the kingdom of Korea, which for centuries acknowledged the suzerainty (in foreign affairs especially) of the Chinese Empire. But China could no longer protect its borderlands. In one decisive battle in 1894, the new Japanese navy destroyed Chinese naval forces. The Chinese government once again had to accept a humiliating defeat. Victory in war gave the Japanese control of Korea (which

it soon made a colony) and the island of Formosa. Earlier, the Russian Empire had taken over an enormous territory on the northern edges of China. In the last half of the century, the French Empire gradually extended its conquest over the southern region that it called Indochina. In the early twentieth century, even the Buddhist leaders of the mountainous land of Tibet, on the southwestern borders of China, turned to British protection to escape Chinese rule. China was falling apart.

The crisis propelled frightened Qing leaders into desperate action. They gave support to a secret anti-foreign and patriotic society that in 1899 prepared a popular uprising directed against foreign settlements, traders, and missionaries, and against Chinese converts to Christianity. The leaders of this so-called Boxer Rebellion (from the name of one of the secret societies that supported the revolt) appealed to their followers to "Support the Qing, destroy the foreigners." But the rebel militia were too poorly armed and disorganized to withstand attacks from organized Western troops. A coalition of forces, mainly from Russian, British, and Japanese armies, defeated the Boxers. They ordered the Chinese government to punish its leaders and occupied the capital city of Beijing (also written "Peking"), whose foreign settlement had been under siege for weeks. In the process, they burned and looted large parts of the city. Shortly afterward, the Chinese government, in a last-minute, desperate effort to reform the state, set about creating a modern administrative system, Western-type schools, and a well-equipped modern army. But it was too late.

The Qing dynasty's most serious opponents came from within the country. Even the generals charged with setting up the "new-style" army had lost faith in its leadership. In coastal cities, a new Chinese middle class, enriched largely by the booming overseas commerce, turned against the traditional Chinese system. They were sympathetic to the aims (if not the methods) of revolutionary nationalists. These rebels organized the Guomindang (Chinese Nationalist Party), under the leadership of Sun Yat-sen, a doctor trained in the new Chinese medical schools. This movement called for the end of the empire and the creation of a democratic republic. In 1911, an ambitious general seized control of the government, taking the infant emperor prisoner. The next year the Nationalist Party proclaimed the creation of the Chinese Republic. The Chinese Empire, with no one to defend it, disappeared.

◀ SPOTLIGHT: The Empress Dowager of China ▶

The Empress Dowager (1835–1908) was the last powerful ruler of the oldest empire of the world. She became the "dowager" when in 1861 her husband, the emperor, died. His death placed in her hands the care of their son, the heir to the Chinese throne. She had come to the court as one among the emperor's many wives. It had been her good fortune to give birth to his first son and heir. In the imperial court, as in all important families of traditional China, a wife became a noteworthy person when she produced a male heir. The Empress Dowager acquired her initial position of influence by giving the empire its future ruler.

Her responsibility for the well-being of the infant after the emperor's death brought her directly into the highest court circles of the imperial dynasty. She took the name of "Empress of the West" (*Cixi* in Chinese). Her political activities began in the following years, when she proved her determination to protect the dynasty and to ensure the survival of the empire. She pursued that goal with determination until her death in 1908. Three years later, the empire collapsed.

Her personal accomplishment is remarkable when set against the forces undermining the empire. Her own imperial court was deeply divided by personal rivalries and by opposing programs for the defense of the Chinese Empire. Her country confronted powerful foreign states, also called empires but organized, equipped, and led very differently from her own. The Russian, English, and Japanese empires had seized Chinese territory and forced her government to grant their citizens special economic and legal privileges in China. Their armies and navies were equipped with deadly modern weapons capable of overwhelming Chinese forces in war. Their emissaries in China were scornful of the Chinese for their lack of scientific knowledge and technical skills and for their traditional customs. Western diplomats and visitors to Beijing mocked the Empress Dowager as the "dragon lady" (the dragon was the symbol of the empire), believing the rumors that told of her corruption and brutality.

The Empress Dowager herself had little education and had to rely on the advice of court officials in dealing with the crises that confronted her country. She had no confidence in the emperors, first her son and, after his death, her nephew. She believed them to be weak and irresolute, and she was right. Her loyalty went entirely to the dynasty and to the Chinese imperial tradition to which it was heir. She was prepared to be ruthless to defend that cause, even though it seemed virtually hopeless. The foreigners moving into her land brought new, alien customs. She distrusted them both because they challenged sacred Chinese ways and because they threatened her dynasty. The backing that she secretly gave in 1900 to the Boxer Rebellion was a measure of her despair at the decay of the Qing dynasty and decline of the empire.

The defeat of the Boxers forced her to renounce her commitment to traditional Chinese imperial rule. For the first time, she received foreign guests. She allowed a Western photographer to take a picture of her dressed in her imperial finery. Most important, she finally accepted the advice of court officials urging fundamental reforms of her empire. But it was too late to save the Chinese Empire from collapse.

The Empress Dowager of China, 1903 (*Cixi, Empress Dowager of China, 1835–1908, Photographs. Freer Gallery of Art and Arthur M. Sackler Gallery Archives, Smithsonian Institution, Washington, D.C.: Purchase. Photographer: Xunling, negative number SC-GR 252*)

The Decline of the Ottoman Empire

At the western end of the Asian continent and in the same decades, the Ottoman Empire confronted similar threats from Western empires and experienced internal turmoil nearly as great as the Chinese Empire. This ancient empire had existed since warrior tribes from central Asia had conquered the lands of the Byzantine Empire. These tribes spoke a Turkic language and were ruled by descendants of their first great leader, Osman (deformed in English as "Ottoman"). Ruling from the ancient city of Constantinople (later renamed Istanbul), the Ottoman emperors governed an enormous territory that at its peak stretched from the Hungarian plains in central Europe to the borders of Persia and from the northern shores of the Black Sea and the Caucasus Mountains to the Atlantic shores of Morocco. In their lands lived peoples of many different cultures, languages, and religions. The emperors adopted the Muslim religion, which became the religion of state. The Ottoman rulers' political title was "sultan," to which they later added that of "caliph." This title was taken from medieval Arab Muslim empires and elevated the sultan to the rank of titular leader of all Sunni Muslims. The empire permitted non-Muslim religious communities to practice their rites and customs at the price of a special tax. This policy amounted to religious toleration and was a remarkably humane practice at a time when Western states still persecuted non-Christian religions.

The strength of the empire lay in its fighting forces and in the extensive commerce that passed through its lands. Ottoman armies and navies were the best in the entire Mediterranean basin in the sixteenth century. But by the nineteenth century, their armies had suffered defeat after defeat at the hands of modern Western forces. Its economy flourished until Western seaborne trade replaced the caravans that had carried goods from Asia to Europe, and until Western industrialization turned out products far more cheaply than any Ottoman subjects could produce. By the middle of the nineteenth century, the Ottoman leaders confronted a military and financial crisis.

As in the case of China, conservative forces within the imperial court and among Muslim clerics stood in the way of reform. The Ottoman Empire was tightly bound to traditional Muslim values. These were defended by religious leaders ready to condemn any cultural and social innovations, especially those inspired by Western practices, as violations of Muslim law and customs.

The sultan and his court proved unable to undertake fundamental reforms of the state. They lived in isolation from the outside world, assured sumptuous comforts in the great palace of Topkapi in Istanbul. It also housed the sultan's enormous harem, gathered from influential Ottoman families and allied princely families. This absence of leadership in the face of the mounting crisis placed responsibility for reform on the army. It also opened the way for uprisings and nationalist movements among its minority Christian peoples.

The empire's decline came from military defeats at the hands of Western empires. Its lands in southeastern Europe were a tempting prize for neighboring Christian empires, no longer fearful of Ottoman might. The rulers of the Russian and Austro-Hungarian empires claimed the right to protect Christian subjects of the sultan. They even enlarged their claims to include small areas of Jerusalem, holiest of Ottoman cities, where Christian churches stood on sacred sites. Wars along the borders of the Ottoman Empire had by the late nineteenth century reduced Ottoman territory in Europe to a tiny portion of the Balkan peninsula. In North Africa, the French Empire had conquered Algeria, and the British Empire had made Egypt its protectorate. The British had moved military forces into Egypt to protect the Suez Canal, a vital new link for its imperial commerce and communication. By the end of the century, Western leaders were openly laying plans for destruction of the empire and the partition of its lands.

Disagreement on this issue among the European governments became a source of diplomatic conflict. In 1877–1878, the Russian Empire waged a brief war on the Ottoman forces. It produced such a crushing defeat of the Ottoman Empire that Russia's army almost reached Istanbul before war's end. In reaction, leaders of all the other major European states intervened to prevent the Ottoman state from falling under Russian domination. By then, the sultan's regime was so impoverished and indebted to Western bankers that it had to accept Western control of part of its tax revenues to pay back its debts. The very existence of the Ottoman Empire was in doubt.

In this growing crisis, members of the ruling Ottoman elite concluded that radical reform was the only salvation for their state. Army officers claimed that they held the secret for restoring Ottoman might by learning from Western states. They observed that these countries relied on their national communities to contribute voluntarily to public needs. It seemed clear to them that their own Turkish-speaking community could become the national core of a reformed empire capable of mobilizing its people against the threatened collapse and conquest.

Internal opposition to their reform program came from all sides. Islamic religious leaders were bitterly opposed to their plans, which were inspired by secular (that is, nonreligious) ideals. They viewed the empire as the center of Islam, within whose borders Muslim pilgrims could restore their faith and the purity of their practices at Mecca, holiest of Muslim sites, and at the religious centers in Istanbul. Secular reform appeared to them a greater danger than foreign enemies.

Non-Turkish peoples also resisted the reformers' program. To create a Turkish national community meant favoring Turks at the expense of its other peoples. Their protected status had ensured them some degree of security; Turkish nationalism threatened to destroy the delicate ethnic balance there. The Armenian community, concentrated within the empire's northeastern territory (as well as in the neighboring Russian lands), reacted to the nationalist program of Turkish reformers with their own nationalist movement. Ethnic antagonism, stirred up by nationalist claims, brought attacks on Armenian communities from surrounding Turkish (and Kurdish) Muslims. Reforming this multi-ethnic, multi-religious empire posed social and religious problems so acute that they could undermine the empire that the reformers hoped to save.

The leaders of this Ottoman reform movement, calling themselves Young Turks, came from the officer corps of the Ottoman army. Organized in secret societies, their goal was to force the sultan to agree to their program of reform. They did not begin with political revolution in mind, but they were prepared to use force to obtain concessions from their sultan, Abdulhamid II. He was reluctant to join them. In 1908, they organized mutinies among army units and threatened to attack Istanbul unless he agreed. The sultan capitulated, accepting the Young Turks' demand that he grant the empire a constitution guaranteeing free elections and representative government. The rebels (including a young man named Mustapha Kemal) took control of the government and set out to reform their ancient empire.

The Young Turks' priority was strengthening the empire. Constitutional rights and the rule of law meant less to them than saving the Ottoman state in the face of recurring insurbian Peninsula to the Muslim Holy Places of Mecca and Medina); German military advisers helped strengthen Ottoman armed forces. At the time, these links with Germany suited the reformers' needs. The consequences ultimately proved disastrous to the empire. After European war began in 1914, they succumbed to German pleas to join the Central Powers. The Ottoman Empire in 1914 was a pale shadow of the once-glorious domain of the conquering Turks.

WESTERN LIBERALISM AND NATIONALISM

Western liberalism and nationalism aroused the greatest interest, and the greatest controversy, among non-Western elites seeking to understand the secrets to Western might. Both were achievable only after the profound political and cultural transformation of traditional societies. They were in these terms a threat to old elites; by the same measure they drew support from reformers. The practices and attitudes that informed these institutions were the product of historical forces peculiar to the West, and yet they did appear transferable and valuable.

The Liberal State

Most Western states recognized in law and practice the liberties that had come to be known as human rights. Great Britain, France, and the United States had evolved over the previous century the institutions of democratic government intended to ensure the protection of these rights. Gradually, more and more states in the Western world followed their example. This process had come at times through reforms granted by hereditary monarchies, who accepted becoming constitutional rulers. At times, it came after revolutions that overthrew monarchs who attempted to

Mustapha Kemal (Ataturk) in Traditional Uniform of Ottoman Officer, 1914 (© *Hulton-Deutsch Collection/CORBIS*)

rections among its subject peoples and new wars with European states. Their leadership lacked popular support; among themselves they could not agree on the vital measures needed to cope with social unrest and political decay. Their survival required outside help.

They turned to the German Empire. Its economy was the most productive in Europe, its army was the mightiest of European forces; also important, the German Empire was hostile to the Russian Empire. The Ottoman reformers welcomed German financial and technical assistance. With this help, they built new railroads (including one down the Ara-preserve their power and to restrict these rights. In 1905, Russian revolutionaries forced their emperor, Nicholas II, to concede some measure of political freedom to his subjects. The struggle for liberty could lead to bitter political conflict. The same situation emerged in colonial lands when these same liberal demands from native subjects met the opposition of their imperial rulers.

The key elements of *liberalism* centered on the rights of the citizen. At its heart was the rule of law, to be embodied in fundamental laws most often contained in a constitution (as in the United States and France). Criminal and civil law codes enforced by the state forbad in principle any legal privilege for any citizens on the basis of class, race, or religion. The state guaranteed religious toleration. Marriage, family, and property relations came under the jurisdiction of the state's laws, which took precedence over the laws or customs of any particular religion. This principle of equality before the law of all citizens is usually referred to as *secularism*. Later it became one of the most controversial reforms in colonial lands, especially among Muslim peoples whose religious laws extended into the family and public domain of the faithful.

The goal of liberal states was to ensure civil and political liberties to everyone. Liberalism promised citizens their civil liberties, including freedom of speech, assembly, and worship. Citizens also enjoyed political rights, principally the right to elect political representatives to whom the powers of government were granted. These powers were limited; legislatures at times chose the executive leadership in the government (Britain's cabinet system), whereas in other countries citizens voted directly for their leader (the presidential system). Courts could reject illegal acts of the government, and regular elections were intended to prevent political leaders from claiming abusive powers and neglecting the needs of their citizens. Finally, law codes protected individual and corporate property rights in an economy that operated in a free market (capitalism).

This nineteenth-century liberal program hid serious problems. One involved the crucial issue of what part of the population should enjoy the full rights of citizens. Voting rights (suffrage) were a major source of disagreement throughout the nineteenth century. Gradually, universal manhood suffrage laws were adopted, largely as a result of the competition of political parties for voter backing. The issue of women's suffrage stirred up particular controversy. Most men still shared the conviction that women, in political affairs, were inferior to men. Consequently, they should aspire only to be second-class citizens. But women's suffrage movements disputed this claim, demanding that the political and civil rights be granted the female half of humanity. They sought "the emancipation of woman as a personality" and labeled their cause *feminism*. Their pursuit of liberty, whose roots lay in the eighteenth-century revolutions, continued into the twentieth century.

A second weakness of the liberal ideology as practiced in the West in the nineteenth century was its reluctance to accept the claim of colonial peoples to the protection of political rights. At a basic level, liberalism did sanction interference in colonial peoples' way of life to ban certain practices, such as slavery, judged violations of basic human rights. Anti-slavery campaigns, led by private organizations and governments, were especially prevalent in the African lands that were once the prime source of slaves for the Americas and the Arab countries.

But most Westerners judged the rule of law and representative government to be unfit for backward peoples. They justified this claim by pointing to what they considered the primitive conditions in their colonies. At best, they offered to these subjects the possibility of attaining some measure of citizenship after a lengthy period of learning, which they as-sumed required knowledge (and apprecia-tion) of the empire's language and culture. The rulers of the British Empire recognized by the early twentieth century that some of their Asian subjects, especially in India, might one day be fit for local self-rule. But they did not foresee that possibility coming soon. Political paternalism, buttressed by pervasive racism, stood in the path of serious political reform of the colonial regimes of the European empires.

A third serious failing of the liberal states was their unwillingness to address the prob-lems of acute social inequality. The widening of political citizenship came far more easily than the reduction of the great disparities of wealth and property that characterized all in-dustrial societies. Nineteenth-century liberal-ism did not recognize social welfare to be a human right. Individual citizens had to sat-isfy their economic needs through their own efforts. That some benefitted while others suf-fered was judged a sort of law of nature. The working classes formed their own parties to compete in elections and sought new laws to protect the impoverished and the laboring classes. Some European intellectuals were convinced that the liberal system itself was so flawed that only its profound transformation would bring the working masses social justice and political freedom. Karl Marx's socialist theories were the most influential denuncia-tion of this failure of liberalism, which he at-tributed to the dominant position of the bourgeoisie (middle classes) in these states.

Despite these flaws, the political ideals of liberalism inspired revolutionary movements in countries outside the Western democracies. The early years of the twentieth century were a period of political unrest in Asia and Latin America. Cuban revolutionaries rebelled in the 1890s against Spanish domination in the name of political liberty as well as national liberation. In 1910, a revolution in Mexico started as a revolt against a dictator in the name of freedom and justice. It quickly turned into a social revolution as well when Mexico's peasant masses found radical leaders to voice their grievances (see Chapter 3). The Russian liberal movement won mass support in the 1905 revolution by demanding that the tsarist regime renounce absolute rule and grant its subjects the rights of citizens in constitutional democracy. A similar set of demands united the Young Turks in their 1908 revolt against the sultan of the Ottoman Empire. Two years earlier in Persia, the shah was forced by his political opposition to grant the country a lib-eral constitution. And in the far-off Chinese Empire, Sun Yat-sen made the promise of democracy as important as that of nationalist renewal in formulating the program for his new Nationalist Party.

These liberal revolutions could not claim to have fully succeeded in bringing freedom and justice to their people. The promises made were unattainable when leaders fought for power or when the new regime lost mass sup-port by failing to address social and economic grievances. These regimes had their greatest chance of keeping that support when liberals clearly demonstrated their commitment to de-fend the nation. Nationalism and liberalism together could remake the political map of the world. But opportunities to do so depended on finding the means of satisfying the press-ing economic needs of the working masses.

Industrial Society

The prosperity of the West in the period be-fore 1914 helps explain the attractiveness of Western liberalism. Social discontent erupted now and then in serious conflicts but none so great as to threaten democratic rule. And to visitors from non-Western lands, the benefits of industrial society appeared real and closely tied to the liberal program. They were correct, at least, in judging industrialism an economic success.

The Industrial Revolution had, in many ways, brought a remarkable improvement in Western peoples' standard of living. The extraordinary productivity of the new technology—applied in agriculture as well as industry—and the factory system provided food and shelter for a European population twice as large in 1900 as in 1800. The greatest hardship—and the areas of massive migration to the Western Hemisphere—were in eastern and southern Europe, where industrialization had just begun. Cities expanded everywhere, their inhabitants enjoying better living conditions than ever before. They attracted migrants from the countryside who sought an escape from rural poverty. Disappointment awaited many new urban dwellers, but still they came. By the first years of the twentieth century, urbanization had created major metropolitan areas throughout the West.

Within these cities, family and class relations experienced dramatic changes. The older business classes were closely tied to industrial production and commerce. At the turn of the century, the fastest-growing middle-class occupations were in professional employment, ranging from bank clerk to doctor and lawyer. New terms appeared, such as *white collar*, to designate a large array of new jobs that required secondary and advanced education. The poor population had little hope of qualifying, for social barriers and inadequate education still stood in their way. A few unmarried women from the middle classes were able to enter educational institutions to acquire advanced training, but most had to accept positions such as schoolteacher or nurse. Even then, custom dictated that upon marriage a woman must immediately abandon outside work. To be a wife was, in that social sphere, synonymous with being a housewife. In the Victorian Age, power and wealth lay in the hands of middle-class men.

Opportunities for individual advancement increased in the late nineteenth century. As the factory system spread, the numbers of employed workers grew, as did that of managers and engineers. Although fewer workers than ever before suffered constant privation, their labor too often stunted their bodies and shortened their lives. Work depended on economic demand and the needs of private businesses. Depression meant unemployment and hardship. In the early twentieth century, governments did little to help those unable to work or who lost their jobs. They still honored the old precept that "God helps those who help themselves." One of the most popular books of the late nineteenth-century, written by the Englishman Samuel Smiles, summed up its how-to-succeed message in the words (and title of the book) "Self-Help."

Profound social and cultural changes were underway among the lower classes in the West. They were beginning to enjoy a share of the benefits of the industrial economy. Adult life expectancy improved, largely as a result of improved diets and hygiene among the laboring classes. Literacy was becoming widespread as a result of universal elementary education. This massive advance of popular education and the emergence of a mass reading public, especially in the cities, were probably the major cultural developments in the Western world in the late nineteenth century.

Worker family life was beginning to adjust to new economic conditions. Improved health and food brought longer life expectancy and lower infant mortality. At the same time, birth-control methods became widely available among the middle and working classes. Birth rates were declining throughout the West by the late nineteenth century as families chose to have fewer children than before. The most obvious explanation for this trend was the widespread confidence that most children would survive to adulthood and would thus be able to contribute to the care of elderly parents. The era when three out of four infants died before the age of ten was gone. Small families could share more easily the family's resources while still giving the parents the satisfaction to seeing several children grow to adulthood. This trend, called the "demographic transition" (the decline in an entire society of the birth and the death rates to a point of relative equality), signaled the end of Europe's population explosion of the previous century. The same demographic process, one of the most important means to balance resources and human needs, began to spread to other parts of the world later in the twentieth century.

In these ways, the faith in progress shared by most Westerners reflected tangible improvements in their lives. Leisure time, once a middle- and upper-class privilege, was becoming available to working classes as well. It opened new opportunities for activities such as organized sports. Europeans favored soccer games; Americans chose baseball. The Frenchman Baron de Coubertin made his dream of international sports competition a reality when, in 1896, he organized the first Olympic Games in Athens, Greece (where they had once flourished 2,000 years before). Only thirteen countries participated, sending 200 male athletes to strive for medals in what Coubertin believed should be a model of peaceful rivalry among nations.

Marvels of technology were a source of wonder. Motion pictures, the new product of the combination of photographic film and electric light, enchanted viewers with escapist tales of romance, comedy, and adventure.

This world of wonders and achievement went on public display at the 1900 World's Fair in Paris. Its organizers celebrated the beginning of a new century in the name of progress and Western civilization. It attracted 50 million visitors before it closed. The subjects of the exhibits, spread out across the city center in scores of new buildings, ranged from giant industrial machinery to the lethal bacteria visible under microscopes that doctors had identified in their fight against infectious diseases. An entire array of displays and sets revealed the curious customs and dress of the colonial subjects of Asia and Africa and included representatives of the native peoples in their traditional dress.

National exhibit halls arrayed along the "Street of Nations" rivaled each other in an effort to impress the public with the achievements of their nation-states. The German Empire's building resembled an enormous medieval town hall. The United States chose the design of a Roman temple (after having rejected the idea of a log cabin). The Russian Empire built a copy of the Kremlin (Moscow's medieval fortress), inside of which was the Trans-Siberian railroad in the shape of a giant map of Siberia and a real railroad dining car. Guests were invited to enter the car and sit at tables, to be served Russian delicacies while watching for thirty minutes through the windows a moving diorama (a very long rolled canvas) revealing scenes of an imaginary train trip from Moscow to Peking. It was, according to observers, the most popular exhibit at the fair. Globetrotting had become a popular attraction.

The World's Fair presented the public with an optimistic vision of *modernity*. This term refers to both industrial society and the cultural attitudes born of an awareness of the profound social and economic transformations under way. Some people saw a darker side to these forces, pointing to the rise of nationalist antagonism among states, the appearance of deadly new weapons of war, and the class conflict and poverty hidden in city slums and in the countryside. Progress and confrontation were two sides to the history of the twentieth century, a time of greater upheaval than ever before in human history.

The "Street of Nations," Paris World Exposition, 1900 (From *"The Paris Exhibition 1900"* [London 1901])

European Nationalism

The presence at the World's Fair of the pavilions of the West's nation-states and empires underlined how important nationalism had become in the political life of Europe. The ideal of the nation-state, formulated first at the time of the French Revolution, was destined for a people sharing a common identity and set of beliefs drawn from their historical experience. This vision hid a profound contradiction. It joined together the state and the people of that state but left open the question of whether the defining characteristic of that union was the political ideals enjoyed by that people or the apparent ethnic unity of one people, either ruling themselves or governed by a ruler speaking in their name. These two differing versions of nationalism, one individualistic and the other collectivistic, were present within all Western countries. They reemerged in non-Western countries as nationalism spread in the twentieth century throughout the world.

Nationalism as a form of human rights is usually defined as *civic nationalism*. It based the nation-state ideal on national bonds that were defined by a shared commitment to the rule of law and to civil and political rights in a democratic nation-state. In other words, it imagined the nation to be open to all who were ready to share the values defining citizenship (hence, the term *civic*). President Lincoln defended this vision when, in his Gettysburg Address in 1863, he proclaimed the United States to be "one nation, conceived in liberty." The people in such a nation-state usually all spoke one language, but it was conceivable for such a nation to be a place of peoples speaking several different languages.

In the nineteenth century, citizens in states such as Great Britain and France appeared to have come closest to achieving this form of nation-state. But even there critics, also claiming to be nationalists, argued that the dominant people, with their own language and culture, should not grant equal rights and power to other peoples. In their view, all citizens needed to assimilate elements of the dominant culture, beginning with its language, before acquiring full citizenship. Their arguments made clear the promise, and the weakness, of civic nationalism. To become truly equitable, the state needed the agreement of its peoples to join in a pluralistic national community. Lincoln's vision of a special American civic nationalism was for a century after the Civil War a tragic failure because the United States was unable to overcome the racism that excluded blacks from the political community.

Nationalism could also define a very different community. It often appeared in political debates and claims to power to refer to one people sharing a collective identity based on common ancestry. Termed *ethnic nationalism*, its intellectual roots lay in the glorification by writers in the nineteenth century of the cultural and historical uniqueness of separate peoples. This definition of *people* stressed the richness of their folklore, language, and history. The term *ethnic* refers to the special inherited traits of that people. Transformed into a political program, ethnic nationalism stressed the need for each people, within their native land, to form their own nation-state.

Each people needed their own state to fulfill their true destiny and to defend their needs. Other peoples living in that territory had to accept the rule by the dominant ethnic group. Most nineteenth-century writers and political leaders who argued for national unification on these terms assumed special laws should protect the rights of national minorities.

Popular awareness of national identity, increasingly defined in ethnic terms, had spread widely throughout Europe in the decades before the First World War. Nationalism drew its strength from mass public schooling and generalized literacy, which gave the population access to accounts of the past of a particular nation as transmitted in histories, the press, and literature. Its principal adherents lived in urban centers, where personal contacts and popular culture made shared national identity a lived experience. The sense of shared identity enriched the lives of people by greatly enlarging meaningful human contacts. It was, however, a destructive influence when it increased distrust and even hatred toward other peoples. Nationalism was a new and potent force in human history, creating a new perception of self and the other, of friends and enemies.

In Europe, nationalism's revolutionary potential to destroy old states and create new nation-states had become apparent during the nineteenth century. Germany and Italy became nation-states in the 1860s as a result of wars and popular uprisings, all in the name of national unification. In central and eastern Europe, large multi-national monarchies remained centers of unrest and violent confrontation between governments determined to defend their unity and nationalist movements seeking to break away into separate ethnic nation-states. Both the Austro-Hungarian Empire of southeastern Europe and the Russian Empire to the east were home to a multitude of peoples. Germans and

Hungarians dominated the Austrian Empire; Russians were the ruling people in that empire. Nationalism among their subject peoples was a revolutionary movement.

The Serb nationalists in the Balkan region of the Austro-Hungarian Empire demanded the creation, partly out of imperial lands, of a nation-state for all the Serbian-speaking people. Serb writers and intellectuals believed that all South Slavs (the most numerous people in the Balkans) belonged in one state. These peoples spoke languages that appeared to be linguistically similar despite significant differences of dialect. Serbian nationalists discounted the lack of a clear common language, just as they discounted the importance of the religious barriers that had created separate communities of Catholics (Croats), Muslims (often referred to as Bosnians, since most lived in Bosnia), and Orthodox people (for whom the term *Serb* was commonly used). They claimed that these peoples spoke the same Serbian language and shared a similar ancestry. By the logic of ethnic nationalism, they all shared a common national identity and all should belong to one (South Slav, or Yugoslav) state. Most Serbian-speaking peoples lived in the Austro-Hungarian Empire. The little kingdom of Serbia, on the southern borders of the empire, constituted the core around which Serbian nationalists hoped to construct this new nation-state. The empire stood in their way, and some Serbians were prepared to use violent methods, including political assassination (terrorism), to triumph. They ultimately succeeded but only after a terrible and bloody war. The transition from empires to nations could not escape bloodshed and violence.

SUMMARY

The stability and might of empires had for millennia rested on the power of their armies, on the cultural and religious traditions that legitimated their authority, and on the economic resources that sustained the enormous apparatus of empire. The fall of the Chinese Empire revealed that ancient empires could not rely on the loyalty of their people in the face of economic hardship and defeat at the hands of foreign states. The success of the Japanese Empire, on the contrary, suggested that the key to survival lay in adapting to a country's needs the political institutions and industrial technology of the Western empires. Japanese leaders had good reason to congratulate themselves on having forced their people to incorporate Western industry, national political institutions, and a modern army and navy.

These new empires had created a new form of imperial rule for their conquered territories. Inventions in science and technology made accessible lands previously beyond their reach. These same tools of empire made possible more intensive economic exploitation of their colonies than ever before and permitted closer political control over the colonial peoples than previously. Their railroads and telegraphs facilitated communication and transportation, drawing together colonies and homeland, and binding together colonial territories. The borders that they drew around their colonies became tangible boundaries to the imperial administrators and to the peoples enclosed within them. The names that these Western officials, ethnographers, and geographers gave to these peoples were often arbitrary, and the authority granted local rulers of tribes bore little resemblance to traditional tribal ways. Yet these colonial practices embedded themselves in the life of the colonies just as firmly as the ports, railroads, and telegraphs that the empires constructed.

The fate of these empires rested ultimately on their ability to settle their conflicts without recourse to war. The First World War was the end of a long period of empire-building in Asia and Africa and of peace within Europe. Though some Marxists argued that the war was the product of the internal weakness and conflicts of the capitalist system, doomed soon to collapse, the immediate origins of the war lay primarily in terrible blunders made by Europe's political leaders. Ultimately, their greatest failure was their inability to understand that war was no longer merely an instrument for achieving national interests. Warfare in the industrial age had become more destructive than ever before. When the new weapons were employed by the nation-states of Europe against one another, war destroyed much that had been the pride of European civilization.

DATES WORTH REMEMBERING

1900	World population about 1.5 billion
1900	Boxer Rebellion in China
1899–1902	Boer War
1901	Discovery of Iranian oil
1904	U.S. policy of intervention in Central America
1904–1905	Russo-Japanese War
1905	First Russian Revolution
1906	Young Turk movement in Ottoman Empire
1907	Great Britain in informal alliance with France and Russia
1910	German military aid to Ottoman Empire
1910	Beginning of Mexican revolution
1911	Fall of Chinese Empire
1914	Opening of Panama Canal

RECOMMENDED READING

Perspectives on Modern World History

*David Landes, *The Wealth and Poverty of Nations* (1998). A forceful analysis (and argument) to explain the West's successful Industrial Revolution.

J. M. Roberts, *Twentieth Century: A History of the World* (1999). A detailed introduction to contemporary world history.

Empires and Nations

*Benedict Anderson, *Imagined Communities: Reflections on the Origin and Spread of Nationalism* (revised edition, 1991). An inquiry into the emergence of nationalism, with special attention to its social-cultural roots.

Raymond Betts, *The False Dawn: European Imperialism in the Nineteenth Century* (1875). A brief but succinct interpretation of the new European colonial empires.

Basil Davidson, *Africa in Modern History: The Search for a New Society* (1978). Study of the impact of European empires on Africa.

*David Headrick, *The Tools of Empire: Technology and European Imperialism in the Nineteenth Century* (1981). A perceptive discussion of the role of new inventions in European colonial expansion; also *The Tentacles of Progress: Technology Transfer in the Age of Imperialism, 1850–1940* (1987), carrying the story into the colonies themselves.

Memoirs and Novels

*Ivo Andric, *The Bridge on the Drina* (1959). Fascinating fictional history of Bosnia, as experienced by a Muslim-Christian community and a 300-year bridge, which brought its peoples together until warring states destroyed it in 1914.

*Joseph Conrad, *Almeyer's Folly* (1895). Sardonic view of Europeans in the East Indies, written by the Western novelist most intrigued by imperialism.

*Rudyard Kipling, *Kim* (1901). The greatest of English colonial novels and a vivid portrait of British India.

___
*Indicates book is available in paperback.

CHAPTER TWO

War and Revolutions, 1914–1930

- War and Peace in Europe
- The Birth of Fascism
- Communist Dictatorship in the Soviet Union
- Revolution in Mexico

Highlight: War and Society

Spotlight: John Reed

The great test of the new empires came in 1914, when a local conflict on the borders of the Austro-Hungarian Empire unexpectedly began a major war among European states. Soon distant Asian empires and then the United States joined in the conflict. At the end of the First World War, several empires in Europe vanished, the victims of war and internal unrest. In the closing years of that war, influential political voices even put in doubt the right of empires to rule colonial peoples—in somewhat timid language by the president of the United States and in violent terms by the leaders of a new revolutionary state in Russia.

Even before war ended in western Europe, a political revolution had begun within the borders of the Russian Empire. The revolutionary changes undertaken by Lenin and his Communist (Bolshevik) Party destroyed, within a few years, the old Russian social and political order. The old institutions of empire were gone. So, too, were the laws, passed during the revolutionary months of 1917, which had laid the foundations for a liberal democracy and a market economy. The Communists anticipated that their revolution would prepare the way for a socialist society in Russia. In those years, their vision of revolutionary transformation extended as well to the entire world.

Revolutionary movements emerged in several countries in those years. European revolutions of the nineteenth century had erupted over issues of democracy and political freedom. Those of the new century brought to the foreground questions of national unity and military glory, most notably in postwar Italy where the term *fascism* first became current. They also involved national unity and social justice, both of which became central features of the Mexican Revolution. The twentieth century was to be an era of social turmoil as well as military conflict.

WAR AND PEACE IN EUROPE

The First World War lasted four years. It was fought in Europe on two major fronts almost until the end. The eastern front pitted German and Austrian forces against the armies of the Russian Empire. Russia's collapse in 1917 brought that fighting to a stop when a new Russian government capitulated. In the West, the fighting continued until the Western Allies had forced Germany to sue for an armistice. The war's terrible damage ensured that Europe's recovery would be slow and painful.

The war's battlefields soon stretched into distant lands. The Ottoman Empire joined the Central Powers to defeat the Russian Empire. It did indirectly succeed, for its blockade on commerce to Russia from the Mediterranean contributed to the internal hardship that led to the Russian Revolution. But the Ottoman Empire had to share in the 1918 defeat of the Central Powers and soon vanished from the map of the Middle East. All the peoples of that region had to rebuild their lives within new states. Even East Asia shared in a small way in the fighting when the Japanese Empire joined the Allies, moving troops to seize German territory in China, and later joining Allied forces sent to Russia to defeat the Communists. That war was international in scope and in impact. Peacemakers attempted to extend their settlement around the world, creating the League of Nations to stop aggressive wars against member states anywhere. Peace, like the war itself, was a global affair.

The Origins of the First World War

Within the largely industrial, partially liberal European world, disturbing signs of conflict had surfaced by the turn of the century. The states of Europe had a long history of war. During the nineteenth century, hostilities had involved few countries and lasted only a short time. By the end of the century this "long peace" was threatened by the very political and economic transformation that had made progress appear so secure. Nationalism appeared to be aggravating antagonism among European peoples. The Industrial Revolution made possible the construction of new, far more effective instruments of war. And the prosperity of the turn of the century gave governments the funds to engage in massive rearmament programs. When new military conflicts erupted, they were fought in ways that observers knew were revolutionizing warfare. The American Civil War had offered European military observers a good opportunity to grasp the changes underway. Until another great war came, however, most army generals never measured the true scale of bloodshed that warfare could extract from nation-states in arms.

The origins of the European conflict lay in unresolved international issues within Europe itself. Relations among the new empires outside the borders of Europe provoked occasional bitter disputes, but all were settled by negotiation. Imperial claims to territory were not essential to the strategic, diplomatic, or economic needs of the European states. These needs defined what diplomats understood as *interests of state* (or *national interests*). The protection of these interests constituted the principal goal of their states' foreign policy.

In the realm of international relations, the independence of these states (their "sovereignty") ensured that their leaders were free to decide what these interests were and how they were to be promoted and defended. No international organization restrained their freedom of action; no effective international law set limits on the use of warfare to resolve conflicts. Certain diplomatic conventions did seek to distinguish between combatants, who might kill and be killed, and civilians, who were theoretically protected from such mayhem on land and on sea. But the responsibility to maintain the peace fell to the leaders of Europe's major powers.

In those circumstances, European diplomats had come to judge the relative strength or weakness of their countries in terms of the *balance of power*, that is, the relative might of their state and allied states as opposed to that of rival countries. Depending on their international ambitions, they might be satisfied with a balance sufficient to deter war or might seek to swing the balance in their favor, by intimidation if not actual war, in order to achieve international gains. None considered war an end in itself. It was the ultimate means that their government or other states might use to attain certain diplomatic objectives. They considered these guidelines to international relations to be the only "realistic" basis for their foreign policies.

By the early twentieth century, the major states of Europe had come together in two antagonistic alliances. The choices of Allies followed from decisions of national interest made in each state. The new German Empire, created in 1871 in a war against France, chose to join forces with the Austro-Hungarian Empire, which was in need of support against rival states (especially Russia) on its southern and eastern borders. This alliance became known as the Central Powers. French leaders, unwilling to accept the loss of its eastern provinces to Germany after 1871, looked for aid to the Russian Empire. Russia, in turn, was prepared to welcome the French alliance to prevent Austria-Hungary and Germany from becoming the dominant powers in the Balkans. Here the conflict lay between the Russian government's goal of preserving a Balkan sphere of influence centered in Serbia, and the Austrian leaders' determination to suppress any separatist efforts by Serbians, from the Serbian state as well as from subjects of the Austrian Empire, which might threaten the unity of their state. Of all the sources of possible war, this one proved decisive.

It was made more likely by the German Empire's unconditional backing of this dangerous Austrian policy. In the beginning of the century, the German emperor, William II, had set his state on what he called a "world policy." By this he meant diplomatic and military efforts to make his country a global power. Germany possessed a highly productive industrial economy and a military leadership more talented than any other European state. Using these assets, German diplomatic and military emissaries established close ties with the Ottoman government, assisting in its rearmament efforts and in the construction of the strategic railroad to the Arabian peninsula.

The German emperor pushed an intensive armaments drive to give his state a navy to rival that of Great Britain and an army capable of overwhelming its potential enemies. This rearmament was to be completed by 1914. By then, German generals had devised a seemingly foolproof military strategy to bring quick victory in the event of European war. Their plan was first to destroy France's armies by an invasion through neutral Belgium and only then to turn their forces against Russia. The German government did not seek war but sought instead global power by using its might in an aggressive manner that included support for Austrian expansion into the Balkans. This policy, called by its critics "power politics" (*machtpolitik*), heightened the risk of war. It also incited the British government to take seriously the likelihood of war with the German Empire.

The British government in the first decades of the century concluded that the principal danger to its imperial interests and strategic defenses was the German Empire's goal of global power and its reliance on power politics to achieve this goal. Germany's ambitious program of a large navy threatened Great Britain's own naval supremacy, and German expansion in the Middle East brought that state close to the Suez Canal and Egypt, already a British protectorate. For these reasons, the British government settled its long-standing grievances with its rivals for empire, Russia and France. Between 1904 and 1914, it quietly put together with them the pieces of an informal alliance against Germany. Both major alliances were defensive in intent. In each case, interests of state dictated the choice of Allies. Still, they became the basis on both sides for war plans intended in case of hostilities to ensure a quick defeat of the rival alliance.

In this tense situation, the event that triggered the war occurred in the city of Sarajevo, capital of the province of Bosnia inhabited both by Muslims and Christians, all speaking the Serbian language. A small group of Serbian nationalists there had organized a secret society called the Black Hand whose goal was union of all Serbs. Political terrorism was their chosen means of action against the Austro-Hungarian Empire, which stood in the way of a "South Slav (Yugoslav)" state. Like other terrorists then and later, they became assassins to publicize their cause and to inspire less committed supporters to participate in their struggle. Few inhabitants of Bosnia were active supporters of their cause. Their terrorism was the desperate, destructive gesture of the weak.

Black Hand's chosen targets for assassination were officials serving the empire. Their best opportunity came in late June 1914, when the Austrian archduke Francis Ferdinand, the heir to the Austrian throne, made a state visit to Sarajevo. Their conspiracy was an amateurish affair that succeeded, after a bomb attack failed, when Gavrilo Princip, a young (18-year-old) member, shot the archduke at point-blank range. They were citizens of the empire, but their loyalties lay with their nationalist cause and their obedience to their terrorist organization. Confrontation was their objective. In this, they succeeded beyond their wildest dreams.

Slightly over a month later, the states in the European alliances were at war. The first move was the decision by the Austrian government, backed by Germany, to end the independence of the Serbian state. The assassination provided Austria with the pretext in late July to declare war on Serbia. Both Austrian and German leaders expected Russia to protest but not to risk war over Serbia. They were only partially correct, for to demonstrate its support for Serbia, the Russian government ordered the mobilization of its army on the western (German and Austrian) frontier. The Russian action was the second step leading to European conflict. The German generals understood only the military implications of Russian mobilization, which threatened to block their own war plans. They convinced their emperor that war was inevitable unless the Russian government stopped its call-up of troops. But the Russian leaders refused to back down. Claiming that Germany was threatened with invasion, the German emperor declared war on the Russian Empire and France. When German troops marched into neutral Belgium in their drive to encircle the French armies, the British government made the momentous decision that its own national security was at risk and joined the conflict on the side of the French. The local

Austrian-Serbian war had become a general European war.

Why had peace in Europe come to an end? The debate over the causes of the First World War began with the first shots and continues to this day. Two general theories have emerged out of the research and interpretations of historians. One places principal responsibility on the conditions that exacerbated international conflict in those years. It points to the aggressive colonial conquests worsening relations among states, to the nationalist hostility dividing peoples of Europe, to the armaments race tempting the best-armed state to prefer war to diplomatic compromise, and to the alliance system creating hostile groups of states. In this perspective, no one state was to blame, for all contributed to the worsening of relations and to the preparations for war. A more persuasive theory isolates specifically the expansionist plans of the German Empire and the dangerous German-Austrian decision in 1914 to destroy Serbia. By identifying aggressive policies implemented by German and Austrian leaders, it holds these governments responsible for the chain of events leading to the outbreak of war.

The events in the weeks and days before general war revealed as well the dangers of power politics to resolve diplomatic conflicts. Political leaders on both sides struggled to resolve the dispute peacefully but used the threat of war to make clear their determination to achieve their objectives. A point was reached when generals demanded the authority to respond to those threats, taking out of the hands of diplomats the decision for war. German and Austrian generals believed war would bring their armies quick victory. Their error was Europe's tragedy. In that sense, the outbreak of the war was an accidental event over which statesmen had lost control. It represented a cautionary tale for political leaders later in the century (including President Kennedy in the Cuban missile crisis of 1962)

seeking to understand how they could avoid unintentionally causing another, even more terrible war.

The European War

The outcome of the great battles in 1914 on the eastern and western fronts frustrated the prewar military plans for quick victory (see map on page 39). All the military offensives failed to attain their objectives. All the armies remained at the end of these battles with sufficient force to continue fighting. Even the little Serbian army succeeded (for a short time) in holding back the Austrian army's campaign to conquer its small border country. Defensive weapons, especially the mobile, rapid-firing cannon and machine guns, proved the real victors. The most accurate image of war by year's end was the deep trenches, where the combatants sought meager protection from massive artillery bombardments and that, ultimately, became graves for millions of soldiers. The loss of human life was enormous, but military leaders everywhere promised that they would soon achieve victory. In the words of one embittered German officer, the First World War became "the grave of nations."

The likelihood of a long war forced war leaders to alter peacetime social and economic practices. Millions of able-bodied men left for the front, many never to return. The acute labor shortage overrode earlier prejudices against women in the economy. Wartime opportunities and patriotic appeals for their help encouraged women to leave their homes to work on the "home front." For many married women, work in factories could not make up for the loss of their husband's income and increased family needs at a time of worsening living conditions. Governments were forced to enact special powers to allocate goods for the war effort and to ensure that the wartime economy functioned as required.

Europe at War, 1914–1918

SPAIN

Triple Entente	
Allies of the Triple Entente	
Central Powers	
Allies of the Central Powers	
Neutral	
Battle Lines	

400 MILES

400 KILOMETERS

ATLANTIC OCEAN

North Sea

UNITED KINGDOM

Yarmouth
London
Dover
Le Havre
Ypres
Arras
Compiègne
Versailles
Paris
Verdun
Toul
Belfort
Geneva
Clermont
Lyons

NORWAY

Christiania
Stockholm
Göteborg

SWEDEN

DENMARK

Copenhagen

NETH.
Amsterdam
Brussels
Liège
Sedan
BELG.
LUX.
Metz
Strasbourg

Kiel Canal

Baltic Sea

Hamburg
Bremen
Berlin
Essen
Cologne
Koblenz
Frankfurt
Mainz
Nuremberg
Munich
Leipzig
Dresden
Prague
Vienna

GERMAN EMPIRE

SILESIA
Breslau
Oder R.
Elbe R.
Danzig
Memel

BOHEMIA
MORAVIA
SLOVAKIA

SWITZ.
Berne

Milan
Turin
Genoa
Marseilles

ITALY
Rome
Naples
Taranto

CORSICA

SARDINIA

SICILY

Mediterranean Sea

FINLAND

Petrograd
(St. Petersburg)

Revel
ESTONIA
LATVIA
LITHUANIA
Katunas
Vilna
Suwalki
Warsaw
Brest-Litovsk
Pinsk
Minsk
Gomel

EAST PRUSSIA

RUSSIA

Moscow

Kharkov
Poltava
Rostov

UKRAINE

Dnepr R.

Kiev

Odessa

Galatz

CRIMEA

Sea of Azov

Black Sea

Constantsa
Varna
Sofia
BULGARIA

ROMANIA
Bucharest
Jassy

TRANSYLVANIA
Hermanstadt
Debrecen
Budapest

AUSTRIA-HUNGARY

Cracow
Lemberg
Corlice

Klagenfurt
Trieste
Fiume
Agram
Sarajevo
Belgrade
Nish

SERBIA
MONTE-NEGRO

ALBANIA
Skopje

GREECE
Gallipoli
1915-1916

Constantinople

OTTOMAN EMPIRE

Angora

CYPRUS

Adriatic Sea

TYROL
Caporetto
Venice

Don R.

FARTHEST GERMAN ADVANCE, SUMMER 1918

SUMMER 1918

DEC., 1917

FARTHEST GERMAN ADVANCE, DEC. 1917

BRUSILOV'S OFFENSIVE AUG., 1916

RUSSIAN FRONT

FARTHEST RUSSIAN ADVANCE, 1914

MAY, 1915

FEB. 1915

SEPT. 1914

WESTERN FRONT

ITALIAN FRONT

BALKAN FRONT

The Western Front: British Raiding Party, July 1917 (*Imperial War Museum/Hoover Institution Archives*)

The results proved satisfactory for the armies, much less so for the working classes. Even Russia's armies were adequately supplied with the necessities of war by 1916. But social conflicts, muted in the early months of the war, returned as the cost of living for the laboring population rose. The price for war production was the decline in the standard of living of the workers. Wage increases lagged behind prices. Farmers preferred to deal in the black market rather than to sell under government regulations. Russia experienced the most serious shortages and, as a consequence, the greatest social unrest. In the winter of 1916–1917, a wave of strikes spread among factory workers in Russian cities. It was sparked partly by food shortages and partly by opposition to the tsarist regime. Female workers, newly recruited to the workforce, took an active part in the movement; they joined in strikes and antiwar demonstrations. In February 1917, women employed in factories in Petrograd (formerly St. Petersburg) went on strike on Women's Day (a special day for the socialist parties of Europe) to demand more food. Their cries of "Give us bread!" attracted the support of other workers. They started the revolution that within two weeks overthrew the Russian Empire.

The failure of war plans to bring quick victory transformed the European conflict into a world war. Battles were fought on sea as well as on land. The British navy quickly took control of the high seas and declared a naval blockade of Germany. German admirals turned to a new arm of naval warfare, the submarine. They counted on this new weapon of war to destroy the British warships and merchant vessels carrying goods to Great Britain and France.

Both the British and the French govern-ments mobilized the labor and the resources of their empires for the war effort. Great Britain declared all colonies and Dominion lands, where the white settlers had received self-government, to be at war with the Cen-tral Powers. Troops from Canada, New Zealand, Australia, and South Africa partici-pated in the battles on the western front and fought in Africa and the Middle East. So, too, did the 1.5 million soldiers of the Indian army. France mobilized one-half million troops from its African and Asian colonies. These multi-ethnic forces constituted visible evidence of the importance of the colonies to the war effort.

The demands placed on colonial peoples produced resistance as well as collaboration. Food and industrial production from the em-pires proved vital to meet war needs but cre-ated serious shortages in the colonies. For the first time, laborers from non-Western lands were needed in the Western economies to re-place the men called to arms. Labor conscrip-tion was imposed on colonial subjects; their reluctance to serve was in places so great it led to open resistance. War demands placed by the Russian Empire on its colonial subjects in Turkestan produced in 1916 a major rebel-lion among settled peoples and nomadic tribes, many of whom fled to China rather than assist the tsarist forces. Similar violence broke out in French West Africa, where a re-volt among African tribes greeted French efforts to mobilize labor brigades.

Both the Allies and the Central Powers en-larged their military alliances. In the fall of 1914, Germany succeeded in bringing the Ot-toman Empire into the war on its side. Ottoman leaders believed the Central Powers would soon win and looked forward to restor-ing their dominance in the Middle East. Their entry into the war opened new fronts against Russia in the region of the Caucasus Moun-tains and against Great Britain in the Middle East near the Suez Canal. The Allies, in turn, were able in 1915 to obtain the support of Italy, whose leaders hoped to conquer territory from Austria-Hungary along the Adriatic Sea. That same year, the Japanese government joined the Allies, declaring war on Germany. It immediately seized German-controlled territory in China and forced the Chinese government to grant it special economic priv-ileges in northern China. Japan found in wartime conditions new possibilities to ex-pand its empire in China. The world war brought into play for the first time a global balance of power.

Governments undertook secret as well as public propaganda efforts to foment conflict within the enemy camp. The German state gave secret financial backing to Russian anti-war revolutionary parties, including Lenin's Communist Party. The Allies for their part aided nationalist parties among Austria-Hungary's minority peoples. Their propa-ganda war had its greatest impact in the Ottoman Empire. In 1915, exiled Armenian nationalists in Russia called on Armenians in eastern Anatolia to rebel against the Ottoman Empire. In retaliation, Ottoman authorities forcibly evacuated 1.7 million Armenians from there, to be settled in Middle Eastern camps. In the course of this violent operation, the Turks were responsible for the death of over a half-million Armenians. These Armen-ian massacres set a pattern, repeated many times later in the century, of mass persecution in wartime motivated by ethnic hatred.

The British government turned the hope of national homelands in the Middle East into a weapon to win the backing of minority peo-ples living in the Ottoman Empire. It sup-ported a national uprising among the Bedouin tribes of Arabia, promising that their victory would lead to an Arab state in the Middle East. The most famous agent in this campaign was the British officer T. E. Lawrence. Bedouin irregular cavalry forces, headed by the Hashemite clan under Hussein Ibn Ali (see "Spotlight," Chapter 3), fought for two years against the Ottomans alongside regular British forces.

At the same time, the British government promised unrestricted migration of Jewish settlers into Palestine. Millions of Jews in eastern Europe had long been the victims of oppression, for anti-Semitism—hatred of the Jews—had a long history in this area where most of the world's Jews lived. Their communities lived an isolated existence, speaking a German dialect (Yiddish) and keeping strictly to religious practices. Only a few Jews had broken out of these communities to obtain a modern education, and even they suffered from laws that limited severely their rights as citizens. One of these emancipated Jews, Theodore Herzl, founded in 1897 a movement to create a Jewish national homeland. It was a national endeavor, for he viewed his fellow Jews as a distinct national community. He called it the World Zionist Organization to make clear that the Jewish homeland had to be in Palestine (the Biblical Zion). He argued that only in that land, from which the Jews had been expelled 2,000 years before, would they be safe from persecution. Palestine was at that time a province of the Ottoman Empire, ruled by Muslim Turks and inhabited almost entirely by Arab-speaking Muslims and Christians. A few Jewish pioneers settled in that region before 1914, but both the Ottoman government and the Arab inhabitants of the region viewed them with suspicion. Until the war began, the Zionist goal of a Jewish national homeland in Palestine seemed an impossible dream.

The British need for wartime allies changed all that. The British government included the Jews of Europe in their propaganda war to mobilize support. After lengthy discussions with Zionist leaders, in 1917 it issued the Balfour Declaration, which made a public commitment for "the establishment in Palestine of a national home for the Jewish people." It did promise to protect the civil and religious rights of the "existing non-Jewish communities," but the declaration's effect was to allow free Jewish immigration to Palestine. In return, the British counted on the backing for their war effort from Jewish leaders and peoples throughout Europe and the United States. But there was a problem. Encouraging both Arab and Jewish dreams of Middle Eastern lands of their own was an inconsistent policy with potentially explosive consequences. At the time, the British leaders placed victory in war above all other considerations.

The confrontation in Europe between the Central Powers and the Allies remained the key to the outcome of the war. The Central Powers achieved their greatest victories on the eastern front. The Russian Empire lacked competent leadership, and its war resources could not match those of the German Empire. In 1915, German armies pushed Russian forces hundreds of miles into the interior of Russia, causing more than 1 million Russian casualties. This victory did not force the Russian Empire to capitulate, but it did heighten political and social opposition to the regime of Emperor Nicholas II. By the winter of 1917, hostility toward the government's conduct of the war had spread throughout the population of the empire, including even the generals in the army. In March 1917 (February by the calendar then in use in Russia), a wave of strikes protesting shortages quickly turned into political demonstrations under banners calling for the overthrow of the monarchy. When Nicholas II ordered his army to repress the uprising, the Petrograd garrison troops mutinied and joined the demonstrators. Even the emperor's own generals chose to support the revolution rather than to protect a monarch in whom they had lost all confidence. Nicholas had to abdicate; the Russian Empire had fallen.

In this political revolution, the war proved crucial in deciding who would in the end take control of Russia. Soldiers in the army and workers from the factories were both disillusioned with the sacrifices demanded by the war. Most political leaders refused a policy of capitulation to Germany. Instead they demanded that the people accept the hardships of war until German forces were driven from Russia. Only the radical socialist movement under the leadership of Vladimir Lenin was prepared to offer the population "peace, bread, and land." That November, the Bolshevik Party (which changed its name in 1918 to the Communist Party) ordered its supporters to seize power by armed insurrection. It was a reckless act, for the party had few adherents and the country already was headed toward economic chaos. The first action of Lenin's regime was to declare an armistice along the entire eastern front and to begin peace negotiations with the Central Powers.

In response, the German military leaders demanded a peace of capitulation. Their terms included the occupation by their armies of all the eastern territories that they had conquered. They also demanded Russian recognition of a new eastern European state, Ukraine. Its peoples had for centuries lived within the Russian Empire. Ukrainian nationalists had taken advantage of the empire's collapse to form their own nation-state under German protection. In March 1918, Lenin had to accept these terms. By then, the Russian army had ceased to exist as a fighting force. The Treaty of Brest-Litovsk reduced the size of the new revolutionary state to the old northern lands of seventeenth-century Muscovite Russia. It made the German Empire the

dominant power in eastern Europe. The Central Powers had achieved their greatest triumph in the war. Their negotiators at Brest-Litovsk had allowed the Communists to hold onto power a little longer, but it seemed a worthwhile risk. They expected a quick victory to follow on the western front, ending the war.

Allied Victory

Instead of German victory, that November the Allies were victorious. The reason for this sudden reversal of fortunes was the presence alongside the French and British forces of a new ally, the United States. Without massive American military supplies followed by hundreds of thousands of fresh troops from overseas, the German Empire would probably have won the struggle for mastery in Europe. With them, the tide of battle changed and so, too, did the diplomatic aims of the Allies. For the first time in its history, the United States became an important actor in deciding the outcome of a foreign war and the shape of the peace to follow.

U.S. involvement in the war began first as a result of economic trade binding America to the Allies. It was propelled forward by the objectives pursued by the new U.S. president, Woodrow Wilson. Nominated for the 1912 elections by the Democratic Party on a reform platform, his program held out an optimistic vision of economic opportunity and political freedom. It won him the presidency that year. When war came to Europe two years later, his emphasis on business interest incited him to protect U.S. foreign trade, crucial for the country's recovery from a recent recession. His democratic ideals convinced him that the United States ought to defend the principles of freedom and the rule of law in the world at large. This vision informed his explanation to the American public why he chose to declare war on the Central Powers in 1917. It also explains why Americans so quickly became disillusioned after the war's end with a world that he had promised would be "safe for democracy."

The outbreak of the First World War ended the isolation of the United States from European affairs. Wilson's first response was to proclaim U.S. neutrality in the conflict. He urged Americans to be "neutral in fact as well as in name, impartial in thought as well as in action." Noninvolvement was difficult to maintain, but for three years he managed to keep the United States out of the conflict. He feared the destructive effects of war on the American political system, warning that entry into the European war would force the government "to take such measures of defense which would be fatal to our form of Government and American ideals." He sincerely hoped that he could mediate an end to the war, offering in December 1916 a plan for "peace without victors" that would end the "struggle for a new balance of power" and "entangling alliances." In their place, he proposed a "concert of power." His proposal failed, for neither side was ready for compromise. But these ideas later became the foundation of his peace plans for postwar Europe.

Despite his efforts to defend U.S. neutrality, Wilson faced the reality of the demand for American goods by the Allies. France and Great Britain took full advantage of the U.S. market and placed enormous orders for food, clothing, and munitions. By 1915, both states had exhausted their own funds and needed U.S. loans to purchase more war goods. Wilson hesitated, for he realized that his approval of the loans was not in the spirit of neutrality. But refusal would amount to support of the Central Powers, for whom Wilson had no sympathy. In addition, the U.S. economy was

just emerging from a serious recession. Farmers, businessmen, and labor leaders all looked to foreign sales to speed the recovery. Wilson approved the loans. The result was that, by 1916, U.S. trade to the Allies had increased four times and the American economy boomed. Complete U.S. neutrality in the war was impossible.

The immediate cause of U.S. entry into the war was the German submarine blockade of the British Isles. Commanders of the German navy ordered a total blockade to begin in February 1917. That decision permitted German submarines to attack and sink even vessels of neutral countries. They had made the wildly optimistic promise to the German government that their fleet of 200 submarines could strangle the British economy and force Great Britain to capitulate. They acknowledged that neutral shipping, including U.S. vessels, would be sunk and that this action would be a legitimate reason for a U.S. declaration of war. But they were confident German victory would come long before U.S. forces could reach Europe. It was a fatal blunder.

That naval blockade was the decisive factor behind Wilson's decision for war. In the spring of 1917, one of every four freighters headed for British ports was sunk by German torpedoes. Among them were U.S. ships. Wilson probably considered the German Empire's efforts to achieve global power a real threat to U.S. security. Still, his convictions and his need to persuade the American public to support his action led him to explain the U.S. declaration of war as a moral issue. In April 1917, Wilson asked Congress to declare war on the Central Powers. He condemned German "warfare against mankind" and pledged that the United States was not fighting for "conquest or domination" but rather for "the ultimate peace of the world and for the liberation of its peoples. The world must be made safe for democracy." His speech presented the war in terms of an idealistic plan for political progress and international peace.

Before Wilson could implement his peace plan, the Allies had to defeat the Central Powers. Their first achievement was defeating the German submarine blockade. By late 1917, the combined forces of the British and U.S. navies had cut shipping losses in half. When the time came to send U.S. troops to Europe, not one troop ship was sunk. An entire year elapsed, however, before the army was prepared to fight in France. Finally, in the summer of 1918, hundreds of thousands of U.S. infantry began arriving every month on the continent. By that fall they formed a separate armed force of 1 million troops. Their presence destroyed the last German hope of victory on the western front.

The military collapse of the Central Powers came that summer and fall. Outnumbered and increasingly demoralized, German troops began a steady, uninterrupted retreat across France and Belgium. Small Allied armies in northern Italy and Greece broke through Austrian defenses that fall. At the same time, British and Arab forces in the Middle East advanced through Palestine to the city of Damascus. By late October, the Central Powers ceased to exist as a military alliance. The Austrian armies broke up into units of the various nationalities of the empire, each prepared to protect its own national territory. The empire quickly fell apart, paving the way for the creation of new nation-states in southeastern Europe. Close to victory that spring, in the fall of 1918 the Central Powers were headed toward defeat and revolutionary chaos. In October the German government asked for an armistice.

The terms of armistice and the plans for peace came principally from the United States. President Wilson's radical plan for a "peace without victors" appealed to an enormous audience in Europe. As important, the economic and military might of the United States forced even those European politicians who were skeptical of Wilson's vision to heed his pronouncements. His principal statement of war aims came in the Fourteen Points presented in January 1918. Three points were central to Wilson's plan: national self-determination for all European peoples, democratic governments, and the creation of an international association of states to protect the peace. Wilson placed the prestige and the power of the United States behind liberalism and internationalism.

Victory on Wilson's terms came in early November. On November 11, 1918, the armistice went into effect. The Middle Eastern lands of the Ottoman Empire were in the hands of Arab rebels and Allied armies. The German and Austrian emperors abdicated and their empires collapsed. Nationalist leaders of the Slavic peoples in lands previously controlled by Germany and Austria-Hungary proclaimed in late October the formation of the nation-states of Poland, Czechoslovakia, and Yugoslavia.

After four years of bloody fighting, the shape of the postwar world to come was much less real than the destruction of the old, prewar life. The casualties of battle, numbering everywhere in the millions, were concentrated among draft-age men. The war resulted in 10 million deaths and another 20 million wounded. No one could anticipate what would be the fate of the territory of the former Russian Empire, where a brutal civil war was already underway between the Communists and their enemies. War and revolution were radically altering the course of human history.

● HIGHLIGHT: War and Society ●

When the Russian Eugene Zamiatin wrote his novel *We* in 1920, he imagined a city that had survived 200 years of war. Called the United State, it is ruled by the Benefactor and his Guardians and is dedicated to bringing Happiness to everyone. They have decreed that individuality impedes the attainment of the good of all; personal needs and emotions have to be subordinated to Reason, on which they have the monopoly. Dissent is unknown because it is unreasonable. Numbers replace peoples' names. Unavoidable sexual needs are satisfied by the use of tickets that permit couples a brief moment together at prescribed intervals. Beyond the Green Wall surrounding the city live the plants and animals, survivors of the long war, existing in a primitive state of anarchic liberty. No one goes there, for it would disturb public order. The hero of Zamiatin's novel, D-503, dreams for a short time of personal love and individual freedom of thought, but he is quickly cured of his illness. "We" triumphs over "I."

Zamiatin's tale was a message of destruction in the name of progress. It is the first of several twentieth-century stories warning of a nightmarish future; these include George Orwell's *1984* (1948) and Ray Bradbury's *Fahrenheit 451* (1953). These novels are called "anti-utopian," for they warn against ideological promises of future happiness for all (such as those made by the Soviet leaders). They portray instead a grim future in which ruthless forces trample on what is most precious to people—their own individual self and the freedom that nurtures it.

Zamiatin's warning came after he had lived through three years of communist rule in the midst of civil war and after the four long years

of Russian involvement in the First World War. The plans put forward by the new revolutionary regime promised progress to society by making class interests decisive. Zamiatin was concerned about the fundamental issue of people so stripped of self-knowledge that they become the willing accomplices in denying individual rights for the sake of an imagined collective good. His portrait of that society is intentionally very exaggerated. The issue, in a much milder form, was one that faced the West as total war and revolutions increased the powers of the state over the individual to a degree never dreamed of in earlier times.

The key wartime policy justifying the intrusion of the state into the lives of its citizens was the mobilization of all resources needed for the war effort. The justification for the collaboration of citizens in this process was patriotic duty. Before the First World War, young men in most Western countries were subject to conscription into the army. They gave up two or three years of civilian life to learn the skills of war before returning to their homes, still subject for many years to be called back to the army in the event of war. Conscription was a complex administrative process, but the practice of conducting regular censuses of the population gave the authorities the means to tabulate and record the needed information. In the short wars of the nineteenth century, no more was needed.

The First World War changed all that. The demands on the population increased enormously. The draft called up all able-bodied men, expected to serve if possible until war's end; shirking one's military duty was treasonous. The public calls for service quickly extended to women. They had to step into jobs that were left empty by the draftees. There was no suggestion that they should be spared dangerous work such as munitions manufacturing. Concerns for individual health had to take second place to the well-being of the war effort. The term *home-front* placed their work on a par with that of the men on the front lines. In all the Western countries engaged in the war, distinctions between public duty and personal choice became blurred as the war dragged on and more and more men left for the war, many never to return.

The mobilization extended beyond human resources to the material resources necessary to continue a war that consumed enormous amount of goods as well as human lives. Decisions about industrial and agricultural production and consumption had previously been the affair of companies and individuals. The movement of prices and the lure of profits were crucial in determining what was produced and what was consumed. The war changed that too.

Governments became directly involved in the economic life of their countries. They fixed prices, allocated scarce resources to industry, and distributed goods by rationing. Special agencies were responsible to oversee and, if necessary, to control crucial economic activities. In the United States, the federal government took charge of railroad transportation to make sure that troops and munitions were moving across the country when needed at the port locations for rapid shipment at Europe. It even set up a Fuel Administration to oversee allocation of scarce coal supplies, and an Oil Division to make certain that this precious commodity was available to military transport and to the navy. In the Russian Empire, fears that food would prove inadequate for the army and for the urban population led to a decree in 1916 establishing a "food monopoly." By its regulations (which the administration proved unable to enforce), peasant farmers had to make deliveries in specified amounts and receive from the purchasers a specified price. In theory, price controls and purchasing orders would ensure that no one went hungry. It did not work but did set an example that the Communists later followed.

Germany confronted the most serious shortages and introduced the most rigorous state economic controls. One German industrialist concluded that his country's wartime state intervention in economic affairs had been "an education in state socialism." The old laissez-faire economic principles, by which government had no business interfering in the market economy, were without force in the midst of the Great War.

The war brought strict censorship and stern punishment for those suspected of disloyalty. Newspapers were no longer free to publish what they pleased. A charge of treason was the punishment for individuals whose actions undermined the war effort. In the United States, the accusation was applied so loosely that, in the 1918 Espionage Act, the protections offered the population under the Bill of Rights were temporarily abandoned to allow arbitrary arrest and detention of anyone suspected of disloyalty.

The First World War was the first conflict in which governments, and peoples, thought to place the label of disloyalty on entire groups of the civilian population. In some Allied countries, the outbreak of war had brought riots directed against Germany, during which even businesses and individuals identified with Germans were liable to be attacked. The Russian High Command went much further. In 1914, it issued a decree that consigned the empire's German inhabitants in cities and in the countryside near the front lines to the category of "enemy alien." They were forcibly deported to interior regions of the empire. Russia's military authorities dealt in a similarly brutal manner with the Jewish population in the western regions during the Russian armies' retreat in 1915. They ordered this "pernicious" people out of their villages and left them to fend for themselves as refugees far to the east. Their policy of assigning collective guilt to an entire ethnic group prefigured the process of ethnic punishment and ethnic cleansing that swept other regions of the world later in the century.

The end of the war brought to a close in almost all belligerent countries these intrusive population policies. Constitutions and rule of law reasserted themselves, the free market replaced "state socialism," and wartime patriotic fervor died away. Yet the war made a profound impact on some countries where wartime deaths had devastated the population. France had suffered the worst in this respect. The missing men left behind great numbers of war widows and other single women in a country whose birth rate was already so low France seemed destined to depopulation. To political leaders in 1920, the answer had to be legislation to promote as many births as possible. Their new idea took the shape of a law placing severe restrictions on any form of publicity encouraging the use of abortion or contraceptive devices. It was not an impressive pronatalist initiative. Its focus on abortion was especially ill-chosen, since it picked women to be the particular target for its restrictive call. In later decades, more effective and less intrusive measures offered financial and social assistance to large families; other European countries adopted similar measures. The state had entered, one way or another, into the affairs of the bedroom.

In the Soviet Union, then in Fascist Italy, and later in Nazi Germany, the war's encouragement to state action did set a pattern for state intervention in public life with much greater impact than anything attempted during wartime. In the 1920s, the Italian Fascists boasted, though with much exaggeration, that their regime was "totalitarian" in its domination of society. In the Soviet Union, the very basis for revolutionary action was grounded on the assumption that the collective label of class identified friends and enemies, patriots and traitors. The civil war witnessed for the first time massive arrests undertaken by the Soviet secret police solely on the basis of peoples' origins as members of propertied or privileged classes. Similar class labels worked with even more devastating effect during the First Five Year Plan period of agricultural collectivization. The alleged hostility of peasant *kulaks*, a term used to identify well-to-do peasants, justified the introduction of repressive policies of class warfare called the "liquidation of the kulaks as a class." In its brutality and scope, it was a first step toward the Great Terror of the late 1930s.

In Nazi Germany, population policy was openly racist. The state arrogated for itself the decision of who should be labeled Aryan and who should be labeled Jewish. The former population was worthy and deserving of reproduction, the latter subhuman and in need of elimination. Nazi leaders, like the Communists, claimed for themselves the absolute knowledge of what was good for the people of their countries and built around that knowledge dictatorial regimes. Their supporters were persuaded that collective (racial or class) labeling was sufficient to know who belonged in their state. The "we" whom Zamiatin had warned of had taken control. It proved a tragedy for their countries.

"The Home Front:" Royal Shell Factory, England (*Imperial War Museum/Hoover Institution Archives*)

THE BIRTH OF FASCISM

The end to the war did not prove the triumph for democracy that Wilson had hoped for. The war had roused nationalist passions throughout Europe. For some veterans and political leaders, it was a lesson in militarism and violence, justified by the need to enhance their nation's might and glory. The postwar period was a time to put these new skills and convictions to the test by remaking their nation-states in a militant, authoritarian model. One group in Germany called itself the National-Socialist Workers' Party, led by a war veteran named Adolf Hitler. The most successful was Italy's Fascist Party, led by another war veteran named Benito Mussolini. There the war left in its wake a political crisis so profound that democratic methods proved incapable of resisting the Fascist drive to seize power.

Mussolini and Italian Fascism

Mussolini was the founder of Italian fascism and the inspiration of fascist movements in other European countries. He was a skillful political demagogue, who turned Italian political life into an arena of violent struggle and, ultimately, dictatorship. In the prewar years an antiwar socialist, the war had transformed him into a fanatical nationalist. He had fought in the Italian army. The experience marked his personality and defined his political philosophy. Demobilized after being wounded, he launched a political movement intended to carry the ruthlessness he had learned as a front-line soldier into civilian life. His choice was followed by many other war veterans in Italy and elsewhere in Europe. One German veteran made clear what others believed when he dismissed "those people who told us the war was over." For him, fighting had become his way of life, for "we are the war. It fascinates us with the enticing urge to destroy" those "traitors" and "Bolsheviks" who threatened the nation. The war provided Mussolini, as it did Hitler, with schooling for political combat on the national stage.

Joined by other disillusioned war veterans, Mussolini preached a message of militaristic renewal of the Italian nation. He called for the expulsion of the "corrupt" politicians from government, the end of labor strikes and agitation, and the defeat of the "subversive, internationalist" Communists and Socialists. He scorned the ideal of liberty, preferring "discipline" for the Italian nation. In place of a parliamentary regime, he proposed a strong state purged of all democratic parties under a strong leader. Fascism in its original Italian version was more a set of nationalist slogans and images of masculine valor and violence than a clear doctrine. Mussolini's fertile imagination and talent as a demagogic orator persuaded many Italians that they were a people with a glorious, heroic past, which he projected all the way back to the Roman Empire. He promised to revive that past. In this way, he manipulated ideas of Italian history and ethnic nationalism. Fascism constituted a vague political ideology for nationalist dicta-

torship, turning the spirit of war into a revolutionary creed.

To defeat his political enemies, Mussolini organized a new type of combat party, the *Fasci di combattimento* (Groups of Combat). From the term *fasci* came the name of his party. The elite of the movement were the "fighters," a paramilitary organization dressed in black shirts with heavy belt buckles useful in street fighting against Communists, labor leaders, and other groups they accused of undermining the strength of the nation. Mussolini glorified war and combat as the true test of a man and of a nation. He cared not at all that his party never won more than 15 percent of the vote in free elections. He believed that he and his followers demonstrated their fitness to lead the nation, not by popularity, but by determination and struggle. In place of a concrete political program, his movement used emotional appeals to national unity, warnings of communist subversion, and attacks on the incompetence and corruption of Italian liberals and the democratic system itself.

Mussolini turned the internal weakness of the Italian state to his advantage in his plan to seize power. For several years after the war, his followers recruited Italians discontented with postwar conditions and eager for radical changes. Italy, like other European countries after the war, seethed with political conflict and strikes largely resulting from disappointment at the failure of reckless wartime promises for social reform and national unity. His Black Shirts fought street battles in Italy's major cities and succeeded here and there in taking control of town government. Some business leaders gave Mussolini financial aid in the belief that the Fascists were useful to repress labor unions and parties that threatened their property holdings and financial interests. The great appeal of Italian fascism lay in its glorification of national unity and its promise to end social discord. The message was attractive to many Italians in the crisis that gripped their country in the years after the end of the First World War.

Mussolini became a national political figure in those years, eager to seize power to put his revolutionary program into action. In October 1922, he ordered his fighting squads to "march on Rome" to overthrow the democratically elected government. His action was largely a bluff, for troops and police forces could easily have dispersed his squads. He counted mainly on the reluctance of the authorities to use force, and he was right. Before his squads reached the capital, the king invited him to become prime minister of the Italian cabinet. He began his rule as the legal head of government.

The Fascist State

Within three years, the democratic Italian nation-state had ceased to exist. Political opponents were intimidated by the Fascists' threats of violence, others were attacked, and some were murdered. Soon Mussolini banned political parties and closed the free press. He placed labor unions under the direct control of the state and outlawed strikes. Although no social or economic revolution occurred, the new regime was radical in its destruction of human rights and democratic government. It promised to ensure the welfare of the people thanks to what it boasted was its "totalitarian" power over society.

Mussolini turned his country into a single-party dictatorship, controlled by the Fascist Party under his absolute control. He encouraged the cult of his leadership and was extolled by his followers as "divine Caesar" and "sublime redeemer in the Roman heavens." Taking the Roman emperors as his model, Mussolini promised Italians that the Fascists would create a new empire as glorious as that of the Romans. For years, these vows remained empty words. The Italian colonial empire

Fascism on Parade: Italian Women's Fascist Group (*Dorothy Thompson Collection/Hoover Institution Archives*)

consisted of an impoverished nomadic population in the desert of Libya. But Mussolini's pompous words and deeds struck a powerful chord later among some European peoples when depression struck. Out of the experience of war and the postwar crisis, he had fashioned a nationalist movement unlike any that had ever existed. Nationalism in its radical fascist form became a revolutionary creed that condemned democracy and glorified war.

COMMUNIST DICTATORSHIP IN THE SOVIET UNION

In Russia, the First World War produced a revolution of a very different type. The fall of the Russian Empire in March 1917 was the result largely of hardship inflicted on the population and of the disillusionment with the emperor's wartime leadership. But new leaders failed in their efforts to keep the country in the war, unable to stop the disintegration of the army and the collapse of the economy. In those conditions of chaos, Lenin's Communist Party was able to seize power in November.

It abruptly stopped the country's halting efforts to adopt Western liberal political and economic institutions. The new revolutionary government defied Russian patriots and Western Allies alike by signing a separate peace treaty with Germany. Enemies of the Communists united in 1918 to fight the new regime in a bloody civil war. In the course of the three years of fighting, peasants took up arms to seize the property of landlords, workers expelled industrialists from their factories and prosperous urban families from their homes, and nationalist movements fought to create nation-states for peoples previously under Russian imperial rule. The fighting that had begun with the First World War carried on during the civil war until the country was in ruins.

In that war, the leaders of the Communist Party forged the instruments of power that permitted the new Soviet state to survive. It was

the key to the triumph of the revolutionary regime. It imposed a new ideological blueprint on Russia and later served as a model for revolutionary movements in other countries. It provided the world the first example of an attempt to create a socialist society for humanity. Like the Fascist Party in Italy, it demonstrated how a small group of political militants could change the course of history.

Lenin and the Communist Revolution

Vladimir Lenin, the undisputed leader of the Communist Party, had in the years before 1917 created a unique radical revolutionary party. He and his followers shared with other socialist movements in Europe the belief that the theories of Karl Marx made clear the reasons for the oppression that humanity had endured over the millennia. They drew from Marx's theories the conviction that history would necessarily end with the triumph of a classless society that satisfied the needs and desires of humanity. Lenin differed from other socialists in arguing that only his party possessed the knowledge and organization to lead the revolution of the masses. When the First World War erupted, Lenin went one step further in predicting that the war had brought the entire Western capitalist world to the brink of revolution. To their political enemies, the Communists appeared a dangerous group of fanatics. After the fall of the empire in early 1917, they appeared to an increasingly large number of Russians a dynamic, disciplined movement capable of leading the country out of its crisis and of creating a just, egalitarian society.

Lenin drew his inspiration directly from Marxism. Its fundamental principles were crucial to his revolutionary hopes. Marx's theories convinced him that the ownership of productive property was not only responsible for wealth and poverty but also determined who controlled the repressive powers of the state. In nineteenth-century Europe, capitalism gave power to the property owners (the "bourgeoisie") responsible for the technological wonders and the productivity of the industrial economy. It also created a vast population of workers without property, the "proletariat," who were deprived of the benefits of this economic system and of the political might to alter this system. Marx argued that workers everywhere would come to realize the necessity of overthrowing capitalism. Marxism gave the Communists a global view of capitalism and class conflict. It convinced Lenin in 1917 that his struggle to seize power in Russia would create the conditions for the collapse of capitalism throughout the Western world.

The Communists were convinced that Marx's theory of violent historical progress should guide their own plans for rule. Marx affirmed that capitalism, like feudalism before it, was fated to collapse in a violent revolution. In its place, the working masses would move rapidly through a stage of the "dictatorship of the proletariat" in a socialist society (with collective control of the means of production) to finally reach the ultimate egalitarian, communist society guaranteeing everyone a satisfactory life. Wealth would be shared following the simple formula: "From each according to their abilities, to each according to their needs." This conviction that a perfect society can be created on earth is called *utopianism.*

Lenin and other Communists like Leon Trotsky were in a hurry to succeed in this historic undertaking. They argued that a "permanent revolution" would carry backward Russia, under their leadership, straight to socialism. To the Communists, this faith justified all the hardships and all the brutality that accompanied their revolutionary crusade to transform Russia.

Their seizure of power in November 1917 came with the support of large numbers of Russia's lower classes. Key to their victory was the backing of workers and mutinous soldiers. In the course of 1917, both groups had organized their own revolutionary assemblies, called by the Russian name of "soviets." In 1917, Lenin's slogan "All Power to the Soviets" was a call for insurrection against parliamentary democracy. On November 7 (October 25 by the Russian calendar), Lenin's forces overthrew the liberal "provisional" government that had briefly ruled Russia after the collapse earlier that year of the tsarist empire. In its place, they founded a revolutionary state they called the "Russian Soviet Socialist Republic." John Reed, an American journalist who had traveled to Russia to support their movement, termed that upheaval "ten days that shook the world." His colorful language was really wishful thinking, for the rest of the world went its own way. Still, the new regime possessed a powerful ideology that gave its leaders, and the followers who came from distant lands such as Reed, the faith necessary to sustain them through the terrible civil war to come.

The Communist State and Civil War

The new regime made bitter enemies within Russia and in the West. Opponents came from all sides. Russian patriots condemned their "sell-out" to the Central Powers in signing a peace of capitulation in early 1918. Liberals warned of their ruthless dictatorship. Peasant farmers fought back when the Communists seized their crops to feed workers and their new revolutionary Red Army. Nationalists from the borderlands of the former empire mobilized their meager forces to resist conquest of their peoples by the Communists.

These opponents were aided by Russia's former wartime allies. The Communists had broken all the ties that had bound Russia to the West. Lenin's regime abandoned the wartime alliance to make peace with the

Central Powers. It canceled the entire Russian foreign debt, totaling several billion dollars, owed largely to Western states and investors. Its acts of defiance gave meaning to its appeal for international socialist revolution. Its very existence challenged the international order that the Allies sought to create following victory over Germany.

By mid-1918, Russia was in the grips of a bitter civil war. The Soviet government lost control of large parts of the country, seized by anticommunist "White" forces intent on overthrowing the revolutionary state. Lenin responded by refashioning his regime into a warfare state. The country's resources had to be mobilized for war to destroy the "counter-revolution." The tsar and his family, state prisoners in the distant Ural Mountains, became victims in this cruel war. In mid-1918, Lenin or-

dered their execution to avoid the risk that they might escape to the Whites. Lenin described his state as a "fortress besieged by world capital" and demanded that it become "a single military camp." His new Red Army grew to 5 million men; a new secret police received the authority to imprison and execute political enemies branded "counter-revolutionaries" and "class enemies." To provide the necessary supplies for the army, an economic policy went into effect that included nationalization (i.e., state ownership) of industry and commerce.

The struggle to win the civil war had a permanent impact on the new regime, for it put in place the basic institutions of communist dictatorship and trained communist militants in the ruthless methods of class war. All political parties except the Communist Party were banned, their supporters jailed or forced

Lenin Addressing Soldiers of the Red Army, 1919 (*Corbis-Bettmann*)

to flee the country. Government policy making and appointments were under the control of the central leadership in a new Communist Party committee, the Politburo. There Lenin and his close advisers such as Leon Trotsky and Joseph Stalin made the decisions that determined the survival of their new state. Their Soviet government, called the Council of People's Commissars, carried out these policies, for its members were all party leaders. Their remarkable leadership ability and the backing of zealous party members were the key factors in the defeat of the anticommunist forces in the civil war. Allied arms and financial aid could not compensate for the incompetence and disorganization of the Whites. In 1920, the Red Army was victorious in most of the areas once part of the Russian Empire.

The Soviet Union and Its Peoples

The end of the Russian civil war left the country in a state of economic collapse. Its population was poverty-stricken, epidemic diseases raged among millions of people with little or no medical care, and large cities had become ghost towns after townspeople fled to the countryside in search of food. No one knows how many died in the fighting or as a result of disease and famine. Industrial production fell to one-fourth of prewar levels. In 1920–1921, crop failure in large parts of the country led to famine among the peasant population. The country could not continue living in such terrible conditions.

Communist dictatorship remained the foundation of the new regime. Still, economic ruin and social unrest forced the Soviet government to temporarily abandon policies (now called "War Communism") that it had believed would immediately create a socialist society. In 1921, the government had to permit private ownership of farm land and small businesses to speed the recovery of the economy, baptizing its concessions to a market economy a "New Economic Policy." It permitted churches to reopen (temporarily) and allowed limited freedom of the press. Government leaders even welcomed foreign industrialists (including the Ford Motor Company) to help rebuild their ruined factories and to train their engineers and workers in modern methods of production. The concessions were distasteful, but they in no way weakened the dictatorship of the Communist Party.

The Communists also had to take account of massive backing among the non-Russian peoples of their multi-ethnic country for national independence. In the course of the civil war, nationalists in some of these areas had created independent nation-states, often under the protection of the Western powers. Ukraine and Finland had received the support of Germany until 1919; small states on the eastern shores of the Baltic Sea (Estonia, Latvia, and Lithuania) were protected by Great Britain; small nation-states in the Caucasus and (Armenia, Georgia, and Azerbaijan) struggled largely on their own to survive. By 1920, the Western Allies had withdrawn their military forces from Russian borderlands, leaving only the British fleet in the Baltic as protection for the new states there. Finally, in 1922 the Japanese government ordered its army out of eastern Siberia. No foreign troops threatened the revolutionary regime.

The Soviet government did, in fact, seize those borderlands where it faced little risk of war with the West. The Red Army brought Soviet power on the point of its bayonets to Ukraine, the Caucasus lands, and the central Asian territories north of Iran and Afghanistan. In the south and the east, the frontiers of the Soviet state resembled those of the Russian Empire.

These ethnically diverse peoples presented the Communists with a serious dilemma. The Marxist revolutionary scenario had assumed that the working masses in a new socialist society were largely factory workers shaped by industrialism and ready to renounce pernicious nationalist passions. Russia and Ukraine had, by 1917, a sizable working class; nowhere else, however, within the new state had industrialization made a significant impact. In these terms, the Soviet peoples were largely backward. Yet in many areas nationalist movements had still won sizable support.

In these circumstances, Lenin and his followers had to rethink their views of nationalism. They came to the radically new conclusion that their revolutionary plans had to include recognition of distinct national communities, whose identities as separate peoples appeared (and then disappeared) as part of the historically determined progress of humanity toward communist society. They decided to accord to the various peoples special (political) recognition in a new federal constitution. Adopted in 1924, it created the Union of Soviet Socialist Republics (U.S.S.R., or Soviet Union). Separate national republics grouped the major peoples of the country, who received their own Soviet "republican" government. Ultimately they numbered fifteen, including Soviet Russia, Soviet Ukraine, Soviet Armenia, Soviet Azerbaijan, and Soviet Kazakhstan. Within these lands, minority ethnic groups were granted small, "autonomous" territories where they too had their own administration, schools, and officially recognized language.

This bizarre (and in the event irreversible) acknowledgment of ethnic communities created a constitutional order in the Soviet Union based on "native" lands (called "ethno-territorial" areas) for each of its peoples. The vast area inhabited mainly by Russian-speaking people was only one of many "ethno-territorial" units. The Communists reconciled themselves to this compromise in the short term, since their leaders in Moscow made all-important decisions for the entire country, and their party followers held the monopoly of real power throughout the Soviet Union. Allowing voters to choose national self-determination was to them as unacceptable as free elections for a representative democracy. These territories could not be called "nation-states," since they lacked real independence. In these terms, the Soviet Union was a new form of colonial empire.

The Challenge of Building Socialism

All Soviet peoples were obliged to acquire the basic knowledge of Marxism-Leninism in their cultural development toward the first stage of classless society that the Communists termed *socialism*. For them, learning was a necessary tool to bring their message of class warfare and social liberation to the masses. They organized a campaign to wipe out illiteracy. Secondary and higher educational institutions were opened to the lower classes through special "worker colleges" to provide rapid remedial training. People of upper-class origins were by law second-class citizens, denied the full rights of this "worker-peasant" state and subject to arbitrary arrest and punishment as "class enemies."

This socialist vision of a new era of human achievement following the fall of capitalism included the end of the unequal treatment of women. Communist leaders protested that they were not feminists—true liberation for women could result only from proletarian revolution, according to Marxism. The Soviet state's new laws did incorporate many ideas from the feminist movement. Marriage became a simple legal procedure and divorce could be obtained on demand by either the wife or husband. Abortions were legalized. Communist writers extolled the "new Soviet woman," equal in her rights to men and free in her decisions on marriage and the family.

In reality, women's places in Soviet society changed slowly, particularly among the peasant population. In areas of predominantly

Muslim population, Communist activists attempted to ban the veiling of women but encountered such opposition that the campaign had to be halted. In the Russian cities and among party members everywhere, women did assert their new rights and active place in society. The wife of Joseph Stalin, Nadezhda Allilueva, was an emancipated woman with both a family and a career in party work. A scandal among many Westerners, the Soviet feminist reforms later became a model for other countries.

In the 1920s, the most serious problem facing the Communist leaders was the choice of political leadership. That issue was linked to the urgent need to find the right policies to bring socialism to their country. Lenin had held sway over the party and state policy making but could not assume a leading role after he suffered several severe strokes in 1922–1923. His death came in early 1924. Leadership passed to his colleagues on the party's governing committee, the Politburo. Among the contenders for power was Joseph Stalin, by nationality a Georgian from the southern region of the Caucasus Mountains. But his colleagues were deeply troubled by his ruthless methods, which were apparent in his dealings with colleagues and in his role as Commissar of Nationalities in the Soviet government. Even Lenin, who had earlier supported him, warned in 1922 that Stalin's personality and methods of rule were "brutal" and destructive. But after Lenin's death, Stalin brought the other Communists to his side. He promised to correct his errors and won their backing on a program to end quickly the remnants of "capitalism" and to create, first of any country in the world, a socialist society. After five years of uncertainty, Joseph Stalin emerged as Lenin's successor. He was eager to take on this task. In 1929, the Politburo recognized him to be the new leader of the Communist Party. He was Lenin's heir.

The New Economic Policy that the Communists had put in place in the early 1920s proved successful in restoring agricultural production and raising the standard of living of the population. Its very success proved how strongly rooted free-market practices remained, especially among the peasant population. Industry continued to be run by the state, dependent on state subsidies for reconstruction and expansion. The Soviet government formed a State Planning Commission to provide the "scientific guidance" for state economic policy. How was wealth to be channeled toward industrial growth? The Communists knew an industrial economy was the real material base for socialism. But in their country, the peasant farmers controlled the land as private farms, and their produce remained crucial to Soviet economic fortunes.

In the Communists' eyes, the peasant farmers' presence represented the major obstacle to building a socialist society where property belonged to everyone. They debated these questions at length, searching for the guidelines by which they could plan their country's economic future. They realized that no help was available from outside and that they, as one of their leaders stated, had on their own to "build socialism in one country." Stalin's task at the end of the 1920s was to resolve this fundamental dilemma. His choice was to launch a new revolution "from above." This slogan in fact signified a war on the peasantry and a campaign to rapidly industrialize the economy, no matter what the cost in human lives. The Russian Revolution had not yet ended.

The Communists' attention was directed in those years as much to international as to internal affairs. Their ideological view of global relations blurred the lines between the two, for their vision of revolution recognized no state boundaries. They organized a new international revolutionary organization, the Communist (Third) International, to assist foreign revolutions. They confronted a world that, in their opinion, was dominated by the imperialist Western powers. They expected another war against capitalist states, whose antagonism toward their regime was as inescapable as the class conflict they foresaw in industrial societies. The Communist International grew rapidly in size as revolutionary Marxist parties from around the world acknowledged Soviet revolutionary achievements, taken as models for their own countries. Its members accepted the leadership of Moscow and on Soviet orders reshaped their parties into centralized, disciplined "Leninist" movements.

In colonial lands beyond the Soviet borders, the Soviet leaders gave encouragement and support to nationalist movements seeking to end imperial domination. In their view of the conflict with the Western states, this growing resistance to Western colonial rule signaled a new stage leading to the collapse of world capitalism. They sponsored in 1920 a Conference of Oppressed Peoples, held in Baku, a Soviet city on the Caspian Sea between Europe and Asia. It was the first time Asian and African socialists gathered in one place, and the spirit of the meeting was revolutionary. The delegates urged the peoples of colonial lands to rise up against their imperialist rulers. They were committed to the defeat of all colonial empires. It placed the Soviet regime firmly on the side of nationalist revolutions in non-Western lands.

 SPOTLIGHT: John Reed ▶

John Reed (1887–1920) is buried next to the Lenin Mausoleum in Moscow, side by side with leaders of the Communist Party of the Soviet Union. He is the only foreigner so honored there. Trained as a newspaper reporter, he was drawn in searching for stories to places around the world where he saw working people struggling against oppression. He went to factories in the United States where workers were on strike, to Mexico during its revolution, and finally to Russia when Lenin's Communist Party took over the government in the November 1917 revolution and struggled to hold onto power during the civil war. His fame came from his accounts of these conflicts. He entitled his most famous report *Ten Days That Shook the World.* That book purported to recount the turbulent days when the Communists seized power in Russia. It really was a hymn to their glorious revolution. No wonder the Soviet leaders judged him worthy of being buried alongside their own heroes of the revolution.

His upbringing destined him for a life of ease. He was born to a wealthy family in Portland, Oregon, and educated in private schools and Harvard College. His real education began when he joined the rebellious bohemian community of intellectuals in New York. In the early twentieth century these writers and artists were in revolt against the complacency, conformism, and arrogance of America's capitalist society. In their personal lives they shunned marriage and preached (and practiced) free love; their political convictions placed them on the side of America's working people. Reed made their style of life, and their rebellious beliefs, his own. He found his calling in writing of the struggles of ordinary people.

In his early years as a reporter, he cared little about the principles, or lack of principles, that fired these conflicts. The misery of striking women workers in silk-weaving factories of New Jersey gave him the inspiration to write the dialogue for a pageant dramatizing their struggle and damning their bosses and the police who fought—and broke—their strike. In 1914, he traveled to Mexico to witness that country's revolution by riding with the cavalry forces of Pancho Villa. Though he recognized the hunger for power that lay behind Villa's revolt, his book *Insurgent Mexico* portrayed the rebel leader in the garb of fighter for the oppressed Mexican masses. His real heroes were the peasants who fought with Villa. He had come to understand social conflict in terms of class war and placed himself wholeheartedly on the side of the downtrodden, not just in Mexico but wherever he found signs of class conflict.

These convictions gave him the insight to understand political conflicts and social struggle in terms of progressive versus reactionary forces, good against evil, white and black. Increasingly he thought of his own government from this perspective, judging its policies for its harm or benefit to the masses. He foresaw correctly that the Mexican people would resist as best they could President Wilson's ill-conceived military intervention in 1914 to establish "constitutional" government. When the First World War began, he traveled to both the western and eastern fronts to view firsthand the terrible battles. But he appraised its impact largely for its effect on social revolution. He was persuaded that the upsurge throughout Europe of militarism instilled in the masses "blind obedience" and stifled the revolutionary upsurge that he hoped for. The war had made Europe "the world well lost." He was absolutely opposed to U.S. entry into the war in 1917.

His pessimism at the course of world events suddenly vanished later that year when he traveled to Russia. He went there looking for some reason to hope that social revolution was still possible and found it in Lenin's revolutionary movement. Though he had scarcely any knowledge of the Russian language, he threw himself into the whirlwind of meetings, demonstrations, and debates that marked the weeks of September and October when the Provisional Government was falling apart and the Communists were building their mass support among the soldiers and workers. He attended meetings of the Petrograd Soviet, where the Communists were mobilizing forces to seize power. He watched the insurrection in Petrograd on November 7, then traveled to Moscow to observe the street fighting there between Communists and army units supporting the liberal government. And when he wrote of those "ten days that shook the world," he was writing of this revolution.

His mission afterward was to defend that revolution. In early 1918, he returned to the United States and immediately threw himself into the anti-war movement. His weapon was his pen. Though he was arrested several times for "subversive activities," the Bill of Rights' guarantee of freedom of speech was his successful defense. Completing his account of the Communist revolution was his real accomplishment. It appeared in early 1919, telling of the "ten days" from his eyewitness perspective. He dramatized that revolution, as he had in writing of the struggle in Mexico, by placing in the foreground the ordinary soldiers and workers fighting for Lenin's cause. They appeared in his tale as the revolutionary masses for whom the Communists were leading the way to justice and equality. They believed, as did he, that the future of the world depended on their success. He became one of the founding members that year of the American Communist Party.

But that faith was shaken once he returned to the Soviet Union in late 1919. He seems to have believed that his place was there, not in the United States where political reaction, not revolution, set the tone of public life. Once he found himself among the Soviet Communists, he became less and less persuaded that he had found humanity's salvation. The cruelty of the Red Terror and the misery of the population were everywhere to be seen. At the request of party leaders, he agreed to travel to distant Baku to attend the "Conference of Oppressed Peoples." At the conference he spoke as a fervent opponent of capitalism and imperialism. Traveling there and back through a land crushed by years of war stripped him, though, of his fervent belief in the real benefits to the masses of this revolutionary cause. He died of typhus shortly after returning to Moscow, before he could write of his recent experiences. His burial by the Kremlin walls consecrated his heroism as defender of the revolution. It was an honor that he might not himself have desired.

John Reed, 1916 (*Corbis/Bettman*)

REVOLUTION IN MEXICO

The political turmoil that spread across parts of Europe in the years after the First World War was paralleled by a prolonged period of political and social upheaval in Mexico. Its roots lay in Mexico's own past, not in the war, and its revolutionary impact drew upon the social forces unleashed among the masses by the conflict. Yet in its outcome it bore a strong resemblance to the radical reforms brought to Russia by the Communists. In its peculiar way, what Mexicans proudly called their Revolucion fore-

told other political and social revolutions that occurred later in Third World lands.

A period of violent, revolutionary turmoil began there in 1910, when Mexican liberals organized a rebellion to end the long rule of a political dictator. It appeared to end seven years later with the emergence of a nationalist, populist regime. But subsequent leaders carried forward a series of socialist reforms inspired by ideals born of the revolution. These radical policies did not end until the mid-1930s. In the process, the Mexican regime successfully defied U.S. military intervention and overthrew the century-old governing elite of landowners and the military.

The "Revolucion"

The Mexican Revolution began in 1910 as a political struggle for power. For over a quarter century, the country had been ruled by a benign military dictator, Porfirio Diaz. His power rested on the support of the wealthy landowners and industrials, the Catholic Church, and the neighboring U.S. government. He was not a "client" of the Yankees, but he was prepared to cooperate in opening his country to U.S. investors. Opposition to his rule came first from liberals demanding representative government and political liberty. They found their backing among the country's middle classes but appealed as well to the poor rural peasantry in the name of the "nation" and "class struggle." In 1910, they organized an armed insurrection that succeeded in forcing Diaz to accept new presidential elections. In 1911, their candidate won and Diaz withdrew from politics. But his conservative followers in the army, the Church, and the landowning class continued to resist the new democratically elected government and its social reform program. More fighting soon erupted. "Revolucion" became, as it did later in Russia, a cause for which more and more Mexicans were taking sides. The political revolution was becoming civil war.

By 1913, Venustiano Carranza had become the voice of this powerful revolutionary movement. He identified "militarism" and "clericalism" (i.e., the Catholic Church) as enemies of the people. Mexico's "class struggle" justified rebellion to bring social justice as well as political liberty to the masses. His revolt against a new military dictator became a social revolution when Mexican workers and landless farmers joined forces against the elite of the country. They found leaders adept at articulating their demands for social equality and at organizing large volunteer armies to fight for their cause. Their presence alongside political liberals changed dramatically the character of the Mexican upheaval.

Mexico's Social Revolution

Alongside Carranza appeared new fighters for the "Revolucion." A rebel movement under Emiliano Zapata took control of much of the south, while Francisco ("Pancho") Villa's army occupied northern territories. They confiscated the large landed estates that had once dominated the countryside and proclaimed their determination to fight for a new Mexican nation. They were not socialists, but their action spoke to an ideal of social justice. These guerrilla armies turned the revolution into a bloody civil war. Rival armies waged major battles in a struggle that cost hundreds of thousands of lives. For a time, Mexico seemed destined to fall apart. By 1915, the revolution had left Mexican society prey to roving militia and armies.

The conflict deeply disturbed Mexico's Yankee neighbor. The U.S. president, Woodrow Wilson, believed deeply in liberalism, not just for his country but for the world at large. Watching the turmoil in Mexico, he became convinced that his government had an obligation to take the side of the constitutionalist political movement in Mexico. He also heeded the calls from American investors, who had for a half century poured funds into Mexico to purchase mines, ranches, and oil fields and feared for their companies. Social justice in Mexico was not high in the U.S. government's priorities, but democratic rule was. In 1914, Wilson sent U.S. military forces to intervene in the Mexican conflict on the side of liberal forces. John Reed, reporting that year from Mexico, predicted that the Mexicans "will take up their guns and with reckless bravery resist us desperately in the streets and at the doors of their houses." He was right. The action was unsuccessful in ending the civil war

Revolutionary Warrior: Francesco (Pancho) Villa (*Clendenon Collection/Hoover Institution Archives*)

and succeeded only in arousing Mexican nationalist resentment at U.S. intervention.

In 1916, Wilson concluded that the real threat to Mexican democracy was Villa's army. Villa, for his part, was prepared to fight. His raid on a U.S. border town in Arizona brought the war for a brief moment within the borders of the United States. Like the civil war in the Soviet Union, the conflict in Mexico provoked foreign intervention seeking to protect liberal economic and political institutions. Wilson sent U.S. infantry forces into Mexico to capture and punish Villa. But the only notable result of Yankee meddling was to endow Mexico's social revolutionary forces with the aura of defenders of their nation.

That was probably Villa's aim. He did not seek to conquer U.S. borderlands that had once been part of Mexico. He hoped to unite behind his army all Mexicans who believed in the nationalist cause. Mexicans from all sides immediately condemned this Yankee intervention. Even the far-off German Empire, expecting war with the United States that winter, believed Mexico a possible ally and en-

couraged its ambassador to seek an alliance. This was a misguided act that found no support among Mexican leaders and stirred up a wave of protest in the United States. After a year, the U.S. army withdrew, having failed to capture the Mexican rebel.

This phase of the Mexican Revolution ended in 1917 with the triumph of the constitutionalist forces. Losing his popular backing, Villa gave up his fight. The civil war ended. Mexico emerged from that bloody time with a new nationalist leadership that recognized the powerful desire of its people for social justice. Over the next years, it gave Mexican peasants much of the land seized from landowners during the civil war. They became committed supporters of the new regime which, for its part, remained committed to social reform.

In the early 1930s a new radical leadership decreed that the government take possession of the foreign oil companies. The action gave it ownership not only of the vast petroleum reserves of the country but also the refineries that U.S. corporations had built and controlled. Nationalization of this key resource brought the government directly into the industrial sector of the country and was in its own way as dramatic a socialist reform as the Soviet Union's appropriation of the country's industrial plants. The U.S. government protested but refrained, in the name of its new "Good Neighbor Policy," from a forceful effort to compel the Mexican leaders to return the nationalized oil industry to the former owners.

In those same years, the regime set up a comprehensive primary educational system, one of whose key elements was a glorified history of the achievements of the Mexican Revolution. To embody this vision of Mexico's past,

it built an enormous monument, called simply the "Monument to the Revolution," filled with images of the great battles and heroes who had contributed to Mexico's new regime.

By the mid-1930s, the revolution's social achievements had altered Mexico's economic, social, and cultural life. These included redistribution of the land, nationalization of key industries, and a campaign against the Catholic Church that included the expropriation of much of the property of the Church and a system of secular (i.e., nonreligious) schooling. This new system emerged from Mexico's own revolutionary experience,

Diego Rivera, An Artist's Vision of Mexico's Revolutionary Heroes and Villains, fresco. National Palace, Mexico City. (*Bertram Wolfe Collection/Hoover Institution Archives. © 2006 Banco de Mexico Diego Rivera & Frida Kahlo Museums Trust. Av. Cinco d e Mayo No. 2, Col. Centro, Del. Cuauntemoc 06059. Mexico. D.F. Reproduction authorized by the Instituto Nacional de Bellas Artes y Literatura.*)

owing nothing to the example of the Soviet Union. But the two countries did pass through similar phases of revolution and civil war. In Mexico, too, politics soon came to be dominated by one party (ultimately known as the Institutional Revolutionary Party, or PRI).

The Mexican experience prefigured the social revolutions of the years to come in other parts of the world and that marked much of the twentieth century as a revolutionary era. At the same time, it revealed how powerful nationalism could become, especially when a country was faced by U.S. intervention. The country's independence was real. Mexico, alone among the Latin American countries close to the United States, was able to escape domination by its powerful northern neighbor.

SUMMARY

The global impact of the First World War was so great that the year of its outbreak, 1914, marks the beginning of a new era in human history. Its destructive force undermined the well-being of European countries. Their governments' desperate search for the resources to fight that war brought them into greater involvement in the daily affairs of their citizens than ever before. The Allied plans to spread their imperial domination into the Middle East after victory began Western meddling in the complex politics of the Arab lands that has endured to this day. The decision of the U.S. government to become directly involved on the side of the Allies launched the United States in world affairs, altering the outcome of the war and bringing to the peace negotiations a message of internationalism for peace among states never heard before.

The world was moving in new directions in the wake of the terrible war. The leaders of the Soviet Union never doubted that their "proletarian revolution" placed them in the forefront of this process, which they proclaimed the path of human progress. By the

1920s, their country had recovered from war and a terrible civil war, and the political institutions of the communist dictatorship were firmly in place. Led by Joseph Stalin, the revolutionary regime was ready to begin the radical social and economic reforms that they believed would bring to life in their land a socialist society. Their vision was utopian, and it inspired communist movements throughout the world. Revolutions had erupted elsewhere and had taken on a nationalist character. Fascist Italy was the model of this extremist nationalism. But nationalism could also serve to unite a people around the cause of social welfare, as the Mexican Revolution revealed. The history of the twentieth century was evolving in unpredictable, often troubling ways.

DATES WORTH REMEMBERING

1910	Beginning of the Mexican Revolution
1914	Outbreak of First World War
1915	German military victories on eastern front
1916	Battle at Verdun
1916	U.S. army intervention in Mexico
1916	Arab revolt against Ottoman Empire
1917	U.S. entry into war
1917	Victory of Mexican Constitutionalists
1918	Defeat of Central Powers
1917	Russian Revolution
1918–1920	Russian Civil War
1918	Collapse of Austro-Hungarian Empire
1931	Mexican government's nationalization of oil industry

RECOMMENDED READING

War and Peace in the West

David Fromkin, *Europe's Last Summer: Who Started the Great War of 1914?* (2004). A new analysis of the issue of the war's origin based on the most recent scholarship.

Hew Strachan, *The First World War: A New Illustrated History* (2003). A brief but comprehensive survey of the war.

Edmond Taylor, *The Fall of the Dynasties: The Collapse of the Old Order, 1905–1922* (1963). The history of the fall of the Austrian, German, Russian, and Ottoman Empires and the war that destroyed them.

Arthur Walworth, *Wilson and His Peacemakers: American Diplomacy at the Paris Peace Conference* (1986). Generally favorable interpretation of Wilson's role at the Paris peace negotiations.

European Fascism

Robert O. Paxton, *The Anatomy of Fascism* (2004). An eclectic survey of Europe's fascist movements by the outstanding historian of the subject.

*Denis Mack Smith, *Mussolini* (1976). A critical view of the Fascist leader.

Communism in Russia

*Orlando Figes, *A People's Tragedy: A History of the Russian Revolution* (1997). A careful, thoughtful interpretation, based on recent historical research, of the origins and consequences of the Russian Revolution.

*Sheila Fitzpatrick, *The Russian Revolution, 1917–1932* (3rd edition, 1999). A succinct survey of early Soviet history linking Lenin's 1917 insurrection and Stalin's revolution.

Eric Homberger, *John Reed* (1990). A thoughtful biography emphasizing Reed's talents as a brilliant journalist as well as political activist.

Revolution in Mexico

Thomas Benjamin, *La Revolucion: Mexico's Great Revolution as Memory, Myth, and Reality* (2000). The story of the upheaval that remade Mexico, viewed through the eyes of the Mexicans who made the "Revolucion" their own.

*Friedrich Katz, *The Life and Times of Pancho Villa* (1998). Saga of one of the leaders of the Mexican Revolution, who went from outlaw to revolutionary to nationalist leader.

Memoirs, Novels, and Visual Aids

*Boris Pasternak, *Doctor Zhivago* (1958). The classic Russian novel of a helpless individual swept along in the tumult of war and revolution (a melodramatic film version is also available).

*John Reed, *Ten Days That Shook the World* (1919). A dramatic tale of good triumphing over evil in the Russian Revolution.

"Red Flag." Excellent 1993 documentary, in the series "People's Century," on the Russian Revolution, including interviews with participants.

http://www.lib.byu.edu/~rdh.wwi/ An excellent web site on the First World War, including both documents and photos from all combatant countries.

---

*Indicates book is available in paperback.

CHAPTER THREE

Postwar Europe and Its Empires

- Europe's Postwar Revival
- Western Empires in the Middle East and Africa
- New Empires in East Asia

Highlight: Petroleum and the International Economy

Spotlight: Hussein Ibn Ali

The years that followed the close of the First World War were a period of recovery for the Western world. Just as no one could have anticipated the extent of destruction wrought by the war, no one could have foreseen the historic changes set in motion by the war. The world was in many respects a different place. The cultural and economic influence of the United States remained a potent heritage of the late war years even after its political leaders retreated from European politics. The war had undermined international economic relations to such an extent that, after a few years of prosperity, a severe economic recession began in the late 1920s. The yearning for a return to prewar conditions was great, espe-

cially within Great Britain and France. Their empires emerged from postwar negotiations larger than ever, but their human and material resources proved inadequate for the diplomatic and imperial challenges that lay ahead.

The end of the First World War resolved the question of which states would dominate Europe. Gone were the German, Austrian, Ottoman, and Russian empires. The Western powers were victorious. They set the terms for peace that leaders of the defeated states were forced to accept. Wilson's peace plans had little chance to succeed when in the early 1920s the United States withdrew from active participation in political life in Europe. Its absence from the League of Nations seriously weakened hopes for international peacekeeping. The peace established by the victory of the Allies was built on fragile foundations.

Western expectations for a return to prosperity rested on the recovery of their industrial economies after the dislocations of war. Success depended as well on the capacity of the world economy to function again as a free market. But the European war had devoured too much wealth for these wishes to become reality. Disagreement over war reparations from Germany and the repayment of war loans from the United States unsettled economic reconstruction for years after the war. The United States possessed the most prosperous economy of the world. The U.S. government's refusal to lower tariffs seriously hampered free trade and set severe limits on the expansion of European foreign commerce. In the mid-1920s, U.S. private banks and investment institutions took a direct hand in European economic recovery. When U.S. investors threw away much of that wealth in the speculative boom and bust of the late 1920s, the United States retreated from the world economy. The absence of the United States from international economic affairs worsened and deepened the global depression of the 1930s. The Western world could not return to the comfortable conditions that it had enjoyed before the First World War.

Leaders of the Western empires came slowly to the realization that their powers were in decline. One of the fruits of victory that they claimed was overseas territory previously ruled by their defeated enemies. In the short term, the Allies had concrete plans for expanding their control of the non-Western world. They redrew the political map of large parts of the Middle East where the Ottoman Empire had once ruled. Imperial administrators in Western colonial empires grudgingly acknowledged that their "sacred trust," as the British referred to their relations with colonial peoples, included preparing these peoples for self-rule. In Africa, the German colonies passed under Allied "mandate," authorized by the League of Nations. Gradually in the postwar years, the interior territories of the colonies in Africa, last of all the continents to fall to Western empires, came under the effective administration of colonial officials. Their presence brought improvements to the lives of their subject peoples, in the form of railroads, ports, and military garrisons responsible for ending the old practice of tribal raiding. These innovations were primarily intended to create conditions for economic development, but in most countries private investment was meager. The Western empires were not prepared to expend their scant resources on these distant lands.

In the Far East, the victorious states introduced a new formula for international collaboration. There the ideal defended by the League of Nations for an end to power politics seemed in the 1920s to become reality. Treaties signed in 1920–1921 among several major powers included the renunciation of their spheres of influence in Chinese and Russian lands and the drastic reduction of their naval armaments in the Pacific Ocean. For a time, the treaties brought Wilson's internationalist ideals to life. They came about through decisions made in Tokyo, Washington, and London regarding peace and political power. The fate of the peace was in Allied hands.

EUROPE'S POSTWAR REVIVAL

The postwar peace treaties did not provide a final settlement to the bitter divisions created by the First World War. In distant Turkey, nationalists refused to allow the Allies to partition their country, as provided in the treaty signed with the Ottoman leaders in 1920. They fought for and created a new nation-state whose presence forced the Allies to accept new borders set by the Turks' own armies. Their victory forced the Allies to renegotiate a new peace treaty. Within Europe, the reparations issue proved the source of greatest dispute in the years after 1919. It lay at the heart of the difficulties confronting the West in establishing a new international financial system. Security within Europe required a new treaty, signed in 1924. Only then could Europeans hope that they were finally at peace.

Peacemaking and the League of Nations

President Wilson's goal of a "peace without victors or vanquished" called for a spirit of compromise and a readiness among Allied leaders to accept an idealistic plan to preserve the peace. His vision for the postwar world called for the creation of nation-states for all large ethnic populations by the democratic process of national self-determination. His hope for a just settlement rested on the assumption that peoples who were granted national and democratic rights would never again support militaristic leaders. With the assistance of an international organization that would coordinate the collective resistance to aggression, states would trade freely among themselves and prosper without fear of war. Wilson looked to an end to international relations based on the principle of balance of power to ensure real progress for humanity. His goal was a system, often called "internationalism," based on joint collaboration among states and respect for democracy (see "Internationalism," Chapter 6).

But other leaders of the victorious Allied powers held firmly to the idea of a peace of victors. In their view, the defeated states would have to sacrifice territory and wealth to ensure the permanence of the settlement. The principle of international relations that they adhered to was the crude but clear demand: "To the victors belong the spoils." Great Britain and France looked forward to dividing between themselves the Middle Eastern lands of the Ottoman Empire and Germany's African colonies. Japan had seized German-controlled territory in China. Issues of national self-determination had a secondary place in this peace program. The bitter debates among Western statesmen reflected in large part the profound difference dividing them on the very nature of peace.

The peace negotiations were dominated by the American delegation. Wilson went to Paris determined to "fight for what is right." His influence there was great, for he was at the peak of his popularity in Europe. Behind the scenes, European statesmen knew also that the economic aid from the United States was essential for the first steps of postwar recovery. The American Relief Administration (ARA) brought public and private assistance to the war-ravaged economies of central Europe. It provided food to millions and made available technical assistance to reopen coal mines and railroads. The head of the ARA, Herbert Hoover, ran the operation with a combination of practical engineering efficiency, charitable concern for social hardship, and faith in the ultimate triumph of free enterprise. He argued that his aim was "to prevent Europe from going Bolshevik," but his larger vision looked forward to the restoration of a prosperous Europe and markets for U.S. goods. The popularity of the ARA revealed the importance to Europe of U.S. help in the recovery from war.

The peace provisions proved in the end to be more conciliatory than punitive. They reflected the complexity of the territorial questions and incorporated the conflicting objectives of national self-determination, security against Germany, and collective peacekeeping. Four provisions of the treaties embodied the major features of the compromise reached after months of negotiations. These were (1) a weakened but still united German nation-state; (2) new Polish and Czechoslovak nation-states in central Europe; (3) German reparations for war damages; and (4) the formation of the League of Nations.

The fate of Germany dominated all other issues. Germany had to cede to France territory on the Rhine it had seized in 1871 and had to give up eastern lands to the new Polish state. Still, the new Germany emerged almost as large as the prewar German Empire. The German industrial and agricultural economy was still potentially the most productive in Europe. Its population remained the largest of any European country except Soviet Russia. French acceptance of these provisions came only after the negotiators agreed to limit the size of the German army to 100,000 men and to "demilitarize" the Rhineland region of western Germany, that is, to forbid the German army to occupy the area. Wilson promised that the United States would participate in a defense treaty with France and Great Britain. He made this commitment to satisfy French demands for help in maintaining the new balance of power. In return, the French government collaborated in the formation of the League of Nations. In his eyes, this was the real promise of future peace.

Two new nation-states in eastern Europe received special consideration at the conference. Both Poland and Czechoslovakia bordered on Germany. Both governments claimed territory on their western borders that, though inhabited by Germans, they believed vital for protection against future German expansionist wars. Poland received a "corridor" of territory extending from Polish-inhabited lands to the Baltic coast. The German port city of Danzig (Gdansk) was its outlet to that sea and became an "international city." Out of the northern provinces of the Austro-Hungarian Empire emerged the state of Czechoslovakia. Grouped separately in one nation-state, Slavic peoples (Czechs and Slovaks) were granted the right to govern themselves in lands with large minorities of Germans and Hungarians. Czechoslovakia's borders, like those of Poland,

represented a compromise between the principles of national self-determination and security. It, too, could survive a new war with Germany only with the military backing of the Western states.

National self-determination also set the boundaries of Yugoslavia. Its core was the prewar state of Serbia, defeated in the war but resurrected by the Allied victory. Its goal of a state for all southern Slavs became reality, though only after Wilson had settled a bitter dispute with Italian negotiators during the peace negotiations. They had insisted Italy be rewarded for its war effort on the side of the Allies by receiving territory along the eastern shores of the Adriatic Sea, where once the lands of the Venetian Republic had extended. But the area was settled largely by Slavic-speaking peoples, and Wilson insisted it go to Yugoslavia. Nationalists in Italy (including the leader of the new Fascist Party named Benito Mussolini) were outraged, and in protest the Italians left the Paris conference.

Of all the issues that aroused public debate, reparations for war damages provoked the most controversy in the immediate postwar years. The Allied states all agreed to seek reparations from Germany, a centuries-old practice by which the losers in war had to make financial payment to the victors. In private, they realized European economic recovery and heavy German reparations were incompatible. They sought U.S. financial aid in rebuilding their countries' devastated areas. Their first request was that the American government reduce the size of their war debts, which totaled more than $15 billion. Wilson's refusal to consider making what he called this "gift" forced the Allies to use reparations in place of U.S. aid for reconstruction. From this decision began a long and bitter controversy with Germany. The reparations requirement and the loss of territory in the east appeared to many Germans to be proof that the Versailles Treaty was an unjust, punitive peace. In 1919,

German leaders could do nothing to alter the peace settlement. Their country was occupied by Allied troops and was still under naval blockade. Despite their bitter opposition, they had to sign the treaty.

Wilson's plan for an international peacekeeping organization took the form of the League of Nations. He believed the project to be the key to peace. He thought that collaboration among states committed to peaceful relations could replace the balance-of-power system of alliances and armaments. His plan was visionary in its treatment of colonialism and even more so in its new approach to peacekeeping. Wilson's principle of self-determination appeared to nationalists from colonial lands to signify the end of European colonial rule. It only began that process, however. The Covenant, or binding agreement among League members, stipulated that the territories of the German colonies in Africa and the Ottoman Empire's Arab lands were to be administered temporarily by Allied states as "mandated territories." The Allied governments were responsible for preparing these peoples for self-rule to come sometime in the future. The Covenant said nothing about the colonies of the Allied empires. In these terms, it was a compromise between European colonialism and the new principles defended by Wilson.

The heart of Wilson's plan to end militarism and war was contained in Article Ten of the League Covenant. It declared that each signatory to the document would "respect and preserve against external aggression the territorial integrity and political independence of all members of the League." Governments were to act together to stop aggression by declaring war on the aggressor if necessary. This key provision required that states decide the question of war not only in conformity with their own national interests but also in accord with the security of other states. It tied the League to the defense of the provisions of the treaties drawn up that year, including the new frontiers and the restrictions on German military power.

Nowhere was Wilson's internationalist idealism more clearly revealed. Article Ten introduced a radical new concept into international relations—the idea of a community of states bound together by a moral commitment to peace and to collective action, regardless of their immediate interests, to protect all independent states against aggression. This vision of a new international order represented to Wilson "the hope of the world." But later in 1919, he failed to win the backing of his own Congress. A large number of U.S. senators were hostile to his concept of international peacekeeping and believed that U.S. security and national interests should remain the fundamental guideline of U.S. foreign policy. When Wilson refused any compromise, the Senate rejected the entire Versailles Treaty.

That action represented only one step in the resurgence of isolationism in the United States. Among political leaders, domestic issues became their paramount concern. Business came first for the Republican Party, triumphant in the 1920 elections. International debts had to be paid, even if the debts were incurred in a war that the United States had made its own. International commerce provided a means to promote the sales of American goods abroad. To appease domestic producers, the government enacted in 1922 a protective tariff law to restrict foreign imports, though the restraint on trade made it more difficult for European states to repay their war debts. In those years, anti-foreign pressure among Americans led the government to enact the first restrictive immigration act in American history. The United States applied to international relations the shortsighted precept that private American interests assured the public good.

Foreign alliances had no place in these isolationist policies. The U.S. government never ratified the Versailles Treaty, never joined the League of Nations, and never became a member of a defensive alliance with Great Britain and France to protect them against Germany. With hindsight, it is clear that the withdrawal of the United States from European affairs crippled attempts to rebuild a stable system of international relations. The government's decision to treat war debts and trade relations solely from the perspective of U.S. short-term interests was just as damaging. The United States, having altered profoundly the outcome of the war, left the preservation of the peace to the European states.

Peacemaking in Europe

The damage caused by German armies in western Europe in the course of the war gave Allied governments the grounds to demand reparations, that is, payment for the material destruction, from the new government of the German Republic. The Versailles Treaty included a provision requiring that Germany pay but did not specify the total amount. Under Allied blockade of their ports, the German leaders had to agree but protested that their economy was terribly weakened by the war and that, in any case, responsibility for the damages (and for the war itself) lay with the government of the German Empire that they had overthrown. But the issue was not negotiable. Too many lives had been lost and too much nationalist passion aroused among the Allied countries. After a long delay, the International Reparations Commission agreed in 1921 that Germany should pay France, Great Britain, and Belgium a total of $35 billion. It presented the Germans with a collective mortgage on their financial future.

The German government refused to accept this decision. For two years, the conflict grew until in 1923 French military forces reoccupied the Ruhr valley, a key industrial region of western Germany. Germans organized a re-sistance effort, financed by the government and at the cost of allowing a hyperinflation that destroyed the value of the German currency and wiped out the savings of middle-class Germans. Both French and German leaders understood that they could not afford the human and economic price exacted by the dispute over reparations. Conciliation was the only path to a stable peace. The conflict over reparations involved all European governments, which were determined to avoid another war. It hurt investors and banking interests in Europe and the United States. Their plans for economic expansion and profitable financial investments were disrupted by the political crisis and the uncertainty caused by the Ruhr occupation.

The Republican administration in Washington finally realized that its war debts would be paid only when German reparations payments flowed regularly to the Allied states. It encouraged U.S. bankers to take part in the formulation of a workable reparations plan. The entire settlement depended, in fact, on the participation of the American financial community, called upon to join in a sort of "dollar diplomacy" in Europe.

Charles Dawes, an American banker, agreed to head a commission to prepare the plan. Presented to a conference in London in 1924, this Dawes plan set up a regular schedule of yearly German payments, starting at $250 million. At the same time, it provided for a massive loan of private funds, mostly from U.S. banks, to assist the German government in making its first payments. In effect, the Dawes plan put in place a cumbersome system for international financial exchange. German reparations flowed primarily to France and to Great Britain. These countries applied the funds to regular payments on their war debts to the United States. American investors continued their profitable short-term loans to Germany, and from there the dollars returned once again in the form of reparations.

Dollars sustained the system. This, in turn, reassured international financial interests. Until 1928, high German interest rates attracted U.S. investment, which by then totaled nearly $3 billion. U.S. loans dwindled after investors in 1928 decided that Wall Street stock market speculation was more rewarding. Then the financial system began to fall apart. While it worked, governments avoided conflict, and U.S. dollars fueled the growth of the international economy.

The second part of the new European agreement on peace put together in the mid-1920s consisted of a security treaty among all the major European states. In 1925, leaders of the German, British, and French governments met in Locarno, Switzerland, to negotiate a comprehensive diplomatic settlement. The Locarno Treaty was a compromise. Europe's major powers recognized the permanence of the western frontiers of Germany, and Germany accepted the permanent demilitarization of the Rhineland. It left that region bordering on France and Belgium free of its troops (and soon of any foreign troops as well after the occupation forces left). Germany was admitted to the League of Nations. It was an act that symbolized the country's restored status as a major power in Europe.

In those years, the League of Nations still held out the hope that, as Wilson had promised, it could function as a collective force to protect peace. In the absence of the United States, Great Britain and France became the most important participants. Their leaders collaborated in debates of the executive council, where proposals emerged to settle peacefully conflicts among smaller states. As long as no great power was involved, the League appeared capable of preventing war. The World Court, made up of jurists elected by the League, offered its assistance to settle international disputes when the quarreling states accepted outside mediation. A third important component to the new system was the Inter-

national Labor Organization, whose purpose was to improve working conditions around the world. "Social justice," proclaimed the charter of the organization, was the only sound basis for "the establishment of universal peace."

All three organizations operated on the principle that war was avoidable, that the causes for disputes among states were subject to discussion and compromise, and that statesmen would agree to international cooperation to protect the interests of their nations. The activities of the League represented a new direction in international affairs. Still, it lacked important participants. The consensus among delegates rested on its narrow membership, excluding the United States, the Soviet Union, and colonial peoples. Its promise to resist aggression sounded hollow in the absence of the most powerful Western state, the United States. The ideal of the peaceful resolution of international disputes had become a European affair.

Germany's ability to become a liberal democracy was crucial to the success of the postwar system. The founders of the new republic, whose capital was in the city of Weimar, created a constitutional order modeled somewhat on the French system. A majority of German voters indicated throughout the 1920s that they preferred political parties committed to democratic rule. Conservative politicians, originally hostile to the Weimar regime, came to accept its existence. Enthusiasm for freedom appeared less noticeable than satisfaction at improved economic conditions of the mid-1920s.

In 1925, the first popular election for the president of the republic attracted candidates from conservative, liberal, and socialist parties. It also drew the candidacy of the war hero Marshal von Hindenburg. A majority of German voters, drawn more by memories of past national glories than by hopes for a restoration of the old monarchy, chose Hindenburg. Despite his monarchist background, he was faithful to his presidential oath to uphold the democratic constitution. It may well be, as one

German historian claimed at the time, that "a secret Germany" longed for "its emperors and heroes." If so, the yearning did not disrupt the political stability of those years. In the prosperous years of the late 1920s, political and social hostility was muted and the parliamentary government was able to ensure political stability. Germany appeared a part of the new European system.

The International Economy in Prosperity

Called by exuberant Americans the Roaring Twenties, the ten years following the end of the war gave peoples in the industrial world reason to hope that peace and prosperity had returned. Scientists explored uncharted areas of the natural world; inventors added basic discoveries to the technological marvels of the industrial economy. Pessimistic voices did warn of darker human forces of destruction. Some writers extolled the glories of violent struggle and national supremacy, carrying into the years of peace the rhetorical violence that had characterized wartime. The German philosopher Oswald Spengler singled out the postwar "revolutions of stupidity and vulgarity" to prove that Western civilization had, like Roman civilization long before, entered its inevitable final stage of decline. His major work, *The Decline of the West*, was especially successful among fellow Germans, many of whom were deeply pessimistic about the future of their country.

While these debates reverberated within the world of intellectuals, technological developments produced startling changes in everyday life. The automobile emerged as a vehicle for individual transportation, cheap enough in the United States to be accessible to the middle classes. Mass production of automobiles, led by Ford Motor Company, sparked new industries in the West and increased global demand for raw materials such as oil and rubber. The boom in road transportation made gasoline a vital commodity. The international economy of 1900 was gradually evolving into an interdependent global economy.

Architects raised skyscrapers to greater and greater heights. New York, a new center of the international economy, proclaimed its economic prominence by constructing the Empire State Building, the tallest building in the world. Electricity spread through cities and into homes in rural and urban areas. With it came the radio, a new form of communication bringing global events almost instantaneously within reach of individuals. The plane, used extensively first as an instrument of war, became in years of peace a means of rapid transportation across continents and even oceans. Of all the public events of the 1920s, Charles Lindbergh's solo flight in 1927 across the Atlantic aroused the greatest enthusiasm and captured best the popular vision of the future. Acclaimed throughout Europe and America, he appeared the new civilian hero who used the power of technology for the conquest of space, not territory, and whose exploit dissolved national frontiers. In this respect, as in others, the "old" continent looked to the "new" for inspiration.

Economic prosperity was the foundation on which rested postwar recovery from the material and psychological damage of war. The world economy grew rapidly in the mid-1920s. The bulk of international trade and finance remained concentrated in Western hands. The war had left its traces here, too. Great Britain, drained of much of its international investments, no longer coordinated and stabilized investments and international trade. Japan and the United States enjoyed the highest rate of growth in exports. New York, not London, became the financial capital of the West. The United States, once a debtor nation to European investors, became the major creditor, lending more than $6 billion to foreign countries between 1924 and 1929. Great Britain, by contrast, lent half that amount.

The weakness of European finances and investment led governments there to assume greater responsibility than before for economic growth. They took steps to stimulate commercial exports, disrupted by the needs of war. They raised tariffs to protect their own producers from foreign competition. Only Great Britain returned to free trade and to the gold standard (assuring free purchase and sale of gold) to ensure a stable value of the pound sterling. The new states of eastern Europe, which suffered from the decline of international food prices after 1925, raised tariff barriers on industrial imports. Increasingly, trade and financial policies tended to reflect national interests at the expense of the international economic growth. Under these conditions, global recovery from war remained unstable.

In those same years, new economic and social trends were appearing in non-Western countries, both colonial and independent. Two key developments emerged then that continued into the postcolonial era. First, these lands were becoming the source of vital minerals and of agricultural produce in the international economy. Second, the gradual diffusion of medical care and improved food supplies were improving living conditions to a level permitting a global population expansion. For the first time, the rate of population growth in Asia and Africa rose above that of Europe. Terrible famines and epidemics, previously the principal natural limits on growth, declined in severity. By 1930, the estimated world population had reached 2 billion, up from 1.5 billion in 1900. The basic improvements in the standard of living suggested by population growth were barely perceptible. Still, they heralded a gradual change in attitudes of peoples, whose fatalism in the face of seemingly unstoppable catastrophes gave way to the hope of better conditions for themselves and their offspring. These trends signaled a profound "revolution of rising expectations."

These non-Western countries were increasingly dependent on the international economy. More and more small farmers were raising cash crops for sale, entering for the first time a regional or even foreign market. In Africa, crops such as cotton and cocoa spread through the countryside, and the high prices on these commodities promised farmers a good income until the late 1920s. At the same time, Western mining corporations were expanding their exploitation of the rich mineral deposits of certain African regions, providing employment for African labor. African workers migrated from great distances to work in the copper mines of the Belgian Congo, in the tin mines of Niger, and in the gold mines of South Africa. Employers welcomed their arrival, since they accepted wages far below those of white workers. Gradually an African working class was beginning to appear around these European-owned enterprises.

In Asian lands, an industrial economy, launched by wartime demand, continued to expand in the 1920s. Japan had the most developed economy. Even coastal cities in India showed signs of modernization. In both lands, textile manufacturing had grown rapidly during the war, and its production continued to rise in the 1920s.

The principal characteristic—and the greatest weakness—of most Asian and the African economies was their dependence on the export of raw materials. Their markets lay elsewhere, and the prices received for their goods depended on global forces of supply and demand over which they had no control. Until the mid-1920s, prices on these commodities continued to rise. Those good years came to an end when world prices began a long, steady fall. By the end of the 1920s, rubber had lost two-thirds of its value; economies in Latin America and Asia dependent on rubber sales experienced a severe depression. Farmers and laborers whose well-being was tied to the production of a single commodity were the first to suffer. The economic decline of non-Western regions hurt, in turn, international industrial exports and, even before the 1929 financial crisis, pointed to the coming global depression.

The economic recovery of Europe brought national incomes to prewar levels by 1925. Industrial growth continued at a steady, though slow, pace for three more years in Europe and North America. The United States played a key role in the economic prosperity of those years. It provided the bulk of the investment funds for public and private lenders. It was also the single most important foreign market for European and Japanese manufactured goods.

U.S. political leaders relied on the impersonal operations of the capitalist, free market system to ensure that economic growth continued. They ignored the reckless speculation on the U.S. stock market and intervened in economic affairs only to raise tariffs to protect farmers and manufacturers. Protective tariffs and stock speculation appeared profitable to American investors in the short term. Economists would later conclude that these aspects of U.S. domestic policy seriously undermined stable world economic growth. The United States failed to provide the leadership that Great Britain had once given the global capitalist system. The prosperity of the Roaring Twenties was not built on solid foundations.

● HIGHLIGHT: Petroleum and the International Economy ●

Lighting lamps with kerosene first made the oil industry an important part of the international economy. Bringing light to homes was the dream of nineteenth-century Westerners still forced to rely on candles once night fell and on the moon for uncertain outdoor illumination in town and countryside. It was also a lure to enterprising inventors and investors who dreamed of the mass market ready to purchase a bright, reliable source of lighting. Knowledge of the potential uses of the dark, gluey product called oil had existed for centuries, and it was accessible in a few known locations where it bubbled out of the earth. Bringing together the petroleum in a refined form and the mass consumer was the work of a few fortunate Americans in the middle of the nineteenth century. A few decades later, oil became an effective way to power motors useful throughout the economy. This demand for petroleum products proved insatiable and dramatically altered the global economy.

In the early years, political and strategic considerations had no part in the development of the oil industry. U.S. inventors counted on future profits in gambling that they could draw oil from beneath the surface of the earth and refine it to make a product fit for lighting. In 1859, drilling in the Pennsylvania oil fields was finally successful when the drill of an oil rig penetrated a major deposit and the pressure from the trapped fluid drove the oil out of the rig in an abundant, messy flow. The refining process in special factories was quickly mastered, putting on the market a product called kerosene. The oil industry was born.

Sales were assured, but production was a wildly speculative process as oil flows had a way of drying up once a particular field's reserves had been tapped. This instability proved a boon for an ambitious businessman named John D. Rockefeller, who used his funds and his unscrupulous skill at buying out rivals to create in 1865 the first major oil refining and sales corporation, called the Standard Oil

Company. It quickly reached out to markets beyond the United States for its kerosene and other oil derivatives. By the 1880s it was one of the first corporations operating on an international scale, with profits to match.

These alluring rewards drove other investors to look for the precious natural resource wherever in the world it could be located and successfully extracted. For millennia people on the western shores of the Caspian Sea had noticed the dark liquid bubbling to the surface. With the conquest of the area by the Russian Empire and the arrival in the 1870s of capitalists seeking oil, Baku became an oil boom town. It was far from European markets, so inventors devised special tank cars to carry the oil products by railroad to the Black Sea and special tankers to complete the voyage by sea to the West. Distance was no consideration for a product in such great demand. In the 1880s, oil fields had begun production as far away as the Dutch colony of the East Indies. There a company called Royal Dutch had made the gamble that its kerosene could compete in the international market with that of Standard Oil. The oil industry reached around the world by the end of the century.

By then, it had also found a new and very promising source of demand for its products. The internal combustion engine was proving to be the best means of automotive locomotion; the "horseless carriage" had an irresistible attraction for increasingly mobile Western societies. It was just as well for the petroleum industry that this invention came when it did, since electric lighting was rapidly cutting back the demand for kerosene. When Henry Ford launched in 1908 his "Model T" car for middle-income consumers, it was an instant success. The U.S. market sold nearly 1 million cars by 1914, and the demand for gasoline soared. Adding to the de-

mand was the use of fuel oil in the boilers of factories, trains, and ships. British naval experts recognized quickly that their fleet, the greatest in the world, would have to adopt the new technology, offering far greater power and mobility to their ships than the old coal-powered engines. "Oil fuel," exclaimed Admiral Fisher in 1901, "will revolutionize naval strategy." Major issues of national strategic interests entered directly into the affairs of the international petroleum business.

In the decade before the outbreak of the First World War, discoveries of new oil fields kept an abundant flow of petroleum into the global market. The United States remained the major producer, supplying enough for its own needs and satisfying two-thirds of the demand for oil outside the country. Europe's other sources were the Caspian oil field in the Russian Empire, and the Dutch East Indies, where Royal Dutch-Shell controlled production. The situation was not to the satisfaction of Winston Churchill, placed in charge in 1913 of the British navy. In melodramatic tones, he warned the British Parliament that their country was being subjected to "the long steady squeeze by the oil trusts all over the world." His answer was to ask the British government to assert "the power to regulate developments according to naval and national interest." In real terms, he proposed that his government purchase a controlling interest in a petroleum company that had uncovered vast oil reserves in Persia, where British diplomatic influence was already great. Churchill got his wish. From this decision emerged the company ultimately called British Petroleum. And Great Britain had become a player in the great game of international petroleum production.

This action came just in time, for the First World War proved conclusively how vital oil was to winning (or losing) a war. When in

1914 the French army needed to move an army division from Paris to stop the German offensive headed toward the city, its solution was to mobilize the entire taxi fleet of Paris for troop transport. This stopgap solution made very clear that the "foot soldier" would have to have his own motor transportation. The invention of the tank (built on the motor that had driven farm tractors) reinforced that elementary truth. And on the seas, the British navy had desperate need, for its fleet, of increasing amounts of oil, still coming largely from the United States. In mid-1917, supplies were running so short that the British government warned Washington that, unless more petroleum reached the British Isles quickly, the shortage would put "the fleet out of action." The experience drove home to the Allies that the future might of their countries, militarily as well as economically, depended on having direct access to petroleum, wherever it might be located. This included the Middle East territories of the Ottoman Empire.

That consideration played a large role in the outcome of negotiations between French and British governments on the postwar partition of this enemy empire. Information was already circulating among oil corporations and official circles of the likelihood of vast oil reserves located in the region of the province known as Mesopotamia, especially around the town of Mosul in a region inhabited largely by the seminomadic Kurdish people. One powerful British official let his colleagues know that "control over these oil supplies is a first-class British war aim." British troops had moved north to Damascus at the close of the war. Though the two governments had not completed their discussion of spheres of influence there, some of these troops soon occupied Mosul. The new state of Iraq, placed under British control as a mandated country, found its borders extend-

ing around the entirety of the Mosul territory and stretching as far north as Turkey. The Kurds did not have a serious chance at obtaining their own nation-state.

The actual discovery of the extraordinarily abundant and high-quality petroleum deposits of the Middle East came in the next two decades. First, though, the major oil corporations made a determined effort to keep control over oil exploration. In 1927, their negotiators drew a "red line" around the former Ottoman lands and the new kingdom of Saudi Arabia to establish clearly where they (and no one else) would have the right to collaborate in Middle East oil exploration and production. It amounted to a claim to their own economic "sphere of influence" and signaled how powerful they (and the governments under which they worked) had become in global petroleum affairs. In the following years, the drilling of their geologists produced "gushers" (great fountains of oil created when a drill hits a major oil deposit) first in the Mosul region of Iraq, then in the Persian Gulf principalities of Kuwait and Bahrain, and then—the biggest find of all—in the kingdom of Ibn Saud. The estimated reserves of Middle Eastern oil totaled by the end of the 1940s over three-fourths of the world's petroleum. When to these were added the oil fields discovered in Mexico and Venezuela and the new fields found in the western United States, the world seemed to be awash in oil.

But the price of petroleum did not collapse. One reason was the boom in demand for gasoline and fuel oil. Roads spread across the developed world, and cars and increasingly trucks appeared to fill them to capacity. The United States remained the champion of automobile transportation; its gas consumption in the 1920s alone more than doubled. By the end of the Roaring Twenties, oil amounted to one-fourth of the country's total energy consumption. The depression and yet more petroleum discoveries brought a decline in prices so severe that oil production regulation became a part of the New Deal policies of the Roosevelt administration. By ordering limits on production across all the oil-producing states, the U.S. government forced prices up sufficiently (to more than one dollar per barrel) to ensure profits to the oil corporations. Those limits in turn helped sustain prices on the world market. Government and petroleum corporations were even more closely linked than before.

Then war came again, and the need for vastly increased amounts of petroleum became a national priority among all the belligerents. At times, the course of the war itself seemed determined by petroleum. When the United States and the Netherlands cut off oil sales to Japan in mid-1941, the action pushed the Japanese government to accept the plans for war in the Pacific to obtain by force of arms access to the petroleum denied it by the embargo. When Japanese planes failed to destroy the Hawaiian Island's oil reserves, they ensured that the remaining U.S. aircraft carriers would be capable of entering the war against their fleet the next year. And when in 1942 Hitler ordered his armies on the eastern front to attack across southern Russia to the Caucasus Mountains in conjunction with the drive by General Rommel headed across North Africa to the Middle East, he and his advisers saw at the end the oil fields of Baku and Iraq. The failure of these campaigns in turn placed severe limits on the war-making capacity of the Axis in Europe.

The U.S. government understood very clearly the simple geopolitical truth that oil was power. U.S. reserves were dwindling at the very time that the demands for gasoline and fuel of its armed forces were growing.

Early in the war, the government included gasoline among the items rationed for all nonessential civilian uses. American drivers discovered that their cars had become a liability. President Roosevelt and his foreign policy advisers paid careful attention to good relations with those countries where petroleum was in abundance. The oil of the Middle East was, one adviser wrote enthusiastically, "the single greatest prize in all history."

At the end of the Yalta Conference in early 1945, Roosevelt made a very demonstrative display of goodwill by inviting King Ibn Saud of Arabia to visit him on a U.S. warship in Egypt's Suez Canal. The Bedouin king, for whom this was his first trip ever outside the Arabian Peninsula, arrived with his own tent and Persian carpets to sleep on the ship's deck. In their conversations, Roosevelt did mention his government's support for a Jewish homeland in Palestine but let pass the king's reply that the surviving Jews make a homeland in Germany. The significance of his invitation to Ibn Saud was spelled out by his successor, President Truman, who informed the Saudi king just after the war that "no threat to your kingdom could occur which would not be a matter of immediate concern to the United States."

The dilemma created by U.S. eagerness to support Saudi Arabia (and other cooperative oil-producing Arab states) at the same time as it welcomed the settlement of Jews in the Middle East would come back to haunt the government in the years to come. And in the years just before and after the beginning of the twenty-first century, the U.S. government became directly involved in wars in the Middle East over issues that arose out of its interests in oil. By then, some leaders had decided that Middle Eastern oil was worth fighting for.

Ibn Saud, King of Saudi Arabia
(*Philip McConnell Collection/Hoover Institution Archives*)

The Global Depression

The economic decline that began at the end of the 1920s damaged all the industrial economies of the world as well as the areas supplying food and raw materials to the West. It had the characteristics of earlier recessions, including a severe decline in production and trade, a rapid rise in unemployment, and a drastic fall in the standard of living of the population. Businesses declared bankruptcy; banks were unable to make loans and many were unable to pay their debts to depositors; and food prices fell so low that farmers let fields lie fallow although the urban poor went hungry. The recession began in 1929 in the United States and gradually spread throughout the Western world and into East Asia. By the early 1930s, it had become a global economic depression, far worse in its impact and extent than any previous slump. It represented a human tragedy of monumental proportions, creating hardship and suffering, destroying confidence in governments, and undermining hope in the future. It led in many countries to a serious political crisis.

The American economy led the way in recession after having launched the prosperity of the 1920s. By early 1929, U.S. industrial production had begun to decline, with the new automobile industry the first to suffer. Declining demand for industrial goods represented an important factor in triggering recession. Added to this condition, however, were other grave problems of American finance and trade that complicated and prolonged the international effects of the recession. Inflated stock values in 1929 reflected speculative dreams, not economic reality. This fact led some major investors to abandon Wall Street in late 1929 for less risky ventures. Their decision, coupled with financial problems in London, burst the speculative bubble and started massive selling by small and large owners of securities. By the winter of 1929, stock prices had declined by one-third, and many speculators who had borrowed heavily faced bankruptcy and ruin.

When they failed to repay their loans and banks raised their interest rates, investment funds for industry dwindled by almost one-half. Factories cut back production even more. The decline in sales of U.S. goods and rising unemployment led to political pressure to keep out foreign goods. In response, in 1930 the U.S. Congress enacted the Smoot-Hawley tariff law. It set tariff barriers 50 percent higher on imports and spread the harmful effects of declining demand to industrial producers in Europe and Japan.

The impact of the American recession on other economies was critical. In the first place, the United States ceased making sizable investments in foreign countries. The financial crisis caused by the Wall Street crash of 1929 penetrated deeply into the world economy. U.S. foreign investments fell two-thirds by

1932. European manufacturers curtailed factory investments. At the beginning of the depression, financial orthodoxy in ruling circles still dictated balanced budgets and high interest rates to attract foreign money. Both policies were severely criticized later for hindering recovery. The United States, center of world financial dealings since the war, could not provide those funds. The entire system of foreign investments in Europe fell apart as creditors called in their loans.

The long-term effect of the U.S. financial collapse produced a major banking and financial crisis in Europe in 1931. Banks in Germany and Austria defaulted on their own loans; Germany forbade withdrawal of funds to other countries. In Great Britain, the flight of money abroad forced the British government late that year to abandon once and for all the gold standard. It ended its guaranteed exchange of British pounds for gold at a fixed value, renouncing its effort to protect stable international finances. In 1931, Great Britain and France stopped repaying their war debt to the United States. In retaliation, the U.S. Congress prohibited purchase of British and French government securities by U.S. investors. No other country besides the United States had the economic resources to restore world financial stability. U.S. investors had recklessly gambled away their funds, and their government sought primarily to protect American banks and investments.

The U.S. response to the recession contributed directly to the global economic decline as well in its reckless decision to impede the import of finished goods. Instead of opening its market to foreign products falling in price, the U.S. government raised tariffs (a form of taxation on goods) across the board. Recovery in earlier recessions had come in part because goods at lower prices in one country attracted buyers in foreign countries.

The United States did not permit that process to occur. Its prohibitive tariff of 1930 helped reduce foreign imports by almost one-half. Country after country retaliated by raising their tariffs; even Britain abandoned free trade in 1931. In the next two years, world trade declined by one-third. Most countries exporting food and raw materials lost much of their foreign sales by the early 1930s. Japan, dependent on exports to pay for imports of vital raw materials, saw its American market suddenly contract and its total exports decline by 50 percent. The standard of living of its workers fell by one-third. Japan's vulnerability to the international depression encouraged its political leaders to consider East Asia their special market. And the economic decline revived plans by Japanese generals to conquer Asian territory. Economic crisis and war were closely linked.

By 1932, industrial production had declined by one-fourth worldwide and by one-third in Europe. In concrete terms, only three-fourths of the quantity of the manufactured goods once available were still produced. The wealth of the industrial world was shrinking. The economic crisis was particularly acute in the most heavily industrialized countries. Germany was especially hard hit, losing the bulk of its American loans, experiencing a severe bank crisis, and suffering a fall in exports after U.S. tariffs were raised in 1930. As a result, production fell by 40 percent. One out of every four German workers was unemployed and many others were surviving on lower pay. The German liberal government, to which employers and workers looked for help, appeared at a loss to devise new remedies to the crisis. The extremist parties claimed to have easy answers. The Nazi Party's rise to power came in the midst of that economic crisis.

The economic depression undermined the international financial and commercial network of the capitalist economies. States increasingly relied on their own internal markets for recovery. A major international conference gathered in London in 1933 to attempt to put the international trade and financial system back together. European leaders turned to the U.S. government to guarantee a stable dollar, to serve as a source of new investment funds, and to open its economy to increased imports. The new U.S. president, Franklin D. Roosevelt, refused to cooperate. He feared that an international program to promote economic growth would worsen the depression in his own country. The conference was a failure. International cooperation gave way to shortsighted national interests. The entire process of recovery from war was undermined by the severity of the depression. International collaboration collapsed, political confidence in democracy was shattered, and hopes for peace and prosperity vanished. The harmful effects of the depression were pushing the world toward renewed instability and conflict.

The Decline of Western Democracies

The lure of fascism in the 1930s arose largely from the profound crisis caused by the depression. The capitalist system's promise to provide people with work and to satisfy their needs had failed miserably. Gradually after 1932, industrial production did begin to rise, but in many countries it remained below the level of prosperity of the late 1920s. The underlying obstacle to global recovery was the lack of free movement of investment funds, and of consumer and producer goods, across state borders. The international financial system of the 1920s had disappeared, replaced by "autarky," a nationalist system of self-reliance and rivalry with competing economies. "Beggar thy neighbor" was the motto of the day. The free market left economic resources and labor idle. It was only partly the consequence of the inadequacy of old-style political liberalism, but democratic government did suffer terribly in some countries. Conservative fiscal policies did not offer an adequate solution to the crisis. In the years of the depression, political leadership in the Western democracies did not respond vigorously and effectively to the crisis.

Critics of conservative policies condemned state inaction and classical economic theory that relied on the "laws" of supply and demand to ensure prosperity. This view appeared in all democratic countries. Franklin Roosevelt, Democratic Party candidate for the U.S. presidency in 1932, rejected the argument of his Republican rival that the economy would improve on its own. "Economic laws are not made by nature," he argued, "they are made by human beings." His conclusion was simple and straightforward: since "men and women are starving," the state had to take action. The crisis in the United States, in his opinion, called above all for strong leadership.

A long-term solution to the depression required a fundamental revision of economic thought. The most promising ideas came from a British economist, John Maynard Keynes (see Chapter 6, Spotlight), who proposed a radical new theory to deal with the crisis. He argued that the free market was inherently unstable. It was incapable of ensuring long-lasting recovery and full employment. By itself, the long-term demand for producer and consumer goods could not rise sufficiently to meet these objectives. Instead, he proposed that governments use their own financial means to invest, spending if necessary during hard times more than they collected in taxes to compensate for the inadequacy of private consumption and investment. His call for government intervention in the economy encountered vehement opposition among conservatives, for it violated deeply cherished beliefs in the limits to government powers and in the benefits of the free enterprise system.

Keynes's controversial theories were slow to win sufficient political backing. In the United States, Great Britain, and France, leaders improvised policies to meet the needs of their people. In every case, their governments became more active than ever before in helping to alleviate the social hardship caused by the depression. Under strong pressure from their citizens, they expanded the meager aid previously granted the unemployed, the aged, and the sick and granted new rights to labor unions to protect the interests of the workers. The new policies to assist the needy were called "social welfare." Once considered socialistic by liberals and conservatives alike, they became important not only to protect the welfare of the poor but also to ensure the democratic consensus on which the political stability of these countries depended.

In the United States, Franklin Roosevelt's victory in the 1932 election began a period of sweeping social and economic reforms. On becoming president in early 1933, he launched a program for recovery that he called the "New Deal." It started with immediate government action to save the banking system, in a state of collapse at the time, and to revive the economy. His first period of reforms emphasized assistance to producers. It included efforts to save the farmers from foreclosure and businessmen from bankruptcy. Federal regulatory agencies were set up to prevent the abusive action of speculators, judged responsible for the stock market crash of 1929. His major effort to assist the poor at that time was a massive public works campaign. Later in the 1930s, his administration launched the Social

Security System to provide pensions for retired people, with funding from obligatory contributions by employers and employees. Conservatives called Roosevelt a "socialist" for using federal powers to regulate and limit the powers of business. Roosevelt answered that he was trying to save the capitalist system from collapse. In 1936, the voters showed their support for his policies by giving him an overwhelming victory in the election that year.

Still, Roosevelt's reforms had only limited success. Recovery from the depression was incomplete, for millions remained unemployed. Even the introduction of government spending measures in 1937, inspired by Keynes's theories, was not sufficient. Only the beginning of intensive armament production in 1940 restored full employment. Domestic measures for economic growth, even in a country as large as the United States, were not sufficient. A new system of global economic expansion was needed, but Roosevelt and his government had no plans for such measures. Political leadership and the majority of the population were as isolationist as ever in those years.

Social and economic reforms in Great Britain and France had similarly meager results. Voters in these countries, as in the United States, remained loyal to democratic parties, refusing to back authoritarian and fascist movements. Improvements in living conditions were slow, and political leadership was increasingly preoccupied by the threat of war. British and French leaders, like their people, desired nothing so much as peace. They collaborated in the policy, known as "appeasement," of conciliating the expansionist fascist states. Inspired by the Italian fascist state, the spirit of war animated Europe's fascist movements, whose motto was "might makes right." Fascism seemed the wave of the future. Seeking peace above all, the democratic governments of France and Great Britain proved powerless to resist the fascist pressure until, too late, they revived defensive alliances like those before the First World War. The great tragedy of that time was that the world was no longer, as Wilson had so optimistically forecast in 1917, "safe for democracy."

WESTERN EMPIRES IN THE MIDDLE EAST AND AFRICA

The First World War had destroyed the old order in the Middle East. British and French secret treaties had allotted each state a sphere of influence in the area once ruled by the Ottoman Empire. But at the same time, the British government had given Arab forces a role in the war effort, and to do so had appealed to Arab hopes for a nation-state of their own. During the war, Arab tribesmen under the Hashemite clan, headed by Hussein Ibn Ali, had organized— with the assistance of the British—a revolt against Ottoman rule. They had extended their conquest as far north as the city of Damascus, capital of the Syrian province whose borders extended from the eastern shores of the Mediterranean to the province of Mesopotamia.

Hussein and his followers had fixed their ambitions on the creation of a large Arab state in the Middle East. It was a vision inspired by the great Arab empires of the Middle Ages. But in the twentieth century the Arab-speaking population was divided into many religious and clan groups. Muslims were split into five separate sects, of which the Sunni were the most important (see Chapter 12, "Highlight: Islam and the Nation-State"); the smaller Christian population was divided as well. These divisions prevented the emergence of a united nationalist movement and permitted the Allied states to divide and rule separate parts of the area after the war.

◀ SPOTLIGHT: Hussein Ibn Ali ▶

The Bedouin tribes of Arabia helped transform the Middle East in the course of the First World War. These Arab-speaking nomadic peoples had once before emerged as a force for historical change. In the seventh century they had united under the leadership of their prophet, Mohammed, to carry the Muslim faith on the point of their swords in conquering a vast empire. Their leader in the First World War was Hussein Ibn Ali (1854–1931). His family (the Hashemites) traced its ancestry back to Mohammed. In the mid-nineteenth century, it had received from the Ottoman sultan the right to rule the most holy places of Islam, Mecca and Medina, in the area of the Arabian peninsula known as the Hijaz.

His was not the only powerful clan in Arabia. Further to the east, Ibn Saud had become sheik (the leader) of a large group of Bedouin tribes. His authority rested on his skill in organizing his followers for successful raids on their neighboring Arabs, bringing them the plunder that was one of the main sources of livelihood of the Bedouin. He also headed a militant Muslim movement, the Wahabis, who claimed that they alone understood the revealed religious truths of Islam. Ibn Saud and Hussein were bitter rivals for power. In the course of the war, Hussein found a new claim to dominance in winning British backing for the creation of an Arab nation under his leadership.

In 1908, Hussein received from the Ottoman sultan, as his father and grandfather before him, the eminent (and profitable) post of sharif of Hijaz. Its great shrines were the destination each year of hundreds of thousands of Muslim pilgrims from around the world. Hussein took his religious obligation seriously.

His post was the basis of his claim to be leader of the Arab peoples (most of whom were Muslims). At that time, a few Arab nationalists had begun forming secret organizations dedicated to the creation of an Arab nation-state in the Middle East. Hussein knew of their subversive activities, for which they risked death at the hands of their Ottoman Turk rulers. Even before the war he revealed to them his desire to support, even to take the lead, in this pan-Arab movement. He may well have sympathized with their dream; he also saw in it the chance to become king of the Arabs.

The war between the Allies and the Ottoman Empire created the opportunity that he was seeking. The British Empire had responsi-

Leader of the Arab Revolt: Hussein Ibn Ali (*Imperial War Museum/Hoover Institution Archives*)

bility for the war against the Ottoman forces. It had few troops, mostly from its India Army, to send to the Middle East. To generate more support, British agents went to the Bedouin tribes with offers of generous financial backing if they supported the Allies. This was an alluring offer to the poor nomads and provided leaders such as Hussein the means to build up their military forces. The Bedouin nomads were skilled at cavalry attacks, on horseback or camelback, traveling rapidly through the desert to attack their enemies. Hussein's son Faisal was a skilled leader in war. In 1915, Hussein informed the British that he was prepared to champion the cause of "the whole Arab nation" and would lead the Arabs against the Ottoman Turks. He admitted later that the claim was of his own making. Without his leadership the Arabs were lost, he told his British agent privately, since they were "ignorant and disunited." In return, he demanded "the independence of the Arab country." That vast land was to be his kingdom.

His goal appeared for a time to be within his reach. The British government accepted his lofty title of Arab champion. It sent him generous funds, munitions, and a talented agent to collaborate in the Arab revolt. This was T. E. Lawrence, who had in the prewar years studied the history of the Arabs and learned their language. The war changed his life as dramatically as that of Hussein. He believed in the Arab national cause and saw in Hussein and his Bedouin warriors the instrument to forge Arab unity under British (and his own) guidance. After a U.S. war correspondent publicized his exploits in that war, he became known as "Lawrence of Arabia."

In 1916, Hussein launched the Arab Revolt. It took the form of a proclamation promising to "serve Islam and to reclaim the glory of Muslims." He was the inspirational leader of the uprising. His son Faisal, aided by T. E. Lawrence, led the military campaign. The two men fought against forces far larger and better armed than their own. The appeal to Arabs launched by Hussein brought only a smattering of backing. Most Arabs in towns and farming villages distrusted the Bedouin fighters and remained obedient to their Ottoman rulers. The Bedouin had to fight a guerrilla war in the first years, for they were isolated from the British troops defending the Suez Canal. Hussein's prospects brightened when Faisal and Lawrence, campaigning with the Bedouin cavalry in a Bedouin robe, successfully defeated the Turks along the rail line from Medina to Jerusalem. They joined forces with the British, who by then were moving up the Mediterranean coast.

The campaign proceeded slowly until, in late 1917, the combined British-Arab army captured Jerusalem. The city whose holy sites were sacred to Muslims, Christians, and Jews had become a prize of war. In the course of the next year, Arabs and British forces fought their way north until they reached Damascus, capital of Syria and (to Hussein's supporters) of the future Arab state. The Allied victory in November of that year over the Ottoman Empire seemed to promise the achievement of Hussein's dream of his Arab kingdom.

Peacemaking proved for him a terrible disappointment. His son Faisal accompanied Lawrence to the Paris peace negotiations. They already had learned that the British government had in the course of the war promised a homeland in the Palestinian province to the Jews. Great Britain had as well signed with the French government an agreement to partition the lands of the Fertile Crescent (created by the Tigris and Euphrates rivers). Hussein faced for the first time the realities of great-power politics. The treaties that settled the fate of the territories of the Ottoman Empire came without his participation or agreement. They did not create a single unified state for the Arabs. Instead, several smaller states, "mandated" to the French and British governments and armed forces, emerged in its place. The British created thrones in two of these countries, Iraq and Jordan, for Hussein's sons Faisal and Abdullah. They left Hussein himself with only his original territory of Hijaz, to which he received the title of king. It was a sorry reward. When the British requested that Hussein officially approve the Paris peace treaties, he refused. His fortunes owed nothing to the peacemaking.

Hussein's deception was partly caused by Allied betrayal, partly by the flaws in his own grandiose project. His Arab Revolt had never won the backing even of all the Bedouin tribes of Arabia. Hussein was right in deploring the disunity of the Arab-speaking peoples of the Middle East. But he deluded himself into be-

lieving that his own prestige and authority could overcome these divisions. He refused to accept the consolation prize offered by the British of king of Hijaz. He came to believe that he could capitalize on his religious eminence as ruler of the Muslim Holy Places. When in 1924 the Turkish government abolished the position of caliph, held previously by the sultan, Hussein claimed the title for himself. His effort to become religious leader of the enormous Sunni Muslim community in the Middle East appeared impious to fervent Muslims. It gave Ibn Saud the excuse he needed to launch his Bedouin forces against Hussein.

Hussein could not even win that small war. In 1925, he fled the Hijaz, leaving Ibn Saud to create the kingdom of Saudi Arabia. His life ended in exile at the court of his son Abdullah in the kingdom of Jordan. Arab unity was a lost cause; so, too, was his dream of becoming king of the Arabs.

The Allies in the Middle East

During the Allied peace negotiations, the British and French governments put in effect their secret wartime treaty to partition that part of Ottoman territory extending south from Turkey to the Red Sea and Persian Gulf and west from the Mediterranean Sea to the borders of Persia. Their claims followed in the tradition of the earlier imperial scramble for colonies. They were not bothered by the wartime promises made by the British government to support the creation of an "Arab nation-state" in that territory. But Wilson's plans for a new world order that included the right of colonial peoples to self-rule stood in the way of their sphere of influence in the former Ottoman lands.

The Paris peace negotiators reached a compromise by creating the "mandate" system of territories, under the nominal authority of the League of Nations. The policy was applied to

all non-Western lands that had previously been colonies of the defeated Central Powers. In the Middle East, Great Britain and France assumed responsibility in "mandated" territories to provide, as the League required, "advice and assistance" until the peoples there could rule themselves. French and British troops and colonial administrators took, in one form or another, indirect control of these governments. French troops moved into the former Ottoman province of Syria, expelling Hussein's forces from Damascus and setting up the state of Syria and a new country called Lebanon, where most Christians lived. The British controlled the mandated states of Iraq and Transjordan (the area between Iraq and the Jordan River, later called the Kingdom of Jordan). The Arab-speaking peoples were a majority in all these countries.

Other peoples received no recognition. The Armenians' dream of a large state in eastern

Europe and the Middle East after the First World War

Anatolia, where their medieval kingdom had once flourished, was crushed when the Soviet Union and Turkey agreed to a common frontier. The Armenians were left with only a small republic within the Soviet Union. Leaders of the Kurdish people, who lived in the mountains of the northern Middle East, also presented to the League their case for a separate Kurdistan. Lacking the support of any Western state, they failed completely. Their people found themselves a minority group scattered among the new countries. State-building in that region could not avoid creating multi-ethnic lands with governments that lacked strong popular support.

In all these territories Arabs enjoyed a small degree of political autonomy on condition that their political leaders collaborate with the Western empires. The presence of large oil fields, discovered and exploited first in Persia then in Iraq and Syria, made a sphere of influence in the region a question of vital strategic importance to Western governments. Real independence remained a vague promise. Arab revolts against Western rule broke out in both Iraq and Syria, but they were too weak to defeat French and British army forces and were repressed. These new states suffered as well from internal political and social conflict among rival ethnic and religious groups. No Arab leader enjoyed the support of the masses as Gandhi did in India; no one could prevent the partition of this region by the Western powers. This proved the permanent inheritance of postwar peace-making in the Middle East.

The Problem of Palestine

In the territory of Palestine, the peace settlement led to a deeply divided population, split between Arabs and a growing Jewish community. The 1917 Balfour Declaration had promised a "national home for the Jewish people." The British government hon-ored the pledge, allowing Jews to migrate to that coastal region from which twenty centuries earlier they had been expelled by the Roman Empire. The number of Jewish settlers, most from eastern Europe, rose slowly to 180,000 at the end of the 1920s. In those years, Arabs (Christians and Muslims) totaled 750,000. British leaders set limits on Jewish settlement and assured the Arab population the protection of their political and economic rights. But the Arabs in the region were adamantly opposed to Jewish settlement and refused to cooperate in governing the mandated territory as long as Britain supported this policy.

The key to understanding Arab opposition to the presence of Jewish settlers lies in the ethnic differences dividing Arabs and Jews. Ottoman rulers had not practiced religious persecution, treating both Jews and Christians as inferior subjects free to observe their religious customs. They had resisted the Zionist Organization's request to permit large-scale Jewish immigration. The British readiness to open Palestine to Jewish migration altered drastically the ethnic balance there. The postwar influx of Jewish migrants created in the midst of a large Arab population a growing community of settlers of European culture, often well educated, economically enterprising, and nationalistic. The Jews bought Arab property to set up businesses and to establish their communal farms (called in Hebrew *kibbutz*). The Arab-speaking Muslims of the area remained closely bound to their communal customs; many still kept a pastoral way of life and were unable to compete economically with the Jews. Religious disputes over access to the Holy Places of Jerusalem brought to a head conflicts whose roots lay in the deep social and cultural differences separating the two communities.

In the absence of strong Arab leadership in Palestine, the leaders of rival Arab clans all declared publicly their opposition to the creation of a Jewish homeland. With their encouragement, anti-Jewish riots erupted first in 1921 and were repeated on a much larger scale in 1929. The Zionist Organization formed its own armed security forces. Palestine was becoming a land of communal antagonism and sporadic ethnic conflict.

The British had no choice but to rule the Palestine mandate themselves. The Arab leaders refused to collaborate, and the British could not encourage the Jewish minority to assist in rule without provoking Arab violence. A British high commissioner governed with the assistance of imperial military forces. His task became increasingly difficult as Jewish migration accelerated in the early 1930s. The persecution of Jews in Europe forced increasing numbers to abandon their homes. The United States accepted only a relative handful following passage in the 1920s of a very restrictive immigration law. Palestine was the Jews' last haven as well as their religious homeland.

This rapid increase in Jewish settlers set off in 1936 the most serious Arab revolt since the war. It lasted until 1938, with Arab guerrilla forces operating in the countryside and Jewish defense forces protecting their settlements from Arab attack. Before the uprising ended, several thousand lives (Arabs and Jews) were lost. By then, British leaders were seriously considering partitioning Palestine into separate Jewish and Arab regions. The proposal was unacceptable to Arab leaders. They denied the right of Jews to a Palestinian homeland, demanding that all Palestine be placed under Arab rule. The two communities were irreconcilable.

Independence for Egypt

Arab nationalism was strongest in the one state in the area untouched by the Paris peace settlements. At the outbreak of war, Great Britain had severed Egypt's ties to the Ottoman Empire, formally declaring the state a British protectorate. During the war, resistance grew there to British rule. This nationalist movement encouraged Egyptian political leaders to appeal to the Allied peacemakers in 1919 for independence. When the British refused to allow the Egyptian delegation to leave the country, violent protest broke out in several cities. The nationalists formed their own party and organized a mass campaign to demand Egyptian national independence.

Confronted with this opposition, the British leaders in 1923 proposed independence on the condition that the Egyptian government allow its military forces to remain in the Suez Canal Zone. The canal remained as vital as ever to the security of their Asian empire. Still, granting Egypt its independence was a sign of Britain's declining imperial might. The Egyptians agreed to the compromise. Their state remained closely tied to Great Britain, but they were free to govern themselves.

Egypt became a constitutional monarchy. The king possessed very limited influence over policy, for real power was held by a cabinet drawn from parties represented in the parliament. These leaders came largely from the wealthy landowning elite possessing most of the farming lands along the Nile River. They were strongly influenced by Western (especially French) culture. They embodied a future in which progress for Egypt came from Western secular practices, not from the Muslim religion or Egyptian traditional ways. Many Egyptians were troubled by the influx of Western culture. One young nationalist student of the 1930s, Gamal Abdul Nasser, recalled later that "our spirits were still in the thirteenth century" but everywhere "the symptoms of the nineteenth and twentieth centuries infiltrated" Egyptian society.

This Westernized way of life of Egypt's elite offended the country's Muslim leaders. The most militant among them set about organizing a popular movement to defend the practices and laws of the Muslim faith. Such an effort to enforce strict adherence to Islam was called "Muslim fundamentalism." Finally in 1928, these religious conservatives agreed to form the Muslim Brotherhood, whose goal was to uphold religious authority and Quranic law (the *Shari'a*). Their basic goal was to oppose those Egyptians who supported secular education, civil marriage, and women's rights, which threatened religious customs by introducing "secular" (i.e., state-controlled) rules and institutions for society. The Brotherhood's methods of resistance included enforcing Muslim practices on the population and promoting religious education. It also organized mass street demonstrations to protest the government's efforts at secular reforms and even backed the assassination of dangerous political enemies. The Brotherhood appeared later in the century in other Arab lands where the introduction of Western secular practices and values challenged Islamic ways.

After 1923, Egypt was freed from direct British control and became the leading independent Arab state in the Middle East. Its people experienced, also in advance of other Arab nations, the cultural and social tensions in their daily lives created by the attraction exercised by Western secular culture and individual liberties.

Postwar Colonial Empires in Africa

The Allied peace settlements reached beyond the Middle East into sub-Saharan Africa. The European colonies there had become involved in the war, partly as a result of the acute need of the Western states for African raw materials and workers, partly because fighting took place there between German and Allied forces. Then and after the war, Western industrial demand for minerals stimulated the expansion of mining, centered in South Africa and the Katanga (Shaba) area of the Belgian Congo. The recruitment of African workers from tribal areas to work in the mines and in other industries was enlarging the African labor force. Slowly Africa too was evolving under the impact of Western empire-building.

The economic and social progress of Africans created a political problem for white rule in South Africa. In that country more than anywhere else in Africa, the demand for raw materials was bringing Africans into an industrial economy. But this force for integration confronted the racism of the Afrikaners (Boers). Shared to a lesser degree by other European migrants, it had produced a society as deeply divided between whites and blacks as the southern United States. To control these migrants, the South African government augmented its segregation policies to include a "pass" system. It required South African blacks to carry internal passports, which the government used to severely restrict their right to residence in towns. The Afrikaners were not ready to abandon their convictions of racial superiority in the face of social pressures created by the international economy.

Western colonial rule in Africa altered little in the years following the war. The Allies took control of all German colonies. Under the League's mandate system, they became "trustees" for the peoples there. In effect, these areas were integrated into the colonial system established by the Western empires in Africa before the war. A handful of Western administrators governed vast territories, relying largely on African tribal leaders to carry out their orders. Both the French and the British made a concerted effort to make their subject peoples pay for colonial rule, levying taxes throughout their lands though the population remained very poor and the economy dependent on agriculture. They encouraged Africans able to obtain Western education to work in their colonial administration. This small, educated, and bilingual elite constituted an important new group in the political life of Africa. Western medicine spread slowly beyond the cities into rural areas, providing

Mining for Gold in South Africa, approx. 1925 (*Stark Collection/Hoover Institution Archives*)

assistance against the endemic tropical diseases afflicting the population in those lands.

The bulk of the African population had little contact with Westerners. The outside world did make itself felt as cash crops penetrated the traditional village economy. These altered the daily lives of farmers, making them more dependent than before on the market for their livelihood. An abiding hostility toward Western-imposed changes colored relations between colonizers and colonized. "They have given us a road we did not need," recalled one African tribal chief in the Belgian Congo, bringing "foreigners and enemies into our midst, making our women unclean, forcing us to a way of life that is not ours, planting crops we do not want, doing slaves' work. [They send] us [Christian] missions to destroy our belief." His was a voice of opposition to colonial rule, which was undermining his authority among his subjects. The presence of the

Western colonial states created a clash of cultures that irrevocably altered the way of life of Africans.

The social and psychological stress of colonial rule opened the way to large-scale religious conversion to Christianity and to Islam. Muslim missionaries offered Africans a rigorous set of religious practices and a strong religious community led by African Muslim scholars and teachers. The Islamic faith spread rapidly in the postwar years into the northern regions of both East and West sub-Saharan Africa. In many areas over half the population was Muslim.

Christian missions, both Protestant and Catholic, usually worked with the backing of Western colonial officials. They offered the Africans who came to their centers basic social services, medical care, and schooling, as well as instruction in the Christian faith. In the years after the First World War, Christian missionaries were successful, as never before, in winning great numbers of converts to their churches. Imperial conquest had undermined the credibility of the old animistic beliefs and made Christianity the religion of the conqueror. Allegiance to the Christian faith provided a sort of cultural baggage for those Africans eager to learn and to profit from new economic and political conditions. Gradually, they too began to assume positions of leadership in their church communities.

Under the pressure of Western colonialism, the old bonds of tribal unity were gradually dissolving. The cultural and social void was filled very slowly with new institutions and ideologies. Religion itself became a source of dissent. The high plains of west Africa were centers of Islam, while the peoples living in the coastal regions were more likely to convert to Christianity. The very process of conversion provoked dissension within the African community. The Nigerian writer Chinua Achebe, whose father had converted to Christianity during British colonial rule, remembered that as a child he and all those in his church community called themselves "the people of the church" and referred to all the non-Christians around them as "the heathen" or even "the people of nothing." Later in life he condemned this prejudice, but it remained a real source of divisiveness. The drama and tragedy of postimperial Africa had their roots in the unsettling impact of the West.

NEW EMPIRES IN EAST ASIA

The rivalry among Western states and Japan in East Asia led to a diplomatic settlement as important in its own way as the Paris treaties were for Europe and the Middle East. The end of the war left the Japanese Empire in a more powerful position than ever before. Its navy had the largest fleet in the eastern Pacific; its army was stronger than either the forces of the new Chinese Republic or the Soviet Red Army. At the beginning of the war, it had joined the Allied coalition, although its army and navy had taken no direct role in the European conflict.

The New Japanese Empire

Those war years were a time of Japanese expansion onto the Asian mainland. During the war, Japanese leaders forced the Chinese government to accept a Japanese sphere of influence in north China and Manchuria. They were subjecting their weakened neighbor to the same humiliating treatment as the Western states had imposed earlier. Further north, the Allied decision in 1918 to intervene in the Russian civil war gave Japanese military leaders the opportunity to move troops into the far eastern regions of the former Russian Empire. In those years, the Japanese Empire was becoming the major power in East Asia.

The Japanese Army took the initiative in pushing Japanese expansionism in those years. The feudal traditions glorifying conquest and military valor had reemerged in Japan's modern army. The emperor himself lent his prestige and semidivine stature to this "imperial way." Expansion was also in the economic interest of industrialists eager to seize new markets and mineral resources. The seizure of territory and recognition of commercial privileges came at a price. Many Chinese bitterly protested Japanese expansion into their country. In 1919, Chinese nationalists declared a trade boycott of Japanese goods to express their opposition to Japanese imperialist claims. Their boycott proved a great success, for it drew upon the nationalist loyalties of urban Chinese and in particular upon their hostility toward the country's new imperialist enemy.

The year before, Japanese military forces had occupied eastern Siberia, which was far beyond the reach of the weak Soviet government. The Russian civil war and Western intervention on the side of the Communists' enemies made this region a tempting territorial prize for imperialists in the Japanese army, who claimed originally to be acting in the interests of the Allied states. Japanese political leaders were less persuaded than the army of the benefits of this adventure, for it was costly and gave Japan no direct benefits. But even after the last Western troops had left Soviet territory, the Japanese troops remained.

The Washington Conference

In 1920, the government ordered a halt to the army's plans for Asian conquest. Its decision was a dramatic act of resistance to the imperialists in the military. It achieved this result by reasserting direct control over the Japanese High Command, ending (until the 1930s) the "autonomy of command" used by army leaders to act without the approval of civilian leaders. Its action came as a result of its decision that year to accept the offer of the U.S. government to join an international conference in Washington to settle the struggle for mastery in East Asia.

The Japanese readiness to negotiate came after the concerted efforts of the U.S. government to halt Japanese imperial expansion. American economic and strategic goals made an isolationist foreign policy there an impossibility. U.S. trade flourished in the region, and the Philippines remained a U.S. colony and military base. These conditions required a U.S. policy to contain Japanese influence in East Asia. The U.S. navy was Japan's only serious naval rival in the Pacific. In the postwar years it had expanded its Pacific fleet to counter Japanese imperial ambitions. Japanese business interests had their own good reason to support the negotiations. The United States had become an important customer for Japanese goods and was also a source of vital raw materials such as petroleum and iron ore. The economic importance and naval might of the United States brought an end (temporarily) to Japan's expansionist policies.

At the initiative of the U.S. government, a conference gathered in Washington to discuss the East Asian crisis. It introduced into Asian international relations a model of collective peacekeeping similar to that taken by the U.S. negotiators in Paris in 1919. The Republican administration came to the 1921 conference as eager as Wilson once had been to abandon spheres of influence and power politics, for war with Japan held no appeal to this economy-minded U.S. leadership. It was determined to continue the long-standing policy of the United States to protect China from foreign intervention and to keep its market open to American goods, but preferred negotiation to confrontation with Japan. The other major powers were prepared to accept the U.S. proposals for an end to the diplomacy of power politics in the Far East. Great Britain and France collaborated because they were weakened by the war. Japan's civilian leaders hoped that cooperation with the United States would bring to their country economic prosperity and lessened expenditures for its army and navy.

When its work was finally completed in 1922, the conference produced a remarkable set of agreements. The most important was the treaty to restrict the total number of warships of each empire. It fixed among the participating states a ratio of the relative number of capital ships they were permitted. Great Britain and the United States were left with the largest navies, followed by Japan, then France and Italy. To meet the treaty restrictions, Great Britain, the United States, and Japan all scrapped a large number of naval vessels—thirty-two for the United States. The British and the Americans promised not to establish any new military bases in the Pacific or to strengthen fortifications in their existing bases at Singapore and at Corregidor in the Philippines. In exchange, the Japanese military withdrew its troops from Soviet territory. For a few years, the treaties effectively ended power politics in the Far East and stopped the naval armaments race. Like the Locarno Treaty in Europe, the Washington treaties held out the hope of a peaceful era in Asian international relations.

The treaties' success depended, above all, on continued cooperation between Japan and the United States. Misunderstanding over their terms came easily, for these agreements embodied in Japan and the United States very different approaches to global politics. American leaders assumed that a common interest in peace had to be the overriding concern of all states, large or small, and that a treaty, like a contract, was inviolable. At the same time, they had a low opinion in general of "Oriental" peoples, whom they expected to defer to their own wishes and needs. The disdainful attitude of so many Americans toward the outside world led their leaders to seek, and to believe they had achieved, a self-regulating peace in East Asia.

Japanese historical experience gave its people a very different perspective on their country's place in the world. Centuries of isolation, followed by the remarkable revival of Japanese might, bolstered the conviction that their empire was unique and that its national needs and interests were of far greater importance than those of other East Asian lands. The governing elite of Japan interpreted their active role at the Washington Conference and in the League of Nations to be proof of Western recognition of their country's stature as a great power. The civilian government of Japan adopted wholeheartedly the American program of international cooperation. It had to justify its policy to the industrial and military elite by pointing to direct benefits to Japan. The unstated Japanese condition in signing the Washington treaties and withdrawing from the Asian mainland was economic prosperity and the expansion of U.S.-Japanese trade. When prosperity ended and trade declined at the end of the 1920s, so, too, did Japanese compliance with the treaties. The result was the collapse of the security treaties and the renewal of war in East Asia.

SUMMARY

The decade of the 1920s appears, in hindsight, to have been a time of transition toward a new and even more terrible war. The "normalcy" acclaimed by one U.S. president of the 1920s had only a short time to survive. The success of the French and British empires in extending their control into the Middle East could not hide the difficulties both states confronted in ruling colonies where nationalist movements were beginning to emerge. The new order put together by European statesmen represented a timid effort to find new solutions to the problems of international conflict and economic growth. We may judge these men shortsighted, but we should recognize that their powers were limited and that their peoples were exhausted by war and fearful of "Bolshevism" as much as of another war.

The world appeared to them in many respects as it had been before the war. Rid of German "militarism," the British, Americans, and French could look out on empires and spheres of influence that extended far across the world. The Middle East was now a part of that supra-imperial domain, all the more important in the 1920s since petroleum had come to occupy a crucial place among strategic resources for peace and for war.

The international economy was bringing countries in closer contact than ever before. Far-sighted political leaders realized that economic growth could not endure without the creation of a global economy. In the short term, international cooperation was necessary for economic recovery from the war. But that process was fatally weakened by the readiness of states to place the immediate interests of their people ahead of collaboration. The new postwar order hid grave problems. International financial and economic collaboration collapsed when the depression struck the industrial countries.

The United States bore a major share of the responsibility for the failure of the recovery. Its leaders and most Americans refused to acknowledge the new diplomatic and economic role of their country in global affairs. They made the naive assumption that the complex set of international financial and diplomatic arrangements—the League of Nations, the Locarno agreement, the Dawes plan, the Washington treaties—would function by themselves, leaving the United States at peace behind its ocean frontiers. The depression and wars of the 1930s ended these illusions.

DATES WORTH REMEMBERING

1920	Founding of the League of Nations
1921	Creation of French and British mandated territories in Middle East
1921–1922	Washington Conference on East Asian security
1924	Egyptian independence
1925	Defeat of Hussein Ibn Ali by Ibn Saud
1925	Locarno Treaty
1927	Lindbergh solo Atlantic flight
1929	Beginning of global depression
1932	Election of Franklin Roosevelt to U.S. presidency
1932	Creation of Kingdom of Saudi Arabia
1936–1938	Palestine Arab revolt

RECOMMENDED READING

International History of the 1920s

Frank Costigliola, *Awkward Dominion: American Political, Economic, and Cultural Relations with Europe, 1919–33* (1984). A balanced analysis of the complex impact of the United States on postwar Europe.

Sally Marks, *The Illusion of Security: Europe's International Relations, 1918–33* (1976). A thoughtful interpretation of the failure of Europe's postwar efforts to preserve the peace.

Postwar Empires

Raymond Betts, *Uncertain Dimensions: Western Overseas Empires in the Twentieth Century* (1985).

A thematic study of European colonial empires in the twentieth century.

*David Fromkin, *The Peace to End All Peace: Creating the Modern Middle East, 1914–1922* (1989). An excellent survey of the wartime and diplomatic process remaking the Middle East.

Akira Iriye, *After Imperialism: The Search for Order in the Far East* (1965). A history of Japan's search for its place in East Asia after World War I.

*Efraim and Inari Karsh, *Empires of the Sand: The Struggle for Mastery in the Middle East* (1999). A clear, critical assessment of the historical forces leading to the destruction of the Ottoman Empire and the creation of the modern Middle East.

Economic Prosperity and Depression

*Charles Kindelberger, *The World in Depression: 1929–1939* (1973). Still the best survey of the global origins and impact of the depression.

A. J. H. Latham, *The Depression and the Developing World, 1914–1939* (1981). A survey of the origins and impact of 1930s' depression on non-Western countries.

*Daniel Yergin, *The Prize: The Epic Quest for Oil, Money, and Power* (1991). An excellent history of the emergence of petroleum in international politics and economy.

Memoirs and Novels

*Isak Dinesen, *Out of Africa* (1937). Story of a failed European plantation owner in Kenya (and subject of an excellent film).

*T. E. Lawrence, *The Seven Pillars of Wisdom* (1926). Lawrence's memoirs and meditations on his life as "Lawrence of Arabia"; his story is also told in vivid color in David Lean's movie *Lawrence of Arabia* (1962).

*George Orwell, *Burmese Days* (1934). The disillusioned story of the author's years in Burma working in the British colonial service.

*Erich Maria Remarque, *The Road Back* (1931). The grim story of a German veteran, told by one of Germany's finest twentieth-century novelists.

---

*Indicates the book is available in paperback.

CHAPTER FOUR

Nations Versus Empires in Asia

TURKEY, INDIA, CHINA, 1918–1941

- The Forging of the Turkish Nation
- British India and Indian Nationalism
- Civil War and Foreign War in China

Highlight: Colonialism and Nationalism

Spotlight: Mohandas Gandhi

In the two decades following the First World War, nationalism brought new life to old civilizations all across Asia. No major battles occurred in India or in East Asia. The peace settlement left intact there the prewar colonial possessions of the Western empires. But that war proved a critical moment in the history of Turkey, China, and India. Turks were mobilized by their Ottoman sultan on the side of the Central Powers and suffered a defeat as devastating as that experienced by the Austro-Hungarian and German empires. Indian soldiers fought with the Allies after the British viceroy proclaimed India at war with the Central Powers. The sacrifice made by India encouraged nationalists in the National Congress to demand

self-rule for their country. The new Chinese Republic joined the Allies in hopes of gaining international recognition, only to discover that the Japanese Empire was its most dangerous enemy.

Wilson and Lenin had, each in his own way, presented peoples beyond the borders of Europe with a vision of liberation from colonial rule. At the same time, the First World War had brought together workers and soldiers from the colonies mobilized by the Western empires in a common cause. It gave them the opportunity to learn of new political ideologies such as socialism and to appreciate their own potential role in ending colonial domination. Everywhere hopes were raised for better economic conditions and for the recognition of national rights. Revolutionary visions of social liberation of working masses and of colonial liberation from imperial rule, propounded by the leaders of the new Russian state, echoed throughout the world. The war and the Russian Revolution marked the beginning of the decline of colonial empires.

The victory of the Allies fatally undermined the Ottoman Empire. Allied forces occupied Turkish lands. In reaction, officers from the former Ottoman army, led by Mustapha Kemal (later Kemal Ataturk), brought together their followers in a nationalist movement to rid the country of foreign troops and to save their country from partition. Their goal was the creation of a unified Turkish nation-state. To do so, they had to become traitors to the Ottoman Empire, condemned in their eyes by its feeble leadership and defeat in war. The authority of the sultan crumbled after he chose, in hopes of preserving his throne, to collaborate with the Allies. Conservative religious leaders tried but failed to arouse Muslims against the nationalists. Modern, secular reforms became the foundation for the new Turkish nation. Within a few years, Turkish leaders had abolished the sultanate, ended the legal supremacy of Islam, and defeated all the foreign invaders. For the first time, the crucible of war forged a new nation-state, the Republic of Turkey.

The First World War had involved the peoples in India more deeply than ever in the affairs of the British Empire. Indian industrial production grew rapidly to meet imperial needs; the Indian army fought on front lines in Europe and the Middle East. The British recognized that these new conditions required political concessions to Indian nationalism. But their idea of limited self-rule failed to satisfy the major nationalist movement, the Indian National Congress. The remarkable leadership of Mohandas Gandhi turned this small party of intellectuals into a mass movement by identifying liberation from British rule with the needs of the Indian masses. Having begun the process of introducing self-

government into India, the British viceroy found himself under increasing pressure from the National Congress to make more and more reforms. While India remained a British colony, by the late 1930s it was headed for complete independence. India occupies a central place in the study of Asian nationalism, for it produced one of the most effective reformist independence movements of the twentieth century.

The 1919 peace settlement aroused in China an unprecedented upsurge of nationalist protest. The collapse of the Chinese Empire in 1911 had been followed by the disintegration of central rule and civil war. Army generals, called "warlords," had in the following years carved out territories where they ruled with their troops like feudal barons. Their presence stood in the way of the efforts after 1919 by Chinese nationalists to create out of the vast territory of the fallen empire a new nation. During the war, Japanese troops had occupied German-controlled areas in northern China. Chinese opposition to the Japanese sphere of influence and commercial privileges was so strong that it produced the first nationalist mass movement in the country's history. Out of this struggle against foreign and internal enemies, Chinese patriots forged their own Nationalist Party and army. By the end of the 1920s, the Nationalists appeared close to dominating their country. But a new rival, the Chinese Communist Party, had appeared to claim the mantle of revolutionary leadership of a new China. With the onset of the depression, Japanese troops returned to dispute control of coastal areas of the country. Internal and foreign enemies still stood in the way of Nationalist plans to be heirs to the empire and the founders of the Chinese nation-state.

THE FORGING OF THE TURKISH NATION

The Ottoman Empire could not long survive the defeat of the Central Powers in 1918. The

sultan and his conservative religious and political supporters bore the brunt of the blame
for defeat. Reformist officers had before the
war sought to mobilize the empire to end the
growing Western domination of their country.
These "Young Turks" had put aside their radical political program during the war. Officers
such as Mustapha Kemal proved courageous
and skillful in holding back Russian offensives
in the east and in defeating in 1915 the forces
of the British Empire seeking to conquer the
straits between the Mediterranean and Black
seas (the Dardanelles campaign). But they
could not succeed in stopping the British offensive coming up the Mediterranean coast
from Egypt. By 1918, British and Arab forces
had pushed Turkish troops out of the Middle
East. The empire faced yet another defeat by
its European enemies.

The collapse of the empire's allies, Germany
and Austro-Hungary, was the final blow to the
Ottoman forces. The sultan capitulated. Allied
troops took over key areas in the empire. The
Young Turks concluded that imperial decay was
irreversible; only the overthrow of the Ottoman
Empire would permit the national resurgence
of the Turkish people. The harsh lessons of war
pointed to the need for political revolution.

The Fall of the Ottoman Empire

After the Ottoman Empire surrendered to
the Allies in November 1918, much of its territory was occupied by Allied military forces.
British troops and their Arab allies controlled
the Fertile Crescent, the area from the Tigris
and Euphrates rivers to Palestine. Greek troops
took control of the islands of the Aegean Sea
and the Anatolian coast around the port of
Smyrna, where half a million Greeks lived. The
straits linking the Black Sea and the Mediterranean, including Istanbul (Constantinople),
were under Allied military and naval occupation. The wartime plans for the partition of the
empire became the central feature of the peace

treaty drawn up in 1919. Presented to the sultan for his approval, it left only central Turkey
in a shrunken Ottoman Empire.

The fate of the empire and its sultan mattered
less to the Turkish officers of the sultan's army
than that of the Turkish people. If implemented,
the treaty would have left many Turks under
foreign (and Christian) rule, some incorporated
in an Armenian state, others in the Greek state.
Refusing to bow to Allied terms or the sultan's
orders, the officers gathered around a military
commander, Mustafa Kemal (later to take the
name Kemal Ataturk), to organize a nationalist
movement of resistance. Their aim was to create a Turkish nation-state and to form a Turkish
army to defend their people from the threatened partition of their land.

Mustafa Kemal's extraordinary achievements occurred in the chaos of war and the
collapse of the Ottoman Empire. They made
him the leader of the Turkish people. He was
born in 1881, the son of poor peasants who
lived in the Balkan area of the Ottoman Empire. His early years were shaped by the opportunities offered by service within the
Ottoman Empire. He chose the career of officer in the sultan's army, where his family's
poverty mattered less than his remarkable talents. He was a skillful and brave officer.
Alongside his career in the military, he (like
other officers) became deeply involved in
plans for the reform of the declining empire.
He was one of the conspirators calling themselves "Young Turks" who, in 1908, forced the
sultan to accept a reformed, constitutional
monarchy under their leadership. Their first
attempt at political leadership was short-lived.
The sultan had strong allies, including Muslim religious leaders who backed the monarchy. The world war ended temporarily
Kemal's political activity, but the empire's defeat in 1918 renewed his struggle for reform.

The next year, the sultan's ordered his army
to submit to the Allied treaty that partitioned
the empire. Kemal refused, committing what

National Leader of the Turks: Kemal Ataturk in Modern Military Uniform, approx. 1925
(© *Hulton-Deutsch Collection/CORBIS*)

amounted to an act of treason. He called together representatives of the Turkish people to form a National Assembly. Its task was to create the new nation-state of Turkey. He organized a new Turkish army whose mission was to expel the foreign invaders and to unify the Turkish people. The sultan and the Muslim authorities ordered his execution, but he had the support of growing numbers of the population. They found in him a dynamic leader whom they came to admire for those mysterious qualities of leadership we call "charisma." He himself later called 1919 "the year of my birth."

The task of defending the new state was made easier by the weakness of the sur-

rounding states and the unwillingness of the Allies to mount a major offensive against Turkey. In the east, the Turkish army encountered the forces of the newly created Republic of Armenia. It had emerged in 1917 amidst the ruins of the Russian Empire on its Caucasian borderland. Its leaders held firmly to their own nationalist vision of a state whose borders would extend far into eastern Turkey, where the bulk of the Armenian population had lived for thousands of years. They created their own army, though it was small and poorly armed. In the last year of the war, a few British troops protected their area. But Great Britain had more pressing concerns than the defense of faraway Armenia.

Beyond the Armenian forces were the Soviet Union and its Red Army. The Turkish nationalists did not support communist revolution. In fact, in the early years of their republic they would arrest and execute the leaders of the Turkish Communist Party. Sharing common enemies, however, the two young states overlooked political differences; their leaders preferred cooperation to war. After Soviet troops seized in 1921 the territory of the Armenian Republic, the two states reached an agreement useful to both. Turkey accepted the Soviet seizure of the Armenian Republic's land near the Caucasus Mountains. In exchange, the communist regime provided military aid to the Turkish army and agreed on a new frontier to separate the two new states.

There was no place for any other independent state in that area. Neither "Kurdistan" nor a "Republic of Armenia" could find room there. Despite support in the League of Nations, the Armenians stood no chance to create their own independent state. Kemal's explanation of their failure was cynical but accurate: the Westerners such as "poor Wilson" failed to understand that "a frontier which is not defended with bayonets cannot be secured by any other principle." His nationalist revolution had mobilized armed followers ready to die for their homeland, and he was prepared to use them to expand the borders of his "native land" as far east as his treaty with the Soviet Union permitted.

Having come to terms with the Soviet state, the Turkish army turned west to attack the occupation forces of Greece. In 1919, Greek leaders had ordered their troops to occupy large areas of western Turkey. They believed that their nation should incorporate the territory that 2,000 years before had belonged to the ancient Greek city-states. It was a fantastic, destructive dream. They realized that a Turkish nation-state stood in the way of their vision of Greater Greece. But they underestimated the vitality of Kemal's nationalist movement. Their decision to take possession of Turkish lands across the Aegean Sea proved a political blunder and a tragedy for their people.

In the Greek-Turkish war of 1920–1922, the new Turkish army succeeded in expelling Greek forces from all Asia Minor. The distrust that had long divided Greeks and Turks turned to violent hatred during the war. Of the 1.3 million Greeks living in Anatolia, many died in the course of the fighting. Others, fearful of reprisals by the Turkish forces, abandoned their homes to flee to Greece when the Greek army retreated. After the war, the two governments agreed to the repatriation of all remaining Greeks in Turkey and the emigration (in effect, expulsion) of the half-million Turks (including Kemal's own family) living in Greek territory to settle in Turkey. For the first time, nation-building was accompanied by the flight of millions of refugees to escape rule by another people. Ethnic nationalism was a two-faced cause, presenting on one side an image of strong bonds of trust and solidarity among the people of one nation and on the other the ugly mask of hatred toward other peoples.

The Nation-State of Turkey

By 1922, the Turkish army had successfully conquered the entirety of the Anatolian penin-

sula, the core territory where the Turkish population lived. The next year, nationalist leaders formally abolished the position of sultan and with him the remnants of the Ottoman Empire. They could take enormous satisfaction in the victory of their Turkish nation-state. This was Mustafa Kemal's crowning achievement, for which the Turkish parliament later accorded him the name of Kemal Ataturk ("father of the Turks"). His army was a national force, recruited from the Turkish population. Under Kemal's leadership, it embodied the crusade for national unification and was the principal instrument to defend that state. When the sultanate was eliminated, he told his people that "the Turkish nation has put an end to these usurpers and taken sovereignty into its own hands." The Ottoman Empire had ceased to exist, replaced by the Turkish nation-state. In 1923, the Western powers agreed to a new Middle Eastern peace treaty, leaving most of Asia Minor, including the straits, within the borders of the Republic of Turkey.

The Turkish government set out on an ambitious program of internal reforms. Its leaders created a constitutional order including a parliament and elected president. Most radical of all was their decision to remove from their new state the Islamic pillars that had once supported the Ottoman Empire. Kemal lead the attack. He emphasized that he was a faithful Muslim, but he understood the Islamic faith to be a private affair. He believed many Muslim traditions to be a relic of the backward past. He was convinced that religion should not dictate the way of life of Turks or the policies and institutions of the new nation-state. The government ended the legal privileges enjoyed by Muslim religious institutions under the sultan. It ordered the abolition of the title of caliphate, the highest post among Sunni Muslims.

Most important of all, it decreed that civil law (drawn from Switzerland's civil law code) replace Quranic law in the public affairs of

Turkish citizens. Even the alphabet became a subject of reform. The Turkish language had previously been written in the Arabic script, for Arabic was the language of the Quran. The Turkish government ordered that Turkish henceforth be written in the Latin script (used in all Western lands). Literacy for Turks meant fluency with a new set of letters; the Quran now came to them not only in a foreign language but also in an alien alphabet. *Secularism* is the term commonly used to describe this program to create the rule of law extended to all citizens, whatever their religious practices. Many other Muslim states later in the century followed Turkey's example (see "Highlight: Islam and the Nation-State," Chapter 12).

The emancipation of women was a major part of Kemal's crusade to modernize his country. The new laws of Turkey ended the legal subordination of women to the head of the family. Schooling and jobs were opened to them. The government even supported a campaign to persuade women not to wear the veil covering their face when in public. It was the mark in many Muslim countries of women's seclusion and inferior status. In defying religious custom, Kemal believed that he was ridding his country of the dead weight of the past.

Islam remained very influential in the private lives of the Muslim population, but freedom of religion became a part of the Turkish constitutional system. All other religions received the right of freedom of worship. The great Christian church in Istanbul, Hagia Sophia, had been a mosque since the fifteenth century, when the Ottoman Turks had conquered Constantinople; in the 1920s, Kemal had it converted into a national museum to commemorate this architectural marvel of Byzantium. Secularism and modernism were the models that the government held up to the nation. He wished Turkey to be a modern state in all respects.

The Islamic faith was especially strong among the Kurds, a seminomadic people scattered across the lands of Turkey, Syria, Iraq, and Iran. They were fiercely loyal to their clan leaders and to their Muslim spiritual elders (from the Sufi religious societies). Stirred by the Allied calls for national revolt against the Ottoman Empire, Kurdish leaders had emerged by the close of the First World War ready to form a nation-state for their people. But it proved far easier to draw up a map of the northern Middle East with borders for a state called "Kurdistan" than to hold back the nationalist revolution of the Turks, whose new state included a large area inhabited by Kurds.

Kurdish leaders had traveled to Paris in 1919 in hopes of obtaining from the Allied powers the backing for their own nation-state. But they did not obtain the diplomatic support of the victorious states, which were more concerned with their own interests in the Middle East, and they had no army comparable to the Turkish forces. Their campaign was a failure. As a result, the bulk of the Kurdish population found themselves an ethnic minority within the new Turkish state. In 1924, their leaders, hostile to Turkish rule and to Kemal's anti-Muslim reforms, organized an uprising against the new republic. Kemal sent his army to repress the revolt. At the same time, he ordered the suppression of all Muslim religious societies, which he blamed for the revolt. No rebellious people or religious group was to stand in the way of his nation-state.

In achieving this national revolution, the Turks had distanced themselves from the rest of the Middle East. Having once ruled as conquerors, they pulled back into their own land and created new borders that were national and cultural frontiers as well. Kemal was their national hero. In 1925, he took the post of president of the republic. He held the position until his death, fifteen years later. In many ways, he embodied the unity of that new country, ruling with an authority so great that he could have become dictator. But he was satisfied to be recognized "father of the Turks."

The army that he had created remained the defender of national unity and the bastion against the revival of Islam in the country. Out of the ruins of the Ottoman Empire had emerged a unified Turkish state.

BRITISH INDIA AND INDIAN NATIONALISM

The long history of India made it a very unlikely prospect to become a nation-state. It was one of the oldest civilizations in the world. Over that long period, the subcontinent had become a vast and diverse array of peoples, customs, and religious practices. Many different languages were spoken among the 300 million people who came under British colonial rule, with Hindi and related languages such as Bengali dominant in the north and a very different family of languages (such as Tamil) in the south. The British conquest of the subcontinent, completed by the mid-nineteenth century, had left in place hundreds of principalities. Some large, some minute, each was governed by its own prince in conformity with its own traditions. Along the coast, merchants and manufacturers produced and traded as capably as any Western entrepreneurs, while elsewhere peasants eked out a miserable existence by farming with primitive implements.

Religion and culture emerged in the colonial period as the principal social and cultural bonds among the peoples of the subcontinent. Two thousand years before, the Buddha had preached there his message of spiritual salvation through meditation and renunciation of personal pleasures. His sacred shrines in India remained places of pilgrimage from followers in lands such as Tibet and China, but the religion itself had faded from Indian spiritual life. In its place, Hinduism had come to mark Indian society both by its spiritual values and by the caste system. Later, the Muslim religion spread widely throughout Indian society. India's development during the period of British rule accentuated the differences between these two religious communities. Until the end, that conflict remained confined within the colonial borders drawn by the British Empire. Those borders enclosed the territory of the colony; they later defined the land the Indian nationalists wished to remake into the independent nation-state of India.

Hinduism and Islam in India

Hinduism lay at the core of Indian civilization. It gave most of the area's inhabitants their religious faith, their cultural inheritance, and the precepts for daily life. It was an extremely complex religion, with no single sacred book or organization of spiritual leaders. It included the worship of a large number of deities, no one of whom stood out as the principal god. Hinduism emphasized perpetual change, as the wheel of life transported souls through incarnation from one body to the next, as birth was followed by death. Through this cycle of life, souls carried with them the moral consequences of acts of the individuals previously inhabited by these souls. No merit went unrewarded in the end, no sin unpunished. As a result, individuals, in principle, had to accept the life that fate had prepared for them.

A second important aspect of Hinduism was the caste system. It divided the population into hereditary groups according to status and social responsibilities. It translated the moral duty of each Hindu into specific personal obligations and social bonds. The structure included hundreds of separate castes (only some of which might be present in one community), all of which belonged to one of the four major orders of Hindu society. The orders, once actual occupations—priests, warriors, merchants, farmers—had long since become merely social ranks, of which the Brahmins were the highest. The Hindu social hierarchy included one other group: the untouchables, or the "unclean," segregated from all recognized castes and condemned eternally to perform the most degrading, menial tasks. They represented a sizable group, perhaps 15 percent of the population. Taboos governed behavior, including eating, among castes; beef was forbidden to most groups because the cow was sacred. Marriage had to remain within the caste. The customs and taboos governing the caste system had existed for many centuries and were closely bound with the spiritual values of Hinduism.

Before the arrival of Western empires, the most influential outside force had been a new religion, Islam. Carried by merchants and warriors from the Middle East, the Muslim religion had spread through the subcontinent. It embodied a radically different set of spiritual values and social practices. Worship demanded submission by the faithful to one God, Allah; His word was contained in one sacred book, the Quran. The Muslim religion forbade the segregation of the faithful into castes and rejected the lowly status of outcasts or untouchables. It condemned absolutely the worship of any other deity but the one God. Pork, not beef, was forbidden food. In a multitude of practices and habits of daily life, Islam and Hinduism were radically different creeds and communal bonds.

The populations of the two communities had lived for centuries side by side throughout the subcontinent. The greatest concentration of Muslims lay in the Indus River valley to the west and, in the east, in Bengal. Everywhere, though, village life mingled the two groups, which on a daily basis lived at peace and worked alongside one another in the harsh struggle to survive. Yet their communal identities, shaped by religious doctrine and social custom, created invisible but potent barriers. These differences could become the source of dispute, even confrontation. In the late colonial period, "communal violence," that is, attacks by members of one religious community upon members of the other, became increasingly common. Until the mid-twentieth century, no one imagined, however, that the Muslims, a minority among Hindus, would form a separate state to protect their faith and to defend their community.

One other important religious community had emerged out of the interaction and practices of Hindus and Muslims. In northern India, the Sikh religion joined Hindu philosophy with the Muslim worship of one God. Many Sikh men had, during the years of British rule, served in the Indian army, adopting their traditional respect for the warrior to the military code of a modern army. They were concentrated around their holy city of Amritsar, located in the northern province of Punjab, where they lived among large Muslim and Hindu populations. For Sikhs, as for Hindus and Muslims, their lives were held within strict communal limits, which defined their own identities and their daily existence.

British India

Ruling over this vast population was the British Empire. India was its prize colony. The British monarch was India's emperor. India's colonial borders extended around the entire subcontinent, from Afghanistan in the west to Burma in the east, from the Himalaya Mountains in the north to the island of Ceylon in the south. The British found tangible benefits to colonial rule. It provided them with economic profits and manpower for their imperial armies. Its economy was open to British goods. Its soldiers served loyally in African and Asian colonial wars and in the First World War. Political authority over the colonial subcontinent lay in the hands of the viceroy, appointed by the British monarch (on advice from the cabinet). His powers in India in the early twentieth century were vast, for no parliament or constitution limited his authority. He declared war and set taxes, approved laws and mobilized troops.

In practice, important restrictions tempered the viceroy's absolute authority. Large areas remained under the rule of Indian princes. They had proven their loyalty to Great Britain by supporting the empire; they were rewarded by the assurance of dominion over their territories as long as Britain governed India. They ruled in great splendor, but all had to accept British advisers at their courts. British power over Indian subjects was curtailed as well by the colonial administration's decision, largely for fear of popular protest, to leave in place most of the local laws and customs.

British rule imposed an institutional structure and internal economic bonds that left a permanent mark on Indian public life. For one thing, the British organized an Indian army, staffing it with regular British officers and joining one regular British brigade with two Indian brigades to form integrated regiments. They trained the soldiers in Western military techniques and promoted more and more Indians into the ranks of noncommissioned officers. The army proved its value in both world wars; by the 1940s, Indians had become full officers.

The Indian civil service played an important role in British colonial rule. This body of state administrators slowly expanded in size as the British took on new responsibilities in the areas of public works, public health, and state railroads. Indians had long regarded state service as high-status positions. They took advantage of these opportunities for advancement in the colonial civil service. By 1914, one-fifth of the high civil servants were Indians. A few had even become high court judges, responsible in the English tradition for enforcing the rule of law. One of these men was a Brahmin named Motilal Nehru, father of the future prime minister of independent India. Gradually the colony acquired a political elite trained in Western methods of administration, ready to move into positions of political responsibility when India won its independence. All through the turbulent years

when the Indian nationalist movement issued calls for resistance to British colonial rule, these servants of the British rulers remained loyal to the empire.

The empire's extensive program of public works in India was a third important legacy of the colonial era. By the early twentieth century, the British network of roads and railroads had become the largest and best internal transportation system of any Asian country. The railroads, at first a military necessity for the movement of troops, facilitated extensive commercial and industrial growth. They served British economic interests and increasingly were used by Indian traders and workers as the Indian industrial and commercial economy expanded. Irrigation was another key element in British plans for the development of India. The imperial administrators sought crops of benefit to British industry, such as cotton, and food sufficient to alleviate hunger in India. An extensive network of canals opened for cultivation in large areas in northern India. It brought water from the complex river system flowing out of the Himalayas to the parched plains of the Punjab province and elsewhere. By 1940, this irrigation system accounted for one-fifth of India's arable land.

In these and other ways, measures undertaken by imperial administrators to strengthen their own rule opened the country to new economic development. Britain found a vast market for its industrial goods, and as a consequence traditional sectors of the Indian economy suffered. Many small clothing enterprises were ruined by the competition from cheap British cotton products. Gradually Indian entrepreneurs emerged to take advantage of the new industrial technology and the growing market for their goods. During the First World War, the increased demand among the Allies for iron and steel led to the development of the largest metallurgical enterprise in Asia, owned by an Indian family. One small part of Indian society adapted Western capitalist practices; a far larger group became an urban labor force.

India gradually began the transition toward an industrial economy.

India's political life evolved rapidly under the British *raj* (the Indian term for "rule"). Colonial domination had provoked occasional rebellions. The most violent and massive of these was the Indian Revolt of 1857, when Indian soldiers and a sizable number of princes had set out to expel the British and to restore the rule of their Mogul emperor. British forces crushed the rebellion, punishing the rebels but also reforming the colonial administration. The British government set out to train Indians in English administrative, legal, and political practices. At a distance, the example of the British state exercised a powerful attraction for Indians, both opponents and collaborators in imperial rule. Colonial rule altered irreversibly, for good and ill, the history of the subcontinent.

By the twentieth century, Indians opposed to the British had put aside the goal of restoring the ancient empire of the Moguls. Most agreed that India's future liberation had to produce to a democratic, multi-ethnic nation-state. And if Indians were to successfully expel the British, they had to do so by learning British skills, and acquiring Western knowledge. Upper-caste Indians such as Motilal Nehru earned public esteem even while adopting a Western style of life and making a place in the new Indian administration. Nehru himself did not reject the goal of Indian independence; on the contrary, for years he was one of the most outspoken Indians calling for self-rule for his country. For him, as for his son (and future prime minister of India), independence was attainable through the acquisition of Western learning and the adaptation of British democratic values and practices to Indian society.

The educational efforts of the British rulers in India strongly shaped the attitudes of the Indian social elite. By the First World War, few educated Indians denied that Western industrial and scientific achievements had the capacity to transform and improve the life of the people. The network of English-language secondary and higher schools in India provided trained personnel to staff the civil service, courts, public health agency, and railroad administration. Grants were available to a few Indians to study in England; families also helped their sons make the trip. Young Mohandas Gandhi traveled to London to study law in the 1890s with the aid of his family (though under the threat of ostracism from outraged relatives). These Indians desired particularly modern scientific knowledge and professional training. Part of their Western education had to include mastery of the English language. These "England returned" were bilingual, fluent in their own language and in English. Their knowledge in two cultures made it possible for them to bring together elements of both in their own personal life and in their plans for the future of their country. This experience also distanced them from the Indian masses, whose lives remained bound to their villages and to their religious communities.

India's First Steps toward Freedom

The center for Indian nationalist resistance to Great Britain was the Indian National Congress. Formed in 1886, it evolved after the First World War into a mass political movement seeking a free, democratic India. In effect, the Congress borrowed from England the structure and practices of a political party. At first it emphasized collaboration with the British administration to bring self-rule in India. After 1918, it made its objective liberation from Great Britain and national independence.

Although conflicts with the colonial authorities broke out with increasing frequency, the National Congress retained its respect for English rule of law and democracy. It accepted time and again dialogue and collaboration in reforms for regional and then national self-government. The British, for their part, slowly and grudgingly conceded to their colony greater self-rule and democratic liberties. As Congress pushed for more and more freedom for the Indian people, the British repeatedly made compromise proposals leading to greater responsibilities for elected Indian leaders. Both the British and Congress, on the surface bitter enemies, in fact continued to collaborate in the gradual move toward Indian independence.

The struggle for independence brought out the rift in political objectives between Muslim participants in the National Congress and its other members. In the early years of the twentieth century, a group of Muslims created a new organization, the Muslim League. They sought to ensure that the political rights and cultural values of their minority religious community would not be neglected by the National Congress, whose members were predominantly Hindu. Representatives of the League took their place alongside other Indians in the National Congress. Both Muslim League and Congress leaders believed that they had to collaborate in the struggle for self-rule. But the formation of the League proved to be the first step toward the political crisis among Indians that ultimately tore the country apart.

Disagreement over the future of the colony had deep roots in the differences separating the two religious communities. Until the late 1930s, the Muslims supporting the League anticipated that the two great religious groups would coexist, not blend together, in a future independent India. They feared, with some reason, that a Hindu majority in a democratic state might become the persecutors of the Muslims. When, in the 1920s, the British extended self-rule to its Indian territories, serious Hindu–Muslim rioting broke out during the electoral campaign. A unified Indian nation-state faced serious obstacles arising from the religious and social diversity of its people.

India's participation in the First World War proved the key event in the emergence of the National Congress as a mass political party.

The leaders of the National Congress were encouraged in their hope for self-rule by Allied policy statements and by revolutionary events in Russia. They read President Wilson's Fourteen-Point program for peace, which called for recognition of the "interests of the populations" in colonies and for national self-determination. They watched the communist revolution in Russia and read Lenin's appeals for the united struggle of proletarian and colonial peoples. War and revolution in Europe were shaking the foundations of Western colonial power.

The British government had itself recognized that Indian mobilization for war required concessions for self-rule. Yet the institutions and habits of imperial domination remained in place. In 1917, the cabinet issued an official declaration promising "the gradual development of self-governing institutions, with a view to the progressive realization of responsible government in India as an integral part of the Empire." But a year later, the Indian viceroy introduced new repressive laws to combat nationalist agitation. In April 1919, a peaceful meeting of 10,000 Indians in the city of Amritsar ended in bloodshed. Its leaders had defied a British ban on meetings to gather their supporters in protest against these new restrictions. Imperial authorities brought in colonial troops to forcibly disperse the "mob," shooting into the crowd and killing hundreds of unarmed Indians. The National Congress proclaimed that "all talk of reform is a mockery" and organized a national campaign of protest. It had a new leader to carry the movement to the people— Mohandas Gandhi.

In his early adult years, Gandhi joined the ranks of India's new Westernized elite. After legal studies in England, he practiced law in South Africa, where many Indians had emigrated in search of work. There he faced racial prejudice from the European population and discovered his true vocation, political protest and spiritual reconciliation. Caught between Indian and Western culture, Gandhi set out on a spiritual quest to reconcile Indian religious values and Western individualism, which together would give him the ethnic principles for resistance to injustice. He sympathized deeply with Western socialist demands to improve the lives of the poor and oppressed. At the same time, he remained faithful to the Indian belief in spiritual rejuvenation through meditation and to the principle of nonviolence. Gandhi attached great significance to Christ's message in the Sermon on the Mount that violence be met with love by "turning the other cheek." He studied as well Henry David Thoreau's theory of civil disobedience to resist unjust laws. In this long search, he looked for the common humanitarian message that transcended culture and ideology.

Gradually he put together a unique political creed drawn from these readings, Indian religious values, and his own compassion for the sufferings of his fellow Indians. He demanded of his followers that they willingly and peacefully accept imprisonment from their oppressors rather than obey unjust laws or resort to violence. He relied on an innate sense of justice and what he called the "law of love" among all people to achieve the reforms he demanded. His political crusade in South Africa succeeded in temporarily ending the discriminatory legislation imposed on Indian migrants by the government. He returned to India in 1915 a famous champion of Indian rights.

The crisis that resulted from the Amritsar massacre of 1919 turned the National Congress into a potent nationalist movement. It already possessed an extensive political organization, to which was added Gandhi's inspired leadership and a mass following throughout India. In protest against the massacre and the imperial rule responsible for that outrage, Gandhi organized in 1920 his first movement of nonviolent resistance to British rule. He proclaimed that "cooperation in any shape or form with this satanic government is sinful." But a year later when one group of Congress demonstrators attacked a police station, burning it and the police inside, Gandhi called off the campaign. He would not tolerate violence.

His unique program of mass protest and his opposition to any form of collaboration with the British stirred up divisions within the National Congress. Many of its leaders welcomed the British offer to participate in provincial self-rule through elections to provincial legislatures. The Montford Reforms of 1921 carried out the promises of 1917 for provincial representative government. The British viceroy proclaimed that "the principle of autocracy [i.e., absolute rule by the British state in its colony] has been abandoned." Congress politicians accepted the offer to present candidates for the elections. Gandhi had to adjust his campaign to the electoral interests of the party.

◀ **SPOTLIGHT: Mohandas Gandhi** ▶

In Mohandas Gandhi's long life (1869–1948), he never once sought political office or honors. Yet on his death, he was mourned throughout the world as few public figures have ever been. A lawyer by training, he set his goal to help others find justice; "action is my domain," he once said. Yet his greatest achievement proved to be his philosophy of self-purification and humility. He sought nothing for himself, renouncing all material

Mohandas Gandhi (*Embassy of India, Washington D. C.*)

possessions and even sexual pleasure. He lived and died for the sake of his fellow human beings and, first of all, for his fellow Indians.

They rewarded his efforts with a veneration that earned him the extraordinary title of *Mahatma* (meaning "great soul"). His action was from the beginning aimed at improving the spiritual life of individuals as well as ending the injustices of colonial regime. In his years in South Africa and later in India, his own work included the creation of special communities (called in Hindi *ashram*) for close followers committed to a life of moral purification and social reform.

Beginning in the 1920s, his political campaigns against British rule in India mobilized millions of supporters. He expected of them the same readiness to abstain from violence and accept punishment voluntarily (his principle of *satyagraha*) that he practiced himself. When some turned to violence and bloodshed, he denounced their action. He publicly condemned the personal and moral shortcomings of fellow Indians with as much zeal as the injustices and oppression of the British colonial regime. His philosophy of moral purification placed stern demands on everyone and on himself first of all.

His fervent demands for political and social reform at times irritated his collaborators and infuriated his enemies. Despite widespread prejudice against the untouchable class of India, he insisted that these "children of God," as he called them, be given equal treatment alongside high-caste Brahmins. In 1931, the viceroy invited Gandhi to his palace for negotiations over India's political future. It was recognition from the highest quarters of Gandhi's stature as leader of the National Congress. He arrived at the great palace of the viceroy dressed only in a simple tunic and sandals. Winston Churchill, a conservative English politician, was outraged and bitterly protested the presence of this disrespectful "half-naked rebellious holy man" seated alongside the "representative of the King-Emperor." Even Jawaharlal Nehru, Gandhi's loyal disciple and friend, could not accept Gandhi's program, as he described it, for the "salvation" of India through a return to the traditional way of life stripped of "railways, telegraphs, hospitals, doctors." Gandhi's approach to politics, as well as to personal conduct, was moralistic, not practical.

Gandhi's remarkable personality, combined with the goodwill that he showed everyone around him, remained to the end the foundation on which his vast popularity rested. When he was in England in 1932 to continue the negotiations for Indian independence, he chose to live in a poor section of London and to visit textile workers whose jobs were threatened by cottons manufactured in India. They, like most English people, welcomed him with respect and admiration. Nehru remained close to him throughout their decades of collaboration, finding in him moral inspiration and personal reassurance. After his death, a grieving Nehru told the Indian people that "a light has gone out of our lives and there is darkness everywhere."

Until the day of his death, Gandhi's message to Indians stressed the need for respect and toleration. Even when Muslims had created their own state, ending his dream of a unified India, he continued to demand equality of treatment for all Indians no matter what their religion. Gandhi's tragedy, like that of his country and other lands whose peoples were deeply divided, was that the hatred of a few could destroy in a short time the good deeds of generations. A fanatical Hindu assassinated Gandhi, blaming him for his pleas to an end to the bloodshed that partition of his land had provoked. The assassin preached violence, not reconciliation. His brutal solution to interethnic relations found imitators in many other countries in the decades to come. Gandhi's struggle for peace and tolerance remained a vital cause long after his death.

Nehru and Indian Independence

Provincial self-rule did not weaken the Indian nationalists' determination to obtain freedom for their country. In the next decade, the conflict worsened between the National Congress and India's colonial rulers. In 1928, the Congress voted formally for a motion stating "the goal of the Indian people to be complete national independence." This radical new program was the work of a talented young party leader, Jawaharlal Nehru. He had joined the National Congress following an upbringing deeply influenced by British culture. His eminent father provided him with tutors, then with the best English education. Having earned his law degree in London, he returned to India in 1912 prepared to take up a law career modeled on that of his father. An aristocrat by birth and education, he believed deeply in the cause of Indian independence and joined the National Congress. Working for Gandhi gave him, for the first time, an awareness of the social exploitation of his fellow Indians, whom he called "this vast multitude of semi-naked sons and daughters of India."

In the 1920s, he began his own search for the solution to social injustice. He looked first to British socialism, then to Marxism-Leninism as practiced in the Soviet Union. In 1927, he traveled to the Soviet Union in time for the tenth anniversary celebrations of the 1917 revolution. Nehru's understanding of the Soviet revolutionary experience gave him the conviction that the struggle against imperialism had to be joined to the struggle against capitalism. He drew the line at violent revolution, however, rejecting both the Leninist tactics of armed insurrection and the Stalinist methods of single-party dictatorship. He remained faithful to

Gandhi's message of nonviolence and to the goal of a democratic India. He began in the late 1920s a militant campaign for liberation of his country, which he envisioned as both democratic and socialist.

Gandhi remained the sole leader capable of holding together Congress's mass following. In 1930, he called for a campaign against the salt tax. It proved the most effective and dramatic protest movement of his entire career. Touching the poor directly and symbolizing British domination, the tax provided the ideal target against which to unite in opposition well-to-do Congress supporters and Indian peasants. Nonpayment of the tax demanded only the will to resist. By the summer of that year, the nonviolent resistance movement had spread throughout the country. Gandhi himself walked halfway across the land to the Indian Ocean to publicize his readiness to use salt taken from the sea in defiance of the law. The Indian army and police

Nehru's "Semi-Naked Sons of India": Field Workers Winnowing Rice, South India (*Indian National Congress Collection/Hoover Institution Archives*)

briefly arrested demonstrators, including Nehru and Gandhi. The campaign lasted another three years before dying away.

During that time, negotiations continued between the National Congress and the British government. In 1931, Gandhi traveled to London, along with other Indian leaders, to seek Dominion status for his country. The British government had that year created an association of independent former colonies, the Commonwealth, whose members (Dominions) governed themselves yet accepted a common tariff among all associated states, pursued a common foreign policy, and recognized the British monarchy. But Gandhi failed in his mission to include India within the Commonwealth. It remained an association of British settler colonies under white rule (Canada, Australia, New Zealand, and South Africa).

But after several years of hesitation, the British government gave in to most of the National Congress's demands. The depression had weakened Great Britain's power to dominate its colonies, and Congress's resistance was unwavering. In 1935, the British Cabinet issued new laws for Indian self-government—the Government of India Act. This statute created the legal structure of Indian political life until independence. It gave India the institutions of a self-governing state, restricted by special powers for the viceroy only in the event of war or internal emergencies. That part of India under the direct rule of the British, eleven provinces in all, received a federal structure somewhat resembling the state of Canada. An Indian central government had its own cabinet, responsible to a federal legislature. The viceroy, representative of the throne, provided the direct link between Great Britain and the Indian government.

The elections in 1937 for an Indian legislature posed a familiar dilemma to Congress leaders: continued struggle against the vestiges of British colonial rule or collaboration in the implementation of self-rule in peaceful elections. Among those members of Congress who argued against compromise were some admirers of the fascist regimes in Europe and others who found in the Soviet Union the inspiration for an Indian revolution. Between these two extremes, Nehru spoke for moderation. After some hesitation, he chose electoral collaboration. He concluded that "we have no choice but to contest the elections." His moderate policy won the support of the National Congress. Nehru proved in that election to be Congress's outstanding political leader, campaigning throughout India. His party won a resounding victory, gaining control of eight of the eleven provincial governments.

The Muslim League and the Idea of Pakistan

That victory proved ultimately a defeat for the cause of a united India. The Muslim League had presented its own electoral candidates on a program of cooperation with Congress. When the provincial cabinets were formed, Congress leaders refused to appoint Muslim League members to ministerial positions in these cabinets. They were firm believers in Gandhi's warning that India must not allow religious separatism to weaken the goal of a multireligious, multi-ethnic Indian nation. In response, the leader of the League, Muhammed Ali Jinnah, declared that "Islam is in danger." He warned that a unified democratic India represented a menace to the Muslim faith and to the very existence of the Muslim community. In place of one India he proposed two states, one of which would be Pakistan.

The vision of a separate state for the Muslims of the Indian subcontinent was the work of a small group of Muslim intellectuals. In 1930, they had proposed a totally new concept of a nation based on religious affiliation. It addressed in its own way the problem of ethnic-religious diversity by separation into distinct territories. The new state (or states) could not possibly gather together all India's Muslims, but only those areas where Muslims constituted a majority of the population. The name that these visionaries gave to their imagined new state, "Pakistan," came from the first letters of the largest of those areas. *P*, *A*, and *K* referred to lands in the northwest of the subcontinent—Punjab, Afghanistan (not even a part of the British Empire), and Kashmir. It was an improbable idea and a unrealizable national project in its entirety (of the three regions, only one-half of Punjab and a tiny section of Kashmir ultimately became a part of the new state). But this visionary proposal made a permanent mark on Indian history.

The campaign for partition was inevitably controversial. No clear territorial limits separated the followers of the two religions. The large Muslim community of Bengal shared with Bengali Hindus a culture and language different from the language and culture of the Muslims of the Indus River valley in the west. Many Muslims remained committed to Gandhi's vision of a secular, multi-ethnic nation-state of all inhabitants of the Indian subcontinent, and some continued to hold influential positions in the National Congress. Still, fearing Hindu domination and determined to protect their religious practices and culture from Western secular influence, a growing number of Muslims were drawn to the idea of a distinct Muslim political community. Their search for cultural unity fused with the Muslim League's struggle to defend its political influence alongside and in opposition to the National Congress.

Nationalist dreams had produced two very different projects for India's future. Gandhi would not compromise on the principle of national unity. But his commitment to a civic nationalist creed blinded him to the fears of Muslims that majority rule meant oppression for them. Less moralistic, more ambitious leaders on both sides used religious differences to promote their political aims. Mohammed Ali Jinnah himself was a thoroughly Westernized

Indian lawyer who spoke only English. He did not practice the Muslim religion and did not even speak fluent Urdu, the language of most of his Muslim followers. The defense of Muslim political and social needs, not a religious quarrel, lay at the heart of his commitment to the creation of this Muslim state.

Political interests and nationalist programs are not a sufficient explanation for the growing rift among Indians over the future of their country. Communal hostility increasingly split Indian society, and the introduction of democratic institutions appeared only to worsen this ethnic schism. Antagonisms were worst in urban areas such as Calcutta where poverty heightened religious and social hostility. The growth of violence between the Muslim and Hindu communities made real national unity increasingly an illusory goal. Perhaps there was still time to avoid the tragedy of partition through wise leadership and compromise. But war intervened, and the time never came.

That war began for India, as for Great Britain, in 1939. The Indian viceroy proclaimed India at war with Germany. Although it backed the English cause, National Congress refused to be the agents of the British government in a war imposed on India. All Congress provincial ministers resigned their positions, as did those in the federal cabinet in Delhi. At the invitation of the viceroy, Muslim League members took their place. Jinnah proclaimed a Day of Thanksgiving for all Indian Muslims at their deliverance from "Hindu" rule. Muslim deputies became members of provincial cabinets throughout India. The League still looked to the liberation of India from British colonial rule, but not as a unified state. In 1940, the Muslim League agreed on a formal statement, called the Lahore Resolution, calling for the creation of an "independent state" for India's Muslim peoples. As the time of independence drew nearer, so too did the likelihood of conflict between India's great religious communities.

● HIGHLIGHT: Colonialism and Nationalism ●

The Western empires lasted but a brief moment compared with the great empires of Rome and China. Still, their legacy proved as influential as that of earlier imperial states. Most important of all was the impulse their presence gave to nationalism among the peoples over whom they ruled. This process unfolded in spite of and against the wishes of imperial rulers. But when their empires collapsed, out of these ruins emerged the nation-states of the late twentieth century.

Colonialism directly contributed to this momentous change. First, the opposition of subject peoples to imperial rule led them to forge national bonds of loyalty around which to unite in resisting Western rule. Second, non-Westerners searching for an ideological cause to focus and organize an anti-imperialist movement in their land had visible proof in recent Western history of nationalism's ability to unite leaders and their people in a common cause for national unity and respect. Third, Western imperial rule forged new colonial territories within whose borders administrators, military forces, economic activities, and education created centers of public life. This experience gave these territories a tangible presence in the daily experience of the peoples living there. Nationalist movements emerging within these lands directed their efforts to overthrowing colonial rule but left in place the colonial frontiers.

These borders proved tenacious as well because of the distrust among neighboring peoples. The Italian colony of Eritrea, on the shores of the Red Sea, disappeared when the Allies defeated Italy in the Second World War. The large neighboring inland state of Ethiopia absorbed that desert area, claiming that the land had centuries before belonged to the Ethiopian monarchy. But the history that mattered most to the Eritreans, largely Muslim, was their separation under Italian rule from the peoples of Ethiopia, who were mainly Christian and spoke very different languages. After a half-century of federation, in 1993 they voted overwhelmingly to reestablish their independence. Eritrea reappeared on the map of Africa; its borders were those drawn by the Italian Empire.

Everywhere Western overseas colonies forced diverse peoples to live together in a single territory. These colonies extended at times over enormous distances. The island archipelagos of the eastern Pacific were conquered by European states in the sixteenth and seventeenth centuries. Spanish conquest of the Philippines and Dutch control of the East Indies gave territorial unity to peoples divided both geographically and culturally on islands scattered across hundreds of miles of ocean. Dutch in the East Indies and Spanish in the Philippines became the state languages. In each colony, one local language came to predominate among all the dialects and languages spoken there—Tagalog in the Philippines, Malay in the East Indies. Nationalist movements that emerged there in the nineteenth and twentieth centuries set their objective on ending colonial rule but retained the common local language and the boundaries, both a permanent heritage of the imperial era.

Colonialism had to contend with the internal religious and tribal divisions in existence long before Western conquest. European conquerors moved into lands divided among a multitude of peoples with their own tribal or princely leaders. Administrators drew borders that often disregarded the boundaries separating these peoples. The size of their territories created colonies with many distinct ethnic populations. *Ethnic* is the term we use to refer to a people sharing a collective identity based on their belief in a common ancestry. The African colonies seized by European states in the nineteenth century were the homes of many different peoples. Scholars later counted more than 250 separate ethnic groups in British Nigeria, among whom four were very large. The Fulani and Hausa peoples in the north both practiced the Muslim religion. In the south were the Ibo and Yoruba peoples, among whom Christian missionaries made many converts. A colony such as Nigeria was, thus, multi-religious as well as multi-ethnic. Frequently, ethnicity and religious allegiance overlapped, reinforcing the differences among these peoples.

European administrators needed the collaboration of colonial peoples in governing their lands. With only a handful of Europeans filling the most important posts, they had to recruit local officials, police, and even military forces. Faced with diverse peoples often hostile toward one another, their solution usually was to recruit their collaborators from one particular group. In Nigeria, the British preferred to select soldiers from the northern Fulani or Hausa peoples. In their small central African colonies of Burundi and Rwanda, the Germans (and after the First World War the Belgians) turned for assistance to the Tutsi people, who had for centuries held power and enjoyed greater wealth than the much more numerous Hutu people living there. Material wealth mattered most in precolonial times, when possession of more cattle might even earn Hutu families the right to call themselves, and be called, Tutsi. Those who lost their possessions might end up labeled Hutu. The two ethnic terms, in other words, were marks of superiority and inferiority. Memories of supposed different ancestral roots remained alive, though the two peoples lived close by one another and even intermarried. The two groups also came to share a common religious faith, since most of the population converted to Christianity during the colonial period.

The Belgian administrators made the ethnic differences more tangible by giving preference and power to Tutsi soldiers and administrators, then in ordering the entire population to acquire identity cards (internal passports) on which everyone had to identify themselves by their ethnic origins. Ethnic groups, there as in other colonial lands, assumed in this process a far greater awareness of (and potential hostility toward) other peoples than ever before. The ingredients for ethnic conflict were in place.

In these conditions, successful nationalist movements sought to avoid linking their anti-imperialist goals with the objectives of any particular ethnic or religious group. By necessity, they had to establish bonds based on some form of *civic* nationalism, that is, a nationalist ideology promoting shared cultural and political values, not on ethnic or linguistic uniqueness. They retained the borders created by the former colonial rulers, partly for fear of inciting interminable conflicts among peoples and with neighboring states along their frontiers, and partly in the belief that the political future of former colonies had to be multi-ethnic states. The Nigerian writer Chinua Achebe was ready to "give the [British] devil his due: colonialism in Africa disrupted many things, but it did create big political units where there were small, scattered ones before." In his judgment, Nigeria was a more promising homeland for all the peoples living there than the "hundreds of separate communities" that it brought under its rule.

In India, the largest of the British colonies, the internal divisions were probably greater than in any other European-ruled territory. Nationalists seeking an Indian nation-state for the entire population had to propose a formula based on new principles of unity. These principles and ideas had to offer the population substantial reasons to prefer Indian unity to ethnic or religious separateness. Gandhi and the Indian National Congress confronted a daunting task. Their ultimate failure was a tragedy for India.

The historical past of lands such as Turkey, India, and China became the source of unifying national ideals. In India, Gandhi wrote and spoke of the great historical tradition created by the major religions of his country—Hinduism, Islam, and Buddhism. From this tale of spiritual collaboration he drew his inspiration for a doctrine of Indian national solidarity. In China, the political unity and the great civilization that the empire had forged during its 2,000-year existence became points of historical reference to the Nationalist Party of Sun Yat-sen. Its leaders looked to a new Chinese nation, within the borders of the former empire, whose achievements would some day equal those of earlier periods of Chinese greatness. The Chinese Communists had much less sympathy for this tradition, but they too assumed that Chinese political unity was a necessary stage in their revolutionary plans for the Chinese people.

The search for a "useful past" belonging to a particular nation was similar to the efforts earlier by political leaders and intellectuals in Western lands to rewrite the history of their peoples' origins. In some cases the story they told was a generous one, though none came as close as Gandhi to attributing religious humanism to an entire people. Abraham Lincoln sought, in his Gettysburg Address, to make democracy the historical bond of all the peoples of the United States. His speech asked Americans to consider the American Revolution the time when a "new nation [was] conceived in Liberty." This civic nationalism was, in theory, open to all people, no matter what their ethnic or racial origins.

But the new national histories were often written with one ethnic group in mind. Some Western nationalists had shown the way in making history proclaim the superiority of one group of people over others. *Ethnic* nationalism in colonial and semicolonial lands looked to the past to give one people a better claim on power and territory than others living in the same land. Ataturk and his fellow Turkish nationalists glorified their people by praising the Osmanli Turkic tribes, invaders from Central Asia who had long before conquered the land he called Turkey. He traced the nation's roots to this conquest. By implication, other peoples in Turkey, such as the Armenians, were second-rate members of the new nation-state. These nationalists were convinced that their people were endowed with unique qualities, which had appeared long before and had been passed on from generation to generation. Their goal was the creation of political and cultural symbols around which to unify the population in one national community. These national stories of ethnic groups conveyed a potentially dangerous message, for they could become the justification for racism. History, in this telling, was a story of "blood and belonging." Nationalism was a powerful ideology, both creative and destructive.

One scholar has labeled the ideal of a nation-state an "imagined community." The nation, intended to be the basis of a sovereign state, is so large and so remote from people's everyday lives that it can only be imagined. Yet it still relies on the solidarity of a people believing themselves part of one large community.[1] The political community imagined by nationalists was often a fragile creation, contested by other movements and minority peoples living in the same territory. Colonial empires shaped the borders of lands in which these movements took shape; the fall of these empires put the promise of nationalism to the test in every former colonial land.

---

[1] Benedict Anderson, *Imagined Communities: Reflections on the Origin and Spread of Nationalism* (New York, 1991), pp. 6–7.

CIVIL WAR AND FOREIGN WAR IN CHINA

The Chinese path to national unification began with the overthrow of the Chinese Empire in 1911. It did not end until the Communist Party's seizure of power in 1949. Once an integrated empire and social system, China went through a prolonged period of disorder and struggle. Foreign and civil wars wrought terrible destruction and hardship, adding to the perennial sufferings of the population. Supporters of the Chinese Nationalist Party looked to Western states in laying their plans for a new China, while the Chinese Communist Party conceived of a revolutionary society on the model of the Soviet Union. Deeply divided by political ideology, they both distanced themselves from the traditional Confucian order. Bitter enemies, each anticipated that it alone was destined to construct a renewed, unified China. Until the 1940s, the Chinese Nationalist Party appeared the chosen leader.

The Rise of the Chinese Nationalist Party

In 1911, the most powerful commander in the imperial army declared his allegiance to a Chinese Republic. The last emperor, still a child, was taken prisoner and the empire fell without resistance. Supporting this rebellion were intellectuals and students educated in Western schools, ready to devote their lives to bringing Western political rights and national unity to their own country.

In the years after the empire's collapse, ambitious Chinese generals in command of sizable armies seized control of large provinces. One of them took over the entire region of Manchuria, where he governed like a petty prince. These so-called warlords depended on their armies and the taxes on their poor subjects to control their territories. They rarely had a reform program, were unwilling or unable to create new political institutions, and fought among themselves in small-scale wars that worsened the suffering of the civilian population. Within ten years of the 1911 revolution, China was a united republic in name only. Central government institutions and functions fell into decay. Foreign states kept their concessions and spheres of influence by dealing directly with these petty military rulers. The rule of the warlords became the major political obstacle to national unification.

Two revolutionary parties claimed the right to create that Chinese nation-state. One was the Nationalist Party, the other the Communist Party. Their organizers were all intellectuals educated in "new schools" that taught Western languages and knowledge. Often they had gone abroad, to Japan or to the West, to learn of the modern world. The most influential of these radicals was the veteran

China at War, 1911–1949

revolutionary, Sun Yat-sen. He had abandoned Confucianism, converting to Christianity, and had given up his medical career
to organize a secret nationalist movement. His
ideals were summed up in a set of Three Principles: (1) nationalism, by which he meant
freedom from imperialist domination;
(2) democracy, which to him represented
Western constitutional government; and
(3) socialism, which he understood as an industrial economy and equality of land holdings for the Chinese peasant farmers. He
realized that to achieve these goals China required a modern political party. He called his
new movement the Nationalist People's Party
(in Chinese, *Guomindang*). For him as for other
radicals, national liberation and unification
were China's sole hope for progress and independence.

Events at the end of the First World War
brought his party the mass support that it
needed to lead the Chinese nationalist movement. The news that the Paris peace negotiators had granted the Japanese Empire
territorial rights to northern China set off a
wave of protest in Chinese cities, where even
business classes joined a boycott of (that is, refusal to purchase) all Japanese goods. Sun Yat-
sen and his Nationalist Party took the lead in
organizing the boycott. This "May Fourth
movement," so named since the news from
France reached China on May 4, 1919, gave
Sun's party the broad base of support that it
needed to challenge the rule of the warlords.
The Japanese government soon agreed to
withdraw its forces from most Chinese territories. The mass backing that Sun Yat-sen had
obtained set his party on the path to unify
China.

The Nationalists soon found a valuable foreign ally. Their opposition to Japanese expansion and to Western imperialism was shared
by the new Soviet Union. The Soviet leaders
considered nationalist revolutionary move-

ments in colonial lands to be an important
part of their global struggle against Western
capitalism. The two groups shared common
enemies. Some Chinese radicals found in the
revolutionary experiment under way in the
Soviet Union a model for their own country.
They constituted the core membership of the
Chinese Communist Party, created in 1921.
Sun Yat-sen did not share their faith in the dictatorship of the proletariat and the inevitable
triumph of communism. He did, however,
recognize the practical benefits of an alliance
with the Soviet Union. For one thing, the Nationalist Party needed a centralized organization like that of the Soviet Communist Party to
organize and lead the forces necessary to
unify China. For another, he realized that his
movement required military aid to defeat the
warlords. The Soviet Communists had set up
an effective army in their fight for survival
during the civil war. They could furnish Nationalist armies with the needed military
training for the conquest of China.

In 1923, the Soviet state and the Communist International agreed to provide political
and military assistance to the Chinese Nationalist Party. Soviet advisers helped to organize a Chinese "party army" and Chinese
officers, including Sun's aide Chiang Kai-
shek, went to the Soviet Union to learn from
Red Army officers the skills of modern warfare. Soviet assistance proved very effective,
widening the base of support for the Nationalists and strengthening their party organization and army.

In 1926, the Nationalist leadership was
ready to launch its military offensive against
the warlords in northern China. Its troops,
from their base in the south and commanded
by Chiang Kai-shek, moved up the coast.
Their objective was the imperial city of Beijing. The success of this "Northern Expedition" was probably the greatest triumph of
the Nationalists. Warlords surrendered rather

than fight. In 1928, the Nationalists captured Beijing. This military victory was of particular benefit to Chiang Kai-shek. He had become leader of the Nationalist Party following Sun Yat-sen's death in 1925. His authority depended largely on control of the army. It was as much a political as a military instrument of power. For the rest of his life he relied primarily on his armed forces for political as well as military backing. Chiang resembled in this respect the warlords. He did preserve Sun's Nationalist Party and adhered to its program of reform. His military victory conferred on him the mantle of Sun's legitimate heir. In 1928, he appeared to have achieved Sun's dream of a new China unified under Nationalist leadership.

In those years, Chiang set out to eliminate his principal political rival, the Chinese Communist Party. In 1927, his military forces and police suddenly arrested large numbers of Communists, as well as labor union organizers and other suspected radicals; many of them were soon executed. Urban support for the Communists declined as a result of the repression and of the workers' disillusionment at the collapse of the party. In a misguided effort to thwart Chiang's anticommunist campaign, the Communist International ordered the Chinese Communists to organize a large-scale insurrection. It failed miserably. This painful experience gave some of the survivors, including Mao Zedong, a bitter lesson in Moscow's inability to understand the Chinese revolutionary struggle.

Mao Zedong and Chinese Communism

The crushing defeat of the Chinese Communist Party proved the turning point in its history. Its efforts to imitate the Soviet Communists' path to revolutionary power by building working-class backing had proven misplaced and self-defeating. The party's strategy, even ideology, had urgent need of revision. This became the work of Mao Zedong. He had joined the Communist Party after years of searching for a political blueprint to remake the Chinese state and society. A student at the time of the 1911 revolution, he shared with other Westernized radicals the conviction that the old order in China had to be destroyed. He had spurned his father's wish that he return to help run the family farm, preferring the life of an activist scholar. In those years he wrote that the "four evil demons of the empire" were "religion, capitalism, autocracy, and the Three Bonds" (obedience of wife to husband, of son to father, and of subject to emperor). Moving to Beijing in 1918, he discovered the cause to which he devoted his entire life. Some Chinese intellectuals that year were praising the communist revolution in Russia as the "victory of the spirit of all humanity." He joined a Marxist study circle to understand Lenin's theory of revolution. By the time the Chinese Communist Party was founded in 1921, he was a dedicated Marxist-Leninist.

The period in the 1920s of collaboration with the Nationalists gave Mao invaluable experience in revolutionary organization. He devoted his effort to mobilizing Chinese peasants for political action in the campaign against the warlords. He became convinced of their capacity for revolutionary action in the Chinese tradition of rural rebellion; his experience also taught him how to win the peasants' backing. Most peasants were tenant farmers, subject in those years to exploitation by landlords and tax collectors and to looting and murder by marauding bands of robbers or soldiers. Their only recourse, as in past centuries, was banditry and mass rebellion. In the years of collaboration with the Nationalists, Mao became convinced that China's poor peasants could be mobilized to take up arms against their exploiters and against foreign enemies. He had created his own version of communist revolutionary theory and practice.

The destruction in 1927–1928 of the urban forces of the Chinese Communist Party led Mao to seek refuge among his peasant followers. By 1929, he had carved out a small area in a south China province where he and his peasant guerrilla army were able to construct a "Red Base," the center of his operations. He organized and expanded his territory in spite of repeated "extermination" campaigns by Nationalist troops. The survival of his Red Base required an army capable of holding back the Nationalists, and its soldiers had to be recruited among the peasantry. Mao first proved his revolutionary genius in those difficult years. By 1931, his "liberated area" had expanded to include a population of 3 million under the control of a Red Army of 100,000 guerrilla fighters. That year he formally proclaimed it the Chinese Soviet Republic. The proclamation was an act of defiance and a claim to leadership in the Republic of China. He was convinced that the most powerful revolutionary forces of his country were in the countryside, and he was right.

The success of his movement depended on the support of the Chinese peasantry and the organization of military forces capable of sustaining long and arduous guerrilla warfare. Mao's soviet republic gave the poor peasants what they most desired—their own land. His party supporters forced landlords and rich peasants to redistribute most of the property to the landless farmers. The land and its harvest belonged to individual peasants. They depended on Mao's soviet republic to retain their farms. They had good reason to support their communist rulers. Many became the recruits in the Red Army, on whom the survival of the republic depended.

The army was the military arm of Mao's revolutionary movement. He and his followers sought to convince the soldiers that their real enemy was "feudalism." This term, in the vocabulary of Chinese Communists, referred to China's oppressive traditions. In fighting the Nationalist forces, his soldiers believed that they were contributing to the historic progress of China. Over the years Mao devised a unique strategy of guerrilla combat, summed up in a simple formula that every soldier learned: "The enemy advances, we retreat; the enemy camps, we harass; the enemy tires, we attack; the enemy retreats, we pursue." Mao had no assurance of ultimate victory save his unshakable faith in the might of the world proletarian movement. He had no protection from his Chinese enemies besides the rifles of his peasant soldiers. In those years of brutal repression of the Chinese Communists, the very survival of Mao's soviet republic was a remarkable achievement.

China between Nationalists and Communists

In the late 1920s, the Nationalist Party consolidated its leadership of China. For a few years the country enjoyed relatively peaceful times. The Western powers made their peace with Chiang, renouncing the special privileges they had forced on the Chinese Empire. They were unwilling to maintain strong military forces to protect their territorial concessions. Besides, they knew that the Nationalists did not threaten their interest in trade and investment. The Chinese Republic took over control of tariffs, taxes, and postal services, previously run by Westerners. The foreign concessions disappeared; Chinese law extended throughout the country. The Nationalist leaders could fairly claim to be Sun Yat-sen's true heirs in ending Western domination of their country. They promised an end to old abuses. They banned the cruel practice of footbinding, though they had little power to enforce this policy.

Despite Sun's promise of constitutional democracy, the Chinese Republic under the Nationalists was an authoritarian state. Under the command of Chiang, its army was the dominant political force in the country. He held semidictatorial powers, calling his regime a "guided democracy" for the young Chinese Republic. His claim to be the head of a unified China was an illusion. Many areas escaped his control; Manchuria remained in the hands of its warlord, who only pretended to support the Nationalist regime. Korea and the southern Manchurian coast were under Japanese control. Japanese generals were increasingly eager to extend their power into China. They mocked the Nationalist government's claim to govern all China but in private worried that China might once again become powerful. Manchuria was their most tempting target, and in 1931 they undertook to conquer the entire region.

Japanese army officers stationed in the Japanese concession in southern Manchuria claimed (falsely) that Chinese terrorists had attacked Japanese property and military forces. The reality was the reverse. They had decided to take over the province before the Chinese Nationalists could do so. In 1931, the Japanese army invaded Manchuria north of the coastal zone it already occupied. Its forces encountered only weak resistance from the troops of the Manchurian warlord. By early 1932, it had conquered the entire province. Japanese occupation authorities turned it into a satellite state, called Manchukuo. In a mockery of "national self-determination," they claimed to have liberated the Manchu people. They even accorded this phantom state its own monarch, placing on the throne the last Qing (Manchu) emperor. He was in fact their puppet ruler.

Chiang made only token gestures of opposition. The Japanese campaign touched a peripheral area, destroying the power of another warlord. He agreed to an armistice, which resembled a capitulation. He realized that his forces could not defeat the Japanese army and secretly rejoiced at the defeat of the Manchurian warlord. He preferred instead to turn his own troops against his internal enemy, the soviet republic controlled by Mao's forces. It was the stronghold of his most dangerous rival for power.

In the early 1930s, he launched four separate military offensives against the Communists. He turned for help to German military advisers, who taught his troops the methods of encirclement and siege operations. By 1934, his forces had drawn a noose around Mao's troops. They were slowly strangling the soviet area. The Communists' only hope of survival lay in fleeing their enemy and abandoning their soviet republic.

The "Long March" of Mao's army has become a legend in Chinese history. As such, official accounts of the yearlong trek mingle fact and fancy. It started out, in Mao's own words, as a "headlong flight" of about 120,000 soldiers, forced to leave behind their families and possessions and setting out without any clear destination. They were pursued by Nationalist troops seeking their annihilation, through mountainous areas inhabited by peoples hostile to all Chinese. After several months of dissension and debate within the Communist Party leadership, Mao took control.

In that period, he earned the reputation of heroic "helmsman" for the Chinese Communists. They revered him as their courageous warrior carrying the revolutionary torch. Mao made the Long March's destination the remote northwestern province of Shaanxi (old spelling, Shensi). It offered refuge for his forces, since it was the center of another small "liberated area." The choice was a gamble, for Shaanxi was located at an enormous distance and required that Mao and his followers cross a vast mountainous terrain where few supplies could be found (see map, p. 117). Hunger and disease accompanied the marchers all the way. Those who survived required great moral and physical strength. The legend claims that only 8,000 arrived in late 1935 at their destination of Yanan, a city in Shaanxi. Whatever the actual number of casualties, the Long March proved the revolutionary commitment of Mao and his followers. It forged the leadership that led the party to victory fifteen years later. Mao had saved the core of his movement and found a secure base to continue his struggle.

Recognition of his remarkable achievement came from Moscow. In those years, the Soviet leaders had special need of Mao's help. The Comintern had ordered foreign communist parties to mobilize against Germany and Japan, both threatening war on the Soviet Union. In 1935, it sent orders to the Chinese party to organize an anti-Japanese coalition. This was to include Chiang's troops, better equipped than Mao's forces and supported by the West. For Stalin, the strategy promised to divert toward China the Japanese forces that by then had moved as far north as borders of the Soviet Union and Mongolia (a Soviet satellite state). Mao supported the new tactics wholeheartedly. He was himself a Chinese patriot, deeply committed to the defeat of China's enemies. In the following years, his party gained the sympathy of many Chinese attracted by its nationalist zeal as much as by its Marxist revolutionary program.

The communist base of operations became northern China in the poor highland region of Shaanxi. Its military forces, numbering in 1936 about 30,000, were strong enough to defeat a new Nationalist encirclement campaign. Almost completely cut off from the outside world, its very existence was a mystery to the West until the American reporter Edgar Snow visited the area and described it in a flattering book called *Red Star over China*. The new soviet republic had to rely solely on the resources of the region. The Soviet Union provided no military or economic assistance.

Soviet leaders preferred dealing with the Nationalist government, whose strength they overestimated, and still had little grasp of the strength of Mao's "peasant" movement. When, in 1937, the Soviet government began delivering military supplies to China, it sent them to Chiang's forces.

Mao could count only on his own military forces and his political movement. He applied in his territory the same policy of peasant reform and guerrilla war that he had learned earlier. He explained to his followers in 1936 that their "revolutionary war" remained the struggle to destroy imperialism and feudalism in China, embodied in the "counter-revolutionary" regime of the Nationalists. Chiang's forces were very strong, however, and they were weak and small. The Communists' first task consisted of the defeat of the Japanese imperialists; revolution came later.

War against Japan

The alliance between the Communists and the Nationalists finally became reality in 1937. Chiang had resisted joining the coalition until one of his own generals took him prisoner, keeping him hostage until he agreed to the "united front" with the Communists. It was one of the most bizarre and humiliating experiences in Chiang's career. But the alternative was much more unpleasant. His captor might well have shot him; it is likely that Mao himself insisted on methods of "gentle persuasion" until Chiang gave in. The Nationalist leader ended (temporarily) his campaign against Mao's soviet republic and accepted joint military operations against the Japanese forces. As his reward, his state obtained military supplies from the Soviet Union (more than the United States gave his state in the period before 1941). The Chinese Communists for their part acknowledged their place in the Chinese Republic, renaming their soviet republic the "special regime of the Republic of

China" and baptizing the Red Army the "Eighth Route Army" of the republic. Both sides remained deeply suspicious of the other. Only the distance separating their core territories and the conflict with Japan kept them at peace. The two rivals for power made a fragile partnership.

War with Japan gave them a common enemy. Later in the summer of 1937, full-scale war between Japan and China began. No one yet knows exactly how the military conflict started in an area near Beijing where Japanese troops were stationed. Communist and anti-Japanese Nationalist troops apparently started small-scale military operations against the Japanese there. In retaliation, Japanese generals resolved in a reckless move to crush all the Chinese forces and to make coastal China another "client state" of the Japanese Empire. Major Japanese offensives began that year in the northern and central regions of China. Japanese troops pushed farther and farther into China in an effort to crush Chiang's forces.

The Chinese Republic could not match the military might of Japan. By 1939, the Japanese controlled the principal coastal areas of China, where they set up puppet regimes governed by Chinese collaborators. Chiang had to retreat far into the interior, placing his capital in the mountainous city of Chongqing (Chungking). He had kept his regime in existence, but only by husbanding his forces and placing strict controls on the offensive operations of his troops. He preferred to hold what territory he could by defensive fighting, avoiding bloody attacks on the Japanese. He feared the Communists nearly as much as the Japanese, using his forces to hold onto the remnants of the once great Republic of China.

Mao's armies moved into large rural areas of central and northern China behind the Japanese lines. By 1941, their Eighth Route Army totaled 400,000 men and held areas with a combined population of 44 million people. Their guerrilla forces proved more successful than Chiang's armies in seizing Chinese territory from the Japanese. That year the Japanese army attempted to destroy their liberated areas. Japanese forces applied to the guerrilla areas the simple, brutal policy of "burn all, kill all, loot all." The Communists suffered severely, their army declining to 300,000 and the civilians in much of their territory were uprooted or forced to submit to Japanese rule. The Japanese occupation forces could not destroy the Communist insurrection, however, nor could their armies destroy the Nationalists. Neither Communists nor Nationalists by themselves could expel the enemy from China. To end the stalemate, their only hope was military help from a foreign ally.

The only ally capable of providing that assistance was the United States. Since 1937, the Soviet Union had given the Nationalists substantial military aid. But when Germany attacked the Soviet Union in mid-1941, even those supplies ceased. In 1937, the U.S. government made a diplomatic gesture of support for the Nationalist regime. President Roosevelt praised the "magnificent defense of China." Subsequently, he allowed Chinese purchases of military equipment despite U.S. neutrality laws banning aid to foreign belligerents. The U.S. press publicized Japanese brutality toward the Chinese, denouncing the massacre in 1938 by Japanese troops of the population of the Chinese city of Nanking. But American isolationism blocked any major U.S. effort to aid China. A growing naval conflict with Germany turned the attention of the United States toward the war in Europe. Until the Japanese regime's expansionist policies took its troops further into East Asia, the Chinese had to fight alone.

SUMMARY

In the two decades following the end of the First World War, nationalist movements in Asian countries began the historic process of ending colonial rule and creating new nation-states. These developments proceeded then, as later, along paths unique to each country. Different cultural traditions, colonial institutions, and nationalist visions gave the history of these lands their own distinct character. The outcome everywhere was the decline of Western imperial influence.

The Turkish national revolution took the path of rejection of the Ottoman institutions and the Muslim way of life. The struggle included war with Greek invaders, and the repression of internal revolts by minority peoples. Out of this bitter, bloody conflict emerged a Turkish nation-state. It adapted modern secular laws and Western institutions to the needs and character of the Turkish people. Its creation was a national revolution.

The Indian National Congress, after long years of political struggle, won from the British the promise of self-government for the entire subcontinent. The British Empire lacked the resources and the determination to maintain for much longer its hold on India. The leaders of the National Congress pressed forward their campaign for independence with zeal, adhering to Gandhi's commandments for peaceful methods of struggle. They could not, however, overcome centuries of distrust between the Muslim and Hindu communities. Whether the Indian subcontinent would in fact remain united depended on the moderation and realism of the Muslim League and the National Congress. Its fate also rested with the millions of Muslims and Hindus, already in serious conflict.

The rise of the Nationalist Party of Chiang Kai-shek brought a superficial appearance of national unity to China and ended finally the most humiliating aspects of Western domination. There, too, the future of the country rested partly on the outcome of an internal conflict, pitting Communists against the Nationalist regime. Each had its own programs for China's resurgence; each had good reason to distrust the goals of the other. The Nation-

alists proved less capable than the Communists of implementing their ambitious plans to improve the lot of China's impoverished masses. They were strong enough to contain Mao's revolutionary forces and to survive the Japanese invasion. But they lacked the resources to expel the Japanese invaders. The Japanese Empire, though still at war in China, had grown larger and mightier at the expense of the Chinese. The age of empire had not yet come to an end in East Asia.

DATES WORTH REMEMBERING

1919   Gandhi leader of Indian National Congress
1919   Amritsar massacre in India
1919   Kemal Ataturk leader of Turkish nationalist movement
1920–1922   Greek-Turkish War
1921   Provincial self-rule in India
1921   Creation of Chinese Communist Party
1923   Founding of Republic of Turkey
1925   Abolition of Caliphate by Ataturk
1928   Successful conclusion of Chinese Nationalists' Northern Expedition
1929   National Congress vote for Indian independence
1930   Anti–salt tax movement in India
1931   Japanese invasion of Manchuria
1934–1935   Long March of Chinese Communists
1935   Government of India Act
1937   Triumph of Indian National Congress in national elections
1937–1945   Sino-Japanese War
1940   Muslim League decision to seek independent state of Pakistan

RECOMMENDED READING

Modern Turkey

Andrew Mango, *Ataturk* (1999). A detailed biography of the founder of Turkey.

*Bernard Lewis, *The Emergence of Modern Turkey* (2nd ed., 1968). A comprehensive analysis of the upheaval that produced modern Turkey.

Indian History

Judith Brown, *Gandhi: Prisoner of Hope* (1989). The best biography of the inspirational, spiritual, and political leader, with a critical view of his message.
Michael Edwardes, *British India, 1772–1947* (1968). A thoughtful survey of British rule in India.
*Stanley Wolpert, *A New History of India* (4th ed., 1993). A broad survey of pre- and post-colonial India, very critical of the British impact on their colony.

Chinese History

*James Sheridan, *China in Disintegration: The Republican Era in Chinese History, 1912–1949* (1975). The story of the failed hopes and plans of the Nationalist Party in its years of rise and fall from power.

*Jonathan Spence, *The Search for Modern China* (1990). An interpretive history of China, stressing its rich, complex cultural tradition.

Memoirs, Novels, and Visual Aids

Ved Mehta, *The Ledge between the Streams* (1984); *Daddyji* (1979); and *Mamaji* (1975). A vivid multi-volume account of growing up in a Hindu family divided between its respect for tradition and the attraction of modernity.
Han Suyin, *The Crippled Tree* (1965). The memoirs of a young Chinese girl, later a famous novelist, whose European father and Chinese mother made the conflict between East and West a personal drama.
Gandhi. A somewhat idealized film biography (1982) of the great Indian leader.
The Last Emperor. Film dramatization (1975) of the tumultuous life of Emperor Pu Yi, who survived war, revolution, and Mao Zedong.

_____

*Indicates the book is available in paperback.

CHAPTER FIVE

Despotic Empires of the 1930s

NAZI GERMANY, SOVIET UNION,

JAPANESE EMPIRE, 1930–1941

- Nazism and Adolf Hitler
- Stalin's Soviet Union
- The Japanese Empire

Highlight: Communism and Joseph Stalin

Spotlight: Admiral Yamamoto

Hopes in the 1920s for peace and progress faded in the next decade. Economic prosperity gave way to pervasive world depression. In its wake came bitter political conflicts and violence. Extremist prophets in lands hard hit by the economic decline proposed drastic political solutions to the anguish and hardship experienced by the population. In Germany, their hunger for power and their popular support gave them the chance to put in place a brutal dictatorship. In Japan, Japanese generals and civilian politicians, promising imperial might and conquest, transformed a relatively democratic country into an authoritarian, expansionist state. The aggressive foreign policies of these two despotic states

heightened international tensions and pointed the way to a new war. The depression did not produce these changes, but it created the breeding ground for the extremism that afflicted public life in many parts of the world. Despotism, not democracy, appeared to hold the answers to the crisis of those years.

One model for dictatorship was Italian fascism. It had turned nationalism into a creed of totalitarian dictatorship. The triumph of the Nazi Party in Germany represented the most spectacular victory of fascism. On the other side of the globe, Japanese military leaders took over key positions in government and imposed on the country an ideology of militaristic nationalism so severe that it resembled fascism. A militant ideology set the tone for public life in all three states. It glorified the image of the warrior and military conquest. All three regimes pursued expansionist foreign policies by diplomatic intimidation and war. The empires of Italy, Germany, and Japan destroyed hopes for a new era of peace. For a few years, their conquests seemed to bring the world into a new age of imperialism.

At the other political extreme, the Stalinist regime of the Soviet Union announced to the world that its revolutionary deeds and ideology pointed the way to human progress and deliverance from economic hardship. In the years after the 1917 revolution, the Communists had put in place a one-party dictatorship. Stalin took this process one step further, creating a dictatorial regime as despotic as that of Nazi Germany. The message from the Soviet Union affirmed that a new, socialist society had emerged there, freer than any society in the world. The Communists boasted that they had achieved this marvel by means of a "revolution from above." They kept in place a system of elections for Soviet government but allowed only one candidate to appear for each office. They retained a system of justice with trials and defense lawyers, but in the shadows existed a parallel system of repression in the hands of the secret police. The peoples of the Soviet Union submitted to this perverse "democracy," since prison or death awaited anyone who disagreed with the regime.

Soviet foreign policy had to contend with the expansionist threat from Germany and Japan. Stalin, perhaps the most cynical of the political leaders in those years, considered global politics a "jungle" in which only the ruthless could survive. When the opportunity to annex new territories arose at the end of the 1930s, he seized the chance. His state, which ruled over the lands once in the Russian Empire, expanded into western territories whose population had for a few years lived in free nation-states. In this sense, the Soviet Union was an expansionist empire.

NAZISM AND ADOLF HITLER

The character and political ambitions of Adolf Hitler, the founder of the Nazi Party, bear striking similarities to Benito Mussolini. Both leaders were front-line soldiers in the First World War. Both emerged from war believing that they were chosen leaders for their nation. Both men transformed wartime nationalism into a justification for political revolution. Both extolled the brutality of the warrior as proof of the virility of a nation and turned that spirit into the inspiration to seize power by force or by intimidation. Both denounced the alleged decadence that democracy and modern life had spread among their people. They blamed toleration of diversity and individualism for these ills. Both scorned human rights and glorified national solidarity and combat. In mass democracies, they turned the liberties guaranteed citizens into the means to create political dictatorship.

But Nazism was unique among fascist movements in Europe. Most important of all, it made racism a central feature of its nationalist ideology. All fascist parties glorified a particular ethnic nation, appealing to the myth of a glorious ancestry and condemning present-day enemies of their people. None took the idea to such fanatical lengths as did the Nazis. In particular, Nazism turned hatred of the Jews into the central feature of its ideology. At the same time, it elevated the fascist ideal of the warrior to become the driving force behind its plans for Germany's expansion. The restoration of German might in Europe was to be the first step to world power. No other fascist movement so thoroughly turned nationalism into a message of conquest. Nazism combined despotic nationalism and racism in a brutal, destructive message of repression and war.

The Nazi Party and Hitler

The National Socialist (Nazi) Party was Adolf Hitler's chosen instrument for his movement. He became leader of this tiny ultra-nationalist party shortly after leaving the German army at the end of the First World War. Within a short time, he had surrounded his position with an aura of authority like that Mussolini had created. The concept of "leader" was as important to the Nazi movement as it was to Mussolini's Fascist Party. One of his supporters later proclaimed at a party rally, "Hitler is the People, the People is Hitler!" In concrete terms, the party program became whatever Hitler judged best. He understood the term *National Socialist* to mean someone "who knows no higher ideal than the welfare of the nation." The Nazi program offered no real promise of social reform. It allied conservative, middle-class values with revolutionary nationalism. The party and the leader were most important of all.

During the 1920s, the movement acquired its unique militaristic character. Hitler formed within the party a special paramilitary group, the Stormtroopers (the SA), composed largely of war veterans dressed in a special uniform and prepared for street battle to defend the party against its enemies. Later he added an elite bodyguard dressed in black uniforms called the Schutzstaffel (SS). He demanded of the SS a loyalty greater than that of any soldier in the German army. The SS members had to present documents proving their "racial purity" and had to take a personal oath of loyalty to Hitler, promising to obey him unquestioningly—"the word of Hitler has the force of law."

The party became a mass political movement in the early years of the depression. It spread its sections throughout the country. By 1932, party membership totaled 800,000, and the SA had enrolled a half-million men. Many were war veterans or people who had found a sense of purpose in the national community of wartime. They became the warriors in the struggle against German democracy, the Jews, and Germany's foreign enemies.

Economic hardship and disillusionment with democratic parties drove millions of German voters to the party. By 1932, the Nazis received the backing of one-third of all German voters. The only other movement that gained votes substantially in those years was the Communist Party, though it never attracted more than 17 percent of the voters. Together the two extremist parties attracted over 50 percent of the total vote. This extraordinary electoral shift revealed a mood of protest among Germans, not only against the ineffectiveness of government policies but also against the entire democratic system so recently adopted.

According to parliamentary rules, after its triumph in the 1932 parliamentary elections the National Socialist Party had earned the right to take charge of the German government. It had the largest group of deputies in the legislature (Reichstag). Yet it was an avowed enemy of democracy. Hitler had stipulated that his party would agree to have members accept appointment as ministers in the cabinet only if he himself became its leader (chancellor). The German president, Marshall von Hindenburg, relied on the judgment of his closest advisers, including army generals and conservative aristocrats. Unable to understand the Nazis' ruthless ambition and fanaticism, they thought that they could control Hitler easily. They disregarded the brutality and violence of the Nazi Party, seeing in it a mass movement dedicated to nationalism and conservatism. In January 1933, Marshall von Hindenburg yielded to their arguments and appointed Hitler chancellor of the German Republic. Germany had taken a long step toward Nazism.

The Nazi Dictatorship

Taking the law in its own hands, the Nazi Party moved during the winter and spring of 1933 into positions of power. Hitler's armed militia, the SA and SS, intimidated and terrorized Nazi opponents at will. The Berlin building that housed the parliament burned in late February (possibly an event engineered by Nazis). Hitler blamed the Communists and persuaded the president to grant him extraordinary powers "for the protection of the people and the state." He suspended individual liberties, including press and assembly, and obtained parliamentary approval for the Enabling Act that authorized the cabinet (that is, Hitler) to rule without constitutional restraints. With the passage of this law, he was virtual dictator.

During the next several years, the Nazis extended their control over the entire country. In July 1933, the cabinet proclaimed that the Nazi Party "constitutes the only political party in Germany." Other parties were banned; the members of the German Communist Party were arrested and sent to newly created prison camps. The country had become a one-party dictatorship. Nazi organizations reached out to all groups of the population, including youth, labor, and professional associations. Even the churches came under state control or made their peace with the Nazis. Individual religious leaders who dared to protest Nazi injustices were imprisoned. By 1934, the voices publicly opposing Nazism had fallen silent.

The German army still remained beyond Nazi control. Its officer corps retained the traditional solidarity of the old German army. The Nazi movement came to power with its own paramilitary forces, the Stormtroopers, whose leaders believed that their movement should become the core of a new Nazi army. Hitler chose to side with the army against the SA. He promised the generals an expanded army and protection from reform. To end the SA threat, he secretly organized the removal by force of the SA leadership. During the "night of the long knives" in June 1934, SS squads seized and executed over seventy political leaders whom Hitler wanted eliminated. Hitler justified the executions by claiming that he made the law, for he was "responsible for the fate of the German people." By their silence, the army generals condoned this blood purge. They were satisfied to see the SA leaders disappear.

That September, Hitler obtained his reward. At the time of the death of President von Hindenburg, he proclaimed himself head of state and commander-in-chief of the armed forces. Germany's generals made no objection. In a special oath, each soldier and officer in the army swore "unconditional obedience to the Leader of the German State and People, Adolf Hitler," and vowed "as a brave soldier, to stake my life at any time for this oath." Police terror and absolute loyalty to Hitler constituted two central features of the Nazi state.

By then the Nazi regime had created, hidden behind from public view, a potent instrument of political repression. This was the "SS state," a system of brutal, arbitrary rule dedicated to absolute, unquestioning obedience to Hitler. It did not abide by ordinary laws nor were its personnel at all like those of the regular state administration. The Nazi Party embodied the new principles of despotic authority. It orchestrated giant party rallies in the medieval city of Nuremberg to display the awesome might of the new regime. It was the source of recruits to the two key groups in the SS state—the SS, expanded in numbers and power after June 1934 to supplant the SA, and the secret police, called the Gestapo, which was soon incorporated into the SS organization. The powers of the SS extended to the jails for political prisoners and concentration camps for the "reeducation" of "undesirables."

This SS state enjoyed unrestricted power to arrest and to punish. Its only law was the simple command: "The will of the Leader has the force of law." Hitler's dream of a new German

Nazism on Display: Hitler Addressing Party Rally, approx. 1935 (*National Archives and Records Administration*)

nation took the form of a warfare state, led by warriors and supported by the efforts of the entire population in a new empire, the "Third Reich" (Empire). It would, he proclaimed, last for a thousand years.

There was no place in this empire for its Jewish population. Nazi hatred of the Jews became the inspiration for a policy of racial segregation and persecution. First, in 1933, came the expulsion of Jews from any position in the German administration. Then came sweeping measures of discrimination contained in the Nuremberg Laws of 1935. All Germans with at least two Jewish grandparents lost their German citizenship. Marriages between Ger-

mans and Jews became illegal. The goal was the physical expulsion from Germany of Jews, who had assimilated generations before into German society. In the wake of these laws, municipalities issued edicts forbidding Jews entry into their cities, posting signs proclaiming themselves "Free of Jews [*Judenrein*]."

By 1938, over 100,000 Jews had emigrated from Germany. They had to surrender everything they owned to obtain the right to leave. Among them were outstanding intellectuals such as Albert Einstein. Even more Jews fled after the violent attack on Jews and Jewish property throughout Germany in November 1938 ("Crystal Night"), during which all the country's synagogues were burned. In a country Westerners believed an enlightened, civilized society, blind racism had become law. The foundations for the policy of genocide were in place.

To Germans supporting the new regime, those years before 1939 were good times. They were expected to demonstrate public approval of Nazi policies and to serve the nation in the spirit of Nazism. In return, Hitler promised to put Germans back to work. In its social and economic policies, the Nazi regime proved, as the Italian Fascists had earlier, to be a conservative force. Hitler needed a strong German economy for his rearmament plans. He knew no economic theory; he did believe that people had to be employed, even if the state lacked sufficient tax revenues to pay for work programs. His financial advisers were shocked by his deficit spending, used for public work projects, public housing, and other major building projects. The unemployed were required to enroll in the German Labor Service, which enforced the slogan (also applied to concentration camp inmates), that "Work makes one free."

These government economic policies, plus the rearmament program, spurred economic recovery. A Four-Year Economic Plan introduced in 1936 sought to make Germany economically self-sufficient (and, hence, better able to wage war). Nazi planners collaborated with and guaranteed profits to Germany's industrialists and financiers. Such economic methods had nothing in common with the command planning introduced in the Soviet Union in the same years. By the middle of the decade, Germans had work and security, and most did not ask for more.

The Expansion of the Nazi Empire

Both expansionist and militaristic, Nazi Germany within a few years destroyed the system for European peace put in place after the First World War. Hitler stated in 1937 that "Germany's problem can only be solved by force and this always entails risk." He dreamed of turning his nation into a great world power. His vision of Germany's place in the world was grandiose and pitiless. He had written long before taking power of an extraordinary "battle of the continents" that the German Empire under his command would wage against the United States for "world domination." He had no precise plan of conquest. He had learned in his political career how to take advantage of circumstances and did the same in the pursuit of his goal to make Germany a continental and world power. His foreign relations were an extreme form of power politics, relying on warlike threats and intimidation.

In the three years that followed the Nazi seizure of power, the German government destroyed the peace settlement of the 1920s. In late 1933, it abandoned the League of Nations. Then it ended the Versailles treaty's restrictions on its military might. In March 1935, Hitler renounced the limits set in the 1919 treaty on the size of the German army. Nazi Germany immediately increased its army to a half-million men and began a program of rapid rearmament. Hitler justified his action by insisting his country deserved "equality of rights" with neighboring states. Then came the German occupation of the Rhineland in 1936. This frontier area on the northeastern French and eastern Belgian borders had been kept free of German troops. In the 1930s, however, no Allied occupation forces remained there. The only assurance that Germany would honor this restriction on its sovereignty was the Locarno Treaty. Should the German state violate this treaty, the other participants had the right to send their forces back into the Rhineland and, if necessary, to declare war.

Hitler chose to take that risk. His army was still small and his generals warned that German troops would have to retreat immediately if France chose war. He later admitted that "if the

French had marched into the Rhineland we would have had to withdraw with our tail between our legs." He dismissed the fears of his generals, however, for he was persuaded that the British and French leaders had lost faith in the peace settlements and that no Allied state had the determination to enforce their provisions. He was right. He possessed an extraordinary talent for picking out the weaknesses in his adversaries. German military reoccupation of the Rhineland in March 1936 took place peaceably, to the cheers of the Rhineland population.

The Spanish civil war revealed the profoundly different attitudes toward war of the Western democracies and the European dictators. In July 1936, a military uprising led by General Francisco Franco attempted to overthrow the Spanish Republic. He and his supporters were enemies of the Popular Front government just elected that year. This reform coalition had laid plans for land reform to aid the poor and for new laws granting political autonomy to the non-Spanish peoples of the country. In the social turmoil of that year, the Republic's leaders were powerless to prevent some of their followers from attacking the property of the Spanish Catholic Church. General Franco's proclaimed goal was an authoritarian regime protecting private property, the Church, and the unity of Spain. He was not a fascist, though he accepted help from the Spanish fascist movement, the Phalange. The Popular Front government found its support among liberals and Marxists, workers and peasants. Spain began a bloody civil war.

Mussolini, eager to create an Italian empire in the Mediterranean, immediately sent troops and military equipment to Franco. Hitler also supplied military aid to Franco's rebels. Included in this help were German fighter bombers and pilots, responsible for the brutal bombing of the Basque city of Guernica (the subject of the most famous antiwar painting of the century, by the Spanish artist Pablo Picasso).

The Soviet Union led the international opposition to their intervention. Once German and Italian support for Franco began, the Soviets sent military aid and helped organize international fighting units, the International Brigades, to assist the Republic. Many Westerners concluded that the conflict in Spain was part of the European-wide struggle between popular democracy and fascist dictatorship. The civil war became an international cause. Volunteers from the Western democracies joined the Republic's military forces.

Joseph Stalin probably anticipated that Great Britain and France would also intervene in the civil war on the side of the Republic. Instead, the British and French governments, as well as the United States, adopted a nonintervention policy of strict neutrality, refusing arms to either side. The practical result was to deny aid to the Republic. Their objective was to avoid widening the conflict and risking war with the fascist states. This was a matter of greater concern to them than the defense of the Spanish Republic. Appeasement remained their highest priority. In early 1939, the civil war ended with the triumph of Franco's forces. The Spanish state, like many other European countries in those crisis years, became a dictatorship.

Strengthened by its rearmament, the Nazi regime set out on the dangerous path of territorial expansion beyond its southern and eastern borders. There small states that had emerged out of the ruins of the Austro-Hungarian Empire were weak and easily dominated by neighboring aggressive states. In early 1938, Hitler proclaimed that the Austrian people had to join his Greater Germany. When the Austrian government refused, he sent German troops to seize the country by force. Austria became a province of the new German Empire. The second step came when Germany demanded the annexation of the area in western Czechoslovakia known as the Sudetenland. The proclaimed purpose was the protection of "oppressed" Germans living there. The real objective was to destroy this new state, which was a major obstacle in the path of Germany's eastward expansion. Hitler was ready for war that year. He probably anticipated, though, that the West would once again prefer conciliation.

He threatened, in September 1938, to invade the Czech lands unless his demands were met. In response, Italy proposed a four-power meeting of Germany, Italy, France, and Great Britain in Munich, Germany. The Western states grabbed the olive branch, though both the Soviet Union and Czechoslovakia were excluded from the negotiations. Hitler set the terms. The Munich Treaty that resulted from the conference gave Hitler all he wanted. Great Britain and France forced the Czech government to give up the Sudeten territory to Germany, fatally weakening Czechoslovakia. Their desperate effort to preserve peace in Europe was condemned later as "appeasement," that is, capitulation to aggression.

Neither France nor Great Britain was prepared militarily or psychologically for war. Why, asked the British prime minister on returning from the Munich conference, should his country's soldiers have to go to war for a "far-off place inhabited by people of whom we know little." The treaty itself resulted from years of Western wishful thinking regarding Nazi moderation. It was an illusion to which Western statesmen and citizens clung in the fervent hope that European war would never recur. A tragedy for Czechoslovakia, the Munich agreement proved a diplomatic disaster for the Western world.

In 1939, the Nazi leaders took the next steps toward becoming Europe's supreme continental power. That spring, they removed the state of Czechoslovakia from the map of Europe by annexing the western half of the country and creating a puppet government over the eastern half (Slovakia). To the northeast lay Poland, situated between Germany and the Soviet Union and including territory taken

from both states. Its "Polish corridor" was a strip of land in western Poland, situated between German territory and leading to the German city of Danzig, made an international city by the 1919 peace treaties. The return of the area to Germany had constituted an objective of German policy ever since the 1920s.

Hitler publicly demanded no more but, as had been the case in Czechoslovakia, his larger goal was domination of Europe. His method of achieving this objective remained force and intimidation. In March 1939, an appeal from President Roosevelt for peaceful compromise evoked from Hitler only ridicule of the distant Americans. Boasting that he, "who twenty-one years ago was an unknown worker and soldier of my people," had "reestablished the historical unity of German living space," he mocked Roosevelt's concern for "the fate of the world." He could easily afford to do so, since isolationism prevented the United States from exercising any real influence in world affairs.

The Soviet Union presented a more serious problem. Hitler had for years treated the Soviet state as Germany's enemy, yet it possessed the largest army in eastern Europe. That spring, the British government finally abandoned its policy of appeasement and refused any further revision of the Versailles treaty. Instead, it pledged military alliance with Poland in the event of war with Germany and began, with the French, to negotiate a military pact with Moscow. If Stalin decided to join the Western democracies to protect Poland, he could force Germany into another two-front war.

Reluctantly Hitler chose to negotiate. He presented Stalin with an offer of spoils of war—eastern Poland—in exchange for Soviet collaboration in the destruction of the independent Polish state. Stalin accepted, and in August 1939 the two states secretly agreed to divide Poland between their two countries. The German-Soviet Nonaggression Pact opened the way for German war on Poland. In September 1939, Hitler's army invaded Poland. Two days later, in a desperate effort to contain German expansion and to save the Versailles settlement, Britain and France declared war on Germany. A new European war had begun.

The immediate cause of the new war was obvious. Nazi militarism and expansionism drove Europe into the conflict. For all their defects, the Versailles treaty and Locarno Pact had dealt in a fairly equitable manner with the problems of security and national self-determination for Germany. From the perspective of 1939, in fact, they were too fair. They had left Germany with the territory, population, and resources sufficient under Nazi leadership to mobilize for war. No one in 1919 had conceived of a German state so fanatical and brutal as the one instituted by the Nazis in 1933.

STALIN'S SOVIET UNION

In the midst of the global depression of the 1930s, the Soviet Union became a powerful industrialized country governed by a brutal centralized dictatorship. Events unfolded there unlike any other country in the world. In 1929, Stalin had become Lenin's heir and undisputed ruler of the Soviet Union. He was responsible for transforming the country under conditions of turmoil and hardship. The most important changes consisted of (1) the rapid development of the Soviet industrial economy; (2) the forcible seizure of all farmland, brought together in collectivized, state-controlled farms; and (3) the expansion of the repressive powers of the party and the secret police to perpetuate a system of terror, that is, of arbitrary arrest and punishment unhindered by legal restraints. The transformation of the Soviet Union was so radical that historians have termed that period the "Stalin revolution."

The revolution of 1917 had put in place a communist dictatorship in a largely agricul-

tural country whose land was held and worked by peasant farmers. Stalin created a one-man dictatorship and ended private farming, extending the powers of the state into all areas of the economy and society and developing Soviet industry at an extraordinary pace. He claimed that the social and economic transformation of his country raised Soviet society to the historic stage of socialism. Critics called his regime despotic and condemned his policies as inhuman.

The Stalin Revolution

The weakness of the Soviet regime in the late 1920s and Stalin's own political ambition were the key factors in his rise to power. In those years, leadership rested in the hands of the members of the Politburo, the governing Communist Party committee that set state policies in that single-party dictatorship. Stalin was only one of its members and was also General Secretary of the party with extensive contacts among key party officials. The communist "vanguard" consisted of a small ruling elite controlling a vast country and fearful of hostile Western states.

Their country was weak and internally divided between a small working class sympathetic to communist aims and peasant farmers determined to keep possession of their land. The Communists had implemented in 1921 what they called the New Economic Policy (NEP) to raise farm production and to restore the country's dilapidated factories and decaying cities. It succeeded partially, raising farm production sufficiently to feed the population. But it did not provide adequate means to finance the rapid industrial growth necessary to build a strong modern army and create the economy of abundance of which the Communists dreamed. Two considerations, one practical and the other utopian, impelled the party leadership in 1927 to end NEP and to put in motion a plan for rapid industrialization. Their dream of building socialism remained central to their revolutionary plans; no serious campaign to mobilize the country to achieve this goal was possible under the conditions of free market. Industrialization could not in practical terms succeed without expensive investments. These could come only from the state, which in 1927 demanded of the peasantry that it sacrifice a large part of their income and resources, through taxes and low prices for farm produce, to support industrial growth. The peasants' refusal to cooperate on these terms, apparent in 1928, threw the country into its most serious crisis since the civil war and opened the way for Stalin's dictatorship.

The crisis took the form of an acute shortage of agricultural produce, needed for the urban population and for export. The state, which purchased almost all farm production, had lowered the price it paid for major commodities, and many peasant farmers refused to sell their crops. The decline in sales was so severe that in 1928 food rationing appeared in the cities. Soviet agricultural exports, essential to pay for the import of industrial machinery, nearly collapsed. To Western observers accustomed to free markets, the explanation was simple—the shortages resulted from faults in the market economy. The peasants demanded incentives, especially good prices for their crops and consumer products at cheap prices, which the Communists refused to grant them.

Soviet leaders understood the crisis very differently. They were suspicious of the peasants as a "petty bourgeois" class and were prepared to return to the brutal methods of the civil war to deal with these "class enemies." Their solution was to blame prosperous peasants (*kulaks*) for seeking to undermine their Soviet state. Stalin was their spokesman. He put in words their fears of peasant opposition

and of imperialist war, warning in the spring of 1928 that "we confront enemies outside the Soviet Union [and] we confront enemies within the Soviet Union." That year he imposed a simple, ruthless solution to the food crisis, ordering police and party officials to take the surplus produce from the peasants, if necessary by force. Moderate leaders were appalled at his brutality. One even accused him of being a new Mongol Genghis Khan, introducing Asiatic despotism in place of proletarian dictatorship.

That year marked the first time Stalin set state policy. He claimed to be defending the revolution in the spirit of Leninism. The consequences of his action, however, were to launch a new revolution. Most Western historians believe his personal ambition was fixed upon the goal of taking Lenin's place. He turned the crisis of 1928 to his own advantage. We know little of his inner thoughts and motives, for he was a secretive man. His life had been one of escape from poverty and of political combat in the name of proletarian revolution, which he appears to have associated with his own renown. He learned of class conflict and oppression, of the inevitable fall of capitalism, and of the future blessings of socialism through his study of Marxism. We need not question his faith in these basic ideological precepts, for they gave him the essential conviction in the rightness of his cause and the necessity for conflict. His understanding of Marxism, in other words, fit his combative personality. Lenin was his teacher and leader in that period of learning and fighting. He remained loyal to Lenin through the years of underground agitation and then of war and revolution. All he achieved, including his position as general secretary, he owed to Lenin.

Like the rebellious son, however, in the early 1920s he came to think himself worthy of taking Lenin's place. His political methods were harsh, a fact Lenin discovered too late. Even before

Lenin's death in 1924, Stalin began exploiting his key party responsibilities to build up a following among the party cadres who played the key role in choosing new leaders and carrying out policy. They were sympathetic in 1928 to his harsh methods of dealing with the food crisis. With their support, he removed all his rivals from leadership positions in the Politburo. By 1929 he dominated that body and through it the Soviet Union. On his fiftieth birthday late that year, his backers proclaimed that "Stalin is the Lenin of today!"

That year Stalin began what he himself boasted was a "revolution from above." In the Stalinist vocabulary, "revolution" described the transformation of the economy and society at the command of the Communist Party. It took shape through two separate policy decisions. One consisted in the adoption of a Five-Year Plan for industrial production, which was to triple by the early 1930s. The other was the party decision taken late in 1929 to force the 100 million peasants off their private farms and into "collective farms" (referred to usually by the abbreviated Russian term *kolkhoz*), that is, producer cooperatives.

In theory, "collectivization" of farms strengthened socialist cooperation. In reality, it gave the state direct access to agricultural production, because state officials were able to control the administration of the new farms. These measures marked the end of NEP and of conciliation of the peasantry. Their implementation required that the communist dictatorship expand the repressive powers of the secret police. Ultimately, Stalin's ambition and the vast increase in arbitrary police power came together to turn the Soviet regime into a despotic regime.

Industrialization in the First Five-Year Plan combined revolutionary dreams and the need to increase the state's military might. The production goals of the plan were fixed by the guidelines set out in plans elaborated by the State Planning Commission (Gosplan). In a burst of optimism, Stalin ordered the attainment of the plan's objectives by the end of 1932; the slogan was "The Five-Year Plan in four years!" The spirit of Soviet industrialization was warlike; workers had to "storm" ahead and "conquer fortresses" to build socialism. Economists in Gosplan who objected that such extraordinary economic growth would lead to chaos were dismissed or arrested. Under this system of command planning, officials and managers in the state enterprises had to meet production targets set by the Planning Commission or risk being fired or arrested for "wrecking."

These cruel policies met the need to equip a modern army more effectively than they did the goal of creating a socialist society. To Stalin, the former objective was more important. The "tempo" of industrial growth "must not be slowed," he told a meeting of factory managers in 1931. The reason was simple: An advanced "socialist system of economy" would make Russia strong, ending its "backwardness." Stalin warned his audience that the world was still ruled by the "jungle law of capitalism," which he understood to be the simple rule of "beat the weak but be wary of the strong." Speaking more like a Russian ruler than like a Communist, he recited the long list of foreign enemies who had defeated the Russian state in past centuries, from the Mongol Khans in the thirteenth century to the Japanese in the twentieth (omitting the Germans for diplomatic reasons). He demanded that the "socialist homeland" catch up to the capitalist countries in ten years, "or they will crush us." Without realizing where the real danger lay, he anticipated the terrible war that was to come.

The campaign of industrialization proved as chaotic as the skeptics in 1929 had predicted. Russia needed to import foreign machinery and technicians to set up new industries. Among the imports was an entire tractor and truck factory built by the Ford Motor Company. German machinery for steel mills went to the new industrial city of Mag-

Art in the Service of Stalin's Revolution: Poster for Film *Turksib*, 1929 (*Poster Collection/Hoover Institution Archives*)

nitogorsk in the Ural Mountains. The worldwide depression lowered the price of agricultural commodities and raw materials, major sources of Russia's foreign exchange with which to pay for these imports. The government chose to export more food, though part of the population starved in 1932–1933. Within the country there were not enough railroads, not enough skilled workers, not enough housing, and not enough steel and cement for all the new factories. The Five-Year Plan served primarily propaganda needs, cajoling and threatening workers and managers. A priority system similar to wartime decided where the most pressing needs lay and where scarce resources should go.

The most spectacular accomplishments of the industrial plan consisted of giant industrial projects. Accompanied by great publicity, a 1,000-mile railroad, the Turksib, linked the Turkic soviet republics in Central Asia with central Siberia. A mammoth dam on the lower Dnieper River in the southern part of the Ukrainian Soviet Republic generated hydroelectric power to speed the growth of the region's heavy industry. The mountainous region around Kuznetsk, north of Mongolia, became one of the country's major sources of coal. On the parched southeastern slopes of the Ural Mountains, a giant iron and steel complex named Magnitogorsk emerged to extract the rich iron ore deposits of the "Magnetic

Mountain." To these building sites went the machinery, foreign experts, and raw materials necessary for rapid construction. Key party leaders personally supervised the work to ensure that the tempo never slackened.

The greatest burden fell on the great numbers of workers brought voluntarily or by force to these construction sites. Members of the Young Communist movement believed the projects to be a socialist crusade. Workers traveled thousands of miles to join in the campaign. One Soviet writer observing them at work asked why they worked so hard in such primitive conditions. Their answer was simple: "We're building socialism. The entire world is looking at us." Alongside them, however, were peasants fleeing the brutal collectivization campaign and misery in the countryside. They worked simply to escape hunger. Hundreds of thousands of prison laborers, mostly peasants arrested for resisting collectivization, served out their sentences on these sites. They lived in tent camps under police guard. The total size of the industrial labor force doubled by the end of the First

Five-Year Plan. Workers' living conditions were miserable. Housing was inadequate, and food supplies were in such short supply that rationing remained in effect during the entire period. Like it or not, the Soviet people had to accept great sacrifices in Stalin's industrialization drive.

The Soviet state needed an army of specialists to supervise the work. It inherited from tsarist Russia a small core of well-trained engineers. Their middle-class ("bourgeois") origins made them suspect in Stalin's communist state. To force them to work for the new regime, the police arrested many of these engineers, whom they accused of sabotage in the pay of capitalist enemies. No evidence was required, for arrest by the secret police was equivalent to conviction. In 1930, two "show trials" in Moscow put on display for public condemnation engineers accused falsely of "counter-revolutionary" activities. All were forced to confess, and then were sent as prison labor to work in the industrial projects. "Justice" had become another tool to manipulate key segments of the population.

The "City of Iron": Magnitogorsk, approx. 1939 (*National Archives and Records Administration*)

The atmosphere in the country resembled that of a besieged fortress, filled with enthusiasm for battle and with fear and suspicion of saboteurs and spies. Part of that battle consisted of the rapid training of "Red specialists," who were Communists from worker backgrounds given technical training on the job. By the end of the First Five-Year Plan, over a half-million people had received promotions to managerial and technical positions through this Soviet "affirmative action" plan. Among them were Nikita Khrushchev and Leonid Brezhnev, future leaders of the Soviet Union. These people owed their careers to the party and to Stalin, becoming the new Stalinist elite of the Soviet Union.

By the end of 1932, industrial production had soared. New industrial plants in Siberia were beginning to turn out great amounts of iron and steel; their total output doubled between 1928 and 1932. Oil production also doubled, while electrical power output increased three times. In the same years, the urban population's standard of living plummeted, for it had the lowest priority in Stalin's revolution. The urban housing shortage became so severe that most families had to crowd into single rooms of "communal apartments," forced to share a kitchen and bathroom with all the other tenants. Food remained rationed until 1933. Early in 1934, Stalin proclaimed the first Five-Year Plan a success. The price paid by the population, however, was terribly high.

The peasant farmers suffered worst of all. In November 1929, the party leaders ordered mass collectivization of private farms to begin. Stalin refused any compromise with the "capitalist way" of private farming; the "socialist way" of collective farms had to triumph. The party expected resistance and authorized the use of "administrative measures," that is, of repressive police action, to punish those who resisted. The prime target was the so-called "kulak" group of prosperous farmers. In January 1930, Stalin approved orders for the "liquidation" in the entire country of 1.2 million peasant households (approximately 6 million individuals). These peasants, the best private farmers in Russia, were excluded from the new collective farms, forced to give up all their property and exiled to distant areas or even shot.

This organized class war represented a monstrous act of retribution against peasant farmers condemned for their presumed hostility toward the communist regime. By early 1932, collectivization was complete in the principal farming areas of the country. At the Seventeenth Party Congress in 1934, Stalin proudly announced the creation of 200,000 producer farm cooperatives. The regime had "eliminated capitalism" among the peasantry.

The price for this social revolution in the countryside was hardship and famine. The enormous state bureaucracy used its power over agriculture to extract the greatest amount of produce at the lowest possible price. It removed incentives from farming at precisely the moment when administrators on the collective farms were struggling to set up "cooperation" in farm work. Peasants had slaughtered nearly half their livestock rather than let it become the property of the collective farms. As a result, draft animals were in terribly short supply, and the state had precious few tractors to replace them. Peasants on the new farms worked halfheartedly. All these factors led by 1932 to a fall in farm production. In late 1932, it was clear that collectivized agriculture was not producing enough both to satisfy the needs of industry and to feed the rural population. Stalin chose to continue state procurement, ordering severe punishments for any officials who failed to deliver their food quota.

Although never publicly acknowledged by the Soviet state, hunger spread through the countryside, leading to famine, epidemics, and the death of untold millions of peasants. Word of the tragedy reached the cities, where even loyal Communists were horrified at the betrayal of their hopes for a better life for all the people. Stalin's young wife, Nadezhda Allilueva, shared those dreams and experienced the disillusionment at the suffering inflicted on the population. In November 1932, in the midst of the celebrations of the fifteenth anniversary of the Bolshevik Revolution, she had a bitter quarrel with her husband. Afterward, she shot herself in their Kremlin apartment. Her suicide made her another casualty of the Stalin Revolution.

Even Stalin's colleagues in the Politburo concluded that his leadership had led to serious abuses of power. In the spring of 1933, these moderates, including one of his close aides, Sergei Kirov, put in place new policies to end mass terror, to regularize the conditions of the collective farms, and to set reasonable goals of industrial growth in the Second Five-Year Plan. They hoped to revive the practice of collective leadership of the pre-1929 years and to curtail Stalin's own authority. The man they supported to lead this effort was Kirov.

But in December 1934, an assassin murdered Kirov in his office. His two personal bodyguards had mysteriously withdrawn just before the event; both men died soon after under mysterious circumstances before they could be interrogated. The Soviet leadership immediately launched a witch-hunt for the supposed "counter-revolutionaries" responsible for the assassination. Stalin took the lead. Though clear proof is lacking, he was in all probability a party to the secret police plot that brought about Kirov's death. It freed Stalin from the restraints put on his rule. He soon implemented a system of police terror that continued until his death.

Stalinist Terror and Soviet Despotism

The five years that followed were marked by an enormous number of arrests, execu-

tions, and public denunciations of supposed traitors. The period appeared to outside observers a time of "Great Terror." Its bloody methods exceeded by far the Communist Party's brutality in the civil war. Mass repression had already appeared during the collectivization of the peasantry, and it extended now to all members of the population. Historians are still searching to understand the secret process by which police terror installed itself in Soviet life. The growing power of the secret police facilitated Stalin's task. After Stalin's death, Soviet leaders pointed to Stalin's "cult of the personality," that is, his unrestrained belief in his own infallibility, to explain the ease with which he unleashed police terror. They omitted to mention the backing that he received from large numbers of Communists whose careers were linked to his. These "Stalin-generation" Communists were collaborators in terror.

The Stalin terror was based on unlimited repressive powers, exercised by the secret police and controlled by Stalin himself. At his personal orders, immediately after Kirov's death the secret police received the authority to arrest, judge, and shoot or imprison anyone guilty of "counter-revolutionary activity." Because the police alone were the judge of the existence of this activity, they obtained in effect arbitrary powers to punish at will those whom they considered enemies. To Stalin's suspicious mind, all Soviet officials, party members, and plain citizens whom he suspected of thinking or acting in a manner to question his leadership and his policies were traitors. The Kirov assassination was followed by a wave of arrests of anyone remotely connected with opposition to his rule.

Stalin justified his reliance on terror by alleging the existence of a vast network of class enemies and foreign agents operating within the Soviet Union. He argued that "the further we advance toward socialism" the greater will be the "fury of the broken, exploiting classes."

Pitiless vigilance and repression alone could deal with these enemies, whom he perceived everywhere. So great was his suspiciousness that historians have suggested he was mentally deranged. Yet his ruthless supervision of the Terror revealed the careful, calculating mind of a despot. He turned the secret police into his chosen agents of rule.

Mass repression knew no limits for a few years. The unrestricted power enjoyed by the secret police (known then by the initials of the People's Commissariat of Internal Affairs, NKVD) permitted Stalin to decimate the ranks of party cadres, of the state bureaucracy, of the engineers and managers of nationalized industry, and of intellectuals in literature and the arts. Over half of the Communist Party's high officials vanished in the mass repression. His most dramatic action consisted of the arrest, trial, and execution of almost all the "Old Bolsheviks," Lenin's collaborators in the first years of the revolution and frequent opponents of Stalin in that period. Beginning in 1936, they went on trial in three major "show trials," the last of which was held in early 1938. All confessed after months of interrogation and torture to supposed (and completely fictitious) "crimes against the state." All were convicted and shot, their names removed from party histories, their faces eliminated from group portraits of party leaders. Leon Trotsky, whom Stalin had expelled from the Soviet Union in 1929, was tracked down in Mexico by NKVD agents and assassinated. No party leader was left to criticize the dictator.

Stalin and the secret police also singled out for repression the leaders of the national republics that made up the Soviet Union. They claimed that "bourgeois nationalism" had infected the leadership of the non-Russian borderlands; mass arrests hit these regions immediately afterwards. An accusation of lack of loyalty to Stalin and to the Soviet leadership in Moscow was sufficient. Veteran non-Russian party activists, intellectuals, and professionals who had played a vital role in putting in place the multinational system of the Soviet Union disappeared into prison camps or mass graves. The country was now a communist empire governed by Stalinists.

In an action that undermined the efforts to strengthen Russia's military might, the Great Terror extended even to the Red Army. At first Stalin had supported his generals in their effort to turn the army into a professional, highly trained military organization equipped for tank warfare. He appears to have become afraid later of their political influence over his foreign policy. No real evidence ever appeared to substantiate the accusation that these officers had plotted against Stalin. Evidence was irrelevant. Even confessions proved unnecessary to convict, for Stalin and the police had judged the officer corps guilty in advance. The terror in the army began in 1937 with the secret trial of five outstanding generals, including the army commander-in-chief, Tukhachevsky. They were convicted and shot as spies for foreign powers. All officers then fell under suspicion, and one-third of the entire officer corps within a year was arrested. Many were executed and the others sentenced to long terms in prison camps. At a time of growing foreign danger, Stalin gambled his country's security for the sake of his brutal dictatorship.

Out of the terror emerged an enormous secret police empire. It consisted of prisons and a vast network of prison camps extending across the country, especially in the northern and eastern regions of Siberia. Millions of prisoners worked there, a large number dying in inhuman living conditions. In their brutality and hardship, the camps appeared to inmates an extreme form of the police rule that dominated the entire country. The camps constituted a world unto themselves, though, where prison officials reigned as petty despots.

During the Great Terror the secret police became the most powerful political institution in the country. Stalin, probably aware of the potential threat it posed to his dictatorship, had its chief and his followers arrested in 1938, to be shot in their turn for alleged and fictitious "crimes against the state." He tolerated no potential rivals. The new police chief, Lavrenty Beria, remained at the head of the secret police until Stalin's death thanks to his absolute subservience to the dictator. The terror declined in intensity after 1938, but the system remained in place as long as Stalin lived.

The dictatorship extended into all areas of Soviet cultural life. The encouragement for experimentation and the tolerance for artistic diversity that had existed in the 1920s vanished. State-run organizations of writers, artists, musicians, and educators controlled the publication and diffusion of cultural works. Their censorship left little room for individual creativity. Instead, official canons dictated the form and substance of cultural activity. The style of "socialist realism," that is, of art reflecting the imaginary "reality" of Soviet socialist society, was imposed in literature, painting, and cinema. The only new theme was the glorification of Russian nationalism and of Russian military and political leaders from the tsarist past. Tsar Ivan IV (the Terrible) received especially kind treatment, for Stalin viewed very sympathetically his success in eliminating internal enemies and defeating hostile neighboring states. Learning in schools became a dogmatic exercise in memorization stressing simple truths. Among these the most important was the Marxist-Leninist-Stalinist ideology. Teachers were again, as in tsarist times, the absolute authority in the classroom. Pupils once more dressed in uniforms. Culture was in the service of the Stalinist state.

Judgments on the transformation brought about by the Stalin Revolution aroused bitter controversy. Some observers argued that its greatest achievement was to raise the So-

viet Union to the rank of the third-greatest industrial economy in the world. The economic statistics prove this claim correct, though they cannot convey the true measure of human hardship endured in that effort. Others emphasize the social revolution achieved by the elimination of private industry, commerce, and farming, pointing to state ownership of the means of production in all areas of the economy as evidence that a new social system had appeared. Communists called it the first "socialist society" in human history; critics called it an administrative-command system ruled by a new class of party bureaucrats.

The most critical condemnation stressed the police dictatorship by which Stalin and his supporters controlled the party, the state, and the entire population. In some respects, it resembled Nazi Germany. The two regimes were both labeled "totalitarian" by some Western observers to emphasize the extraordinary powers of the state and its leaders over the population. But Stalinism, like Nazism, could not totally dominate society. George Orwell's novel *1984*, based largely on the author's observations of the Soviet regime in the 1940s, provides a nightmarish image of the brutal world of Stalinism.

The Soviet Empire

The new Soviet leadership demanded obedience not only from its own population but also from all communist parties around the world. Stalin had a low opinion of foreign Communists. He valued the Communist International primarily for its service in defending the Soviet Union. He demanded that its member parties help repel the new enemies of the Soviet Union. He ordered the Chinese Communists to organize armed resistance to Japanese forces in northern China to divert Japanese armies away from Soviet territory. These foreign Communists were

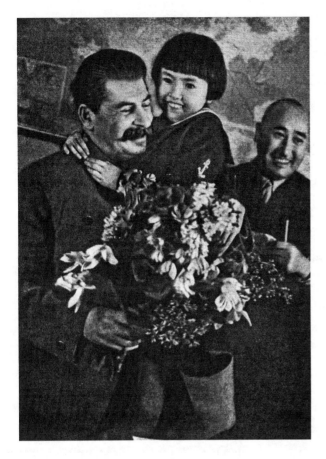

Father of Soviet Peoples: Stalin, 1936
(*Bertram Wolfe Collection/Hoover
Institution Archives*)

under orders to assist the "socialist home-land," the Soviet Union.

Stalin followed a simple set of rules to guide Soviet foreign policy in the dangerous world of the 1930s. Judging Western ideals of collective peacekeeping and conciliation a sham, he adopted for his state what he believed to be real Western practice—power politics. He repeated again in 1934 his conviction, first voiced in 1931, that "in our times it is not the custom to respect the weak; only the strong are respected." States used their power, he argued in 1939, to create around their territory "spheres of influence" in which they dominated smaller states for their own protection and profit.

The "jungle law of capitalism," which he had identified in 1931, dictated that, in international relations, might made right. A state's success at this pitiless undertaking brought it more territory, by annexation of bordering states or by an enlarged sphere of domination. By that elementary rule, the Soviet Union had for its own sake to "respect" other strong states by accepting their spheres of influence. He was persuaded that the "capitalist camp" of Western states would inevitably once again, as in the civil war, attack the Soviet Union in an effort to end the communist threat to their way of life. But that was in the long term. The immediate threat of war would arise when states, no matter what their ideology, disagreed on the borders of those spheres. This simplistic, brutal picture of world relations guided Stalin's conduct of Soviet foreign policy for the rest of his life.

In the 1930s, both the Japanese Empire and Nazi Germany threatened the Soviet Union. In each case, Stalin had to prepare for possible war but welcomed agreements that would, even temporarily, avoid conflict and safeguard Soviet security interests. In 1931, Japan had invaded Manchuria; later in the decade, its troops launched several attacks on Red Army forces both in eastern Siberia and in Mongolia (a Soviet satellite state). The Red Army repelled each Japanese attack, inflicting heavy losses on the enemy forces. After the outbreak of war in 1937 between Japan and China, the Soviet government sent large amounts of vital military supplies to the Nationalist Chinese government. In doing so it adopted the time-honored balance-of-power rule that "the enemy of my enemy is my friend."

The real escape from Asian war came in 1941 when the Japanese government concluded that its most important military objectives lay in the Pacific and southeastern Asia, not in northeastern Asia. That spring the Japanese foreign minister offered the Soviet government a neutrality treaty. Stalin accepted immediately. He cared not at all where Japanese forces might attack in other areas; he asked only that his country be spared.

Nazi Germany proved in the end the greater danger. Hitler's hatred of "Bolshevism" resonated in all his speeches. Stalin, on the contrary, stated publicly in early 1934 that he did not consider ideological differences between fascism and his state to be a serious obstacle in dealing with the new German regime. "It is not a question of fascism here," he argued. "If the interests of the U.S.S.R. demand good relations with one country or another which is not interested in disturbing the peace [that is, not attacking the Soviet Union], we will adopt this course without hesitation."

But Hitler refused the invitation. Stalin had good reason to believe that Germany would move east again, as in the First World War, and that its goals would be the seizure of territory and the destruction of his regime.

To protect the Soviet Union from another war with Germany, Stalin attempted to follow the precedent of the pre-1914 Franco-Russian pact. He agreed in 1935 to a defense treaty with France. It never became the foundation for a Soviet collective security policy, however. At best it offered the possibility that Germany might have to fight first in the west. Soviet aid to the Spanish Republic in 1936 sought to encourage Western resistance to Germany. But the French government clung to its appeasement policy until 1939.

By then, Stalin had returned to his earlier objective of reaching an agreement with Nazi Germany. He seems to have believed that he understood the basic reason for the expansionist policies of Hitler. He judged the Nazi leader a believer, though in an extreme form, in the "jungle law of capitalism." Since the two states dominated eastern Europe, by his reasoning they could avoid war by dividing the region between themselves. He, therefore, accepted Hitler's offer in the summer of 1939 of a nonaggression pact. It contained secret provisions for the partition of Poland and for Soviet domination of the small eastern Baltic states. Stalin interpreted the agreement to mean that his state could expand into these territories. Having signed the pact in August 1939, he sent the Red Army to seize eastern Poland, quickly annexed that fall to the Soviet Union. The next year his forces invaded the Baltic states, which he turned into soviet republics in an enlarged Soviet Union. His objectives were territorial control and peace with Germany, if only for a few years. A German war against France and Great Britain did not concern him. Stalin's dictatorship made the Soviet Union within these limits an expansionist empire.

● HIGHLIGHT: Communism and Joseph Stalin ●

Communism had its roots in the nineteenth century. Karl Marx's socialist philosophy spelled out a revolutionary program of action based on his theories of the economy, society, and history. It became the inspiration for European socialist parties, which ultimately sought social reforms by working within, not in opposition to, liberal democracies. Marxism also provided the core ideas for revolutionary socialism, whose adherents anticipated that only violent revolution would end capitalism and begin the liberation of the working masses.

In 1917, Vladimir Lenin converted this revolutionary approach to Marxism into a concrete program of insurrection. His theory of the vanguard party, which he argued had to lead the proletarian revolution and take sole control of the state afterwards, became an integral part of the communist ideology. His main achievement was to seize power in Russia.

Stalin's contribution was the revolutionary transformation of the country's economy and society. He declared that the radical economic and social changes that he had forced on the people of his land fulfilled Marx's forecast of the social and economic conditions of equality under the dictatorship of the proletariat. The Soviet Union's socialist society, he claimed, marked the advance of his country to the highest level in human history. (The communist society would appear only when the state itself withered away, no longer needed by people who governed themselves.) Stalin's methods of social revolution, his dictatorial regime, and the principles by which he justified his rule constituted the central features of

communism as it was understood by his supporters and enemies alike in the decades that followed. In this way, Stalin made communism his own creation.

His changes to the Leninist ideology consisted of three main features. These were revolution from above, constant struggle with internal enemies, and the priority of the interests of the socialist homeland. He and his supporters argued that the historical progression forecast by Karl Marx from capitalism to the next stage, the socialist society, had come about in the Soviet Union thanks to the powers of the state itself, controlled and guided by the Communist Party. Marx had never provided a blueprint for progress beyond the proletarian revolution. Marxists had expected that this dramatic social leap forward could come only through collective efforts of the working classes once they were the most numerous group in society. To them, the state was an instrument of political domination; its methods of repression were incompatible with the ideals of a socialist society. Lenin disregarded this warning, claiming that his Communist Party had to step in to lead the small laboring class of Russia. Stalin turned the Marxist formula on its head. Instead of curtailing the powers of the state, his Communist Party vastly enlarged these powers.

This revolutionary state had several tasks. Its major responsibility was to implement the basic economic reforms that assured the "breakthrough" from the capitalist to the socialist society, that is, the society where productive property belonged (in theory) to all the people, not to private interests. Stalin announced in 1934 that his country had at last "cast off its backwardness and ignorance" thanks to the progress—made under state command planning—of its nationalized industry and collectivized agriculture. Critics rejected his claim that this new order constituted a socialist society but did not deny that he and his followers had created a unique economic system, usually referred to as a "command economy" (see Chapter 9, "Highlight: Revolution and Command Economies").

Communism became the guide by which the Soviet state took in hand the cultural life of the country. It entailed pervasive state controls of all realms of public speech, writing, and artistic expression. Cultural creativity had to conform to the dogmatic proclamations of Stalin and his followers. They were the proper guides to uncovering the principles of truth, beauty, and goodness, all supposedly grounded in Marxist-Leninist ideology. Art and literature glorified the ideal socialist society and the idealized people. Religious faith and practice were repressed and relegated to a superstitious past.

Taken altogether, communism claimed an all-encompassing role in the life of the Soviet Union. As developed during Stalin's rule, its powers extended throughout state and society. Its extraordinary scope can be summed up as the "three monopolies": the monopoly of power (the single-party state), the monopoly of property (nationalized industry, collectivized agriculture, state-run commerce), and the monopoly of truth (Marxism-Leninism).

Communism also promised to ensure the well-being of the population. Public education, housing, and health care came at almost no cost to the people. What in the West was called social welfare became integral to Soviet socialist society. Though the quality of services was generally low and the peasantry received few benefits, the system remained a key aspect of the communist system. In exchange, the people had to perform a wide array of social duties. The most important of these was working for the Soviet state economy regardless of personal sacrifice and hardship. The population was required to participate in necessary social activities, volunteering (whether willingly or not) for tasks that in other societies were salaried. Idleness was condemned and unemployment unthinkable in a workers' state. Those who refused to work could be sentenced to prison for the crime of "parasitism."

The second important tenet that Stalin incorporated in the communist ideology was the idea that class enemies remained a constant threat to the socialist society and communist state. Marxist theory had assumed that the fall of capitalism ended class antagonism. Stalin's view, repeated throughout his quarter century in power, was that the successful construction of a socialist society incited the Soviet Union's enemies to terrorism and subversion. He expected capitalist states to make every effort, including war, to destroy the Soviet Union, since it was the bastion of world communism and the most progressive society in the world. Temporary alliances might ease relations, but the fundamental antagonism between the two systems was inevitable.

For the citizens living in the socialist society, Stalin's most sinister idea was that class enemies and agents of foreign states remained hidden in their midst. These enemies were more dangerous than ever, he believed, for their "desperate methods of struggle are the last resort of the doomed." Enemy agents and wreckers were everywhere, and only the utmost vigilance, denunciation of suspects, and stern police powers could protect the great communist achievements. No evidence was needed once the police arrested a suspected "counter-revolutionary," for their word was final. Their work was so important and their methods so reliable that arrest alone was sufficient indication of a person's guilt. Failure to denounce enemies was suspect, and families and friends of convicted counter-revolutionaries were immediately subject to arrest and imprisonment. Even members and leaders of the Communist Party might succumb to evil thoughts and become "enemies of the people."

This paranoid fear of enemies was at the heart of the system of police repression and prison camps that existed throughout Stalin's years in power. A similar reign of terror reappeared in China under Mao Zedung at the time of the so-called Great Cultural Revolution in the late 1960s and early 1970s. It emerged in Cambodia when in the late 1970s the communist Khmer Rouge took power and executed hundreds of thousands of their subjects. Each time, the brutal search for supposed enemies reached unbelievable proportions. And each time the terror slowly died away, as had witch-hunts at moments of religious frenzy in the West in earlier centuries. Its disappearance was followed soon by the decline in the faith and solidarity that sustained communism.

The third ingredient in communism that Stalin introduced was the subordination of all foreign communist parties, and later states, to the needs of the socialist homeland, the Soviet Union. Lenin had launched an organization intended to sustain the international communist revolutionary movement. This Communist International became in Stalin's time a weapon for the defense of the Soviet Union, not for the advancement of communist revolution outside his state. His argument was simple: The achievements of the Soviet Union were of such momentous historical importance that no other communist movement could claim equal significance. After communist regimes appeared in Europe and Asia in the years following the Second World War, he forced their leaders to honor this principle. They were expected to serve the interests of the Soviet Union and to obey the orders of the Soviet leaders. Most obeyed; the Yugoslav Communists rebelled, refusing to submit to what they called the "Soviet empire."

Later, the entire communist world split apart when the Chinese communist state under Mao's leadership demanded that the interests of their revolutionary state come first. Like a vast religious movement, communism was splintered by accusations of heresy as rivals charged each other with betraying the true faith. Ultimately, communism vanished from its original homeland, Russia, when the entire system collapsed in the early 1990s. Russians searching to understand their Stalinist past brought from the West the term *totalitarianism*. It seemed to capture best the nature of the extraordinary dictatorship that once ruled their land and whose fantastic claims to be the most progressive society in the world masked the reality of a despotic empire. That faith vanished, leaving behind the decrepit relics of an enormous failed experiment in human engineering.

THE JAPANESE EMPIRE

Japan joined the ranks of the despotic empires in the 1930s. It underwent far-reaching political changes in the years that followed the onset of economic depression. From a democratic regime it became militaristic; its foreign policy shifted from international collaboration to expansionism. The conditions leading to militarism had their roots deep in Japan's political and cultural past. The immediate cause of the decline of civilian rule lay in the economic collapse of the early 1930s. The global depression undermined the foundations of Japanese democracy and encouraged plans for Asian war.

Prosperity and Japanese Democracy

In the 1920s, the country appeared set on a path of peace and prosperity. The sweeping political and economic reforms begun in the late nineteenth century had time to become firmly established. In scarcely more than a generation, Japan had developed an industrial economy equipped with up-to-date industrial technology and organized to compete on the global market. The formula for success, devised and implemented by an elite group of reformers, emphasized the adaptation to Japanese society of Western skills and capitalist methods. These joined with Japanese commitment to hard work and savings, and with a high rate of government investment, to create a Japanese form of capitalism. Giant corporations permitted a few powerful business leaders to control production in key industrial sectors. They also enjoyed an influential voice in political affairs. Obliged to import vital raw materials—especially petroleum and iron—manufacturers turned their industrial skills to profitable ends, exporting much of their output to foreign lands and thereby paying for further imports.

The First World War had been a boon to Japanese industry. Western exports had dwindled. In their place, Japanese businessmen offered their products to the foreign markets once controlled by European firms. Textile exports doubled and so did the size of the Japanese merchant marine. Foreign earnings poured in so rapidly that Japan ceased being a debtor country. For the first time, its capitalists owned foreign investments of greater value than their own debts to foreign creditors (the United States was the only other

country with similar war profits). Japan's gold reserves, still a key measure of national economic well-being, grew to six times the pre-war level. The population expanded to over 50 million, and the standard of living, though still far below that of Western societies, gradually improved.

Prosperity strengthened the democratic leadership of the country. Political reforms, copied largely from British and German models, gave Japan the institutions and laws of a Western constitutional regime. In the 1920s, new electoral laws introduced universal manhood suffrage. By then, the influence of the political parties in the Japanese Diet (legislature) was similar to Western democracies. The agreement of a majority of the legislators was required to appoint the cabinet, which gave leadership to the state and the country.

Though it resembled a Western cabinet system, the Japanese government had certain unique characteristics. Behind the scenes, power lay in the hands of a few individuals: party leaders, advisers to the emperor, and military leaders. The key decisions of cabinet appointment came from advisers to the emperor; cabinet ministers only then turned to their political parties for support in the Diet. Successful politicians relied on the financial backing of the giant corporations, whose large campaign contributions made deputies and cabinets careful to heed the wishes of the business elite. The Japanese army and navy command retained control over their own operations and periodically assumed "autonomy of command," allowing them to take military action without approval from the civilian government. These three small groups made up the real political elite of Japan.

The Japanese political system consisted of a delicate balance between elite rule and popular democracy, between business interests and military expansionists. All agreed on the importance of defending national interests and economic markets in East Asia. The emperor was the symbolic leader and, behind the scenes, still an important participant in key policy decisions. He remained the object of religious veneration that the Japanese believed rightfully belonged to the descendant of the sun goddess. Their devotion became a form of obedience when he sanctioned important government policies. In the "empire of the rising sun," power lay in the hands of the small group of civilian and military leaders who served him.

In the 1920s, the balance swung toward party rule and economic interests. Since the 1890s Japan had built up a small overseas empire, extending from Korea and southern Manchuria through occupied areas in China south to Formosa. Its navy possessed bases in the East and South China seas, where it was the dominant naval power. After the First World War, its military forces had moved into eastern Siberia in the midst of the Russian civil war. But a large army and strong navy represented a heavy and unproductive burden on the economy, and foreign conquest aroused the opposition of Japan's most important trading partner, the United States.

In the 1920s, economic interests and strategic concerns prompted Japan's government to halt military expansionism and to cut back expenditures for the military. The Japanese representatives at the Washington Conference of 1921–1922 decided that the country's interests dictated agreement to limit the Japanese navy to almost one-half the size of either the British or American navies, and to order the withdrawal of Japanese troops from northern China and eastern Siberia. In exchange, they obtained Western promises not to fortify new military bases in the Far East and won international recognition of their state as the major power in East Asia (see Chapter 4). These agreements permitted the Japanese cabinet to drastically cut the size of the army and navy. For the time being, Japanese imperialism was halted.

As long as the world economy expanded, the Japanese government and business leaders could restrain the army. They had solid grounds to argue that peace, not war, best promoted the country's interests in East Asia. Political leaders looked to the needs of the industrial economy and the urban population, ignoring social ills and the farm poor. Their motto might have been borrowed from one American president at the time, who argued that "the business of politics is business." The 1920s were good years for most Japanese, in spite of the terrible Tokyo earthquake of 1923 which killed 130,000 people and caused enormous property damage. Industrial production doubled and exports boomed, with 40 percent going to the giant U.S. market. Another 25 percent went to China, particularly to the relatively prosperous region of Manchuria where Japan established close economic ties. The giant corporations expanded their operations to such an extent that they represented probably the largest economic enterprises in the world. One vast enterprise employed almost a million people in Japan and another million overseas and controlled hundreds of individual companies. The urban population grew to include almost half the country's inhabitants, and the real wages of workers rose by about one-half. In economic terms, Japan enjoyed good times in those years.

Depression and Japanese Militarism

The world depression put an end to Japanese prosperity, to civilian rule, and to peaceful foreign relations. The economic and social signs of hard times appeared in all areas of Japanese life. Exports, a key indicator of Japanese economic success, fell to 50 percent of their level of the 1920s. The U.S. market no longer absorbed an abundance of imports. Then the 1930 U.S. tariff cut the market still further by raising rates on Japanese products by 50 percent. The workers' living conditions worsened.

By 1931 their wages had fallen by one-third. Farm incomes declined even more severely as rice prices fell to below production costs and silk prices collapsed. One-half of Japan's rural population worked as landless laborers. Their living conditions, precarious in the best of times, became tragic.

These grim economic trends brought out the old weakness of civilian government and revealed new opposition to democratic rule. The politicians' close ties with business interests discredited their policies when economic decline set in. The small circle of powerful political figures around the emperor was less inclined to back civilian rule. Old class antagonism between rural and urban poor and the wealthy revealed itself in popular support for the army, a traditional escape from poverty.

The traditional glory attached to the exploits of warriors and the attraction of expansionist policies grew once again to provide old answers to the economic crisis. In the same period, patriotic movements whose militant nationalism closely resembled European fascism appeared in the country to give new meaning to war and imperial conquest. Their followers called for discipline and national unity. They condemned democratic leaders and even attacked military leaders who counseled foreign restraint. They demanded that the country be led by "men of spirit" who possessed the willpower and ruthlessness to enforce national solidarity and to strengthen Japan's overseas empire. These patriotic societies began a campaign of political assassination, murdering political leaders and moderate officers in the army and navy whom they denounced as "traitors" for betraying Japanese honor and renown.

Their nationalist ideology became an inspiration for the militarist leadership of the 1930s. Japanese militarism drew its strength in the 1930s both from traditional sources and from new mass support for authoritarian leadership

and imperialism. In those conditions, the political pendulum swung toward military rule. The Japanese invasion of Manchuria in 1931 revealed how influential the Japanese army had become. Crowds welcomed the news of conquest. The government abandoned any effort to limit the military operations. It defended the army's offensive into Manchuria by arguing that Chinese troops were guilty of attacking Japanese forces and pointing out that no war was officially declared.

The League of Nations condemned Japan for aggression and called on its members to enforce sanctions against the guilty state. The Japanese government's response was to withdraw from the League. The U.S. government was still not a member. Clinging to its isolationist policies, it refused to collaborate in this League decision. It did publicly denounce Japan's conquest of Manchuria, which it called a violation of that state's treaty commitments. The gesture was theatrical and futile, a measure of the weakness of U.S. policy.

Later the Japanese government renounced the limitations it had accepted at the Washington Conference on the size of its navy. The peace settlement of the 1920s in the Far East collapsed even before that in Europe. In 1933, Manchuria, renamed Manchukuo, became a puppet state within the Japanese Empire.

Militarism came to dominate Japanese political life. Civilian government never completely disappeared, becoming window dressing for imperialist policies. For a few years, political violence remained the tool of ambitious officers and fanatical patriots. Their attacks reached a peak in 1936 when junior officers mobilized over a thousand troops in an attempt to overthrow the civilian government. The country's military leaders chose to oppose the insurrection, preferring to work through the cabinet and, in their own way, maintaining the appearance of constitutional rule. The rebellion was suppressed and its leaders executed. In 1937, national elections showed that a majority of the voters supported civilian parties opposed to military rule. The wishes of the people had no influence on the government, however. Power had passed out of the hands of the parties into those of the generals. Civilians continued to run important ministries. In debates on foreign policy they spoke out in favor of peace and compromise. Yet their voices carried less and less influence in policymaking. In late 1941, General Tojo became prime minister, a post he held for the next four years. The military ruled Japan.

This new direction in Japanese policies and leadership was evident by the mid-1930s. The new Japanese regime can best be described as militaristic. The term *militarism* refers to a state in which military leaders are dominant, which pursues a policy of military expansion, and which glorifies a warrior culture. All three traits marked Japanese public life by the late 1930s. This momentous retreat from democratic rule was the work of army generals and naval admirals, backed by Emperor Hirohito, and supported by the great corporations producing Japan's war arsenal. The spirit of militarism spread through public life in a campaign glorifying discipline, order, and sacrifice for the fatherland.

This militaristic regime differed greatly from the political leadership of the 1920s, yet the changes came slowly and without great fanfare. It did resemble in some respects Italian fascism, yet it lacked the essential traits of a charismatic dictator and one-party rule. The Japanese people obeyed their new leaders and responded loyally when called on to sacrifice their lives and their well-being for the sake of their country and their emperor. Patriotism was a powerful bond among the Japanese. So too was respect for military valor. The two together constituted the cement that held together the population under the new military regime.

Japanese Imperialism

Japan's foreign policy reverted to expansionism in the 1930s. Its objective was the creation of what Japanese policy makers called a "pan-Asianist regional order" under their leadership. It included both Japanese economic penetration of China and Southeast Asia, and military domination of the entire region, on land and on sea. Japanese leaders emphasized publicly the benefits of their plan for the other countries. They explained later

Japanese Militarism for School Children: Tokyo High School Students at National Spiritual Mobilization Week, approx. 1938 (*Hoover Institution Archives*)

that they sought a "Greater East Asia Co-Prosperity Sphere." Asians, rid of their Western oppressors with Japanese assistance, would aid one another in a vast enterprise of free trade and economic development.

The principal goal was the expansion of Japanese military and economic might. The plan offered the Japanese army and navy a vast territory, never clearly defined, for conquest and glory. It emphasized Japan's strategic interests and, up to a point, the limits to Japan's means to wage war. This program did not seek domination of all Asia and the Pacific. It did risk conflict with the Soviet Union and the United States, both of which were great powers whose security interests were directly threatened by the Japanese plans for an enormous East Asian empire. Most dangerous of all, this policy expanded the powers and encouraged the ambitions of the army and navy until at a certain point their conquests served no purpose save further military victories. The military leaders' ambition for imperial expansion failed to take account of the limits of their country's real power. After ordering them in 1945 to accept surrender, Emperor Hirohito observed that they "had placed too much significance on spirit and were oblivious to science." By then, they had reduced Japan to ruins.

The first step toward Pacific war came in 1937 with the Japanese invasion of China. No decision to conquer Chinese coastal areas was made by the Japanese government. The move by field officers to defeat Chinese forces set in motion a process of military mobilization and offensive operations organized and led by army generals. They would accept nothing less than Chinese capitulation. By 1939, they had conquered all the major populated areas of coastal China as far south as the border of Indochina. They created in these areas puppet regimes, administered by Chinese collaborators, resembling their Manchukuo satellite state.

Yet they failed in their principal objective. They could not force Chiang Kai-shek to surrender and dislodge the remnants of his army from their refuge in the interior of China. There Chiang clung to his position of national leader and military commander of China's patriotic forces. The Japanese invasion provoked Chinese nationalist resistance among the masses in the occupied areas. Many of them participated in or supported communist guerrilla operations against the Japanese army of occupation. The Japanese military forces retained control of the cities and rail lines but found they could not extend their control over the vast rural population in the countryside. They were caught in an endless war.

Their solution to the dilemma was more war. They were encouraged in this by the German defeat of the Netherlands and France in 1940 and by Great Britain's military weakness. Late that year, Japan joined Germany and Italy in the Tri-Partite Pact, a defensive alliance that strengthened Japan's war party. Western colonies in the Pacific and in Southeast Asia became a tempting prize to the militarists. French Indochina, on the southern border of the Chinese Republic, was strategically located, for it provided the one land route for military supplies from the West to reach Chinese Nationalist areas. The Dutch East Indies (later Indonesia) was valuable particularly because of its oil fields. The Indonesian peoples had lived for three centuries under European colonial rule, and some among them were already prepared to support an anti-imperialist, anti-Western revolt. The defeat of France and the Netherlands in 1940 left these colonies defenseless.

Eager for conquest and determined to end China's resistance, Japanese generals in 1940 moved troops to occupy northern Indochina. Their immediate goal was to cut off supplies from that region to Nationalist Chinese forces. The next summer their forces seized the remainder of Indochina. Militarily the operation proved a simple matter. The French colonial authorities had few troops and immediately capitulated. Diplomatically, the

RUSSIAN EMPIRE
(U.S.S.R. 1922)

KAMCHATKA
(RUSSIA)

SAKHALIN
(1905)

MANCHURIA
(1931)

OUTER MONGOLIA

KURIL IS. (1875)

MANCHUKUO
(1932)

JEHOL
(1933)

Mukden

Peking

LIAOTUNG
PENIN. (1905)

KOREA
(1910)

Port Arthur

Seoul

Tsushima
Straits

Tokyo

Yellow R.

CHINA

JAPANESE EMPIRE

Yangtze R.

Nanking

Shanghai

RYUKYU IS.

0   200   400   600 MILES

0   200   400   600 MILES

Canton

OKINAWA

TAIWAN
(FORMOSA, 1895)

Hong Kong
(BR.)

PESCADORES
(1895)

	1895
	Treaty of 1905
	1910
	Manchuria 1931, Manchukuo 1932
	To Manchukuo, 1933

PHILIPPINE IS.
(TO U.S., 1898)

The Formation of the Japanese Empire

move proved the greatest mistake the Japanese military made.

The Japanese conquest of all Indochina finally aroused U.S. resistance to Japanese expansion. This was a risky and costly move. By then, the balance of power in all East Asia had shifted toward Japan. President Franklin Roosevelt considered military and economic aid to Great Britain in its war with Germany to be the principal U.S. priority. In early 1941, he had moved naval forces from the Pacific to the Atlantic to form the Atlantic fleet. The U.S. Navy had begun a program to expand its fleets, but more ships in the Pacific would not be ready until 1942. U.S. Army units in the Philippines were isolated and weak. Great Britain, desperately fighting

German air and naval attacks, had no forces to spare for a Pacific war. At a time of impending conflict with Germany, a war with Japan might force the United States to wage a global war on two remote fronts. Realism suggested U.S. acceptance of Japanese conquests. Stalin did just that in signing a neutrality pact with Japan early in 1941.

But U.S. internationalist policy and strategic interests in East Asia dictated opposition to Japan's flagrant aggression. Only U.S. diplomatic, economic, and (potentially) military power stood in the way of Japanese domination of all eastern and southern Asia and the eastern Pacific areas. Ever since Japan's attack on China, some of Roosevelt's advisers had urged him to place an economic embargo on shipments of vital raw materials to Japan. This was a crucial step, since the Japanese economy—and military—depended on these supplies to continue their war effort. Until 1941, Roosevelt opposed the embargo for fear of Japanese retaliation. There existed good reasons both for appeasement and for resistance to the Japanese.

In 1941, Roosevelt chose the policy of resistance. He believed that the United States was forced to take action by the Japanese conquest of southern Indochina. From there, Japan's troops were in a position to attack Western colonies throughout Southeast Asia. That summer, Roosevelt approved a total embargo on all exports to Japan, including petroleum. Dutch authorities in the East Indies ended their oil sales to Japan as well. The U.S. secretary of state declared that his country would not lift the embargo until the Japanese "acts of aggression" had ended. He demanded that Japan withdraw, not only from Indochina but also from China.

The Japanese military rulers had to face the consequences of their reckless expansionist policies. The oil embargo on Japan cut petroleum imports to 10 percent of their previous level. Japanese officials warned that their entire oil reserves would run out within two years unless new foreign supplies were found. The Japanese naval commanders proposed a military solution: invasion of the Dutch East Indies. This step would succeed only if accompanied by the defeat of British and American Pacific forces. Japanese diplomats made one last effort to avoid war. They proposed an agreement with the United States to lift the embargo in exchange for Japanese withdrawal from all Asian areas except northern China. But the U.S. government refused to end the embargo without Japanese agreement to withdraw from all of China. Even while these unsuccessful negotiations were under way, the Japanese military was planning its combined naval and land offensive against American, British, and Dutch colonies and bases in the Pacific. On December 7, 1941, their attacks began, bringing world war to East Asia.

◀ SPOTLIGHT: Admiral Yamamoto ▶

He became known under the name of Yamamoto, though Isoroku was his real surname. He became famous as the Supreme Commander of the Japanese navy who conceived the Japanese plan of war on the United States, though he personally believed the war a mistake and victory unlikely. Isoroku Yamamoto (1884–1943) was one of the Japanese Empire's most gifted military leaders during the years when the country's leadership passed from the hands of politicians into those of militarists. Yet he was for years a target for assassination by the patriotic societies, which doubted his zeal to conduct expansionist war. His life offers insight into the reasons for Japan's rise as a great power and the contradictions and failings that led to Japan's catastrophic defeat in the Second World War.

His family had for many generations belonged to Japan's warrior class (the *samurai*). They had served their great lords well. When in the late nineteenth century the emperor's advisers decided to create a modern army, Isoroku's father was among the losers. He lost

Admiral Yamamoto, Commander-in-Chief of Japanese Fleet, 1943 (*Stevenson Collection/Hoover Institution*)

his military standing and the wealth that came with it. Isoroku, the youngest son, had to make his own way in the world. He chose the modern route laid out by the Meiji reformers, attending the new Naval Academy and becoming an officer in the new navy. He had preserved the family tradition of military service. In doing so, he had obtained the education and skills needed to operate the great battleships of a modern navy. Japan's success in its rapid modernization owed much to the collaboration of people such as Yamamoto.

He proved an extraordinarily talented naval officer. He first served his emperor in the Russo-Japanese war, fighting in the great naval battle at Tsushima Straits where the Japanese fleet sank the entire Russian naval squadron. He was seriously wounded and awarded the highest medal for valor. In the following years, he returned to advanced naval staff college. There part of his training was studying English and learning as much as possible of the American navy. His superiors already anticipated that their next great rival for power was the United States.

His success as naval commander earned him the respect of one of the great noble families, the Yamamoto. They lacked a male heir and proposed to adopt him into their family. In Japanese society, such an offer was a great honor. He accepted, taking their family name and immediately marrying an acceptable noblewoman for the sake of offspring who would be the family heirs of the next generation. He respected and honored his new family, just as he honored his emperor and his "empire of the rising sun." Japan appeared to outsiders a "family-nation." Yamamoto was very much a member of that tight community.

Politics as well as ability determined the next major step in his rise to the top of the Japanese navy. In the early 1920s, the government chose to collaborate with the Western naval powers in signing the Washington Treaties and agreeing to reduce the size of its navy. Some commanders were bitterly opposed, calling themselves the "fleet faction." Others, the "treaty faction," agreed with the new policy. Yamamoto was among the latter.

His career took a new turn in those years. The government favored officers of his persuasion, appointing him naval attaché to the Japanese embassy in the United States. He was keenly interested in the innovations in naval armaments and strategy under way in the U.S. Navy. Airpower was the source of greatest controversy and debate among American naval strategists. Battleships, with cannons capable of firing shells over many miles, had been the latest word in naval fighting in earlier decades. Now U.S. naval strategists argued that their day had passed. Large ships with flat tops the size of small airfields could carry airplanes far across the seas to attack targets many hundreds of miles away from the naval forces. Yamamoto soon became the principal proponent of making the aircraft carrier the core of Japan's future navy.

He returned to Japan convinced of two basic truths about Japan's place in the world. One was that it could never defeat the United States in a prolonged war. He had seen with his own eyes the tremendous economic might on which the U.S. military could rely. The other was that Japan's military influence in the eastern Pacific area would grow only by building aircraft carriers and planes and by training the pilots and skilled naval personnel capable of giving Japan the most powerful navy in the Pacific Ocean. He successfully argued the case for aircraft carriers in the years that followed. He even learned to fly, piloting the new Zero fighter planes that Japanese engineers had created. But he could not persuade his superiors, the government,

or the emperor, that the United States was unbeatable.

In the 1930s, his career advanced rapidly. In those years of Japanese military expansion on the Asian mainland, the army won glorious victories while the naval commanders prepared for war with the United States. Yamamoto became admiral in 1930, at the age of forty-six. His task was rebuilding the navy. His emperor had ordered him to join in the preparations for war. His duty, as a patriot and an officer, required him to obey. In private, he continued to warn of the dangers of confronting the United States. But when the European war broke out in 1939 and the Japanese army chose to invade Indochina, he realized that a Pacific war was imminent. His task as Supreme Commander of the Combined Fleets of the Japanese Empire, the post to which he was appointed in 1939, was to devise the means to win that war.

His plan was ingenious. He learned that the U.S. fleet had been concentrated at the naval port of Pearl Harbor in the Hawaiian Islands. The site was many thousands of miles from the Japanese archipelago and Japan's naval bases. Yet he believed that a carrier fleet from the eastern Pacific could, with great care, proceed undetected to within striking distance of the U.S. naval base. From there, its attack planes and torpedo bombers would deal such a destructive blow on the U.S. forces that the United States would have to capitulate within a few months. He did not anticipate that the feeble military forces of the British, at Singapore, or those of the Americans in the Philippines, would offer any real resistance. He nearly succeeded, but that was not good enough.

His plan represented an enormous gamble, and one he would have preferred never to make. When ordered in 1940 to plan for the surprise attack, he explained to a close friend that "to fight the U.S. is like fighting the whole world. But it has been decided and so I will fight to my best. Doubtless I will die on board my flagship and Tokyo will be burnt to the ground." His personal convictions did not matter. Brought up in a society where absolute loyalty to the emperor was expected, he knew no way to resist and, like all Japanese subjects, believed the emperor's decisions to be final. Militarism in its extreme form had no place in his life, yet his career was bound to the brutal expansionist policies that the militarists had imposed on their country. He had, as he understood moral choice, no other way. He died in the war, not on his flagship but in an aircraft shot down in 1943 by U.S. fighter planes. He was right about Tokyo; it was burned to the ground in a terrible air attack and firestorm in 1945.

SUMMARY

The Western world had undergone great political changes in the ten years since the depression began. Two powerful dictatorships had emerged in Nazi Germany and the Soviet Union. Their collaboration in the war on Poland signaled a remarkable shift in the European balance of power. These two states, whose ideologies presented diametrically opposed plans for humanity's future, strongly resembled one another in their structure and operations. Both concentrated political power in one party dominated by a dictatorial leader, both gave broad authority to a secret police, and both demanded absolute obedience of the population.

Perhaps common forces were at work shaping these two regimes. The cult of violence that both cultivated, each in their own way, provides one link. Stalinism and Nazism glorified violent struggle and the self-styled political warriors who were responsible for the violence. Both Stalin and Hitler mobilized a mass movement to support their own political ambitions. Finally, both turned the institutions and methods of a bureaucratic state and modern technology into instruments to dominate an entire society. Although both talked of freedom, the word as they used it really meant obedience. Rivals for international power, their totalitarian regimes were deadly enemies of liberal democracy.

The peace settlements laboriously put together by the Western statesmen had vanished by 1939. The European states chose not to enforce these agreements, partly out of reluctance to risk a new war, partly because their countries were terribly weakened by the depression. The war that began that year would not be ended by the European countries but by great powers on either side of these states. The new world war diminished their power and influence so substantially that they lost control of their Asian empires. The war in Asia was as important to the new balance of power as the war in Europe.

The rise of the German and Japanese empires, and the expansion of the Soviet Union, marked a new phase in the era of empires. These lands were ruled by despotic regimes, whose treatment of conquered peoples was far more brutal than that of the Western colonial empires. They pursued the single-minded goal of strengthening their dictatorial regimes and homelands. The Nazis included in this policy the exclusion of Jews from their lands and ultimately the extermination of the Jewish population. The Stalinist regime physically eliminated by imprisonment or execution supposed class enemies and counter-revolutionaries. Virulent condemnations of Western imperialism occasionally emerged in their public pronouncements. The Japanese claimed to promote the anticolonial movement of national liberation in Asia. The Stalinist leaders announced that their country's federal system of national republics brought to these peoples real national liberation and was a model for colonial peoples everywhere. But the reality was quite different. These lands all had fallen under the domination of despotic empires.

DATES WORTH REMEMBERING

1922	Fascist regime in Italy
1928–1932	Soviet First Five-Year Plan
1929	Stalin dictatorship
1931	Japanese invasion of Manchuria
1932	Withdrawal of Japan from League of Nations
1933	Nazi rule in Germany
1933	Withdrawal of Germany from League of Nations
1935	Nazi Nuremberg Laws against Jews
1936–1939	Spanish civil war
1936	German reoccupation of Rhineland
1937	Japanese invasion of China
1938	Munich Agreement on Czechoslovakia
1936–1938	Stalin's Great Terror
1939	Soviet-German Non-Aggression Pact and partition of Poland
1940–1941	Japanese conquest of Indochina
1941	Soviet-Japanese Neutrality Pact
1941	Japanese attack on British and U.S. forces in Pacific

RECOMMENDED READING

Hitler and Nazism

*William S. Allen, *The Nazi Seizure of Power: The Experience of a Single German Town* (2nd ed., 1984). Fascinating close-up view of one small town that became a Nazi bastion.

*Joachim Fest, *Hitler* (1973). The best study of Hitler's role in the creation of Nazism.

*Richard Overy, *The Origins of the Second World War* (1990). An excellent short analysis of the causes of the world war that proved to be the last.

Stalin's Soviet Union

*Robert Conquest, *Stalin: Breaker of Nations* (1991). The best short biography of the secretive dictator, stressing his political life.

*Stephen Kotkin, *Magnetic Mountain: Stalinism as Civilization* (1995). The extraordinary story of one of Stalin's gigantic industrial projects and, in capsule form, an excellent glimpse of the agony and enthusiasm of the Stalin Revolution.

The Japanese Empire

Ian Buruma, *Inventing Japan: 1853–1964* (2003). A brief, interpretive survey of Japan from the Meiji reforms to postwar period.

Herbert Feis, *The Road to Pearl Harbor: The Coming of the War between the United States and Japan* (1950). A comprehensive study of the growing conflict between the United States and Japan in the 1930s.

Edwin Hoyt, *Yamamoto: The Man Who Planned Pearl Harbor* (1990). A vivid, sympathetic account of the life of Japan's greatest naval commander.

Memoirs and Novels

*Lydia Chukovskaia, *Sofia Petrovna* (1991). A deeply moving story of the destructive impact of the terror on one ordinary Soviet woman.

*John Scott, *Behind the Urals: An American Worker in Russia* (1942). Memoirs of a young American who volunteered to work at the new Soviet industrial center of Magnitogorsk.

*Alexander Solzhenitsyn, *A Day in the Life of Ivan Denisovich* (1964). A fictional account of the Stalinist prison camp experience, written by a survivor of the camps and Nobel Prize–winning author.

_____

*Indicates book is available in paperback.

CHAPTER SIX

The Last World War, 1939–1945

- The Empires of Germany and Japan
- The Formation of the Grand Alliance
- The Defeat of the Axis Empires

Highlight: Internationalism

Spotlight: John Maynard Keynes

The Second World War was truly global in its scope and impact. It came closer than ever before in human history to uniting peoples of the world in one vast, terrible, human endeavor. Countries from every continent became involved. Its battlefields were scattered across Europe, Africa, and Asia and the islands of the Pacific Ocean; its naval battles extended over (and under) the Atlantic, Pacific, and Indian oceans. Heroism was no longer the sole privilege of soldiers in battle. Resistance movements in countries occupied by the Axis powers (Germany, Italy, and Japan) kept alive visions of a better life to follow liberation. For the first time, armies opened their ranks to women, who were not yet warriors but were no longer merely tem-

porary workers and protectors of the home. New military technology restored mobility to armies and made aircraft the key element in naval battles and the means to carry the war far behind the front lines. At the end of the war, one single explosive device revealed the capacity of atomic energy to lay waste to an entire city. Human ingenuity put fantastic weapons of destruction in the hands of statesmen and their military commanders.

In the first years of the war, German and Japanese victories destroyed the old balance of power. Their conquests marked deeply the population within those areas, obliterating old frontiers and overturning established governments. The Nazi New Order in Europe and

159

the Asian empire of Japan both sought supporters among their conquered peoples. The Nazis recruited fascists and sympathizers in the conquered areas for military service and administration, while the Japanese selected anti-Western nationalists to govern former European colonies. Their success in recruiting military and civilian personnel from the conquered peoples added a new term to our vocabulary of war—*collaborators*, that is, those who gave assistance to the occupying German and Japanese forces.

United in opposition to the Axis empires was an international coalition of Allied states. Their alliance was the result of Axis aggression; their war aims emerged out of the necessity to crush their enemies. Allied military victories proved, in the end, easier to achieve than political agreement on the postwar peace. By 1944, these victories had made clear that the forces of Great Britain, the Soviet Union, and the United States would soon defeat the German and Japanese empires. The war leaders of these nations—Churchill, Stalin, and Roosevelt—agreed on the short-term objective of complete destruction of the Axis, summed up in the term *unconditional surrender*.

Their wartime discussions revealed the great difficulties that they faced in shaping a stable peace. Later, Western critics condemned the failure of British and American leaders to force Stalin, deeply suspicious of his Western Allies, to accept the restoration of prewar governments in Europe. But these critics overlooked the limits to Western power, the wartime might of the Soviet Union, and the powerful revolutionary movements that emerged in formerly occupied lands. As the war drew to a close, a new boundary was taking shape that divided the lands freed by Soviet troops and those freed by the Western Allies. The peace, like the conflict that preceded it, bore no resemblance to the First World War. With hindsight, we now realize

that it was the twentieth century's last world war; at the time, it seemed possible that it, like the war before it, was a prelude to a yet greater global confrontation.

THE EMPIRES OF GERMANY AND JAPAN

The shape of Europe was unrecognizable by 1942. A new German Empire had emerged by force of arms and by ruthless domination of the subject peoples. Old borders of nation-states ceased to have any real meaning, except to the governments-in-exile that had fled German invasion to keep alive the hope for a rebirth of their occupied countries. East Asia was equally transformed by Japanese conquests. There too, old borders were obliterated by a new empire. Former Western colonies became independent states under Japanese tutelage, though in reality their leaders had to collaborate with new imperial lords. The United States entered the ranks of the Allies following the Japanese attack on Pearl Harbor in late 1941, but its forces had little impact on the course of the war in the year that followed. That period was the high point of Axis power in the world.

The Conquest of Europe

The first phase of the European war, from 1939 to 1940, began with rapid German military victories. Assured of the neutrality of the Soviet Union, German troops easily defeated Polish forces by the end of September 1939. Britain and France had declared war on Germany but were incapable of offensive military operations to save Poland. In the spring of 1940, Hitler directed his military forces against the Western states. In another rapid victory, German troops conquered western Europe, defeating France in six weeks. By early 1941, Nazi Germany controlled a continental empire that stretched from Norway to the

The Second World War in Europe and Asia

borders of Spain, from the Low Countries to the borders of the Soviet Union.

Great Britain fought on alone, a beleaguered country relying on its navy and air force to hold off a German invasion. Its new prime minister, Winston Churchill, promised a battle to the end, "on the sea, on land, and in the air." The Battle of Britain, waged that fall and winter in the skies over England, left the Royal Air Force the victors and discouraged Hitler's plans for an invasion of the British Isles. Still, Great Britain remained in a desperate situation. Its merchant shipping was being sunk in appalling numbers by German submarines. Its maritime communications with its Asian empire were nearly broken. The British could expect at best to sustain the war for a year or two unless new allies took up the war on Germany.

German domination of Europe grew with Italy's entry in the war in 1940. Small states from eastern Europe also joined forces with the Nazis. The third Axis power, Japan, signed a defensive pact late that year with the fascist states. The German conquests in eastern and western Europe made the Nazi state the most powerful military empire in the Western world.

The United States: Between Neutrality and War

Gradually U.S. isolationism weakened as German power grew. President Franklin Roosevelt had never shared the revulsion felt by many Americans at U.S. involvement in the First World War. He began his political career as a supporter of Wilson's domestic and war policies and had been active in the war effort as secretary of the navy. He held to the belief, first defended in the early 1900s by his elder cousin Theodore Roosevelt, that the United States had to take an active role in world politics. Like Wilson, he considered Great Britain a valuable ally whose defeat in war would

constitute a disaster for the United States. He was not as ardent an internationalist as Wilson, however. He appears to have judged collaboration among the leaders of great powers more important to peace than international forums like the League of Nations. A skillful politician and public figure, he learned from the U.S. Congress's defeat of Wilson's peace treaty the necessity to heed the wishes of Congress and the American voters. He continually sought to reconcile attainable and desirable objectives in foreign policy. Until the late 1930s, his attention was directed to domestic reform and the political struggles arising from his New Deal program. Foreign affairs constituted a secondary matter until European conflict once again intruded on American security and economic activity.

The first year of war in Europe forced Roosevelt to confront the consequences of American isolationism. The initial reaction of the U.S. Congress to the outbreak of war in 1939 was to repeat its commitment to the policy of noninvolvement in European conflicts. Earlier in the 1930s, Congress had passed neutrality acts banning the sale of U.S. military supplies to, or the use of U.S. shipping in trade with, any warring countries. Roosevelt had to declare the United States neutral in the 1939 war.

As German conquests multiplied, Roosevelt began to speak out against isolationism and in support of the British war effort. He feared the strategic threat to U.S. security, especially after German victories in western Europe in 1940. He warned that "if Great Britain goes down, the Axis powers will control the continents and will be in a position to bring enormous military and naval resources against this hemisphere." In 1940, he ordered peacetime conscription to build up once again the U.S. Army. In early 1941, he created the Atlantic Squadron. It was the first U.S. naval force in the Atlantic since 1918, and had to be made up largely of ships taken from the Pacific fleet.

Early that year, Roosevelt obtained the approval of Congress to provide armaments to Great Britain on the Lend-Lease Program. The choice of this term, suggesting a straightforward business transaction, was needed to appease the powerful isolationist movement in the United States. The program in essence was a desperate attempt to shore up the feeble British war capacity with U.S. military supplies (ultimately, the British government did make payments to the U.S. government for the value assigned this war materiel). In the spring of 1941, the U.S. Navy extended its maritime war zone far into the North and South Atlantic. This permitted its vessels to protect U.S. ships bound for Britain from German submarine attacks. That fall, Roosevelt authorized U.S. destroyers to attack and destroy German submarines operating in the Atlantic. The United States was headed toward an undeclared naval war with Germany.

Roosevelt's warlike measures against Germany were based primarily on considerations of security and power. Yet all that time he lacked sufficient political backing for war in defense of Great Britain. The American public understood far more readily the rhetoric of internationalism than that of balance of power. His most successful speeches on international affairs discussed the war in Europe in idealistic terms. To win popular support for his policies, Roosevelt spoke out against the threat that Nazism posed to "religion, democracy, and good faith among nations." He pledged U.S. support for a "world founded upon four essential human freedoms": religion, speech, security, and freedom from want. Roosevelt, like Wilson before him, talked of the European conflict in terms that emphasized the defense of democracy and omitted issues of U.S. national security. In the summer of 1941, he obtained Churchill's approval for the Atlantic Charter. It committed both nations to "a better future for the world" following the "final destruction of Nazi tyranny." The charter did not constitute a military alliance, however. A majority in Congress still opposed war on Germany. Many Americans considered the growing danger of conflict with Japan to be of greater concern to immediate U.S. interests than the European war. The British had to fight on without the United States.

The German-Soviet War

The Soviet Union became Britain's first important ally. Although it had collaborated with Germany in the 1939 defeat of Poland, the two states were ideological enemies and rivals for power in eastern Europe. Stalin took full advantage of the secret agreements signed in 1939 with Germany (see Chapter 5). Annexing eastern Polish territory and seizing the independent Baltic states were only part of his preparations for the war he anticipated in a few years. In the south, he forced the Romanian government to allow his state to annex Moldavia and Bukovina. To the north, in the winter of 1939–1940, Soviet forces attacked Finland after its government refused Stalin's demand to cede eastern territories to the Soviet Union. Though the Finnish army was tiny by comparison with the Red Army, it fought skillfully to withstand repeated offensives. Its heroic resistance saved Finland from being joined by force to the Soviet Union (as happened later that year to the Baltic states), but Soviet forces ultimately gained the upper hand. The Soviet-Finnish peace treaty required that Finland abandon Karelia to the Soviet Union. These military operations gave Stalin a false sense of security from the German invasion that he expected, once Hitler had defeated the Western powers.

In the short term, Stalin sought by all means to appease Nazi Germany. In 1940, his government signed a trade agreement with Germany providing for Soviet shipments of vital raw materials, including petroleum, that the German military needed for its war in the west, in exchange for German military materiel. The Soviet Union carried out the agreement to the letter; the Nazis never delivered the goods that they had promised. In addition, Soviet border forces in the west were ordered to do nothing to provoke the German army. Stalin believed the German generals to be the principal fomenters of war in the east. The Soviet dictator dismissed as "British provocation" reports in the spring of 1941 from Soviet spies and from Great Britain of a planned German offensive against the Soviet Union. He could not imagine that Hitler, still at war in the west, would attack his country that year. The Red Army was the largest land army in the world and was backed by a productive industrial economy. Stalin, imagining Hitler practiced this sort of realistic power politics, could not believe that war was imminent. Because his word was law, the Soviet Union was caught unprepared for the greatest military offensive in history.

In fact, none of the factors arguing against war that year on the Soviet Union swayed Hitler. His fanatical hostility toward communism was as great as that toward the Jews. In the fall of 1940, he ordered that the vast resources of the German Empire and its European allies be mobilized for a "lightning war" (*blitzkrieg*) against the Soviet Union. It was to be waged along a 2,000-mile front with more than 4 million soldiers spearheaded by 10,000 tanks and supported by 5,000 planes. Plans called for victory in three months. On June 22, 1941, Axis armies invaded the Soviet Union.

The attack initially succeeded beyond the German commanders' wildest hopes. Within two weeks Soviet frontier defenses were crushed and German tank forces had penetrated deep into Soviet territory. Along the way they captured hundreds of thousands of Red Army prisoners. The Soviet air force was destroyed. Many of the remaining Soviet divisions had been reduced to small groups desperately fighting or demoralized and ready to

surrender. Rail lines were paralyzed by air attacks, leaving hundreds of thousands of refugees trapped in the war zone. By early fall the Axis forces had captured Ukraine's major city, Kiev, were on the outskirts of Leningrad, and were closing in on Moscow. The German blitzkrieg apppeared close to victory.

In early July, when the scale of the military disaster became clear, Stalin finally assumed active leadership of the Soviet war effort. He took the position of head of government (chairman of the Soviet Council of Commissars) and created an emergency War Council (previously he had held only the position of General Secretary of the Communist Party). In a radio broadcast (his first), he begged the Soviet people, whom he addressed as "comrades, brothers and sisters, dear friends," to make every sacrifice in what he described as their "Great Patriotic War."

Patriotism was the force on which he had to rely to win the support of the peoples of his country. The mechanism of the police state was there to punish those who did not heed his call. He ordered Soviet soldiers to stand fast against the German offensive; "not a step backward" was his command. Soldiers who shirked their duty by surrendering were judged traitors. He made no effort to save the life of his eldest son, who had been taken prisoner by the Germans that summer when his fighter plane was shot down. When later in the year he received an offer from the Germans for a prisoner exchange of his son for several German high-ranking officers in Soviet captivity, he refused. He made no allowances in that war for human weakness, pity, or compassion.

The German offensive continued until late fall. By October, all of western Russia and Ukraine had fallen. The Russian losses were enormous, totaling perhaps 2 million casualties; most Soviet tanks and aircraft were destroyed. Yet the Red Army found new reserves, drawn from Siberia where war with

Japan no longer threatened. In addition, bitterly cold winter weather had become the Red Army's ally, slowing the German advance. In December, Soviet troops launched a successful counteroffensive on the central front. Moscow was saved, and the German army had suffered its first defeat in the Second World War. The Axis had failed, like Napoleon 150 years earlier, to achieve a quick victory. But the front lines remained far inside Soviet territory.

The spirit of global war possessed Hitler. Although deeply committed militarily on the eastern front and under no diplomatic obligation, he linked the European and Asian wars by declaring war on the United States three days after the Japanese attack that December on the U.S. naval forces in Pearl Harbor, Hawaii. His action ensured that Roosevelt's hope to join Great Britain in the European war came true. In the west, the war on Great Britain included submarine warfare around the British Isles and frequent bombings of British cities. In North Africa, General Rommel's divisions came to the aid of Italian troops fighting the British in Egypt. In early 1942, Rommel's forces began an offensive intended to seize the Suez Canal and to establish German satellite states in the Middle East.

The eastern front remained the principal European battlefield. Military operations extended along a front from the Arctic Circle southeast to the shores of the Black Sea. The Germans and their allies maintained 1 million troops on that front; the Soviet combat forces, though weakened by the defeats of 1941, numbered more than 2 million and their size was growing. The ferocity of fighting left no room for compassion. Many of the Soviet troops taken prisoner in 1941, left with little or no care by the Germans, died in their prison camps. The German blockade of Leningrad sought to starve the city into surrendering. That winter it became a frozen wasteland, without food or heat, in which hundreds of thousands of its inhabitants died of starvation and cold.

In a renewed effort in the summer of 1942 to achieve victory against the Soviet Union, Hitler ordered his generals to prepare an attack from central Russia toward the Caucasus Mountains and the Caspian oil fields. South lay the Middle East where he hoped General Rommel would be victorious and would link up with the northern armies. The plan, baptized Operation Blue, exhibited a visionary concept of military operations so far beyond German capabilities that it bordered on the insane. When it began, German fighting ability, coupled with the weakness of the Red Army, achieved the initial objectives. By September, Axis military forces had reached the Caucasus Mountains while others had reached the edges of the city of Stalingrad, on the lower Volga River. They had not, however, destroyed the Soviet armies on the southern front, most of whose troops had retreated beyond the Volga. Victory remained elusive, yet Hitler would settle for no less against his hated enemy. The city of Stalingrad acquired for him symbolic importance. He chose to make its capture, though not originally an important objective, the goal of the offensive. The war of movement became a war of street fighting in a city far to the east of the main German front. The battle of Stalingrad dragged on into the winter.

The German Empire

By the end of 1942, almost the entire European continent had fallen under the domination of Nazi Germany and its Allied states. From the shores of the Atlantic Ocean as far east as central Russia, from the Arctic Ocean to the Mediterranean Sea, a German New Order reigned. It relied in part on the collaboration of allied states and of political movements sympathetic to Nazi Germany. Until 1943, fascist Italy constituted Germany's most important ally, its troops fighting in North Africa, the Balkans, and Russia. In France, a small group of French political leaders collaborated with the Germans, who left them a state in southern France with its capital in Vichy. Most French people in the first years of defeat were resigned to German domination. Similar collaborationist regimes existed in the Netherlands and Norway.

In eastern Europe, some states had allied with Germany as soon as or before the war began. Romania, Bulgaria, Hungary, and Finland aided the German war effort. In these states conservative nationalists, who were bitter enemies of the Soviet Union, hoped to share in the spoils of a German victory. Fascist parties provided collaborators in the German administration. Volunteers for the SS armored divisions appeared in increasing numbers. National and political hatreds dividing eastern Europeans helped the Germans as well. Ukrainians assisted Germany as police, administrators, and soldiers to fight the Communists, who had inflicted great hardship on them before the war. In Yugoslavia, the Nazis encouraged Croatian nationalists to join them with the promise of an independent Croatia after the war. This collaboration never attracted more than a small minority of these national groups. Opposing them were resistance forces that fought the Germans in forested and mountainous areas and provided assistance to the Allies. Still, the collaborators served the Germans well in helping to control occupied Europe.

The dominant trait of the German New Order was exploitation of the conquered lands. All Europe lay at the disposal of the Nazi leaders. French agriculture helped feed German armies and sustain a comfortable standard of living in Germany. The industrial production of occupied Europe augmented German economic resources and supplied military equipment to German armies. The German authorities considered the working population of Europe to be available for their

needs. German workers had to serve in the armed forces. In their place, the Nazis deported laborers from other countries to work in miserable conditions on German farms and in factories. From the Ukraine over 1 million men and women were transported to German lands, from Czechoslovakia more than 300,000, from France 1 million—in all, 5 million forced laborers. Germany turned the conquered populations into its subject peoples.

This repressive policy hit the Polish nation and the European Jews with the greatest brutality. Poland once again ceased to exist. Much of its western territory was annexed by Germany and the Polish inhabitants forced to abandon everything to move to the east. The central region became simply the Government-General, an area open to exploitation by German businessmen provided with Polish forced labor. The economic resources of the area went to Germany, leaving, in the Nazi leader Goering's words, only the "absolute minimum for the maintenance at a low level of the bare existence of the [Polish] inhabitants."

These racist policies reached their most inhumane level in the extermination of the Jews of Europe. Nazi anti-Semitism constituted a powerful bond among all party members and found supporters among peoples in eastern Europe, where most of Europe's 6 million Jews lived. The Nazis searched for the swiftest way to destroy this hated people. Forced Jewish resettlement in ghettos began in 1940, but Hitler judged unsatisfactory the slow death there by disease and starvation. On the heels of the German troops sweeping through the western Soviet Union, special SS death squads spread through the area, executing hundreds of thousands of Jews. Yet these methods too appeared to him insufficient to make Europe "free of Jews."

The Nazi solution was to order the systematic mass extermination of an entire people. In late 1941, Hitler gave his approval to the policy called by Nazi leaders the Final Solution. Its implementation began in 1942. Their instrument for this insane policy was at hand—the SS organization, whose members were sworn to absolute obedience. The entire Jewish population of occupied Europe was to be shipped by train in cattle cars to special camps in Polish territories. These were extermination camps, organized according to the same standards of industrial efficiency as slaughterhouses for animals. The trains, arriving at the camps usually at night, poured out their loads of men, women, and children. Most of them were immediately herded into special sealed buildings to be killed by poisonous gas, their bodies incinerated in enormous ovens. All that was left were mountains of clothing, gold teeth, hair, and other items taken from the victims. A few prisoners survived for a time to work as forced laborers, only to be killed in their turn.

When reports of the existence of these camps began to reach the West in 1942, they aroused disbelief at first, even among Jews. Allied leaders, in the face of mounting evidence of mass killings, issued public warnings to Germany to shut down the death camps. Their priorities of war took precedence, however, over military efforts to save the Jews. Until late in the war, no Allied bombing raids were directed against the facilities or rail lines of the camps.

The Final Solution remained in operation to the end of the war. What little Jewish resistance occurred could not stop the SS. The 1943 uprising of the remaining inhabitants of the Warsaw ghetto constituted an act of hopeless, heroic desperation. By the end of the war more than 5 million Jews had been exterminated, the victims of insane Nazi racism and the moral cowardice of Germans. Historians still debate the circumstances and causes of this policy of genocide (the extermination of an entire people). It is a phenomenon so complex and terrifying that it defies adequate ex-

planation. Germany's New Order tore apart the old Europe, its peoples and its states. Nothing could return the continent to its previous condition.

The Japanese Empire

The Japanese war leaders pressed forward their war, pushed by the need for the petroleum of the East Indies and drawn by visions of a great victory in the eastern Pacific. They set in motion on December 7, 1941, their plan of military conquest. It called for a series of surprise attacks by Japanese naval aircraft to destroy the Pacific fleets of Great Britain at Singapore and of the United States at Pearl Harbor, Hawaii. Subsequently, Japanese land forces were to invade the Philippines, the British colonies in Southeast Asia, and the Dutch East Indies. The attack on Pearl Harbor put the bulk of the U.S. Pacific fleet out of action, missing only the three aircraft carriers sailing on maneuvers at the time. That same day, Japanese planes sank two British battleships that were the sole naval protection for the fortress of Singapore. For the next year, the Japanese navy controlled the Pacific Ocean from the Aleutian Islands south to the Coral Sea near Australia.

Naval victories opened the way for the military offensives of the Japanese army. The great British fortress of Singapore fell to a surprise attack in February 1942. The surrender of the garrison eliminated British rule in Southeast Asia and left the Japanese with 90,000 prisoners, many of them soldiers from the Indian army. That spring, Japanese troops completed the conquest of the Dutch East Indies. In May, the last American forces in the Philippines surrendered in the single greatest military defeat ever suffered by the United States. The Japanese military dealt harshly with the captured Western troops, whom they treated as virtual slaves to be deprived of adequate food and employed for forced labor. Japan's forces swiftly conquered Thailand, Malaya, and Burma, where its army prepared to attack British forces in eastern India. In half a year, it had conquered a territory with 140 million people, destroying in the process the Western empires of Southeast Asia.

The Japanese government ruled these areas with occupation forces and local political leaders ready to collaborate with their conquerors. Throughout Southeast Asia nationalists administered these occupied lands in place of the vanquished Westerners. The Dutch East Indies became Indonesia, whose administration was led by the Indonesian nationalist leader Sukarno. Burma became a model Japanese satellite, receiving formal independence in 1943. Throughout the Philippines the Japanese found influential political leaders from the land-owning elite ready to collaborate in governing the population. They offered Indian prisoners of war, captured when Singapore fell, the opportunity to join an Indian National Army to fight British imperial forces on the Indian front, promising them that victory would bring independence to India. Thousands of Indian prisoners volunteered, many simply to escape death in the prisoner-of-war camps. Assurances of national liberation and the military triumphs of 1942 won for Japan the collaboration of nationalists from every conquered land.

China remained the major prize, but victory proved beyond the reach of the Japanese forces. The Japanese regime had put in power collaborationist Chinese governments following their conquest of the coastal areas of northern and central China. Renegades from the Chinese Nationalist government accepted Japanese offers to become figurehead leaders of the central Chinese puppet state, whose capital was located in the one-time Nationalist capital of Nanking. In 1942, further Japanese military triumphs incited several Chinese generals commanding about one-half million troops to abandon the Nationalists and join the Nanking regime. Its army grew in size until it numbered almost 1 million soldiers by the end of the war. It assisted the Japanese in their operations against both the Nationalist army and the Communist Party's guerrillas. In this respect, the war in China constituted another chapter in the civil war that had followed the fall of the empire in 1911.

Japanese plans for their Asian empire extended over this entire conquered area. The Tojo government extended to China, along with Indonesia, the Philippines, Burma, Thailand, and Indochina, the invitation to participate "through mutual cooperation" in an "order of common prosperity and well-being based on justice." The promise never became reality. Waging war occupied first place in the Japanese priorities. The resources of its empire and of the lands ruled by collaborators served the needs of the Japanese military. Indonesian petroleum fueled the Japanese navy, and food supplies went to the army and to the Home Islands. This economic exploitation alienated the population and fueled resistance movements that sprang up in every country. Later, trade among the conquered lands dwindled when the American submarine war on Japanese shipping made the sea a battlefield and isolated the various countries from one another. The war against the Allies, not "co-prosperity," was the dominant feature of Japanese occupation policy.

Despite the impressive victories of their armies and navies, the Japanese High Command could not bring the war to a successful end. By mid-1942, the U.S. Pacific fleet had recovered sufficiently to launch its own attacks on Japanese naval forces. In China, Japanese campaigns against communist-held regions did not end the guerrilla war. The Japanese continued their offensives against the Nationalist armies. One-half of their overseas forces were tied down in that war in China. Chiang Kai-shek, still out of reach in his mountain capital of Chongqing far up the Yangtze River, would not surrender. Neither the German military triumphs nor the great conquests of the Japanese army and navy gave these empires the final victory their leaders had sought.

THE FORMATION OF THE GRAND ALLIANCE

The alliance opposing the Axis states came together at the end of 1941. The German declaration of war against the United States gave Great Britain and the Soviet Union the ally that they needed in the European war. Great Britain and the entire British Empire were at war with Japan as well, but their major effort

had to be the defeat of Germany. The "Grand Alliance" was complete.

The Western Allies and the Soviet Union were unlike one another in many respects. They fought on different battlefronts, they pursued separate war aims, and their political systems were the product of opposing ideologies. These differences created barriers to understanding and were the cause of serious disagreements. Gradually, though, through meetings of foreign ministers and international conferences, the Allies agreed on a set of common objectives. These goals set the guidelines for military collaboration and for the postwar reconstruction of Europe and East Asia.

● HIGHLIGHT: Internationalism ●

The dream that peace should reign among countries has existed for as long as modern states have waged war. In the nineteenth century, Western writers and political leaders committed to human rights and democracy formulated a new project for ensuring peace among nations. Their internationalist theory became the basis of President Woodrow Wilson's peace proposals to end the First World War. The tragic destruction and loss of life brought by that war convinced many Westerners that such a conflict must never again occur. It had to be "the war to end all wars." But for the dream to come true, it had to be based on a new system of international relations. Despite Wilson's failure to win the backing of the U.S. Congress for his plan, President Franklin Roosevelt revived in a modified form this view of a world at peace. It guided him in laying plans for the postwar international order.

Roosevelt's peace proposals drew inspiration from the core arguments of international-

ism. With some reservations, he was ready to support a postwar settlement that rejected the principles of balance of power and "reason of state" that had governed diplomatic relations since the seventeenth century. To change this system meant altering the very process by which states settled disputes and maintained peaceful relations among themselves.

Those who defended the traditional system called themselves "realists." They claimed that the foreign policy of states had to center its attention on the real power possessed by independent countries, not on visions of universal peace. They observed that the process of international relations was often a struggle among sovereign states, since no higher law or binding moral code restrained the behavior of states. A government might hope for goodwill and cooperation from other states, but it had to be prepared for the possibility that one or several of them would prove a threat to its well-being.

The reasons for war that these realists cited were, first, that some leaders are always tempted to abuse their political power, particularly at the expense of foreign countries. Second, each state has a certain array of special needs and objectives that at times compete with those of other states. These interests of state dictate the guidelines of the foreign policy of any country, which is bound at times to have to confront another country whose interests clash with its own. A government might hope that negotiation and compromise would settle these disputes, but the ultimate defense of its interests and, first of all, the defense of its people and territory had to depend on its ability to defend itself in war. Realists for centuries had argued that individual states had to be the final arbiters of these interests. What they called "reason of state" was the only rational foundation of international relations. They recognized that a powerful, aggressive state might seek to dominate or even destroy other states by using the brutal methods of "power politics," that is, threatening to use or using its military might to wage a war of aggression. To counter this danger, they believed that alliances among states opposing this dangerous state would maintain a stable balance of power, that is, counterbalance the might of the dominant state and dissuade it from its aggressive policies. Still, war remained an eventuality for which states had to be prepared.

Internationalist critics judged this defense of war intolerable and immoral. Even before the First World War had proven the destructiveness of modern war, they had condemned the realists for assuming that states were forever destined to struggle among themselves. They found inspiration in the ideology of liberalism, especially its emphasis on human rights, and in economic trends of the nineteenth century that strengthened trade and financial cooperation among states. The First World War reinforced their conviction that they had to succeed in bringing to a halt wars that had become so destructive there could be no real victors or vanquished. Their belief in democracy persuaded them that most human beings were reasonable and capable of understanding the importance of common interests shared by states and peoples. If the right democratic institutions and obstacles to aggression were put in place, wars could be prevented or, at least, limited in scope. Modern states had brought an end to feudal wars; internationalists proposed to do the same for wars among states.

The nineteenth century had given them special reasons to believe that their project was realizable. The spread of democracy placed power in the hands of masses of voters. They argued that the people had solid grounds to oppose a political leader who plotted military aggression, since their own lives and property would suffer most in the event of war. Internationalists believed that the interests of economic leaders also lay in the preservation of peace, particularly in conditions of a growing international economy. They expected that economic interests and common sense would combine to create an enlightened public opinion throughout Western countries. Generals or dictators, unaccountable to the people, were the likely source of conflict. They had to be restrained, but the means to that end was international cooperation. All peaceable states ought to agree among themselves to ensure the security of each state, for by standing together, they would dissuade aggression. They had to be prepared to act collectively, however. Their individual sovereignty (the right to act independently) would at times have to be subordinated to the need for collective action against aggressors. The preservation of peace among nations was certainly worth this sacrifice.

President Woodrow Wilson had been the first leader of a great power to make internationalism the core of his foreign policy. When at the close of 1916 he had called on the warring European states to end their fighting, he made clear his vision for the future. A "just and secure peace," he had argued, would end the "organized rivalries" sustained by reliance on conditions of balance of power to keep peace among states. Most important, new principles of international relations had to recognize the right of peoples to choose their own governments, whose "just powers derive from the consent of the governed." "National self-determination" was the foundation for peaceful governments. Finally, these governments had to be prepared to cooperate in an organized "community of nations" charged with settling international disputes. It was an extraordinary proposal, called for by the catastrophe brought upon the West by the war.

Wilson had formulated a visionary plan that did not vanish with his political defeat after the war. The League of Nations struggled to make his ideas come alive. *Wilsonianism* was the term by which political leaders in the United States often referred to internationalism. Franklin Roosevelt revived its essential elements. He appealed in the name of world peace to the American people to accept the terrible sacrifices of the new war. He promised that its victorious outcome would restore freedom and allow peoples around the world to proceed with the creation of their own nation-states. The League ceased to exist at the outbreak of the Second World War, but the Allies agreed to create at war's end the United Nations (U.N.). Once again, the

United States took the lead. At the founding of the U.N. in 1945, President Truman reaffirmed his state's commitment to internationalism, which meant that "no matter how great our strength, we must deny ourselves the license to do always as we please" in deciding issues of war and peace.

Wilson's vision appeared closer than ever to fulfillment in the reordering of global relations that followed the defeat of the Axis powers and the disappearance of Western empires, then the end of the Cold War. The U.N.'s membership grew rapidly with the entry of the new nation-states. The vision of an international concert of states to protect peace seemed closer than ever to reality when, in the last decade of the twentieth

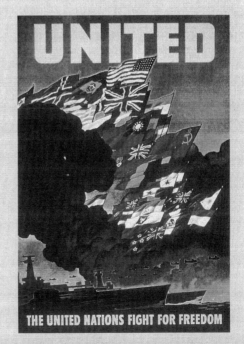

"United Nations" at War: Poster, 1943
(*Courtesy of the Library of Congress*)

century, peacekeeping forces operating under the United Nations' flag and at the orders of the Security Council appeared in country after country where civil wars or regional conflicts threatened the lives of the population and the security of the region.

The United Nations' most ambitious peacekeeping effort came in Iraq. Following Iraq's defeat in 1991 by a coalition of states fighting under the U.N. flag, it took charge of destroying Iraq's weapons of mass destruction and supervising the economic embargo placed on the country's foreign trade until a

peace treaty was signed. The 2003 U.S. war against Iraq ended that attempt at international containment of an aggressive state. Claiming that the United Nations was incapable of controlling Iraq's armaments of mass destruction and that Iraq was a threat to peace, President George W. Bush ordered U.S. armed forces (aided by those of Great Britain) to invade Iraq to overthrow the regime of Saddam Hussein (see Chapter 14). At the beginning of the twenty-first century, internationalism was still a contested doctrine for international relations.

The United States in the Grand Alliance

With U.S. entry into the war, the global conflict found a central focus. Decisions made in Washington were crucial to the course of the war in Europe and Asia and to the elaboration of the diplomatic aims of the Allies. This situation was the result primarily of the global military presence of U.S. forces and of the economic aid provided by the United States to its allies.

The United States soon came to possess the greatest array of modern armaments of any belligerent. By 1943, the U.S. fleets counted the largest number of fighting vessels ever to sail under one flag. The naval construction program, begun by Roosevelt in 1940, produced quick results, replacing the ships sunk at Pearl Harbor even while expanding the Atlantic fleet. Only the United States had access through its naval forces to the shores of every continent and island where the war was being fought. The U.S. Air Force grew in size to sur-

pass that of Great Britain. By 1943, the combined forces of the two states controlled the skies over Germany. In the Pacific, the planes of U.S. aircraft carriers overwhelmed the carrier-based planes of the Japanese and by late 1943 had sunk most of the Japanese carriers. Only on land was the U.S. Army outnumbered by another ally. The Soviet Red Army constituted the largest land army in the world, a fact of crucial importance for the ultimate fate of the states of eastern and central Europe.

Another reason for U.S. wartime leadership lay in its enormous economic resources. After remaining partially unused throughout the depression, factories and farmlands resumed full operation when war production began. The 9 million unemployed in 1940 found jobs, and business boomed. The home front needed women to return to work; the patriotic posters of women in war production factories were a vivid appeal for women to enter the labor force. Mobilized for a two-front war, the U.S. economy equipped its own military forces on land, sea, and air. It also provided great quantities of supplies to its allies. Roosevelt had started a program of military assistance to Great Britain even before the United States entered the war. This Lend-Lease aid began to go to the Soviet Union shortly after the German invasion of Russia.

When the United States became a belligerent, all previous political obstacles to military and economic aid vanished. The only barriers were the consequence of the war itself. Help could reach the Chinese Nationalists only by air throughout most of the war, as long as Japan controlled Burma. As a result, China received a small amount of wartime aid. German submarines and air force blocked direct access to the Soviet Union. Ultimately, the path taken to ship massive aid to Russia passed through Iran, whose territory was occupied jointly by the Soviet Union, Great Britain, and the United States. They built roads and railroads from the Iranian coast to the Soviet border. In 1943, supplies began to pour into the Soviet Union, providing $11 billion in aid, principally food, aircraft, and military vehicles. The single greatest recipient of U.S. assistance, though, was Great Britain. Together with the Commonwealth countries, it received $30 billion in Lend-Lease supplies.

The United States and Great Britain had for half a century formed a working diplomatic partnership based on shared interests and objectives. It had become a wartime alliance once already in 1917–1918. Churchill and Roosevelt had begun forging new ties even before Pearl Harbor. The diplomatic objectives of the two governments were not identical. While the U.S. leaders championed the cause of independence for colonial peoples everywhere, including India, Churchill sought to retain as much imperial territory as possible. But his country was terribly weakened by two years of military defeats. In the winter of 1941–1942, the combined U.S.-British Atlantic fleet had to

keep supplies flowing to Great Britain. Its convoys could barely cope with the German submarine attacks, which reduced to critically low levels the food and fuel supplies reaching the British Isles.

Both countries depended heavily on the military contribution of their Soviet ally. Throughout the war, Roosevelt was guided in making strategic military decisions by the conviction that he must minimize U.S. war casualties as much as possible. He preferred building up vast armaments before risking major land offensives. The invasion of northern Europe had to wait. Until 1944, only the Red Army prevented total German victory on the European continent. Without an eastern

U.S. Home Front Recruitment Poster: "She's a WOW: Woman Ordinance Worker" (*Poster Collection/Hoover Institution Archives*)

front, the Western Allies would face the bulk of German forces when they finally attempted their European invasion.

The U.S. government believed the alliance with the Soviet Union indispensable also for military victory in East Asia. The Red Army appeared to them the only military force in position to undertake the invasion of Japanese territories in Korea and China. In both the European and Asian wars the Soviet Union was an extremely valuable ally.

In the first years the U.S. and British governments could do little to take the enormous burden of fighting off the Red Army. Stalin continually reminded his Western Allies of this fact, begging them in 1942 to open a western front to relieve his armies retreating once again before the German offensive. But Roosevelt agreed with Churchill that their military lacked both the naval power and infantry forces capable of staging a successful cross-channel invasion. In 1942, the Soviet Union had to continue fighting alone in Europe.

In that situation, a diplomatic gesture acquired special significance to prove to Stalin that the West valued the Soviet alliance. The United States and Britain promised in early 1943 not to accept any peace terms from Germany except "unconditional surrender." The real meaning of the declaration was that under no circumstances would the two powers negotiate a separate peace with Germany. Obtaining Stalin's agreement to the policy signified to them that the Soviet Union would remain in the war, even without a second front in the west. Stalin's regime was a vital yet mysterious partner in the Grand Alliance.

The Soviet Union at War

Western statesmen realized from the start that the Soviet Union would occupy a dominant position in central Europe when Germany was defeated. The greatest mystery for Westerners surrounded the international objectives pursued by the Soviet Union. In the 1930s, Stalin had conducted Soviet foreign policy on the principle that whatever was in the interest of Soviet territorial security and power had first priority for his country and for world communism. He used the Soviet-German nonaggression pact of 1939 to expand Soviet territory in eastern Europe. He later made known to the Allies his determination to retain those lands after the war. He protected the Soviet Union and its sphere of influence in East Asia by signing the 1941 neutrality treaty with Japan. He abided by the treaty until four years later. As he had promised Roosevelt, the Red Army entered the Asian war three months after the conclusion of war in Europe. He did so with the promise of substantial territorial rewards in East Asia for joining that war. Revolutionary expansion played no part in these foreign dealings. In appearance the Soviet Union was a revolutionary communist regime, but its policies were those of a great power. In both respects, it constituted a troubling presence in the coalition.

Since the outbreak of war with Germany in mid-1941, Soviet objectives concentrated on the defense of the country. The war had begun with disastrous military defeats and the loss of most of western Russia and the Ukraine. Faced with this crisis, the government mobilized the country for total war. Stalin took direct control of political and military affairs. He followed the actions of his generals closely, and reorganized the nationalized economy for war. His dictatorial powers obliterated the distinction between political and military leadership. They permitted him later to adjust military operations to diplomatic interests of state.

The vast powers of the state and the Communist Party were turned to the war effort. The apparatus of the police state remained in place. Its energies during the war were directed to stiffening the will of the population to fight. Its arbitrary powers of arrest were used against suspected collaborators and traitors as well as against those who dared criticize Stalin.

Army deserters were shot. The prison camps remained in place, though their inmates were at times ordered to the front on suicide missions; the few survivors received their freedom. Stalin's demand that the people of his country "must fight to the last drop of blood" became the overriding feature of Soviet life.

The war required the mobilization of all the economic resources of the country. German victories in 1941 had deprived the Soviet Union of some of its most important industrial areas and most productive agricultural regions. The Siberian industrial economy proved its real defense value in that period. The Red Army was still poorly equipped in 1942, but the new armaments it did possess came from the eastern factories. People had to survive on the meager food supplies remaining; many were hungry and in some areas famine set in. Food aid from the United States began to appear in that year, and at times the one meat dish available to civilians came from a can from "Amerika" bearing the unusual name of Spam.

The population responded with extraordinary patriotic fervor, though the sentiment was not universal. People in the western regions seized by the Red Army in 1939 and 1940 welcomed the German invaders. Non-Russian nationalities in the southern Soviet areas provided a sizable number of collaborators for the Germans. Among the Russian population, though, the war against Germany became a national cause. The population of the blockaded city of Leningrad endured inhuman conditions of hunger and cold in a spirit best described as collective heroism. Over a million lives were lost before the Red Army forces brought an end to the Axis siege in early 1944. The Great Patriotic War, as the Russians called the war with Germany, demanded and received widespread support.

The greatest sacrifice came from the front-line soldiers. In the first two years, the Red Army lacked sufficient military equipment and skilled officers to match the powerful German army, since many of the older, more experienced Soviet officers had died in the Great Terror. This weakness was particularly apparent in the first summer of fighting. Military defeat and encirclement of whole armies

"To the West!" Soviet War Poster (*Hoover Institution Archives Collection*)

led soldiers to surrender in enormous numbers. This remained the case in 1942 as the German offensive swept through southern Russia to Stalingrad. Soviet generals replaced the missing armaments by demanding suicidal heroism from their soldiers. Front-line infantry could hope at best to survive one month of battle before suffering serious wounds or death. By war's end, Soviet military dead had reached 8 million.

In these desperate circumstances, Soviet authorities ordered Communists in the occupied areas of Europe to organize anti-Nazi guerrilla forces wherever possible. Their feeble military operations were useful to weaken the German war effort in the east. In eastern Europe, and in France and Italy as well, communist resistance groups made effective guerrilla forces. They proved most successful in Yugoslavia. Tito, leader there of the Communist Party, built a guerrilla army that gradually took control of the mountainous regions of the country. Though he received substantial military aid from the Western Allies, Moscow remained for him and his followers their Mecca, and revolution was their ultimate goal.

Soviet military operations began to achieve some measure of success in the battle of Stalingrad. After stubbornly defending a small area of the city on the very banks of the Volga River, in November 1942 a major Red Army counteroffensive encircled the German forces there. Two months later, the remnants of the German army surrendered. The Red Army lost probably half a million men in the battle, but the Germans lost nearly as many. The German army retreated to central Russia. In the summer of 1943, the eastern front still lay deep in Soviet territory.

The battle that decided the outcome of the German-Russian war occurred that summer on the plains of Russia. Hitler attempted one last major offensive. It was the biggest tank battle in the entire Second World War. This time, the Red Army was prepared with equipment,

troops, and competent generals. In the end, the Soviet military machine proved mightier than the German army, beaten and in full retreat. By the late fall, the German withdrawal had reached western Russia. Victory was at last becoming a tangible reality for the Soviet leaders.

Allied Cooperation

In those conditions of newfound military strength, Stalin was ready to negotiate a real diplomatic alliance with the Western powers. At the conference of Teheran in the fall of 1943, he finally met with Churchill and Roosevelt. The Western leaders for their part were able to make the firm commitment of a second front in France in the spring of 1944. That conference marked the high point of good relations among the Allies. The three leaders agreed on the basic terms of their Grand Alliance, focusing on three important objectives. First, they repeated their intent to pursue the war against Germany to total victory. Following German surrender, the country would be divided temporarily into occupation zones. Policies of demilitarization, denazification, and reparations payments would be imposed on the German population.

The Western leaders accepted Stalin's demand that the Soviet Union retain its new western lands. Informally, they also agreed that Poland, having lost eastern territory to the Soviet Union, would receive German lands along its western border. They reluctantly accepted Soviet territorial annexation and new Polish frontiers for the sake of the alliance. In doing so, they contributed to the creation of a new postwar Soviet sphere of domination in eastern Europe.

Stalin, for his part, consented to enter the Asian conflict following victory in Europe. Roosevelt, heeding the words of his military advisers, was convinced that only the aid of the Red Army would end the war against Japan quickly. Stalin's promise of military assistance consti-

Leaders of the Great Powers: Stalin and Roosevelt at the Teheran Conference, 1943. (*National Archives and Record Administration*)

tuted a major achievement for the U.S. president. For its sake, he was prepared to agree to Soviet Union territorial gains and a new sphere of influence in Europe and East Asia.

The great battles of 1944 made the Alliance's power apparent to Allied and Axis states alike. In June, the combined naval and land forces of the Western Allies opened a front on the Normandy coast of France. After weeks of fighting, American armored columns were able to begin a rapid offensive through central France, capturing several hundred thousand German prisoners. In August, Allied forces liberated Paris. But the hope that Allied armies would be able to penetrate German territory was frustrated by the failure of the British offensive that fall to reach the lower Rhine River in the Netherlands. Germany had suffered a major defeat in the west, but the war remained still outside German territory.

In the east, German forces suffered a defeat as overwhelming as the Normandy battle. That summer, Stalin assisted the Allied invasion by ordering a major Soviet offensive along the entire central front, located in western regions of his country. Hitler's instructions to the German army were to fight without retreat, a hopeless task but one that his generals obeyed. The Red Army was able to defeat and to encircle most of the German military forces along the front, approximately 300,000 men. The destruction of the central front opened the

Soviet path to Poland and to eastern Germany. By August, its advance divisions had reached the outskirts of Warsaw.

The approach of the Red Army triggered an uprising in Warsaw by the underground noncommunist Polish Home Army. Its leaders were intent on capturing the city before the Russians reached it, fearing that otherwise they stood no chance of forming the new Polish government. Then the Red Army stopped. For months, it remained east of Warsaw while a German division slowly suppressed the uprising and destroyed the city itself. Only in January 1945 did the Red Army resume its offensive there. Historians still debate whether the Soviet halt was a military necessity or political expediency. It is certain that German annihilation of the Polish National Army forces in Warsaw ended the principal obstacle to Soviet political domination of Poland.

These great military victories triggered the collapse of the Axis alliance. One of the Axis powers had capitulated even earlier. The Allied landing in southern Italy in 1943 had finally roused Italy's generals to join the opposition to the Fascist state and to Mussolini. They and most of the Italian people had no desire to pursue further a hopeless, destructive war. With the help of the Italian king and leading Fascist politicians, they succeeded in removing Mussolini from power in mid-1943 and in signing an armistice with the Allies. Immediately afterward, however, German armored divisions occupied the country and replaced the Italian troops on the front lines. The fighting in Italy, never an important theater in the war, dragged on for another two years. Nazi Germany more than ever provided the real force in the Axis coalition.

By 1944, the German air force could no longer protect the country from continual Allied aerial bombardments. Massive British and American bomber attacks using explosive and incendiary bombs turned some cities to ruins, with the loss of hundreds of thousands of German lives.

The worst "firestorm" occurred in early 1945, when the city of Dresden suffered a bombing attack that resulted in civilian losses estimated at between 50,000 and 80,000 lives. Despite Nazi fanaticism and the grim determination of German troops, Axis defeat was by then inevitable. But the war continued, for Hitler and his Nazi followers preferred death in battle to defeat.

THE DEFEAT OF THE AXIS EMPIRES

In early 1945, the wars in Europe and Asia were drawing rapidly to a close. The future of the occupied European states and Asian colonies depended in large measure on the policies of the victorious Allied powers, working either together or separately. The Grand Alliance promised cooperation both for war and for the peace to follow. More important for Europe than agreements among the Allies was the movement toward central Europe of Soviet and Western armies. Behind them Soviet and Western occupation authorities began reconstruction; the results diverged greatly between eastern and western regions. A kind of partition of Europe had already begun to emerge. The fate of Asia was decided soon after, when the world entered the era of nuclear warfare. American military might decided that war. There too communist forces occupied a separate sphere; Korea itself was divided by partition similar to that of Germany. The war's outcome was in the hands of the Allies.

The United States and the Liberation of Western Europe

Among the Western statesmen, Roosevelt had the greatest influence in laying plans for the rebuilding of postwar Europe. The American political system placed the formulation of foreign policy in his hands alone, though it left to Congress and the voters the decision to allocate the funds needed for foreign ventures. An astute politician who had lived through the hopes and the deceptions of Wilson's internationalist policies, Roosevelt anticipated that U.S. wartime influence would not extend into peacetime. The American people, through their elected representatives, would demand an immediate return to peacetime conditions—the demobilization of U.S. troops and an end to foreign aid. The best Roosevelt could achieve would be a peace that was self-enforcing, that is, one that did not require permanent U.S. military commitments. Wilson's internationalism shaped his vision of the future peace. He held out the promise of national self-determination for lands occupied by the Axis, even if these areas had previously been Western colonies. He looked forward to collaboration among the Great Powers within the framework of a new international peacekeeping organization, to be called the United Nations.

His plans modified Wilsonianism in two ways. For one thing, his advisers and the British government worked for the establishment of an international economy based on free trade and a stable financial system. U.S. leaders hoped to see global economic expansion after the war; this would benefit the war-torn countries and the American economy as well. Meeting in the United States in late 1944, British and American officials reached agreement on U.S. financial support for international trade and financial affairs. The so-called "Bretton-Woods system" promised a reinvigorated global market economy, buttressed by U.S. economic wealth.

Roosevelt looked forward to peacetime collaboration among the Great Powers. Their leadership in world affairs mattered more to him than the institutional projects of the United Nations. They were to take primary responsibility for the introduction or restoration of democratic government in small nation-states and for collective action to resist aggressive governments. He assumed that American isolationism was still a force in U.S. foreign policy and sought a policy that would require only limited U.S. involvement

in global affairs. In his speech to Congress after his return from the 1943 Teheran Conference, he made clear how much importance he attached to a new postwar spirit of cooperation. "Britain, Russia, China, and the United States and their allies," he declared, "represent more than three quarters of the total population of the earth. As long as these four nations with great military power stick together in determination to keep the peace there will be no possibility of an aggressor nation arising to start another world war."

He referred to their collaboration as the work of "Four Policemen." He insisted that these states be granted special powers (the "veto") in the Security Council of the new United Nations. It required wishful thinking on his part to imagine Nationalist China capable of becoming the "policeman" of East Asia. Only Roosevelt's deep optimism (and the euphoria of wartime cooperation) justified his hope in continued agreement with the Soviet Union. The alliance had to endure, for he saw no other hope for an enduring peace.

As Allied forces moved toward central Europe, the key role of the occupation authorities became evident. France was the most important country liberated by the Normandy invasion. It had lost all real independence during the war. Its economy had been in the service of the German war machine and its people had been subject to German exploitation. As the years of occupation passed, opposition to the Germans grew and underground resistance forces gathered together in the Free French movement. Its leader, General Charles de Gaulle, was a traitor to his army in 1940 when he refused to accept the armistice with Germany and fled to London. His dedication and eloquence in the cause of French freedom soon placed him at the head of the forces resisting the Germans. As liberation drew near, even the Communists acknowledged, albeit reluctantly, his leadership.

De Gaulle had much greater difficulty obtaining the recognition of Roosevelt. The American president believed that "national self-determination" meant the choice of new leadership by free elections, not by self-proclamation. Yet de Gaulle was the major noncommunist political leader in France and was committed to free democratic government. This agreement on basic political principles, plus the popularity of de Gaulle among the French people and Resistance forces, fi-

nally earned him the diplomatic backing of the Western Allies shortly before the Normandy invasion. In the months that followed he reached agreement with the French Resistance forces on democratic elections to form a new constitutional republic. In return, he had to agree to their demand for substantial reforms in what they hoped would be a new France. In a manner consistent with the principle of national self-determination, France recovered its independence.

◀ SPOTLIGHT: John Maynard Keynes ▶

Until the Englishman John Maynard Keynes (1883–1946) revolutionized economic theory, economists devoted themselves to the scholarly study of what was known as the "dismal science." Classical economics had no role to play in public life, and its specialists sought no place there. They referred to their theory as "laissez-faire" (meaning to "let alone") capitalism, since they believed that the laws governing economics operated, and had to operate, without any outside intervention. Prosperity and depression followed one another in a natural cycle as inevitable as the seasons. When depression hit, bankruptcies and unemployment spread widely. But recovery would follow, as day followed night. It would again lead to renewed prosperity, businesses would again prosper and the laboring population would enjoy better times. No one could alter the cycle.

Keynes challenged that theory and made economic well-being a central concern for governments. He was a rebel in his chosen career, just as he was a rebel in his personal

life. He belonged as a young man to the Bloomsbury circle of bohemian intellectuals in London, who defied Victorian moral conventions for the sake of personal liberty. Among them, Keynes had no need to hide his homosexuality. His brilliance as an economist earned him a place among English negotiators at the Versailles peace settlement in 1919. Afterwards, he taught quietly at Cambridge University, marrying a Russian ballerina and now and then speculating (and usually winning) on the stock market.

His real achievement came when he sought to explain the fundamental economic problems caused by the depression of the 1930s. In those grim years he challenged classical economical theory by arguing that the cyclical evolution of capitalist economies did not necessarily (or even ordinarily) lead to full employment and long-term stability. The promise of laissez-faire capitalism to restore prosperity after major declines in economic activity was false. He spelled out his own theory in a book titled *The General Theory of Em-*

ployment, published in 1936. It created an uproar among economists, for it proposed that governments had the responsibility to use their financial resources (and the advice of economists like himself) to reform the imperfect capitalist system. His theory quickly attracted political leaders looking desperately for a solution to the social crisis caused by the depression. Like President Roosevelt, Keynes sought to protect the freedom of the market economy and liberal democracy on which it depended. At a time when communism and fascism were attracting supporters everywhere (including students at Cambridge University where he taught), he wished to find a "middle way between the anarchy of laissez-faire and the tyranny of totalitarianism."

The Second World War carried him one step further to consider the entire global eco-nomic system. Recovery from depression and war required a new system of international trade and financial cooperation. The United States had to occupy the central position if the postwar world was to avoid the chaotic, destructive protectionism and economic stagnation of the 1930s. The British and U.S. governments welcomed his help. He was, they recognized, a "true genius." At negotiations in 1944 during the Bretton-Woods conference in Washington, he played a key role in bringing agreement on the international institutions to stimulate reconstruction and multilateral trade after the war. That system did not begin full operation until after his death. It grew in importance to become a central feature of the global economy of the late twentieth century. Keynes had helped build that "middle way" on which the Western world depended.

The Economist among the Diplomats: John Maynard Keynes Addressing the Bretton-Woods Conference, 1944. (*UPI/Corbis/Bettmann*)

Soviet Triumph in Eastern Europe

Although the Western leaders were committed to national self-determination throughout occupied Europe, Stalin accepted it only where it suited Soviet power politics. His objectives and methods of building peace differed fundamentally from those of Roosevelt. The difference lay in the use of state power. While the U.S. government set out to create a new world order that would require the least possible U.S. international intervention, the Soviet leader proceeded to deploy his military power to ensure diplomatic or political domination in the areas around the Soviet Union liberated by the Red Army. As in the 1930s, Stalin honored the law of power politics to "respect only the strong" and retained his suspicious view of the "capitalist jungle." The war against Germany had temporarily allied capitalist states and the Soviet Union, but in his opinion the fundamental antagonism between the two social systems remained. In Stalin's worldview, applied even more ruthlessly in his dealings with fellow Communists, no one could be trusted of their own free will to work for the common good. He recognized only political and military power.

Stalin was true to these convictions in his dealings with his wartime allied states. He had to respect the might of the West, especially the United States with its undamaged productive economy, multi-ocean great navy, and enormous airpower. The Soviet Union had been bled dry and strained to the utmost to support the Red Army. For that very reason, he assigned first priority to the strengthening of his country's international power. During the war his spies in the United States had passed on word of the development of an American nuclear bomb; even before the defeat of Germany, Soviet scientists had begun work on nuclear weapons. And his improved relations with his wartime allies had done nothing to dissuade him from creating a Soviet sphere of domination around his country.

By 1943, Stalin had begun to assemble the political and diplomatic parts to a postwar protective zone on the Soviet western borders. Its essential condition was the agreement by the small neighboring states to renounce their independence in international affairs. The Czech government-in-exile in London understood the future shape of central Europe. In 1943, it proposed to the Soviet Union a diplomatic agreement by which the Czechs accepted postwar Soviet international leadership in exchange for internal self-rule. Stalin agreed to the proposal. When the Red Army liberated Czechoslovakia, it passed control over to this government, which proceeded to create anew a parliamentary democracy similar to the prewar regime. In 1945, Stalin looked for diplomatic recognition of Soviet power, not communist revolution in Czechoslovakia. In 1944, he applied this Czech model in his peace treaty with Finland. Realism, not communist ideology, dictated these agreements.

Where communist forces enjoyed substantial power Stalin was prepared to accept their rule, on the condition that they too submit to Soviet domination. By 1945, Yugoslavia had come under the control of Tito's guerrilla forces. From their mountain bases, they proceeded to occupy the country following the passage of the Red Army. Implementing their revolutionary plans, they immediately set up, on the Soviet model, a one-party dictatorship and a federal state to govern their multi-ethnic population. At Soviet insistence they accepted economic agreements providing cheap raw materials from their land for the reconstruction of the Soviet Union.

Events in Poland clearly revealed to the West Soviet aims in eastern Europe. The reconstruction of Poland provoked the greatest controversy among the Allies even before war's end. A Polish government-in-exile in London claimed the right to reconstruct the

Polish nation-state, demolished by the Nazis. The Soviet leaders began negotiations with the London Poles. But in 1943 they broke off talks when Polish officials requested an investigation of reports that Soviet secret police in 1940 had massacred thousands of Polish officers captured in the 1939 war. That the reports were true mattered not at all to Stalin. To him, the Polish request damned their government as disloyal and unreliable, unfit to govern in the Soviet sphere.

From that moment, he set about forming another Polish regime out of the remnants of the Polish Communist Party, most of whose leaders his police had executed in the Great Terror. When the Red Army reached Polish territory in 1944, the Soviet occupation authorities immediately began eliminating the noncommunist Polish Home Army. At the end of the year they set up a Polish provisional government. Its leaders were Communists; the London Poles were excluded. The U.S. and British governments protested this mockery of national self-determination in Poland but to no avail.

When the Allied leaders met at Yalta in February 1945, they had to discuss the future peace as well as measures to end the war. Agreement on the disposition of German lands, once the Nazis were defeated, posed no problem. Zones of occupation for the four European powers (including France) had emerged from discussions the previous year. Berlin was also to be divided among the Allied forces, though the city itself lay far within the Soviet zone of eastern Germany. Regardless of where troops from east and west met at war's end, these zones set the limits to the area they would subsequently occupy.

The issue of war in East Asia also brought no serious disagreements at the Yalta Conference. In exchange for a Soviet offensive in Manchuria and Korea, Stalin requested Japanese territory (Sakhalin, the Kuril Islands) and concessions in northern Chinese territory (the same as those the Russian Empire had possessed until the Japanese victory in the 1904–1905 war). Roosevelt promised to obtain agreement from Chiang's Nationalist government to these concessions. He had once again become Stalin's collaborator in satisfying the Soviet leader's territorial demands. Even the question of Soviet membership in the United Nations did not create serious problems. Stalin probably concluded that Roosevelt's project, though useless to Soviet interests, posed no real threat. To this extent, the Grand Alliance continued to function effectively.

Its limits were apparent when the Allies discussed the fate of the countries liberated by the Red Army. Roosevelt asked for Soviet acceptance of the principle of national self-determination and democratic elections. Stalin did agree to a Declaration on Liberated Europe promising free elections. But the statement left so many holes for Soviet evasion that, as one of Roosevelt's advisers told him, "you can drive a truck through it." Soviet backing for the Polish communist government, which was the real issue and the principal source of the divergence of Allied views, could not be undone by diplomatic declarations. Roosevelt asked for no more, however, so important to him was Soviet collaboration in the war against Japan. Historical debate continues on the failure of the United States to ensure a free Poland at the Yalta Conference. Some critics later called its decisions a "sell-out" to the Russians. Yet the imposition of a Soviet-backed communist regime in that country was not negotiable. The failure of Stalin to compromise at Yalta on this issue revealed to what extent he was prepared to ignore Western protests to impose a Soviet client state on the Polish people.

He assumed that the Western powers would lay claim to their own spheres of influence. He ordered the Communists in France and Italy to surrender their weapons to the Allied occupation forces. By his understanding of power politics, that area fell in the sphere of the West, and Communists there should bend to Western "bourgeois" democracy. So too did Greece, where communist guerrilla forces ended (temporarily) their armed insurrection. The same logic applied in his view to China. These communist parties' rise to power had to follow the path of social and political struggle, not violent revolution. When Roosevelt talked of a world of peace and great power collaboration, Stalin understood hegemony and spheres of domination. No real meeting of the minds or permanent understanding could exist between statesmen of such differing views.

In the spring of 1945, Allied armies proceeded to defeat the remaining German forces. German generals kept the bulk of their troops in the east in an effort to halt the Soviet offensive. By April, Western armies were advancing rapidly through central and northern Germany. Churchill, already foreseeing competition with the Soviet Union over European spheres, urged that Western troops occupy Berlin and Prague. These were politically important cities far within areas designated for Soviet liberation. General Dwight Eisenhower, Supreme Allied Commander, refused to alter his military priorities to make room for political calculations. In April, Roosevelt died. He was replaced by his vice president, Harry Truman, an inexperienced former senator from the Midwest. The only course of action open to the new president was to follow Roosevelt's guidelines. After Hitler's suicide in early May, German war leaders surrendered to the Allies. The European war ended with Soviet troops in Berlin.

In July, Western troops in eastern Germany pulled back to allow the Soviet army to occupy its occupation zone. Carrying out their part of the agreement, Soviet authorities gave Western forces access to western Berlin. Demilitarization and denazification started, and arrange-

ments for the imposition of reparations began in all areas of the defeated land. The German state had ceased to exist. What took its place depended on the four occupying powers, for the time being cooperating still as Allies.

Victory in East Asia

The war in the Pacific followed a very different course. It continued to be primarily a naval war to the very end. In early 1945, the British finally launched an offensive from India into Japanese-occupied Burma. The Indian army had continued through the war to fight loyally for the British Empire, defending India and fighting in the Middle East and Europe. The Indian civil service had performed its duties as expected. Operating from India, the supreme commander of Southeast Asia, Lord Mountbatten, prepared for offensives to retake the lost British colonies in Southeast Asia. Before his forces could proceed beyond northern Burma, the Red Army invaded Manchuria and the U.S. Air Force dropped atomic bombs on Hiroshima and Nagasaki. Japan capitulated, and the Asian war came to an unexpected sudden end.

The U.S. naval offensive had begun in 1943. The previous year, U.S. naval forces, in battles in the Coral Sea and west of Hawaii near Midway Island, had defeated Japanese attempts to destroy U.S. naval power in the Pacific. Instead, the Japanese fleet suffered serious losses when U.S. carrier-based planes sank most of the enemy aircraft carriers. In that far-flung naval war, the United States held the decisive advantage. By 1943, the U.S. Pacific fleet was superior in number and power to the Japanese naval forces. Gradually, U.S. naval and marine forces moved westward across the Pacific, "island hopping" to establish ports and airbases closer and closer to Japan. In 1944, they controlled the seas as far west as the Philippine archipelago. That year, Army divisions

Allied Victory in Europe: Soviet Red Flag Atop the Reichstag, Berlin, May 1945 (*Hoover Institution Archives*)

under General Douglas MacArthur's command reconquered that country. MacArthur's next objective was the invasion of Japan itself, where bitter fighting was expected before the Japanese surrendered.

By the end of 1944, the U.S. Air Force controlled the skies over the Home Islands and operated from bases close enough for massive bomber attacks of Japan. Japanese cities lay open to the same firestorms that had destroyed German cities. In the spring of 1945, Tokyo was consumed in a raging fire provoked by incendiary bombs, leaving nearly 100,000 people dead. That summer, most Japanese urban centers were in ruins. U.S. submarine warfare had effectively destroyed Japanese maritime commerce, depriving Japanese armies of supplies and preventing

vital raw materials from reaching the industrial economy of the Home Islands.

In July 1945, the Japanese war cabinet began to consider peace negotiations. Military leaders, backed by Emperor Hirohito, defended war to the death to uphold the honor of their country. The civilian cabinet members eager for peace negotiations counted on continued Soviet neutrality and on Soviet mediation to obtain a compromise peace with the United States. Japanese leaders were misguided on all counts. Stalin was preparing for Asian war and the United States adhered to its demand for unconditional surrender.

The U.S. war in the Pacific was in its own way total war. Hatred of the Japanese was high, particularly after stories were published of Japanese mistreatment of Allied prisoners of war. In the island battles of 1944 and early 1945, most Japanese soldiers fought to the death, refusing to surrender in the face of hopeless odds. Their suicidal determination further strengthened the U.S. policy of total war, for it heightened expectations for prolonged fighting when U.S. troops invaded the Home Islands. Allied military planning called for a massive Red Army offensive in northern China to coincide with a U.S. Army invasion of Japan. But in the summer of 1945 the U.S. Air Force suddenly acquired a new weapon of unimaginable power.

American development of the atomic bomb had first begun out of fear that Nazi Germany would develop the bomb. Germany's defeat in May and the successful testing of the bomb in July 1945 presented the U.S. leaders with a very different choice. A weapon of unprecedented power was available for use in the war on Japan. The issue was no longer deterring the enemy but rather destroying an opponent defenseless against air attack and prepared to fight a land war to the death. The U.S. government chose with little hesitation (only some of the scientists advising restraint) to authorize use of the atomic bomb by the U.S. Air Force. On August 6, one bomb obliterated the city of Hiroshima, killing more than 100,000 people; a second bomb destroyed much of Nagasaki on August 9. The world had entered the age of nuclear war.

The Soviet land war against Japan ended almost as soon as it began. On August 8, the Red Army invaded Manchuria. Stalin had respected to the letter his agreement with Roosevelt at the Yalta Conference. Japanese forces were overwhelmed by the Soviet invasion, which swept down Manchuria and into Korea. Despite inevitable defeat, a week elapsed before the Japanese war cabinet accepted surrender. On August 14, Emperor Hirohito personally ordered the empire's armed forces to capitulate for, in his words, "the unendurable must be endured."

The Soviet offensive and the nuclear bombing had brought that war to an abrupt end. The planned U.S. invasion of the Home Islands proved unnecessary. The debate still continues whether the use of the atomic bomb was needed to avoid that invasion. Historical evidence now suggests that it was. The emperor and his advisers, in whose hands lay the choice of war or peace, continued to reiterate their demand that the Japanese people "smash the enemy nations." Their appeal to carry on

End of the Second World War:
Japanese Surrender, August 1945
(*Hoover Institution Archives*)

the war resembled Hitler's refusal to accept defeat. The Japanese population appeared ready to obey. The two atomic bomb attacks, coupled with the Soviet invasion of Korea and Manchuria, forced the emperor to change sides and to order the surrender. The concern of American military experts was well founded that, without use of the bomb, the war might endure for months, bringing with it enormous U.S. casualties.

The capitulation of the Japanese Empire brought the Second World War to a close. The Allied countries had defeated the mightiest military empires in history but at a terrible cost.

SUMMARY

The Second World War completed the slow process, begun in the previous war and the depression, that ended the era of empires. The defeat of Japan brought down its overseas empire, but not before it had fatally weakened the Western overseas empires in East and Southeast Asia. Japanese authorities had exploited and mistreated the peoples of their empire, but they destroyed as well the authority of the Western colonial administration that had once ruled these lands. In August 1945, little remained of the Dutch and French empires. The British Empire was weakened and discredited in the eyes of many of its former subjects. The capitulation of the Japanese Empire was complete. Everywhere its troops prepared to leave the conquered lands where they had ruled. A vacuum of power opened up in that enormous area, and no one knew what its future would be.

The destruction produced by Nazi rule in Europe and Allied conquest was appalling. Many millions of people had been reduced to misery, and governments lacked the means to help them. Nearly 50 million civilians and military personnel died in the war. It was one grim measure of the scale of devastation. The United States, which suffered

relatively few casualties, emerged the most prosperous and powerful country in the world. The Soviet Union, despite the suffering of its peoples, possessed the military and diplomatic strength of an international power. The war had produced a global division of influence between the two states, each with very different plans for a new global order.

Hopes and dreams of a new world to be built on the ruins of the old emerged out of the passions and hardship of war. These visions were nurtured among the resistance movements. The inmates of the concentration camps and the hordes of refugees and displaced persons hoped for little more than survival and a new home somewhere. The anti-German and anti-Japanese guerrilla fighters were moved by the desire to free their nations and also to bring to their countries a better way of life than what they had known before the war. The hope for progress did not die, though in the midst of the war the numbers arrested, tortured, and executed were so great the effort appeared often hopeless. Great expectations for political change and national liberation from colonial rule constituted one heritage of the war. Conflict between the Great Powers was another.

DATES WORTH REMEMBERING

1937	Sino-Japanese War
1939	German invasion of Poland
1940	German invasion of western Europe
1941	German-Soviet war
1941	U.S. entry into European and Asian wars
1942–1943	Stalingrad battle
1942–1945	Nazi extermination camps
1943	Teheran Conference
1944	Normandy invasion by Allied forces
1944	Warsaw uprising
1944	Bretton-Woods Agreement on international trade

1944	Liberation of the Philippines
1945	Yalta Conference
1945	Soviet war on Japan
1945	Hiroshima atomic bomb
1945	End of Second World War

RECOMMENDED READING

War in Europe

Robert Devine, *Roosevelt and World War II* (1969). A brief study of Roosevelt's wartime foreign policy.

Lloyd Gardner, *Spheres of Influence: The Great Powers Partition Europe, from Munich to Yalta* (1993). Despite the lurid title, a careful study of European diplomacy from 1938 to 1945.

Charles Hession, *John Maynard Keynes: A Personal Biography of the Man Who Revolutionized Capitalism and the Way We Live* (1984). A respectful life history of the great economist.

Raul Hilberg, *Perpetrators, Victims, Bystanders: The Jewish Catastrophe, 1933–1945* (1992). A thoughtful examination of the human dimensions of the Holocaust, by the outstanding historian of this dreadful event.

John Keegan, *The Second World War* (1989). A succinct military history, magnificently illustrated, of the war in Europe and Asia.

*Voytech Mastney, *Russia's Road to the Cold War: Diplomacy, Warfare, and the Politics of Communism, 1941–45* (1979). The best study of Stalin's wartime foreign policy.

War in Asia

Herbert Bix, *Hirohito and Modern Japan* (2000). A new, very critical account of Emperor Hirohito's responsibility for the Japanese war.

*John Toland, *The Rising Sun: The Decline and Fall of the Japanese Empire, 1936–1945* (1970). A critical history of the Japanese military's effort to conquer and hold an East Asian empire.

Memoirs, Novels, and Visual Aids

*Thomas Keneally, *Schindler's List* (1982). The dramatized history of the ordinary German manufacturer at Auschwitz who became a hero to the Jews (subject of an excellent 1993 movie).

*Primo Levi, *Survival in Auschwitz* (1959); and *Moments of Reprieve* (1986). Memoirs of one prisoner's terrible year at Auschwitz.

Guy Sajer, *The Forgotten Soldier* (1971). The vivid memoirs of an Alsatian volunteer in the German army, who survived the army's great retreat from Russia to the Baltic.

Saving Private Ryan (1999). The best movie version to date of the Normandy landing and the chaos of the enormous battle that followed.

The World at War. Outstanding BBC series (in 26 episodes) on the Second World War (available through www.shop.pbs.org).

---

*Indicates book is available in paperback.

Part 2: The Era of Nations

CHAPTER SEVEN

The Cold War and the West

- The Cold War in the West
- The New Soviet Empire
- The New Europe

Highlight: The Cold War in Outer Space

Spotlight: Eleni Gatzoyiannis

The Second World War left in its wake the ruins of empires. Across much of the world, recovery from war meant rebuilding lives, rethinking human relations, and reconstructing economic and political institutions on new foundations. The human scale of suffering defied imagination, and its impact was felt throughout Europe. The political disorder at war's end called for new solutions. In those tumultuous years, reform and revolution dominated political life in Europe.

The vacuum of power left in Europe after the collapse of the Axis states opened the way for the United States and the Soviet Union to take the lead in reordering European relations. In eastern Europe, reconstruction proceeded in large measure according to the wishes of Soviet authorities and the political goals of communist parties. In western Europe, severe economic shortages and fears of Soviet domination combined to make these countries diplomatically and economically dependent on the United States. Political and human conflicts added to diplomatic insecurity to complicate enormously the peacemaking.

Gradually, western European lands redefined their interests and needs. The colonial possessions proved to be of much less concern to Europeans than economic recovery and political unification. The process of decolonization (freeing of the colonial territories) occurred over a period of decades and occasionally came only after colonial wars of liberation, but it was the logical result of the priority for homeland reconstruction and social welfare. By the 1960s, western Europe had moved toward consumer societies, whose states were increasingly linked by bonds of economic community.

Latent fears of a global communist revolutionary conspiracy reemerged in the West, replacing the idealized wartime picture of a loyal Soviet ally. In the Soviet Union, official pronouncements revived the specter of the capitalist-imperialist menace from the Western states. On both sides, the reappearance of this hostile language indicated the breakdown of wartime good relations and reinforced the barriers standing in the way of constructive agreements for postwar peacemaking.

The new conflict between the Soviet Union and the United States produced its own grim vocabulary. The term *Iron Curtain* suggested that an impenetrable wall divided Europe, split apart by the Soviet sphere of domination in eastern Europe. The overwhelming military and economic superiority of the United States and the Soviet Union in their respective spheres earned them the label of *superpowers*. Soon the expression *Cold War* captured the ominous character of the hostile relations between the two sides, not actually at war but mobilizing their military and diplomatic forces in anticipation of a new conflict in Europe. This global confrontation presented U.S. political leaders, little experienced in power politics and global relations, with complex questions. What was the nature of the conflict? Was the threat communism or was it Soviet power? What areas constituted a vital interest to the United States, and where should U.S. support be directed?

The U.S. response to these new circumstances was a peacetime strategy of foreign involvement in the diplomatic and economic reconstruction of Europe and Asia. Baptized "containment," it set the guidelines for U.S.

diplomatic and political policies for more than forty years. The Cold War fueled an arms race between the two superpowers. Although the acute phase of hostility ended in the mid-1950s, the failure of postwar peacemaking and the continued U.S.-Soviet rivalry in later decades gave a warlike character to the relations between the superpowers for almost a half century.

THE COLD WAR IN THE WEST

The hopes nurtured during the years of war for rapid peacemaking proved short-lived. They rested on the assumption that the Allies would continue to cooperate once victory was won. The United States under Roosevelt had anticipated that a modified version of internationalism would govern relations among the victors, that is, that they would recognize a common goal in collaborating both to encourage national self-determination in liberated lands and to work within the United Nations to help preserve the peace. The Soviet policy of a postwar sphere of influence depended for success on Western agreement for communist domination of an area around the Soviet Union so vast it resembled a new Soviet empire. Neither plan was effective. The alliance fell apart and conflict replaced cooperation.

At the close of the war, the Soviet Union was second only to the United States in military might. It was at the head of an international communist movement more vigorous than ever before. Its victory over Germany gave its leaders enormous influence in lands liberated by the Red Army. Revolutionary zealotry was not Stalin's approach to postwar global politics. Western observers imagined that Stalin ruled like a tyrant over the foreign communist parties as he did over the Soviet Union. It was a mistaken assumption but appeared justified by Stalin's ideological bombast and by the communist uprisings in Europe and Asia. The war, however, had weakened terribly the Soviet people and their country. These two contradictory features—Soviet international strength and internal weakness—dictated Soviet international and domestic postwar policy.

The Making of the New Soviet Empire

Victory created the conditions for Soviet expansion, limited only by the strategic priorities of the Soviet Union and Stalin's recognition of U.S. military might. Recovery from the devastation of war called for massive Soviet investments and brought economic exploitation of the Soviet sphere as well as the continued sac-

Postwar Stalinist Propaganda Poster "For Peace, For a People's Democracy," approx. 1949 (*National Archives and Records Administration*)

rifices of the Soviet people. Stalin's determination to maintain Soviet military and diplomatic power was as great as before.

Although Stalin does not seem to have had a master plan for Soviet expansion in the period between 1945 and 1947, he did have certain minimum objectives. These included diplomatic domination in the states along the new Soviet western and eastern frontiers. Soviet policy was expansionist within these limits. Stalin's foreign goals were opportunistic as well, for he was prepared to take advantage of communist revolutionary gains.

Stalin remained deeply suspicious of the "capitalist camp." The United States had become, at war's end, the most powerful country among the democratic states. The techniques of power politics, that is, reliance on Soviet military and political might to secure the Soviet sphere of domination and deal with the West, continued to guide his foreign policy. He remained convinced, as he had stated first in 1931, that the "law of the jungle" dictated relations between the West and the Soviet Union. His country had emerged victorious in the war, and for this reason he had grounds to hope that the capitalist states would acquiesce in his new zone of domination. His policies unsettled the balance of power in Europe and Asia and forced the Western states to reconsider their wartime practice of collaboration. In these terms, his policy of power politics worked against his own hope for Western acceptance of his sphere of influence.

In those years, Stalin had to take account of the political strength and revolutionary militancy of foreign communist parties. In Yugoslavia, Tito's forces immediately set up their single-party dictatorship and openly flaunted their admiration for Soviet socialism. Twice they attacked Western military planes flying over their western frontiers; Stalin suggested this was imprudent but said no more. Tito lent active support to the Greek Communist Party in its guerrilla war, despite Stalin's warnings of possible conflict with the West. In the early postwar years, Stalin gave only general guidance to foreign communist parties, some of whose leaders behaved in a far more revolutionary manner than he. Crucial to his cautious action were his knowledge of the devastation that the war had caused his country and his determination to protect his country's newly won dominance on its western and eastern borderlands.

In Greece, the Cold War began with the revolutionary uprising by the strong guerrilla movement of the Greek Communist Party. In 1946, it mobilized its troops, armed and trained in the war against the Germans, in a civil war to seize power from the conservative government. The Greek Communists took inspiration and received military aid from Tito's communist regime in Yugoslavia. The Greek government obtained military and economic aid first from Great Britain, whose troops had fought there in the war. Then, when the British government concluded in late 1946 that it lacked the means to help, the Greek leaders turned to the United States. Stalin had serious doubts about the uprising. On his geopolitical map, Greece belonged within the Western sphere. In early 1947, he privately warned visiting Yugoslavs that the Greek Communists were foolhardy to attack a government that could rely on "the most powerful nation in the world."

Stalin's expansionist ambitions extended to states on the southern borders of the Soviet Union. Immediately after the war the Soviet government demanded of Iran and Turkey special territorial concessions—land in northwestern Iran, and in Turkey control over the straits from the Black Sea to the Mediterranean Sea. Land on the Iranian border would open to the Soviet petroleum industry greater access to the great oil fields of the southern Caspian. Forcing Turkey to give Soviet authorities oversight on ship passage through the strategic sea passage would satisfy a centuries-old tsarist objective. The leaders of both countries begged for support and aid from the Western Allies against their powerful northern neighbor. In 1946, Western protests ended Soviet pressure in Iran; soon Stalin backed away as well from his demands on Turkey. Soviet interests there were not important enough to risk conflict with the West.

Stalin's confidence in Soviet postwar might was undermined by the successful construction and deployment by the United States of the atomic bomb at the close of the war on Japan. Faced with a potential enemy possessing such a devastating weapon, he no longer assumed that his armies could guarantee control of the new Soviet sphere in Europe and Asia. The lesson he drew from the Hiroshima explosion was a simple one. Gathering in August 1945 the Soviet scientists who had already begun nuclear weapon research, Stalin exclaimed: "Hiroshima has shaken the world. The balance [of power] has been destroyed." Their secret instructions were to build a Soviet bomb immediately. The chances for peaceful relations between the former allies were dwindling even at the close of the war.

Stalin's preoccupation with maintaining Soviet foreign might sprang in part from his awareness of the enormous damage that the war had caused his country. Soviet loss of life was so great no one has ever been able to calculate accurately the total. The figure of 27 million civilian and military dead, commonly repeated now, suggests the extent of suffering inflicted on the country. Large areas of western Russia were devastated, the cities reduced to rubble, the countryside stripped of its livestock, the mines flooded. So scarce were food reserves that when the 1946 harvest failed in eastern areas of Russia, famine swept the area. The Soviet government had to request Western food shipments (provided by the United Nations Relief and Recovery Administration) to feed its people.

Recovery required workers for rebuilding. Millions of men never returned from the war or came back disabled and unfit for work. One-half of the draft-age men had either died or been seriously wounded in the war. Soviet troops, eleven million strong in 1945, were rapidly demobilized to provide labor for reconstruction. The Red Army declined to three million in 1948, smaller than Western observers believed at the time but still by far the largest army in the world. Stalin ended hopes in 1946 for better living conditions for the Soviet population when he proclaimed rapid growth of heavy industry the first priority. Industry was power, coming before material comfort of the population. Women had to take on the heavy physical work of men in the cities and in the countryside. Collectivization of all arable land remained the basis of Soviet agriculture, permitting the Soviet state to drain the resources of the collectivized farms *(kolkhoz)*. Industrial growth did begin again but at great cost to the people.

The lands occupied by the Red Army or dominated after the war by the Soviet Union had to provide resources for Soviet economic reconstruction. Before reparations ended, East Germany alone furnished approximately $5 billion in agricultural and industrial supplies. Factories in the northern Chinese province of Manchuria, seized in the Soviet war against Japan, were dismantled and shipped back to the Soviet Union before the Soviet troops withdrew in 1946, leaving behind an industrial wasteland. The states within the Soviet sphere had to accept Soviet purchase of their raw materials such as coal at prices far below cost. The Soviet authorities imposed a policy of economic exploitation within their sphere of domination regardless of whether the country was a former enemy, such as East Germany, or a postwar ally, like Poland or Yugoslavia.

Partition of Germany

The acute problems of reconstruction in central Europe brought together the human, political, and diplomatic conflicts that led to the division of postwar Europe. The hatred of other Europeans toward Germany extended beyond Nazism to the Germans themselves. Throughout eastern Europe, the new governments forcibly expelled in 1945–1946 most Germans who had not already fled. The total number of German refugees probably exceeded ten million; most of them sought refuge in the western zones of Germany. At the same time, the millions of forced laborers taken into Germany during the war sought to return to their homelands or to emigrate to a new country. The Jewish survivors of the extermination camps looked to Palestine, while most Ukrainian and Russian deportees hoped for a new home in the West. These destitute peoples were concentrated in central Europe. Their care fell on the United Nations and the occupying powers, who were also obliged to prevent the inhabitants of the ruined German cities from dying of hunger and cold.

In 1945, the victorious Allies set about destroying the Nazi political and military system before constructing a new Germany. The wartime agreements included the dissolution of the Nazi movement, demilitarization, and an unspecified amount of reparations. The most prominent Nazis were put on trial in Nuremberg in the winter of 1945–1946. Accused of crimes against humanity, all were found guilty by an international tribunal and most were executed.

The first serious East–West disagreement arose over issues of reparations. In their eastern zone of Germany, Soviet authorities claimed the region's agricultural production and mining output for their own desperate needs. Having seen their own palaces and museums destroyed and their contents shipped to Nazi Germany, they proceeded to seize as war booty valuable art collections belonging to German museums and to civilians. They demanded that Western authorities deliver to them large amounts of German industrial equipment as well. In the spring of

1946, the impoverishment of the German economy and growing suspicion of Soviet policies combined to convince the Western powers that they should refuse the Soviet authorities any additional goods from their zones. This conflict over the economic spoils of war revealed the importance each side attached to Germany. It was becoming less the enemy and more a front line between East and West. The zones were becoming territorial divisions.

In these circumstances U.S. authorities decided in 1946 to alter their German policy from punishment to reconstruction. This sudden change resulted both from their growing awareness of Soviet power in central Europe and from the economic burden of occupation. The cost of administering the zones grew as German living conditions worsened. A barter economy, in which cigarettes and soap were the most widely accepted medium of exchange, provided the essential items for those Germans with anything at all to trade. Prostitution flourished as desperate German war widows turned to the well-nourished occupation troops to find food. The high cost of supplying Germans in the American zone with minimum food, clothing, and heating— $700 million in 1946—made restoring German economic production an urgent affair for the U.S. government. The British state, faced with near bankruptcy later that year, agreed to the new objectives.

In early 1947, the British and American occupying authorities united their two zones into one economic unit. Later that year, the French brought their zone in as well. The Western governments put into place a new economic policy for reconstructing that part of Germany under their control, disregarding the vehement objections of Soviet occupation authorities. That year the U.S. government declared that "an orderly and prosperous Europe requires the economic contribution of a stable and productive Germany." One-fourth

of the country was excluded from that new policy. Translated into plain language, the new policy of the Western Allies effectively partitioned Germany and marked the end of cooperation with the Soviet Union.

The paths of eastern and western Germany increasingly diverged. In the east, the Soviet authorities created a one-party regime dominated by the so-called Socialist Unity Party, run in fact by German Communists. Their treatment of their German subjects was brutal. Soviet occupation troops, knowing that no punishment would follow, were responsible for the rape of an untold number of German women. These women were treated as war booty. Elections continued to be held but the Communists, backed by the Russians, held power in their hands.

Political reform in the western zones looked toward restoring parliamentary democracy. In provincial elections in 1947, most voters chose either the Social Democratic Party, which defended socialist reforms and favored a unified, neutral Germany, or the Christian Democratic Party, which advocated free-enterprise capitalism and reliance on the Western powers to prevent Soviet domination. Political life in eastern and western Germany was increasingly divergent, though in theory the country remained united.

As a result, Allied negotiations over Germany's future collapsed in mutual recriminations and accusations. The foreign ministers from the victorious powers met in 1947 to write peace treaties for the Axis countries. They could agree only on a treaty for Italy, never partitioned into occupation zones. Germany represented, for both the Soviet Union and the Western powers, a position of strength neither would concede. Responsibility for the failure to complete the German peacemaking process was shared by East and West. Neither side originally sought partition. Stalin may have looked forward to a united German state under Soviet influence but, failing that, he resolved to keep hold of his eastern zone. The Western Allies sought a united democratic Germany outside Soviet control. When that goal appeared threatened by Soviet domination in eastern Europe, they clung to their zones. Partition came by default. It was a product of mutual hostility and the very unstable balance of power in central Europe.

Iron Curtain and Containment

In the two years following the end of the Second World War, American leaders became increasingly conscious that their wartime expectations for a postwar settlement in Europe were unrealistic. The U.S. policy of collaboration with the Soviets was incapable of yielding satisfactory agreements. The issue causing particular concern among Western diplomats was the political reconstruction of eastern Europe. They had looked forward to a postwar settlement in which occupation forces would withdraw everywhere to permit democratic elections and the restoration of independent states. But the Soviet sphere of domination in eastern Europe stood in the way of a return to the independent nation-states of the 1920s. The manipulation of democratic elections by Communists in the East also heightened their concern. Communist parties were undermining rival political movements there to ensure their own political supremacy. Both diplomatically and politically, the fate of eastern Europe lay in Soviet hands.

In 1946, Winston Churchill set out to stir up U.S. public concern about Soviet expansion. He came to the United States that year as the guest of the U.S. president, Harry Truman, to speak out against a return to American isolationism. He was by conviction a believer in a realistic foreign policy based on interests of state and balance of power. In his eyes, Soviet political and military might in Europe was so overwhelming that no balance was possible there without a U.S. commitment to help western European countries. A master of the English language, he drew a picture for his American audience of a continent cut in two by an "Iron Curtain" erected by communist forces in the East. His appeal for support won widespread backing among a U.S. public hostile toward communism and increasingly fearful of Soviet military strength. Churchill's aim was U.S. involvement in European affairs to counterbalance the political and diplomatic preponderance of the Soviet Union's armies and allied political parties in eastern Europe. He looked for a new balance of power in Europe in which a major player was the United States.

Churchill's call came at a time when U.S. diplomats in Moscow were proposing a new policy toward the Soviet Union. The most influential spokesman was George Kennan, since 1944 stationed in the Moscow embassy and an outspoken critic of the wartime internationalist policy of conciliation and collaboration with the Soviet state. Kennan proposed a strategy, which he called "containment," to deal with the Soviet Union (see "Highlight" Chapter 8). His assessment of Soviet objectives appeared to fit Soviet postwar diplomacy in places such as Turkey, Poland, and Germany. His proposals coincided with deepening concern among U.S. leaders at the failure of negotiations with the Soviet Union.

In the spring of 1947, President Truman finally turned his back on Roosevelt's internationalist program to implement Kennan's policy of containment. To do so, he needed the approval of Congress and the American people. In those postwar years the public in the United States was immersed in dismantling the economy of war and returning to peacetime living conditions. The economy boomed, and foreign conflicts appeared distant affairs. Isolationism remained a strong presence in the country and in Washington.

Confronted by isolationist resistance, Truman made his public appeal for a new global policy in the spirit of internationalism. He spoke out for the defense of political liberty and self-determination for peoples threatened by "aggressive movements that seek to impose upon them totalitarian regimes." He did not explain what strategic interests required the new policy or what realistic limits he put to U.S. intervention in distant lands. He emphasized Western internationalist objectives, not U.S. national security, because of his need to win public and congressional backing for the new policy of containment. Its implementation required an end to isolationism and the readiness by Congress to approve peacetime foreign alliances and massive amounts of foreign aid. The American public remained more attuned to issues of democracy and self-determination for oppressed peoples than to problems of global balance of power. Nothing like Truman's policy of foreign alliances and aid had ever occurred in U.S. history.

In concrete terms, the new policy sought two diplomatic objectives. One was to strengthen particular states that were of strategic importance to the West and in need of outside economic and military assistance. In March 1947, President Truman proposed a program of foreign aid to the Greek and Turkish governments. Greece was in the midst of a civil war in which the Greek Communists were gaining ground. Turkey was threatened by Soviet diplomatic and military pressure. His "Truman Doctrine," intended to protect a Western sphere of influence, took on the appearance of a battle for democracy and against communism, not at all what diplomats such as Kennan sought. It did win public support, and the funds were voted quickly.

The second objective was the economic reconstruction of Europe and Japan. Speaking in mid-1947, Secretary of State George Marshall proposed that the United States, for the first time in its history, offer foreign aid to countries devastated by war. That year, the economic recovery of western Europe was progressing but

at such a high cost it could not continue without outside help. The poor living conditions of the population there contributed significantly to social unrest, an important factor in the electoral strength of communist parties. In 1947, Japan and western Germany looked like important front-line areas along the borders of the Soviet Union's sphere.

The immediate goal of providing aid was economic recovery for containment of the Soviet Union. The larger aim was to encourage the stabilization of economic conditions in independent states within a global economy. Marshall proposed that the United States provide large sums of monetary aid as well as economic supplies to those governments ready to meet certain conditions. The most important was that they coordinate their use of the U.S. funds and supplies and make public their financial and economic needs. The Marshall Plan committed the United States to the expansion of the international economy and to the improvement of economic conditions of distant countries without any specific diplomatic rewards or expectation of repayment. The new policies turned the United States away from isolationism and toward involvement in the international affairs of Europe and Asia.

Although the U.S. Congress did not approve the Marshall Plan until mid-1948, the offer received immediate support from all Western countries. It was even extended to the Soviet Union and its satellites, though the requirement for publication of economic conditions was one that the secretive Soviet Union could not accept. Both the Polish and Czechoslovak governments, under communist leadership, at first publicly accepted the U.S. offer, but shortly afterwards had to bow to Soviet orders for refusal. The Marshall Plan was not overtly anticommunist; the Truman Doctrine was. Together they altered the very basis of relations with the Soviet Union. They brought the economic resources and potential military might of the United States to bear on areas where the line between Soviet and Western spheres of influence remained ill-defined. The rejection of Marshall Plan aid by eastern European states made clear that Europe was split in two.

By the winter of 1947–1948, nothing remained of the Grand Alliance. Negotiations had ceased and had been replaced on both sides by public denunciations. The United States launched a massive program of economic aid to Europe, coupled with shipments of armaments to Greece and Turkey. Stalin remade the Soviet sphere of domination into a Soviet empire, where all important policies were decided in Moscow. Actual military conflict did not occur, but the talk was of war between the superpowers. From the perspective of several decades later, we know that Stalin never intended a military offensive against the West. To that extent, Western fears were exaggerated. He did, however, use the international position of strength acquired in the German war to impose the diplomatic and political domination of his state beyond its borders. In pursuing this expansionist policy, he bore principal responsibility for the failure of the peace.

Western fears of Soviet military aggression played a part as well in the growing hostility between East and West. American leaders magnified Soviet military strength beyond its real level and argued that it, plus Soviet communism, was proof of Soviet aggressive intentions. Partly because they needed to win American support, partly because they mistook Soviet power politics for revolutionary communism, their new policy appeared a global struggle against communist expansionism. Out of this climate of hostility and fear emerged military alliances and the arms race.

Soviet Satellites and the Berlin Blockade

The new U.S. containment policies of 1947 brought a swift reaction from the Soviet Union. Predictably, Stalin pronounced these initiatives to be a threat to Soviet security. He responded by drastically strengthening Soviet control over the states in his sphere and by calling on other communist parties to resist the "aggressive" U.S. initiatives. Late in 1947, Soviet leaders organized a meeting of European communist parties, ostensibly to create a new international organization, the Communist Information Bureau (Cominform). Its real purpose was to make clear Moscow's somber view of the new threat from the West and to mobilize communist parties and governments within and outside the socialist camp for action. Reviving the rhetoric of war, Stalin's aide Andrei Zhdanov called for opposition to the Marshall Plan and to the "expansionist and reactionary policy" of the United States. He warned that a new "struggle against the Soviet Union" had begun. His warning was clear: War by the capitalist powers on the socialist camp was possible. Communists had to rally to the defense of the socialist motherland.

The mobilization of international support for the Soviet Union moved in three directions. It brought Soviet control over communist parties and governments; it led to the elimination from power in the eastern European governments of the remaining non-communists; and it produced uprisings by communist guerrilla forces elsewhere to launch their own revolutions. Czechoslovakia experienced the most dramatic political transformation. In February 1948, the Czech Communist Party forced the democratic parties in the coalition government out of power, destroying parliamentary democracy and creating a single-party, communist dictatorship. It happened at the orders of Moscow. Behind the Iron Curtain, there could be no national self-determination.

Increased Soviet power within its sphere brought with it a secret campaign to dominate the communist parties in the area. It succeeded everywhere except in Yugoslavia. In that country the Yugoslav leaders understood national independence to be the fundamental condition of their revolution. Tito had protested in 1946 that his state was not part of anyone's "sphere of influence," though he did explain later that, of course, he did not have the Soviet Union in mind. The Yugoslav Communists were revolutionaries, committed to one-party dictatorship and social revolution. They were also nationalists, unwilling to accept Soviet domination. When, in early 1948, Stalin's agents attempted to replace Tito with a compliant Yugoslav leader, they were powerless against a united Yugoslav party leadership. Failing in his secret maneuvers, Stalin made the conflict public. In the spring of 1948, the Soviet Union withdrew its economic and military advisers from Yugoslavia. It was a warning of Moscow's displeasure.

That summer the Cominform expelled the Yugoslav party from its membership. It accused Tito of confusing Soviet international policy with "the foreign policy of the imperialist powers" and of "boundless ambition, arrogance, and conceit." Its goal was the overthrow of the Yugoslav leader. Stalin privately boasted that "I will move my little finger and Tito will fall." He did more than that, for the Soviet Union and its satellite states imposed an economic blockade on Yugoslavia. The Yugoslav party rallied around Tito, defeating Stalin's campaign to dominate their country. For the first time, Communists loyal to their own country had defied Stalin and the Soviet Union. It was an unequal conflict that Western observers compared to the biblical contest between David and Goliath.

Germany was the location of the first open conflict between the United States and the Soviet Union. The dispute originated in the new Allied policy toward the three western German zones. In 1947, their occupation authorities joined the three to make one economic unit. This union was an important step in their efforts to revive the western German economy. It was still suffering from the de-

struction of war, serious shortages of food and other vital goods, and an inflation so rampant that the German currency ceased to have real value. No longer were economic policies formulated for all Germany; negotiations with the Russians had broken down. The Western Allies' ultimate objective was the creation of a new German state (leaving aside the problem of Berlin). To achieve this, they were prepared to disregard the wartime agreements on Germany. In the spring of 1948, the Western occupying powers announced the introduction in their zones of a new German currency. This was an important step toward an independent West Germany.

West and East had split in the middle of Europe. The West was in the process of rebuilding a new Germany. Even without the eastern German lands this state would have a population of fifty million and an industrial base sufficient to make it a major economic power in Europe. Supported by the United States, it became a front-line region. The Western occupation forces no longer protected the Allies against Germany. Instead, they protected the German areas they controlled against the Soviet Union.

Stalin opposed the creation of a unified western Germany as strongly as he objected to an independent Yugoslavia. Once again, he turned to the methods of economic blockade to get his way. To stop unification required halting the currency reform, and to achieve that goal he ordered the Berlin blockade. When the new currency first appeared in June 1948, Soviet troops stopped all rail, road, and canal traffic into west Berlin along the three narrow land passages from the western zones. They cut off electric power from the east to the 2.5 million inhabitants of west Berlin. The Soviet objective was not to seize all Berlin, which was only a pawn. Stalin's goal was to block the formation of a united western Germany by imposing hunger and cold on West Berliners. They had become hostages in the

Cold War. They were completely dependent on supplies from the West. Stalin expected that, faced with the suffering of helpless Berliners, the Western powers would abandon their unification plans in exchange for an end to the blockade.

He did not take into account the capabilities of modern air transport, since his state had few of its own. The Western powers kept supplies moving along the air corridors, which the Soviets could not block without an act of war. The airlift worked. At its peak that winter one plane arrived every two minutes in Berlin. The blockade failed, and in May 1949, Soviet officials finally opened the passages to Berlin. Neither side had used military force, for both sought to keep the conflict within political and diplomatic limits. Yet the blockade greatly heightened Western fears of war. Stalin's clumsy policy had succeeded only in accelerating the unification of the western zones and the formation of a Western military alliance.

Containment and Military Alliances

In 1948, the U.S. government moved beyond its containment policies of military and economic aid to consider rebuilding its own military arsenal. Western European leaders encouraged this reversal of postwar U.S. demobilization to overcome, in George Kennan's words, "their own military helplessness" and their "lack of confidence in themselves." Military conscription began again in the United States. In 1949, U.S. international obligations widened with the creation of a collective security pact uniting North American and western Europe states. The North Atlantic Treaty Organization (NATO) obligated each member to assist in the defense of the others against any aggression. The presumed enemy was the Soviet Union, and the principal defender of the NATO states was the United States.

Large amounts of U.S. military supplies were already going to the Greek government to help in its civil war against the communist-led guerrillas. Outnumbered by the regular Greek army and deprived after 1948 of Yugoslav support, the insurgents finally gave up the struggle in 1949. Their leaders and the remnants of their army fled to Soviet satellite countries, taking with them thousands of Greek civilians. Western military and economic aid was probably the decisive factor in preventing that country from becoming a communist dictatorship and Soviet satellite.

Primarily political and diplomatic in 1947, the U.S.–Soviet rivalry focused in the next years increasingly on issues of military balance of power and the development of new nuclear weapons. In the context of the Cold War, scientists became warriors and laboratories the key places where future wars were planned. Neither side envisioned this armaments race to be the means of launching an aggressive war, but each feared the power that new weapons would give the other side. This logic was as true in the Soviet Union as in the United States.

In 1949, the Soviet Union exploded its first atomic bomb. Soviet scientists had succeeded, far more quickly than anyone in the West anticipated, in carrying out Stalin's orders in 1945 for the development of Soviet nuclear weapons. They already had begun research on the hydrogen bomb. The destructive capacity of this weapon exceeded by a thousand times that of the atomic bomb. In those years they set out to develop ballistic missiles as well. These rockets were capable of carrying nuclear weapons in a matter of minutes from the Soviet Union to the United States and were a vast improvement over long-distance bombers, of which the Russians had very few. Each new Soviet step heightened pressure in the United States for new armaments in a cycle that appeared endless.

Deeply suspicious of Soviet intentions, the U.S. government undertook an intensive program to expand its armed forces in 1950 (even before the outbreak of the Korean War). Its crucial ingredient was to be an enormous arsenal of nuclear weapons, including the hydrogen bomb. U.S. military leaders ordered above-ground tests of nuclear bombs on Pacific islands and in the western United States. They turned the tests into experiments in destructive might, positioning entire naval fleets near the Pacific bomb sites and building mock towns for the land tests. They encouraged U.S. citizens to build backyard air raid shelters and to lay in supplies to survive weeks below ground. A third world war became an imaginable event.

Convinced of the aggressive intent of Stalin, the U.S. government decided that national security lay in military superiority over the Soviet Union. In Allied countries near Soviet borders, the United States built air bases for its Strategic Air Command, whose bombers were in position to attack the Soviet Union. By the early 1950s, military preparedness came to dominate U.S. Cold War thinking. Tragically, both Soviet and U.S. leaders could find no other way to ensure their countries' ultimate protection than to apply nuclear power to military use.

 SPOTLIGHT: Eleni Gatzoyiannis

The tragedy of Eleni Gatzoyiannis (1912–1948) was to find herself on the front lines of the Cold War. She knew that she and her children were caught in the middle of a civil war, but phrases such as "socialist camp" or the "Truman Doctrine" meant nothing to her. The communist guerrillas occupying the remote mountainous region of northern Greece where she lived believed their real enemy to be the forces of capitalism, not the Greek government troops in the valley below. In such a war, everyone had to join the battle, and those who disobeyed had to be punished. Eleni understood the struggle differently and defied their orders. She did so to save her children but at the price of her life.

The village where she lived was close to the borders of Albania and Yugoslavia. The Greek king and his government were far away in Athens. Politics had no place in the lives of the mountain villagers. Living was very hard there, and the men of the village traveled far away, even to America, to earn enough to support their families. Her husband made his living

working in America. He came back often but never for very long. He was scarcely more than a visitor with gifts and stories about a faraway land. In the first eight years of their marriage, they had five children, four girls and a boy. It was the law of the village that wives and children stay behind. The stern moral code of the mountain people dictated that women care for their children and serve their own parents, keeping together the family while the men were away. Eleni obeyed that code.

When the war came to Greece in 1940, her family helped her stay alive. Her husband could not return and could not even continue sending money since mail from America no longer reached their village. Her father brought the food that kept the family from starving. Young men from her village joined the guerrillas fighting the Germans. German army units swept through the area, pursuing the guerrillas and burning the villages suspected of helping them. She was lucky, for her farmhouse survived while many others around it were destroyed. At war's end, she had kept her family intact. Peace returned, and Eleni begged her husband to bring the family to America. He promised to do so, just as soon as he had saved enough money. In the meantime, she had to stay.

And then the civil war began. In 1945, the communist guerrillas had fled to Yugoslavia to escape the army of the Greek government. Then in 1946, they came back. War, not political campaigns and elections, was to be their path to power. They followed the example of the Yugoslav Communists, who helped train and provided arms to their forces. Their Democratic Army faced a strong Greek army trained and equipped by the British and the Americans. They were not strong enough to move out of the mountains. In 1947, with Stalin's encouragement, they organized their own provisional government in what they called their liberated area of northern Greece.

The villagers became the citizens of this tiny, infant state and its unwilling laborers. Children learned in school to salute the portraits of Stalin, and to sing "Onward to the struggle for our precious freedom!" The Communist Party promised the villagers to protect "our friends who work with us" but swore punishment for any who collaborated with the "monarcho-fascist" enemies. The only immediate change to the villagers' well-being was the loss of grain that the new government collected as taxes and the time they had to give to work brigades organized by the new authorities. Eleni herself was often ordered to work harvesting the grain in the fields that the guerrillas had taken for themselves.

Soon, the Communists ordered young women to serve in their army. Eleni saved her eldest daughter from that service by pouring boiling water on her foot and then burning it with a hot branding iron. The local authorities suspected her of having defied them. There was nothing she could do, without being arrested, to prevent her second daughter from being conscripted. It was harder and harder to protect her children.

Then in the spring of 1948, the Communists decided to transport to Albania and Yugoslavia the children between five and fourteen years old living in the villages in their territory. They called it the "gathering up of children," explaining that they only wished to provide a haven from the devastation of war. But it was really their way of forcibly enlisting new followers for the long combat to come. Their struggle was not going well. Their leaders refused to admit defeat, though, and anticipated retreating north beyond the Greek borders to find a refuge for themselves and their followers in nearby communist-controlled countries and to prepare for new war. They knew parents would resist the abduction of their children. Their police had to seize the children by force. Within a few months they had rounded up 25,000 involuntary young refugees.

Eleni refused to let this happen. The front lines of the government forces were just a few miles away, and behind the lines were her parents and brothers. Secretly, she and neighboring women found guides to take a group of twenty women and children down the mountain and through the front lines to the valley and safety. Just before they were to leave, the guerrillas ordered her again to work in the fields. She had to go, for had she tried to join the fugitives the security police would have been alerted and caught them. So in the end she had to abandon her children.

The authorities were furious that so many people had escaped. They had never trusted her, calling her the "Amerikana." They blamed her for conspiring with the enemy and put her on trial. They tortured her to make her confess and forced neighbors to testify against her at the little show trial in the village organized by the chief of the area. They had decided in advance that she was guilty. She was shot by a firing squad two months after her children had fled.

Escapees from the "Gathering Up of Children": Greek Refugee Children and Mothers, Athens, 1948 (*Christopher Emmett Collection/Hoover Institution Archives*)

THE NEW SOVIET EMPIRE

In eastern Europe, Stalin ruled the small communist countries on the Soviet Union's western borders through his ambassadors and secret police officials. These governments became "satellites," that is, states whose decisions on leadership and key policies were made in Moscow. These countries resembled an "outer" empire of a Soviet Union that itself governed its own peoples in a communist-style imperial manner.

The "Outer" Empire

In the years after 1948, all were miniature replicas of the communist regime in the So-

viet Union. Their leaders ruled with the same dictatorial power as Stalin, employing similar repressive police methods. In some countries, little "show trials" put on display leading Communists accused of "national deviation" and "Titoism." These mockeries of justice repeated the experience of the Soviet trials of the 1930s. All the accused confessed their guilt, and most were executed.

The Soviet socialist model was applied by force to eastern European societies. Industry and commerce were nationalized. Peasant farmers were forced to sell their produce to the state at low prices. State plans set ambitious targets for industrial growth, achieved at the cost of miserable living conditions for the population. The Stalinist literary style of socialist realism was imposed on writers and artists who had to glorify Soviet socialism and Stalin's "genius." A gray uniformity colored public life, forced into the Stalinist mold.

Of all the eastern European states, only Yugoslavia escaped Stalinist domination. The expulsion of the Yugoslav Communist Party from the Cominform in 1948 was followed by the political and economic isolation of the Yugoslav state. Its trade with all other communist states ceased, and Soviet and all eastern European states broke diplomatic relations. For a year, Tito continued to claim his fidelity to Stalinism and to Soviet socialism. Finally disillusioned, he took apart bit by bit the framework of Stalinism that he had used to guide Yugoslavia's foreign and domestic policies. He joined the leaders of newly independent Asian states in founding the so-called nonaligned movement of countries refusing to join either Western or Soviet military alliances. But the Yugoslav one-party dictatorship remained, a remnant of his years of loyalty to Soviet communism.

His country kept its constitutional order as a federation of national republics (modeled on the Soviet Union). Tito maintained peace among the many peoples who lived there by giving each a small degree of political autonomy. The Serbian people were the most numerous and the peoples living in the north of the country (Slovenes and Croats) were the most prosperous. His government implemented polices to redistribute part of the northern peoples' income and economic resources to the poorer south. His authority and the power of his party made this formula work. A rebel against Stalinism, he even loosened slightly his dictatorial powers in the early 1950s. Among the satellite countries, his state alone enjoyed real independence and his people were spared Stalinist terror.

Despite Tito's public defiance of Soviet hegemony, Stalin chose not to invade Yugoslavia. Although Red Army forces surrounded Yugoslavia and made threatening moves, they never attacked. Perhaps Stalin feared prolonged Yugoslav resistance; perhaps he was determined to avoid any risk of war with the United States. In matters of European security, the dictator pursued a very cautious policy. Tito's revolt did not disrupt Soviet domination elsewhere along its borders. After 1949, the Soviet Union could deploy nuclear weapons, but it remained militarily inferior to the United States. It possessed only a few long-range bombers and its navy was little more than a coast guard protecting its shores. Whether through prudence or fear, Stalin pursued a foreign policy of domination but not aggression.

The Soviet leader was growing old. In 1949, he celebrated his seventieth birthday, receiving so many gifts from within the Soviet Union and around the world that they filled two entire warehouses. He continued to rule with dictatorial powers, feared by his subordinates within the ruling party circles. His successor, Khrushchev, remembered later how Stalin could "without warning turn on you with real viciousness." His suspiciousness remained acute. Violent public denunciations of "Zionists" foretold a worsening of Soviet persecution of the Jews, more numerous there than in any other country. These signs of a new wave of terror suddenly ceased in March 1953. That month a cerebral hemorrhage brought Stalin's life to an end (hastened, perhaps, by his advisers' willful delay in ordering emergency medical care). His death closed an extraordinary, terrible period of Russian history and of Soviet communism.

Post-Stalinist Soviet Union

Stalin's death in 1953 ended his brutal rule but not the communist dictatorship that he had put in place in the Soviet Union and in eastern Europe. His heirs, a handful of men in the Communist Party's Politburo (then called the Presidium), reverted to the methods of collective party leadership that Lenin had created. They vied among themselves for leadership of the country until, in 1955, Nikita Khrushchev managed to take control of the party and state.

For the next decade, Soviet foreign and domestic policies were shaped by the policies and institutions in place since the 1920s and by the personality and aims of the new Soviet leader. Born into a poor peasant family, Khrushchev rose through the ranks of the Communist Party in Stalin's years to become a member of the leadership group around the dictator. He, like his colleagues in the Presidium, never doubted the fundamental truths of Marxism-Leninism, namely, the historical superiority of their command economy and egalitarian social system, the inevitable collapse of capitalism and the global triumph of Soviet socialism, and the necessity for communist dictatorship. Their attitudes and methods of rule were formed in the harsh world of Stalin's personal dictatorship. This political culture nurtured in them a suspicious, antagonistic view of the West. It sustained their dogmatic conviction that they knew what was best for the Soviet people and for the "socialist camp" of satellite countries.

They broke with the Stalinist system on one crucial issue. The entire party leadership understood that they had to end Stalin's terrorist methods of rule. The enormous power of the secret police threatened their own political dominance and violated the Leninist system of single-party rule. They proceeded to remove from office and to execute for "crimes against the people" the head of the secret police, Lavrenty Beria. The laws authorizing terror were abolished, and thousands of Stalin's victims were released from jail or prison camps. This quiet "destalinization" did not proceed fast enough for Khrushchev. In early 1956, he publicly denounced Stalin's crimes and the "cult of the personality" that had surrounded the dictator with an aura of infallibility. Soviet citizens opposed to all forms of Stalinism took heart when they heard of his speech. Peoples in eastern Europe looked forward to an end of the Stalinist sphere of domination over their lands.

In fact, the Soviet leaders had not renounced the use of repressive measures when needed to protect their system. They kept the secret police, now called the Committee of State Security, or KGB, to suppress political dissent and religious practices. They still authorized the state censorship committee to enforce the monopoly on truth of Marxism-Leninism. They were determined to keep intact the "socialist camp," by force if necessary.

Khrushchev himself remained in power only as long as the collective party leadership was in fundamental agreement with his policies. He undertook a series of economic and social reforms to improve the poor living conditions of the Soviet people. In 1961, he even promised them that they would live in conditions of abundance within a few years. His vision of "communism in our generation" took the shape of a grandiose welfare state, offering its inhabitants free housing, schooling, transportation, and health care. To him, a communist society (the highest stage of history, according to Marx) meant egalitarian living conditions for all guaranteed by state programs in support of collective consumption. The Western individualistic consumer society of private cars, stereos, blue jeans, and rock-and-roll music embodied the evils of corrupt capitalism. He was equally opposed to the privileges that the communist elite of his country had come to enjoy. He blamed officials in the state and even in his own party for the corruption spreading throughout the country. He dreamed of reviving the revolutionary zealotry of Lenin's years. In a real sense he was the last communist dreamer of the Soviet regime. But when he attempted to end their comfortable, secure positions of power, they turned against him.

His colleagues were not prepared to let him undermine the privileges that they enjoyed or the stability of their one-party dictatorship. Khrushchev failed in his efforts to end the abuses of bureaucratism. He could not understand that bureaucratic institutions constituted the essential mechanism by which the party retained its strict controls over political power, productive property, and public culture and information. Critics called this system "USSR Inc." Even his own colleagues finally turned against him, voting in 1964 to send him into early retirement. They undid many of his reforms and ended public denunciations of Stalin's crimes. Dogmatic in their ideological views and fearful of reform, they kept tight control over the population, the vast state-run economy, and the Soviet empire. This modified Stalinist system remained in place for another twenty years until, too late, another party reformer attempted to remedy its grave defects.

In those years, the Soviet leadership's confidence in this system was bolstered by its popularity in other parts of the world. Khrushchev and his successors looked upon the Third World as an arena where capitalism and socialism contended for dominance. Their Marxist-Leninist convictions assured them that their side would win. In the short term they were prepared (as Stalin had not been) to provide economic assistance to noncommunist regimes in Asia, Africa, and Latin America that were sympathetic to their socialist ideals. They did require that these countries be "nonaligned" in the Cold War conflict, that is, not become allies of the United States.

They found a sympathetic audience among Third World leaders around the world. In late 1959, Cuba's new revolutionary leader, Fidel Castro, found a warm welcome when he appealed to Moscow to help his new government construct socialism in Cuba. In Africa,

socialist regimes in Angola in the west and Ethiopia in the east obtained in the 1970s not only Soviet aid but also assistance from Cuban armed forces in defeating their internal enemies (who themselves received help from the United States and its allies). When, in 1977, a group of Afghan Communists seized power in their country, Soviet economic assistance came immediately.

The balance of power was in those years as much a concern of Soviet as of U.S. leaders. Their new global policy sought to swing the world's balance in their favor. Soviet intermediate-range missiles reached Cuba in 1962, primarily because Khrushchev judged Soviet strategic interests would benefit. The arms race occupied an important place in this new Soviet world policy. Power politics had become more than ever a part of the Cold War.

Unrest in the Soviet Empire

Khrushchev and his successors were resolved to keep the communist regimes of eastern Europe in power. They recognized the urgency of ending the terrorist system of rule and the policies of economic exploitation that Stalin had put in place there. They altered the terms of trade between the Soviet Union and the satellite countries to allow improvements in the peoples' miserable living conditions. They made concessions to the deep-seated longing of these peoples (as well as Soviet peoples) to develop the cultural and historical traditions of their nations. But they were prepared to use military force to prevent these countries from freeing themselves from Soviet domination.

In 1956, Soviet leaders acted quickly and forcefully to quell revolution in Hungary. Late that year illegal demonstrations by Hungarian students and workers, protesting political and economic oppression, quickly turned into a mass uprising against Stalinism. Hungarian

The Arms Race on Parade: November 7th Celebration in Red Square, Moscow, approx. 1965
(*Patty Ratliff Collection/Hoover Institution Archives*)

reformers, supported by the entire population, announced their intent to end the communist dictatorship and break their military ties with the Soviet Union. They took their inspiration from Khrushchev's denunciation of Stalin, who had imposed Soviet rule in their land. The Hungarian army joined the protesters and reform Communists took over the government. Destruction of a giant forty-foot statue of Stalin in the middle of the capital Budapest revealed the depths of hatred toward the Soviet dictator and his satellite system. The uprising was successful in bringing to power an independent government. It introduced re-forms to restore civil and political liberties and declared their intention to make Hungary a free, neutral state.

Its plans clashed with Soviet insistence on military control in eastern Europe and on the preservation of communist dictatorship. Khrushchev did not permit desertion from the "socialist camp." A week after the uprising began, Soviet troops invaded the country. They crushed the rebellion and put in power Communists loyal to the Soviet Union. Hungarians lost their chance for national independence, but not their hostility to communist rule.

Europe's most dangerous and visible border divided the communist and noncommunist countries into two enemy camps. That line ran through the middle of Germany. To the east, fifteen million Germans in the German Democratic Republic were under communist rule. The discontent of East Germans at their political and economic plight was evident in the flight of hundreds of thousands of refugees to West Germany each year. The drain on the economy of the Soviet satellite was so damaging that Soviet leaders had to take forceful action or see the East German population literally slip away. Their ultimate objective was the withdrawal of the Western powers from West Berlin, which would fall under East German control. But the West refused to make any concessions.

In 1961, Khrushchev took the risk of a major international crisis and possible war by allowing the East German regime to build an impenetrable physical barrier around West Berlin. Suddenly that August, East German workers protected by Soviet troops encircled West Berlin with concrete walls topped by barbed wire and guarded by East German border troops. The "Iron Curtain" had descended on the last small opening between East and West. The U.S. government preferred not to challenge the Soviet action for fear of provoking a military confrontation. Europe remained divided between Soviet and Western military alliances, between communist and democratic states. The Berlin Wall became, to many Europeans, the symbol of the failure of postwar peacemaking.

The Arms Race and Cuban Missile Crisis

By the 1950s, U.S. containment policies included a policy of nuclear deterrence, that is, the development of armaments so devastating that Soviet leaders would never consider launching an offensive war against the West. U.S. military forces possessed by the middle of that decade both atomic and hydrogen bombs. Technological advances gave them ever more effective and expensive means of destroying the Soviet Union.

By the end of the decade, the U.S. armed forces commanders had put in operation their key strategic weapons. They relied on three methods of launching nuclear bombs on Soviet targets, one from supersonic bombers stationed on airfields around the globe; a second from nuclear-powered submarines, equipped with ballistic missiles, that patrolled the Soviet coastlines; and a third from land-based intercontinental ballistic missiles (ICBM) in the United States capable of striking any region of the Soviet Union. Their "triad" of armaments was crucial to U.S. policy of deterring a Soviet attack in Europe or Asia. Seeking to maintain military superiority over the enemy, U.S. strategy was a spur to the escalating arms race.

After Stalin's death, Soviet leaders continued his development of modern armaments. Their nuclear scientists and engineers proved as capable as U.S. specialists in mastering the skills needed to produce the most powerful bombs ever created. They too realized that these weapons were so devastating that nuclear war was inconceivable. Still, they were convinced that their country's security and influence in the world depended on matching the military might of the United States. Khrushchev announced in 1956 that, contrary to Stalin's grim forecast, war with the capitalist states was not inevitable. His (relative) optimism was based on the argument, identical to that of U.S. leaders, that his country's military advances held in check the Cold War rival.

His claim to strength included a recognition of the terrible consequences of modern war. The previous year Soviet scientists had exploded their first hydrogen (thermonuclear) bomb. In 1957, they launched into space the first satellite, which they called *Sputnik* (meaning "little traveler"). The exploit dramatically confirmed Soviet technological skill. It also demonstrated that Soviet military scientists had developed long-range ballistic missiles (rockets capable of carrying nuclear weapons distances of several thousand miles). In the mid-1960s, the Soviet military forces expanded still further to include for the first time a multi-ocean navy possessing nuclear submarines capable of launching ballistic missiles on distant targets. The United States and the Soviet Union by then each had the awesome capacity to destroy the other country many times over. The cost of the weapons buildup was terribly high, especially for the Soviet economy. The United States spent 5 percent of its yearly national income on defense expenditures, whereas the Soviet economy, which was less than half as wealthy as the United States, had to commit 20 to 25 percent of its output to its military program. Secret cities in the Soviet Union were entirely devoted to weapons development.

Those terrible armaments came close to being deployed in late 1962. The Cuban missile crisis of that year had its roots in Castro's revolution and U.S. opposition to Cuban communism (see Chapter 11). Castro's pleas to Soviet leaders for military protection brought help, though not in the shape of a military alliance. In the spring of 1962, Khrushchev proposed stationing a complete Soviet missile division on Cuban soil. It would be so close to the United States that its intermediate-range ballistic missiles could strike any part of the United States. The reasons for his reckless offer are still not clear. The most likely explanation is that he anticipated from this move an enormous boost to Soviet global power and influence. He did not, however, allow the Cubans to control the nuclear weapons on their soil. This foreign initiative was strictly a Soviet undertaking.

When the U.S. government discovered the missile installations in Cuba that fall, it demanded their immediate withdrawal. President Kennedy and his advisers all agreed (as did the U.S. Allies in Europe) that this Soviet move would represent a devastating diplomatic and political defeat for the West. The Cold War had its own peculiar logic of victory and defeat, measured by the relative diplomatic and military power of each side. Kennedy's advisers disagreed on the proper response. Decisive action was vital, and some U.S. military and political leaders argued that it had to begin with the invasion of Cuba. If the Soviet forces responded with nuclear weapons, or Soviet troops invaded West Berlin in retaliation, war was a certainty. Kennedy put off the invasion, preferring to use a naval blockade of Cuba to stop additional Soviet ships from reaching Cuba while leaving the opportunity for negotiation open for a few days. His caution was rewarded.

With only a day left before the U.S. invasion of Cuba was to begin, Khrushchev accepted the compromise solution worked out in secret between U.S. and Soviet leaders. He agreed to withdraw his missiles from Cuba in exchange for a public commitment by the U.S. president not to authorize an invasion of the island. As important to the compromise was Kennedy's secret agreement to withdraw U.S. medium-range ballistic missiles from Turkey. Both leaders spoke in private of their overriding resolve to avoid nuclear war. Khrushchev, explaining to his colleagues in the Soviet leadership why he chose to back down, was brutally frank: "Once you begin shooting, you can't stop." In the language of the time, nuclear deterrence pushed both sides to settle the conflict peacefully.

End of the Cuban Missile Crisis: U.S. Destroyer Inspecting Soviet Freighter Carrying Soviet Missiles Back to USSR, November 10, 1962 (*UPI/Corbis/Bettmann*)

● **HIGHLIGHT: The Cold War in Outer Space** ●

Soviet–U.S. rivalry extended into outer space. The dream of exploring space had for long inspired novelists and visionary scientists. At the time when explorers were mapping the last unknown regions of the world, the French novelist Jules Verne had laid out in his 1865 story *From the Earth to the Moon* a fantastic tale of human space travel and exploration of the moon. One hundred years later, this dream was a reality. It was the product of the competition between the Soviet Union and the United States for military might and global prestige.

It reached that far initially when rockets became a reliable means to transport nuclear weapons to any point in the globe. Military rockets had first appeared in the German arsenal during the last months of the Second World War. The threat that this weapon posed at the time was not great, since German research into nuclear weapons had led nowhere and Allied armies were rapidly advancing on Germany. The U.S. and the Soviet governments were both aware of the enormous military potential of this German technology.

U.S. armed forces, the first to reach the German rocket center, seized all the German V-2 rockets. The German space scientists had fled but soon surrendered to U.S. authorities.

Brought back to the United States, this live "war booty" became the founders of the new U.S. rocket program. Extremely expensive, the program proceeded slowly for the next ten years. Air Force visionaries were more interested in experimenting with manned flights by rocket-powered aircraft (the "X" series) capable of attaining speeds that would carry them into space and ultimately would permit them to orbit the earth.

Soviet rocket developments in the late 1950s altered the U.S. space program's pace and direction. The Soviet military had an urgent need for missiles to carry its nuclear weapons, since it lacked adequate long-range bombers like those in the U.S. Strategic Air Command. Stalin himself had given the Soviet program highest priority at war's end. He had personally ordered the release of the country's outstanding rocket engineer, Sergei Korolev, from the prison laboratory where he had been serving a twenty-five-year sentence for "counter-revolutionary activities." Working in absolute secrecy, Korolev proved one of the most inventive and successful scientists working for the Soviet military. His achievements were comparable to those of physicist Andrei Sakharov, who was responsible for developing the Soviet hydrogen bomb (see "Spotlight," Chapter 13). By the mid-1950s, Korolev and his research team had tested long-range liquid-fuel rockets capable of carrying cargo into space. If that cargo was a nuclear weapon, it could reach any region in the United States within an hour. The intercontinental ballistic missile was a devastatingly effective new weapon of war.

It appeared to Nikita Khrushchev a dramatic means to demonstrate the great accomplishments of the Soviet socialist system to the whole world. At his orders, the first public demonstration of Korolev's rockets came in the form of a small metal ball containing a tiny radio. In the fall of 1957, Korolev used his new rocket to launch into orbit around the earth the very first artificial satellite named *Sputnik*. It attracted enormous attention, all to the benefit of the Soviet Union. It marked the real beginning of the space age. It also set the Cold War in a new direction.

The U.S. military program for missiles had also developed powerful rockets. It still had nothing that could rival Korolev's inventions. Accused in 1957 by members of Congress and the press of "losing the Cold War in space," the U.S. government immediately set out on a crash program to launch its own space satellites. The first, hasty efforts produced the predictable fiascos. Observers baptized the failed U.S. launchings later that year "Kaputniks." Urgency grew as Soviet rockets successfully carried still heavier payloads into space. The "Chief Designer," as Korolev was known in the West (his name remained secret until after his death), seemed capable of miracles. If his rockets were so effective, then they could even carry a human cargo into space orbit. The fact that the United States did put reliable rockets into operation and in 1958 placed in orbit satellites that made notable scientific discoveries only accelerated the momentum of the "space race."

That race took four important, distinct directions. In the early years, the most visible public achievements came from the determination of both Soviet and U.S. political leaders to accomplish space exploits to enhance the global standing of their political systems. But this propaganda competition hid the very important, and largely secret, military use of space. Then governments and industrial enterprises found in communications and navigational satellites an invaluable and economically profitable use of space in the electronics age. Finally, the pursuit of scientific knowledge remained an important part of space developments. It produced an enormous array of new discoveries made by manned space stations and voyages and by unmanned probes of outer space.

Aroused by the first satellite launchings, public expectations and political priorities in both the United States and the Soviet Union quickly centered on placing a human cargo in orbit. Beyond that was the enticing prospect of sending that cargo to the moon and back. The Soviet "Chief Designer" flaunted the competence of his rocket team when a space capsule containing the first "cosmonaut," Yuri Gagarin, circled the earth in early 1961. Within a year,

several other Soviet cosmonauts, including a woman, had proven the capacity of humans to survive the rigors of brief space travel.

At an early moment in this series of Soviet victories, the U.S. president, John Kennedy, concluded that the United States could no longer be "second best" in space. He promised that the United States would "land a man on the moon" by the end of the decade. The new National Air and Space Administration (NASA) found itself suddenly with a yearly budget of several billion dollars to carry out this plan. It faced a public and government demanding that it produce immediate results.

Winners of the Race to the Moon: Astronaut Nelson Aldrin and U.S. Flag, Moon, 1969 (*NASA/Johnson Space Center*)

The first U.S. "astronaut," Alan Shepard, was launched into space late in 1961. His capsule returned immediately to earth, rising beyond the earth's atmosphere and then rapidly descending like a human cannonball. NASA had an enormous and complex task before it.

Its success in the moon project represented an extraordinary engineering achievement. The secret Soviet program to land a cosmonaut on the moon was a failure. Korolev died in 1965, and his research team was unable to create the reliable rocket and guidance systems necessary for the daring space voyage. In those years, U.S. space engineers designed a giant rocket (the Saturn) thirty-six stories high. It had sufficient capacity to send a spaceship with three astronauts into orbit around the moon, plus a landing craft. The first moon landing took place in 1969. The "first steps for mankind," announced by Neil Armstrong when he set foot on the moon, brought the United States its greatest space triumph. His companion Edwin Aldrin followed him out of the craft to plant a U.S. flag in the moon's soil. NASA won the race to the moon.

That achievement was the high point of manned space probes. The United States in those years confronted serious domestic and international problems, and the government had made major financial commitments to expand social welfare programs for the American people. The disillusionment that some Americans felt at the space program appeared on a placard, held later that year by a demonstrator in front of the White House in Washington, which read "You Promised Us Food, but You Gave Us the Moon." Funds to NASA dwindled, and the final lunar landing occurred in 1972.

The military use of space proceeded with great speed. The possibilities for surveillance of Earth from space created the alluring prospect of uncovering military secrets, such as rocket installations, weapons, and troop movements, without complex spy projects or risky high-altitude flights. The U.S. military's previous efforts at air reconnaissance of the Soviet Union from jet planes had provoked a serious international incident. A Soviet ground-to-air missile had in 1959 shot down a U-2 spy plane flying 10 miles above Russian soil. The Soviet government put the U.S. pilot on public trial after he parachuted to earth and was taken captive. His confession broadcast one of the secrets of the Cold War to the entire world.

Satellites performed far more effectively than any pilot. Placed in orbits passing repeatedly over enormous areas of the globe, their highly accurate cameras made even objects 10 feet square clearly visible on the photos sent back to earth. Both the Soviet and U.S. military had by the late 1960s achieved marvels of technological perfection in their spy satellites. The nuclear arms limitation treaties (SALT I and SALT II) were trustworthy documents because each side possessed all the photographic evidence needed to confirm any violations, not because they believed the other's promises to respect its provisions. Ironically, the space race produced the means for more effective peacemaking between the superpowers than could ever have been imagined when the Cold War began.

Still, military leaders continued to look upon space as an arena of war. Ballistic missiles acquired extraordinary accuracy by the 1980s. The technology and engineering skills necessary for building ballistic missiles became sufficiently easy to master so that other governments whose military acquired nuclear weapons had their own rockets for use in the event of a possible nuclear war. Space appeared to some U.S. scientists and to President Ronald Reagan the place for the ultimate defense against ballistic missile attacks.

At Home in Space: Soviet Orbital Station Saliut-7, 1985 (*Russian Space Agency*)

The "Star Wars" program wasted enormous funds in the vain expectation that satellites equipped with powerful laser beams could destroy all incoming missiles before they ever reached the United States. The plan was expensive and unrealistic. An impenetrable space shield covering the United States proved unattainable, since precision space targeting on such a vast scale was impossible to achieve. Research on the program continued in the 1990s but on a very reduced scale.

The Soviet *Sputnik* satellite had transmitted signals from a tiny radio solely to let everyone on Earth know that it was flying overhead.

The lesson was not lost on governments and businesses involved in communications. Suddenly possibilities opened up for instantaneous radio and television signals to reach the remotest parts of the earth. Microwave signals, containing words, numbers, music, or voices, could travel to satellites in a fixed position relative to the earth (approximately 22,000 miles high) and return to waiting receivers ("satellite dishes") so small and inexpensive by the 1980s that consumers could afford them. Industries that relied on the new electronics technology viewed space as a new frontier for economic expansion and profits.

Global television networks appeared, such as the American CNN and the British Star networks, that broadcast commercial programs around the world twenty-four hours a day. People in countries where state censorship severely restricted television programming, such as China, began buying their own satellite dishes to watch uncensored entertainment and news. Businesses engaged in international financial transactions were able to communicate with branches and conduct their affairs instantaneously throughout the world. Satellite communication made the earth a much smaller place.

Governments, especially in the Third World, that relied on radio and television to spread among their peoples their message of national loyalty and solidarity understood as well the benefit of satellites. By the 1980s, the Indian and Indonesian states possessed their own communication satellites that permitted the state-run radio and television networks to transmit their programs throughout their vast countries. The U.S. global positioning system (GPS) used navigation satellites to give exact longitude and latitude positions to ground stations. Used at first solely for the military, it soon served the needs of shipping companies and sailors seeking reliable information on the

position of their boats. Using a small electronic navigation device, GPS became an essential piece of equipment for navigators, whether on giant supertankers or small sailboats. Useful knowledge, financial investments, and national propaganda all moved through these satellites. By the 1990s, they numbered about five hundred (with the debris of another thousand still in space). What appeared as shooting stars in the night skies was often their reflected light.

Scientific discoveries accumulated as a sidelight to the propaganda and military exploits. After the frantic space race that ended with the moon landings, the scientific programs of both states became more prominent and received more attention. In many ways they were linked still to Cold War competition. Scientists obtained financing in part for the potential military benefits that might emerge from their research. The Soviet government directed its resources toward the creation of a permanent space station, where its cosmonauts discovered the possibilities and limits of human life in outer space. These Soviet space stations first appeared in the early 1970s. They expanded in size and complexity in the next decades. They were maintained constantly even throughout the period when the Soviet Union ceased to exist and the Soviet space center in central Asia suddenly became the property of a newly independent country (Kazakhstan). Cosmonauts remained on board for seven and eight months at a time. Space for them became a temporary home.

The U.S. scientific space efforts moved in two directions. Its space probes increasingly relied on unmanned satellites filled with equipment that automatically recorded scientific observations. This information brought to light geophysical conditions not only on Earth, revealed through space photographs, but also on the moon and planets of the solar system. Satellites reached Mars and Venus in the early 1960s, and ten years later they circled Jupiter. The first U.S. satellite to touch the soil of another planet was the Mars landing of 1975. The most ambitious astronomic experiment was the launching in 1990 of the Hubble Space Telescope, a giant precision instrument capable of viewing and photographing distant galaxies with a clarity many times greater than the best earth-bound telescope. It revealed no military secrets and only later, after serious technical problems were corrected, did it prove its capacity to uncover hidden secrets of the universe. Its achievements belonged strictly to a world beyond the Cold War.

Space shuttles were the second new area of U.S. space developments. The old Air Force dream of a plane capable of going into orbit and returning to land on Earth was partially realized when NASA launched the first *Challenger* shuttle in 1981. These spacecraft were sent up "piggyback" on enormous rockets and kept in space for several days before returning to land like an airplane. The shuttles became orbiting laboratories in which astronauts carried out missions to test materials, to take photographs of Earth, and to repair other satellites. Each launching and landing of U.S. space shuttles attracted a large audience. Space continued to hold some

of the mysterious attraction that Jules Verne's novel had created among its readers. The success of the missions became the guarantee of NASA's continued funding. When in 1986 one of the shuttles exploded shortly after launching, killing the astronauts on board, NASA was blamed for haste.

After the fall of the Soviet Union, NASA joined in the new international era by collaborating with the Russian space agency. U.S. space shuttles linked up with Russian space stations. In 2000, the International Space Station became the first multi-state endeavor to permanently sustain human activity in space. Construction of the station itself drew on Russian experience. U.S. space shuttles brought the equipment for the station and provided regular transportation from and back to Earth for astronauts and cosmonauts. The space station embodied a post–Cold War view of space exploration. The urgency that the Cold War had given to space exploration declined, yet the public interest in and scientific rewards from space probes remained. Viewed from space, the earth appeared a colorful but very finite and tiny object floating in an incredibly vast universe. The ultimate moral lesson from space exploration was humility.

THE NEW EUROPE

While the Soviet Union was expanding its empire to lands in eastern Europe, the empires of France and Great Britain had begun their collapse. The real victors in the war, the United States and the Soviet Union, were opposed to colonial empires. They had given encouragement to anticolonial movements during the war. When they joined in helping create the United Nations (U.N.), their representatives insisted on full representation for non-Western states. They both repeated, in

very different terms, their support for the liberation of the colonies of the Western empires. Their cooperation quickly ended, but the impetus to decolonization remained.

The End of Western Empires

The remaining Western empires lost their colonies one after another in the postwar period. The dramatic change came swiftly in Asia, more slowly in Africa. Pressure for decolonization came from the colonial peoples, from Soviet and U.S. political leaders, from the United Nations, and from within the imperial states themselves. After centuries of power, the British and French colonial empires disappeared. The long-term consequences altered the very nature of global relations.

The United Nations became, in the years after its formation in 1945, a forum for defenders of national liberation. It came into being through agreement among the Allied states. President Franklin Roosevelt was instrumental in obtaining the cooperation of the Allies for this undertaking. His views on decolonization guaranteed that the preamble of the U.N.'s charter recognized formally the "equal rights of nations large and small" and repeated the commitment, made by the League of Nations, to support "self-government or independence" for the mandated (now called "trustee") territories. Roosevelt did, however, insist that the charter give special powers (the veto) to the major states seated on the Security Council. Roosevelt hoped that cooperation among the Allies would ensure a long-lasting peace.

Although Roosevelt died before the United Nations came into existence, President Truman carried forward his initiative. Peacekeeping responsibilities belonged to the Security Council. There, Soviet and American delegates, along with the other permanent members, decided on key U.N. policies. These policies could also be proposed by the General Assembly, where delegates from all the world's sovereign states had seats. When the British government decided in 1946 it could no longer govern the Middle Eastern area of Palestine (a "mandated" territory), it let the U.N. decide how Palestine should be divided between Jewish and Arab states. Nationalist movements in non-Western lands found a sympathetic audience in the United Nations.

But the U.N. was vulnerable to antagonism between the Soviet Union and the Western states. The veto power given to the Security Council members (enabling any one of them to block U.N. action) opened the way for the U.S.-Soviet rivalry to paralyze the United Nations. Its only effective action to stop aggression came

Decolonization of Western Empires since 1945

in 1950 when the Security Council, minus its Soviet member, condemned North Korea for its invasion of South Korea. Soldiers from twenty states fought North Korea under the U.N. flag, with the goal of keeping the Communists out of South Korea (see Chapter 8). U.N. intervention placed it squarely on the side of the West in the Cold War.

The recovery from war of the Western states created pressures as well for loosening colonial ties. The participation of the U.S. government in that reconstruction gave U.S. leaders an influential voice in the foreign policy of these states. The reconstruction of countries that had been liberated by the Western Allies lay in the hands of their elected governments. Western postwar policy in Europe rested on the principle of national self-determination, that is, that self-rule and political liberties offered the right path to stable recovery from war. It did not dictate the social and economic reforms that these governments should introduce and assumed that outside powers ought not meddle in their internal affairs. But U.S. foreign aid, especially the Marshall Plan launched in 1947, was a potent means to influence their foreign affairs. The government of the Netherlands discovered this unpleasant fact after it had launched a military campaign in the East Indies to defeat nationalist forces and restore colonial rule there. The United States threatened to cut off all foreign aid to that war-torn country unless the Dutch negotiated a peaceful withdrawal from their most valuable colony. For a few years, U.S. leaders made decolonization one of their highest priorities. Seeking to help create a new world order, they enlarged Wilson's 1919 internationalist program by insisting that colonial peoples should enjoy the "right to national self-determination."

Among the Allied governments, sympathy toward colonial peoples (and reluctance to continue imperial rule) was strong at war's end. Before the war, the United States had promised independence to its Philippines colony. In Great Britain, the Labor Party won national elections in 1945 on a program that included freeing colonial peoples of the empire. Similar views emerged in France. Defenders of imperial glory and power, such as Britain's elder statesman Winston Churchill, condemned this "betrayal" of empire. In France, the opponents of decolonization were able to call a halt (temporarily) to colonial liberation. Within European countries, opinions were deeply divided on the pace and even desirability of freeing colonial peoples.

Both Great Britain and the United States intended that independence come to their Asian colonies by treaty agreement with their colonial subjects and that the population be given the opportunity to vote on new leaders. In other words, liberation was to come according to Western principles of national self-determination. In Burma, a unified nationalist movement (strengthened by Japan's recognition of Burmese independence in 1942) accepted the offer of the British government to participate in the process. A similar situation existed in the Philippines, where supporters of independence agreed on the terms proposed by the United States.

The British discovered quickly that their withdrawal from colonial areas could bring bitter conflicts. The difficulties arose partly from an animosity toward the British imperialists, partly from deep divisions among the population on the future of the independent state. Palestine became an arena of irreconcilable disagreement between Jewish settlers, seeking a homeland there, and the Arab population that was opposed to any Jewish state (see Chapter 12). The British departure in 1948 left in its wake the makings of war between Arab states and the new state of Israel. Similarly, the British negotiators in India could not bring the two major nationalist parties, the National Congress and the Muslim League, to agree on terms for independence (see

Chapter 10). Unable to keep the peace, the British forces left their great colony in 1947 in the throes of civil war.

Yet these tragic sequels to negotiated decolonization were no more destructive than the colonial wars of European states attempting to hold onto Asian colonies. The Netherlands had governed the East Indies for four centuries; its state-owned oil company, Royal Dutch, had discovered vast petroleum deposits there. In 1946, the Dutch were not prepared to yield this valuable colonial possession and sent troops to reoccupy the vast archipelago. Indonesian nationalists organized guerrilla resistance; a colonial war dragged on for three years until the Netherlands accepted the inevitable, granting Indonesia its independence in 1949.

Twice France became embroiled in similar colonial conflicts. The first erupted in the French colony of Indochina, where nationalists and communists had in 1945 renounced all ties to France. Negotiations began with the French government, but in 1946 French military forces, backed by pro-empire politicians in France, set out to destroy the independence movement. That war lasted until 1954, when in its turn the French government acknowledged that it could not defeat the communist rebels. France's second and bloodiest war was still to come. The Algerian war, begun in 1954 to repress an anticolonial rebellion, was the last attempt to preserve one small part of the French Empire. France's army generals were so committed to this cause that they became key players in organizing a revolt against their own government when they learned of negotiations with the Algerian rebels in 1958. Their rebellion ended the short life of the Fourth Republic, created in 1945, and brought back to power Charles de Gaulle.

Wartime leader of the French struggle against Germany, General de Gaulle agreed to return on the condition that the French parliament write a new constitution for a presiden-

tial regime (somewhat like the U.S. system). Once this Fifth Republic began to function, he turned to the Algerian war. De Gaulle was convinced that this colonial conflict undermined French unity and international prestige, both crucial to his plans for a new France. He sought for his country the stature of great power in Europe and Africa, welcoming collaboration among nationalist leaders in France's colonies where he could find it, renouncing efforts to forcibly retain ties to lands where nationalists held power. In 1960, de Gaulle's government launched plans for a "French Community" among France's African colonies, most of whose leaders agreed to cooperate in exchange for independence. In North Africa, he concluded that, since his army could not defeat the Algerian rebels, he had to accept their demand for complete independence. Despite terrorist attacks by settlers and attempted revolts by forces within the French army, de Gaulle carried out his project to end French rule in Algeria in 1963.

Decolonization of the once-mighty European overseas empires continued until the 1970s. Colonial lands in Africa were last to reach the point of massive decolonization (see Chapter 11). The reason lay partly in the weakness of nationalist movements there and partly in the reluctance of European imperial leaders to accept the possibility that African peoples were prepared for independence. One British colonial official painted a bleak picture of a population scarred by "ignorance and poverty, disease and widespread malnutrition, primitive cultivation and harsh natural conditions, hopelessly inadequate revenues and need for services of every kind." His argument was in many ways justified, but it was also a self-serving claim to continued colonial rule. Without intending it, he revealed how inadequate imperial rule had been to meet the human needs of these colonies.

But international and economic priorities in Europe dictated liberation for all the colonies, even those in Africa. In 1961, Belgium abandoned its Congo colony, largest of all African holdings. Great Britain and France pulled out of Africa in the same period. The Asian and African holdings of the Portuguese Empire, the earliest of Europe's overseas empires, were the last to obtain independence. Ruled by a dictator, General Salazar, until 1975, the Portuguese government had refused to bow to the "winds of change" sweeping away the colonial rulers. Portugal had sent troops to suppress nationalist rebellions in its African colonies of Angola and Mozambique and in its East Indies colony of East Timor. But when a democratic government took over from Salazar in the mid-1970s, one of its first acts was to free these lands. By then, the only reminder in Europe of that imperial age was the presence of migrants from their former colonies. They left their homes in search of better jobs in Europe with, as their most important entry card, a knowledge of the languages of their former colonial rulers. Slowly, in conditions of either peaceful negotiation or war, the European colonial empires in Asia and Africa gave way to nation-states.

Western European Recovery

At war's end the European peoples had to turn their principal efforts to their countries' recovery from war. The terrible destruction left in the wake of liberation called for ambitious reconstruction, not just of the physical framework of an industrial economy but also of social relations in a more humane society. Hopes and plans looked to a better life for the entire population, and political leaders sought to satisfy these expectations for social welfare. As a result, labor obtained a greater voice in industrial affairs. Women became active political leaders and new family policies provided state support for child care. The postwar economic

Ruins of European War: Budapest, Hungary, 1945 (*Hoover Institution Archives*)

reforms in countries such as Great Britain and France created what is known as "mixed economies," that is, productive property partially nationalized (i.e., state owned), partially in private hands. Expensive in the best of times, these reforms exceeded the financial resources of their still impoverished populations. Yet political leaders could not back down. They deeply believed in social justice for their people, whose demand for a "new deal" brought strong pressure for quick action. In those postwar years the governments in western Europe were concerned above all with rebuilding their own countries.

The destruction of western Europe had appeared so serious and its consequences so threatening to the political stability of the West that the U.S. government had promised massive economic assistance for reconstruction in 1947. The Marshall Plan was an extraordinary event, not only in the foreign relations of the United States but also in the relations of the European states among themselves and with their former wartime ally.

European governments had agreed to collaborate in making crucial decisions about how vast sums of aid were to be spent. The U.S. government set strict conditions on granting European states billions of dollars of aid (ultimately more than $13 billion). Most controversial was its requirement that all participating governments make public their economic needs and their financial condition. A European-wide committee, called the Commission on European Economic Cooperation (CEEC), united representatives of all the western European countries in administering the Marshall Plan aid. It decided on the priorities in recommending where U.S. aid was to go. European integration was an alluring dream in those years. The Marshall Plan's approach to unification came with an immediate payoff.

The aid proved effective beyond the highest hopes of its planners. By 1952, the Marshall Plan had supplied more than $10 billion

in financial and economic assistance to European countries, the largest shares going to Great Britain ($3.2 billion), France ($2.7 billion), and West Germany ($1.5 billion). Each government chose the appropriate use of the aid. In Britain, it helped rebuild old industries. In France, it provided the means for modernizing French industry and transportation. The West German government used the funds to lay the foundations of a free-enterprise industrial system (called the "social market economy"), in which the state encouraged capitalists to reinvest their profits and asked workers to accept low wages and long hours. The result was what came to be known as the German economic miracle. By 1952, German production climbed to 50 percent above the prewar level.

By then, western European economic growth averaged 5 percent a year. This growth came with large imports from the United States and increased trade among the European states. The European and U.S. economies were becoming increasingly interdependent. Gradually they adapted to the new system of international monetary exchange, conducting foreign trade in dollars. The U.S. formula for economic aid to promote political stability and industrial expansion among western European countries proved a resounding success.

The collaboration between the United States and western Europe ensured that these countries would restore their market economies. The Bretton-Woods system (see Chapter 6) had created a set of institutions to ensure that countries within the global free market could count on international assistance to keep trade flowing and to encourage them to work to lower trade barriers. This system included an international bank, the World Bank of Development, to be a source of long-term loans to nations requiring assistance for economic growth. It also provided a special reserve of funds, held by the International Monetary Fund (IMF), to facilitate trade through short-term loans to states lacking adequate foreign currency to pay for needed imports. The system's international currency was the dollar, just as its principal banker had to be the United States. Although the Bretton-Woods plans were of less help in postwar recovery than U.S. economic aid, they did become a permanent part of the new global economy of the following decades.

In the postwar years, European governments became more deeply involved in economic affairs, principally through nationalization of private companies and state forecast planning for economic development. But their economic and financial powers never extended to the elimination of the market economy. Its key criterion of success was productivity (the efficient use of resources as measured by output and price). That measure remained a fundamental reality in the economic reconstruction and development of Europe. Ultimately, the failure of nationalized industries to meet that test caused European governments to sell off completely or reduce drastically their nationalized enterprises in the 1980s.

European consumers found more and more goods available as production increased and wages rose. Employment remained at a very high level during the three decades after the war, and personal income increased rapidly along with the standard of living. By the 1960s, leisure became a reality in long weekends and yearly four-week paid vacations. Families traveled to inexpensive vacation resorts such as those created by the new "Club Mediterranee" company. The automobile became a purchase accessible to a majority of the population. The first "dream" car was a Cadillac, but later the German Mercedes-Benz cars claimed that honor. The hardships of depression and of wartime destruction became distant memories.

The social and economic reforms introduced in the postwar years succeeded remarkably well in overcoming divisions and

in uniting the peoples of western Europe. The details of the reforms varied substantially from country to country, but at their core was the goal of guaranteeing to all the people a substantial measure of social welfare and security. Postwar socialist movements promised that state ownership would ensure employment and good wages. These and other reform movements came to believe deeply in the responsibility of the state to contribute to its people's basic social needs, including inexpensive or free medical care, free and accessible higher education, and decent housing. They proposed to pay for these expensive programs by high taxes on the well-to-do and on private enterprises. Extremes of wealth and poverty among the population appeared to them a social injustice. In this sense, all hoped to promote some type of "social democracy" among their people.

In Great Britain, the close of the war marked the beginning of momentous political and social changes under the leadership of the Labor Party. It called on British voters in 1945 to "face the future" by supporting its plan for democratic socialism. In the national elections that year, it overwhelmed the Conservative Party led by Winston Churchill. It took power at a critical time, for the war had resulted in the death of a million British citizens and had caused tremendous property loss, both to foreign investments and to domestic capital. A year later, it had to ask Washington for a $4 billion loan, most of which paid for food and fuel imports. By the winter of 1946–1947, the British government faced such a serious budgetary crisis that it could no longer pay for both its domestic reforms and its foreign obligations in India and the Middle East. Decolonization came, in part, out of this near bankruptcy. Social welfare and nationalization of basic industries had highest priority for the Labor government. Domestic interests came first.

Similar reform movements took power in other western European countries. The need to care for the health, education, and welfare of their populations put a heavy burden on their budgets and required careful planning. Foreign aid from the United States began to arrive by 1948, but it had to be spent with great care. In several countries, the urgent need for guidance in reconstruction led to greater government intervention in economic life than ever before. In France, this took the shape of state forecast planning. It did not seek, as in the Soviet Union, to replace free market forces by state command planning. Instead, its goal was rational use of the scarce resources for optimal economic growth. Railroads had to be rebuilt and became the property of the French state. Their reconstruction followed the guidelines for modernization and electrification spelled out in the plan. Capitalism and state-run industries operated side by side in this new French mixed economy.

In the 1960s, the United States finally joined in the move toward comprehensive welfare programs and greater state supervision of economic affairs. The election in 1960 of John F. Kennedy to the U.S. presidency began a period of extensive social and political reforms, carried on by Lyndon Johnson after Kennedy's assassination in 1963. The "Great Society," as Johnson named his 1964 reform platform, included new laws to protect the civil and political rights of all citizens. The goal was an end to the century-long segregation and oppression of blacks. Reforms also brought new welfare policies for a "war on poverty," in spirit and intent resembling the social welfare measures introduced in Europe after the Second World War. No private enterprises were nationalized. Still, the government's yearly budget and the controls over banking and interest rates exercised by a federal agency (the Federal Reserve Board) guided the country's economy in a manner inspired by the ideas of John Maynard Keynes.

The most extraordinary postwar political recovery occurred in the German Federal Re-public. It came into existence in 1949. German politicians and lawyers wrote the constitution under Allied supervision. It gave West Germany a federal structure under parliamentary rule. In the first national elections of 1949, the Christian Democratic Party obtained the majority of the votes and selected the Republic's new chancellor (head of the government). He was Konrad Adenauer, a prisoner during the Nazi years and a strong believer in Germany's rightful place within a unified Western political and military community.

Gradually the West German state recovered its full sovereign powers. In 1951, Adenauer obtained full control over German foreign policy. He was instrumental in bringing his country within the European Common Market, alongside Germany's age-old enemy France. By the 1960s, his country's industrial economy was the most prosperous of Europe. West Berlin, built up as a beacon of prosperity under continued Allied military occupation, turned into a magnet drawing East Germans. They took advantage of the open border between East and West Berlin until 1961 to migrate to West Germany. By then, more than three million refugees had abandoned the communist East to make a new life in West Germany. There they were welcomed as refugees and helped to create new lives in the Federal Republic.

By the 1960s, West Germany's working-age population was still unable to meet the economy's growing need for workers. Migrants arrived to fill these jobs from poor lands in southern Europe, especially Yugoslavia, and from Turkey. Like migrants to Europe's other prosperous countries, they lived as second-class citizens. They enjoyed economic and social benefits, including access to the welfare system, but they were excluded from active political participation (in Germany, they were denied the right to citizenship). Countries like West Germany were becoming multi-ethnic and multi-religious, for their prosperity was bringing Third World peoples within their borders.

The division of Germany was the last great unresolved problem left by the war. In 1955, West Germany entered the Western military alliance, the North Atlantic Treaty Organization (NATO), and obtained the right to build a new German army. A nationalist and a conservative, Adenauer did not recognize the legality of the new western borders of Poland, far within old German lands, nor did he accept permanent partition of German lands. In his opinion, West Germany had to speak for the real German nation, for its people were free to decide the fate of the country. The Adenauer government had no way of ending the partition, however. It was a helpless observer in 1961 when the East German government, backed by Soviet tanks, constructed a wall around West Berlin. The refugee flow was cut off, except for the handful of daring individuals who attempted to break through the barrier. Most were shot down by communist border guards. West German television broadcasts kept alive enticing images in the East of Western prosperity and the hope among viewers that their lives might somehow, sometime, change for the better.

In 1969, a new West German government decided to recognize the partition. It was headed by the Social Democratic Party, which had once been a strong defender of Marxist socialism. German prosperity and its electoral weakness forced it to renounce this program. Its new goals emphasized expanded social welfare policies and improved relations with communist countries. The Social Democratic government put this "Eastern policy" in motion immediately. It signed a treaty recognizing East Germany and another with Poland renouncing any claim to the German lands annexed after the Second World War by Poland. Through a number of separate agreements, a kind of informal German peace treaty emerged, confirming the division of the German nation into two states. The former Allies regarded the partition of Germany and Berlin as a permanent part of the new European international system. They foresaw no alternative for peaceful relations between East and West. Eastern Europe remained within the Soviet empire, its peoples ruled by communist dictatorships.

Western European Unification

The peoples of western Europe had, first of any region of the world, acquired a strong awareness of their national identities. Their nation-states and the nationalism that glorified these states and their peoples became a model for other peoples in the twentieth century, for good and ill. Both the promise and the defects of nationalism had entered the fabric of European life. The solidarity that emerged within these national communities created enduring bonds of loyalty. The terrible world wars that had pitted nation against nation left no doubt how destructive nationalist fanaticism could be.

The end of the Second World War proved the turning point in their histories. Their leaders agreed to cooperate in supranational institutions for the sake of economic development and, most important, to create indissoluble ties among the previously warring states. Europe's governments sacrificed the principle of the absolute independence of their nation-states to overcome nationalist enmity. Their new institutions for unity (ultimately called the European Union) were the outstanding achievement of Europe's postcolonial age. Europeans searching for a stable peace realized that bonds had to be forged among nation-states and that a federation of European states might undo the damage that ethnic and nationalist conflict had caused. The most serious hurdle was the abiding hatred for Germans still shared by many Europeans.

The experience of collaborating in the distribution of Marshall Plan aid demonstrated that economic cooperation was feasible.

The first serious proposal for unification came from the French leader Jean Monnet. A former banker, he made his mark in postwar France as the head of the state's economic planning commission. He grasped the simple truth that a unified Europe could be reached only by stages. He concluded that economic unification was the first practical step in that direction. He proposed in 1950 the formation among Europe's democratic lands of a tariff-free "common market" for iron, steel, and coal. It required that western European states agree to abolish all tariffs among themselves on trade in those products. They would create a supranational commission, that is, a governing body whose policies no member state could veto, to coordinate production and wage plans among the enterprises in these key economic sectors.

The European Coal and Steel Community (ECSC) became a reality in 1952. Six states in western Europe—Italy, West Germany, France, and the Benelux countries of Belgium, the Netherlands, and Luxembourg—signed the treaty creating the ECSC. This unprecedented agreement emerged out of discussions among the political leaders of Italy, Germany, and France, all of whom belonged to Christian Democratic parties. Their commitment to a Christian concept of peace and humanitarian values created a shared ideal for reconciliation among nations and, in particular, for the reintegration of Germany within Europe. The specific agreement that they reached was a practical rather than an ideological undertaking. It sought new ways to speed the recovery of their economies. The Labor government of Great Britain refused to join, clinging to the dream of British "splendid isolation" and suspicious of the important role that business interests would play in the ECSC. Although political unification remained a distant dream, the ECSC was a historic event in the relations among European nations. It was a first step toward integrating Germany into an association of Western countries.

Then Monnet proposed a far more radical reform to speed the creation of an economic union of western Europe. He proposed that a "common market" unite the member states in free trade for all industrial, commercial, and agricultural transactions. Thanks to the success of the ECSC, agreement came quickly. In the mid-1950s, the six governments in the European Coal and Steel Community, led by France and West Germany, accepted Monnet's plan for a European Economic Community (EEC). It was to begin in 1958. The shift to a free-trade area was complex, for it entailed the dismantling of tariffs on trade among these states, the coordination of subsidies to disadvantaged manufacturers and aid to the unemployed, and the formation of a unified financial market. It represented a momentous step toward Monnet's dream of a politically united Europe.

The barriers on commerce declined dramatically and far more quickly than the treaty signers had expected. By the mid-1960s, western Europe had begun a new era of economic collaboration. The Common Market operated on the basis of market competition, whether conducted by private or state-owned enterprises, by small farmers or agribusiness. All the major political parties in western Europe agreed on the desirability of economic unification.

SUMMARY

The Cold War could not provide a permanent settlement to the Second World War. Stalin's intent to create a diplomatic and political sphere of domination around the Soviet Union ensured a partition of Europe that followed the approximate line of farthest advance of Soviet armies. His warning after 1946 of the inevitability of war with the capitalist powers kept his country in virtual wartime conditions. Privately he admitted that this war would not come soon. "Respecting the powerful" dictated that he avoid risky actions that might provoke the mighty United States, for his country would take years to recover from the terrible wartime destruction. West Berlin was blockaded, not seized, by his troops; Yugoslavia was isolated, not invaded. Although political leaders in the West feared the diplomatic and military might of the Soviet Union, Stalin was intent on consolidating his new empire on the Soviet Union's borders, not on launching a new war. But the Soviet dictator's limited expansionist aims stood in the way of enduring peace treaties and undermined a stable balance of power in Europe. Peace could not be ensured under these conditions.

The U.S. policy of containment encouraged the formation of politically and economically strong Allied states in strategic areas around this Soviet empire. In these terms it constituted a creative and ultimately successful global strategy. But the U.S. government's exaggerated fear of Soviet aggression focused efforts on the creation of military alliances in place of diplomatic policies of containment. It rebuilt its own armaments and supported anti-Soviet military alliances even where the Soviet Union posed no real threat. This revision of the containment policy accelerated the nuclear arms race and led to the creation of military alliances that gave the United States hegemonic influence so great that it seemed to be building its own global empire.

Both the massive destruction of war and international tensions contributed to the emergence of two distinct new global systems in the decade after the war. In the East, one-party regimes imposed command economies on their lands, following the Soviet model of collectivized agriculture and nationalized industry run by a mammoth state and party bureaucracy. In the West, countries were bound together through trade and investment in an international capitalist economy. The United States was the center of this Western system. The dollar was the stable currency of exchange, and U.S. technology provided key tools of modern production. U.S. foreign aid and private investments were vital ingredients for economic growth in foreign lands. The economic crisis of the depression appeared resolved for the time being. The new challenge was to avoid a war between the superpowers, each possessing nuclear weapons whose use would bring civilization to an end.

In the background to the Cold War, new political and social forces were reshaping the world. Both superpowers proclaimed that the age of colonial empires had ended. Yet in a real sense the Soviet victory in the Second World War had brought that country an enlarged empire around its borders, where national frontiers were meaningless divisions within a vast territory governed from Moscow. The old age of empires had disappeared in the turmoil of the Second World War. The new world of nations had yet to fully emerge.

DATES WORTH REMEMBERING

1945	Formation of the United Nations
1945	Partition of Germany
1945	Victory of Labor Party in British elections
1946	Philippine independence
1946–1949	Greek civil war
1946–1949	Dutch colonial war in East Indies
1946–1954	French colonial war in Indochina
1947	Indian independence
1947	Marshall Plan and Truman Doctrine
1947	Start of Cold War
1948	Communist seizure of power in Czechoslovakia
1948	Yugoslavia resistance to Soviet control
1948–1949	Berlin blockade
1949	Creation of North Atlantic Treaty Organization
1949	Creation of German Federal Republic (West Germany) and German Democratic Republic (East Germany)

1953   Death of Joseph Stalin
1957   Creation of European Economic
         Community

RECOMMENDED READING

The New Europe

*Raymond Betts, *Decolonization* (1998). A useful
essay surveying the process by which Europe's
overseas empires vanished.

Anthony Sampson, *Anatomy of Europe* (1968). A
close-up view of European peoples and issues
by a very perceptive observer (also entitled *The
New Europeans*).

The Cold War

*John Lewis Gaddis, *We Now Know: Rethinking Cold
War History* (1997). New thoughts on the Cold
War in light of secret Soviet documents from the
Cold War period, from the outstanding histo-
rian of the subject.

William Walter, *Space Age* (1992). A beautifully illustrated history of space exploration, focusing
on the civilian aspects.

*Tom Wolfe, *The Right Stuff* (1979). An ironic view
of the space frenzy that possessed the United
States when it confronted the first Soviet space
exploits.

*Daniel Yergin, *The Shattered Peace: The Origins of
the Cold War and the National Security State*
(1977). A study of the disturbing transformation of U.S. political life under the impact of
the Cold War.

Soviet Foreign Policy

Max Frankel, *High Noon in the Cold War* (2004). A
succinct history of the Cuban missile crisis using
newly opened U.S. and Soviet archival materials.

*David Holloway, *Stalin and the Bomb: The Soviet
Union and Atomic Energy, 1939–1956* (1994). The
engrossing story of the start of the nuclear
weapons race from the Soviet side.

*Voytech Mastny, *Cold War and Soviet Insecurity: The
Stalin Years* (1996). A convincing interpretation
of Stalin's postwar foreign policy.

Memoirs and Visual Aids

*Milovan Djilas, *Conversations with Stalin* (1958).
Unique personal record of three secret meetings
between Yugoslav communist leaders and Stalin
between 1944 and 1947.

*Nicholas Gage, *Eleni* (1983). The story of a Greek
mother as told by her son after he had become
a correspondent for *The New York Times* and had
returned to Greece to reconstruct her life and
tragic death in the Greek civil war.

*Robert Kennedy, *Thirteen Days* (1968). Memoirs of
one of the key participants in the Cuban missile
crisis; also film version (2001) with the same
title.

*Czeslaw Milosz, *The Captive Mind* (1953). En-
thralling real-life portraits, by an eyewitness
(later emigre) Polish poet, of intellectuals who
collaborated in the formation of communist
Poland.

---

*Indicates book is available in paperback.

Cold War and Revolutions in East Asia

- The Victory of the Chinese Communists
- The Korean War
- Wars and Revolution in Indochina

Highlight: Containment and Anticommunism

Spotlight: Ho Chi Minh

Like Europe, the lands of East Asia became an arena for the Cold War, but they did so not in the presence of Soviet troops. These troops withdrew after they had completed their duties as occupying forces in Manchuria and northern Korea. Cold War hostilities there originated in the upsurge of revolutionary movements that claimed allegiance to Marxism-Leninism-Stalinism and that took up arms to achieve the radical transformation of their lands like that they believed had occurred in the Soviet Union.

China, Korea, and Indochina had once belonged to, or had been under the domination of, outside empires. The last of these was the Japanese Empire. Its occupation of part or all of these countries provoked nationalist resistance. By their skills as guerrilla fighters against the Japanese, the Communists made the most forceful claim to the right to construct new nation-states while building socialism. Following war's end, they sought to defeat their enemies by force of arms. Though the influence of the Soviet Union over these communist parties was substantial, Soviet leaders did not control the course of these wars.

In the early postwar period, the U.S. government considered these conflicts to be part of the collapse of the colonial empires. The containment strategy did extend across the Pacific Ocean, but only as far as the Japanese islands. That view changed dramatically when North Korean troops invaded South Korea in 1950. U.S. leaders extended the front lines of the Cold War onto the Asian continent in Korea and in Indochina and came to view the victorious Communist regime in China with the same hostility as it treated Stalin's Soviet Union. While no actual fighting between Communists and non-communists ever occurred in postwar Europe, East Asia was the scene of wars in Korea and Vietnam (one of the states formed out of Indochina) that brought U.S. troops face to face with communist forces. The Cold War took on a violent, bloody character in that part of the world.

The new states in Korea and in Indochina were shaped by these wars, partly civil wars pitting peoples of these lands against one another and partly foreign wars in which the United States played a leading role. The settlement of the Korean conflict left that country partitioned between communist and non-communist states, like Germany a reminder of the Cold War. In Indochina, on the contrary, the war lasted far longer and had a very different outcome. For three decades civil war and foreign intervention tore apart the former French colony. In the end, the military triumph of the Vietnamese Communist Party made it the ruling force throughout that land, still separated from its neighbors by the borders drawn by the French in the nineteenth century. The existence of these frontiers was one visible sign of the permanent impact of the West on East Asia.

THE VICTORY OF THE CHINESE COMMUNISTS

In China, the Nationalist government had claimed sovereign powers in the Republic of China ever since its victory in the Northern Expedition in 1928 (see Chapter 4). Chiang Kai-shek, president of the republic and heir to Sun Yat-sen at the head of the Nationalist Party, was more determined than ever to take control of the entire country. He had enjoyed the backing of the United States during the Second World War and had received substantial amounts of military and economic aid. President Roosevelt's plans for postwar East Asia relied on Nationalist China to be a regional center of stability and authority. He hoped China would become one of the "four policemen" collaborating in a new world order. His plan was wildly unrealistic. Chiang's forces had failed to win any major battles against the Japanese and remained confined at the close of the war to the mountainous interior. Communist guerrilla forces had conquered large rural areas within the Japanese puppet states on the coast. Their struggle against the invader had endowed them with the mantle of defenders of the Chinese nation.

The Decline of Nationalist China

In 1945, the U.S. government made substantial efforts to strengthen the Nationalist government of China. President Truman ordered 50,000 marines to the northern coast of China to keep order while U.S. planes and ships transported Nationalist troops into the areas being evacuated by the Japanese. He also made available surplus military supplies worth $1 billion to the Nationalists. In no other war-torn country did the United States become so directly involved in the task of postwar recovery.

The burden of rebuilding China lay in the Nationalists' hands. It proved a task they could not handle. Behind a facade of power, the Nationalist state was weak. Chiang's government was incapable of administering the country in an efficient manner. Nationalist generals in command of newly reoccupied provinces conducted their affairs like the old warlords, interested above all in enhancing their own power. They did little for the people. The ineffective Nationalist government and expensive army proved an obstacle to economic recovery. Exorbitant government spending fueled rapid inflation, which became ruinous in the postwar years. The most serious weakness of the Nationalist regime was its inability to win the confidence of the Chinese people. Corruption and abuse of power discredited its claim to national leadership. Its failure to implement land reform for the peasantry deprived it of support among the masses of the population.

The war had swelled the power and authority of the Communists. Their army had grown to one million and their liberated territories held a population numbering fifty million. Mao Zedong and Chiang had been rivals for power in the decade before war began with Japan, and they resumed their contest as soon as peace returned. The U.S. government, faithful to the same principle of national self-determination that it followed in Europe, encouraged the two sides to form a coalition government. It was an arduous task. The U.S. secretary of state, General George Marshall, traveled personally to China to persuade the two leaders to reach agreement.

He had the assistance of Joseph Stalin. The Soviet leader practiced the same strategy of power politics in Asia as in Europe. He considered that China belonged to the U.S. sphere of influence. In late 1945, he signed a ten-year treaty of friendship with the Nationalist government. In exchange, he obtained important economic concessions in Manchuria (including control of a seaport). With these spoils in hand, he urged the Chinese Communists to give up their hopes of seizing power by force and to accept instead a political coalition with the Nationalists. He later recalled that, when a Chinese Communist delegation came to Moscow in 1945, "we told them that we considered the development of the uprising in China had no prospect, and that the Chinese comrades should join the Chiang government and dissolve their army." The combined pressure of the United States and the Soviet Union

brought together the former enemies. In January 1946, the Nationalists and Communists signed a cease-fire and began discussions to form a joint government.

The agreement quickly collapsed. The influence of the superpowers was incapable of effacing the bitter rivalry between the two contenders for power. The United States could not force Chiang to put aside his deadly hatred of the Communists. The Soviet Union had no means to impose on Mao Zedong the dissolution of his peasant army and the abandonment of his liberated areas. These were twin elements to the policy on which Mao had based his revolutionary hopes ever since 1928. At the end of 1946, fighting between Nationalist and Communist troops began again over the perennial issue of territorial control. Manchuria was the prize, occupied by Soviet troops until late that year. Their withdrawal began a contest between Nationalists and Communists to take over that once prosperous region.

In the battle for control of Manchurian cities, the Nationalists had the initial advantage. The Communists, less well equipped and fewer in number, had to retreat to the countryside to resume guerrilla war once again against their old enemy. In late 1946, the United States finally abandoned efforts to bring the two sides together. General Marshall declared impossible an agreement between, in his words, "the dominant reactionary group in the [Nationalist] government and the irreconcilable Communists." By late 1947, communist forces were two million strong and had succeeded in cutting off northern China from the central regions. Only force of arms would decide the victor.

Communist Victory in China

That conflict became one of the greatest wars of the twentieth century. On one side was the Nationalist state, with more than three million troops equipped with U.S.

Chinese Communist Leaders (far right, Mao Zedong; far left, Zhou Enlai) with General George Marshall in Yenan, 1945 (*Philip Sprouse Collection/Hoover Institution Archives*)

armaments. It appeared the dominant political movement in the country, but its strength was rapidly declining. The weaknesses apparent in 1945 became more serious with each passing year. The army was poorly led and, with the exception of several crack divisions sent to Manchuria, consisted of conscripts who deserted at the first opportunity. The population was increasingly hostile to the Nationalist government, incapable of assuring public order and of preventing the collapse of commerce and industry. When forced to choose, more and more Chinese turned to the Communists.

Their forces were fewer in number in 1948 than the Nationalists, but the balance was shifting in their favor. Social, political, and military factors explain their increasing power. The party leadership under Mao Zedong proved effective and skillful in mobilizing popular support and in forming a military and political organization capable of governing large areas of the country. The Communists had to rely on their own resources, for no aid came from the Soviet Union. They fixed their own political objectives, paying polite attention to Stalin's recommendations but never obeying him blindly.

In 1947, Mao began a social revolution in the rural areas under communist control. He may have been encouraged in this radical shift by the Soviet support that year of aggressive "anti-imperialist" action by the international communist movement, but Mao's communist crusade drew primarily on his own vision of a revolutionary China. Farms of landlords and wealthy peasants were confiscated and the land was redistributed among poor peasants. The Communists banned the hiring of labor and promised all peasants a modest amount of land. A new revolutionary order was emerging in the Chinese countryside, and support among the masses of the peasantry grew correspondingly. Ten years before, Mao had proclaimed that "political power grows out of the barrel of a gun." That gun was held in the late 1940s by peasants who believed that they were fighting for their own land as well as for a liberated Chinese nation.

The communist cadres enforced these reforms ruthlessly, often brutally. Still, they proved effective administrators capable of maintaining order in the "liberated areas." After decades of war, firm and orderly rule appealed to many Chinese. Another factor behind the growing strength of the Communists was military leadership. The commanders of the People's Liberation Army (PLA) had, after years of guerrilla fighting, learned to lead massive army groups in battles increasingly resembling a regular war. They proved superior to the Nationalist generals. Their soldiers (among whom were growing numbers of Nationalist deserters) remained disciplined, increasingly confident of victory and convinced of the justice of their cause. The power of the Chinese Communists lay principally in their morale and leadership, not in numbers.

In 1948, the communist objective became the conquest of all Manchuria. That spring communist armies blockaded Nationalist garrisons throughout the region. In mid-1948, they began the systematic destruction of the best troops the Nationalists could field. By the end of 1948, the Nationalists had lost thirty divisions. Half these forces had deserted or surrendered without fighting. All Manchuria lay under communist rule, and panic was spreading among Chiang's troops in China.

In early 1949, the balance of military force between the two sides had swung toward the Communists. The U.S. government had done as much as possible to help the Nationalist government with economic and military aid. President Truman refused to send U.S. troops to fight in place of Chiang's demoralized army. The Communists, unaided by the Soviet Union, obtained most of their arms from American supplies captured from the Nationalists. The U.S. government condemned the military offensive of the Communists, and Stalin may have warned the Chinese comrades to show caution, but to no avail. In the Chinese civil war, no outside powers could contain the conflict.

In the winter and spring of 1948–1949, the PLA launched massive military offensives all through northern and central China. One Nationalist army, surrounded in the capital city of Beijing, surrendered in January 1949, with the loss of half a million troops. A few months earlier, armies of the Communists, numbering 500,000 soldiers, attacked the main defensive line protecting Nationalist areas in central China. By February 1949, the defenses there were breached and the Nationalist armies routed. Between the spring and fall of 1949, Mao's forces moved south across the Yangtze River and into southern China. That summer entire Nationalist armies, generals as well as troops, deserted to the Communists. By the fall of 1949, no important areas of resistance remained.

The Chinese People's Republic

In October 1949, the Communist Party leadership proclaimed in Beijing the formation of the Chinese People's Republic. The most populous country in the world, land of the world's oldest civilization, had passed under communist rule. A successor state had taken power, ending the long period of disorder in China following the fall of the Chinese

Empire in 1911. The Communist Party leaders did not consider the war at an end until they captured the island of Formosa (Taiwan), where Chiang and remnants of his Nationalist forces had fled. Their People's Liberation Army prepared for an amphibious invasion of the island, planned for the summer of 1950. Nothing appeared to stand in its way.

The U.S. government had no clear idea of the intentions of the new Chinese leadership. Seeking to make clear what part of East Asia lay in its security zone, it publicly outlined in 1949 its military forces' "defense perimeter." This strategic area included Japan; it excluded all lands on the Asian continent (including Korea) as well as Formosa. That statement made clear at that moment where U.S. foreign policy extended in the eastern Pacific and which areas were key for its containment strategy. Beyond these areas the United States made no commitment to send its own military forces to fight communist armies. At the same time, new Asian nationalist regimes from South Korea to the Philippines obtained U.S. economic and military aid sufficient to strengthen their armies. Early in 1950, the U.S. government agreed to assist the new Indochinese state of Vietnam, largely a French creation, to win the backing of nationalist groups in the war with the Vietnamese communist guerrillas. These anticommunist policies did not appear in late 1949 to exclude recognition of the new People's Republic of China. Secret talks began that winter between Chinese leaders and the United States in preparation for the possible opening of diplomatic relations.

To Mao Zedong, the Chinese People's Republic needed first of all to establish good relations with the Soviet Union. He traveled to Moscow in the winter of 1949–1950 on his first trip outside China to begin lengthy and difficult negotiations with Stalin. The Chinese Communists requested a military alliance, economic assistance, and the end to Soviet occupation of

Chinese territory. These Soviet-controlled areas included a port and railroad in Manchuria and a large area of Chinese central Asia. The Chinese were in effect requesting the end to Soviet imperial domination in East Asia. The Chinese and Russians shared a common Marxist-Leninist ideology, and Mao revered the wisdom and achievements of the Soviet party. Though the Chinese desperately needed Soviet help rebuilding their war-torn country, they were determined to obtain Stalin's recognition of their new revolutionary state.

For his part, Stalin persisted in treating China, even though communist, as a subordinate member of the Soviet sphere of influence. He apparently distrusted the Chinese Communists, whose independent behavior must have reminded him of the Yugoslav Communists. Mao later recalled that "Stalin feared that China might degenerate into another Yugoslavia and that I might become another Tito." Stalin certainly was concerned at the possible weakening of the Soviet sphere of influence in East Asia, which extended from Inner Asia through Mongolia to North Korea. Alongside the Chinese leaders in the negotiations were Communist representatives from these lands. The negotiations dragged on for two months.

In the end, Stalin agreed to Mao's request for a military alliance and economic aid. He promised the end of Soviet territories in Manchuria in a few years. In exchange, Mao had to recognize the independence (under Soviet protection) of Mongolia and to tolerate the existence of a special autonomous region in Manchuria under a Chinese communist leader taking orders from Moscow. Between these two enormous states, relations remained friendly, and the Chinese honored Stalin's ideological leadership. To the outside world, the two leaders of world communism appeared united in their revolutionary goals and in their hostility to the capitalist-imperialist West. Yet Communist China did not join the ranks of Soviet satellites.

Stalin and Mao: Fragment of 12′ x 16′ Painting "Signing of Sino-Soviet Treaty of Friendship," 1950 (*Hoover Institution Archives Collection*)

THE KOREAN WAR

The border dividing the superpowers in the Cold War reached as far east as the country of Korea. In 1945, Soviet invasion forces had taken control of Korea just as the Japanese Empire capitulated. They had withdrawn into the northern half of the peninsula, respecting the wartime agreement with the United States. This partition of Korea between U.S. and Soviet occupation troops was to end when an Allied peace treaty with Japan authorized the restoration of an independent, united Korean state.

Partitioned Korea

The desire for national unity was strong among Koreans after a half century of Japanese rule. But the occupation zones became an insurmountable obstacle to unification. U.S. authorities opened the southern half of Korea to exiled nationalists under the leadership of Syngman Rhee. In 1948, he became head of the Republic of Korea. U.S. armed forces withdrew from their zone of occupation. Their military base was to be Japan, which the U.S. government made into its East Asian strong point in the Cold War. Rhee governed South Korea with dictatorial powers, suppressing the Korean Communist Party and its labor unions in his country and damning the Communists as traitors to the nation. He vowed that national unification would be his doing, warning that his army was prepared to seize by force the northern half of the peninsula unless the Communists agreed to his terms for unification. The U.S. government, as opposed there as in China to becoming directly involved in civil war, took seriously the threat of war. To restrain Rhee's nationalist fervor, it provided the South Korean army with only defensive weapons.

Soviet occupation authorities in the north created a civilian government under the control of the Korean Communist Party. Following the example of the United States, in 1948 they permitted the Communists to create their own state, the Korean Democratic People's Republic, and withdrew their occupation forces. North Korea's leader was Kim Il Sung, a veteran Communist who had learned his revolutionary lessons in Moscow in the 1930s, then had acquired military skills fighting alongside the Chinese Communists in the war against Japan. He admired Mao's revolutionary exploits, especially his defeat of the Nationalists and his unification of all China. Kim hoped to do the same for Korea, for (like Mao and Ho Chi Minh in Vietnam) he was a nationalist as well as communist revolutionary. But unlike these other Asian Communists, he could not on his own begin a war for Korean unity. His devotion to Stalin was reinforced by his reliance on economic and military aid from the Soviet Union. North Korea was a new Soviet satellite.

Armed by the Soviet Union, his army was ready for war. He still needed Stalin's approval to undertake the conquest of southern Korea. His army had already fought in the Chinese civil war and was better armed than the South Korean forces. He assured Stalin that military victory would come in four weeks. All Korea would be under the Communists. The moment was right. Though Rhee talked of war against the north, his military forces were weak. Unstated but understood by both Kim and Stalin was a revolutionary vision: What the Chinese Communists had already achieved, Kim's forces should be permitted to do in their turn. Revolution was his goal, and no U.S. troops stood in his way.

China, Stalin, and the Korean War

The bonds uniting communist China and the Soviet Union became a military alliance in the Korean War. Soviet, Chinese, and Korean Communists launched and sustained a local conflict that deeply marked the Cold War and postwar East Asian history. Throughout the winter of 1949–1950, Kim Il Sung had begged Stalin to approve an invasion of South Korea, bombarding Moscow with telegrams begging for the Great Leader's backing. Without Stalin's word he could not act. In his telegrams to the Great Leader, his arguments emphasized the strength of his army, capable in his opinion of victory within a few weeks. Even if the United States did reverse its policy of keeping troops off the Asian mainland, he was sure of a rapid conquest, making it unlikely U.S. forces could intervene in Korea in time to prevent communist victory. That spring, Stalin gave his consent. In June 1950, North Korean troops invaded South Korea. A unified Korea, like its neighbor China, seemed destined to become another triumph for revolutionary communism.

Stalin's readiness to allow that war came only after he had obtained the support of the Chinese Communists. Mao showed no hesitation in backing his Korean comrades. Moved by a sort of revolutionary conceit, he seems to have believed that his forces could conquer Taiwan that summer, and North Korea could conquer the south, without U.S. military opposition. He too credited North Koreans with sufficient armed might to quickly overwhelm their enemies in the south.

The Korean conflict ceased being a local war two days after the invasion, when President Truman declared that his country would defend South Korea. This sudden reversal of U.S. policy resulted principally because U.S. leaders realized then that a communist Korea would extend the ring of Soviet satellites to within a short distance of Japan, the kingpin of U.S. Asian defenses. Perhaps as important was the consideration that U.S. failure to resist the North Korean offensive would convey a message throughout the world that the policy of containment hid military weakness. The U.S. government feared reviving memories of

the 1930s' appeasement policies by Great Britain. Having emphasized the military dimension of containment, the United States had to prove its readiness to resist military expansion backed by the Soviet Union. The new U.S. policy of military intervention in Korea altered the course of that war and of the Cold War as well.

The Korean fighting quickly became a full-scale war. The North Korean army routed the South Korean forces. If U.S. intervention was to succeed, the United States had immediately to send troops from Japan to stop the offensive. The U.S. government appointed General Douglas MacArthur, in charge of U.S. occupation personnel in Japan, to be its commander of the forces in Korea. He fought under the United Nations' flag when the U.N. Security Council (minus the Soviet representative, away protesting the failure of the United Nations to seat the representative of the People's Republic of China in place of the Nationalist delegate) approved the defense of South Korea in a formal motion condemning North Korea's aggression. U.S. troops did succeed, at the last minute, in halting the march of the North Korean forces to the end of the peninsula. Kim Il Sung's prediction of quick victory was wrong.

MacArthur's own vision of the war extended as far as the ultimate destruction of communism in the Far East, in China as well as Korea. The U.S. government lent some support to that idea when in July it reversed its decision not to defend Taiwan. U.S. naval forces of the Seventh Fleet sailed into the Straits of Formosa to block Chinese troops preparing to invade the island. The communist regime in China had entered the ranks of U.S. Cold War enemies.

U.S. objectives in the Korean conflict did not become clear until late that fall. General MacArthur's immediate goal was the defense of South Korea. Two months after the invasion, U.N. troops launched a surprise landing

Korean War, 1950–53

in the middle of the peninsula, forcing the North Korean army to flee north to escape encirclement. Supported by President Truman, MacArthur pushed U.N. troops beyond the line of partition that September into North Korea. His forces quickly reached the very borders of China. His goal was complete military victory and the capitulation of North Korea. The U.S. government had already received Chinese warnings of military intervention if U.S. land forces approached Chinese territory. MacArthur dismissed these warnings, believing mistakenly that his armed forces could defeat Chinese troops (and perhaps welcoming the possibility to bring the war into China).

The Chinese leaders carried out their threat. Their reasons for intervening appear

New War in Asia: U.S. Counteroffensive against North Korean forces, Sept. 1950 (*National Archives and Records Administration*)

mainly strategic. U.S. troops occupying territory on the very borders of their country constituted a serious threat to the stability of their new regime. In November, 300,000 Chinese troops attacked the U.N. forces, which were quickly overwhelmed and forced to retreat back into South Korea. There the front soon stabilized in the region of the old border. The war had turned into a struggle of endurance. In 1951, the U.S. government dismissed MacArthur from his position of commander-in-chief. His dreams of military victory and his efforts to undermine the containment strategy—he publicly proclaimed that "there is no substitute for victory"—were out of touch with the limited objectives of U.S. foreign policy. U.S. military leaders insisted that MacArthur's plans would "involve us in the

wrong war, at the wrong place, at the wrong time and with the wrong enemy." The U.S. government sought only to protect South Korea, refusing to use its nuclear weapons in a war for the containment of North Korea, not its conquest.

The Korean War dragged on for another two years. It was marked by bloody, inconclusive battles that failed to break the stalemate. The United States suffered more than 30,000 dead, but for the Koreans the war appeared total. South Korea's casualties numbered 1.3 million, and its capital city Seoul was reduced to rubble in the fighting of 1950–1951. The United States sought to force the war to a close by an intensive bombing campaign of North Korean cities. These too were reduced

Chinese Communist Anti-U.S. Poster
"Extinguish Fire of War, Save Peace!" 1952
(*Hoover Institution Archives Collection*)

to rubble, with enormous casualties, but supplies continued to reach the North Korean front lines. Estimates of dead and wounded there reach 1.5 million. The war was destroying the two countries.

Responsible for the outbreak of hostilities, Stalin apparently prevented a compromise settlement. The Korean conflict confirmed his grim view of the inevitability of capitalist war and forced communist China to depend on the Soviet alliance and Stalin's leadership. In 1951 the first peace negotiations began, only to stall over the issue raised by the Communists of forcible repatriation to the north of their prisoners held in the south. Shortly after his death in 1953, the prisoner issue no longer

mattered to North Korea's negotiators. Stalin's disappearance made possible the end to the Korean War (and soon the French war in Indochina). Chinese and Soviet governments undoubtedly knew of the threat by President Eisenhower's new administration to increase its military effort in Korea. They probably heard the rumors (spread intentionally by the U.S. government) that it was even considering the use of nuclear weapons. Ending the costly war suited their interests. The Korean War ended in 1953 in an armistice leaving the border between North and South Korea approximately where it had been in 1950. That was sufficient for the Chinese, Soviet, and U.S. negotiators. The leaders of North and South Korea had to accept the decision.

North and South Korea

North Korea remained under the rule of Kim Il Sung and the Communist Party. For the next half century, he forced his country to conform to a dogmatic Stalinist ideology. Kim became North Korea's Great Leader and the subject of public adulation. He maintained a brutal dictatorship and kept industry and agriculture in a rigid command economy, modeled on that of the Soviet Union. The army prospered, sending infiltrators over the demilitarized zone into the south and periodically threatening to resume the crusade for national unification. The Communists forbade any communications with the south. Stalinism had a secure home in North Korea.

North Korea remained frozen in the communist mold long after it was abandoned in China and even after the fall of the Soviet Union in 1991. The result by the 1990s was impoverishment and periodic famine for the population. The collective farm system was incapable of providing adequate food. Nationalized industry barely functioned, with only armaments factories receiving substantial state subsidies to keep operating at full capacity. No foreign investors, except a few South Korean banks and the South Korean state, were prepared to risk their funds in that bankrupt economy. Only massive foreign aid, consisting of food and petroleum from China, and food and financial contributions from South Korea, kept the country from collapse. That awful possibility, with the resulting massive exodus of refugees, made both governments unwilling supporters of North Korea's Stalinist leadership.

Yet even after Kim Jong Il took his father's place in 1994 as dictator, his government continued to parade well-armed troops through the central square of the capital to impress foreign dignitaries. It publicly proclaimed in 2003 that it had acquired the capacity to produce nuclear weapons. These, it claimed, were needed to defend the land from "U.S. aggression." Behind this facade of power, the country was a pathetic relic of the Soviet experiment in state socialism.

At the end of the war, the south lay under Syngman Rhee's authoritarian rule. After his death in 1965, a series of military rulers seized control of the government. By then, the recovery from wartime destruction was complete. They threw the country's meager resources into building a modern industrial economy to replace the backward agricultural

economy of prewar years. Their statist methods of "guided capitalism" closely resembled the Japanese model. To increase savings (and funds for investment), they imposed stringent controls on consumption, even forbidding Koreans to take their vacations outside the country. By the 1980s, their methods and the people's industriousness succeeded in creating a South Korean "economic miracle."

In the mid-1980s, democratic opposition forces were strong enough to oblige this authoritarian regime to abandon power. For the first time in South Korea's history, free elections for parliament and the president gave the country's voters the chance to select a leadership of their choice. One of the first acts of the new, democratic government was to end the freeze on factory wages, allowing the pay for workers to increase rapidly for another decade. By then, the standard of living among Koreans was comparable to that of Spanish people. Still, the Cold War had left a scar across their landscape. Their troops, assisted by an entire U.S. Army division, were permanently stationed along the demilitarized zone that separated their state from communist Korea. The division of the globe into rival armed camps was a visible part of the Korean peninsula.

● HIGHLIGHT: Containment and Anticommunism ●

The Soviet Union appeared to many Westerners a mysterious and threatening presence among the victorious powers of the Second World War. Its history had followed a very different path from that of the liberal democracies. Its leaders explained international relations using a language of class conflict completely unfamiliar to the Western public. Winston Churchill had been so puzzled in 1939 by So-

viet policies that he called the country "a riddle wrapped in a mystery inside an enigma." Its actions remained equally difficult to understand after the defeat of the Axis powers, when it became a key player in global politics.

One solution to the riddle pointed to the role of communist ideology in Soviet politics. Communist leaders extolled Marxism-Leninism-Stalinism as the source of truth in history, politics, and human relations. Revolution was, in theory, the only path to progress. Since 1917, enemies of communism in America and elsewhere in the West had warned that the Soviet Union was the homeland of a revolution that, unless resisted, would destroy Western civilization. Their anticommunist persuasion made them fear an inevitable confrontation between the Soviet Union and the West. Preparations were urgent to resist the revolutionary offensive of the Soviet state and its supporters. It was not clear whether that attack would come from Soviet armies or a series of communist political conspiracies and insurrections. Whatever methods the communists used, the threat remained real as long as the Soviet Union existed. The anticommunist theory of Soviet international behavior foresaw inescapable conflict, even war, with the homeland of communism.

Another answer to the mystery of Soviet expansion came from lessons drawn from the history of the rise and fall of empires. In the past, aggressive new states had expanded by conquering and taking control of territories and peoples beyond their borders. Their leaders sought power and wealth through territorial aggrandizement and were prepared to use threats and force to achieve this goal. But these great empires had invariably met obstacles to their aggressive growth. Other states had by diplomatic or military means put up barriers to their rise to power, and their own internal weaknesses had with time forced them to contract and ultimately to fall. From this historical perspective, the Soviet Union had acquired the might and size of a great empire because its leaders were expansionist, like others before them. The communist ideology strengthened their suspicion of other states but was not the explanation for Soviet territorial expansion. Their foreign policy did

constitute a threat to the security and interests of independent neighboring states and to the hope for a stable peace. But a historical approach suggested that the reasonable response, as in earlier times, was to put together diplomatic and political restraints to contain this new imperial power.

The historical explanation of Soviet aggressiveness was the key idea behind the new U.S. foreign policy of containment. It appeared in the late 1940s at a time when Franklin Roosevelt's policy of collaboration and conciliation (termed *internationalism*, since it relied on international negotiation and peacekeeping) had failed to bring fundamental agreements with the Soviet Union on peace in Europe and Asia. George Kennan, the principal architect of the new policy, argued that the old internationalist approach could not possibly produce satisfactory results. His observations and understanding of what he called "Soviet conduct" convinced him that Soviet leaders were deeply suspicious of the West and fanatically determined to overcome the perils that they believed threatened their rule.

In Kennan's opinion, the origins of their hostility lay in the historical experience of Russia. It had, time and again, confronted aggressive foreign enemies, whom only military might could repulse. He never made clear how the memories of this long past had shaped the suspicious world view of Soviet leaders. At times, he argued that their communist ideology bore a large measure of responsibility for their particular antagonism toward the capitalist states in the West and that Stalin's own ruthless personality shaped Soviet political life. But his understanding of the Soviet Union drew above all on his conviction that it showed the historical traits of an expansionist empire. It relied on despotic authority within its borders and was prepared to expand its diplomatic and political influence beyond those borders whenever weaknesses appeared in neighboring states.

Soviet hostility and expansionism stood in the way of a permanent peace settlement. Conciliatory gestures from the West had no chance of moderating the Soviet leadership's suspicions. They relied only on their country's military and diplomatic might, not international agreements, to protect Soviet interests. They were unresponsive, in Kennan's words, to the "logic of reason." But his long years of study of Soviet conduct convinced him also that they were not "adventuristic" in seeking to expand the power of their state and were prepared to avoid "unnecessary risks" when they encountered resistance. In other words, they understood the "logic of force." This formula gave Kennan the key to formulating a new long-term U.S. policy less appeasing than Roosevelt's internationalist approach but less belligerent than the anticommunist agenda.

In the short term, his containment strategy called for resistance to, not conciliation of, the Soviet leaders' efforts to expand their sphere of domination around the borders of the Soviet Union. Kennan had seen firsthand the consequences of appeasement of Nazi Germany in 1938 (he was stationed in Czechoslovakia during the Munich crisis). Containment was his answer to the danger of appeasement. It called for U.S. diplomatic backing and economic aid to certain strong, independent states that were capable of resisting Soviet expansionism. With U.S. support, these countries would become secure allies of the West and centers of regional stability. They included states in western Europe, the Middle East, and Japan. Kennan believed that the threat from the Soviet Union was not military aggression. He was persuaded that

Soviet leaders recognized their military and economic weakness relative to the United States. He urged that diplomatic alliances and economic prosperity become the principal barriers to contain the Soviet Union. But when North Korea invaded the south in 1950, he too supported U.S. military intervention, limited to the defense of South Korea. His policy of containment did come with a military price.

Still, his policy did not promise a quick solution to the conflict with the Soviet Union. International peace, as he understood the term, was a dream that could never be fully achieved. The protection of human rights was an ideal that for him ought not prevent collaboration with authoritarian states vital to containment. Allies ought not be excluded on grounds of their internal politics. But Kennan did not believe that U.S. foreign policy had to respond to the communist ideology with an anticommunist crusade. He disagreed with anticommunists about the nature of the Soviet threat, and he disagreed with them as well about the correct U.S. response. His policy was in some respects too realistic. Presidents Wilson and Roosevelt had promised that the U.S. involvement in foreign wars furthered the cause of democracy and national self-determination. In other ways it was too restrained to win complete approval. Some U.S. leaders were sympathetic to the warnings of the anticommunists, convinced that war was inescapable and pushing for a vast rearmament program and a system of global military alliances.

Yet his program remained the core of U.S. policy toward the Soviet Union. Despite moments of anticommunist fervor—like that following the Korean War—and crises that threatened nuclear war—like the Cuban missile crisis of 1962—the U.S. government did not attempt to force a Soviet retreat and resigned itself to the existence of a vast Soviet sphere of domination. In the 1950s, U.S. leaders drew the line of military containment around North Vietnam in the mistaken assumption that it was a puppet of Moscow, but when war came there, resisted (as earlier in Korea) calls for total victory over the enemy. Later, it initiated or accepted negotiated agreements to limit the dangerous nuclear arms race. Kennan had foreseen the day when this patience would be rewarded by the internal decline of Soviet power. Forty years after he proposed his policy, that decline began. It culminated in 1991 with the complete collapse of the Soviet Union and the end of the Cold War. Containment succeeded beyond his wildest dreams.

WARS AND REVOLUTION IN INDOCHINA

On the southern edges of China, the land that the French had named Indochina passed from the French to the Japanese Empire in the early years of the Second World War. In the late nineteenth century, the French had created in the region one colony made of many peoples, among whom the Vietnamese and the Khmer were the two largest ethnic groups (and had been bitter enemies). Indochina was also divided by religion, with many Buddhists but also an important Catholic community. Like China, its economy was based primarily on agriculture with extensive large estates owned by a few wealthy landowners (many of them French) and worked by a poor peasant population. It resembled other colonial lands in the fact that, by the middle of the twentieth century, some of its people were prepared for nationalist revolt against colonial rule.

The French Colonial War

The colonial conflict in Indochina began in earnest at the end of the Second World War. The struggle was centered in the populous coastal region known as Vietnam. It provided the recruits for the Vietnamese Communist Party, whose founder and leader was Ho Chi Minh. He became an international agent in East Asia of Moscow's Communist International, helping the Chinese Communists and then creating in 1929 what he first called the Indochinese Communist Party. From that point on, his cause was independence and communist revolution for Vietnam. Like Mao Zedong, Ho Chi Minh firmly believed in the inevitability of global proletarian revolution, one chapter in which was the fight against imperialism. He honored the leadership and wisdom of the Soviet Communists, but, also like Mao, he and his party were an independent revolutionary party in the world communist movement.

The immediate objective of the Vietnamese Communists was the liberation of all Indochina from foreign rule. His armed struggle had started with the war against Japan. In 1940, Ho organized and took charge of guerrilla war against the Japanese occupation forces. The jungles and mountains of Vietnam were the refuge of the guerrillas, while Japanese troops held onto the cities and coastal region. Before surrendering at war's end, the Japanese commander had, in a gesture of defiance toward the Allies, proclaimed Vietnam's independence. The withdrawal of his forces permitted the Vietnamese Communists, who were the principal anti-Japanese resistance force, to assume leadership of the Republic of Vietnam.

Prepared to negotiate with the postwar French government, Ho traveled to Paris in 1946. Had an agreement been reached there, Vietnam would very soon have become a communist state. While talking of eventual freedom for Indochina, French officials and military commanders there were adamantly opposed to granting power to the Vietnamese Communists. Resolved to restore some form of French colonial authority, in 1946 they attacked the communist-occupied areas in Vietnam and quickly moved their troops into the inland regions of Cambodia (land of the Khmers) and Laos. The Communists and their nationalist allies retreated to the countryside, where they, like their Chinese comrades to the north, resumed guerrilla war.

In its first years, it was a French colonial war. The war did not go well for French forces. They attempted to win the backing of nationalists there by creating in 1949 the independent states of Vietnam, Cambodia, and Laos. They still had to bear the principal burden of the bloody fighting. French generals promised quick victory against the communist guerrillas but could not end the insurrection. Their army, made up of colonial forces as well as French soldiers, occupied key urban areas, but the countryside lay beyond their control.

In 1950, the conflict in Indochina entered the Cold War when the U.S. government intervened on the side of the French. It had previously judged the conflict to be a French effort to restore an outdated empire. The Cold War in Asia changed that view. By 1950, U.S. leaders had expanded the containment policy to include those colonial areas where communist insurrections were under way. In effect, they incorporated the Indochinese war into the global battle between the free world and communism.

U.S. leaders concluded that Ho's victory in Indochina would constitute a triumph for global communist forces. That was a misguided and ultimately tragic judgment. Its origins lay partly in the growing influence of anticommunist political forces within the United States, outraged at what they considered the "loss" of China. They were so committed to organizing the combat against communism that they paid no attention to the human and material cost that intervention in a colonial region like Indochina would entail. In the background was the pervasive fear of Stalin's expansionism. North Korea's aggression had appeared proof of this faulty idea. As a result, the French colonial forces found an ally in the U.S. government.

The United States began to provide France with military and economic aid for the war in Indochina. In return, it demanded of the French that they suppress the communist guerrillas. Not only was the French army unable to do so, but in the attempt it suffered a major military defeat. By 1953, its forces were overextended and weakened by its campaign to wipe out the communist insurrection. It could not protect its mountain fortress of Dienbienphu, encircled that year by the Communists. The surrender of the fort and its 10,000 troops in early 1954 ended the French efforts to retain control of Indochina.

That year a new French government concluded that its military forces could not win the Indochina war. Its army had suffered 100,000 casualties in a conflict draining the wealth of the French economy for control of a distant country of no vital importance. The glories of colonial dominion in Asia no longer attracted France. Although the French army still occupied much of Indochina, the French government in 1954 agreed to negotiate with the Vietnamese Communists.

At that point the U.S. government expanded even further its involvement in Indochina. It was one of the participants at the Geneva conference that negotiated the end to the war. Representatives from the Vietnamese Communist Party, from the new Republic of Vietnam, and from France were there, as were delegates from China and the Soviet Union. Peace in Indochina was an international affair. The French and American negotiators sought a partitioned Vietnam, limiting the Communists to the northern half of the country where their centers of strength were located. Under the circumstances, they sought more territory than the French actually controlled.

The Vietnamese Communists came to Geneva expecting a treaty granting them a unified Vietnam. But Ho's delegates found no support, even from the Soviet Union and China, for their demand for the formation of a single Vietnamese communist state. The Soviets and the Chinese, determined on a quick settlement to the war, promised Ho that he would soon attain his goal of national unification without further fighting. They assured him that his forces, still the only strong, organized political movement in northern and southern coastal areas of the country, would easily win all Vietnam in the elections that the peace negotiators planned to hold in 1956. Communists in other lands had proven adept, through intimidation and violence, at manipulating elections. Ho and his followers expected to do the same. National self-determination, the principle guiding this peace settlement, offered the Communists an apparently easy opportunity to take control of all Vietnam. Ho accepted the temporary partition of Vietnam, and in 1954 the French war in Indochina came to an end.

North and South Vietnam

The U.S. government was determined to prevent the Communists' seizure of the south. Although observers warned that South Vietnam had a slim chance to survive, the United States brought out of exile a nationalist leader, Ngo Dinh Diem, to become ruler of the new state. U.S. agents from the new intelligence service, the Central Intelligence Agency (CIA), began to organize the hunt for Communists in the southern half of Vietnam. U.S. military advisers took over the task of forming a new Vietnamese army. U.S. economic and military aid poured into the country. By 1960, South Vietnam had received more than $1 billion in American assistance. This was vital to the very functioning of its state and economy. The result was the emergence of a U.S. satellite state under client nationalist leaders who could not survive without American aid. In President Kennedy's words, South Vietnam was "our offspring."

That effort at creating a noncommunist Vietnamese state represented an audacious gamble, probably doomed from the start. In a land divided by political rivalries and with no strong institutions or outstanding noncommunist nationalist leader to guarantee the stability of a new political order, state-building was in the best of circumstances a daunting task. Nearly one million refugees had fled from communist rule in the north, including large numbers of Catholics fearing Ho's political dictatorship and repression of their religion. Most of the south Vietnamese were poor peasants, reluctant to support either the Communists or the Diem regime for fear of persecution by the other side. Diem's main interest lay in strengthening his personal power. Like Syngman Rhee in South Korea, he was persuaded that by building an authoritarian regime he could defeat the communist underground movement (called the Vietcong) in his infant country. With U.S. encouragement, he refused to hold the elections on Vietnam reunification scheduled for 1956. Instead, he built up his police and army, which were used primarily as instruments for internal repression. They proved effective in weakening the Communist Party in the south. By 1958, many of its members had moved to the north or were in prison.

Diem's plan for South Vietnam was a conservative government protecting landowners and businesses and receiving economic and military aid from the United States. A similar political formula had worked in South Korea at the end of the war there. But Diem had much less chance of making it work in his country. South Korea's leaders had in their favor their claim to be the rightful national heirs to the long history of a Korean state. Their regime had been independent since 1945. Diem lacked popular support among the

Vietnamese and, more importantly, confronted a dynamic revolutionary movement determined to rid the country of what it called the "Western imperialists and their puppets."

After 1954, the North Vietnamese Communists quickly remade their country into a Soviet-style regime. They created a single-party state, eliminating all political opposition. With Chinese and Soviet socialism as their model, they forced the peasant farmers into collective farms. In doing so, they disrupted agricultural production and, by their own later admission, permitted the party and police officials to use brutal repressive measures against the rural population. Ho Chi Minh pursued his revolution from above with a fanaticism equal to that of Stalin and Mao.

In 1959, civil war came to South Vietnam. That year, Ho concluded that conquest of the south would come only by guerrilla war. Communist cadres returned south along the secret Ho Chi Minh trail, built on Cambodian territory. It brought military supplies and new directives to supporters to the south. The Communists' first targets were local rural officials on whose shoulders rested the stability of Diem's rule in the countryside. Political assassination and in-

timidation destroyed the regime's control in many areas, where the communist underground established new bases of operations.

The weakness of the South Vietnamese state quickly became apparent. Peasants preferred submitting to the communist agents, who protected those who helped them. Diem's officials feared for their lives (2,500 were assassinated in 1960) and retreated into fortified camps. By the end of that year, the communist insurrection had spread widely, and U.S. officials were warning that Diem's state was in serious danger. U.S.-sponsored state-building had not succeeded.

The new insurrection, begun in 1959, gathered strength from the widening circle of South Vietnamese enemies of Diem and the United States and from the readiness of North Vietnam to commit all its resources to the struggle. Supplies for the guerrillas came partly from captured government materiel, partly from North Vietnam. Central leadership and party cadres came south to aid and direct the southern Communists. Still a conflict among Vietnamese, the fighting was in 1960 essentially a civil war that the Communists were close to winning.

◀   **SPOTLIGHT: Ho Chi Minh**   ▶

Secrecy was an integral part of the life of Ho Chi Minh (1890–1969). During his long years as head of the underground Vietnamese Communist Party, his anonymity protected him from arrest by the French colonial authorities. It also kept his private life hidden from the public, to whom he appeared entirely devoted to the cause of Vietnamese independence. The very name by which we know him was only the last of the aliases that he used to hide his identity. It means "Ho the Bringer of Light," and be-

came his name in 1940 when he helped to create a nationalist resistance organization to fight the Japanese occupation forces.

The struggle for the liberation of Vietnam from foreign powers remained the goal of his life as a revolutionary. He grew up and was educated in Vietnam, where he received both a traditional Vietnamese education and acquired a fluent knowledge of the French language. In 1911, at the age of 21, he left for Europe to seek a new life, working first as a cook on a French steamer and then moving in 1917 to France to work in positions such as gardener and waiter. His real life was that of a political activist.

He had discovered his calling as a socialist and as a Vietnam patriot. In 1919, he presented a petition to the Paris Peace Conference calling for the independence of Indochina, signing the document "Ho the Patriot." In those same years he, like Mao Zedong, became persuaded that the liberation he sought for his people had to come through the revolutionary communist movement. He became an active member of the Communist International, serving wherever

Ho Chi Minh (*David Barrett Collection/Hoover Institution Archives*)

Moscow ordered him. Founding in 1929 the Indochinese Communist Party was just a part of his plans to work for world revolution.

His highest priority was national liberation of his country. By that he understood that the creation of an independent state of Vietnam was to be the work of his Communist Party, for he believed liberation to include social revolution as well as the overthrow of the colonial yoke. He was a convinced Leninist-Stalinist. Violence was the necessary path to revolutionary emancipation, and his new regime had to be a single-party dictatorship that would achieve socialism by revolution from above.

His first attempt to create a new Vietnam almost succeeded. In 1945, the Japanese authorities had allowed him the opportunity to set up a new state. In Hanoi that year, he held an independence celebration at which he read passages from the American Declaration of Independence. He had no intention of imitating the American Revolution, only to convince the American forces in East Asia of his reliability. But the French returned to take control of Indochina, and he had to flee to the mountains and jungles of his country to continue the battle. He did not live to see the day of final victory.

What he did achieve was the defeat of the French and the formation in northern Vietnam of the Vietnamese People's Republic in 1955. He was its president as well as the head of the Vietnamese Communist Party. He was the initiator of the violent campaigns that began then to wipe out class enemies and to construct a system of state socialism. The revolutionary society that he planned had no room for other political parties, just as it had no place for private farmers or merchants.

When the southern half of Vietnam escaped the political control of his followers there, he called again for guerrilla war. The enemy this time was, besides Vietnamese anticommunists, the United States. His skills as a revolutionary and the authority that he enjoyed among his followers ensured that he remained their unquestioned leader through more long, terrible years of war. Like Mao Zedung, he never doubted that the sacrifices would lead to victory and that a united, communist Vietnam would prove the salvation of his people. He was right about the outcome of the war with the United States. He was wrong about the future of his country. His communist faith proved in the end an illusory vision of progress but one that absorbed his entire life.

U.S. War in Vietnam

By the late 1950s, opposition to communist China had become a central feature of U.S. containment policy in Asia. U.S. leaders did not consider the fighting in Vietnam to be merely a local conflict. To them, it appeared as another step in global communist aggression. If not stopped in Indochina, they feared that other Southeast Asian states would fall to communist insurrection "like a row of dominos." The new administration of President John Kennedy, elected in 1960, judged the South Vietnam civil war to be part of the Cold War struggle to prevent, in the words of one U.S. official, "China's swallowing up Southeast Asia." Overly confident in the power of the United States, Kennedy and his advisers anticipated that greater military and economic assistance would assure Diem's victory. Increased military aid seemed the way to avoid direct U.S. involvement in the war while still ensuring South Vietnam's victory.

U.S. intervention in the conflict proceeded in two stages. In the first four years (1961–1965), it came in the form of very large amounts of military supplies to reequip the South Vietnamese army, which was responsible for the actual fighting. This policy permitted the doubling of the army's size by 1963. It was trained by 15,000 U.S. military advisers, not yet combatants but close to it.

But the political weakness of the South Vietnamese state was far more serious than the problems confronting the Vietnamese army. Increasing numbers of South Vietnamese were opposed to Diem's authoritarian rule. His political ambitions did not match the actual strength of his regime, and he appeared incapable of winning popular support and reforming his corrupt state. In 1963, the United States backed a military coup in a desperate attempt to find leaders capable of governing a viable South Vietnamese state. Vietnamese generals, with the tacit approval of U.S. officials, stepped into the internal political struggle. They seized control of the government and assassinated Diem (only a few days before President Kennedy's assassination in the United States). The U.S. officials in Vietnam hoped that the generals would restore order, end corruption, and strengthen the Vietnamese forces fighting the Vietcong.

Military rule only increased the internal disorder of the Vietnamese state. Within two years, ten different generals had stepped forward to rule the country in a self-destructive struggle for political leadership. The most serious consequence of this instability was the inability of any of the generals to halt the expansion of communist-controlled areas, which extended over entire provinces by late 1964. Guerrillas had even encircled the capital, Saigon, while Communist Party cadres operated freely in the city. The South Vietnam government had lost its claim to Vietnamese national leadership. Unless the United States itself took drastic action, within a few months the insurrection would succeed.

War in Vietnam

The prospect of "losing" South Vietnam was unacceptable to the U.S. government. President Kennedy's successor, Lyndon Johnson, won the 1964 elections primarily on a program of extensive domestic social and civil rights reform. Despite his commitment to what he called America's "Great Society," he had to turn his attention to Vietnam. Faced with impending communist victory, he declared that he could not become the "first president to lose a war." U.S. leaders were motivated both by the belief that communist con-

quest of the land would be a serious defeat for the containment policy and by the conviction that U.S. military might was invincible in a local war. This tragic overconfidence led one U.S. senator later to judge his government guilty of "arrogance of power."

The second stage in U.S. intervention in Vietnam began in 1965. Johnson's advisers guaranteed quick victory if U.S. land and air forces joined the war. Persuaded by their arguments, Johnson set about organizing direct U.S. military participation in the Vietnamese civil war. He expanded enormously the presidential war-making powers, permitting him to avoid any interference from the U.S. Congress. In early 1965, Johnson used those powers to order American combat forces into action in Vietnam. For the second time since the end of the Second World War, the United States entered a land war in Asia. The conflict did not resemble the Korean conflict, however. In guerrilla combat there existed no front lines. The enemy was everywhere, easily confused with civilians. The only clear separation was that distinguishing Americans and Vietnamese. The Indochina war posed problems the U.S. military had never confronted before.

The formula for victory included two separate military operations. The U.S. objective remained limited, as in the Korean conflict, to the defense of the territory not already part of the organized communist state to the north. U.S. land forces were responsible, in collaboration with South Vietnamese troops, for the "pacification" of the south, that is, for the suppression of Vietcong guerrilla operations. At the same time, the U.S. military began aerial bombardment of North Vietnam in the ex-

pectation that the damage would be so great that it would force its leaders to agree to end the communist insurrection in the south. The U.S. Air Force undertook the most intensive bombing campaign in its history.

The bombing failed to bring victory. North Vietnam, an agrarian economy, did not offer targets vital to its economic life, and its people were prepared to endure enormous suffering in that war of national liberation. At no time did the bombardment stop the movement of supplies south to the guerrillas or force North Vietnam to seriously consider abandoning the war.

The land war in the south failed as well to achieve its main objective of suppressing the guerrilla forces. By 1968, the United States had more than 500,000 troops in South Vietnam, nearly as many as the South Vietnamese Army. Assisting infantry operations, the U.S. Air Force conducted intensive bombing attacks in rural areas of South Vietnam. The immediate result of massive U.S. military involvement was to prevent a Vietcong victory. The Communist guerrillas lacked the equipment and numbers to defeat the combined U.S.-South Vietnamese forces. They

Fighting the Invisible Enemy: U.S. Naval Forces in Action in Vietnam, approx. 1968 (*Official U.S. Navy Photograph, Courtesy Freda Utley Collection/Hoover Institution Archives*)

attempted in early 1968 one major offensive to seize urban areas in the south (the Tet offensive), only to suffer a crushing defeat. Their military strength dwindled by one-third, from 300,000 to 200,000, as a result of the bloody battles. North Vietnamese forces assumed the principal role in the fighting. The guerrillas dug hundreds of miles of underground tunnels, some 30 feet below ground, to escape the U.S. bombardments. Many soldiers died, but more took their place.

The diplomatic, political, economic, and human price of U.S. intervention in the Vietnam War grew to the point where it far exceeded the importance of victory to the United States. The most obvious result was heavy casualties among the South Vietnamese, helpless victims caught in the fighting between the two sides. As serious for Vietnam society was social disorder on a monumental scale. This was the direct consequence of the war. It brought the destruction of organized village life in many areas, a fall in agricultural production resulting from the bombing and the massive use of herbicides to defoliate forested regions, and the influx of four million refugees to the cities. The human suffering of the Vietnamese appeared out of all proportion to the limited war aims.

The cost to the United States, although it did not compare to Vietnam's hardship, was sufficient to undermine the commitment to intervention. The total expense of air and ground fighting plus the aid granted the South Vietnamese government raised the price of war to more than $150 billion. Before war's end, the fighting left more than 50,000 U.S. soldiers dead. Within the United States, bitter political conflict arose when predictions of quick victory proved wrong. Many Americans recoiled at the brutality of the war, revealed to them by instant television coverage. The diplomatic price of U.S. intervention proved high as well. The war deflected attention and resources from larger issues of great power relations, such as Soviet-American arms control and the worsen-

ing conflicts in the Middle East. The very continuation of the Vietnam War represented a defeat for the United States.

In 1968, the combination of these factors forced the U.S. government to turn again to South Vietnamese armed forces to defeat the insurgents. The next year it began the withdrawal of U.S. troops. "Vietnamization" meant passing responsibility for the war to the South Vietnam government, more dependent than ever on U.S. military and economic aid. At the same time, the new Nixon administration began peace negotiations with the North Vietnamese government.

The new policy also brought one final effort to end the flow from the north of supplies to the guerrillas. The Ho Chi Minh trail passed through the neighboring neutral state of Cambodia. Years of secret U.S. bombing had failed to prevent traffic, carried on any vehicle on wheels including bicycles, from moving along the jungle road. To end the flow, in 1970 American forces invaded Cambodia. The United States became the protector of an anticommunist military government there.

The only effect of this escalation was to widen the conflict. North Vietnamese supplies continued to reach the south, for the jungle lay largely beyond the reach of U.S. infantry. Cambodian insurgents (Khmer Rouge) took over large areas of their country, with the military support of the North Vietnamese Communists. The immediate result of that invasion was to bring Cambodia directly into the war. The Khmer Rouge began their own war of liberation against the United States and its Cambodian allies. Still the U.S. withdrawal from Indochina continued, until by 1972 no combat troops remained in Vietnam or Cambodia.

The disappearance of U.S. forces doomed the South Vietnamese regime. The United States and North Vietnam did negotiate a compromise peace settlement in 1973, but it left the way open for a communist victory. The Vietnamese Communists accepted the existence of the U.S.-backed government in South Vietnam. In exchange, the U.S. negotiators agreed not to demand the withdrawal from the southern territory of all North Vietnamese troops. The continued presence of substantial North Vietnamese forces in South Vietnam gave them the bases from which to launch a new offensive when the right moment arrived.

The South Vietnamese leaders recognized the danger, refusing initially to sign the treaty. President Nixon overcame their opposition by secretly promising to send in U.S. military forces if North Vietnam did attack. The promise proved worthless, however, after Nixon's resignation from the presidency in 1974 in the Watergate scandal. The South Vietnamese leaders were no more successful than before in forming a strong nationalist regime. Nothing the United States did could ensure a strong, noncommunist nation-state in South Vietnam.

In 1975, the Communists were finally victorious throughout the lands once called Indochina. That year North Vietnamese troops launched their final offensive. They overwhelmed the southern forces in two months, and along with the army the South Vietnam state collapsed. Soon afterward the Communists joined South Vietnam to their People's Republic. At the same time, the Khmer Rouge defeated the U.S.-backed military regime in Cambodia. Their revolution proved as brutal as any previous communist regime. In a three-year period, they imprisoned and executed millions of Cambodians. In the end, the revolutionary violence of the Khmer Rouge caused their downfall. In 1978, their troops invaded a border region of Vietnam that they claimed for Cambodia. This action provoked in return a Vietnamese military offensive, which easily overthrew the Khmer Rouge government. For a few years, the Vietnamese Communist Party ruled all of former Indochina.

In the end, the victory of the Vietnamese Communists did not prove the catastrophe for Southeast Asia as predicated by the U.S. war party in the 1960s. Though it was a bitter hu-miliation for many Americans, U.S. diplomatic influence in Asia did not suffer. The major international event in East Asia in the early 1970s was the restoration of good relations between the United States and communist China. In global perspective, the Vietnam conflict turned out to be a sideshow.

Even the Vietnamese Communists' dream of bringing all Indochina under their rule collapsed in the face of anti-Vietnamese nationalism in Cambodia and the decay of Vietnam's command economy. Civil war in Cambodia continued for years between the new government, controlled by Vietnam, and a coalition of forces hostile to Vietnam. In 1990, Vietnam's forces finally abandoned in their turn that ruinous war. The government of Vietnam agreed to leave the country in the hands of a new Cambodian government.

In Vietnam, the failure of the command economy and the cost of military intervention in Cambodia produced an economic crisis that Vietnam's leaders could not blame on the decades of war. By the 1980s, the standard of living of the country had declined so severely that it ranked as one of the poorest societies in the world. In desperation, hundreds of thousands of Vietnamese fled the country, many by boat, in the hopes of finding refuge in the West. The communist revolution there was in human terms a calamity. The monuments erected in Vietnam and in the United States to the war dead marked the real price of the ruinous struggle for Indochina.

SUMMARY

Wars and revolution had profoundly altered the history of East Asia. Japan no longer possessed either a great empire or a powerful military. Having occupied a vast area of East and Southeast Asia, it had to abandon all its conquered territories. Japan's defeat opened the way to revolution and the emergence of new nation-states in that vast area.

The internal transformation of East Asian lands depended in large measure on forces unique to each country. In China, nationalism fused with communist ideology to sustain a long revolutionary war. Korea's continued partition after the war owed its tenacious hold on the country to the strength of the two authoritarian regimes that emerged out of the Allied occupations in the years after the Second World War. The extraordinary economic success of South Korea, becoming one of the countries called the "Four Dragons" of East Asia where prosperity came in a generation, was due to the skills and commitment of the Korean people. There they had the relative liberty of economic choice and made it the password to open the door to a modern economy and society. The imported Stalinist regime of North Korea, by contrast, left the country impoverished.

The success of the Vietnamese Communist Party in defeating both French and U.S. forces was also a product of the commitment and sacrifice of its followers. While the United States could land a man on the moon, its military confronted an indomitable opponent in these guerrilla forces. The destruction and bloodshed of the decades of Indochina war left behind a legacy of united Vietnamese and Cambodian nation-states and memories of communist heroes as part of their official national histories. In Vietnam, the communist regime kept hold of dictatorial power even after the command economy had collapsed. It too was a relic of the war.

DATES WORTH REMEMBERING

1945   Partition of Korea
1946–1954   French war in Indochina
1946–1949   Civil war in China
1949   Creation of Chinese People's Republic
1950   Formation of Vietnam, Cambodia, and Laos
1950–1953   Korean War
1954   French withdrawal from Indochina

1955   Creation of North and South Vietnam
1959   Communist insurrection in South Vietnam
1961   Beginning of massive U.S. military aid to South Vietnam
1965   U.S. military intervention in Vietnam
1972   Withdrawal of U.S. troops from Vietnam
1975   Communist conquest of South Vietnam and Cambodia

RECOMMENDED READING

The Chinese Communist Revolution

Susanne Pepper, *Civil War in China: The Political Struggle, 1945–1951* (1978). A thoughtful assessment of one of the critical wars of this century.
Jonathan Spence, *Mao Zedong* (1999). A short, critical reassessment of the life of this great revolutionary leader.

Korea's War

Sergei Goncharov, John Lewis, and Xue Litai, *Uncertain Partners: Stalin, Mao, and the Korean War* (1993). The best study to date of the murky origins of the North Korean invasion.
William Stueck, *Rethinking the Korean War* (2002). A judicious analysis of that forgotten Cold War conflict.

War in Indochina

William Duiker, *Ho Chi Minh* (2000). A lengthy critical biography of the communist leader.
*George Herring, *America's Longest War: The United States and Vietnam, 1950–1975* (2nd edition, 1986). A succinct discussion of America's failed experience in state-building and anticommunist war in Vietnam.

The Cold War and Containment

*John Lewis Gaddis, *Strategies of Containment: A Critical Appraisal of Postwar American National Security Policy* (1982). A very perceptive study of U.S. containment policy from its origins to the late 1970s.

Anders Stephanson, *Kennan and the Art of Foreign Policy* (1989). An intellectual biography of the diplomat, stressing the cultural forces that shaped his world view.

Memoirs and Visual Aids

*Robert McNamara, *In Retrospect: The Tragedy and Lessons of Vietnam* (1995). Thoughtful and frank autobiography by one of the key actors in the U.S. Vietnam War.

*Bao Ninh, *Sorrow of War* (1993). A vivid North Vietnam novel about the human misery of the Vietnam War.

Platoon (1986). A brutal film view of the Vietnam War, as seen from the perspective of the ordinary U.S. soldier.

---

*Indicates book is available in paperback.

CHAPTER NINE

The Resurgence of China and Japan, 1950–2000

- Revolution to Riches in Communist China
- Japan's Recovery from Defeat

Highlight: Revolution and Command Economies

Spotlight: The Fourteenth Dalai Lama

Last of the empires in East Asia, the Japanese Empire lost all its colonial lands in the cataclysm of defeat at the end of the Second World War. Its troops departed from the Asian mainland, abandoning Indonesia, Burma, Indochina, China, and Korea. Left with only their archipelago of main islands, the Japanese people had to remake their lives in the ruins of cities and under American occupation. In many respects East Asia had to be remade.

The countries of the region retained the boundaries drawn by Western imperial powers. The revolutionary armies of the Chinese Communist Party never recovered all the outlying lands that the empire had once ruled, but the new state did keep by negoti-

ation and force of arms the bulk of its territory and population. It was still a multi-ethnic country, with large Turkic and Tibetan minorities in its western regions. The preponderance of Han-speaking people gave it greater claim than ever before to be the land of the Chinese nation. Still, its size and diversity left it in appearance like the old empire, whose lands the new communist rulers still hoped to recover. The new China was in many ways an empire-nation.

The Soviet Union and the United States were a constant and important presence, both by the influence they exerted and by the opposition they encountered, in the evolution of the East Asian countries. Chinese Communists depended in the early years of their revolution on the Soviet Union for ideological inspiration and military support. Later, they denounced their Soviet neighbor for abandoning "true" communist ideology and failing to support them in their confrontation with the United States. This conflict led to a profound alteration in the Asian balance of power. The United States played a key role in the reconstruction of Japan, both as an occupying power and as a source of economic aid, until for a time the Japanese economic "miracle" became a model for American industry. To understand the evolution of East Asia, we must pay attention both to internal political forces in each country and to the policies of the two superpowers. Their global ascendancy made post-1945 world history in some measure a product of their actions.

REVOLUTION TO RICHES IN COMMUNIST CHINA

In 1950, the future of China, the oldest existing civilization in the world, had become the responsibility of the Communist Party. The long years of civil war had divided the population and devastated much of the country. Despite the destruction that the Japanese war had produced, it proved a unifying influence. The Communists' struggle against a hated foreign enemy brought the party the support of Chinese patriots and nationalists. It paved the way for political unification of the country following the military victory of the communist forces. Mao Zedong came to power both as the "Great Helmsman" of his party and as the heir to an ancient imperial state.

Mao Zedong and Communist Dictatorship

The Chinese Communist Party undertook after 1949 the revolutionary task of transforming the Chinese state and society and of re-

making the behavior and attitudes of the Chinese people. Mao Zedong's influence had grown until he became the object of a semireligious cult resembling the hero worship in the Soviet Union surrounding Stalin. His dominance infused Chinese communism in its first decades with unique revolutionary traits. Ever since the 1920s, Mao had placed his hope for revolution in China above all in the peasant masses. He preserved that faith when he set about, as he explained in his peculiar Marxist vocabulary, to "destroy feudalism" and to "build socialism." What to skeptics appeared impossible was attainable, he believed, since "the masses of the Chinese people" were capable of "miracles," provided they received correct communist inspiration and party guidance. This extraordinary confidence in the Chinese masses remained with him throughout his years in power and inspired grandiose—and ultimately disastrous—experiments in Chinese communism.

Mao believed that his understanding of communism and socialist revolution offered the country a unified body of revolutionary wisdom. The message incorporated two principal lessons: (1) The revolutionary ideology of Marxism-Leninism had to be adapted to Chinese conditions; (2) Mao possessed the creative knowledge to discover the Chinese path to the socialist society and to lead the party and the country to this glorious life. He gave to the People's Liberation Army (PLA) a special and crucial place in the Chinese communist movement. It had been the spearhead of the party in the seizure of power. He believed that its discipline and dedication set the model for the whole revolutionary vanguard, of which it was, in some respects, the elite. No earlier communist movement had placed such heavy responsibilities on its military organization in the struggle for political power. Taken as a whole, these fundamental precepts of Chinese communism define what is called "Maoism." Mao's beliefs were utopian. For a quarter century they marked China's path to the future.

In the early years, the Chinese Communists conceived of their country's immediate future as a literal repetition of the construction of socialism in the early decades of Soviet development. They idolized Soviet achievements and made the Soviet Union their model of political dictatorship and economic revolution. They believed (although not for long) that the Soviet Union had successfully built a socialist society. China's revolutionaries had to follow the Soviet model on its own road to socialism. Mao declared on his visit to Moscow in the winter of 1949–1950 that Soviet farm collectivization, nationalized industry, and command planning were "models for construction in New China." While the Japanese were in those same years reconstructing their state and economy on the basis of Western democratic and capitalist institutions, China's path followed that of Soviet communism.

Revolutionary China

The Chinese leaders faced enormous problems implementing their revolutionary plans. They had extensive experience governing comparatively small areas during their years of guerrilla war. Suddenly they found themselves in control of a land larger than the continental United States with a population approaching 600 million. Among these people were many who had fought for or supported the Communists' enemies. Political convictions and self-interest had incited many Chinese to work with the Nationalists, while others had collaborated with the Japanese. China remained an impoverished country, severely damaged by decades of war, whose new leaders dreamed of building a socialist society of abundance and equality. The revolution had a great distance to go, and some of its leaders, especially Mao, were very impatient.

The formation of a new state came first. The borders of the new state followed closely those of the Chinese Nationalist state and of the Chinese Empire before it. Tibet became Chinese once again after its occupation in 1950 by communist troops. Tibet, with a tiny army and primitive weapons, was an easy conquest. The Communists claimed to have "liberated" Tibet from the imperialists. But their conquest and subjugation of the land resembled the policies of a conquering empire. They brought to the Buddhist people of Tibet their own version of modernity. It included war on religion, the end to monastic rule, and the exploitation of the natural resources (including uranium) hidden in the remote region. The life of Tibetans was never the same again. The far western region of Xinjiang ceased being within the Soviet sphere of influence with the withdrawal of Soviet troops that same year; Chinese authorities moved in immediately afterwards. Only the island of Taiwan remained outside the control of the People's Republic, for its Nationalist government-in-exile was under the protection of U.S. naval forces.

The ruling organs of the Chinese People's Republic copied the Soviet one-party system. When the new constitution went into effect in 1954, it gave the Chinese state a National Assembly, chosen by popular election, whose responsibilities included selection of the president of the Republic and of the Council of Ministers. The new order formally acknowledged the existence of national minorities by creating an "autonomous region" for each non-Han people. Tibetans, Turks, and Mongols possessed (in theory) the right to their own local government, schools, and culture. Behind this democratic facade lay, as in the Soviet Union, the monopoly of power of the Communist Party. All candidates to elected political positions had the advance approval of party authorities. Only one candidate for any office ever appeared on electoral ballots. Voters merely registered their approval of the party's decisions. Communists appointed in Beijing kept firm control over the autonomous regions, where units of the PLA were ready to repress national unrest. This "people's democracy" meant in fact that the leaders of the Chinese Communist Party could claim to speak for the people in deciding what was best for the revolution and for their own power.

The Communist Party itself followed the Leninist principle of centralization of command in the hands of the Central Committee and the Politburo. Mao Zedong was chairman of these powerful committees. He held also the positions of president of the Republic and head of the People's Liberation Army. Taken altogether, these responsibilities confirmed his preeminence over the state and the party. His authority was uncontested in those years. Like Stalin, whose power and eminence Mao admired, he set the guidelines for state and party policy. The fate of China lay in his hands, to the extent that any man could exercise supreme power in so enormous and complex a country. Around the great square in Beijing were hung the portraits of the intellectual giants of revolutionary Marxism, beginning with Marx and Engels, then Lenin and Stalin, and finally Mao. This picture of the "apostolic succession" of world communism elevated Mao to the rank of world leader.

Making a socialist revolution on the ruins of the oldest civilization in the world required the purging of enemies and the elimination of rival ideologies. The Communists began the "repression of the enemy classes," conducted by the army, the courts, and the secret police (the National Security Forces). In 1951, a new law against "counter-revolutionaries" called for mass meetings and public denunciations of anticommunists. No one knows the number of Chinese arrested and sentenced; moderate estimates mention one to three million executions. A vast system of prison camps emerged in remote parts of the country to "reeducate" the prisoners, many of whom spent decades

as forced laborers. The party-state did not tolerate diversity of religion or political persuasion. Following the Soviet example, it imposed its own ideological mold on the country's intellectual and cultural life.

The social reforms undertaken in those years were directed against the "five bonds" that had constituted the core of imperial Chinese society. The Communists' attack on old China included among their targets the traditional family, which was the bastion of Confucianism and ancestor worship. They championed the principle of the equality of rights of women. Applied to Chinese society, it required the abolition of the old marriage practices, including infant and forced marriage, concubinage, and infanticide. Divorce became legal, as did abortion. The new regime wiped out the practice of foot binding, which had been a symbol of women's subjugation and a relic of that "feudal" past whose destruction was key to the success of the revolution. All these reforms were contained in the family law of 1950. It challenged the customs of centuries.

These reforms became effective only after massive propaganda campaigns and new edicts drove home the message that the revolution would not spare the family. In those years, the regime promoted birth-control methods to limit the rapid growth of the population. Other new social policies included a ruthless campaign against drug addiction, which was virtually wiped out within a few years. Political dictatorship and sweeping social reforms brought the power of the new state and of the party into the personal lives of the Chinese population.

The Great Leap Forward

Stalin's death in early 1953 opened a new period in Soviet relations with China. The new Soviet leaders publicly acknowledged China's status as an equal in the socialist camp. They renounced the special territorial concessions that Stalin had obtained. They expanded their economic aid program, providing China in the following five years with machinery, credits, and technical assistance worth billions of dollars. These years were a honeymoon in the relations between the Soviet Union and China.

Using the Stalinist economic system as their model, the Chinese leaders adopted the principal institutions of the Soviet command economy, that is, command planning, collectivized agriculture, and rapid development of nationalized industry. In 1955, they launched their First Five-Year Plan for economic development. That same year Mao ordered the party to begin a rapid campaign for farm collectivization. In 1955, the state nationalized the remaining private commercial and industrial enterprises. Imitating Soviet practices, the Chinese leaders strictly limited peasant consumption in order to turn agricultural production to the benefit of the cities and the industrial population.

By 1956, the entire Chinese economy was under state control. Mao expected miracles of socialist development, pointing to the Soviet experience to justify his claim. "The Soviet Union's great historical experience in building socialism inspires our people," he wrote that year, "and gives them full confidence that they can build socialism in their country." Never again did he refer in such glowing terms to Soviet socialism.

Within a year Mao denounced (at first in private, then publicly) the Soviet leaders for abject failure in their commitment to socialism. It is not clear what brought him to that startling reversal of opinion. He revealed later that he judged the Soviet leadership guilty of permitting the existence in their country of substantial inequalities in salaries and incomes. To him, this amounted to the revival of capitalism and the decay of socialism. He attacked the Soviet bureaucracy, whom he believed guilty of corruption and profiteering.

In Marxist terms, he was right on both counts, but later events proved that his own utopian socialism was equally flawed.

The dispute between the two communist states quickly assumed the proportions of a religious schism. In the spirit of a Protestant church reformer challenging the Catholic papacy during the Reformation in sixteenth-century Europe, Mao believed that he, better than any other Communist, understood how to achieve a just, egalitarian socialist society. The conflict began in the tones of a doctrinal quarrel. United until then by their universal vision and shared ideals, they proceeded to condemn each other as sinful heretics.

In early 1958, Mao set out to prove that the Chinese way to socialism was the correct path. He based his hopes on his conviction that the Chinese masses were capable of such prodigies of work, of such superhuman efforts, and of such radical improvements in their collective institutions that their willpower and his leadership would bring to China in a few years both abundance and social equality. He wrote that the "600 million people of China" were like a "clean sheet of paper" on which "the newest and most beautiful pictures [could] be painted." He asked that they assist him in a "Great Leap Forward."

His spectacular vision for his country required that it abandon the Soviet-type economic policies that it had just adopted a few years before. Command planning had to end, for it was misguided and harmful. He argued that in a year Chinese workers and peasants could by their own efforts raise economic production by 100 percent, could complete enormous dams and flood control projects, and could transform collective farming into communal-type farming. He demanded the creation of "people's communes" in the countryside, relatively few in number and grouping up to 100,000 peasant households, to replace the collective farms. They were to be organized on egalitarian principles, with no special benefits to good workers and no separate garden plots or private houses. Families would conduct their lives collectively, with meals and child care provided by the commune. Mao wrote just before the campaign got underway that "there is no difficulty in the world" the masses cannot overcome "if only they take their destiny into their own hands." The party's need for help from the masses even led to the abandonment of birth control (it did not return until twenty years later when the country's population had grown by another 300 million). The Great Leap Forward revealed Mao's extraordinary revolutionary populism and utopianism.

The reality was disaster. The worst consequences resulted from the radical reorganization of agriculture. Peasant farmers lost the incentive to work, were taken from their farming for great irrigation and flood prevention projects, and spent long hours in political indoctrination meetings. Agricultural production in 1959 and 1960 declined so seriously that famine spread throughout the Chinese countryside. The full extent of the catastrophe of the early 1960s became public knowledge decades later. Despite severe rationing and the decision in 1961 to import large quantities of grain, millions of Chinese rural inhabitants died (recent estimates suggest more than 40 million) as a result of famine and disease. Mao's disastrous experiment in mass mobilization was the cause. The crisis gave Mao's opponents in the party leadership the incentive to force an end to the Great Leap Forward. They publicly criticized "guerrilla methods" in governing the country. They took control of the government, pushing aside Mao despite his complaint that he was being treated like a "dead ancestor." He was, temporarily, dethroned. Still, his authority as Great Helmsman of the Chinese revolution ensured his stature in the party. For a few years, he had to suppress his dissatisfaction with the course of his coun-

try's development. His vision of egalitarian socialism no longer set policy, and his influence dwindled among the party leadership.

His revolutionary policies hastened the breakup of the Sino-Soviet alliance. Many issues of national interest were a source of disagreement between China and the Soviet Union in the late 1950s. Disputes over territorial questions and differing policies toward the United States were bound to strain the ties between the two most powerful communist states. In 1960, Mao accused the Soviet Communists of betraying Leninism and selling out the cause of world revolution by not promising its military backing in case of war with the United States over Taiwan. In retaliation, the Soviet leaders stopped all Soviet assistance, refusing any further help in Chinese nuclear development and breaking the economic aid agreement. Within a few weeks, all Soviet technicians left and factories being built by the Russians stood abandoned. To Soviet leaders, good relations with neutral Third World countries became as important as their relations with China. At about the same time as their quarrel erupted with China, they agreed to sell arms to India. In the circumstances, it was a hostile act toward China.

India and China were divided by a longstanding territorial dispute on their long Himalayan frontier. In 1950, Chinese troops had conquered and annexed the kingdom of Tibet. Rebellious peoples, Turkic in western China (Xinjiang) and Tibetan in the southwest, lived on this borderland of the new state. The Chinese government wanted rapid access to these lands in the event of unrest. It began building a strategic highway linking Tibet and Xinjiang through mountainous territory claimed by India. In 1959, the Tibetan people did rebel against the Chinese, requiring prolonged military repression. Tibet had become a Chinese colony. The strategic highway's use in keeping together this new Chinese Empire was clear.

The Chinese government was determined to establish its control over the strip of territory claimed by India. By 1960, the quarrel turned into a military confrontation. The Indian government refused to cede the area needed and began to move its own troops there. The Chinese leaders prepared for war. In 1962, their troops, operating in difficult mountainous areas all along the Indian border, attacked and defeated Indian forces in a brief border war (see Chapter 10). Having occupied the area along the highway, they halted the war. Without any outside support (the Soviet Union remained neutral), the Chinese regime had proven that it was a major power in Asia.

◀   SPOTLIGHT: The Fourteenth Dalai Lama   ▶

For most of his life, the Fourteenth Dalai Lama, born in 1937, has been a political refugee. He remains the legitimate leader of the Buddhists of Tibet, though he had to flee the country in 1959 to escape imprisonment by the Chinese Communists who rule his land. He, like many millions of other political refugees in the twentieth century, became the victim of war and revolution.

As practiced in Tibet, the Buddhist religion had for many centuries formed the core of the life of the population in that remote mountainous kingdom. The Dalai Lama is the name given to the person, chosen while still an infant, who is believed to be the reincarnation (reappearance after death) of the spirit of the Buddha himself. The Fourteenth Dalai Lama was the spiritual descendant of the First Dalai Lama of the sixteenth century, when this Tibetan Buddhist practice began. Monks in Tibet's many monasteries preserved the religious teachings of the Buddha. They regarded the Dalai Lama as the source of wisdom and guidance in religious and political affairs. Until the twentieth century, these monasteries were the center of Tibetan life and the source of law and public order. The Dalai Lama was, in effect, the absolute ruler as well as a religious leader, a "God-King." For a time, Tibetan leaders had recognized Chinese suzerainty (political authority) over the country. Still, nothing that the Chinese Empire did threatened their way of life and religion.

When the Western world (in the form first of British explorers) discovered Tibet, they brought with them tools of modern life unknown to Tibetans. Electric power and steam engines suddenly became tangible and desirable items. The Tibetan rulers had need of a foreign policy, ambassadors, and a postal system. In 1911, the collapse of the Chinese Empire was their chance to proclaim Tibet an independent country. That peaceful period ended when the Chinese Communists invaded their land in 1950.

In the first years of Chinese rule, the Fourteenth Dalai Lama (still a young man) tried to conciliate the Communists and to preserve Buddhist practices. He had had little contact with foreigners but had begun to learn of the world beyond the Himalayas from occasional visitors (and from two German prisoners-of-war who had fled captivity in India). India was Tibet's other powerful neighbor and a land where respect for the Buddhist religion was widespread. The Dalai Lama could expect moral support from Indians and even might hope for diplomatic backing from the Indian government. Until the border war erupted between India and China, the Indian leaders discouraged him from challenging the Chinese invaders. He had become a player in the "great game" of power politics in those crisis years.

Mao's Great Leap Forward brought the full force of the Communists' antireligious campaign to Tibet. In early 1957, Chinese Communists and PLA soldiers began systematically weakening Tibetan Buddhism, attacking the monasteries, expelling the monks, destroying religious relics, and tearing down the ancient buildings. The Dalai Lama's deepest religious and political convictions required that he speak out against these vicious measures. They aimed, in his words, at the "extermination of the religion and culture of the Tibetan race." He publicly condemned the anti-Buddhist measures, though he risked his own life in doing so. In 1959, Tibetans joined in a massive revolt against their Chinese rulers. The PLA

was there to suppress the rebellion. But it took the occupation forces fourteen years to do so.

The Dalai Lama could no longer remain in his country. In the midst of the violence, he secretly fled across the high mountain passes to India. There, with more than 100,000 Tibetan refugees, he asked for political asylum. Although the Chinese Communists protested India's "imperialist" intervention in their affairs, the Indian government agreed to his request. The Chinese victory in the Sino-Indian war of 1962 ensured that the Dalai Lama's exile would last for a long time.

He and his followers created what they called "Tibet in exile," located in one of the old British hill stations in the Himalayan foothills. He continued to act as the true leader of the Tibetan community, heading a government-in-exile and receiving foreign statesmen. Prime Minister Nehru was the first to visit. His was a discouraging message, for the Indian government would not back the cause of Tibetan independence. Secret messengers kept the Dalai Lama in touch with

XIVth Dalai Lama (*Stillwell Collection/Hoover Institution Archives*)

Tibetans living in Tibet. He devoted his time largely to religious matters, but politics kept intruding in his life. The agonies of the Buddhists during Mao's Great Cultural Revolution brought from him expressions of sympathy and pleas to the Chinese for religious toleration, all to no avail. Tibetans again revolted against the Chinese and for several years fought a desperate guerrilla war. But the Chinese were too strong.

In 1974, the Dalai Lama begged his followers to cease armed resistance. He pre-sented to Tibetans a pacifist program of opposition, arguing for nonviolence in defense of the rights and liberties of his people. At first, he called for a neutral Tibet that would take no part in the power politics of Asian states; later he asked only for full autonomy for Tibet within the People's Republic. For his courage and moral strength, the Dalai Lama won the Nobel Peace Prize in 1989. The Chinese leaders paid no attention to his proposals and denounced his "subversive" activities. Exile was to be his fate.

The Cultural Revolution

The years between 1960 and 1966 were a period of temporary calm before Mao and his supporters launched a new and even more violent revolutionary offensive. The people's communes were disbanded and smaller collective farms reinstalled. The recovery of agriculture required a large investment of state funds, allocated in those years according to pragmatic criteria of need and productivity.

Although powerless to prevent these changes, Mao refused to compromise. He rebuked his colleagues for their "bourgeois" spirit. He publicized his version of revolutionary communism—and his cult—in a little red book entitled *Quotations from Chairman Mao*. Its distribution was assured by the People's Liberation Army, which printed one billion copies to make sure it was available to the entire Chinese population and to foreign supporters. Its most ardent readers were China's youth, among whom admiration for the Great Helmsman was deep and unquestioning. Mao welcomed what he called their "socialist education" and their support for his ideals.

In the mid-1960s, he seems to have become convinced that his revolution was caught in an ongoing conflict between forces of evil—his enemies—and of good—the masses, the army, and the students. He imagined Chinese youth to be uncorrupted by avarice or ambition and ready for combat against the "enemy classes" that he believed had penetrated his country. His immediate objective was to end the "counter-revolutionary restoration" of those he called a new "exploiting bourgeoisie," including well-paid professionals, intellectuals, and party bureaucrats. In a manner recalling Stalin's Great Terror, he prepared to undertake a new class war against his own party and the educated elite of his country.

The decade of turmoil that began in 1966 had no parallel in the history of earlier revolutions. It involved both the Chinese state and society. It undermined party institutions and rule, produced a prolonged upheaval in education, industry, and agriculture, and destroyed precious works of traditional Chinese culture. So chaotic were conditions that the full story remains obscure. In 1966, Mao was still the revered leader of his people, able to mobilize supporters among the students, workers, and soldiers to participate in what he referred to as a Cultural Revolution. That year he made clear whom the enemies were, warning that "the bourgeois agents who have infiltrated the party, the government, the

Cult of Mao: Bust of Mao Zedong, 1970
(*Hoover Institution Archives Collection*)

army, and all sectors of cultural life constitute a gang of counter-revolutionary revisionists."

Mao's principal weapon in this class war was a mass movement to promote what he baptized his "Great Proletarian Cultural Revolution." His immediate goal was nothing less than the destruction of the old party leadership and the creation of a new revolutionary regime, consisting of "revolutionary mass organizations" running a country rid of greedy bureaucrats, profit seekers, and egotistical intellectuals. Somehow he managed to win sufficient backing from party leaders to begin a campaign that they must have known threatened their policies and their power. In 1966, he obtained the authority to create and to lead a special committee charged with organizing his Cultural Revolution. This organization started a propaganda campaign in mid-1966 calling on all 700 million Chinese to "destroy the old world." The first recruits for the Cultural Revolution came from the student youth, organized in units called Red Guards. That fall all regular university and high-school studies ceased (the interruption lasted nearly ten years). Students had better things to do than to study, for Mao called them to lead his new revolution.

The Red Guards were the revolutionary organization of Chinese youth. Their appearance coincided with Mao's emergence at the head of the Cultural Revolution. That August, he gathered together one million Red Guards at the Gate of Heavenly Peace in Beijing, appearing before them just as the sun rose in the east. His message was simple: "Destroy the old and construct the new." That fall and winter, violence swept the country as these self-proclaimed revolutionaries organized mass demonstrations, attacked alleged counter-revolutionaries, imprisoned party officials, and destroyed old monuments and precious relics of China's past. Centers of resistance emerged when party officials mobilized their own supporters to oppose this children's crusade. Street demonstrations often degenerated into open fighting between rival political factions.

The next ten years were a time of extraordinary turmoil. Serious disorders accompanied the attack on party officials and factory administrations. Rival groups of Red Guards fought for leadership and battled with worker organizations claiming to defend the true Maoist line. Punishment inflicted on "class enemies" included public humiliation, exile to the countryside, imprisonment, even death by beating. Cities like Canton and Shanghai experienced so much violence that the conditions there resembled civil war.

Soon units of the People's Liberation Army began to intervene to enforce a minimum of public order in China's cities and towns. In 1968, Mao authorized the army to supervise the economic and political affairs of the provinces. The army commanders did not seek to militarize the Chinese state. Instead, they organized revolutionary committees, grouping representatives of workers, students, and the military in very disorderly and unstable coalitions. They replaced the old regional and city party committees, which were a prime target in the Cultural Revolution. The guiding principle of action of these committees was the "three loyalties": loyalty to the "person, the thought, and the policies" of Mao Zedong. Maoism was the very essence of the Cultural Revolution.

Mao's revolutionary regime proved incapable either of governing the country effectively or of establishing new institutions for socialist revolution. The PLA became by default the backbone of political rule throughout the country. At a party congress held in early 1969, the head of the PLA, Lin Biao, who was second only to Mao in political power, proclaimed that the Great Cultural Revolution had triumphed. The reality was endemic disorder and continued witch-hunts of supposed enemies. PLA provincial military commanders held onto meager remnants of political authority in the country. The tasks of industrial construction, training of professionals, and scientific research had all been abandoned in the upheaval. Hundreds of thousands of scientists, specialists, and teachers were forced to accept "reeducation" by performing menial tasks in agricultural communes. China had entered a period of permanent revolution from which it did not finally emerge until after Mao's death in 1976.

In those years, relations with the Soviet Union became so strained that war appeared likely. Mao's supporters treated the Soviet Union as if it had become the principal enemy of China. The Chinese press published maps that claimed for China most of eastern Siberia (the Chinese Empire had exercised a remote and sporadic suzerainty over these lands be-

fore the nineteenth century). Pitched battles erupted with Soviet forces on the Manchurian border in 1969; sporadic confrontations occurred all along the enormous Chinese-Soviet frontier that year and the next. The Soviet government concluded that Mao was as dangerous and aggressive as Hitler had once been. They believed the threat of war with China so serious that they moved large military forces, including nuclear missiles, to their eastern region bordering China. The conflict between the Soviet Union and China became a new cold war.

Gradually other party leaders, appalled by the internal turmoil and foreign danger Mao had created, brought an end to the period of revolutionary zealotry of the Cultural Revolution. Zhou Enlai, the chairman of the council of ministers and the most influential moderate party leader, resumed his role in policy making. The process by which power changed hands again remains unclear. In 1972, the party leaders formally disbanded the Red Guards. Most of its members were sent to work in the countryside, where they could no longer champion Mao's Cultural Revolution. But as long as Mao remained alive, no one challenged his utopian vision of Chinese socialism, and no new reforms appeared to remedy the havoc that his policies had created.

"To Get Rich Is Glorious"

In the late 1970s, this Maoist revolutionary order fell apart. The event that opened the way to sweeping changes in China's economic system was Mao's death in 1976. He received all the honors due the founding father of the new China. He was elevated to the status of "venerated ancestor" for citizens of the People's Republic. His heirs could do no less, for their power ultimately rested on the revolution that he had launched. But Mao's successors had learned by painful experience from their leader's terrible utopian experiments. Abiding poverty for over one-half of the population, who still had barely enough food for survival, was too great a price to pay for socialist egalitarianism. The future development of China, and their own authority, depended on putting China on the road to economic growth.

By 1978, all Maoist supporters had fallen from power. A new party leadership, headed by Deng Xiaoping, was in a position to bring to an end the quarter century of Mao's destructive revolutionary experiments. That year Deng declared publicly that Maoism was "wrong in its theories, policies, and slogans." After a quarter century of utopian experiments, communist dreams ceased to have any role in economic policies.

The new leadership sought pragmatic reforms that would give the Chinese population the opportunity and incentive to get to work. Support for education, science, and technology became a high priority. Command planning was drastically weakened. Foreigners obtained the right to open their own businesses. Private stores could offer goods that consumers desired and at prices that the market could bear.

Deng drew the line at nationalized industry. He was unwilling to abandon the enormous network of state-run factories. These remained a foundation of China's socialist economy and an assurance of worker support. Their guarantee of work, housing, and welfare to their employees and workers created what observers called China's "iron rice bowl." Deng did order that these nationalized enterprises, notoriously inefficient, earn profits on their production. Events proved his hope to be misplaced, for the factories continued to lose money, surviving only on state subsidies.

Deng's immediate concern was to give to the Chinese rural population the economic incentive to raise food production. China's very survival depended on their efforts. In 1978, the new leaders revised so thoroughly the regulations that had kept farmland under state supervision that they in effect returned this land to individual ownership. Prices on farm produce were largely freed from state control, permitting the farmers to make profits from their work. In the years that followed, the government opened private commercial networks to bring to the countryside consumer goods desired by the farmers. These soon included expensive durable items such as refrigerators, television sets, and motorcycles imported from Japan. The formula was remarkably successful.

The end of collective farming had an enormous impact on the lives of the Chinese masses, most of whom still lived in the countryside. Within a short time, Chinese farmers were able to double the country's agricultural production. They introduced new, highly productive strains of rice and wheat that had been developed a decade before in the West as part of the "Green Revolution." By the mid-1980s, China had a surplus of food for export. By then, the economy was expanding by the remarkable rate of 9 percent each year. At the end of the decade, only one-tenth of the population (100 million people) were still living in poverty. Deng Xiaoping himself proclaimed that the motto for the new China was: "To get rich is glorious!" It was a slogan that bore no resemblance to Maoism. Later, the communist leaders toned down his exuberant message to promise Chinese people the more attainable goal of "a moderately well-off society." It was still a far more appealing ideal for the Chinese people than Mao's permanent revolution.

Chinese socialism survived in the rhetoric of the Communist Party. Most important of all, the party-state was sacred. Its powers grew even greater when in 1980 it dictated a birth-control policy restricting each family to only one child. Penalties for violations were very strict, at times brutal. At the extreme, local officials could force a pregnant woman who had exceeded the limit of children to have an abortion. The leaders could find no alternative to controlling the rapid rise in population, which by then had passed one billion.

The Chinese Communist Party possessed the repressive apparatus of a dictatorship. The secret police operated when need be outside the law; prison camps in remote regions kept prisoners in miserable conditions for long periods; when disorder threatened, the state called upon the military might of the PLA. China's leaders were prepared to wield these brutal methods when their power was challenged by the democracy movement in the late 1980s. The supporters of democratic reforms, drawn largely from China's intellectual elite and student population, asked for representative government and free speech. They drew their ideas from Western liberal institutions and from the political reforms under way in the Soviet Union (see Chapter 13). The movement grew so powerful that in the spring of 1989 its supporters organized massive demonstrations in Beijing against the party dictatorship. They were backed by many workers but had no encouragement from the country's rural population. Political liberty remained an affair of China's urban population. Symbolizing their goal was a statue baptized the Goddess of Democracy, which demonstrators constructed in the center of Beijing, in Tiananmen Square.

The party leaders refused any compromise with those they considered "counter-revolutionaries." They could not conceive of any weakening of the communist dictatorship. It was the essence of their power, and they still claimed, like Stalin and Mao, that history was on their side. In early June 1989, they called in reliable army units to disperse the demonstrators, thousands of whom were killed or injured.

The leaders insisted that the Communist Party alone possessed the wisdom to lead the people to socialism. But no one claimed to know what a real socialist society was or when it would emerge in China. The Chinese government increasingly emphasized its nationalist program for a united China. Chinese migrants moved, with state support, into borderland territories of non-Han peoples in the western regions of Tibet and Sinkiang. The influx of ethnic Chinese threatened to overwhelm these peoples, but resistance met with immediate repression. The Chinese government demanded that Great Britain cede Hong Kong, Britain's small colony on China's southern coast. The British complied, handing the territory to the People's Republic in 1995. The Chinese Communists continued to insist that their leadership alone was "truly" Chinese, threatening periodically the small Chinese Republic on the island of Taiwan. Asserting that the People's Republic was the legitimate heir to the Chinese Empire, the Communists claimed the right to be the champions of the Chinese nation.

After Communism: China in the Global Economy

In the People's Republic of China, the economic reforms launched by Deng Xiaoping in 1978 gradually opened the country to a market economy. Later, his successors made the protection of business property a constitutional right. Chinese cities became the center of the country's booming economy, while the countryside (where two-thirds of the population still lived) lagged behind. In the next twenty-five years, China's per capita national income grew seven times, perhaps the most rapid massive increase in wealth in human history.

By then, the communist leaders were firmly committed to collaborating in the global economy. They welcomed foreign investors, who poured billions of dollars into the country. Their economy acquired direct access to the wealth of Hong Kong, financial center of East Asia, when Great Britain returned the tiny territory to China in 1997. Years before, wealthy Hong Kong business interests had become the major investors in the People's Republic. The products of these new enterprises found markets in the global economy, especially in the

United States, which had become the major trading partner of China.

The biggest problems faced by the Chinese economy resulted from rapid population growth; by the early twenty-first century, the population was estimated at 1.3 billion. Millions of rural migrants left their villages to seek jobs in the coastal cities' rapidly expanding industrial economy. An increasing number joined the flood of illegal migrants bound for Europe and the United States, going deeply into debt to smuggling gangs and risking death on the long trip in sealed trucks and ship containers. Those who stayed in China's cities found air and water contamination there as bad as the worst polluted urban areas in the world. Groundwater was in increasingly short supply in northern China as a result of wasteful industrial and agricultural use. Without severe restrictions on water usage, the Chinese Academy of Science warned that later in the twenty-first century large areas of the country would face severe, prolonged drought.

Rising demand for energy to power the economy was raising prices on the global oil market and altering China's landscape. In the early years of the twenty-first century, the country's needs for imported petroleum made it the second largest market (after the United States) in the world. The shortage of electric power persuaded the Chinese government to begin construction, in 1995, on the Yangtze River, of the single largest hydroelectric dam in the world. Its reservoir was so vast that five million people had to be displaced and millions of acres of productive land were lost. The communist government gambled that it could find work for the country's enormous population only by pursuing economic modernization, no matter what the cost.

The post-Mao leaders redefined their foreign policy goals in those years to place national interests above world revolution. By the end of the century, the United States had become the most important market for China's exports. Economic expansion through sales on the world market became the Chinese government's primary concern. It was prepared to play by the rules of the international market economy, joining the World Trade Organization in 2001. Peaceful relations with their neighbors mattered as well. The Chinese ended their quarrel with the Soviet Union as well, although the two states never returned to the earlier alliance. Maoism was dead, and communist ideals, though not forgotten, did not get in the way of interests of state. By the first years of the twenty-first century, China was the major power in East Asia. The Chinese state remained a single-party dictatorship in which party leaders clung to Marxism-Leninism in political speeches for their source of truth. In reality, the country no longer bore any resemblance to Maoist China.

● HIGHLIGHT: Revolution and Command Economies ●

When after the Second World War nationalist leaders took control of their new nation-states in Asia and Africa, they immediately searched for the policies that in the shortest possible time would give their countries a modern industrial economy. The market economies of the West offered one model but left much initiative to private investors and gave little assurance of rapid economic growth. The command economy of the Soviet Union was their other model. Stalin repeatedly proclaimed that his country was well on its way to the "shining future" of socialism. His prestige was at its peak in those years. He and his supporters had no doubt that Soviet victory in war had come thanks to the socialist system that he and his party had imposed in the 1930s. History, they announced, was on their side. The argument made many converts among nationalists in former colonial lands who repudiated Western capitalism along with Western imperialism.

The great attraction of the Stalinist reforms lay in their apparent ability to ensure rapid economic growth and their commitment to social justice and equality. In other words, they were both a means to industrial development and a socialist end in themselves. The term *command economy* best describes the Stalinist economic system, since the state possessed the powers to control all economic activities—in industry, commerce, and agriculture—and issued the commands that set production, price, and wage targets. The goal was to maximize resources for economic development. When the communist regimes in China, North Korea, and Vietnam set out to bring economic revolution to their peoples, they recreated the institutions and policies of this command economy. Many nationalist regimes in Asian and African countries also introduced important aspects of this system. During the half century after the Second World War, the economies of countries throughout the Third World resembled more closely that of the Soviet Union than Western capitalism.

Two characteristics of the command economy were particularly important in its operations. The first was the ownership and supervision by the state of all productive property. The second was the control by the state of all trade with foreign countries. Taken together, these powers brought state administration into the economic affairs of the population to a far greater extent than existed in capitalist countries. Nationalization was an essential step in creating a command economy. In the Soviet Union, as later in communist China, the government issued decrees soon after the seizure of power dispossessing all the owners of industrial enterprises and commercial businesses. Even agricultural production came under the supervision of the state after collectivization of private farms.

The only private property left in the hands of individuals were their personal possessions and, in the countryside, the houses and surrounding plots of land where the peasants lived (and at times even these were taken away). Private production and profit making became illegal. The authorities denounced these institutions as vestiges of capitalist behavior. Illegal private trading never disappeared from the command economies, since their inefficient distribution system and endemic shortages created a ready market for scarce goods. But the state declared this private trade the work of criminals to be punished by imprisonment and, in extreme cases, even death. The command economy of the communist regimes justified the repression of activities that in free-market economies brought profit and praise.

All foreign economic operations also fell under the supervision of the state. Governmental agencies were responsible for the purchase of goods and services from foreign countries. Other agencies decided whether and what amounts of goods from its country should be sold abroad. The command economy permitted the state to isolate its people from the outside world more completely than Western countries had ever attempted, even during the 1930s' depression. No international corporation or bank could make decisions that directly helped or hindered its plans for economic growth. The fluctuations of international prices could not block the import of items its leaders judged useful or desirable. At a time when Western economies were moving toward an interdependent global economy, communist regimes kept tight reins on all foreign transactions. They were protected from capitalist interference and were also cut off from the technological innovations of the Western economies. Most important, these controls assured the political leadership enormous power over the economies of their countries.

These economies operated at the command of the state. In countries such as the Soviet Union or the People's Republic of China, the state in turn was under the control of the Communist Party. Its political dictatorship extended into all areas of economic activity, in theory governed by the plans created by state planning agencies. The so-called science of command planning made fulfillment of the yearly plans the key measure of the success of economic activity. Managers of the state enterprises executed the orders of their ministries, while workers followed the orders of their factory bosses. No labor unions were permitted to hinder production by calling strikes, which were illegal.

The consumers whose living conditions depended on this tightly controlled economy had to take what goods they could find, at prices fixed not by supply and demand but by state ministries. The socialist society guaranteed jobs to workers and (usually) a minimally adequate standard of living for all consumers. Choices were few, but everyone enjoyed a certain measure of security. Leaders like Mao Zedong altered important elements of the system but never considered abandoning it. A socialist society for them was unthinkable without maintaining the essential qualities of the command economy.

Yet this system hid fundamental flaws so serious that by the 1990s it had vanished from almost all the countries where it had dominated economic life. These defects included the inability to assimilate effectively and rapidly technological innovations, the disregard for the choices of the population, a very low level of agricultural productivity, complete indifference to the environmental damage caused by economic projects, and incompetence of the officials who ran the system. In effect, the command economic system turned the entire economy of a country into one great corporation, whose board of directors consisted of the political leaders of state, whose employees worked in a vast bureaucratic network of ministries, and whose products enjoyed a monopoly on the market.

Nowhere in the system did there exist any incentive to take risks, such as introducing more productive farming, experimenting with more productive methods of manufacturing, or offering new products for consumers. Beginning in the 1950s, Western economies undertook a vast retooling as electronic, telecommunication, and computer technologies brought revolutionary new methods of production and communication. Nothing comparable happened in the communist countries.

State ministries continued to prescribe gigantic economic undertakings that fulfilled the plans but wasted scarce resources. These projects were of little use to consumers, whose most effective means to acquire new products was the black market. They also did grave damage to the environment, for no organizations or laws forced the ministries to take account of environmental costs. But the flaws that ultimately undermined the entire system were the unfitness and corruption of the political and economic leaders. They held in their hands the wealth of their country but had little interest and no training in how to use that wealth productively.

The all-powerful state bureaucracy was increasingly tempted to profit from its economic power and influence. These officials lived in seclusion in conditions immeasurably more comfortable than any ordinary citizen. Large numbers of officials took bribes in exchange for personal favors, extending even to illegal, black market operations. In the 1950s, one eastern European critic of the command economy called the communist bosses a "new class" that exploited their economies as ruthlessly as nineteenth-century capitalists. They failed to keep the promise of socialism and were incapable of achieving the economic performance of the capitalist countries. In economic terms, the command economy proved ultimately to be bankrupt.

JAPAN'S RECOVERY FROM DEFEAT

In August 1945, the Japanese imperial government surrendered unconditionally to the Allies, accepting American military occupation and the imposition of peace terms decided by the Allies. The defeat was complete, both militarily and psychologically. The Japanese people heard their emperor in his first radio broadcast accept in his name the surrender and the loss of independence, a humiliation "unendurable" and "insufferable" but nonetheless inescapable. For another six years, American occupation authorities governed this defeated empire. Only the position of emperor reminded the people of Japan's imperial past. Like Germany, Japan was only a ghost of its former self.

U.S. Occupation of Japan

The treatment accorded the two defeated states was not identical, however. Japanese occupation was the sole responsibility of the United States. Its navy and air force had played the key role in the defeat of the Japanese Empire. American military forces alone occupied the country following the surrender. General Douglas MacArthur, U.S. Army commander-in-chief in the Pacific theater, became the Supreme Commander for the Allied Powers in Japan. He held absolute power in that country and was accountable only to the U.S. president. The territory he governed remained intact. The Soviet Union requested a separate occupation zone; MacArthur refused, and no Soviet occupation forces reached Japan. An Allied council had nominal authority to oversee MacArthur's work; in fact, it merely approved policies the supreme commander had already decided upon. Japanese occupation was a U.S., not an Allied, affair. Late in 1945, Stalin complained to the U.S. ambassador in Moscow that the Soviet general on the Allied council in Japan "was treated like a piece of extra furniture," but his protest was halfhearted. He accepted the fact that Japan was in the U.S. sphere of influence.

The fact that the United States exercised such extraordinary control over Japan led to a second important feature of Allied occupation. A central Japanese government carried out the orders of the supreme commander (in Germany no national government existed at any time during the occupation). The symbol of Japan's unity remained the emperor. Despite his purely titular political role, the Japanese continued to treat him as a semidivine person.

When MacArthur assumed his post of supreme commander in late 1945, Emperor Hirohito made a brief ceremonial call, placing himself at the mercy of the victors. He informed General MacArthur that he wished to assume "sole responsibility for every political and military decision made and action taken by [his] people in the conduct of war" and to be judged for their conduct. Although the U.S. government was determined to punish Japanese war criminals, MacArthur decided not to hold Hirohito responsible. He preferred to obtain the emperor's backing for his occupation policies. His decision spared the Japanese people the humiliation of seeing their emperor tried like a common criminal. Hirohito's responsibility for the conduct of the war was left a state secret. Japan maintained its political unity and its imperial monarch, under American orders.

The country over which MacArthur assumed command was in ruins. Total Japanese casualties numbered nine million. All major Japanese cities had been destroyed—most by massive U.S. bombing raids, Hiroshima and Nagasaki by single atomic bombs—and millions of civilians were homeless. The merchant marine had lost almost all its ships. Most of the textile factories and coal mines had ceased to function, and food production had fallen to nearly half its prewar level. To add to the miseries, more than six million Japanese who had lived in overseas imperial territories had fled to or were forced to return to Japan.

The destruction went much deeper than life and property. Respect for Japanese military leadership had vanished with the humiliating defeat. American ascendancy over the Japanese state and people undermined national pride and deference to the old elite. The Japanese empire-nation had lost its guiding code of behavior, leaving many of its people in a state of collective shock.

Ruins of Asian War: Hiroshima, Dec. 1945 (*James Watkins Collection/Hoover Institution Archives*)

Their psychological response to surrender played an important part, albeit difficult to define, in the success of the American occupation. The most unusual aspect of the adaptation of the Japanese to the conquerors was their readiness to cooperate in the building of the new order imposed by the Americans. It reflected, in the opinion of a Japanese historian, a deep-seated hope that "something [could] be done" despite the terrible destruction and a widespread conviction that Japan's "path to future greatness lay in absorbing America's technological civilization."[1] The victors, in other words, held the key to recovery.

Reinforcing this attitude was the enormous respect General MacArthur enjoyed among the Japanese. His imperious manners, disliked by many Americans, embodied in the eyes of the vanquished Japanese the traditional authority of the warrior, displayed with remarkable American informality. Although he traveled daily in an open car to his headquarters, at no time in his six-year reign was he the target of an assassination attempt. The emperor had publicly accepted American rule and demonstrated his willingness to collaborate in the occupation. The Japanese people did the same.

During the years of occupation, U.S. authorities imposed a sweeping set of fundamental political reforms on the country. These included a new constitution, the introduction of universal suffrage, legal protection of women's rights, and the expansion of the entire educational system. More than 200,000 former officers and politicians were to be punished for wartime activities. Many individuals subject to purges vanished temporarily, however, only to reemerge in new positions of authority when the U.S. occupation ended. The purge included the trial and conviction of war criminals. Among the condemned was General Tojo, held guilty of

launching the war, and the military commander of the Philippines. Many Japanese, unaware of the brutality of Japanese treatment of defeated peoples, found the principles applied in these trials to be a conqueror's justice. From a global perspective, the trials were a manifestation of Western confidence in an international code of law to govern war.

The new constitution was the principal political reform introduced during the occupation. MacArthur took direct responsibility for the constitutional reform. He presented the Japanese government with the document he expected them to approve. When translated into Japanese, its passages sounded to one Tokyo newspaper commentator "exotically like American English." MacArthur also insisted that it include an introduction stating that "never again shall we be visited with the horrors of war through the action of government." No other constitution in the world made pacifism a political principle. It was another clear indication of the extraordinary circumstances of U.S. military occupation. Despite its exotic aspects, the constitution fit well the expectations and past democratic practices of Japanese citizens. It drew heavily on the British cabinet system and did not differ substantially from Japanese parliamentary democracy of the 1920s. A popularly elected parliament held sovereign power, choosing the cabinet headed by a prime minister. It became with relative ease the fundamental law of the land.

U.S. economic reforms were intended to restructure Japanese businesses and property holdings. They touched agriculture, industry, and labor. The new laws on farming property produced the most important and enduring changes in economic life. The American occupation authorities ordered the massive redistribution of farmland. It was taken from absentee landlords who were paid a price so low that their land was, in reality, confiscated. Over one-third of all Japanese arable land was transferred to five million farmers, pre-

[1]Masataka Kosaka, *A History of Postwar Japan* (Tokyo, 1972), p. 35.

viously tenants without their own land. The reform was so extensive that it resembled the initial land reforms in communist China and earned MacArthur the reputation of a radical. Some American critics called him a "socialist." As a result, the farmers became a major conservative political force in the country, supporting the new order that had given them their own farms.

U.S. efforts to encourage small business and labor proved much less successful. The spirit of these reforms resembled Franklin Roosevelt's New Deal reforms of the 1930s. This American version of free enterprise did not take hold among the Japanese business and political elite. An industrial reform broke up several of the giant economic firms, the *zaibatsu*, blamed by Americans for collaborating in the Japanese war effort. The U.S. occupation authorities passed laws intended to "tear down the concentration of economic power" in Japan. They promised that capitalist entrepreneurial opportunities would be "redistributed peacefully" among small enterprises. Conditions became more favorable for new business activities. Very large Japanese business firms, however, reemerged within a few years and soon dominated the country's industrial economy.

For a few years new laws protected and encouraged labor unions for factory workers and state employees. This led to a labor militancy unexpected by the reformers. Workers turned to socialist and communist union organizers and activists. Many unions came under the control of the Communist Party. Continued labor discontent, fed by shortages of basic goods and exploited by communist labor leaders, produced bitter strikes in 1946 and 1947. When the unions called in early 1948 for a nationwide strike, MacArthur used his exceptional powers as Supreme Allied Commander to forbid the strike.

By then the U.S. authorities in Japan had decided that economic reconstruction and so-

cial stability had to be their highest priority. They sided with Japanese management and withdrew their support for labor unions. This conservative social policy set the pattern for Japanese capitalism in the decades to come. The U.S. occupation authorities installed in Japan a type of democratic, free enterprise system that promoted political and economic practices closely resembling those in Japan of the 1920s.

The new Japanese political leadership, apparently subservient to the occupation authorities, in fact had an important role to play in the introduction of this new order. Japan had a strong socialist movement, though split into several parties, and the labor unions attracted millions of members on promises of fundamental social improvements. These groups proposed reforms far more extensive than the measures backed by the U.S. occupation authorities. They had no real opportunity, though, to introduce their reform projects. In the 1947 elections, the Socialist Party, with the largest vote, obtained only 25 percent of the total. It set up a coalition cabinet. U.S. occupation authorities' hostility to the Socialist Party was decisive in ending this first (and only) left-wing government in Japan's postwar history. They were very suspicious of any socialist reforms. As in Germany, they judged political conservatives best suited to Cold War policies. Political power shifted to the right, organized in the coalition of the Liberal and Democratic parties (soon to become one party). Their leader was Shigeru Yoshida.

Backed by the U.S. authorities, Yoshida became the dominant force in Japanese politics for the following decade. Dissension among the left-wing parties assured the Liberal-Democratic coalition control in parliament and leadership of the cabinet. The goals of the conservatives were to encourage Japanese business interests and to hasten the end of U.S. occupation. Rising Cold War tensions pushed the U.S. authorities to rely increasingly on the

Liberal-Democrats to assist them in their new containment policies. In 1948, Yoshida became the Japanese prime minister.

In a major policy change (paralleling that in Germany), the U.S. government set out to hasten Japanese economic recovery by all possible means. The reform of Japanese economic and social institutions became a secondary consideration. MacArthur declared in 1948 that he wished to make Japan a "self-supporting nation" capable of resisting Soviet pressure from abroad and radical political agitation from within. In 1949, he used his occupation powers to force the Japanese government to drastically cut its expenses and to reduce the budget deficit to bring down inflation. This fiscal conservatism was essential to the country's economic growth under a free enterprise system.

Yoshida cooperated, for he welcomed the end to social reform policies. His collaboration had the strong backing of Japanese business and financial leaders, who were key supporters of his party. He also assisted in the creation of an anticommunist labor union movement and in the purge of Communists from administrative and union jobs. The new industrial unions cooperated with management, which held down wages and increased investments (a formula for recovery applied also in West Germany).

Yoshida's collaboration made him a valuable ally for the United States. It also advanced the political fortunes of his party and the conservative program it supported. By 1950, the labor union movement had declined, torn by battles between Communists and non-communists and weakened by conservative U.S. occupation policies. The primacy of business interests, the weakening of labor, and conservative political rule by Yoshida's Liberal-Democratic cabinet remained the dominant trends of Japanese internal politics in the decades ahead.

Japan in the Cold War

Once the enemy, Japan became a close ally of the United States in the Cold War years. The Korean War turned Japan into a major East Asian base for U.S. military forces. Its geographical position on the eastern borders of the Soviet Union made it a desirable location for air bases for the U.S. Strategic Air Command, and its ports provided harbors to the U.S. Navy. The basic reforms had gone into effect, and Japanese political leadership was in the hands of conservatives. In 1951, the U.S. military ended its occupation of Japan, signing a peace treaty with the Japanese government. The peace treaty left Japan in possession of its Main Islands. It lost the Kuril Islands and Sakhalin to the Soviet Union. Taiwan was independent, and Okinawa was occupied by the United States. Japan began reparations payments to the countries conquered during the war (except communist China, with whom it had no diplomatic relations).

The Japanese government had little choice in devising its own foreign policy. Its margin of maneuver was small, for it was caught on the front lines of the Cold War and near the borders of the new People's Republic of China. Some Japanese nationalists hoped to restore Japan to a position of independent East Asian power, protected by its own army and navy and free to set its own course between the superpowers. Antimilitarists and pacifists, on the contrary, urged the neutralization of their country. They argued that Japan should take no part in the Cold War and should refuse the presence of any military forces, either its own or American, on its territory.

Prime Minister Yoshida chose a compromise between these two positions. In the U.S.-Japanese Security Treaty of 1952, he accepted a military alliance with the United States, permitting U.S. military bases in Japan and leaving his country (like West Germany) under the protection of the U.S. "nuclear umbrella." He agreed to comply with U.S. Cold War policies. Among the Japanese, the most controversial policy was nonrecognition of communist China. It was a decision imposed by the United States. For another twenty years Japan had no official relations with its powerful neighbor. Yoshida refused, however, to give in to repeated requests from the U.S. government that Japan rearm beyond the minimum level of its self-defense forces. In those years his country was a disarmed state, relying on U.S. military protection and free to devote its energies and resources to economic growth.

The U.S. alliance aroused bitter controversy in Japan throughout the 1950s. The Security Treaty set the terms of this uneven union between the mightiest military power in the world, the United States, and its former Asian enemy. Opposition to its terms came principally from the Socialist Party and from a very strong pacifist movement. In 1959, when the treaty was being renegotiated, political opposition and street demonstrations grew so violent that the government was for a time paralyzed. This was the most serious crisis that Japan's parliamentary regime had confronted since the war. In the end, the Japanese public turned against the violent tactics of the opponents to the new treaty. It was ratified virtually by force in parliament that year. In return, the conservative prime minister resigned to quiet protests at his undemocratic handling of the crisis.

The "Economic Miracle"

Japan's phenomenal economic expansion began ten years after the war. First the country had to pass through a period of painful recovery from wartime destruction and the loss of colonial territories. Japanese businessmen remained in the postwar years reluctant to begin real reconstruction of the economy.

They lacked foreign markets, had no domestic shipping industry, and feared the consequences of worker unrest and U.S.-imposed social reforms. By the early 1950s, these issues had been resolved to their satisfaction. The political conservatism of Yoshida and the ruling Democratic-Liberal coalition protected and reassured investors, and labor agitation subsided. Beginning in 1950, large U.S. purchases of goods for the troops in Korea gave a strong boost to the Japanese economy. The U.S. government permitted Japanese goods unrestricted entry into the American market. It began a major program of economic aid, the Dodge Plan (comparable to the Marshall Plan for Europe), encouraging the use of these funds for the modernization of the Japanese economy. Finally, it made U.S. modern technology accessible to Japanese entrepreneurs. Little did it expect the extraordinary success of these businesses in using that technology to build a great new industrial empire.

These favorable financial, commercial, and technological conditions laid the foundation for what became known as the Japanese "economic miracle." Per capita national income reached the prewar level in 1956. At about the same time food rationing finally came to an end. Japanese families still had to content themselves with a very modest standard of living. Surplus wealth went primarily into economic expansion. The Japanese people put into savings an average of 20 percent of their income (in the United States, savings averaged only 7 percent in the early 1960s). Industries went heavily into debt, using the savings of the Japanese people to invest in new products, new machinery, and the formation of commercial companies engaged in foreign trade. By the late 1950s, the economy was growing at the extraordinary rate of 10 percent a year; national income doubled every seven years. No Western capitalist country had ever matched that rate of expansion.

Foreign and Japanese observers debated the causes of this remarkable turnaround in the economic fortunes of the country. Some emphasized the superior educational level of the Japanese, highly trained and able to adapt easily to a new industrial era of complex electronic technology. Others underlined the favorable international conditions, including U.S. free trade and technology and the rising demand for products in Asia and the West. Everyone agreed that collaboration between government officials and leaders of industry had proven successful in their joint effort to expand Japan's share of the global industrial market. The conservative government committed financial resources, decreed legal protection, and created public agencies for the development of Japanese commerce and industry. The principal instrument of this free-enterprise planning system was the Ministry of International Trade and Industry (MITI). Its officials used their extensive authority over the country's financial and trading activities to oversee Japanese economic development.

The Japanese business and government elite put in place an economic system that came to be known as "guided capitalism." Bureaucrats in MITI gathered economic data to forecast international trends in technology and industry. With this information they recommended economic objectives for big business. The government used tariffs to create protectionist hurdles to foreign imports competing with Japanese goods. Businesses producing profitable exports received state subsidies in the form of low-interest loans. Guided capitalism cemented the alliance of conservative politicians, state officials, and business leaders. The Japanese respected democratic procedures, but behind the scenes, real political power depended on what one Western observer called Japan's "authoritarian institutions and techniques."

A quarter century after its crushing defeat, Japan had emerged as one of the most productive, prosperous countries in the world. Its form of capitalism was studied and imitated by other Asian states. In the 1970s, the formula proved remarkably successful in South Korea, Taiwan, and Singapore, which together with Japan were labeled the "Four Dragons" of East Asia. Their economies boomed. With growth rates of nearly 10 percent a year, all four doubled their economic wealth every ten years. Many Asian leaders heralded guided capitalism as the "Asian way" to economic prosperity.

New industries sprang from the enterprise of Japanese businessmen. They proved remarkably capable at turning Western technology into reliable, inexpensive products. The story of some of these entrepreneurs reveals important characteristics of the Japanese "economic miracle." In the late 1940s, a young Japanese mechanic, Sochiro Honda, began to make motorcycles at a price far below Western imports. By the end of the 1950s, his firm was the largest maker of motorcycles in the world, with markets throughout Asia and in the West. He enjoyed even greater success when his factories shifted to automobiles. When electronic inventions in the West opened up a new consumer market for television, a Japanese electronics engineer started a small firm in 1958 with $500 and seven workers to make some of these electronic items. His firm, Sony, became one of the principal world producers of television equipment. Recognition of new opportunities and quality work were important factors assuring the success of Japanese entrepreneurs offering new products for consumers in the expanding global economy.

Individual initiative combined in Japan with the old techniques of giant corporate management and government support. The major enterprises, called by the Japanese "business communities," brought banking, transportation, and sales operations into one firm, with branches extending into Asia and the West. Their employees and workers, grouped in company unions with guaranteed lifetime employment and high wages, were the aristocracy of the labor force. They were far better off than those workers in small businesses, where labor was poorly paid and unemployment a constant threat.

Deprived of its overseas empire by defeat in war, the Japanese state made its economic might the foundation on which it built up a regional sphere of influence. The United States remained the major market for Japanese exports. Soon Japanese investors and exporters established important business connections in Southeast Asia. Japanese-owned factories appeared throughout the region, assembling products made with inexpensive labor and Japanese technology. With the government's encouragement, Japanese businessmen invested in the new electronic industry. By the 1980s, Japan was a global center of computer manufacturing. Rapid expansion of the country's nuclear-power industry was another key decision of the Japanese government. In an era of Middle Eastern oil crises, it was determined to free the country from dependence on imported petroleum and coal. Until the 1990s, guided capitalism remained Japan's key to economic success. Then it lost the capacity to generate rapid growth as competition from other East Asian economies cut into its overseas market, still the major source of sales in a country where the population lived modestly, and continued to save a substantial part of their income.

By then, the U.S.-Japanese alliance had become an unusual, awkward partnership. U.S. diplomatic and military influence remained great, but Japanese financial and technological achievements gave its banks and industrial corporations an important role in the U.S. economy. Each year Japanese exports brought in tens of billions of dollars in foreign earnings. A part of these funds was reinvested in the U.S. financial and real estate markets. Each country depended on the other. The Japanese economy was earning profits on a par with U.S. businesses. The

Japanese population had reached a standard of living equal to that of Americans. Although Emperor Hirohito's death in 1989 briefly revived memories of the war and Japanese military defeat, by then it seemed part of a distant past.

SUMMARY

War and revolution had profoundly altered the history of East Asia. Japan no longer possessed either a great empire or a powerful military. Having occupied a vast area of East and Southeast Asia, it had to abandon all its conquered territories. Its defeat opened the way to revolution and the emergence of new nation-states in that vast area.

The victory of the Chinese Communists transformed the political landscape of East Asia. Although Mao's vision of utopian socialism brought the country two decades of political and social turmoil, the Communist Party dictatorship was unshakeable. The Chinese Statue of Democracy, erected by supporters of democratic reform on Tiananmen Square in 1989, fell that June when the tanks of the PLA crushed the protest movement. Ten years later, Japan's new Statue of Liberty (copied from the U.S. statue) was a tourist attraction as well as a symbol of Japan's postwar transformation. Japanese national pride suffered terribly in the aftermath of defeat, but the nation's ability to collaborate in the new economic endeavor brought Japan back among the great powers of the world.

Behind the diversity of historical experiences are apparent important similarities in the recent history of that region. This pattern repeats itself in different ways in other parts of Asia, the Middle East, and Africa. Movements for national independence became powerful political forces. The goal of economic development became an integral part of political action and of popular hopes. In China, unheroic but effective programs for economic growth replaced Mao's utopian campaigns of communist equality. The overriding goal was to raise production and to improve the people's standard of living and well-being.

East Asia became more, not less, involved in global affairs after the fall of the great empires. The superpowers extended their rivalry into the region, and governments there looked to the West or to the Soviet Union for economic aid and for military support. Global markets lured manufacturers and governments to compete on an international scale. National independence and global interdependence constituted two inextricable facets of the postwar history of East Asia.

DATES WORTH REMEMBERING

1949	Creation of People's Republic of China
1950	Chinese conquest of Tibet
1951	End of U.S. occupation of Japan
1956	Beginning of Japanese economic boom
1959–1971	Tibetan revolt
1958–1960	Great Leap Forward in China
1959	Flight of Dalai Lama to India
1966–1975	Great Proletarian Cultural Revolution in China
1975	Death of Mao Zedong
1978	End of collective farming in China
1980	Introduction of "one child" policy in China
1989	Suppression of democratic movement in China

RECOMMENDED READING

Communist China

*John Avedon (1988), *In Exile from the Land of Snows: The Dalai Lama and Tibet since the Chinese Conquest* (1984). A sympathetic history of contemporary Tibet and its leader.

Stanley Karnow, *Mao and China: Inside China's Cultural Revolution* (1985). A careful study of the most destructive years of Mao's reign.

*Jonathan Spence, *The Search for Modern China* (1990). An ambitious effort to place China's communist regime within the story of the great historical transformation of the country.

Postwar Japan

*John Dower, *Embracing Defeat: Japan in the Wake of World War II* (1999). A thoughtful study of Japan's painful renewal following defeat.

Akira Iriyi, *The Cold War in Asia* (1974). An international history of East Asia that integrates Japan into the Cold War conflict.

*Edwin Reischauer, *The Japanese Today: Change and Continuity* (1995). A brief survey of recent Japanese social, cultural, and political history by one of the senior historians in the field.

Karl van Wolferen, *The Enigma of Japanese Power* (1989). A critical assessment of democracy, Japanese-style.

Memoirs and Visual Aids

*Orville Schell, *To Get Rich Is Glorious: China in the Eighties* (1984). The perceptive observations of an old China hand watching with amazement the emergence of private enterprise in communist China.

Small Happiness (1980). A close-up documentary film, made by a team of Western anthropologists, of a Chinese village in the 1960s, paying particular attention to the new freedom enjoyed by women.

---

*Indicates book is available in paperback.

CHAPTER TEN

10

New Nations in South Asia

- The New Island Republics
- Independence for India and Pakistan
- The Nation-States of India and Pakistan

Highlight: New Nations and Ethnic Conflict

Spotlight: Sukarno

Within a few years of the end of the Second World War, the Western empires in South Asia had vanished. The Dutch left their colony in the East Indies, the United States gave full independence to the Philippines, and the British granted freedom to India, Burma, and Malaya. The political transition, coming in some cases after centuries of colonial rule, was abrupt. The move to independence was accompanied in some countries by civil war and ethnic conflict, leaving bitter memories and antagonism among the newly freed peoples. Although the Western states had ruled their colonies by force of arms, they also recruited and trained increasing numbers of their colonial subjects for military and administrative service. Lan-

guages in common use in their colonial borders gave ethnically diverse peoples a useful means of communication. Their years of rule had brought economic investment for the extraction of raw materials needed in Western industry, including the construction of railroads and ports. The centuries of imperial rule left their mark on economic and political life in the new states to follow.

Throughout South Asia, the anticolonial movements that took power made national unity the foundation of their plans for independence. It was a generous vision that held together leaders and supporters as long as the immediate aim was the expulsion of Western colonial rulers. It proved a difficult ideal to

279

incorporate afterwards into the life of the new states. Leaders spoke of a nationalism that would transcend the deep internal social, religious, and cultural divisions within their countries, implying that they sought a nation-state of toleration and freedom for all. But they found that ethnic and religious bonds remained a powerful force among their peoples. Separatist movements often emerged whose goal was to defend the interests and integrity of their own community. Ethnic nationalism threatened the newly won unity of these states. Faced with abiding social disagreements and conflict, leaders often turned to authoritarian rule as a substitute for elusive national unity.

Freedom brought within the newly independent lands an awareness of fundamental differences separating them from their former empires and the West. The broadest definition of this uniqueness came from the Indian leader Jawaharlal Nehru. Decolonization had, in his opinion, created the collective need for peace among the liberated peoples of the globe. He sought to distance his country from the international conflicts of the Cold War. Many other leaders shared his view and supported a policy of "nonalignment," refusing to ally with either the West or the Soviet bloc. Nehru described their place in the new world order as the "Third World," separate from the democratic "First World" and the communist "Second World."

The differences were not so great that these new nation-states could ignore the more industrialized countries. Their leaders confronted acute problems of poverty and economic backwardness that required outside help and aid. Their efforts to raise living conditions and to stimulate economic growth relied in some cases on the free-enterprise system of the West, in others on the central government controls resembling the command economy that Stalin's Soviet state had instituted. While often looking to foreign lands for aid and guidance, they adapted and altered these policies and institutions to suit their needs.

THE NEW ISLAND REPUBLICS

The history of the countries of Southeast Asia in the quarter century after the war followed a common pattern. The first years were a period of decolonization, that is, the elimination of political ties to Western states and the first stages of state-building. The new regimes set out to define a new international policy in their relations with East and West, gathering to discuss common problems and policies even when they were deeply divided on the most desirable course to take. Their political development in the following decade shifted toward authoritarian rule, with small groups of leaders controlling elections by means of political followers and clients. Everywhere economic development was an increasing concern. Poverty remained an abiding presence among both urban and rural masses, while business and bureaucratic elites built up great wealth. Social and ethnic unrest erupted at times in spontaneous uprisings, giving support to guerrilla movements organized by revolutionary parties. State-building constituted a complex, often violent, process.

Independence for the Philippines

Liberation of the Philippines from Japanese rule came with the return in 1944 of General MacArthur and U.S. forces. Before the war, the U.S. government had granted the Philippines self-rule in a political system copied from the American constitution, with an elected president and legislature. Dominating the political life of the islands were powerful families. Their power depended on their great wealth, which they used to sustain

Postcolonial South Asia

a political patronage system employing political "clients" to carry out their orders. They
were the real rulers of the Philippines.

Japanese occupation had only worsened
the hardship of the peasant farmers, who
made up the bulk of the population. They

were forced to pay heavy taxes to their conquerors. In protest, a major peasant uprising
had begun in 1943. The rebels attacked both
the Japanese occupation forces and the great
landowners, many of whom collaborated with
the Japanese. This rural unrest, combined with

ethnic hostility among the peoples scattered across the archipelago, remained the major source of conflict in the postwar years.

In 1946, the United States formally granted independence to a new Philippine government. The first elected president had himself worked for a short period with the Japanese. His administration, like the preceding one, made no effort to punish collaborators. The transfer of political power to the Philippine people did not weaken the dominance of landowners and business elites. No revolutionary movement swept in new leaders or offered the peasant population a concrete plan for land reform. Independence came peaceably without upsetting the privileges and comforts of the Philippine upper classes.

Remnants of the colonial order continued to shape the country's economic and diplomatic relations with the United States. Reliance on U.S. leadership in world affairs was a guiding principle of the new Philippine regime. It joined the Western bloc in the Cold War, signing a military alliance with the United States that left in place American naval and air bases in the Philippine archipelago. In exchange, it received military and economic aid from the United States. It remained closely bound to the capitalist system brought by their American rulers, preserving the laws that protected its market economy.

The country's foreign trade was tied as tightly as before to the U.S. economy. Special trade agreements permitted Philippine goods to enter the United States without tariffs, and few restrictions stood in the way of Philippine families who wished to migrate to America. In return, U.S. investors received special financial incentives to create new companies in the republic. Close ties existed between Philippine traders and industrialists and U.S. bankers and manufacturers. The interests of the Philippine government and middle classes were closely bound to those of the U.S. government and economy. Socialist experiments had no place in the new order.

Despite social inequality and ethnic diversity, Philippine leaders were able in a few years to build the foundations of national unity. The greatest danger to the new government was the peasant uprising on the main island of Luzon. By the late 1940s, it had grown into a major rebellion with its own People's Liberation Army. It drew its support from landless farmers, who were bitter enemies of the large landowners. Beginning in 1950, Ramon Magsaysay, the dynamic and popular leader of the army, organized effective resistance to the guerrillas. Initially successful in taking control of large areas of the countryside, the insurgents lost support when the government finally passed reform laws to give land to tenant farmers. Most peasants abandoned the rebellion in exchange for ownership of their own land. Magsaysay proved a charismatic nationalist leader, very popular with the masses. His formula of reform and reconciliation successfully ended the insurrection by 1951. That year Philippine voters elected Magsaysay to the post of Philippine president, which he retained until his death in 1957. For a few years, the new Philippine nation-state enjoyed a period of peace, democratic government, and economic growth.

In the next decade, though, the republic's democratic constitution and representative government became subverted by a handful of powerful political bosses. Democracy turned into elite rule. The Philippine leader Benigno Aquino, writing in the late 1960s, lamented that his land was "consecrated to democracy but run by an entrenched plutocracy," and "dedicated to equality but mired in an archaic system of caste." One of these power-hungry politicians, Ferdinand Marcos, was for a decade dictator in all but name. The Philippines became a land of political intrigue, increasingly torn by civil rebellion.

Elected president in 1965, Marcos had manipulated his legal position to expand enormously his presidential powers. His real backing came from his informal network of supporters whom he had recruited through the system of political patronage. Marcos justified his increasingly authoritarian rule by pointing to the social disorder and ethnic conflicts that continued to mark the country's political life. Muslim groups in the southern Philippines had rebelled against the central government and the presence of Catholics and the Catholic Church on their islands. In northern islands, communist-led guerrilla movements reappeared among the poor peasantry. But Marcos's brutal methods and corrupt regime failed to halt the disorder. Rather than allow new elections, Marcos proclaimed a regime of martial law in 1972. With the backing of the army, he arrested his political opponents and ended the constitutional guarantees of political and civil liberties.

His dictatorship did not resolve any of the major problems confronting his country. His regime was never capable of repressing the communist and Muslim uprisings. It was unable to improve economic conditions in the cities and in the countryside, despite vast amounts of U.S. military and economic aid. He used his authoritarian powers to amass enormous wealth for his family (some estimates after his fall placed his total wealth at more than $1 billion) and to enrich his cronies and his powerful political machine. Power brought enormous benefits to him and to his followers. By the early 1980s, his corruption and political repression had aroused outrage throughout the country. Even the Catholic Church joined the call for his removal from power. In 1986, he had to flee the country when army leaders turned against him. By then the political opposition had reached the proportions of a mass uprising.

His successor as president was Corazon Aquino. She was the widow of a prominent opponent of the regime, Benigno Aquino, whom Marcos had ordered assassinated in 1983. She promised to restore democratic rule and reunite the country, but the heritage of decades of economic decay and authoritarian rule posed enormous problems. The country had preserved its national unity and restored democratic government, but it could not end the

revolt among the Muslim populations on the southern islands. Nationalists could claim victory in their efforts to end the presence of U.S. military bases on the archipelago. In 1994, they rejoiced at the closure of the last U.S. naval base, whose buildings Philippino investors converted into headquarters for start-up computer and Internet companies. The global economy had replaced the Cold War as the Philippines' major link to the outside world.

Sukarno and Indonesia

In the East Indies, years of colonial war between Indonesian nationalists and Dutch forces followed liberation from Japan. Before withdrawing from the East Indies in August 1945, the Japanese occupation authorities had allowed nationalist collaborators to proclaim the independence of their country. No Allied troops reached the East Indies until weeks later. In the interval, nationalists created a government for a state that they baptized "Indonesia." Their leader was Sukarno. For the previous twenty years, he had campaigned against Dutch rule, preaching a semireligious message of Indonesian nationalist revival. His creed proved less important in the independence movement than his charismatic hold over the Indonesian peoples. They found inspiration in his promise of Indonesian rebirth following independence.

When in late 1945 Dutch armed forces reached the islands, they ended this first brief moment of independence. The leaders of the Netherlands had desperate need of their vast colony, whose valuable resources, especially petroleum, were vital for the reconstruction of their war-torn homeland. But years of colonial war that followed failed to reestablish Dutch control over the vast East Indian archipelago. U.S. opposition to their colonial war and their failure to end the insurrection brought the conflict to an end in 1949 (see Chapter 7). The Netherlands abandoned its colonial empire in Asia. Sukarno and his nationalist followers had won.

◀ SPOTLIGHT: Sukarno ▶

In the early twentieth century, most of the peoples who inhabited the main islands of the Dutch colony of the East Indies still lived in isolation from one another and treated inhabitants from other islands as foreigners. The father of Sukarno (1901–1970) was from the island of Java, but because he was one of the Dutch's few well-educated subjects he found work as a schoolteacher on the island of Bali. There he married a Balinese woman, whose parents were so outraged at her choice of an "outsider" from Java for a husband that they expelled her from the family. A half century later, her son became the supreme leader of the new nation-state of Indonesia. It gathered within its borders all the islands of the vast archipelago of some 17,000 islands that the Dutch had gradually conquered over the previous 200 years in forming their East Indian colony. It was an improbable dream of national unity that Sukarno and his followers made happen in the face of enormous obstacles.

Sukarno acquired his nationalist convictions while a student in the schools that the Dutch had founded to provide the colony with loyal native officials. His father was, as most Indonesians, a Muslim but preferred to give his son a nonreligious education. Sukarno's university training drew him away from the narrow, insular identity of an islander from Java, for it gave him the tools to imagine a unique Indonesian nation. As a boy he spoke both Javanese and Balinese. His schooling gave him fluency in Dutch (and later French and English), which opened up before him the literature of European nationalism. There he learned of the glory of national cultures, the dignity of independent, self-governing nations, and the injustice of empires and monarchs. His friendship with the first generation of Indonesian nationalists brought him within the circle of political parties already proclaiming their vision of a free Indonesia and fighting the Dutch rulers to make their dream come true. Sukarno communicated most often in the language of his imperial rulers (just as Indian nationalists relied on English). He also made use of the Malay dialect that was becoming the common tongue among East Indies subjects, including the traders who moved among the islands and the native officials helping the Dutch. Sukarno's nationalism was shaped by the very Dutch imperialists whom he and his followers considered their worst enemies.

His revolutionary activities took shape within the Indonesian National Party, which he founded but whose goal of a nation called "Indonesia" was a creation of predecessors in the Indonesian nationalist movement. He fought the Dutch through his writings and speeches and for that suffered years of imprisonment and exile. He proved himself an extraordinarily successful public figure, attracting a following through the force of his personality as much as through his message of national liberation. Over the years, he gradually codified his own nationalist ideology, which he called the "Five Principles" of Indonesian unity. These were nationalism (opposition to any insular hostility among the islanders), internationalism (acknowledging the rights of other nations), democracy (to him referring to a consensus, not majority rule), social well-being (care for the peoples of the nation), and belief in one supreme God (toleration for all religions). Like other twenti-eth-century revolutionaries, he believed in the power of ideas to produce a radical, progressive change in the way of life of the masses of the population. His was a creed of civic nationalism, adapted to the peculiar conditions of the East Indies (see "Highlight," this chapter). Like the creed that Gandhi formulated for India, it promised the new nation peace and prosperity on the condition the peoples there overcome their ethnic, religious, and social antagonism. In these terms, it appeared a utopian vision. For him, it had the force of a religious faith, for which he sacrificed the security and comfort of ordinary life.

Sukarno struggled throughout his years in the nationalist resistance to make that dream come true. In the course of the Second World War, he collaborated with the Japanese occupiers. They welcomed the help of anti-Western nationalists. In return, he spoke publicly in support of the Japanese requests for Indonesian laborers needed to assist their war construction projects (virtually forced labor). By the end of the war, he was the undisputed leader of the Indonesian liberation movement. With the defeat of Japan in August 1945, he proclaimed the independence of Indonesia. He was the founder of a new nation-state.

In the years after the defeat of the Dutch in 1949, he found that his Five Principles were a poor substitute for effective rule, for which he had little taste. In 1957, he gave in to the temptation to assume dictatorial powers in what he called a "Guided Democracy." Behind him the Indonesian army stood as the guarantor of his leadership and of the unity of his nation-state. His leadership consisted principally in speeches condemning global imperialism and capitalism for his country's ills. His feeble answer to Indonesia's economic decline and ethnic conflicts was to praise the Indonesian Communist

Party's proposals for a single-party state and a command economy similar to that of the People's Republic of China. His awareness of his own inadequacy as a leader is the best explanation why in 1965 he encouraged the communist plot to eliminate their military rivals for power. It was a fatal choice. The victorious generals forced him to resign the presidency, keeping him under house arrest for his few remaining years. His dream of an Indonesian nation-state had come true, but its continued existence depended on a military dictatorship.

Sukarno in World War II: Japanese 1944 pamphlet featuring picture of Sukarno to promote Indonesian labor brigades (*Hoover Institution Archives Collection*)

That year they proclaimed the victory of the independent Republic of Indonesia. Its borders were those put in place by the Dutch colonial rulers, and its state language was the Malay dialect that had become the common language among the subject peoples within the colony. Its new constitution promised parliamentary democracy to the 80 million people of the vast archipelago, whose islands stretched across 3,000 miles. The peoples were divided by great inequalities of wealth, different cultures and languages, and an age-old distrust of peoples of neighboring islands. Most of the population practiced the Muslim religion; within Indonesia's borders lived the single largest Muslim community of any state in the postcolonial world. Buddhism continued to exert a strong influence among peoples in the central islands of Java and Bali, and large Christian communities had emerged in regions where missionaries had been active. Political parties representing the various islands and peoples feuded among themselves, weakening their authority in a state unified only by its leader and by the nationalist liberation movement.

Sukarno was the national hero and became the first president of the republic. His stature rested not only on constitutional power and his nationalist ideology but also on his vast following among Indonesians. Many virtually worshiped him. He was the guarantor of Indonesian national unity. The government, which was a parliamentary democracy, was increasingly the scene of bitter political quarrels. Politicians from areas where Islam was powerful demanded that the state enforce Muslim religious laws among the population. Regional rivalries opposed the leaders of the various islands, many of whose peoples were deeply attached to their local culture. The army was the effective national institution, whose presence ensured the unity of the new state.

Sukarno needed the backing of the army, just as its commanders needed the national legitimacy that he embodied. In the mid-1950s, the alliance between the two became the foundation for authoritarian rule. Like many other leaders of Third World countries, Sukarno was persuaded that the welfare of his new state depended on his personal leadership. In 1956, he declared to Indonesians that he had dreamed of "burying" the old constitutional order and of giving his people what he called a "Guided Democracy" and a "Guided Economy." In 1957, he took command of the state. His dream, when put in practice, translated into political dictatorship, a nationalized economy under state planning controls, and diplomatic nonalignment in the Cold War.

Sukarno's leadership relied more on personal inspiration and favoritism than on coherent policies. His government seized all Dutch and other foreign businesses and estates, nationalizing the great oil fields of Royal Dutch-Shell. It lacked the trained personnel to run these state enterprises, however. As a result of this hasty nationalization, the country's economy passed through several years of painful recession. Sukarno did obtain the economic assistance of both Western and communist states, for the two sides were rivals there as elsewhere in the Third World. To win the backing of the many political factions in his country he offered their leaders positions in the largest cabinet of any country in the world. His one hundred ministers worked largely for their own benefit and that of their followers. Cronyism led to useless projects in the state-run businesses that enriched a handful of corrupt politicans backed by Sukarno. Meanwhile, the country went deeper and deeper into debt, and foreign trade declined for lack of funds to pay for imports.

Sukarno's dictatorship brought with it his own personality cult and nationalist ideology. He received the grand titles of "Permanent President" and "Great Leader of the Revolution." Boasting that his country was "living dangerously," Sukarno declared war on "neo-colonialism" (shortened to *nekolim* in his speeches) in all its forms. He blamed it for the economic hardship that his ineffective and corrupt regime had created. He encouraged the Indonesian army to seize islands on the borders of Indonesia, claiming them for his nation. Unity remained a fragile, contested creation. Sukarno and his army kept the island republic together, but the price was the growing hostility of minority peoples toward Indonesian rule.

Sukarno's nationalist ideology and flamboyant leadership hid serious political weaknesses undermining his state. He himself realized that his personal powers were inadequate to maintain national unity. His solution was to search for a mass movement on which he and his regime could rely. He came to believe that the Indonesian Communist Party, the largest political organization in the country, would provide him with that disciplined popular support. He hoped that its backing would win him the diplomatic and military aid of the People's Republic of China at a time when his government had few foreign allies. His rhetorical sparring with the West and expansionist foreign policy rested on a

National Heros and Imperialist Devils: Indonesian Government Poster "The Five Pillars [of Indonesian National Liberation] Crush All Forms of Imperialism," approx. 1960 (*Howard Jones Collection/Hoover Institution Archives*)

grandiose (and illusory) vision of Indonesia as a great power in southern Asia.

The encouragement that he gave the Communists proved to be his downfall. He became the center of a violent struggle for power. The Indonesian Communist Party and the army were bitter rivals for leadership in the country. The communist leaders seem to have believed that they had Sukarno's backing to seize power. In 1965, they secretly organized an armed uprising, beginning with the capture and execution of several of Indonesia's top military leaders. But the uprising failed, for the surviving generals, led by General Suharto, mobilized their troops to stop the insurrection. At the same time, they appealed to the population to join in resisting the Communists, whom they damned as "godless enemies" of the nation. Political revolt provoked mob executions.

Throughout the islands, crowds, often led by military units or militant Muslim gangs, attacked Communists and suspected allies. Political and ethnic animosity within Indonesia, stirred up by pressures of nation-building, suddenly erupted in terrible violence. It produced a butchering of Communists and their supporters, many of whom were drawn from the country's large Chinese community. Chinese migrants had moved to the East Indies during the centuries of Dutch rule. Many had become prosperous through trading and commerce. In a time of economic hardship, they became an easy target for the discontented, of whom there were many in Indonesia in the mid-1960s. Ethnic discord and political rivalries produced, there as elsewhere among the new nations, the seeds of mass violence. No one knows how many people died in the 1965 massacres. Conservative estimates point to a half-million dead.

In the turmoil, Sukarno's regime fell from power. He was no longer trusted by his generals. The head of the army, General Suharto, took over control of the state. Indonesia remained a neutral, nonaligned country, taking foreign aid from East and West. General Suharto and the army leaders made national unity in the archipelago their highest priority, holding in check the ethnic unrest and denying the political opposition any public forum. Their second priority was economic development. They took apart Sukarno's halfhearted command economy, ending state planning. They sold nationalized enterprises (often to their own cronies) and opened the country to foreign investors (who often had to pay enormous bribes to set up operations). A small group of Indonesian bankers and investors received special favors from Suharto's government. In return, they secretly opened special bank accounts for politically influential individuals, among whom Suharto and his family were the most favored. Military dictatorship bred "crony capitalism" throughout the islands.

Gradually the Indonesian economy began to grow. By the 1980s, its abundant natural resources had become the cornerstone of an economic boom. Asian timber companies moved into the forested regions of Sumatra and Borneo, removing the valuable hardwood trees, burning the remaining forests, and leaving the land for plantation farming (see "Highlight," Chapter 14). By the 1990s, this Indonesian version of the "Asian way" of capitalism had turned the economy into one of the "newly emerging markets" of Asia.

Its reliance on the global economy was also its weakness. The crony capitalism that had flourished since Sukarno's fall had bred reckless financial borrowing. In 1998, those debts became a crushing burden when international financial panic ruined the Indonesian currency and provoked sudden recession. In the chaos and disorder that followed, Suharto abandoned power. In democratic elections, the first in thirty-four years, Indonesian voters chose in 1999 moderate leaders to bring calm to their country. Fundamentalist Islamic parties seeking to create a Muslim state like Pakistan attracted few voters. Indonesia became, at a time when several other states fell under Islamic rule, a model of democracy in a multi-ethnic Muslim land.

Singapore and the Global Economy

The political fate of the island of Singapore depended on its neighboring states, all former colonies of the British Empire. In the territories of Burma and Malaya, the experience of the war years had given nationalist leaders the confidence to demand national independence after 1945. The new leaders of the British Empire made no effort to resist. The British Labor Party, in power after 1945, readily agreed to organize the transfer of power. Nationalists there welcomed the aid of British troops in defeating communist-led uprisings in their lands. In 1948, Burma became an independent state; a decade later, the Malay colonies became the nation-state of Malaysia.

The city of Singapore remained a British crown colony. Its economic and strategic importance far outweighed its minute size. It lay on the maritime path to East Asia and possessed the finest naval port in Southeast Asia. Its largely Chinese population had been instrumental in making it the commercial and financial capital of the region. It was the exception to anticolonialism, a prosperous remnant (like Hong Kong) of an empire surrounded by independent states.

The British government had no wish, or the financial means, to maintain for long even this minute imperial presence in the area. In 1963, it ended its rule over the city, convincing Singapore's leaders to join the Malaysian state in a federation. This new state was a fragile creation, made up of a multi-ethnic collection of disparate regions. The Muslim Malay peoples, largely peasants and lacking the commercial skills of the Chinese, resented the prosperity of Singapore. Their Muslim religious practices

and communal organization constituted a vital part of their lives. Many feared that their way of life would suffer if they were ruled by Chinese politicians. The intensity of ethnic antagonism between the two groups led to riots by minority Malay in the city of Singapore, and political quarrels within the federal government between the Chinese leaders of Singapore and Malay politicians. Malay leaders, fearing that the ethnic conflict would destroy their young state, decided to expel the city from the federation. In 1965, Singapore was forced to form its own independent state, an island of only two million people.

Its isolation proved a blessing. Its leaders were able to create the conditions for an economic boom that rivaled that of Japan. The island-state evolved into an authoritarian regime committed to state-supported economic development. In free elections, a majority of its population approved the program of the People's Action Party. Once in power, its leaders moved immediately to enforce public discipline and rapid economic growth. They virtually eliminated opposition political parties, independent trade unions, and any separatist ethnic movements among the city's Chinese, Malay, and Indian inhabitants. They severely punished all crimes, with small offenses punished by whipping with a birch rod (introduced first by the British). They instructed families to have more children when Singapore's birth rate fell too low. They turned their tiny state into a model of social order, economic productivity, and authoritarian rule. The leader of the People's Action Party and longtime prime minister, Lee Kuan Yew, promised Singapore's citizens an "orderly, organized, sensible, rational society."

This authoritarian regime settled down to guide its tiny state on the path to economic wealth. Its unstated bargain with the population called for their submission to authoritarianism, which it claimed was rooted in Confucianism, in exchange for economic prosperity. It invited foreign investors to develop oil refining and textile and electronic manufacturing, staffed by the island's industrious, educated workforce. It opened the door of the city-state to international banks and welcomed global commercial firms to use its port. On a small scale, it introduced to its island the "guided capitalism" that had succeeded so well in Japan. Not surprisingly, Lee Kuan Yew championed the cause of the special "Asian way" of orderly capitalist countries.

Singapore founded its prosperity on global economic expansion and on its internal political stability. In economic terms, it succeeded extraordinarily well, becoming one of the four East Asian lands called the "Four Dragons" for their booming growth rates. The city's rate of yearly economic growth rose to above 10 percent by the 1970s, remaining at that level for the next twenty years. Soon the population's standard of living was second only to that of Japan among Asian countries. Economic conditions on the island were the envy of surrounding states. Militarily insignificant, its security depended on its vital role in the economic activity of South Asia. It, too, was a nonaligned country, seeking good relations with all countries, communist and noncommunist, conducting financial and commercial affairs with whoever had the means to pay. Although it resembled in size a city-state of Renaissance Italy, it contained within its borders all the dynamic economic forces propelling the global boom of the late twentieth century.

INDEPENDENCE FOR INDIA AND PAKISTAN

The legacy of the Second World War in India differed from that of other countries in southern Asia in one important respect. Japanese armies had never penetrated deeply into Indian territory. The British viceroy, the Indian civil service, and the Indian army remained

the vital forces in the united provinces, while the six hundred princes who had accepted British rule continued to govern their principalities. Only those Indian soldiers who had been taken prisoner by the Japanese in 1942 and who had agreed to join the Indian National Army became collaborators against the British. Their welcome as heroes on their return to India in 1945 proved that opposition to the British overrode all other issues confronting Indians in the postwar years.

The End of British Rule

The National Congress leaders had vowed from the time they began their struggle for independence to preserve the unity that the British had given the subcontinent. They desired national independence and a democratically elected government that respected the rights of the entire population, regardless of religion or social rank. For Mohandas Gandhi, Congress's inspirational leader, special privileges for any religious community were a betrayal of his deepest belief in civic equality for all citizens within a free Indian nation-state. This vision was threatened by the social antagonism (termed *communalism*) that divided the Muslim and Hindu communities and by the demand by the Muslim League for a separate Muslim state. Indian unity and independence were inextricable goals for the National Congress, but only independence proved attainable.

The half century before 1945 had witnessed a rising number of violent incidents and riots pitting Hindus against Muslims. Every province mingled the two communities, though overall Hindus were the large majority. No single territory was exclusively Hindu or Muslim. The population of Calcutta, largest and most industrial of India's cities and the capital of the province of Bengal, was almost equally divided between these two groups. Their very proximity was a cause of friction and political rivalry, for self-rule raised the possibility of one community losing power to the other. Individual rights appeared to many Indians less important than communal solidarity. National independence threatened to tear India apart.

The Muslim League preferred the partition of the subcontinent between Muslim and Hindu territories to one unified nation-state. If a unified Indian state, ruled democratically, placed government in the hands of the National Congress, the League feared that the new rulers would deprive the minority Muslims of civil and political rights, regardless of the promises of Congress leaders. What to liberal idealists appeared democratic safeguards of individual freedom seemed to the League a threat of minority persecution. In the postwar years, it made the achievement of a separate Muslim state of Pakistan its immediate objective. Its leaders did not seek a religious (theocratic) regime, for they considered the label of *Muslim* to be an ethnic marker of social and cultural identity. Their plan was a tremendous gamble, for no such nation-state, organized around Muslim religious loyalty, had ever existed. Still, the followers of the Muslim League were prepared after war's end to resort to communal violence to prevent Indian national unification and to achieve their goal of Pakistan.

Preparing for Indian independence was the first priority for British and Indian leaders. The British Labor government supported freedom for the peoples of the subcontinent as strongly as they did the empire's other Asian colonies. Its postwar financial crisis dictated rapid liberation for India, whose rule placed a heavy burden on the impoverished British treasury. Mass demonstrations and violence were a constant threat. The British proposed new elections to select an Indian leadership ready and able to negotiate the terms of independence.

When those elections were held in 1946, National Congress candidates won a major-

ity in nearly all the provinces. Yet the Muslim League received the support of most Muslim voters. Who then spoke for India? Congress and the League both agreed to negotiations with the British, but each on its own terms. Mohammed Ali Jinnah, head of the Muslim League, demanded that Muslim representatives be granted an equal voice in negotiations alongside the Congress. But Jawaharlal Nehru and the other influential leaders of Congress refused to recognize the right of the League to represent the Muslim community, fearing that to do so would represent a fatal concession to partition. In July 1946, Jinnah concluded that his party could not become the sole negotiator for India's Muslims by legal means. He called on his Muslim supporters to prove forcefully to the British and to Congress their hold over the Muslim population.

The League's Day of Direct Action in August 1946 was the real turning point in the history of postwar India. Jinnah proclaimed that "the only solution to India's problem is Pakistan," that is, partition of the Indian subcontinent into what he referred to as "Hindustan" and his Muslim state. To make clear that civil war was the alternative, he demanded of Muslims throughout India that they join in "direct action," including strikes, meetings, and demonstrations. He and the other League leaders must have known that rioting would accompany the demonstrations and that communal conflict would inevitably result. He accepted the possibility, saying: "We also have a pistol." The Muslim League's agitation did lead to Muslim-Hindu riots throughout the country. Ethnic hostility and fear deepened as the tragic process of partition began.

Bengal was the scene of the greatest bloodshed. Its capital city, Calcutta, saw such violence that observers later called the events of those terrible days the "Great Calcutta Killing." Perhaps six thousand people died in that city alone, most of them innocent Hindus or Muslims attacked by mobs from both sides.

British forces moved into the centers of riot-ing, gradually restoring order. Gandhi, horri-fied at the violence, set out on a personal pilgrimage through Muslim and Hindu areas of Bengal to restore peace and tolerance by his own personal example and teaching. Al-though he risked death at the hands of a fa-natic, he helped calm the population.

It was tempting to blame partition on the League. Nehru himself, without any deep re-ligious feeling and cosmopolitan in his polit-ical ideology, hated the League and all it embodied. He considered the Muslim reli-gious solidarity that the League cultivated to be "medieval," a dangerous anachronism in a "rapidly changing world of industrialism, science, and nuclear power." He repeated over and over his conviction that other religious groups "have nothing to fear from the Hin-dus." After his visit that August to riot-torn areas of the northern province of Punjab, he expressed despair and "shame" that Indians should have betrayed the "great ideals that [Gandhi] has placed before us." That year he and the other Congress leaders persisted in working for a free and united India. But the country was too deeply and bitterly divided. The Muslim League had inflamed, but not created, that bitterness and hostility. Its fault lay in condoning and leading the mob action. Ultimately, religious and social divisions, not political manipulation by the League, decided the fate of India.

Frustrated and baffled by the impasse in negotiations, the British cabinet in February 1947 proclaimed that Great Britain would pull out of India within a year. It was prepared to leave even if it failed to bring agreement among the Indian negotiators on a constitu-tion and the means for the peaceful transfer of power. The statement was a declaration of defeat in the form of an ultimatum. The British government refused to take responsibility any longer for the escalating violence. One British official called the country's ethnic riots to be

the "natural, if ghastly, process tending in its own way to the solution of the Indian prob-lem." Jinnah had made his point. That spring the British government appointed a new viceroy, Lord Mountbatten, to make one last effort to achieve a negotiated settlement. He concluded that partition presented the only solution. The Muslim League, he reported, was ready to "resort to arms if Pakistan in some form were not conceded."

Partition of the Indian Colony

This outcome was impossible without the agreement of the National Congress. It spoke for the majority of India's population. Parti-tion did not have the support of Gandhi, whose entire life and moral preaching had been dedicated to fellowship and toleration. He had pursued national independence be-cause he believed it to be the path to Indian spiritual rebirth. Acceptance of Pakistan meant recognizing communalism and the vic-tory of religious separatism. Although he con-sidered the partition to be destructive and evil, he did not impede the settlement. He allowed Nehru to assume leadership of the National Congress and to take on his shoulders re-sponsibility for Indian independence. That spring Nehru concluded that partition was in-evitable. In June 1947, Mountbatten an-nounced to India and the world the agreement of India's leaders to the plan for the subconti-nent to receive independence not as one but as two states.

Partition cut through the fabric of Indian political, economic, and social life. The provinces with a substantial Muslim popula-tion would go to Pakistan, the rest to India. The territory of two key provinces, Bengal and Punjab, were to be divided in their turn. The Punjab contained within its borders the Sikh religious community as well as Muslims (as numerous as the Sikhs) and a smaller group of Hindus. Provincial leaders reluctantly agreed to the partition of their two regions. A British official secretly rewrote the map of India to draw the boundaries separating the two states. The partition left the Indus River valley in the west and part of Bengal in the east in the new Pakistan state, itself divided into two separate territories. Three-fourths of the subcontinent's population went into India, under Congress leadership.

The partition required the division of land, communities, economic systems, and the institutions of state administration and army. East Bengal's economy, dependent on the export of jute, lost its principal port and center of industry, Calcutta, which went to India. The vast irrigation system in the province of Punjab was disrupted because the frontier cut across its river and canal systems. The Sikh community there was split in two, with its holy city of Amritsar in India and its capital of Lahore in Pakistan. Millions of Hindus remained in Pakistan, and one-third of all Muslims were still in India. August 15 was set as the day of independence.

Nehru spoke to the Indian people on Independence Day. He exulted in the newly won freedom from empire. "We are a free and sovereign people and we have rid ourselves of the burden of the past." Despite Jinnah's objections, his state kept the name of India. Even with partition, it remained one of the most populous countries in the world. The removal of the "burden of foreign domination" was in his eyes a great historic event; it was part of the liberation of colonial peoples in their move to equality with the Western nations. Nehru had ambitious plans for dealing with the "great economic problems of the masses of the people," including industrial development, redistribution of wealth, irrigation, and hydroelectric projects. First, however, the country had to "put an end to all the internal strife and violence."

In the capital of Pakistan, Jinnah spoke to his people. He prayed that "God Almighty give us strength to make Pakistan truly a great nation among all the nations of the world." He urged that Pakistani Muslims respect the rights of his country's Hindu population. That day the exact boundaries of India and Pakistan were made public, revealing the true dimensions of partition.

Centuries of British rule had created a legacy that helped shape the new states. British administrators had formed the Indian civil service, whose authority extended into the rural districts to the level of village life. British officers had trained an Indian army in Western military skills. After independence, Indian administrative and military personnel immediately began to serve in the new regimes, replacing the departing British officials. English had been the language by which many educated Indians communicated among themselves and acquired direct access to Western learning. It became the first official language in both states.

The constitutional origins of self-government lay in the Government of India Act that Great Britain had promulgated in 1935. It had created a federal state that allotted separate legislative powers to the provinces. It had proclaimed the principle of legislative control over the executive in a cabinet form of rule, modeled on the British parliamentary system. This constitution provided the basis of government for both Pakistan and India in their first years of existence. The era of British colonial domination also passed on a valuable economic inheritance. The enormous Indian railroad network and the ocean ports, sinews of an industrial economy, became the property of the new states, as did the irrigation system and hydroelectric dams. The formal transfer of power from Great Britain to India and Pakistan occurred remarkably easily, and the new leaders imagined that their populations would heed their calls for peace and accept the partition as the necessary price for their freedom.

Independence and War

Neither the British nor the nationalist leaders understood the intensity of communal fears and antagonism among Muslims, Hindus, and Sikhs. As a result, they could not foresee the outpouring of anger and panic provoked by the announcement of the new boundaries on August 15. Westernized leaders such as Nehru and Jinnah had built up a vast following among the masses, yet were separated from them by class and education. They did not heed the warning from Sikh leaders in the Punjab that "our swords shall decide if the Muslims shall rule," or note the rising numbers of Sikh men joining armed bands in anticipation of conflict with Muslims. Only Gandhi sensed the tremendous human tragedy that partition had precipitated.

The two partitioned provinces, Bengal in the east and Punjab in the west, were the regions where greatest violence was likely to occur. Calcutta, capital of Bengal, had been the scene of the worst rioting in 1946. At the urging of Lord Mountbatten and with the backing of the leader of the city's Muslims, Gandhi agreed to go there. He was prepared to place his own life in jeopardy to prevent blood from flowing again in the city. He went to live in the worst slums of the city, proclaiming a fast to the death unless the leaders of the religious communities there agreed to collaborate in keeping their peoples from rioting. So great was his moral authority that, almost single-handedly, he maintained peace in Bengal that month.

In the Punjab, however, violence erupted immediately. Refugees began to move across the border, becoming easy targets for mobs. Rumors of atrocities on both sides of the boundaries set Hindus and Sikhs against Muslims in Indian Punjab, while in Pakistan Muslim bands attacked Sikhs and Hindus. The 50,000 troops that Mountbatten had at his disposal could do little to stop the rioting. The number of refugees swelled to a torrent as terrified families and entire villages set out on foot or in trains to find sanctuary, the Muslims to Pakistan, the Hindus and Sikhs to India. They became victims of roving bands of killers and robbers. The violence spread to the Indian capital of Delhi, where Hindu refugees from Pakistan spread stories of massacre, mass rape of Hindu women, and widespread looting by Muslims. In retaliation, Hindus attacked the city's large Muslim population. Mountbatten and Nehru, collaborating closely to prevent chaos from engulfing the country, had to call out the army to keep order there.

In the countryside, order was restored much more slowly. Perhaps a half-million Indians and Pakistanis died that year as a result of the hardship of flight or of mob violence. By mid-1948, an estimated five million refugees had arrived in India and perhaps an equal number in western Pakistan. Independence brought the worst civil strife in Indian history and left in its wake intense animosity between the peoples of the two countries. Nehru attacked the Muslim League as "fascist" and vowed never to let such religious fanaticism destroy the democratic and nonviolent principles of the Congress movement. Two years later he recalled in a sort of self-confession the anguish of those terrible months, when Indian leaders became "slaves of the events that inexorably unroll[ed] themselves before our eyes" and succumbed to "fear and hatred." He shared with his people the anger aroused by mob violence.

Gandhi himself came to Delhi late in the year to continue his crusade for peace and understanding. His efforts were directed toward the leaders of the two states as well as toward their peoples. He attacked fanaticism no matter who preached intolerance, Hindu or Muslim. He received all who wished to talk with him despite rumors of plots against his life.

On January 20, 1948, a Hindu political extremist, outraged at Gandhi's message of peace and conciliation, shot him as he was going to prayer. Gandhi died a martyr's death, another victim of the partition.

Most of the territories ruled still by Indian princes went peacefully, with some strong persuasion by British advisers, to the state in which the principalities were located. But the prince of Kashmir hesitated to join either side. His indecision proved a fatal mistake. In late 1947, Pakistan and India each decided to use military force to bring this land into their state. Although the prince was Hindu, the majority of his population was Muslim. Among them were strong supporters of unification with Pakistan. They had begun violent demonstrations to force their prince to agree to join the new Muslim state. Pakistani troops moved over the border to bring additional pressure on him. But Nehru, whose family was from Kashmir, was determined to keep the mountainous region in his state. That October, Indian troops stopped the Muslim invasion and occupied most of the province. Nehru denied that his state was an aggressor nation and claimed that the Pakistani attack represented "aggression of a brutal and unforgivable kind, aggression against the people of Kashmir and against the Indian Union." In fact, both sides were guilty of aggression, turning to their armed forces for control of the vital Himalayan area.

The conflict over Kashmir escalated into open war between Pakistan and India. Pakistani troops attempted to expel the Indian forces from Kashmir. After several months of fighting, both sides agreed to an armistice, with the front lines close to their original location. The war had succeeded only in partitioning Kashmir by force. The failure to settle this issue left behind a poisonous legacy of Muslim-Hindu hostility in the mountainous province. The final consequence of partition was to turn Pakistan and India into outright enemies. Their conflict endured for the next fifty years and erupted twice in new wars. Pakistan, the weaker state, sought military alliance and foreign aid from the United States; India accepted military aid from the Soviet Union. In the early 1980s, both states secretly developed nuclear weapons for possible use against their neighbor. The division of Kashmir turned that frontline territory, once so beautiful it may have been the source of the myth of "Shangri-la," into a war zone. Partition was a tragedy for the population of the subcontinent and a terrible burden for the two new states.

 HIGHLIGHT: New Nations and Ethnic Conflict

The new states that emerged in the late twentieth century where empires once ruled all presented in one form or another the image of the nation-state. Flags, ceremonies, and heroes (real or mythical) commemorated and celebrated the historical achievements and prestige of a particular national community, united in one state. Leaders claimed that their government embodied special qualities of the people over whom they ruled. This was true in Latin America following the collapse of Spanish and Portuguese empires in the early nineteenth century. It was true in Asia and Africa after the Western empires withdrew from those continents in the decades after 1945. In their early years, these states were weak. Their governments had not, in most cases, had the chance to establish a solid foundation of authority and often were plagued by internal rivalries among ambitious individuals and political movements eager for power. The ideology of nationalism held the promise of a firm bond between the people and their leaders on the condition the new government appeared legitimate and fit to govern the nation-state.

The creed of nationalism could be a trap for new states if politicians misused it. Its crucial shortcoming was the confusion surrounding the idea of a national community itself. The term could refer to all the people within the boundaries of that state, which derived from them a unique civic calling that distinguished it from other nation-states. This ideal of the nation is termed *civic nationalism*. On the stroke of midnight, August 15, 1947, the Indian prime minister, Nehru, welcomed the freeing of "the soul of a nation" given at that moment its independence. Like Gandhi, Nehru believed freedom and tolerance were by themselves bonds that would maintain the unity of the Indian people and their leaders.

But *nation* also could refer to peoples united by their collective sense of ethnic identity, which supposed a common ancestry and usually a common language. Civic ideals constituted a vague moral appeal by contrast with the belief in ancestral nationhood, characterized by one historian as "blood and belonging." This national ideal is termed *ethnic nationalism*. When this form of national loyalty prevailed, the new states confronted the potential of serious internal divisions. All the new states contained within their borders more than one, and often many, separate

groups with strong ethnic ties. Ethnic loyalty became especially meaningful in the lives of the population after independence from colonial rule. It offered the people within a particular community the reassurance of a shared collective identity, the social solidarity needed at moments of political unrest, and the bonds of mutual assistance invaluable in hard times.

These bonds of ethnic unity originated in many sources. Language formed the most prevalent and meaningful marker of ethnic identity. Among the population of India were fifteen separate major languages. After Indian independence, leaders of some of these peoples demanded a territory of their own within the Indian federation, even though other peoples shared that area. Religious practice was another powerful social bond. It was the foundation of the Muslim League's demand for a state of Muslim people to be carved out of the Indian colony. A belief in common ancestry was yet another ethnic link. Leaders of major and even small tribal groups claimed a special place in independent Nigeria because they believed that their own people's uniqueness deserved special territorial recognition. Each time these claims for ethnic recognition appeared, they implied that civic nationalism was less important to some people than their own ethnic identity. That demand, in turn, raised the possibility that the very borders of the new state had to be redrawn or even that the state should not exist as such.

Strife among ethnic groups in these states emerged out of the heritage of colonial experience, postcolonial politics, and economic hardship. The newly freed lands frequently inherited from their colonial past a policy of favored treatment for one particular people. Often the imperial administration had recruited soldiers or subordinate officials to serve their colonial needs. Animosities built up over the colonial decades spilled out in ethnic conflict once independence had lifted imperial control.

This historical experience was only the prelude to the real difficulties created by independence. The new nation-states followed in their first years the democratic principle of popular elections to select their new leaders. Electoral competition created the possibility for political parties to emerge claiming to defend the needs of a particular people. In South Africa, the Inkatha Party spoke for the Zulu people alone and denied the African National Congress's claim to be the true voice of all African peoples there. Voters often preferred candidates from their own people. Voting on the basis of ethnic loyalty ensured that the candidates from the party backed by the largest ethnic group had the best chance of gaining power. Since the winners could use their position to distribute jobs and other rewards only to followers from their people, minority peoples could find themselves outcasts as a result of democratic rule. When the Ibo people of Nigeria believed themselves in this situation in the late 1960s, they rebelled against the central government. The resulting civil war, which lasted three years, nearly destroyed Nigeria.

Ethnic nationalism rested on the belief in a "native land" that belonged by "right" to a particular people. The assertion was based usually on a people's historical claim of having lived there over many generations. It was even made, though, for lands where a people had not lived for centuries. The Zionist movement affirmed that Palestine was the real homeland for the Jewish people, though the Romans had expelled almost all the Jews from there almost two thousand years before. Nowhere did the inhabitants in a particular area all belong to one ethnic group, nor were all those identifying with that group located within one compact territory. The demand to govern one's "own" land meant necessarily that the other peoples there did not enjoy a comparable right. By its very nature, the claim to a native land created ethnic minorities. If these peoples responded by making a claim to the same land, no peaceful resolution could satisfy both sides. The fifty-year struggle between Palestinian Arabs and Israeli Jews emerged out of that dispute.

The search for a way to reconcile civic and ethnic national loyalties led political leaders to promise legal protection of ethnic differences. In many Third World countries, constitutions spelled out minority rights, the most important of which was usually language rights. Often fundamental laws created a federal political system to divide state powers between the center, whose representatives spoke for all the peoples, and regions where particular ethnic groups obtained their own leadership and local rights. This system became the legal foundation of ethnically diverse countries such as India, Nigeria, and, late in the century, the Russian Federation.

It was a fragile compromise, since in theory it denied to the majority people the right to create a nation-state in its image, and by necessity refused to a minority people the right to their own nation-state. When peaceful compromise failed to satisfy ethnic nationalist demands, the result was civil disorder, political repression, and civil war. These conflicts first appeared very early in the postimperial era in Asia and Africa. They continued to erupt, and with increased intensity, later in the century. One reason was the spreading struggle for livelihood among impoverished masses in the Third World. The temptation for them was strong to blame their poverty on other peoples, accused of denying them access to economic benefits. In times of economic hard- ship in the 1960s and late 1990s, the Chinese minority of Indonesia, largely urban and en- gaged in commerce and finance, became a target for other peoples in that republic envi- ous of their well-being.

Civil wars within the new nation-states erupted where these ethnic conflicts became armed confrontation. At times, the spark was the effort of minority peoples to secede and to achieve at any cost their own independent state. Many of these revolts were settled by military means. Though the Indian constitu- tion and federal laws guaranteed respect for ethnic rights, the government turned to extra- legal powers of repression when violent na- tionalist movements among Sikhs in the province of Punjab, then the Kashmir Muslim population, threatened secession and the breakup of India. The Nigerian government triumphed over the Ibo in a brutal civil war that resulted in the deaths of millions of civil- ians, most from starvation resulting from the economic blockade of the region.

Occasionally free elections brought the eth- nic conflicts to an end, usually leading to peaceful secession. In 1993, the Eritrean Peo- ple's Front, after decades of guerrilla war, forced the Ethiopian government to hold an election on independence for the people of the province of Eritrea. Its popular backing was overwhelming, and the new nation-state of Eritrea appeared in Africa. This was a com- promise, and Ethiopian leaders, determined to reunite their state, launched a new war six years later to retake this land. Only Eritrean armed might saved the new state.

The collapse of multi-ethnic communist states in eastern Europe produced some of the worst ethnic conflict in recent times. These states, the most important of which were the Soviet Union and Yugoslavia, had tried to quiet hostility among their peoples by creating "na- tional republics" for the largest ethnic groups. But they too had at times to rely on repressive measures resembling those used by colonial empires. When the Communists lost power, these animosities quickly reemerged. The worst violence occurred in the Balkan state of Yugoslavia. It had created within its federation separate republics for its peoples, among whom Serb, Croat, and Bosnian peoples were the most numerous. Nationalism among these peoples erupted in civil war when the Yugoslav state collapsed in 1991. Hostility to- ward minorities was so great that some na- tionalists were prepared to forcibly expel or murder thousands of innocent civilians living in "their land" who did not belong to their na- tion. This cruel practice, called "ethnic cleans- ing," revealed how inhuman ethnic conflict could become.

In the 1990s, the problem of restraining ethnic conflicts became the principal issue facing the international community. Verbal protests from outside states and the United Nations could not halt bitter ethnic struggles such as the Yugoslav civil war or the 1994 vi- olence in the African state of Rwanda. The in- tervention of foreign troops could for a while restrain the mob rioting and killings. Some ob- servers argued for the moral obligation of out- side intervention to end the bloodshed. At times it seemed that only when the fighting had created a human wasteland did exhaus- tion end the violence. In these places, na- tionalism had replaced epidemics as the great killer of humanity.

THE NATION-STATES OF INDIA AND PAKISTAN

As a result of British withdrawal from the subcontinent of India, it appeared on world maps as a land divided into first two, then three large countries. Their leaders claimed, in their own terms, to govern nation-states. Complicating state-building was the painful task of healing the wounds caused by the partition of British India between Pakistan and India, then again the secession of western Pakistan, now called Bangladesh, in 1971. Within India, small but violent nationalist movements among some of its peoples led to civil disorder and military repression. The promise of peace and civic nationalism that the leaders had originally promised proved difficult or impossible to fulfill.

Nehru and the New India

A new Indian state took form under Nehru's leadership. In the first violent months, he and the head of the National Congress, V. Patel, ruled virtually as a military government. Yet the Indian government put together the elements of a democratic state. The first step consisted of completing the incorporation of the princely states into Indian provinces. In exchange for generous allowances, almost all princes renounced their power peacefully. Only the Muslim prince of Hyderabad resisted, until finally Indian troops occupied his land in 1948 to "restore order" in what was officially called a "police action." The removal of the princes from power amounted to a sort of national revolution, achieved almost without force. Only the unresolved fate of Kashmir continued to remind Indians of the complexity and potentially tragic consequences of nation-

building in one of the oldest civilizations in the world.

The creation of a new administration and army proved relatively painless. Despite Congress's earlier criticism of Indians working for the British civil service and army, the new government accepted willingly their assimilation into the new Indian state. It preferred the stability and efficiency provided by trained administrators and experienced military forces to the dangers of forming a state apparatus from scratch. This personnel proved its worth in those first chaotic months of independence, serving the new state as loyally as they had their former British rulers.

Enormous responsibility for the shape of the new state rested in Nehru's hands. His political authority was virtually unlimited, for he enjoyed immense popularity as father of his country. His political ideal, as he told an American audience in 1949, was to find "some balance between the centralized authority of the state and the assurance of freedom and opportunity to each individual." The National Congress had from the start gathered together diverse groups defending a variety of interests and creeds. The new state had to reconcile these divergent objectives. Nehru valued this diversity, accepting the compromises it forced upon him.

Agreement on basic political goals did unite all factions of the National Congress. Key to their plans was the creation of a liberal democracy in India. In all of Asia, only Japan had successfully adapted Western democratic institutions to its public life. It had the advantage of small size, a homogeneous population, and historical unity. Democratic government in India represented in practice an audacious gamble. It appeared to Congress leaders the best guarantee of toleration and

Jawaharlal Nehru (*Embassy of India, Washington D.C.*)

equal rights to all Indians regardless of religion, language, or caste. To political and civil liberties, Congress added social welfare and state-sponsored economic development, both intended to protect and enhance the well-being of India's impoverished masses. Three objectives—democracy, toleration, and socialism—pointed toward the transformation of one of the oldest civilized societies in the world. The task of the Indian leaders was formidable, and the very democratic institutions and diversity that they wished to protect severely restricted their means of action.

The Indian constitution went into effect in 1950. It preserved and extended the federal structure first introduced by the British in 1935. The provincial states and the federal government were all ruled by ministries, dependent on majorities in their legislatures to retain power. The position of greatest importance was that of prime minister of the federal cabinet, empowered even to dissolve provincial governments (that is, to violate the principle of federalism) if there existed a threat to the unity of India. Nehru occupied that office until his death in 1964. Political and civil liberties were guaranteed to all citizens. Voting was by universal suffrage. The first elections for regular legislative positions took place in 1951. More than 170 million citizens had the right to vote, over half of whom were illiterate. This enormous electorate made India, as Nehru later remarked, the "largest functioning democracy in the world."

Nehru's political stature within India was so great that it might have undermined the very foundations of the free democracy that the National Congress defended. Many years earlier he had written for an Indian journal an anonymous portrait of himself, warning that "in this revolutionary epoch Caesarism [i.e., dictatorial rule like that of the Roman general Julius Caesar] is always at the door, and is it not possible that Jawaharlal [Nehru] might fancy himself a Caesar? Therein lies the danger for Jawaharlal and India." He might have added that the danger existed in all the newly independent Asian and African countries. Sukarno of Indonesia did succumb to the temptation of Caesarism. Nehru's personal commitment to liberty was a key ingredient of Indian democracy.

Democratic Socialism in India

India's path to democratic socialism supposed fundamental social and economic reforms. Nehru's ideal was "a socialist pattern of society which is classless, casteless." His principal concern was the misery of much of the Indian population. One-half of his people were estimated in 1950 to live in abject poverty, lacking adequate food for an active life. He did not attempt a campaign of expropriation of private property, such as occurred in China. Peaceful reform and tolerance of diversity forbade that solution. Instead, he conceived of an economy divided into public and private sectors, with the state exercising substantial regulatory controls over both. India's established industries remained in private hands, as did its farms and commerce.

For the next forty years, the Indian state played a central role in the country's economic development. It claimed ownership of major industrial projects such as steel mills (built with state funds and foreign aid), of public utilities (gas and electricity), and of new irrigation projects. A National Planning Commission guided the development of India's "mixed economy" (part capitalist, part socialist). Its administrative personnel was responsible for crucial decisions on investments, agricultural development, transportation, and foreign trade.

The commission used state funds to guide economic development in a manner best suited (in theory) to improve the living conditions of the people. It relied on a combination of elements of the Soviet command economy, which Nehru admired, and the collaboration of India's capitalists and peasant farmers. Its most ambitious plan for rural development relied on the voluntary efforts of millions of villagers. The Village Development Program granted state funds to village committees for the construction of wells and schools, for minimum health care, and for other measures essential to fight poverty. Within a few years 150 million Indians shared in the benefits of this program. It proved a remarkable success, all the more so as Indian socialism excluded the use of Maoist methods of compulsion and mass mobilization.

Economic planning worked well in those first years. India's agricultural production climbed 3 percent a year, almost twice as fast as population growth. The Second Five-Year Plan, although not as successful as the First, did maintain a comparable level of economic expansion. Industrial production, the great hope of that plan, grew 6 percent annually, a rate that increased to 9 percent in the 1960s. But India's population explosion of almost 2 percent a year frustrated hopes of freeing India from dependence on industrial imports and of ensuring adequate food for the country. The government, to avoid conflict with Muslim religious authorities, made no effort in those years to promote birth control. Improved medical care and social welfare contributed as well to the expansion of the population from 350 million at independence to more than 700 million in the mid-1970s. It was a crushing burden for the economy.

Feeding the population became a problem so critical that only Western help saved the country from famine in the mid-1960s. Western agronomists had developed new, high-yield strains of dwarf wheat and rice. They intended their discoveries particularly for poor agrarian lands. These crops were unknown in those areas and required complex farming techniques. Large amounts of chemical fertilizers were needed to sustain substantial harvests year after year. The governments of both India and Pakistan were initially hostile to these exotic crops. In desperation, India's minister of agriculture, faced with a grave population crisis and stubborn opponents, planted his own garden in the capital of Delhi with the new wheat to prove its value. His gardening experiment, plus a thousand "demonstration sites" around the country, proved his point. In 1967, the government agreed to distribute the wheat seeds throughout India. Indian grain production soared, and by the mid-1970s the country was producing harvests sufficient to meet the needs of the growing population. The use of these crops required extensive application of insecticides and fertilizers, produced at new factories (owned by multi-national corporations) like that outside the city of Bhopal. Famine in India was averted, at least for a few decades.

The "Indian way" of economic development did not produce miracles, but its results were substantial as measured over the first thirty years of independence. Perhaps the best comparison was with China, where famine and economic stagnation followed the Great Leap Forward of the late 1950s. By contrast, India's moderate policies avoided social turmoil and maintained for the first decades a steady rate of economic growth, albeit at a snail's pace.

Improvements also came in health and education. Average life expectancy among Indians doubled between 1950 and 1990, rising from thirty-two to sixty years. It was a phenomenal achievement, resulting from both the relative success of public health and the improvement in the Indian standard of living. Indian efforts to spread education were much less successful. During those same decades basic literacy was in possession of only half of the population. This key skill, which opened access to the modern economy, remained unobtainable for hundreds of millions of Indians. The Indian government was determined not to let this obstacle get in the way of disseminating its news (and national ideals) among the population. To do so, it set up a national television network, launched a communications satellite, and provided villages with television sets (coming before schools in some cases).

Despite these improvements, poverty remained widespread. In the 1980s, over one-third of the total population was still impoverished. Once hidden in the vast countryside of the subcontinent, the poor became far more visible when, in a desperate search for livelihoods, they moved to urban areas. In the 1980s, places such as Calcutta were the goal of a thousand new immigrants each day. India's cities became focal points of human misery. A wasteland around a new pesticide factory near the city of Bhopal became a shantytown for hundreds of thousands of these poor migrants, until an explosion at the plant spread poisonous gases that killed thousands of the inhabitants in 1984. Urbanization in such conditions was a sign not of economic development but rather of the ongoing struggle to survive of hundreds of millions of Indians.

Ethnic Diversity and Secular Democracy

During the same period, the Indian government put into effect laws intended to ensure equal rights for India's multi-ethnic, multi-religious population. *Secularism* was the term used by the National Congress government to describe its program. It was intended to assure the protection of civil law and a common citizenship to the entire population. Customs and entrenched social and religious prejudice built up over many centuries stood in the path of these goals. But Nehru insisted that secularism be achieved "through our own volition, as a result of our own experience," not "through any kind of force or pressure." It was a noble dream.

The constitution itself abolished the social category of untouchables and declared caste restrictions to be illegal. It established the principle of legal equality for all Indians regardless of religion, caste, or sex. To become effective, its principles had to be embodied in laws touching the personal lives of the population. It confronted the deeply rooted customs of marriage and property ownership, bastions of caste exclusiveness, and of the subjugation of women. Caste prejudices continued to divide the Hindu population, and intolerance toward untouchables weakened very slowly despite the special laws intended to protect them.

At the heart of the secularist project was the commitment of the Indian leaders to keep their state neutral in all religious matters. All official discussions and policies had to avoid even the slightest implication of preference for one religion or another. This concern was most acute in the state's relations with the minority Muslim population. They remained apprehensive at any threat to their religious laws and customs. Although it was not originally intended to do so, secularism turned into a form of defense of Islam. The Muslim community retained its own customary laws governing marriage and divorce. In this domain, the civil laws of the state did not reach all the people.

The majority Hindu population did slowly receive legal protection as individual citizens. In the mid-1950s, the Indian state issued basic laws establishing civic equality of rights for Hindu women. The Hindu Marriage Act of 1955 and the Hindu Succession Act of 1956 established the legal basis for equality among Hindu Indians. The Succession Act gave women equal rights with men in inheritance and ownership of property. The Marriage Act declared polygamy and bigamy criminal offenses, permitted divorce, and made provision for alimony. Subsequently, marriage dowry was made illegal. In daily life, this equality of condition spread first among upper- and middle-class women in India. They increasingly shared in the new opportunities for education and work.

Among the remainder of the population, social custom and family restraints continued to hold women in inferior status. "Purdah" (female seclusion) was still widely practiced among Muslims. The Hindu custom of marriage dowries, though illegal, became the source of cruel demands from the husband's family for expensive gifts from the family of the bride. When these were refused, the wife risked beatings, even murder, at the hands of her husband and his relatives. Women's defense groups estimated that in the 1980s between 10,000 and 15,000 women died each year as a result of these dowry murders. Only by comparison with past conditions could one conclude with Nehru that India's secular reforms instituted "equality of status and opportunity" among Indians.

In its multi-religious, multi-ethnic land, the Indian government kept its peoples together with a mixture of concessions to ethnic communities, appeals to civic nationalism, and military repression of movements that appeared to threaten the unity of the country. Ethnic loyalties, based on religion and culture, constituted a powerful force in a country divided by a multitude of distinct languages and cultures. Leaders of ethnic groups organized campaigns for the redrawing of provincial borders to give their peoples their "native land." Their demands posed the threat of partition if they sought to secede from India. Gradually, the government submitted to these pressures. In 1956, several provincial states disappeared, and new provincial territories, each grouping in majority a distinct ethnic group with its own language, took their place. But these concessions opened the way for further agitation among other peoples. India's bond of unity remained fragile.

Still, Nehru's achievements were substantial. He had focused the attention of Indians on national problems and had given them a sense of national pride. He could not possibly have created out of the enormous Indian population one nation in the full sense of the word. Just how important he was to India became apparent after he died in 1964. With only brief interruptions, the National Congress and Indian voters preferred the leadership of his family in the next quarter century. They first chose his daughter, Indira Gandhi, then his grandson, Rajiv Gandhi, to be prime minister. Nehru's personal charisma seemed for a time to have become a family heritage, endowing his descendants with the symbolic majesty of national unity.

Their domestic program differed from Nehru's principally in their gradual dismantling of command economy policies that he had introduced. Indian nationalized industry proved to be inefficient and costly, and the so-called "license state" tied up private enterprises in complicated and unending requirements for official documentation. The new leadership relied increasingly on Indian capitalists and foreign investors for economic development, new jobs, and technological innovation. In the 1990s, educated Indians found well-paying jobs in new centers of the electronics and computer industries, funded by foreign investors such as Microsoft and overseas Indians who had themselves become wealthy entrepreneurs in this "new economy." One small part of the Indian population had entered the electronic age, exploiting and developing this new technology that bound them more closely to the developed world than to the sea of poverty that surrounded them. By then, the country numbered over one billion inhabitants.

Ethnic strife was never absent for long from Indian life. In 1989, Kashmir secessionists yet again rebelled against Indian rule. Backed this time by Pakistan, they demanded for the Muslim population of the province the right to form an independent state. They operated out of camps in Pakistan, where they planned military raids and terrorist attacks on the Indian half of Kashmir. The Indian army was again called upon to enforce Indian unity. Its forces set up a regime of military rule in Kashmir. Occasional border skirmishes with Pakistan troops in the 1990s maintained an unsettled condition resembling low-grade war in the region. By then, both states had acquired the military arsenal for nuclear war. The danger of devastating conflict between the two states was greater than ever before.

Elsewhere in India, basic political liberties and the rule of law were transforming the character of Indian society. The community of untouchables, the most persecuted of India's masses, was no longer excluded from public life. Thanks to the parliamentary system, they used their voting power to elect their own leaders to provincial government. Despite periodic civil strife between Muslims and Hindus, India retained its national unity and democratic freedoms.

War and Peace in South Asia

Nehru understood decolonization to mean the beginning of a new era of international peace and cooperation among new and old nation-states. He shared with Sukarno and other leaders of the newly independent states their opposition to Western political or economic domination, which they called "neocolonialism." Nehru hoped to make India a leader in bringing good relations among the world's states, whether communist or capitalist, former colonies or old empires. He slowly worked out his new foreign policy in the years following independence. It sought peaceful change through cooperation, with its ultimate goal the equitable distribution of wealth and well-being among all the peoples of the world. In a speech in 1949, Nehru stated that his country's objectives consisted of the pursuit of peace, not by joining any major power or group of powers, but through an independent approach to each controversial or disputed issue.

His version of internationalism, reminiscent of President Wilson's approach, rejected the methods of power politics and balance of power in international relations. He refused to take sides in the Cold War, preferring what he called "nonalignment" with either camp. His ideals were those of a visionary who dreamed of an era of peace to come with the liberation of subject peoples.

He counted on his prestige as the Indian national leader and on the influence of his large state to bring together a group of nations committed to his principles. He defended his policies before an international audience at Bandung, Indonesia, in 1955. This Conference of Non-Aligned States, attended by delegates from countries in Africa, Asia, and Latin America, agreed that there should be "no domination in the future" by powerful Western countries in former colonial lands. But the conference par-

ticipants were so deeply divided already over the issues raised by the Cold War that they could not agree on Nehru's program. They merely adopted a vague "Declaration on World Peace and Cooperation."

Nehru's foreign policy for India confronted two immediate obstacles. One was the conflict between his country and Pakistan. The second arose from India's serious border dispute with China. The first conflict brought to South Asia on a small scale the characteristics of the Cold War—military alliances and a nuclear arms race. The second dispute revealed, yet again, that war remained the instrument of last resort in revolving disputes of state security, bringing to the relations of the new nation-states the instruments of power politics. It proved the undoing of Nehru's idealistic foreign policy.

The Chinese Communists supported the theory but not the practice of internationalism. In the 1954 Sino-Indian treaty, India and China agreed on basic principles of coexistence, nonaggression, territorial respect, and nonintervention. Nehru came away believing that the Chinese had accepted wholeheartedly his internationalist foreign policy. The Chinese negotiators considered the agreement an insignificant paper concession to the Indian leader's utopian ideals in return for India's recognition of their conquest of Tibet. Their government had concrete territorial demands along the long Chinese-Indian border and expected the Indian government to agree. If not, they were prepared to rely on force of arms to settle the matter.

The issue was national security, as defined by the Chinese government. It claimed territories in the Himalayan Mountains separating Tibet from Chinese western territories (Xinjiang), where it planned to build a strategic highway to move troops between these areas of rebellious peoples. But the Indian government claimed for itself these regions, through which the British Empire had marked out a vaguely defined border with China the previous century. Nehru did not attempt to confirm the boundary either by military occupation or by negotiations with the Chinese. He chose to deal with the boundary dispute by ignoring it. In the meantime, the Chinese government began to build its road. How could peace be preserved between neighboring Asian states when they confronted intractable territorial conflicts? Nehru had no solution to that problem.

The unresolved border issue and Chinese repression of Tibetans became a source of growing hostility in the late 1950s. By then, the Chinese road between Xinjiang and Tibet was nearing completion. It passed through high mountainous regions (14,000 to 15,000 feet high) where India had no frontier troops. In 1959, the Indian government welcomed the Dalai Lama when he fled Tibet after Chinese troops had quelled a major Tibetan revolt (see "Spotlight," Chapter 9). The Chinese government accused India of "walking in the footsteps of the British imperialists and harboring expansionist ambitions toward Tibet." Chinese and Indian frontier forces moved closer along their long high-mountain border. Nehru acknowledged that China, a "world power or would-be world power," and India confronted a crisis so acute that "for the first time two major powers of Asia face each other on an armed border."

Neither side was prepared to compromise. China was isolated, but its army was well trained and equipped for mountain war. Nehru claimed that justice was on India's side, denouncing China's "unlawful" seizure of Indian territory. He would negotiate with the Chinese on the condition that they concede Indian possession of the disputed frontier regions. The Chinese government refused. In 1962, the Indian army finally began to move troops into the remote areas where the Chinese highway was located. War had become

unavoidable. China would not abandon its vital road link, and India chose to back its claim to the frontier region with military force.

The Chinese knew that military superiority was on their side. Indian troops were still few in number and unprepared to fight at high altitude. In late October 1962, Chinese troops attacked in eastern and western regions of their frontier with India. Everywhere Indian resistance collapsed. Within three weeks, Chinese forces had destroyed Indian frontier defenses and were in a position in the east to invade the Indian lowlands. Nehru accused the Chinese government of violating "all principles which govern normal neighborly relations between sovereign governments" by a "deliberate cold-blooded decision" to invade India. Nonalignment offered no protection at a time of military defeat. Fearing a Chinese invasion of India, Nehru appealed for U.S. naval and air support. The United States agreed, moving ships from the U.S. Pacific fleet into the Bay of Bengal, close to one of the areas of fighting.

Then the Chinese troops withdrew. In the west, they had defeated Indian frontier forces and had established control over the territory along their Himalaya highway. Their commanders sought no more. In the east, they pulled back behind the original border and proclaimed a cease-fire with a twenty-mile neutral zone to separate the opposing sides. The war was over. Although no negotiations followed the end of the fighting, China had settled the border dispute by force of arms. Its army had fought and won a limited war for a specific territorial objective, applying a centuries-old Western principle of using war as a continuation of diplomacy by other means. India was powerless to alter the settlement.

Nation and Islam in Pakistan

The history of Pakistan as a new nation-state differed in fundamental aspects from India's path of development. Islam, not civic nationalism, defined its uniqueness. Dictator-ship, not democracy, became its preferred form of government. Alliance with the United States, not nonalignment, determined its for-eign policy. The first years after independence revealed the fundamental differences between the two countries. In both states, the India Act of 1935 had provided the first elements of in-dependent political life, creating a federal state and establishing the cabinet system of rule for India. But the Muslim League could not nur-ture the political conditions needed for dem-ocratic government in Pakistan. Its problems were enormous. Its support among the coun-try's population was weak, for it had never succeeded, as the National Congress had, in becoming a mass movement. Its leader, Jin-nah, died in 1948. Deep internal social and ethnic differences among Pakistanis thwarted his successors' efforts at state-building.

Only the Muslim religion provided a frag-ile bond among the population. The constitu-tion proclaimed Pakistan to be an Islamic Republic. It was the first state to lay down the principle that the Quran was the basic law of the land. Many Middle Eastern states with large Muslim populations imitated its exam-ple later. A shared Muslim identity was not sufficient, however, to overcome regional and ethnic rivalries. The greatest threat to the unity of the new state was its territorial disunity. Its leadership and strongest supporters were in West Pakistan. In East Pakistan, the Muslim League ruled as outsiders, for the people there were deeply attached to their own Bengali lan-guage and culture. After 1954, East Pakistani voters voted for their own Bengali parties and rejected the leadership of the Muslim League.

Pakistan's parliamentary government proved incompetent and unstable. Prime min-isters succeeded one another in rapid succes-sion, six in the first ten years of independence. That instability and the internal conflicts be-tween East and West Pakistan discredited democratic rule. In 1958, parliamentary

democracy in Pakistan ceased to exist when the army took power. The "Caesarism" of which Nehru had warned became a reality in the Muslim state. A general, Ayub Khan, seized power that year and promised to introduce order and to set up "Basic Democ-racy." The term masked a military dictator-ship. He agreed to a military pact with the United States, for the alliance brought his poor country massive U.S. aid—$4 billion between the late 1950s and late 1980s. He accepted U.S. advisers to encourage individual enterprise and capitalist development. This market strat-egy stimulated economic growth but enriched a handful of successful capitalists and further deepened the country's social inequalities.

Military rule proved no better able to en-sure political unity than civilian government. Opposition to rule from West Pakistan grew steadily in East Pakistan. Its leaders protested the government's inadequate aid for their people, who were considered by economists among the most impoverished in the world. By the late 1960s, the disagreements had be-come so bitter that East Pakistan came under military occupation by forces from West Pak-istan. Bengali political leaders were placed under arrest.

In 1971, the dispute produced civil war. Bengalis demonstrated and rioted against Pakistan rule. Military repression forced mil-lions of Bengalis to flee across the border into Indian Bengal. The Indian government, eager to weaken Pakistan, welcomed the refugees. The conflict was becoming an international crisis. Under pressure from its own Bengal population, the Indian government decided to support the rebellion. When Pakistani forces refused Indian demands to end their military occupation, the Indian army invaded East Pakistan. Once again, India and Pakistan were at war. The fighting ended quickly with Indian victory. The peace settlement required that Pakistan grant its Bengal territory inde-pendence. The rebel leaders proclaimed the independence of their land under the name of Bangladesh.

Pakistan itself retained less than half the population of the prewar state. Its economy depended more than ever on U.S. foreign aid. Poverty and disease were severe. Among the lower classes, many men migrated overseas in search of work. They remained away, some for years at a time, in Europe and the Middle East. The "remittances" that they sent back to their families came to represent a substantial part of Pakistan foreign earnings. England remained the greatest lure. Migrants settled there in large communities, bringing with them their religious practices and social customs.

The great hopes of the first years of independence faded for many Pakistanis. What was left was the ideal of a country uniquely Muslim and the reality of continued internal ethnic quarrels and the threat of war with India. Muslim legal principles became part of the constitutional basis of the state after 1978. Educated Pakistanis who objected to the strict Islamic laws of their country could move to England, for them a place of individual freedom and secular rights.

Backed by the U.S. government, Pakistan provided secret support for the guerrilla uprising in neighboring Afghanistan after Soviet troops invaded in 1979 (see Chapter 13). Its leaders hoped to increase their regional power by extending Pakistan's influence into Afghanistan. The only immediate result was to increase the influence in their land of militant Muslims, including many foreigners eager to join the Afghan "holy war." The Pakistan government chose the dangerous path of giving support to these fanatics (including a Saudi Arabian named Osama bin Laden).

Poverty among a rapidly growing population, combined with hostility to Western culture, encouraged a growing number of Pakistanis to subscribe to fundamentalist Muslim beliefs and practices. Islamic religious schools in Pakistan became centers of political activism by movement seeking still stricter Islamic laws in their country. Their support in the country gave them a majority in the legislature, but once again a general assumed supreme power over the government. He, like military rulers before him, justified his authoritarian regime by warning of the ethnic strife that threatened to destroy his country. The Muslim religion remained a dubious symbol of national unity in a land founded on the idea of an Islamic nation.

SUMMARY

The disappearance of Western empires from southern Asia left to nationalist leaders the responsibility to deal with the acute social and economic hardship of their peoples and to ensure political stability in conditions of ethnic and religious conflict. Did independence improve the lives of these populations? On what grounds does one measure progress in the history of developing nations: national independence, political freedom, economic growth, the lessening of social inequalities, or ethnic and religious diversity safeguarded within a nation-state? All of these goals appeared to a greater or lesser extent in the policies of Third World governments and in the public aspirations of the peoples of those lands. None of them was fully achieved in the decades following independence. The disappointment and anger provoked by these failures led to a search for simple explanations.

Neocolonialism provided one easy answer. Sukarno blamed Indonesia's economic failures and international weakness on the colonial heritage. His search for Western culprits was not, in historical hindsight, convincing. The roots of Indonesia's problems under his rule lay in ethnic divisions, poverty, and the incompetence of his government. His fall from power was caused largely by his own shortsighted efforts to create national unity around his charismatic leadership in a one-party state. It opened the way for army generals to use military force to bring order to the vast territories of the state and to impose their own rule.

Colonialism left a complex heritage that the peoples of the former colonies chose to accept or reject in ways that the concept of neocolonialism does not help us to understand. To enhance their power and glory, European conquerors had created large colonies out of scattered islands and disparate peoples. The Philippines, Indonesia, and India came into existence as unified lands under colonial rule. Imperial methods of rule did not by themselves create ethnic conflict but did make such antagonism more likely to erupt when the empires collapsed.

In the last decades of British rule, Indian nationalists nurtured and enriched the idea of an Indian nation. In Gandhi's national creed, it became a lofty ideal of human solidarity and moral equality. Responsibility for the tragic collapse of that dream, destroyed in the partition of the subcontinent, rests with the political leaders, imperial and national, and with the deep animosities that divided the Indian masses. There, as in other parts of the world, ethnic antagonism aroused latent fears of outsiders, from within as well as beyond the new state borders. Loyalties were never a simple matter of language, culture, religion, or ancestry. In the case of Pakistan, its nascent national unity drew primarily on Islamic solidarity. But the state's partition in 1971 revealed that the unique language and cultural traditions of East Pakistan's Bengal people were more powerful bonds than the Muslim faith that they shared with West Pakistan peoples. The new nation-states were fragile creations.

Authoritarianism was a tempting answer to instability. Generals from national armies came at times to believe themselves the saviors of the state, but they invariably resorted to brutal methods of dictatorial rule to remain in power. Burma (renamed Myanmar), once a model new nation-state, became in the 1980s and 1990s a glaring example of brutal military dictatorship and economic decay. Its generals preferred to seal the country off from the outside world for fear that the free flow of goods and ideas would undermine their regime. National independence and social progress were goals for Asian countries whose means and capabilities could not possibly match their dream.

DATES WORTH REMEMBERING

1946	Philippine independence
1947	Indian partition; independence for Pakistan and India
1947	Nehru prime minister of India
1947–1948	War between Pakistan and India
1950	Sukarno first president of Indonesian republic
1951	Indian federal constitution
1955	Bandung Conference of Non-Aligned States
1962	Sino-Indian War
1964	Death of Nehru
1965	Independence for Singapore
1966	General Suharto ruler of Indonesia
1967	"Green Revolution" crops accepted by India
1971	Indo-Pakistan war and independence of Bangladesh
1981–1989	Pakistan aid to Afghan rebels
1982	Sikh rebellion against India
1989	Revolt of Kashmir Muslims against India

RECOMMENDED READING

Southeast Asia

Theodore Friend, *Indonesian Destinies* (2003). An interpretive history of Indonesia, focusing on the major political leaders Sukarno and Suharto.

*Stanley Karnow, *In Our Image: America's Empire in the Philippines* (1989). A history of the close relations between the United States and the Philippines before and after independence.

C. L. M. Pendus, *The Life and Times of Sukarno* (1974). A critical biography of Indonesia's national hero and deposed ruler.

India and Pakistan

*Larry Collins and Dominique Lapierre, *Freedom at Midnight* (1975). A dramatic history of the personalities and circumstances surrounding the liberation of Britain's greatest colony.

*Patrick French, *Liberty or Death: India's Journey to Independence and Division* (1997). A balanced historical assessment of India's recent colonial past and the tragedy of partition.

Memoirs and Novels

*V. S. Naipaul, *Voyage among the Believers: An Islamic Journey* (1981). A personal voyage of discovery through Asian Muslim countries by a West Indian novelist and essayist.

*Salman Rushdie, *Midnight's Children* (1981). A vivid novel about independent India, viewed through the eyes of an Indian born at the moment of independence.

*Khrushwant Singh, *Train to Pakistan* (1956). A moving fictional account of the tragedy of partition, from the perspective of the people of a tiny Punjab village.

---

*Indicates book is available in paperback.

CHAPTER ELEVEN

Africa and Latin America in the Third World

- Africa's Liberation from Colonialism
- Latin America in the Cold War
- Democracy in Latin America

Highlight: The Third World

Spotlight: Nelson Mandela

Africa and Latin America were distant continents that confronted a similar dilemma in the postwar decades. Both regions were divided largely into small states with meager resources to care for the needs of their growing populations. The difficulties created by this situation provide an important clue to their history in the period following the Second World War.

The liberation from imperial rule occurred in Latin America 150 years before that of African colonies. Almost the entirety of Latin America won freedom from the Portuguese and Spanish empires in the early nineteenth century. It came largely through colonial revolts, whose leaders appealed to the images and symbols of revolutionary democracy and national liberation to explain the justice of their cause. The story of the nation-in-arms became one of the key ingredients by which politicians there created a mythical birth for their new nation-states. The real process of state-building was slow, and political unrest erupted frequently in the next 150 years.

In Africa, imperial conquest began in earnest only in the late nineteenth century and was not complete until the first decades of the twentieth century. European empires retained their territories there for another half century. Suddenly, over a period of twenty years between the late 1950s and the 1970s, they granted freedom to their African colonial

311

peoples. The coming of independence was unexpected for both the colonial rulers and their peoples. It occurred in large part because small nationalist movements in these areas encountered little or no resistance from their empires. The governments of Great Britain and France, which held the largest imperial domain in Africa, had turned their attention to internal affairs after the Second World War. They were primarily concerned with their own economic and social reforms. Africa, in this sense, received freedom by default.

The major tasks confronting Africa's new leaders were similar to those of former colonies in Asia, namely, the creation of stable political regimes and the mobilization of the resources of their country to overcome the poverty of their peoples. Important features of the command economy adopted by the Soviet Union and the People's Republic of China attracted these leaders, looking for a quick road to economic development. The political model that they all sought to adopt was the nation-state. The ideal of national unity informed their political speeches. The ethnic diversity of their populations required, though, that they offer trustworthy guarantees of political pluralism. It was a requirement that few could satisfy. The alternative was civil strife that, when it occurred, was so severe that it undermined the very foundations of organized, normal life. Just who would take these monumental tasks in hand remained a constant issue throughout the vast area. South Africa was exceptional, both because liberation was delayed by a system of colonial domination ("apartheid") that remained in place until its abandonment in the early 1990s and because it remained economically dynamic afterward. Elsewhere, by the last decade of the century, the African continent's new states had achieved a minimum level of stability but in conditions of economic decay and sporadic civil wars.

Political leadership passed quickly out of the hands of those elected leaders who had first guided their peoples on the path of independence. They were displaced forcibly by ambitious officers from the new national armies. By the 1990s, outside states providing valuable economic assistance to African states had begun to put pressure on these dictators to restore some measure of democracy, but the results were disappointing. The crisis of the new African states was especially apparent in the remorseless economic decline that occurred in large areas of the continent. No easy answer could explain the origins of the decay of agriculture and industry. The sad result was clear. Surveys revealed that the living conditions for much of Africa's population were worse at century's close than in the first decade of independence.

In Latin America, political life also involved a struggle for power between political leaders and army officers. There the conflict had persisted ever since independence from Western empires in the nineteenth century, and continued into the late twentieth century. In the decades after 1945, civilian and military governments there, as in Africa, turned to state controls over trade and finance to stimulate economic growth. They set up new social welfare programs for basic improvements in the living conditions of the population. Their efforts proved more successful than those of the African leaders. Gradually the standard of living in most Latin American countries improved. In a few countries, such as Brazil and Mexico, economic growth increased so rapidly it seemed in its own way to be a miracle.

The opposition to military rule in Latin America grew so strong that by the late 1980s these dictators had abandoned power. Unable to govern effectively and confronted by mass political opposition from democratic forces, they yielded power to elected civilian leadership. This political transfer occurred in the same years as governments gradually ended the system of state economic controls introduced at midcentury. This move followed the trend in Africa and Asia. The capacity of the free market to produce ongoing economic development proved everywhere more effective than the techniques of strict state planning and opened up economic opportunities to large numbers of the population. Only Cuba retained the basic features of a command economy. Despite the failure of its Soviet-type regime to realize their goals, the Cuban revolutionary leaders refused to abandon their dream of socialism.

Social inequality remained a pervasive condition throughout the region. Toward the end of the century, migrants left in greater numbers than ever before for North America in the hopes of escaping the poverty of their homelands. Still, the spread of democracy in Latin America was an encouraging sign of the decline of the old system of elite rule. Free enterprise did not bring social justice, but it appeared more suitable than state socialism in extending to a large portion of the population the opportunity to construct a satisfactory life on their own terms.

AFRICA'S LIBERATION FROM COLONIALISM

Independence came quickly to the African colonies of Western empires in the late 1950s and 1960s. This dramatic disappearance of empires in Africa marked the end of Europe's overseas colonial dominion. In the late colonial period, the only independent states in sub-Saharan Africa had been the countries of Ethiopia (under Italian control for a few years in the 1930s), Liberia, which was a small state created as a refuge for liberated slaves in the nineteenth century, and South Africa, granted independence within the Commonwealth by the British in 1910. Suddenly the other peoples of Africa ceased living under Western imperial rule. Their new leaders spoke proudly of their new African nations, even though many different peoples lived in each state, and

they promised a better life for their citizens, though these countries were still very poor.

The colonial past had left an indelible mark on the peoples of this vast continent. European rulers had, there as elsewhere in their vast empires, carved out new political borders to delimit their territories. Each colony acquired its capital city and centers of trading and, to a much lesser extent, manufacturing. Colonial officials encouraged trade where possible in cash crops such as cocoa, palm oil, and peanuts; African farmers were quick to adopt the new crops, which they hoped would increase their income. But in doing so they became dependent on the international economy, whose periods of recession depressed prices on these crops and caused them severe hardship.

The encounter with the outside world brought profound cultural and religious changes. The social and psychological stress of colonial rule opened the way to large-scale religious conversion to Islam as well as to Christianity. Muslim missionaries offered Africans a coherent religious dogma and a strong religious community. The Islamic faith spread rapidly; by midcentury, in eastern Africa and south of the Sahara, over half the population was Muslim. The imperial states for their part supported the work of Christian missionaries who offered the Africans who came to their centers basic social services, medical care, and schooling, as well as instruction in the Christian faith. Conversion was intimately linked to the disruptive impact of colonial rule. Imperial conquest undermined the credibility of the old animistic beliefs and elevated the Christian faith to the status of the conquer's religion. Conversion to Christianity provided social standing and cultural capital to those Africans eager to learn and to profit from new economic and political conditions.

Under the pressure of Western colonialism, the old bonds of tribal unity were gradually dissolving. But the cultural and social void was filled very slowly with new institutions and ideologies. Religion itself became a source of dissent. The high plains of Britain's west African colony of Nigeria became centers of Islam, while the peoples living in coastal regions were more likely to convert to Christianity. The very process of conversion provoked dissension. The Nigerian writer Chinua Achebe, whose father had chosen Christianity during British colonial rule, remembered that as a child he and all those in his church called themselves "the people of the church" and referred to the non-Christians around them as "the heathen" or even "the people of nothing." The nationalist message of resistance to empire and solidarity among African people appeared an alluring solution in these conditions of social and cultural disruption.

Nationalism in Africa

After the end of the Second World War, the British government reorganized its African colonies to prepare them for independence. Its plan for the transition consisted of a long period of self-government, under imperial supervision. Even then, its most optimistic plans foresaw a slow process of liberation lasting several decades. But its timetable proved useless under pressure of movements for colonial liberation and of Europe's reluctance to enforce colonial rule. One British statesman called these forces a "wind of change" sweeping away all the colonial empires. For the first time in African history, mass nationalist movements spread across the continent.

The emergence of African nationalism was a remarkable development. It took shape after educated Africans became familiar with the nationalist ideology of the West and was nurtured within the colonial world by shared enemies and new economic ties. The peoples within the European colonies in Africa were divided by tribal loyalties, by religion, and by language. Agreement among nationalists came from their perception of a common imperial enemy. The presence of European administrators and soldiers ruling the colonies was the tangible symbol of colonialism. The capital cities that flew the flags of the empire and housed the offices of the key colonial officials became sites of nationalist demonstrations and unrest. The struggle for the overthrow of imperial rule was a common bond uniting African nationalist leaders and their peoples.

The areas where effective movements against European rule first emerged were the British colony of the Gold Coast (later Ghana) in western Africa and Kenya, located in eastern Africa. In the 1950s, members of the dominant Kikuyu tribe in Kenya organized a violent struggle against white settlers on their land. They named their organization the Land Freedom Army, but Europeans scornfully called it the Mau Mau. Their nationalist leader, Jomo Kenyatta, united his followers around a program for the end to foreign rule and for distribution among the Kikuyu of the lands seized by Western settlers. Their greatest weakness, one which was apparent in the nationalist movements of other African colonies as well, was the reluctance of other tribal groups to join the Kikuyu revolt.

For four years the British struggled to repress the uprising. In the process, they mobilized other tribes in Kenya to fight the rebels and resettled many of their African subjects in fortified villages. They captured Kenyatta and sentenced him to seven years in prison. The Mau Mau uprising caused 13,000 deaths among the blacks (both Mau Mau followers and British supporters) and 95 among the whites. But in the course of the fighting, the British decided that they had to speed up the introduction of self-government in Kenya. In the end, Kenyatta had succeeded in forcing the British government to begin its withdrawal from eastern Africa.

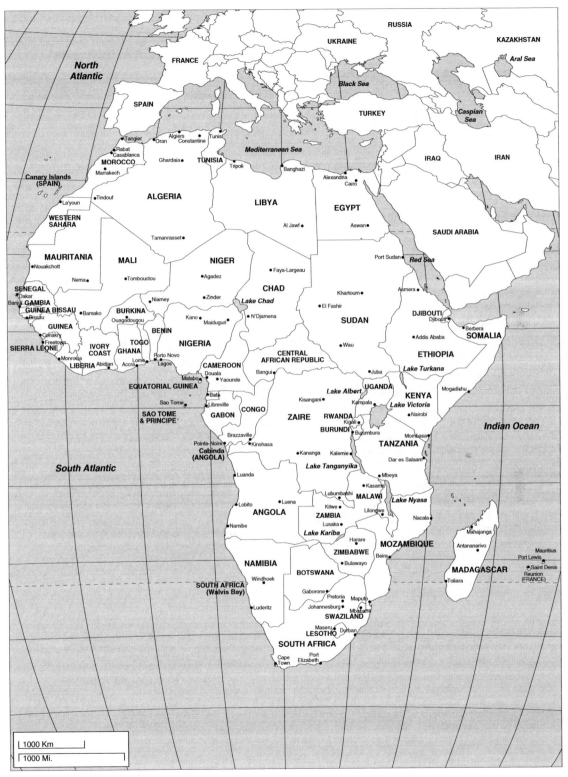

North
Atlantic

RUSSIA

UKRAINE

KAZAKHSTAN

FRANCE

Aral Sea

Black Sea

SPAIN

TURKEY

*Caspian
Sea*

Tangier
Algiers
Tunis
Oran
Constantine
Rabat
Casablanca
Mediterranean Sea
IRAQ
IRAN
MOROCCO
Ghardaia
TUNISIA
Tripoli
Marrakech
Banghazi
Alexandria
Cairo

Canary Islands
(SPAIN)
La'youn
Tindouf
ALGERIA
LIBYA
EGYPT
SAUDI ARABIA

WESTERN
SAHARA
Tamanrasset
Al Jawf
Aswan

MAURITANIA
Nouakchott
MALI
NIGER
Faya-Largeau
Port Sudan
Red Sea

Nema
Tombouctou
Agadez
CHAD
Khartoum
Asmera

SENEGAL
Dakar
Niamey
Zinder
Lake Chad
El Fashir
DJIBOUTI
Djibouti
GAMBIA
Banjul
BURKINA
Kano
Maiduguri
N'Djamena
SUDAN
Berbera
GUINEA BISSAU
Bamako
Ouagadougou
SOMALIA
Bissau
GUINEA
BENIN
Wau
Addis Ababa
Conakry
Freetown
IVORY
COAST
TOGO
GHANA
NIGERIA
CENTRAL
AFRICAN REPUBLIC
ETHIOPIA
Lake Turkana
SIERRA LEONE
Monrovia
Abidjan
Accra
Porto Novo
Lome
Lagos
Juba
LIBERIA
CAMEROON
Douala
Bangui
Lake Albert
UGANDA
Mogadishu
Malabo
Yaounde
KENYA
EQUATORIAL GUINEA
Bata
Kisangani
Kampala
Lake Victoria
SAO TOME
& PRINCIPE
Sao Tome
Libreville
CONGO
ZAIRE
RWANDA
Kigali
Nairobi
Indian Ocean
GABON
BURUNDI
Bujumbura
Mombasa
Brazzaville
Pointe-Noire
Kinshasa
Kananga
Kalemie
TANZANIA
Dar es Salaam
Cabinda
(ANGOLA)
South Atlantic
Luanda
Lake Tanganyika
Mbeya
Lubumbashi
Kasama
Lobito
Luena
Kitwe
MALAWI
Lake Nyasa
Nacala
Namibe
ANGOLA
ZAMBIA
Lilongwe
Lusaka
Mahajanga
Lake Kariba
Antananarivo
Mauritius
Port Lewis
Harare
MOZAMBIQUE
NAMIBIA
ZIMBABWE
Beira
MADAGASCAR
Saint Denis
Reunion
(FRANCE)
BOTSWANA
Bulawayo
Windhoek
Toliara
SOUTH AFRICA
(Walvis Bay)
Gaborone
Pretoria
Maputo
Luderitz
Johannesburg
Mbabane
SWAZILAND
Maseru
Durban
LESOTHO
SOUTH AFRICA
Cape
Town
Port
Elizabeth

1000 Km

1000 Mi.

Contemporary Africa

The first anticolonial campaign to reach its goal of independence took place in the Gold Coast (Ghana), located on the Atlantic coast of western Africa. The pattern of political activism and the difficulties of mobilizing mass support there reveal important characteristics of African independence movements elsewhere in later years. The Gold Coast nationalist leader was Kwame Nkrumah. He was a dynamic and skillful organizer, who used his Western education to formulate his own nationalist creed of liberation and freedom. He began to gather supporters against British rule in the late 1940s. By then a strong labor union movement had appeared among African workers in the colony's port cities, where cocoa beans, the principal Gold Coast cash crop, were exported to the West. The once-powerful Asanti tribes lived in inland areas where the crop was grown. Those commercial links between the coast and the hinterland of the Gold Coast created a bond of common interests and interaction among the ethnic communities. The colony's new market economy, suffering from price fluctuations passed on to growers and workers by the international corporations, became a major source of grievances against British rule.

In 1949, Nkrumah created his nationalist party, the Convention People's Party. It united activists from urban and rural populations from as far away as the Muslim north. He promised that freedom would put an end to the hardships of the Gold Coast peoples and would bring them a new era of progress and opportunity. Using language drawn from the Bible, he told his followers: "Seek ye first the political kingdom and all else will follow." Coupled with these promises he launched a campaign of passive disobedience against colonial laws. He drew inspiration for his anticolonial movement from the example of Gandhi and the Indian National Congress. His party honored those activists whom the British sentenced to prison as the party's "Prison Graduates." By the early 1950s, his movement had won such widespread support that the British government, unwilling to continue its costly and fruitless repression, granted the colony extensive self-rule. A British prisoner at the time, Nkrumah agreed to step into the interim position of the Gold Coast's first prime minister. Both sides preferred to avoid violence by agreeing to political compromise.

Nkrumah's goal was an independent nation-state. In other words, he refused to use ethnic loyalties of any people as the cement for his nationalist cause. But the Asanti tribal leaders in the north feared the rule of the southerners in a centralized government. In response to their concern, the British offered the country a constitution with a federal system made up of separate autonomous territories for the major tribal groups. Nkrumah reluctantly agreed to the new arrangement, though he had not abandoned his goal of creating a unified state. Independence came to the Gold Coast, renamed Ghana, in 1957. It was the first African country freed from colonial rule. Nkrumah was its first president and a hero for African nationalists everywhere.

Nationalist leaders such as he could mobilize widespread support against colonialism, but their coalition of forces relied, for united action, on hostility toward the British enemy. Once the British had withdrawn, these nationalists could no longer count on the continued backing of the peoples in their new state, for they did not have in hand a program for state-building that could satisfy the concerns and interests of their ethnically diverse population. Decolonization in Africa posed problems of state-building more acute than anywhere else in the colonial world.

In the late 1950s, both the British and French governments chose to end colonial rule in Africa as quickly as possible. International pressures played an influential role in accelerating the African decolonization. The leaders of the newly independent states of Asia made the freeing of African peoples an international crusade. Both the United States and the Soviet Union publicly backed freedom for colonial peoples. The United Nations became a public forum where anticolonial speakers denounced Europe's outdated imperial system. The weakness of the British and French empires became cruelly apparent in their failure to regain control of the Suez Canal in the 1956 war (see Chapter 12). That loss deprived them of a strategic imperial possession and demonstrated to them (and to the rest of the world) that they no longer possessed the power to defend their colonies at a time of global decolonization. This event proved decisive in pushing the two governments to grant independence to their African colonial territories. Imperialism was a lost cause.

Independence for African Colonies

Once an area governed by distant European empires, Africa suddenly was transformed into a continent divided into more than forty sovereign states. The process by which liberation came depended, in large measure, on the policies of the imperial states. Great Britain followed the procedure that it had used in Asia of negotiating with nationalist leaders in each colony for the creation of constitutional, democratic governments. After the Gold Coast, Nigeria became independent in 1960. There the leaders of the major tribal groups agreed, as in Ghana, on a constitution guaranteeing federal government as the best means to protect ethnic diversity among its 35 million people while ensuring the unity of the state. Then, in 1963, Kenya became an independent state under the leadership of Kenyatta, freed at last from British prison to move immediately to the presidency of the new government. The constitutional order of the new states resembled British parliamentary democracy. The British considered this Western import best for

Africa. Many nationalist leaders thought of it as a temporary measure useful during the transition from colonialism to full independence. Despite the speed of decolonization, the British and African leaders managed to cooperate and to maintain peace among the population during the transfer of power.

French decolonization differed from the British method in one major respect. In 1958, the French government proposed a transition period of extensive self-government coupled with economic and military advisers and financial aid to all French African colonies. For this purpose, it reformed its colonial empire, called the French Union, to allow African subjects to vote on joining the Union. The alternative offered to Africans was independence outside the French organization and no French support at all. This policy was the creation of Charles de Gaulle, French wartime hero, who in 1958 once again became president of France. His offer of collaboration with African states through the French Union was an effort to maintain close ties between France and its former African colonies.

Most African leaders from France's empire accepted membership in the Union. They dismissed charges from opponents that his plan was a form of "neocolonialism." They believed it a helpful measure in holding onto power, for they faced daunting problems of state-building. They hoped as well to obtain substantial French economic assistance, especially to fund expensive industrial investments and to sustain the value of their new currencies. In 1958, the colonies voted on joining the Union. In each territory, the voters adhered to the recommendation of their nationalist leaders. All the French colonies in Africa save one became members of the Union.

The member states received economic aid, financial advisers and technicians, and a monetary union with France. They obtained as well permanent French garrisons located in strategic locations on call in the event of border conflicts or political unrest. In exchange, they safeguarded French investments in their country. Two years later, the French government took the final, inevitable step of recognizing the full independence of all these former African colonies, who became members of the new "French Community."

The moderate leaders of these new states were effective opponents of radical revolution. They knew it to be a danger to themselves as well as to France's economic interests. One African leader concluded later that "General de Gaulle is the greatest African of our time." His opinion revealed how highly he valued political stability, achieved at the cost of very little social reform. The aid that France provided did bring those countries substantial benefits. Among these, political stability in the early years of independence was the most important.

In the largest of all the African colonies, the Belgian Congo (later Zaire), decolonization became a nightmare of civil strife and bloodshed. The area experienced violent anti-Belgian demonstrations in early 1959 for the first time. The protests were the work of a small nationalist movement supported largely by urban workers in the capital city, Kinshasa (formerly Stanleyville). This brief moment of political opposition was sufficient for the Belgian government to grant its colony independence immediately. In the previous decades it had made no effort to prepare the colony for self-rule. The nationalists themselves lacked a prominent leader supported by the peoples of that enormous country. Swept along by the "wind of change," in 1960 the Belgians freed their colony in the worst possible circumstances.

The results were tragic for the new state and for its population, both African and European. The colonial institutional structure quickly collapsed. The Congolese army mutinied and turned on the white settlers, who fled the country. Tribal groups fought among themselves. The only political leader with a substantial following, Patrice Lumumba,

could not restore order in the army and refused any help from the Belgians. The disorders soon became outright civil war. The southern region of Katanga (later Shaba), which was rich in mineral resources and a center of mining operations owned by Western interests, seceded from the new state and created its own army.

The United Nations agreed to send troops from member states to keep the Congo from complete collapse and anarchy. In the course of the fighting, Lumumba himself was captured and executed by Katanga forces. After a long period of political disorder, a former sergeant of the colonial army, Joseph Mobutu, seized control of the government in 1965. By then the surviving white settlers had fled, the economy of most regions was in ruins, and many thousands of Congolese had died in the fighting and rioting. The Democratic Republic of Congo, renamed Zaire a few years later by Mobutu, had begun its slow decay into a failed state.

The Triumph of Democracy in South Africa

South Africa, the southernmost country of the African continent, had enjoyed self-rule since 1910. The full rights of citizenship were restricted, however, to the white population. A member of the British Commonwealth, South Africa had a privileged place in international trade because of its valuable natural resources. Like a European democracy, its government passed back and forth between conservative and liberal political parties competing to exercise the powers granted by the majority in the country's parliament. Its constitutional order was watched over by an autonomous judicial system, also modeled on British practices. But it excluded the non-European majority of the population from participation in this system and subjected its African subjects to increasingly severe racial discrimination.

This restrictive democratic system opened the way for the country's Afrikaner people (formerly called Boers, the Dutch-speaking settlers) to insert racial intolerance into the constitutional order of the country. They numbered only four million, but their Protestant faith and their war with the British at the beginning of the century had made them a tight-knit community. Their three centuries of life as pioneers and farmers in South Africa had persuaded them that this was their native land. Their religious creed taught them that they were the "chosen people" and that the Africans were an inferior race. Their form of ethnic nationalism was racist at its very core. Their leaders were determined to hold onto this homeland by whatever means were necessary.

The economic wealth of the country, concentrated in gold and diamond mining, was in the hands of the English and other recent immigrants from Europe. Urban commerce was the special domain of Indian migrants, who had traveled there as subjects of the British Empire in search of work in the growing cities. Africans, for their part, had taken up labor in the country's vast mining industry. The Second World War had brought prosperity to the business interests of the country, dominated by the Anglo-American Corporation. Its holdings were extensive; one-half of all the companies in the South African stock exchange were in its possession.

Social inequality was not entirely a product of white domination. Most of the Afrikaners were poor farmers with relatively small plots of land, while some Indians and "Coloreds" (the term used to designate South African people of mixed ethnic ancestry) had prospered in trade. The poorest segment of the population consisted almost entirely of Africans. Still, by midcentury an increasing number of nonwhites were entering the urban economy to meet the needs of commerce and industry. Some Africans had obtained an advanced education and had entered the middle class. Nelson Mandela, later head of the African resistance movement, was a trained lawyer. In those years, the social consequences of economic development were gradually undermining white segregation policies.

By then the government had enacted an increasing number of laws intended to exclude Africans, Asians, and Coloreds from contact with whites. In response, many opponents of racial segregation had become supporters of the African National Congress (ANC). This organization emulated the methods and goals of the Indian National Congress. Formed in 1912, its members agitated peacefully for democratic freedoms and for an end to segregation in all forms. Its growing influence, and the support it received from liberal whites, presented Afrikaners with a serious threat to their domination.

The Afrikaner people had their own political party, called the Nationalist Party. In the late 1940s, it triumphed in national elections in which the principal issue was the place of nonwhites in public life. The Nationalist program called for their complete exclusion. It won sufficient backing from the voters to take control of the cabinet. The new Nationalist government proceeded in the next ten years to put in place a policy of racial domination that it called "apartheid." It excluded nonwhites from all political rights and curtailed their civil liberties. Africans did not even have the right to free choice of residence; they were forced to live in special settlements and permitted into urban areas to work solely as "guests" (the so-called pass system). Only the South African court system continued throughout the years of repression to honor (with major exceptions) the British principle of rule of law, even in trials of opponents of apartheid.

The Nationalists denied that the multiethnic, multi-racial people of their country could possibly form one nation. Nationalism in their understanding existed only as ethnic loyalty. There was no place for the spirit of civic nationalism in their racist program. Their policies intentionally sought to strengthen the divisions among South Africa's African peoples, whom they referred to as tribes. They were responsible for creating a regime of white supremacy in the very years when the African peoples elsewhere in the continent were obtaining political independence.

The African National Congress was encouraged by the success in the 1950s and 1960s of nationalist movements elsewhere in Africa to intensify its fight against apartheid. In 1955, it approved a "Freedom Charter," which spelled out clearly its program for a multi-ethnic, democratic South Africa "belonging to all who live in it." Its Youth League attracted activists impatient with the placid methods of the older members. Young leaders such as Nelson Mandela came forward arguing that the ANC had to fight the increasingly harsh Nationalist racist laws with a new campaign of mass action. Nonviolence remained the basis of their tactics, but the repressive powers of the state were pushing them toward confrontation.

In 1960, the ANC organized large demonstrations against the restrictive pass system. At Sharpsville, an African settlement, South African police fired on the unarmed demonstrators, killing more than sixty. It was a massacre whose principal effect was to mobilize the ANC to directly confront the regime. More demonstrations followed. In response to massive arrests and brutal imprisonment, the ANC leaders agreed finally to a campaign of violent resistance to accompany its political action. Nonviolence was no longer sufficient. The Nationalists had created a political crisis of their own making.

Their response was to resort to still harsher measures of repression. They outlawed the African National Congress and arrested its leaders on charges of treason. For the next three decades their police hunted down all political opponents. The government pitilessly enforced the pass system and all the laws that maintained white supremacy. It created separate "homelands" for African tribes. Africans had no permanent legal residence outside these areas, located in poor regions of the country. The pass laws gave them temporary residence elsewhere in settlements, which became mass ghettos outside the country's major cities. The Nationalists' policies isolated South Africa from the outside world, caused its expulsion from the United Nations, and created a state of emergency in the country.

Resistance came from within and from outside South Africa. The African National Congress retained its mass following and organized itself for survival as an underground organization. Violence within the country erupted frequently as protests were met with repression. In the 1980s, many Western countries joined in an international economic boycott of South Africa. By the late 1980s the government found itself in a grave crisis, facing social turmoil and a serious economic recession. The Nationalist leadership, under a new prime minister, F. W. de Klerk, finally conceded the hopelessness of apartheid. The very survival of South Africa depended on instituting a new political and social order. The only solution had to be real democracy and racial toleration. De Klerk's government gradually dismantled the laws that had enforced segregation. Many Afrikaners protested, but they had no alternative program to resolve the crisis.

In a desperate search for a solution, the reformers turned to the African National Congress. In 1990, they lifted all the legal restrictions that had denied the ANC the rights of a political party and freed all its political prisoners. After a half century of repression, the Nationalist Party recognized the African National Congress as its equal. The leaders of the ANC were prepared to cooperate. The Freedom Program had set out their conditions for negotiation. They had never abandoned their belief in the possibility of a peaceful multi-ethnic land of toleration and freedom. Their claim to speak for all Africans was challenged by a strong political movement among the Zulu people, the largest African tribal group in the country. This Inkatha party, like the Muslim League in India, had no hope of winning in national elections and demanded special recognition to protect the interests of its people. Reluctantly, the ANC agreed to collaborate with Inkatha.

In 1993, negotiations between the Nationalist government, the ANC, and Inkatha produced a new democratic constitution for South Africa. The next year free elections gave the ANC a majority of parliamentary representatives and the right to rule the country. The collaboration of the Nationalists, the ANC, and Inkatha ensured that, despite thirty years of violent confrontation, the transition of power occurred peacefully. This extraordinary, hopeful end to South Africa's political crisis owed much of its success to the remarkable leader of the African National Congress, Nelson Mandela.

◀ SPOTLIGHT: Nelson Mandela ▶

For most of his adult life, Nelson Mandela (b. 1918) was a political prisoner in South Africa. In 1994, he became president of that state. His decades of imprisonment and sudden rise to power were directly linked to the struggle against and ultimate defeat of the white supremacy regime in that country.

His childhood was spent within one of the African tribal groups living in South Africa. He was born to the ruling family of that tribe. The king sent him to an English-language Methodist secondary school to prepare him to become a tribal leader. But Mandela chose not to follow in the traditional path. He broke with the religion of his people, joining the Methodist church. After graduation, he left his tribal area to begin a new life in the booming cities of South Africa. He found work in a law office and ultimately earned his law degree.

In those years, the racial segregation imposed by the Nationalist Party touched him as much as other Africans and nonwhites of South Africa. He chose to make the fight against segregation his calling. When he was twenty-six, he joined the African National Congress, seeking the means to end tribal divisions and unite Africans, in his words, "as one people." He worked for many years with its Youth League to strengthen popular support for the ANC's program of racial equality and toleration. He was a dynamic, charismatic political organizer and forceful writer. He defended the ANC's program of democracy for all of South Africa's peoples. In his first years in the party, he backed the methods of nonviolent resistance to the racist laws of the Nationalist regime. For that work, he was arrested and accused of treason in 1955. "Because of my conscience," he wrote, "I was made a criminal."

His very life was at risk at the hands of the Nationalist government. The courts finally dismissed the charge of treason. When the Nationalist government in 1960 increased its repression against the ANC's political campaign, Mandela decided that the time had come to abandon nonviolent methods of resistance. South Africa had become, he wrote, a "land ruled by the gun." He saw no choice but to resort to intimidation and terror, principally by attacks on state buildings and key economic installations. This became the special task of his new underground organization, the Spear of the Nation. He became a hunted man, able to speak freely in defense of his cause only during a brief trip to Europe in 1962. When he returned to South Africa, he was arrested, convicted of treason, and sentenced to life imprisonment.

Mandela's long years of prison were a time of moral and physical trial, of isolation and hardship. Yet his commitment to democracy for his country did not weaken, and his political stature grew stronger than ever. His determination not to give up in the face of the government's repression became an inspiration for ANC followers. In those years, he emerged as the real leader of the ANC. As the international campaign in opposition to apartheid grew stronger, his imprisonment became a measure of the cruelty of the Nationalist regime's racism. His loyalty to the ANC cause confirmed the inability of its police state to end democratic resistance. In 1980, the Security Council of the United Nations stated that Mandela's release from prison was the first step necessary to permit a "meaningful discussion of the future of the country."

The Nationalists themselves had to concede his prominence as political leader. Mandela had always accepted the principle of peaceful negotiations for the creation of a democratic state granting equal rights to all its citizens. His release from prison in 1990 came because the Nationalists realized that his active leadership of the ANC was their only real hope to end the country's political and economic crisis. Mandela set the terms of freedom, accepting negotiations only after the government had released all South African political prisoners and had abolished its segregationist policies. In return, he made the peaceful transition of

power possible. When the new South African parliament met in 1994 after the country's first free elections, the ANC held the absolute majority. Its representatives elected him to be South Africa's first African president. Mandela had achieved his goal, to which he had subscribed when he joined the ANC, of creating a country that belonged to "all who live in it, black and white." Like Nehru in India, he sought to be the leader of a multi-ethnic nation.

President Nelson Mandela (*Courtesy of South African Consulate General, Los Angeles*)

These political reforms proved irreversible. The racists were defeated, and the ANC government began a concerted effort to make a better life for the country's nonwhites and especially its majority black population. A decade later, the results were encouraging. Its social welfare policies were creating public housing, intended to replace the black ghettoes, and were pushing elementary schooling after decades of disruption caused by social unrest against apartheid. Alongside the white middle class were appearing newly well-to-do blacks, who numbered by the early twenty-first century about ten million. But that left still over half the country's blacks in poverty. Those conditions sustained a massive crime wave, from burglary and robbery to assault and murder, that the authorities seemed powerless to control. South Africa was not isolated from the instability that afflicted lands to the north. Still, it appeared a desirable place to work and live to the hundreds of thousands of illegal migrants pouring in each year from neighboring African states. South Africa, among other African states, was a remarkably peaceful island of democracy, economic opportunity, and interracial collaboration.

African State-Building and Failed States

During the 1960s, the new African states proceeded slowly and painfully along the difficult path of state-building. The experiences of these countries varied greatly, but in the next decade two trends emerged. One was the appearance of authoritarian governments, most frequently under military rule, whose leaders replaced one another in forcible, sometimes bloody struggles for power. The other was economic stagnation and continued impoverishment among the rapidly growing rural and urban population.

Most African leaders quickly abandoned the democratic constitutions adopted at independence. Their peoples had been deprived of the experience of self-rule during the colonial years. After liberation, they valued political unification and economic development more than the creation of a multi-party system of government. Power soon passed into the hands of a political elite, consisting of civilian politicians and ambitious military leaders. One West African politician, whose state was among the best ruled on the continent, explained that "in young countries such as our own, we need a chief who is all-powerful for a certain period of time. If he makes mistakes, we shall replace him later on." He offered his people political stability under strong central rule and believed this the best they could hope for. The experience of other African states suggested that he was right.

In Kenya, Jomo Kenyatta continued in power until his death in 1978. He had no serious political rivals, for his prestige and authority as father of his country were enormous. His political party dominated the government. Violence rarely disrupted public life, though one influential politician from a rival party was found assassinated and his murderers were never captured. Kenya experienced orderly rule and relative prosperity, with white settlers living alongside their former colonial subjects. The army remained small, and the press enjoyed the freedom to report critically on public events. In Kenyatta's lifetime, Kenya represented the best case of independence with a stable government protecting a peaceful society.

Other small African states passed successfully through the period of liberation from colonialism into independence. The key proved to be the collaboration between respected leaders and loyal citizens. The former British colony of Botswana, landlocked and largely desert, enjoyed a few decisive advantages in that transition. The British had left in place the tribal leadership of precolonial times, and independence in 1966 endowed those leaders with new legitimacy as national figures. The desert hid great reserves of diamonds, discovered first in 1969. Their exploitation remained a private business (though with a substantial share of the profits going to the state), which prevented unscrupulous politicians from using the lucrative operations to enrich themselves and their supporters. Democratic government continued to function effectively. By the 1990s, taxes from this industry provided elementary education for all the country's children and adequate health care for a population whose average life expectancy had reached seventy. Along with these benefits, Botswana's citizens enjoyed a standard of living comparable to that of emerging economies in Asia. Key to the country's well-being was effective democratic leadership.

But in most new African states, authoritarian regimes brought only instability and misrule to their people. Ambitious politicians sought ever-greater power by manipulating parliaments, extorting state funds for their personal enrichment, and creating mass parties whose only purpose was to serve and to glorify themselves. Little or no political freedom existed, and enemies of the regime ended up in jail or were assassinated. Events after independence in Ghana illustrate this trend. Nkrumah had promised an era of great reforms when he took power. He set about dismantling the free market system, introducing laws creating a type of command economy. Proclaimed by his party "Man of Destiny" and "Redeemer," he rewrote the constitution to make himself president for life. His greatest ambition was to be recognized leader of all the African nations. He helped to found the Organization of African Unity and spent vast sums of money entertaining visiting African heads of state.

His rule proved disastrous for his people. He lacked the skilled personnel and the personal ability to use effectively the resources at his state's disposal, including large grants of foreign aid. Economic conditions worsened, and the standard of living of the people declined. By 1966, nine years after independence, economic decay and political disorder had undermined his authority. That year his own military commanders forcibly removed him from power. The army, which was the only national institution with a claim to respect among the population, became the backbone of dictatorship; army generals took charge of the government. Ghanaians welcomed his departure, destroying the statues and photographs that had glorified his exalted leadership throughout the country.

The usual pattern in many African countries became government by force of arms. During the 1960s, a total of forty successful insurrections took place among African states. They were the work of small groups of leaders and armed followers. In few African states did a new government come to power in those years in an orderly manner through democratic elections. One African observer sadly concluded: "We will never be at peace again." In the midst of such political unrest, people turned for protection to their tribal leaders. Tribal power frequently determined the winners in the struggle for control of the state; the resulting conflict among tribes became a cause of bitter civil war.

The bloodiest of these wars was the conflict in Nigeria. It began when northern Muslim peoples suspected (without substantial reason) that the Ibo people in the south had acquired a commanding role in the government of the Nigerian federation. They were fearful that their own well-being and security would suffer if Ibo people obtained special favors. The rumors were sufficient to set off bloody riots. Ibo settlers were attacked by mobs in areas where they lived among other tribal groups. The federal government appeared incapable of protecting the Ibo, who fled to their homeland. Ethnic violence led, in a vicious spiral of rumors, riots, and death, to civil war in 1966. An Ibo general convinced his people to secede from Nigeria. He counted on Ibo solidarity, which proved amazingly strong. For three years in the late 1960s, the Ibo people fought to establish their own state, called Biafra. Outnumbered and besieged by the Nigerian army, the Ibo abandoned the struggle only after their land was largely devastated and famine had decimated the population. Even then, their leaders refused to admit defeat and demanded that the people fight to the death. The foreign support that they had counted on melted away when the extent of the suffering became known outside Biafra. Nigeria was reunited, but at a terrible price. State-building in these conditions became a desperate effort to preserve, in the face of bitter ethnic rivalry, a country's meager remnants of civil order and political unity.

For the next two decades, authoritarian regimes headed usually by military officers governed most of Africa's new states. Their claim to power rested on the armed might at their disposal, not on any legitimate legal sanction. New leaders appeared usually after the violent overthrow of their predecessors in a turbulent struggle for power. When one strong ruler managed to remain in control for a lengthy period, the country was spared political turmoil. Invariably, though, the price was widespread corruption and persistent violations of civil liberties. At best, these leaders became aware of the urgent economic and social needs of the country. Their authoritarian practices made it fairly easy to end state economic controls and to allow a market economy to take root again. Ghana experienced a remarkable economic recovery in the 1980s after its military rulers abandoned the command economy that Nkrumah had put in place and opened the way for free trade in farm produce and industrial goods.

At worst, these rulers ravaged the meager well-being of their peoples. In the decades after he seized power in 1965, President Mobutu of Zaire (formerly the Democratic Republic of Congo) accumulated enormous personal wealth while depriving the country's public services of desperately needed state financial support. His personal prestige as leader of the largest state in sub-Saharan Africa brought him the support of Western states. Large amounts of foreign aid poured into his country. Most of the funds were wasted, going into his private bank accounts in Europe. He argued in television messages and public speeches that he was the guarantor of Zairian national dignity and solidarity. His message won him the support of those in his country who hoped Zaire's diverse peoples could be united under a just ruler in a multi-ethnic state. But he failed to satisfy their hopes.

His government nationalized the prosperous mining industry. Instead of reinvesting the profits, he appropriated its income for his own purposes. By the early 1990s, his mismanagement and the growing rebelliousness of his army had produced conditions in Zaire close to anarchy, that is, the absence of a functioning state and widespread lawlessness. The country's administration fell apart for want of funds, the army lacked arms and air transport, road and river transport dwindled, airports ceased operations, and cities lacked police protection, sanitation, and schools. The borders of Zaire remained intact, at least on maps of Africa, and its flag still flew among the United Nations flags. In other respects, Zaire ceased to function as a real state. It had become a "failed state," among those places in the world where the population could no longer rely on their state for law and order and for the most elementary public services.

The Cold War penetrated the African region in the decades after decolonization. It came as a result of competition between the Soviet Union and the United States for allies among African states and for access to the valuable natural resources (including uranium) of the continent. The U.S. Central

Intelligence Agency (CIA) established close ties with President Mobutu of Zaire, sending him secret military support and financial aid to help sustain his regime even after he proved to be a disastrous ruler. When in the 1970s civil war erupted in the former Portuguese colony of Angola, the Cold War rivals took sides in an effort to influence the outcome of the conflict. Soviet advisers and Cuban military forces were able (temporarily) to help their Angolan ally gain the upper hand in that war. Their foreign assistance stopped with the end of the Cold War in the late 1980s. The Soviet Union and the United States had provided assistance to the African states for reasons of state interest, not because they had an abiding commitment to the well-being of African peoples. When that assistance dried up, Africans were left with meager resources to cope with widespread impoverishment and the spread of diseases, old and new.

Effective opposition to dictatorship emerged within African countries from small groups committed to the political and civil liberties promised in their countries' first constitutions. They were encouraged in their efforts by Western governments, whose economic aid was vital to the very survival of some African lands. In 1990, both France and Great Britain announced that their aid would go in the future only to African states that respected their peoples' civil liberties, that permitted voters in democratic elections to select their leaders, and that loosened the state's control over economic life. Many dictators did, in fact, make serious efforts to open political life to parties and permitted elections.

The results were disappointing, however. In Nigeria, the military rulers refused in 1993 to allow the newly elected president to assume office, arguing that they alone could keep the ethnic hostility of the country's peoples from erupting in a new civil war. Another six years passed before free elections finally brought a civilian president to power there

and then in conditions of worsening conflict among the land's many tribal groups. Elsewhere, elections became a moment of struggle among ethnic groups, some of whose political leaders played on the fears of their people to win their votes.

African countries remained deeply divided by religious and ethnic bonds that impeded the formation of strong ties of national loyalty. Nigeria, the most populous African state, was also one of the borderlands where the struggle for power and land pitted pastoral nomads against farmers, Muslims against Christians. This social and religious divide cut across the northern states of sub-Saharan Africa from the Ivory Coast on the Atlantic to the Sudan on the Red Sea. Population growth and the spread of desert conditions heightened the conflict there over available resources, from water to pasture land to farms. Any dispute easily escalated into interethnic rioting, for the social differences were exacerbated by divisions into tribes, among whom some were Christian (usually the farming population) and others Muslim (usually the nomads).

In Nigeria, the early twenty-first century saw repeated bloody massacres across this divide, which ran through the heavily settled central regions of the country. In these circumstances, areas where economic systems, peoples, and religious communities had lived among one another in relative peace saw tribal groups gather together, expelling from their midst the outsiders, burning the mosques or churches of their enemies. The process was a form of "ethnic cleansing," that is, the creation of "pure" tribal areas by the elimination of another people. The writer Chinua Achebe condemned this tribalism in his Nigerian homeland as a form of "discrimination against a citizen because of his place of birth." But his wish for the growth of civic nationalism in his country remained an optimistic vision of the future.

The Failure of Economic Development

Closely linked to political disorder was the failure of many African economies to grow sufficiently to support an adequate standard of living for their peoples. The population explosion in Africa was greater than in any other part of the world, with growth fluctuating between 2.5 and 3 percent a year in the last decades of the twentieth century. Food production fell behind the growing needs of the people. In some areas, farmers chose or were forced to plant crops for export in place of food crops. Many governments monopolized farm exports in an effort to increase state revenues by artificially lowering the purchase price of cash crops and pocketing the profits from foreign sales. In Ghana, the result of the price controls set up by Nkrumah and retained until the early 1980s by later military rulers was a drastic decline in cocoa production. Exports fell by almost one-half, in turn cutting back funds available for needed imports. These price controls kept down the cost of basic foods for the poor migrants flooding African cities, where food riots were a serious threat to the fragile stability of the government.

Social distress and economic impoverishment resulted from a combination of political, commercial, and environmental factors. Where civil wars broke out, the rural population had to flee for their lives, abandoning their villages and fields. In the 1970s and 1980s, the decline in the international price of agricultural products hit African countries especially hard, for it deprived the farmers of income and the states of desperately needed revenue. Environmental degradation of the land became a serious problem as well. It was a visible result of a growing rural population denied adequate state assistance. Soil erosion and soil depletion were twin markers of this decay. In countries just south of the Sahara Desert, this process led directly to the expan-

sion of the desert ("desertification"). The environmental crisis in its turn contributed to a decline in agricultural yields and harvests. These political, demographic, and ecological difficulties produced a critical shortage of food throughout Africa. By the 1970s, the continent was harvesting substantially less food per inhabitant than in the previous decade. The situation worsened in the 1980s. By the end of the decade, overall food production had fallen 20 percent below its 1970 level.

Despite the fact that land had earlier been one of the sources of the continent's wealth, it could no longer adequately feed the population. Malnutrition was a fact of life for half of Africa's population. Economies declined, and families had to migrate to cities within or beyond the borders of their own country in hopes of finding work and food. Fearful of urban disorders, governments continued to keep food prices low to feed its urban masses. They relied in large part on foreign aid programs to supply this inexpensive food. It was all that stood in the way of serious famine.

The agricultural crisis hit even those countries such as Tanzania (formerly Tanganyika) where national liberation had produced stable political leadership. There Julius Nyerere, who enjoyed the prestige as founder of the Tanzanian nation, became president in the first elections in the former British colony and remained in that position until resigning twenty-four years later. His regime put in place an array of welfare programs to improve the level of education, health, and nutrition of the people. He was proud of the relative social equality that his policies had achieved. To further this goal, he took up the cause of collectivized agriculture (rather like the Soviet collective farms). Villages became a part of state-run farms, and the villagers had to join work brigades on the farms whether they supported the reform or not. Farmers resisted the state's coercive controls, and erosion and soil exhaustion resulted from misguided state agricultural experiments. The result of his disastrous policy was a decline of food production in Tanzania by nearly one-half its precollectivization level. Like China under Mao Zedong, the Tanzanian nation could be egalitarian only in conditions of economic decay. In the 1990s, a new political leadership abandoned his unrealistic socialist policies, allowing farmers to cultivate their own land and sell their crops on the free market.

The agricultural crisis was the key to the failure of economic development in Africa. This factor, more than any other, explains why in the decades after independence living conditions of the population scarcely improved and in many regions actually worsened. The economic statistics tell a tragic tale of stagnation and decline. Until the 1980s, the yearly rate of economic growth (domestic product per person) was less than 1 percent. The decade of the 1980s was a period of actual decline, averaging each year about 1 percent, in per capita wealth in Africa. One observer called that time the "lost decade" in the development of sub-Saharan African lands.

Economic aid officials in Western capitals concluded by the early 1990s that they had to cease subsidizing ineffective governments and to put severe conditions on financial assistance to African states. The French government curtailed its support for the currency used in the French Community of Africa. The resulting decline in the value of the member states' money forced their peoples to pay twice as much as before for imports. Officials from the World Bank, as a condition for loans, requested that African governments end their unsuccessful intervention in the economy and abolish policies of price and production controls. They insisted on reforms to establish the basic features of a market economy with free enterprise, free prices, and balanced state budgets.

Private investors gradually returned to Africa in search of profitable enterprises. Outside investors were drawn especially by the mineral wealth of the continent. Zambia's great copper mines had once been one of the world's major producers, next only to those of Russia and the United States. Taken over by the government in the optimistic years of national liberation and command economies, mismanagement and neglect led to the collapse of production. In the late 1990s, the government was forced to sell the mines to a South African mining company. Years of repairs were needed before the mines could produce as before.

A few fortunate countries, especially Nigeria and Angola, possessed abundant petroleum reserves. These states opened their doors to international oil corporations, who in exchange for rights to oil export assured the central governments of a substantial share of the profits. These revenues created what observers called the "spigot economy" ("spigot" standing for both the export of oil and the control of "big men" over this financial bonanza). Political leaders paid off their clients with the funds instead of looking for productive investments. The increase in state expenditures created inflation so severe that it made agricultural production unprofitable. In the worst cases, small-scale civil wars erupted when peoples in the area where oil was extracted protested the failure of the government to return to them their "fair" share of the profits. All these complications prevented the African economy from benefitting adequately from its natural resources. Though the presence of outsider investors and financial advisers was often deeply resented, African governments had no choice but to accept their presence.

For lack of adequate financial resources, state-run social services in African countries fell into decay in the late twentieth century. Education ceased to receive sufficient funds to train skilled labor. Medical care, which had dramatically improved life expectancy and infant care until the 1970s, became inadequate in the face of the population explosion and new epidemics. The most devastating of these was the spread of autoimmune deficiency syndrome (AIDS), carried by war and civil disorder into many African areas. In some countries health experts discovered in the 1990s that one-fifth of the population was infected by the human immunodeficiency virus (HIV) that caused AIDS. By the end of the century, health authorities estimated that about 14 million Africans had died of the terrible disease. African migrants, desperate to sustain the well-being of their families, defied immigration laws to seek work in Europe and the United States. The African crisis was a global concern.

The tragic betrayal of the hopes raised by national independence had many causes. Responsibility lay most directly with incompetent and corrupt rulers who manipulated their governments' resources in a destructive struggle for the spoils of rule. The sudden withdrawal of the European empires left a vacuum of power, which African peoples had little preparation to fill. They became the victims of their leaders' tragic misuse of political authority. The economic misery with which they struggled and the political insecurity of their lives pushed them to rely on clan and tribal ties and to mistrust leaders from beyond their ethnic group or of a different religion.

This tribalism produced ethnic conflict, the flight of refugees, and ugly massacres in country after country in the late 1980s and early 1990s. It had its roots in the failure of African national leadership. New forms of outside intervention appeared in the shape of foreign troops sent on U.N. peacekeeping missions, of bankers advising governments on economic policy, and of diplomats suggesting the means of restoring democratic practices. No better alternative appeared capable of helping Africa out of its misery.

LATIN AMERICA IN THE COLD WAR

The end of empire had come for almost all the peoples of Latin America in the early nineteenth century. Nationalist revolution swept the continent. The weak colonial forces of the Portuguese and Spanish empires were quickly defeated. European settlers had led the rebellions, and they became the rulers of the new states. Their understanding of nation was defined by the administrative borders of their former colonies, by the European languages implanted by the empires, and by the exclusive control over these nation-states by the population of European descent who had settled the New World. They made no place in their new national communities for the Native American peoples.

These "Indians" made a meager living in the countryside as farmers or farm laborers. The Europeans held in their hands the wealth of countries in the form of great estates, mines, commerce, and industry. In Brazil, many tribes in the Amazon basin remained isolated, some completely unknown, for a century or more. Only the Catholic Church, whose faith had spread among most of the population during the colonial period, had in some measure succeeded in breaching the barrier between these communities. In these terms, Latin America's economic and cultural evolution had little in common with lands in Asia and Africa that had just achieved their own national liberation.

Latin America's relations with the outside world were unique as well. Its states were diplomatically and militarily weak. In the early twentieth century, the northern regions of Latin America fell within the sphere of influence of the United States. Occasionally, the U.S. government sent military forces or political advisers to settle civil disorders or political quarrels in the small countries in the area of the Caribbean Sea and in Central America. Only Mexico escaped U.S. domination after its revolutionary upheaval of the 1910s. In the 1930s, President Franklin Roosevelt finally renounced this interventionist policy, promising "good neighbor" relations with Latin American countries.

In the middle of the twentieth century, the United States remained the dominant power in the region. It was the principal source of investments and the major market for the sale of Latin America's raw materials, still its major export and principal source of wealth. The U.S. government expected Latin American governments to recognize the importance of its strategic interests. In the Second World War, many Latin American states joined in the alliance against the Axis powers. In the Cold War, the United States relied on them to oppose the Soviet Union and the international communist movement. Its diplomatic and economic influence in the region was pervasive and at times oppressive.

Latin America fit well the category of "Third World" region. Observers used the term to suggest the social and economic gulf between the underdeveloped lands and the developed countries, capitalist or communist. Living conditions among much of the Latin American population were so poor that they resembled those in Africa and Asia. Political leaders devised new political and economic strategies to deal with underdevelopment. Their hopes centered on state policies for economic development. In these terms, too, the area bore a strong resemblance to countries in Asia and Africa. European and North American corporations controlled major industries, and their banks were an important source of investment funds. Real political and economic independence remained an elusive ideal and achieving it became the highest priority for many Latin American governments.

The Lure of Economic Independence

After the Second World War, a new generation of Latin American leaders came to power who for the first time took an active role in promoting economic development. The war itself had expanded the global demand for Latin American exports; it also opened markets for its manufactured products. These new opportunities for economic growth offered an escape from the dependency of these countries on the United States. Latin American economists argued that this "import-substitution strategy" would raise their countries into the ranks of developed economies and improve the living conditions of the population. Political leaders promised as well extensive improvements of the states' social welfare programs for their peoples. It proved a winning electoral program. But achieving success in both areas was difficult, at times impossible.

An important and controversial innovation in foreign economic relations was the introduction, with U.S. backing, of new policies intended to encourage outside investments for economic development. These offered tax exemptions and cheap labor to international business investors, primarily from North America. U.S. corporations, protected by their state and by Latin American rulers, expanded their ownership of mines, plantations, and industrial enterprises throughout the continent. These investments did not grow as rapidly as expected, however. The disappointing results forced Latin American leaders to continue to rely on their own economic resources to fulfill their promises to the people.

The "import-substitution" plans for development called for active involvement by state agencies in the economic affairs of their country. Officials, working under government supervision, assumed special power over markets to bolster domestic industries whose products would replace foreign imports. State funding made subsidies available for the opening of desirable new industries, such as aviation and automobile. State tariffs and other regulations hindered foreign imports that might weaken these infant industries. The success of these plans depended on wise leadership, difficult to achieve in poor countries torn by political rivalries and confronting rapidly growing populations. The lure of increased independence and economic prosperity was all the greater. Conservative in their social policies, many Latin American governments were prepared to experiment with a limited type of a command economy.

The success of these programs depended, as in most Third World countries, on outside financial assistance. Latin American economies looked to Western banks for loans to stimulate industrial growth. Governments also needed loans and foreign aid to pay for basic public services needed to raise the people's standard of living. But economic boom times, when exports brought plentiful state revenues and abundant foreign loans, were followed by harsh times of international recession, crushing debts to foreign banks, and domestic government deficits. Wild inflation resulted from continued financial payments on popular projects. Too often, governments found that as a result of their bad planning and reckless commitments they lacked even the means to repay their foreign debts.

Populist political movements defended the social and economic needs of the people, accusing their rivals of collaborating with foreign business interests (a common practice) and demanding increased state welfare policies for the poor (for which funds usually were insufficient). Leaders who refused these demands ran the risk of provoking mass protests. Those who supported the populist program bought popularity at the expense of financial chaos. Political strife and economic dependency held Latin America in a tenacious grip in midcentury.

Populism in Argentina, Brazil, and Chile

The political and civil liberties promised in the nineteenth-century nationalist constitutions of Latin America had little chance to be enforced in the midst of the bitter quarrels among political parties and between civilian government and the military. The decade of the 1950s was a time when powerful leaders supported by populist coalitions dominated Latin American politics. Their moment of glory was cut short by army insurrections followed by a return to military dictatorship.

This was the political fate of Argentina, Brazil, and Chile, which were the dominant states of Latin America. In 1946, Juan Peron was elected president of Argentina. He had promised the voters an end to rule by the country's wealthy elite and a massive program of social welfare. With the strong backing of the labor unions, he formed a populist coalition of followers eager to see the country's oligarchy finally dethroned. Argentina was rich in raw materials and agricultural resources. President Peron used his presidential powers and political influence to make sure welfare benefits went to the laboring population.

The political price of his policies was high. In a few years, his government had to curtail spending and cut back social programs. Soon labor unrest grew. In desperation, Peron mobilized his supporters in a campaign against the Catholic Church, which he accused of excessive wealth and support for his political enemies. It was a dangerous move in a country with a strong Catholic population. Argentina's social elite, fearful of Peron's populist program and outraged at his attack on the Church, encouraged ambitious generals to intervene in the political crisis. In 1955, their wish was fulfilled when Argentine military leaders overthrew Peron's regime. Argentina passed rapidly from populist democracy to military dictatorship.

This authoritarian regime remained in power, with brief interruptions, until the 1980s. The generals, claiming to defend the "Western and Christian world," proved to be oppressive and incompetent rulers. Staying in power was their main objective. They were little concerned with using the natural abundance that their country possessed to improve the well-being of the people. The country's opportunity for economic development slipped away and popular discontent grew. Once at the beginning of the century a country as prosperous as Europe, Argentina began a decline into a social and economic hardship that resembled by the end of the century the conditions of underdevelopment. In the 1970s, revolutionary groups fought the regime with bombings, kidnappings, and murders. They, too, were unconcerned with immediate economic issues, for violent revolution in Argentina appeared to them to be their country's salvation.

The military dictatorship responded with a ruthless campaign of mass arrests and executions. Tens of thousands of alleged subversives simply disappeared, their very names erased from the official records. When they left behind small children, the infants were officially classified as orphans and made available for adoption. But repression failed to quell social and political unrest. In the hopes of winning patriotic backing, the generals attempted in 1982 to seize the Falkland Islands in the south Atlantic, occupied by Great Britain in the nineteenth century. They lost the war against British forces. This humiliating failure thoroughly discredited their leadership and doomed their regime. Shortly afterwards, they withdrew from politics, leaving Argentina, once a prosperous land, economically impoverished and politically unstable.

Like Argentina, Brazil was rich in natural resources but plagued by political conflict and extreme social inequality. Its social elite lived in a world far removed from the poor population in the country's coastal cities and interior jungles. Brazilian politics posed specially challenging problems to its government, since the country was the largest and most populous of all Latin America. Its coastal regions were centers of modern urban life, while its enormous interior (especially the rain forests of the Amazon basin) remained largely untouched by modern industry and agriculture.

In the 1940s, Getulia Vargas, a dynamic and charismatic political leader, took up the task of reviving Brazil's economy and improving the living conditions of its people. He mobilized a broad coalition from the middle and working classes to support his ambitious program of economic growth and social welfare. He sought above all the expansion of Brazil's industrial economy. His government used the powers and revenues of the state to subsidize private companies and to create nationalized enterprises in key sectors such as oil exploration, armaments manufacturing, and automobile production. His program produced substantial benefits, and his economic policies set the model for future governments.

After his death in 1954, his political heirs proclaimed their commitment to his vision of a "new Brazil." They made the enormous interior regions, still undeveloped, the object of the greatest colonization drive since the nineteenth-century occupation by white settlers of the North American Great Plains. The state constructed more than 11,000 miles of new roads that penetrated deep into jungle areas where Indians had once lived in absolute isolation. The roads brought settlers who carved out land for ranching and farming from the great rain forest. The Brazilian government spent enormous sums constructing its new capital, Brasilia, in the middle of the wilderness. Intended to be "the capital that [would] unite the whole nation," it was inaugurated in 1960.

The cost of these immense development projects was far beyond the financial resources of the Brazilian government. To pay for them, it had to turn to Western banks, contracting enormous foreign loans whose repayment put a great burden on its budget. As in Argentina, power-hungry generals were the only ones to benefit from the social unrest and political conflict caused by the resulting financial crisis. With the backing of the conservative Brazilian elite, they overthrew the democratic government in 1964, beginning a twenty-year military dictatorship. The prevalence of the military in Latin American political life in the

1960s and 1970s constituted a depressing return to an old form of rule.

The Cold War was a distant event for Latin American countries. Yet the pervasive influence of the United States and the emergence of revolutionary movements inspired by Chinese and Soviet communism brought this global conflict into the political life of the region. The Cold War made its disruptive effects felt most visibly in the Pacific coast country of Chile. Unexpectedly it found itself the center of ideological and political crisis in the early 1970s.

Once a model of liberal democracy, Chile's political parties were split between radical and conservative forces by bitter ideological issues of social reform. With the backing of workers and peasants, a reform government, led by the socialist Salvador Allende, took office in 1970. His political strength depended on a coalition of socialist and communist parties. They had agreed on a radical populist program, including sweeping nationalization of domestic and foreign-owned industries. Their goals resembled those of socialist governments in Asia and Africa. While looking to Third World reformers, they were tempted in particular by the example of Fidel Castro's Cuba to break away from U.S. international leadership. Theirs was a vision of revolutionary socialist change. That spirit spread to the countryside, where peasants began to seize large estates, and to the factory workers who repeatedly went on strike to demand wage increases. Opposition to this program came from business groups, from conservative parties and the military, and from the U.S. government. The country was gripped by bitter political and social conflict.

Determined to restore order, Chilean military leaders led by General Augusto Pinochet plotted to seize power in 1973. They and their followers were persuaded that the country faced a communist revolution. That fear was shared by the U.S. government, determined to crush any communist threat in Latin America. Its CIA agents began secret operations in Chile that year, helping to organize opposi-

tion to the Allende government with funds and promises of U.S. backing. The threat of communist insurgency there was a myth but one that shaped the U.S. global containment policy in those years. Supported by Chile's middle classes and with the encouragement of the CIA, General Pinochet successfully ended Chile's experiment in socialist government. In the course of his insurrection, his army was responsible for Allende's death during its siege of his presidential palace. Arrests of supporters of Allende's regime swept across the country; the army and police executed without trial an unknown number of prisoners. For nearly two decades Chile was ruled by Pinochet's military dictatorship.

Military rule in Chile differed from that in Argentina and Brazil in one important respect. The Chilean generals, in their effort to promote economic development and social stability, opted for the capitalist strategy. In the decade after the insurrection, they invited American economists to be key advisers in implementing free market policies. They pulled the Chilean government out of economic activities and cut back social welfare for the poor. All Allende's reforms disappeared, at the price of serious hardship to the working population and in conditions of prolonged recession. But in the early 1980s, the formula produced substantial benefits to the population when the country began a period of rapid economic growth.

Central America under U.S. Domination

In the 1950s, the U.S. government found its most faithful allies in Central America to be military dictators. Diplomatically, it sought to bring all the countries in the entire region, including the Caribbean islands, within its sphere of influence. The small states there had to adhere closely to U.S. anti-communist and procapitalist policies in their domestic and foreign affairs. The United States took its Central American allies wherever it could find them.

One of these was the head of Nicaragua, General Anastasio Somoza. He had seized power in his country in the early 1930s, capturing and executing his principal rival, the nationalist leader Augusta Sandino. Somoza's rule brought his family great wealth. At the same time, it guaranteed the landowning elite the protection of its comfortable living and en-

Contemporary Central and South America

sured the United States a loyal ally in the Cold War. Rulers such as Somoza were in effect client politicians in their relations with the United States. They faithfully adhered to its diplomatic guidelines and protected American business interests. In exchange, they obtained economic and military aid from the American government and an export market in the United States for their raw materials.

Cuban politics in the 1950s duplicated this pattern of rule. The dominant figure was Fulgencio Batista, an army sergeant who became dictator in the 1930s and then president after he himself introduced a democratic constitution in 1940. Keenly aware of U.S. political and economic interests in Cuba, he bent with the political winds from Washington. In the war years, he heeded the U.S. call for the renewal of democracy. In 1944, he withdrew (temporarily) from politics. The era of democratic government lasted only eight years. In the early 1950s, Batista realized that the United States once again tolerated dictators within its Caribbean sphere of influence, on condition that they back Cold War policies. His appetite for power was as strong as ever. With the support of the Cuban army, he seized control of the government in 1952. Elections scheduled for that year were not held. He banned the Communist Party and ended diplomatic relations with the Soviet Union. The United States asked for no more.

Batista's understanding of U.S. priorities was correct. Like Somoza of Nicaragua, he received generous U.S. military assistance to arm and train his small army. His state kept closely in step with U.S. foreign policy and cooperated with U.S. investors. Sugar, the country's major crop that was sold principally to the United States, epitomized Cuba's continued economic and political dependence on the United States.

Cuba's military dictatorship lasted until 1959. Its economy expanded in those years, for sugar sold well in the United States and foreign tourists flooded the country. Impressed by Cuba's flourishing gambling casinos, one American gambler exclaimed: "The future looks fabulous!" Many middle-class Cubans benefitted substantially during those prosperous years. The Cuban standard of living was among the highest of any Latin American country. Economic prosperity was not sufficient to safeguard Batista's rule, however. He proved to be an incompetent and unpopular ruler. Cuban nationalists condemned the commanding role of the United States in the Cuban economy and accused Batista of neocolonialist subservience to the Yankees. He relied on his army to control popular unrest, but his repression of political opposition served only to provoke more resistance. He had confidence in his military forces and in U.S. backing. He was wrong on both counts.

The man responsible for the fall of the Cuban dictator was a remarkable revolutionary leader, Fidel Castro. Son of a successful sugar plantation owner, Castro grew up in comfortable conditions. He was sheltered from the effects of the depression as a child and given the benefits of an education reserved for well-to-do Cuban youth. But his political convictions were those of a radical nationalist. Trained as a lawyer, he entered Cuban politics in the late 1940s on a program of independence from the United States and social reform. In those years, a period in his life Castro later called his "bourgeois thralldom," he was no different from many other aspiring young Cuban politicians. National legislative elections were scheduled to be held in 1952, and he prepared to campaign for office. But Batista's military coup disrupted these plans. Among the most bitterly disappointed candidates for office was Fidel Castro. Batista's dictatorship transformed him from party politician into a revolutionary leader.

By early 1953, Castro had gathered a group of 150 followers, mostly young factory and farm workers, united in support of what they loosely termed the "Revolution." They pledged themselves to the restoration of the

1940 constitution, to "complete and definitive social justice based on economic and industrial advancement," and to liberation from "any links to foreign nations," that is, to the United States. The emphasis on social reform and opposition to U.S. imperialism constituted the core of Castro's political ideology. It was a romantic mixture of revolutionary fervor, defiance of Yankee domination, and concern for the needs of Cuba's poor. It later became the heart of his revolution. His confidence in his political genius far exceeded his means of action, though. In mid-1953, he led his small band of followers on a reckless assault on Batista's regime. He was convinced that justice was on his side and that Cubans were prepared to rise up under his leadership. He was wrong. His uprising was easily quelled by the army, and he was captured and sentenced to a long jail term.

Castro's determination to overthrow his country's military dictatorship was undaunted. Amnestied by government in 1955, he fled to Mexico to organize a guerrilla force for a second attempt at overthrowing Batista. His revolutionary group, called the July 26th Movement (the date of his first insurrection), sought support among anti-Batista forces prepared to take up arms. A new rebellion was a risky undertaking, for Batista appeared firmly in control of Cuba. In other Third World countries, guerrilla forces had attempted to seize power from authoritarian regimes, and a few had even succeeded. Nowhere in Latin America did a comparable movement exist, and the United States might prove a serious enemy.

Castro's Revolution

In late 1956, Castro and eighty comrades returned to Cuba to begin once more their campaign to overthrow the Batista regime. This time, he succeeded in establishing a guerrilla base in the mountains of eastern Cuba. Opposition to the dictator had grown by then to include political rivals, labor unions, and many farm workers. Within a year Castro had built his tiny army into an organized band of 300 fighters supported by an underground political movement in most Cuban cities. He had alongside him his brother Raoul, a member of the Cuban Communist Party who had become his loyal aide and effective political organizer. With him also was a young Argentine doctor named Ernesto (Che) Guevara, an experienced, longtime revolutionary. They proved dynamic and forceful rebel leaders and found among the Cuban population many supporters repelled by Batista's brutal methods of rule. The guerrilla movement provided Castro with the instrument to seize power. Those who fought with him later became the leaders of revolutionary Cuba.

The U.S. government, suspicious of Castro's revolutionary and anti-imperialist program, hoped that Cubans would find another solution to the growing political crisis. In 1958, it ended its military aid to Batista's regime, clearly a losing cause. It anticipated that a new government would emerge uniting a broad coalition of Cuban parties. But it did not publicly condemn Castro's movement. Its silence helped Castro win the backing of Cubans prepared, for the sake of ending the dictatorship, to ignore his radical reform ideas. The U.S. policy of nonintervention in the Cuban conflict left to Cubans the choice of political leadership. The consequences proved not at all what U.S. leaders had expected.

In 1958, Batista's hold on the government was rapidly slipping away. Castro had by then organized a broad coalition under his leadership. That fall, small groups of his Rebel Army operated in all areas of the country. In the cities, an urban guerrilla force, the Civic Resistance, fought police and army units. In December, guerrillas under the command of Che Guevara moved out of the countryside to attack the capital, Havana. Batista's army melted away, and his generals fled for their lives. Batista found no one to defend his discredited regime. On January 1, 1959, he abandoned power and fled the country. On his heels came Guevara's Rebel Army. Castro arrived a week later, having traveled across the length of Cuba and received a hero's welcome from hundreds of thousands of Cubans. Castro, at age thirty-two, was leader of his country.

A political revolution began in Cuba that was unlike any that had ever occurred in Latin America. An armed insurrection led by a small rural guerrilla army totaling at most 2,000 fighters had ended the rule of a military dictator. Its political leadership, the July 26th Movement, possessed only the outlines of a reform program and exercised little control over its political allies. In a country of seven million, Castro's own forces were few in number. Supporting them was a collection of liberal and socialist organizations and movements. Castro's most valuable ally was the Communist Party, with about 15,000 members and a centralized leadership modeled on the Soviet Communist Party. It shared Castro's opposition to American domination and brought him cadres experienced in organizing mass movements. The coalition of groups that participated in the insurrection shared no common goal. Real unity came from Castro's own leadership. The new regime's ruling cadres came from the Rebel Army. This was the case in 1959, and it remained so in the years that followed.

The revolution that swept Cuba bore some resemblance to other revolutions that had occurred in Third World countries in the postwar decades. But the consequences in Cuba were unique and unexpected. Within three years after Batista's fall, the Cuban economy was run under a system of command economy identical to that of the Soviet Union and the country was governed by a one-party state supported by and dependent on the Soviet Union. Most significant of all, Cuba suddenly found itself on the front lines of the Cold War. Castro's decision to rely on the Soviet Union for economic aid and military protection weakened the U.S. sphere of influence in the Caribbean and led to the most serious inter-

national crisis since the end of the Second World War.

From the first year of his revolution, Castro was the central figure in Cuban politics. Consolidation of political power was his first objective. His second was radical reform to improve the living conditions of Cuba's lower classes. His third was the withdrawal of Cuba from the U.S. sphere of influence. His aims resembled in many ways those of other Latin American populist movements. His program appealed to many Cubans, especially the poor peasant farmers and urban working classes. For them, he was their undisputed national leader. He was determined to maintain political control of the new state. He arrived in Havana in early January 1959, warning that he would not allow the new leadership to behave "like the many revolutionaries of the past [who] roamed around fighting each other." He understood that task to mean the exclusion from power of any groups that might challenge his own leadership.

Within two months he assumed the formal powers of prime minister. Gradually all the important government positions passed to his colleagues in the July 26th Movement. Free elections were never held. In 1961, Castro formally dissolved the constitution of 1940, claiming it was "already too outdated and old for us." In fact, Castro refused to permit free elections and civil liberties to weaken his political domination of the country.

A Soviet-type centralized dictatorship began to take shape. Castro and those around him intentionally modeled their new regime on communist one-party states. Leadership of labor unions, once controlled by Batista's supporters, passed into the hands of Communists. Political opponents were prosecuted by a new security police acting in the name of the "revolution." The state took control of Cuba's press, radio, and television, all placed under strict censorship. Castro called his rule "direct government by the people." Power actually belonged to the former guerrilla leaders.

The conflict between Cuba and the United States began shortly after the revolution. It originated in Castro's early efforts in 1959 to make tangible the ideals, as he understood them, of social equality and economic justice. To aid the urban poor, he had housing rents lowered by 50 percent and electric power rates cut by as much. In May, the new regime ordered the expropriation of all landed estates of more than a thousand acres, including all large sugar plantations owned mainly by foreign companies. Part of the land went to poor and landless farmers, while the largest plantations became collective farms under state control. Nationalization of foreign businesses continued through the rest of the year despite objections from the U.S. government.

The Cuban revolutionaries were determined to liberate their country from domination by the "Yankee imperialists." Castro announced in 1959 that Cuba would adopt a new foreign policy of nonalignment. He condemned U.S. Cold War policies and capitalist exploitation of Cuba's resources. The new Cuban leaders were searching for a way to escape the U.S. sphere of influence, but they realized that their country depended as much as before on sugar exports. These sales brought the income essential to finance their expensive reform program. The U.S. government had for decades supported the Cuban economy (and the state) through regular, massive purchases of sugar at a guaranteed price. In strictly commercial terms, Cuba was dependent on the U.S. economy.

Castro decided to present the U.S. government with a daring, remarkable demand for indirect assistance. His proposal took the form of a request that the United States double its procurement of sugar and agree to a 20 percent increase in price. His demand represented a public claim on the wealth of the Yankee imperialists. It was a reckless move, in contradiction with his denunciation of U.S. foreign policy and typical of his revolutionary zeal to transform Cuba. Unable to believe that the Cuban revolutionaries were beyond

control, the Eisenhower administration refused to renegotiate the sugar agreement and demanded that U.S. businesses receive proper compensation from Cuba for their property losses.

Rather than retreat, the Cuban revolutionaries pushed ahead in their efforts to escape U.S. domination. They turned to communist countries with a request for the economic and diplomatic support denied by the United States. They were successful, for the Soviet leaders welcomed the opportunity to carry their new Third World policy of aid to "bourgeois nationalist" leaders into Latin America (see Chapter 7). In February 1960, the Soviet Union signed an agreement to buy Cuban sugar on a regular basis and to provide Cuba with a major loan to permit Cuban purchase of Soviet machinery, petroleum, and military armaments. Castro considered the treaty a victory for Cuban nationalism. The Soviet petroleum had to be refined in Cuba, and Castro ordered the U.S.-owned refineries to cooperate. After consulting with Washington, the oil companies refused to process this "Red oil." In June 1960, Castro seized their property.

His decision proved the breaking point in U.S.-Cuban relations. The U.S. government halted all purchases of Cuban sugar and later that year declared a complete embargo on trade with Cuba. It had, in effect, begun economic war. Castro responded by seizing all U.S. property. He added to this list all the remaining privately owned industries, banks, and transportation in his country. By the end of 1960, trade and banking, most of industry and transportation, and one-third of the agricultural land belonged to the state.

By then the Cuban leaders had decided to take control of the entire Cuban economy. They viewed the Soviet Union as their model, copying the Soviet command economy system. They introduced laws enforcing command planning, organized collective farming throughout the countryside, and used state revenues to develop nationalized industry. Their decision was made hastily, and they lacked the skilled personnel and the revenues for this mammoth task. They borrowed heavily from the Soviet Union and welcomed Soviet economic advisers to help in constructing a socialist economy on their island. In doing so, they made their country dependent on the Soviet Union both diplomatically and economically.

The U.S. government had already begun plans to end this pro-Soviet state so close to its shores. President Dwight Eisenhower had authorized the U.S. foreign intelligence service, the CIA, to organize anti-Castro Cubans for a possible invasion. In early 1961, John F. Kennedy, just elected president, publicly warned that Cuba was becoming "communism's first Caribbean base." His Cold War strategy remained the policy of containment, enlarged by then to include covert measures against states suspected of allying with the Soviet Union. He approved the CIA plan for a U.S.-supported rebel invasion of Cuba. He believed CIA assurances that Castro was unpopular and that a mass uprising among Cubans would reinforce the small rebel force attacking the island.

Events proved them wrong. The 1,400 Cubans who disembarked from U.S. warships to invade Cuba at the Bay of Pigs in April 1961 were stopped at the landing beaches. The new Cuban army quickly defeated the invaders. In the interior, Cuban police immediately arrested suspected rebel sympathizers. The invasion was in the end a disastrous, futile undertaking. Victory brought the Cuban revolutionaries greater popularity than ever before. They had defeated the forces of the "Yankee imperialists."

Still, their new regime remained terribly weak in the face of their mighty neighbor. They had to anticipate another U.S. invasion, certainly more concerted and massive than the first. That reason alone may have incited Castro to seek a military alliance with the communist states. His understanding of global revolutionary forces had evolved as well. He

believed that his country had joined the Third World's crusade against capitalism and imperialism. The enemy in this confrontation was the United States. Castro concluded that his country belonged both in the Third World and in the communist camp. He made this clear in December 1961, when he announced, "I am a Marxist-Leninist and shall remain a Marxist-Leninist until the day I die." It was an affirmation of faith that contained a direct appeal to the Soviet Union for protection.

The Soviet leaders proposed to him only part of what he sought. He hoped for a Soviet military alliance. Neither the Soviet Union nor the Warsaw Pact (the military alliance of communist states) was ready for this risky move. Instead, in the spring of 1962, the Soviet government proposed to place short- and intermediate-range ballistic missiles in Cuba. These were to be installed and controlled by Russians. Castro agreed, believing that his country was obtaining military protection in the fight against world imperialism. The missiles, accompanied by Soviet technical personnel and anti-aircraft units, began to arrive in great secrecy early that fall. Then U.S. military surveillance penetrated the secret. The United States demanded the immediate removal of the missiles and threatened to invade Cuba if necessary. The Cuban missile crisis began (see Chapter 7).

To end the crisis, the Soviet government agreed to withdraw its military equipment and personnel from the island. It did obtain from President Kennedy a commitment not to organize any future military operations, either with U.S. forces or anti-Cuban groups, to overthrow Castro's regime. The world at large welcomed the compromise agreement, for it avoided nuclear war. Castro did not share in the satisfaction at the settlement. His government received only a U.S. promise of nonintervention. Worst of all, Castro had no voice in the resolution of the crisis. Soviet missiles vanished from Cuba without his approval. From a front-line position in the world struggle against imperialism, his island was reduced to a sideshow.

● HIGHLIGHT: The Third World ●

The term *Third World* appeared in the 1950s to identify a new part of the globe. It was the invention of a journalist who could not have imagined how successful his expression would become. It seemed to him an effective description of the newly independent countries such as India and Indonesia whose situation was unlike either the democratic West or the communist East. Its use quickly spread. Leaders of these new nation-states used it to emphasize their prominence in the postcolonial world. Radical politicians and intellectuals went further still by using the expression to identify all those areas of the globe which had been liberated from Western, "neocolonial" exploitation. In other words, this term became useful in the ideological debates about the future of the peoples of Asia, Africa, and Latin America after the collapse of Western empires.

In the decades that followed, its most meaningful and least controversial message identified the great disparity in economic and social well-being between industrialized and nonindustrialized lands. In the postcolonial world, the peoples in many countries were miserably poor, while a few areas enjoyed relative prosperity. At a time when governments in democratic and communist camps (the "First" and "Second" worlds) each argued that their own social and political ideologies were the best guides to human progress, the Third World urged both sides to look to the crying needs of their peoples.

These needs were defined in a variety of ways. Evidence suggested that about one-third to one-half of the peoples in the countries of Africa and Asia lived in absolute poverty, that is, lacked sufficient food to meet their basic

needs for subsistence. Inadequate medical care for mothers and newborn children meant that one-fourth to one-third of infants in areas of poverty did not live to be one year old. In human terms, conditions of life in these lands truly appeared to belong to another, "third" world.

Economists based their analysis of "underdevelopment" on the obstacles in these countries standing in the way of economic growth and well-being. They emphasized the inadequacy of basic facilities for industrialization such as electricity and roads and the lack of technically trained personnel prepared to maintain public services. They stressed the extremely low productivity of agricultural land, on which most of the peoples in Africa, Asia, and Latin American depended for their livelihood. They warned that countries that relied largely on the export of raw materials, true for most Third World economies in the 1960s, lacked funds to pay for needed imports of industrial goods and new technology. They stressed as well the inadequacy of education in these countries, where at most 50 to 60 percent of the population possessed minimal skills of literacy. These figures painted a picture of countries whose populations faced a future of misery and disease identical to that of their ancestors. Outside help appeared the only possible way to break this infernal cycle.

That need became the basis for economic aid programs in part because of the formation of the Organization of Non-Aligned States. It first met in the city of Bandung, Indonesia, in 1955. India's president Nehru rejected the argument of "some great countries" (referring to the United States and the Soviet Union) that "their quarrels are the world's quarrels and that the world must submit to them." In his opinion, the former colonial lands should not be "aligned" with either side. They had their own needs, the most urgent of which was aid from developed countries, communist or capitalist, for economic development. The United Nations became another forum for political appeals from Third World states. Their numbers grew until they constituted a majority of the membership in the U.N. General Assembly. At their urging, the United Nations launched programs called "Decades for Development." The first of these extended through the 1960s. It invited wealthy countries to contribute at least 1 percent of the value of their yearly national income to economic programs for developing areas. Nothing comparable had ever been attempted.

These calls for help incited a large number of governments to begin programs for aid. They did so partly out of humanitarian concerns, partly in response to Cold War competition for allies among the new states. Western governments made the largest contributions in the 1960s. The U.S. program for Latin America, called the "Alliance for Progress," brought billions of dollars in aid to that region. It came in large measure in response to the Cuban revolution and Fidel Castro's appeal for revolution in Central and South America. The Soviet Union's aid often went to great construction projects, helping to construct a mammoth dam for the Egyptian government on the Nile river at Aswan. Competition among donors occasionally produced unusual results. India obtained at about the same time three separate steel mills, one built by the United States, one by Great Britain, and one by the Soviet Union.

Economic assistance to the Third World grew rapidly through the 1960s and 1970s. The French government's program of economic assistance was directed especially to its former colonies whose new leaders had chosen to join the French Community. The World Bank made major loans at low interest and for long periods to governments that proposed specific projects, such as road building or the construction of hydroelectric dams. In the 1970s, the oil-producing countries of the Middle East became major donors when rising oil prices increased their revenues. Economic aid in the form of grants or loans to Third World countries became a long-term commitment by international organizations and industrialized states.

The efforts by Third World governments and by foreign aid programs to break the cycle of poverty and economic underdevelopment proved in places a remarkable success, in others a sorry failure. We cannot easily attribute these achievements or disappointments solely to foreign aid, for local and private initiatives played a major role. Economic development and public health programs were at times very effective. One example was the work of Western agronomists, notably Norman Borlaug, to create new, highly productive varieties of wheat, rice, and other crops. The success of their research brought an increase in yields so great that observers called the results a "Green Revolution." India's farmers increased their wheat yield by over 500 percent in the two decades that followed introduction of the new crops in the 1960s and did so without putting new land under cultivation. Borlaug warned that, unless India's population explosion was halted, these "miracle crops" would provide that country with sufficient food for no more than three decades. But for the time being, famine was held in check.

Other countries experienced remarkable improvements in industry and commerce. The most amazing transformation took place in small countries in eastern and southeastern Asia. Once poor areas largely devoted to peasant farming, South Korea and Taiwan became by the 1980s important industrial centers selling complex electronic products on the global market. Their growth rates were as high as those in Japan, whose economic example they seemed to follow. They could no longer fit by any measure the model of Third World countries.

Serious obstacles stood in the way of economic development elsewhere. One was the reluctance of the industrialized countries to sustain massive aid programs, since few ever reached the level of yearly aid at or above 1 percent of their national income. A second was the worsening of the terms of trade between industrialized and nonindustrialized countries. Between the 1960s and 1980s, international prices on raw materials fell drastically, sometimes by as much as 50 percent, as poor countries increased production to obtain a greater share of the market. A third barrier emerged when many of the Third World states, having accepted very large loans and grants, were unable to repay these loans. In the 1980s, interest rates on loans rose while prices on exports fell. Third World countries in Africa and Latin America were so deeply in debt to foreign creditors that they could afford only to make interest payments on their loans. In these desperate circumstances, they lacked funds for their own development programs.

Complex Technology for Africa: Irrigation Dam, Republic of Mali (*African Pictorial Collection/Hoover Institution Archives*)

A fourth obstacle proved to be the poor political leadership of many Third World states. Governments introduced risky economic reforms (often versions of command economies) that wasted the resources obtained through foreign aid on unproductive programs. Others were attracted to gigantic projects, such as Egypt's Aswan dam, that consumed tremendous funds that might have been used to cope with more pressing needs. Critics argued that simple technological innovations were in the long run better suited to the population and to the resources of poor countries. "Small is beautiful" was the motto of one economist who favored modest improvements in technology. By the 1980s, it was clear that Third World governments could not produce miraculous economic development through state policies. Their efforts were better directed to achieving what came to be known as "sustainable" growth that brought steady, small improvements adapted to their economies and resources.

The most serious obstacle emerged from the very success of policies combating diseases in these countries. The campaigns to halt epidemics, eradicate disease-carrying insects, and improve health care quickly raised the life expectancy of the population throughout the Third World. The immediate result was a population explosion in these regions, doubling the world's population between 1950 and 1990 (from 2.5 to 5 billion). This increase ate up the slow rise in farm production and industrial manufacturing. It left countries such as India with scarcely more food per capita in 1990 than in 1950.

The Third World was changing in shape. Well-to-do, well-educated, professional and entrepreneurial classes were making their presence felt within countries such as India. They were nearly as far removed from the poor masses as were the prosperous Westerners. The essential problem of a world deeply divided between wealth and poverty, developed and developing, the well fed and the hungry, endured to the end of the century. The Third World remained a dominating presence in global relations.

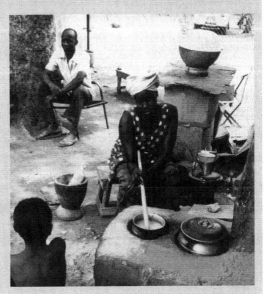

"Sustainable Development" at the Grassroots Level: U.N. Sponsored Technology for Cooking (*UN/DPI Photo by Kay Muldoon*)

DEMOCRACY IN LATIN AMERICA

In the decades that followed the missile crisis, Latin America gradually evolved toward an economically developed region where democratic governments coped, more or less successfully, with the needs of their peoples. Politically ambitious generals proved so incompetent that they were forced to withdraw from power. Economic plans for industrial development set in motion a process for development that raised the standard of living of a large part of the population. Increased well-being led millions of families to have fewer children, thereby slowing dramatically the increase in population. By the early 1990s, the region as a whole no longer belonged alongside sub-Saharan Africa within the Third World.

From Dictatorship to Democracy in South America

In the 1960s, the pressures in Latin America for social reform and economic development came from three new trends peculiar to the region. The Cuban revolution and Castro's stature as revolutionary leader crystallized social opposition to Latin American oligarchies. Castro laid down in early 1962 his guidelines for Third World revolution in his Second Declaration of Havana. He placed Cuba in the forefront of the "upward march of history." Cuba was to be a key player in the forthcoming triumph of socialism, because "the Cuban Revolution shows that revolution is possible, that the people can do it." He held up his revolutionary state as the model for revolutionary insurrection and economic development in all Latin American countries. To counter his program, governments in Central and South America turned their attention more than ever to plans for improving living conditions among their people.

Another reason for expanded efforts at social and economic progress was the decision of the U.S. government, pushed by fears of revolution, to sponsor economic development and social reform in Latin America. President Kennedy's Alliance for Progress, intended to assist all noncommunist states in the region, included a request that they create their own development plans. Governments that complied were assured of U.S. economic and financial assistance, which ultimately totaled $20 billion in the next ten-year period. U.S. advisers strongly encouraged the Latin American leaders to impose heavy taxes on the wealthy to help pay for these programs and to institute land reform to provide farms for the

rural poor and landless workers. The U.S. government also increased its military aid, directed specifically at repressing guerrilla movements like the one that led Castro to power.

A final important factor behind the concern for coping with poverty and social inequality was the decision of the Catholic Church to play an influential role in social reform. Pope John XXIII, elected in 1958, had initiated what he called a "reawakening" of the Church. The Second Vatican Council, meeting between 1962 and 1965, gave the Church's approval to his daring proposals. Many reforms and policies approved there had particular significance for global problems of economic inequality. These addressed the so-called pastoral mission of Catholics to care for the needy and underprivileged. The council looked to the needs of "the whole of humanity," calling on the clergy and the faithful alike to take an active role in social and economic reform to help the poor and oppressed. It welcomed state welfare policies and suggested that the faithful should create special organizations to assist in this enormous task. The Catholic Church was firmly opposed to violent revolution. Its program was meant to be an alternative path to social progress.

The consequences of its call "to all people of goodwill" to work toward peace and social justice had a profound political impact among the Catholic faithful, particularly in Latin America. The Catholic Church had for centuries been an integral part of the daily life of the peoples there. It had exercised a very conservative role, preaching obedience to the state and deference to the social elite. Pope John XXIII's "reawakening" changed all that. To implement the decisions made at the Second Vatican Council, all Latin American bishops met in 1968. In the presence of the pope, the delegates laid down the principles of social action by Catholic priests and laity. The goals were those fixed at the Vatican conference—the need for peace based on justice, human betterment through social action, and major social reforms.

The impact of these decisions was longlasting, though they are not easily measured. Within a few years nearly a million Brazilian Catholics, mainly from the poor laboring classes, had joined religious associations (called "cebs") to undertake local reform measures. In the years of repressive military dictatorship in the 1970s, they were the only mass political movement in the country. The effect among Catholic clergy was equally profound. Although upper-class bishops resisted the reform movement, other bishops and priests began to speak out openly against poverty and injustice, at times at the risk of their own lives. While Castro's supporters called for Marxist revolution, the Catholic Church proposed its own ideology of social reform.

The three decades following the Cuban Revolution were a period of political transition to democracy and economic growth in Latin America. Popular demands for better living conditions focused the attention of military and civilian leaders everywhere on the need for economic development. In the 1960s and 1970s, Latin American economies expanded rapidly, in large measure because prices on raw materials were high, and banks were generous in lending funds. The United States remained a very influential presence, pushing economic development and backing anticommunist foreign policies.

Rule by military dictatorship, typical of the 1960s and 1970s, proved to be short-lived. All the dictators had by the late 1980s vanished. Most were forced to resign as a result of popular opposition to their repressive policies and often as a consequence of their inability to cope with a growing financial and economic crisis. Interest rates rose and international commodity prices fell in the early 1980s. The old formula of raw material exports and foreign loans no longer worked. State subsidies

dwindled and nationalized industries went deeply into debt. Many Latin American governments were so heavily indebted to foreign banks and international lending agencies that they had to default on payments. Their leaders could no longer count on new loans. Lacking outside aid, they had to introduce painful measures of financial and economic austerity. These unpopular measures were beyond the limited competence of the military rulers.

Chile proved the exception, principally because the military regime of General Pinochet had from the start adopted austerity and free market policies. These finally brought substantial economic rewards in the 1980s, the very years when other military regimes faced similar policy choices. Even in Chile the military regime came under growing popular pressure to return the country to parliamentary democracy. Faced with growing foreign and internal opposition to his dictatorship, in 1988, Pinochet finally allowed free elections to take place. The choice was between authoritarian rule and democratically chosen leadership. The voters chose democracy and civilian rule. By then the country enjoyed a level of economic well-being remarkable in a region in the throes of serious economic crisis.

The nature of the predicament appeared most clearly in the crisis that faced Brazil in that decade. The military revolt that ended Brazilian democratic rule in 1964 had come in response to the social unrest stirred up by the civilian government's failure to carry out measures for the redistribution of wealth among the poor. The new military dictators dealt ruthlessly with the revolutionary opposition and cut back on social welfare. Inflation dwindled for a time and foreign debts were paid.

The leaders of the Brazilian military regime did continue the policy of state-sponsored development launched in the 1940s. They offered financial subsidies to industrialists and ranchers and poured funds into state enterprises. They hoped to expand the economic opportunities for conservative Brazilian investors and business interests. They undertook a vast program for the development of the Amazon region, still largely a wilderness inhabited by Indians and a few settlers. In opening the Amazon basin, they anticipated that migrants from Brazil's poorest regions would flood into the area. Social unrest would dwindle, and the country's economy would prosper. Their ambitious plans for economic growth came at enormous cost. But they understood little and cared less about the economic and financial risks that their projects created. Their objectives were political. They hoped to increase the independence and international influence of their state. Their dream was visionary; it was also wildly unrealistic.

Their program did partially achieve its goals. By the mid-1980s, Brazil had developed into one of the major industrial powers in the world. The Amazon basin had attracted large numbers of settlers and ranchers. But the program of Amazonian development led to the uncontrolled destruction of large forested areas opened to colonization. The most powerful new settlers were ranchers eager to acquire vast tracts of open land. In that frontier world, they made the law, even ordering the assassination of outspoken opponents of their land grab. Small farmers came in their wake, ready to extract as rapidly and cheaply as possible what produce they could grow on land that was quickly depleted. The two groups together burned vast regions of the rain forest. The devastation represented a tragedy for the inhabitants of the Amazon basin, particularly the Indians, but also those whose livelihood depended on the forest, such as rubber tappers. Equally as serious was the fact that the disappearance of the rain forest threatened an ecological disaster to a unique and vital environment. By the mid-1980s, the fires had grown so great that the smoke at times shrouded the entire Amazon region. Environmental movements, such as Greenpeace, launched an international campaign to stop further destruction of the rain forest (see Chapter 14, "Highlight: The Global Environment").

The financial, ecological, and social price that the country had to pay for the general's reckless economic policies proved so high that the military regime was ultimately compelled to abandon power. The state went deeply into debt to cover the expenses that it lacked the means to pay for. By the mid-1980s, the resulting budget deficit produced a disastrously high rate of inflation and financial instability. At the same time, Brazil had accumulated an international debt of nearly $100 billion, higher than that of any other Third World country. It could not meet its debts and its attempts at fiscal restraint only heightened popular opposition. The poor population had benefitted little from the country's prosperity. The Catholic Church began to speak out publicly in support of the needs of the poor and backed protest movements in defense of the Vatican Council's reform program. Other political movements also were increasingly active. In the face of this opposition, the military government decided in 1985 to withdraw from politics. It allowed free elections to take place.

A new democratically elected government took over power in Brazil in extremely difficult circumstances. Gradually, it set about dealing with the state's financial crisis and the economy's inadequate performance. Its solution was to allow a full market economy to reappear. Within a few years it abandoned the policies of state-sponsored development, gradually opening the country to foreign imports and privatizing (selling to private investors) nationalized industry. It promised to curtail destruction of the rain forest and in 1992 sponsored the first United Nations Conference on Environment and Development. Social inequalities and political instability still remained a part of Brazilian life, but the crisis appeared at an end.

Mexico's New Democracy

Mexico followed the path of the other Latin American countries toward political democracy and a free-market economy. The authoritarian one-party regime of the Institutional Revolutionary Party (PRI) had been in existence since the 1930s. It had brought stability to the country following the revolutionary turmoil of the early century. The price was the loss of political freedom. One Mexican critic called its regime the "perfect dictatorship," because it "suppressed methodically by whatever means any criticism that threatened its hold on power." In appearance Mexico was a political democracy, with an elected president and parliament, but in reality each president came only with the approval of PRI. Newspapers received secret subsidies from the party and in return published the "news" supplied by the authorities. On the surface, the state was stable and the country calm.

Beneath the surface, the PRI dictatorship, like the communist regime in the Soviet Union, was falling into decay. Corruption spread as powerful gangs smuggling drugs into the United States bribed police and party bosses. Bankers and industrialists found that their businesses could thrive only after bribes to powerful officials. The nationalist fervor that had animated the postrevolution generation of Mexican leaders faded, leaving behind a regime devoted primarily to keeping its monopoly on political power and enriching its supporters.

The Mexican government had followed the same path as other Latin American countries in making the state a key player in the economic life of the country. A state-owned company managed the extraction and refining of petroleum from the country's enormous oil fields. In the 1960s and 1970s, rising foreign sales of petroleum bolstered the state budget and induced foreign bankers to make large loans. The government allocated generous subsidies to important industries and used

tariffs and other measures to hinder foreign competition. The recession in the early 1980s ended those good times, leaving the Mexican economy in crisis and the state unable to repay its foreign loans. The government's attempt at economic independence could not meet the needs of Mexico's rapidly growing population (nearly 90 million by the 1980s). Illegal and legal migration to the United States increased dramatically as Mexicans departed in search of a better life.

Among the PRI leaders were some who, like Soviet reform leaders of the late 1980s, concluded that the welfare of the country required radical political and economic reforms. In those same years, they decided that a free-market economy and the expansion of international trade offered the best hope for Mexican economic recovery. The success of their daring program depended on improved trade and economic ties with the United States. In 1994, the Mexican government agreed to join with Canada and the United States in the North American Free Trade Agreement (NAFTA). The reformers realized the next year how important these ties were when wealthy Mexicans and foreign investors suddenly "dumped" (sold) Mexican currency on the international market. The peso, which had already begun a slow decline, plummeted in value. The Mexican government's salvation from the ensuing financial crisis came from a massive U.S. government loan, saving the Mexican state from defaulting on all its foreign debts. In these conditions of growing financial and commercial interdependence, Mexico entered a new era of cooperation with its former enemy to the north.

The reformers came to the conclusion that they had to open Mexico's political system to free elections if they were to succeed in their program of economic recovery. Their reform program encountered the opposition of PRI officials who had enriched themselves by their easy access to public wealth. They anticipated that the entrenched PRI leaders would lose power when voters had a chance to vote for rival candidates. It was a painful, and at times violent, process. With the strong encouragement of the U.S. government, the Mexican leadership coupled free market reforms with the restoration of democratic rights. PRI reform leaders formally renounced the party's monopoly of political power. In 1997, for the first time in nearly a century, opposition parties won a majority of the seats in the Mexican parliament. Three years later, the winner of the presidential elections of 2000, Vincente Fox, came from a reform political party. PRI had given up its "perfect dictatorship" in what amounted to a peaceful revolution. By the late 1990s, democratic government and a free-market economy had taken hold in most Latin American countries.

Cuba, Central America, and the Yankees

Though Cuba remained under U.S. economic embargo after the 1962 missile crisis, the Cuban regime no longer faced the threat of a U.S. military invasion. Castro was free to pursue his socialist reforms. His path was erratic and the results in the next decades disappointing. His country regularly received large amounts of Soviet foreign aid, including cheap petroleum and wheat vital to the Cuban economy. Soviet yearly assistance totaled nearly $5 billion in the 1980s. The Soviet military assisted Castro's army with arms and advisers. Castro was able to send armed forces to aid Marxist regimes in Africa, first to Angola in 1975 and then to Ethiopia in 1978. These military adventures were his greatest international success, reassuring him that communist Cuba was still part of the "upward march of history."

The social and economic impact of Castro's reforms brought the people substantial social benefits but left many dissatisfied with the dictatorship and with the command economy. Their living conditions improved in the 1970s, and the country did not experience the extremes of wealth and poverty of societies such as Brazil. Women in Cuba enjoyed greater opportunities and rights than women in most other Latin American countries. A revealing sign of the social revolution in Cuba was the fall in the birthrate, lowest in all of Latin America. Women's liberation was not the whole explanation, however, for most women had to work to support their families in an economy plagued by shortages of consumer goods.

The lure of life in the capitalist United States remained great. Many families had relatives who had fled the country after Castro's revolution. Large numbers lived in nearby areas such as Florida; a large part of Miami became "little Havana" for its Cuban residents. When given the opportunity in 1979 to emigrate to the United States, hundreds of thousands more Cubans departed. Small

Cult of Fidel Castro: "Cuban Solidarity" (*Hoover Institution Archives Collection*)

groups continued illegally to flee in small boats, many of which sank in the stormy seas between Cuba and Florida. But Castro remained convinced of the virtues of Marxist-Leninist socialism, even after the collapse of communist regimes in Eastern Europe and the fall of the Soviet Union in the early 1990s. A billboard slogan appeared in Cuba reading "Socialism or Death!"

In Central America, Catholics, reformers, and revolutionaries joined in opposition to the entrenched social and political elites. Each group chose a different path of opposition. Following the 1968 conference of Latin American bishops, the Catholic clergy took the lead in denouncing military rule and economic injustice. When conditions worsened, some even spoke out in favor of insurrection as the only means left to attain freedom and justice. El Salvador's army, fighting revolutionary Marxists in the countryside, turned against these reformist clergy. In 1981, officers assassinated the country's archbishop, Oscar Romero, to silence their critics. In the face of political conservatism and military repression, there was little place for real social reform.

Cuban socialism provided a model for the revolutionary regime that emerged in Nicaragua in the 1980s. The Somoza dictatorship there faced in the late 1970s opposition from a coalition of resistance groups, radical and liberal, calling themselves the Sandinistas (Sandino, a political reformer, had been assassinated by Somoza). The Catholic Church joined forces with Marxist revolutionaries in 1979 to organize a popular insurrection that ended the Somoza rule. The radicals in the coalition refused to share power, however. Much like Castro in 1959, they set out to create socialist institutions under a single-party dictatorship. Their small country lacked the resources to meet their Marxist expectations, however, and they faced the bitter opposition of the conservative U.S. government. The United States gave military supplies and training to an anti-Sandinista guerrilla force called the "Contras" and declared an economic embargo of the country. The revolution aroused widespread opposition from the population, whose living conditions rapidly worsened.

Confronted by a grave economic crisis and social unrest, in 1989 the Sandinistas allowed the people to choose their future leaders in free elections. A majority of the voters preferred the democratic opposition, and the Sandinistas left the government. Their socialist experiment was over, leaving an impoverished population as evidence that their reform program was not the key to social justice or prosperity.

Despite some signs of economic growth, at the end of the 1980s most countries of Central America and the Caribbean remained lands of political instability and economic poverty. The precariousness of their governments opened the way for political extremists and dictators whose actions only worsened economic conditions. Close to the United States, these lands remained subject to U.S. military intervention when American leaders judged their internal or foreign policies unacceptable to U.S. interests.

Twice in the 1980s, U.S. military forces occupied countries in the region. In 1983, they forcibly expelled from the island of Grenada the Marxist government trying to introduce a revolutionary regime there. In 1989, they removed from power Manuel Noriega, the military dictator of Panama. He was involved in international drug smuggling and had recklessly proclaimed his intention to seize the Panama Canal, still U.S. territory. Close to the United States, these small states remained within the U.S. sphere of influence. In the same years, increasing numbers of migrants from these lands left their homes to settle in the United States. Some were refugees from political oppression, but most sought work and better conditions of life. These small countries on the very borders of the United States remained a part of the Third World.

SUMMARY

When the term *Third World* appeared in the 1950s, the areas of the globe it described seemed far removed from the West. The readiness of European states to grant independence to their African colonies arose in large part because their leaders and most of their population were prepared, even eager, to distance themselves from old imperial ambitions and to proceed with the urgent task of reconstruction from war. The fall of these empires created new states separated from and far removed from Europe's immediate concerns. The nationalist leaders of the African states were eager for independence and the freedom to set their countries' future course. The new postcolonial age in the Third World seemed an era of promise beyond the conflicts of the Cold War. The liberation of South Africa from white rule held the hope that there too a better life was open to all the people. In Latin America, nationalism was winning more converts to the idea that real independence from the United States was at last attainable. New leaders everywhere agreed that the path to this goal was economic development.

The obstacles proved to be far more serious than expected. The problems encountered in Africa and Latin America varied from country to country. The most common was incompetent leadership, often from military dictators, far more interested in personal power and wealth than in the welfare of their people. Obstacles also arose from a lack of resources and skills, leaving ambitious economic projects to fall into decay. There was no quick route to prosperity and well-being. The promise of Soviet leaders that their form of socialism was both just and productive proved hollow. The Cuban experience revealed that a small agrarian country remained as dependent on outside powers when it was part of the communist world as when it was within the Western international economy. The experiments in state control over economic development that emerged in Africa and Latin America did initially contribute to short periods of prosperity. Their shortcomings appeared after the initial spurt of growth had ended, when inefficiency, corruption, and lack of productivity became a serious obstacle to continued development. In the end, the Western system of free market production and distribution proved to be less wasteful and disruptive than state-managed economies. The capitalist idea of social justice was confined within a system in which productivity and enterprise received the highest rewards.

In Latin America, the return to market economies gradually yielded results that were impressive and long-lasting. One measure of the impact of a rising standard of living was the dramatic fall in the birthrate in countries such as Brazil between the 1960s and 1990s. More and more families were persuaded that their own resources were sufficient for their old age, and that the survival of every one of their newborn children was, if not certain, at least probable. Their lives no longer depended on a desperate daily struggle for food and their future appeared secure. The continued high birthrates in many countries of Africa revealed, on the contrary, how unsuccessful the efforts there had been to cope with poverty. In most areas of Africa, local economies were in serious decline. These grave problems brought in outsiders to take a hand in economic reforms there. Western intervention came again to parts of Africa where failed states and decaying economies worsened poverty. Increasing numbers of migrants left these areas to search for work in distant urban centers. Some traveled on to cities in the Western world. The Third World was by the 1990s more than ever a part of an interdependent world.

DATES WORTH REMEMBERING

1948	Introduction by Nationalist Party in South Africa of apartheid
1955	Approval of Freedom Charter by African National Congress
1957	Independence for Ghana (Gold Coast)

1960   French Community membership for former French African colonies
1960   Independence for Nigeria
1960   Independence for Belgian Congo (Zaire)
1960–1963   Civil war in Zaire
1961–1993   Imprisonment of Nelson Mandela by South African government
1965–1996   Joseph Mobutu leader of Zaire
1967–1970   Biafran civil war in Nigeria
1993   End of apartheid in South Africa
1994   Nelson Mandela president of South Africa

Latin America

1934   U.S. "Good Neighbor" policy in Latin America
1946–1955   Juan Peron Argentine president
1955   Beginning of Brazilian plan to develop Amazon rain forest frontier
1959   Castro's revolution in Cuba
1960   Completion of construction of Brazil's new capital, Brasilia
1961   Cuban Bay of Pigs invasion
1962   Cuban missile crisis
1962–1965   Second Vatican Council
1964–1985   Military dictatorship in Brazil
1973–1988   Military dictatorship in Chile
1985   Democratic government in Argentina
1985   End of military dictatorship in Brazil
1989   Democratic government in Chile
1992   First United Nations Conference on Environment and Development
1994   North American Free Trade Agreement among Mexico, Canada, and United States
2000   First free elections for Mexican President

RECOMMENDED READING

The Third World

Nigel Harris, *The End of the Third World: Newly Industrializing Countries and the Decline of an Ideol-* ogy (1986). An inquiry into the economic success of East Asian lands and its lessons for "Third Worldism."

Akie Hoogvelt, *The Third World in Global Development* (1982). A historical view of the difficulties of economic development in the Third World.

Independent Africa

*Frederick Cooper, *Africa since 1940* (2002). A thoughtful analysis of the evolution of the continent as it passed from the last bastion of European colonialism to a land of nation-states.

Karl Maier, *This House Has Fallen: Midnight in Nigeria* (2000). A grim picture of Nigeria's struggle to escape the conditions of a failed state.

*Martin Meredith, *Nelson Mandela; A Biography* (1997). The most perceptive, yet still sympathetic study of the life of this remarkable political leader.

Postwar Latin America

*Greg Grandin, *The Last Colonial Massacre: Latin America and the Cold War*, (2004). A critical study of U.S. intervention in Central America in the 1950s.

*Thomas Skidmore and Peter Smith, *Modern Latin America*, 5th ed. (2001). A brief survey of the history of Latin America with separate treatment of major countries.

*Tad Szulc, *Fidel: A Critical Portrait* (1986). A detailed and critical biography of Castro as a personality and political leader.

Memoirs and Novels

*Chinua Achebe, *Anthills of the Savannah* (1985). A story of lost hopes by a Nigerian novelist whose stories chronicle Nigeria's colonial and postcolonial history.

*Nelson Mandela, *Long Walk to Freedom: The Autobiography of Nelson Mandela* (1995). The moving personal reflections on a life that led the author from prison to presidency of South Africa.

*Alan Paton, *Cry, the Beloved Country* (1948). The powerful novel, by one of the country's finest writers, of South Africa's years of brutal racism.

---

*Indicates book is available in paperback.

Nations at War in the Middle East

- Israel and the Middle East
- Nation-Building and Petroleum
- War, Peace, and Islam

Highlight: Islam and the Nation-State

Spotlight: Golda Meir

The history of the Middle East after 1945 is above all a tale of wars, revolutions, and civil strife. More than any other region in the world, it became in those decades a hotbed of political conflict and war. No one state dominated the territories once ruled by the Ottoman Empire. Its collapse after the First World War had marked the first step in the remaking of the Middle East.

In the 1920s, Western governments had taken charge, in one manner or another, of drawing the borders of the successor states. The lands of Egypt and Iran were already well defined, with frontiers historically established and governments nominally independent. Elsewhere the borders and even the names of

states existed only as remnants of Ottoman provinces (such as Syria and Palestine). The territorial outline of these areas became the basis on which the Western powers laid out the frontiers of the new states after the First World War. In that multi-ethnic, multi-religious area, each country gathered peoples of diverse languages, cultures, and clan loyalties within its borders. Later observers called them "states without nations, nations without states."

Sectarian religious quarrels (principally between the Sunni and Shiite Muslims) and rivalries among ethnic groups presented serious obstacles to political unity. Conservative monarchs (such as the rulers of Iran and

Saudi Arabia) relied on traditional fidelity to their throne, but their legitimacy was threatened by their own incompetence, by Muslim fundamentalism, and by social unrest. The vision of a great Arab nation offered one alternative ideology. Arab intellectuals drew their inspiration for this grandiose national community from the medieval Arab empires that had ruled the entire area. After 1945, Arab political leaders frequently called for the creation of a pan-Arab nation. Often, though, such appeals to Arab nationalism were based on the claim by one particular Arab ruler that his leadership was the only basis for Arab unity.

Authoritarian rule proved the most prevalent method throughout the region of dealing with instability. By the 1960s, military dictators had taken power in most Middle Eastern countries. They justified their rule by promoting social reform and, often, by claiming to be defenders of the Muslim faith practiced by most of their peoples. But all the economic indicators of development revealed that at century's end many areas of the Middle East remained sunk in poverty. Only a few oil-rich lands along the Persian Gulf shared widely the benefits from the exploitation of this valuable natural resource. Elsewhere, impoverishment and deep devotion to Islam combined to make an Islamic form of nationalism a powerful magnet to attract popular support. Disunity and the struggle for power among conservative monarchs, Muslim fundamentalists, and ambitious generals sustained conditions of disorder and instability in the political life of these lands.

The violent history of the region was also due to factors outside the Arab community. The Jewish settlers living among the Arab-speaking peoples in Palestine achieved the Zionist dream of a Jewish nation-state shortly after the Second World War. The inflexible opposition of Arab states to the very existence of Israel led to four separate wars between Israel and its Arab neighbors. Pan-Arab na-

tionalism came to mean resistance to Western imperialism and also to Zionism, by which Arab leaders referred to the state of Israel. In later decades, Palestinians entered into the struggle against the Jewish state in an effort to forge their own nation-state. Nationalism was at the heart of the Middle East's turmoil in the last half of the twentieth century.

The recent history of the Middle East is also a story of oil. Its oil fields, concentrated in the area around the Persian Gulf, contained greater petroleum reserves of higher quality than anywhere else in the world. The dependence of the industrial countries on this vital resource brought the pressures of the Cold War to bear on the oil-rich countries. The Soviet Union and the United States kept close watch on the unstable governments there. Each intervened in the political life of these states and used their global might to protect Allied countries. The governments of lands with large oil reserves nationalized their petroleum industry to get direct access to a share of the profits and created an international cartel to set levels of production and prices for this increasingly valuable commodity. The fabulous wealth to be drawn from oil production became the cause of war when Iraq attempted to conquer oil-rich areas on its borders. Internal and international conflict remained the central feature of the postwar history of the Middle East.

ISRAEL AND THE MIDDLE EAST

The Middle East was the birthplace of three major religions—Judaism, Christianity, and Islam. For many millions of people, Jerusalem was the most holy place in the world. It remained a center of pilgrimage and worship for the faithful of all three religions in the twentieth century. It had also been for long the main city in the region known as Palestine. This was the area in which Zionists were determined to create a Jewish national homeland. Their goal appeared attainable after the defeat of the Ottoman Empire by the Allies in the First World War. Their determination to achieve this goal brought them into conflict with the British rulers of the League of Nations' mandated territory of Palestine, then, after the withdrawal of the British, with the neighboring Arab states and the Arab-speaking peoples of Palestine. The new nation-state of Israel extended its borders across a landscape where for centuries Muslim and Christian religious communities had dwelled under foreign rule and worshiped at their own holy sites. National and religious differences combined to make this one small region of the Middle East a cauldron of ethnic conflict and war.

The Struggle for Palestine

The end of the Second World War immediately brought out the long-standing antagonism between Arabs and Jews in the British mandate of Palestine. By war's end, the other mandated territories—Lebanon and Syria, Iraq and Jordan—had received their independence under constitutional monarchs (in the latter two) or elected parliamentary governments. No political movement or leader enjoyed comparable authority in Palestine, where 600,000 Jewish settlers lived among 1.2 million Arabs. Each community sought self-rule to the exclusion of the other. Arab opposition to British occupation and Jewish migration had erupted in a prolonged and bloody Arab revolt in the late 1930s. When British forces finally suppressed the insurrection, the British government had laid plans for the partition of the territory. While the Zionist movement had welcomed the prospect of a Jewish nation-state, even reduced in size, Arab leaders were united in opposition and vowed to resist any grant of territory to the Jews. The prewar deadlock in negotiations for Palestinian independence had raised, as in India, the prospect of civil war. The leaders of each community were resolved to

control a territory that the other group considered its own.

The Second World War deepened the conflict over Palestine. It brought independence to Arab countries, united in their opposition to a Jewish state in Palestine. In those same years, the horrors of the Holocaust united Jewish peoples as never before in support of the creation of their own nation-state. The Zionist commitment to that cause became a crusade. The war temporarily ended all discussion of future Palestinian self-government, Jewish migration, and partition. The British made the preservation of order in Palestine their sole objective, virtually ending Jewish immigration. Yet those were the very years when Jewish persecution in Europe rendered the establishment of a Jewish homeland in Palestine a matter of life and death.

During the war, the British government hardened its political domination of the region. Fighting remained at a distance, but the Axis powers made themselves felt nonetheless. In Palestine, the Muslim religious leader, the grand mufti of Jerusalem, had publicly announced his support of Nazi Germany and had fled to Berlin. He made radio broadcasts to the Middle East calling for Arab revolt against the British. In Egypt and in Iraq, some nationalists appeared ready to welcome Rommel's German divisions when his offensive reached the borders of Egypt in 1942. The vital importance of the Suez Canal and of the region's petroleum gave the British government reason enough to use its forces to repress any signs of possible Arab collaboration with Germany. In Iraq and Egypt, they forcibly installed political leaders sympathetic to the Allies. Palestinian Jews for their part welcomed the opportunity to join in the war against Nazi Germany, sending 30,000 men to serve in the British Army. They later became the core of the Israeli Army.

The Palestinian crisis erupted immediately following the war. The British

150 MILES

150 KILOMETERS

Tripoli

LEBANON

Beirut

Mediterranean

Damascus

SYRIA

Sea

Sea of Galilee

Haifa

ISRAEL

Tel Aviv

Jaffa

Amman

Jerusalem

Gaza

Dead Sea

Nile Delta

Port Said

Damietta

El 'Arish

Beersheba

El Mansura

El Auja

JORDAN

Suez Canal

Ismailia

E G Y P T

Cairo

Suez

Gida Pass

NEGEV

Helwan

Mitla Pass

Kuntilla

Eilat

Aqaba

Nile R.

Sinai Peninsula

Mt. Sinai

△

SAUDI ARABIA

Gulf of Suez

Gulf of Aqaba

El Nabq

Sharm El Sheikh

TIRAN ISLAND

Red Sea

Jordan R.

Golan Heights

West Bank

Gaza Strip

Jordan Water to the Negev

Israel and Its Neighbors

government, caught between Palestinian Arabs and Jews and intent on keeping good relations with the Arab states, refused to open the country to more immigrants. Jewish refugees scattered across Europe looked to Palestine for a new home and were helped on the way by the Zionist organization. Desperate migrants sailed from Europe to the Holy Land in decrepit old boats such as the *Exodus*. Some ships sank before reaching their destination. Others were captured by the British, who placed the passengers in internment camps in Cyprus, prisoners again.

The Zionist movement acquired a valuable ally in 1945 when the U.S. government publicly supported their demand for renewed Jewish immigration to Palestine. American political leaders were sympathetic to the cause of a Jewish state and were under strong pressure from American Jewish organizations to assist in the creation of a Jewish homeland. President Truman's announcement of the new U.S. policy brought the full weight of American international influence to bear on Britain's Palestine problem. It made the crisis an international affair.

The profound disagreement on political objectives and the ethnic strife among the peoples in Palestine made peaceful negotiations impossible. Palestinian Arab leaders all agreed that their land had to become one independent nation-state under the rule of the Arab majority. The Zionists demanded special territorial protection for their people, whom they feared would suffer persecution in an Arab-dominated state. Palestinian Jews began in 1945 a forceful resistance movement to make London heed their demands for immigration and self-rule. Small terrorist organizations even launched attacks against British troops and colonial officials.

Unable to transfer power peacefully to a Palestinian state, the British government turned to outside help. In early 1947, it placed the fate of its Palestine mandate in the hands of the United Nations. It had abandoned the hopeless effort to bring the two sides together and had resolved, as in India, to withdraw quickly. The United Nations had to determine whether Palestine should become one state or two. The United States played the key role in mobilizing the votes needed for approval of the creation of two states, one for the Arabs and the other for the Jews. Even the Soviet Union and its allies backed the plan, hoping in this way to prove their opposition to "British

imperialism." In November of that year, a majority in the U.N. General Assembly voted in favor of the partition of Palestine, to be divided into Arab and Jewish states. As in India, the existence of two deeply antagonistic communities, each intent on defending its own national rights, had led to the creation of new borders around areas to become, somehow, nation-states. Each people had opted for an ethno-territorial nationalist formula, and the United Nations' decision meant international approval for this solution.

This action was unacceptable to the surrounding Arab countries. Opposition to a Jewish state had become a key test of loyalty to the cause of pan-Arab nationalism and to the Palestinian people. An additional factor behind their decision to intervene in Palestine was the competition among Arab leaders for political influence in the Middle East and for control of the Palestinian territory. The king of Jordan hoped to annex lands west of the Jordan River and feared expansionist Syrian plans for a Greater Syria encompassing all the land from Iraq to the Mediterranean. The Iraqi and Egyptian monarchs were rivals for leadership of the Arab countries. They agreed on only one point—the Middle East had to remain Arab. This objective brought them together in 1945 in a regional organization called the Arab League. They proclaimed its purpose to be "coordinating policies" and "strengthening relations" among its members (Syria, Lebanon, Jordan, Iraq, Saudi Arabia, and Egypt). Its immediate objective was to prevent the formation of a Jewish state in Palestine.

Egypt was the founder and leader of the Arab League. It was the largest and most powerful Arab state. Its population had grown rapidly, rising from ten million in the early century to sixteen million. The standard of living of the urban and rural masses probably had stagnated in those years, creating the conditions for serious social disorder. Problems of unrest and political corruption strengthened the role of the Muslim Brotherhood among the Egyptian masses. Its membership after the war increased to more than one million, and it (with considerable exaggeration) claimed to have a half-million Egyptians in its paramilitary force, the Phalanx. No political party possessed such mass support. It alone offered material help and spiritual guidance to the country's lower classes. Its Muslim fundamentalist program made the Islamic faith its guide to social reform and the grounds for its unyielding resistance to a Jewish homeland in Palestine.

In the winter of 1947–1948, Palestine was a land torn by civil war. Jewish and Palestinian military units fought each other for control of villages and towns as the British forces gradually withdrew to the coast. The Palestinians received arms from the Arab League, while the Jews had to take their weapons where they could find them. The day after the last British troops left Palestine in May 1948, Jewish leaders formally established the state of Israel. They had achieved their goal, but enemies on every border endangered their new state. Egypt, Iraq, Syria, and Jordan immediately declared war on Israel and ordered their armies to destroy the new state. The first Arab-Israeli war had begun.

Egypt took the lead. The Egyptian army marched off to fight its first war while volunteers from the Muslim Brotherhood's paramilitary forces joined the Palestinian Arabs. King Farouk ignored the warnings of his generals that his army was poorly prepared and equipped for war. He believed that Arab forces would quickly annihilate the outnumbered and ill-armed Jewish army. He, and most Arab leaders, underestimated the ability of the Jews to resist.

Surrounded on three sides by enemies, the Jewish forces fought for the survival of their new state and for their community. The Palestinians did not share the same nationalist fervor. Many Arabs, fearing for their lives and their religion under Jewish rule, fled the Jewish-controlled areas. Only a few Arab forces could match the fighting skill of the Jews. The Jordanian Arab Legion, led by English officers, seized part of the area on the right (western) bank of the Jordan River and the old city of Jerusalem. The ancient Jewish neighborhood was for months surrounded and under siege before Israeli troops had to withdraw outside the walls of the old city.

The other Arab forces fared poorly. Among the Egyptian officers, some, like Captain Gamal Nasser, fought bravely. Most officers in the army did not share his commitment to the war. The army was badly led and badly supplied by the Egyptian government. The Egyptian attack on southern Palestine collapsed and was followed by retreat from the entire Negev Desert. Lacking any coordinated strategy, the Arab forces conducted separate campaigns and could not prevent the Jews from seizing an area even larger than that granted by the U.N. partition plan.

The failure of the Egyptian offensive was the key to ending the war. In February 1949, the United Nations obtained agreement from all sides to an armistice. Israeli forces occupied the coastal region of Palestine, a part of the Jordan River valley, and the Negev Desert to the shores of the Red Sea. Jerusalem was divided. The armistice line marked a new partition of the Palestinian territory, which was now split between Israel and Jordan. The old city of Jerusalem and much of the Jordan River valley stayed in the hands of the Jordanian forces. The armistice confirmed the victory of Israel, a small, oddly shaped state surrounded by enemies. The flight during the war of most Palestinian Arab inhabitants from Jewish-controlled areas made Jewish settlers the majority of Israel's population. Palestinians found at war's end that they had no state of their own.

The new Israeli government began the process of constructing a Jewish nation-state.

The new state was a parliamentary democracy. It welcomed Jews from any country and made Hebrew, the Biblical tongue not spoken for two millennia, the official language. It bore some resemblance to a theocracy, that is, a state whose inhabitants were inspired by a religious faith. Yet at the same time it was a modern nation-state whose laws protected political freedom and individual opportunity. It introduced social reforms inspired by the socialist movements of Europe. It supported the creation, begun earlier by the first Jewish settlers, of collective farms called "kibbutz." Members of these cooperatives shared the revenues from their crops as they struggled to make the desert fertile.

Though Israel guaranteed freedom of religion to its Christian and Muslim minorities, to many Arabs it was the object of abiding hatred. It had broken apart Palestine. Its legal and social order embodied Western secular values rejected by Muslim fundamentalists. Surrounded by enemies, the Israelis had to arm their nation in anticipation of another war.

The defeat of the Arab League's forces was a public humiliation for the Arab countries. A constant reminder of the defeat was the presence of 750,000 Palestinian refugees, scattered throughout the Middle East but concentrated in refugee camps in Egyptian territory. The Palestinians received little help from the Arab states. A few were able to find a new home for themselves in other parts of the Middle East. Most remained in miserable refugee camps under U.N. care, hoping for the day when Israel would no longer exist and they could return to their homeland. In all respects, the Israeli victory was a disaster for the Egyptian monarchy, unable to unite Arab forces and to organize and lead its army. The months of war proved a bitter lesson for Egyptian army officers. They returned to Egypt convinced that the corrupt political leadership of their country had betrayed them, the Egyptian nation, and the Arab cause.

◀ **SPOTLIGHT: Golda Meir** ▶

Golda Meir (1898–1978) devoted her life to the creation of a Jewish homeland in Palestine. Her family fled the Russian Empire when she was nine years old. By then she had experienced firsthand anti-Semitic hatred, widespread among the population where her family had lived. She had also begun to learn of a new movement called Zionism dedicated to the creation of a Jewish homeland in Palestine. Though she grew up in the United States, she decided when she was twenty years old to make that cause her own. The decision changed the course of her life.

The lifelong service that she rendered to Zionism drew upon her remarkable personal qualities and her commitment to the goal of a Jewish homeland. With her husband, she moved to Palestine in the 1920s. "The Jews must have a land of their own again," she wrote, "and I must help to build it by living and working there." She became a pioneer on a Jewish farm (a "kibbutz") reclaiming desert land. The pioneers laid claim to a Palestinian homeland, in the midst of Arab-speaking Christians and Muslims, by making the land prosper once again. In her words, "only self-labor could make it possible for the Jews to earn a moral right, as well as a historical right," to that land.

Like the other Jewish migrants, she firmly believed that their claim to Palestine was morally and historically justified. The harsh life that she led for the next decades had as its goal the acquisition of a territory belonging to the Jewish people. That land was the birthplace of the Jewish religion, but she did not wish to make it a religious state. The Jews formed a community like other peoples who desired their own nation-state. She believed in toleration for all religions, hoping that the Arabs would "live with us in peace and equality as citizens of a Jewish homeland."

Her dream inevitably meant that those Arabs would have to become a minority nationality in a state of the Jews. Many Muslim Arabs rejected the idea that infidels should govern them and their holy places in Pales-

tine. Their religious convictions excluded the possibility of the Jewish secular state for which Zionists such as Golda Meir struggled. Conflict between Arabs and Jews was unavoidable.

Her own personal life became consumed by her work for the Zionist cause. She admitted later that she had too little time for her marriage and children. She left her family for long trips to Europe and America to encourage Jewish immigration and to raise funds for Jewish settlements, then for the state of Israel. But her greatest contribution lay in political leadership. Along with a handful of other Zionists, she came to embody for many Jews the selfless

Prime Minister Golda Meir Reviewing Israeli Soldiers, 1969. (*UPI/Corbis/Bettmann*)

dedication that had made the incredible dream of Israel come true. When she arrived in 1948 in Moscow to serve as the first Israeli ambassador to the Soviet Union, crowds of Jews celebrated outside the Israeli embassy at the risk of arrest and imprisonment.

She also possessed the talents of a far-sighted political leader. The Zionist movement had always regarded women as equal to men in its work, though bias against women in politics remained strong among some Israelis. Her government believed in and needed her abilities. In 1949, it offered her the position of minister of labor. She proceeded to lay the foundations of the social welfare policies of Israel. Her greatest challenge was to create a shared loyalty among the "flood of Jews from opposite ends of the earth who spoke different languages and who were ignorant of each other's traditions and customs." It was, she remembered, "the most satisfying and the happiest years of my life."

In a real sense, Israel absorbed her remaining years. She moved from her labor post to become minister of foreign affairs in 1956. Thirteen years later she reluctantly agreed to become the prime minister of her country. Why, she asked, should a "seventy-year-old grandmother head a twenty-year-old state?" The answer was that no one else could. Her commitment to a Jewish homeland had carried her as a young woman to Palestine. Her sense of duty to that land elevated her ultimately to the most powerful political position in her country. It was a career that few men could match.

Revolution in Egypt

The Egyptian monarchy was increasingly unpopular in the years after the war. Free elections in 1950 (the last multi-party elections until 1984) revealed to what extent parliamentary politics had become the affair of a small political elite. Few voters bothered to cast their ballots. The state was weakened still more by King Farouk's ambition to control the government. The new cabinet mobilized popular support for an anti-British campaign to oblige the British to withdraw their troops from the Suez Canal zone. These forces had stayed on by agreement with the Egyptian government after independence in 1924. The British refused to negotiate, and the movement grew increasingly violent. In early 1952, riots broke out in Cairo protesting the British presence along the Suez Canal. The king dismissed the cabinet, took over the government, and called in the army to repress the rioting. In doing so, he sealed his own fate.

Egypt's revolutionary officers chose that moment of political chaos to move into action. The leader of this secret opposition was Gamal Nasser. As a student before the Second World War, he had been active in the nationalist movement. For him, as for nationalists in other poor countries, the nation symbolized a new, just community in which "the weak and the humiliated Egyptian people [could] rise up again and live as free and independent men." The son of poor parents, he chose the career of an army officer. It was for him the means to improve his own life and to advance the cause of Egyptian nationalism. In the first years, army life brought him no glory and little opportunity. It did form the bonds uniting Nasser and other officers, including Anwar Sadat (his successor as ruler of Egypt), who later set about remaking Egypt. His political career began after the Palestinian war. He and his colleagues realized, as he wrote later, that "our battle was taking place in Cairo. We knew that we had to liberate our country first, in order to be able to fight." Believing themselves betrayed by the monarch and the parliamentary regime, they resolved to restore Egyptian power and influence on their own. Their military conspiracy pointed to a political revolution in Egypt.

The officers, under Nasser's leadership, organized a secret group calling itself the Free Officers. Founded in 1949, it grew to about a thousand members. When in the summer of 1952 King Farouk ordered the army into Cairo to end the rioting, its members set in motion their plans for a military "coup," that is, the overthrow of the monarchy by military force. They secretly took over command of the armed forces with the help of General Naguib, a senior officer who shared their opposition to the monarchy. Army units surrounded the royal palace and forced the king to abdicate. On leaving the country Farouk warned the victorious insurgents: "Your task will be difficult. It isn't easy, you know, to govern Egypt."

The process of remaking the Egyptian nation-state had only just begun. Few Egyptians regretted the departure of the Turkish king. Several contenders for power aspired to govern the republic. Liberal political parties hoped to preserve constitutional government, as well as to protect the interests of the financiers and landowners who supported them. The followers of the Muslim Brotherhood looked to an Islamic republic to bolster the Muslim religion and to wipe out the social and moral decay that they believed to be caused by Westernization.

The officers were not prepared to tolerate political diversity and dissent. Nasser later referred sarcastically to the "dispersed followers and contrasted remnants, chaos, dissensions, surrender, and idleness" that they encountered in the months after overthrowing the monarchy. It is unlikely that they ever seriously considered sharing the responsibilities and powers of rule. Their response to political rivalries was to eliminate their rivals and to

end parliamentary rule. They dissolved parliament and the cabinet, replacing them with a Revolutionary Command Council (RCC). It consisted of the leaders in the Free Officers conspiracy, under the chairmanship of Gamal Nasser. The council abolished the constitution and in early 1953 disbanded all political parties. Lacking a mass following, the liberal parties disappeared from public life. The small Communist Party became the target of outright repression and its leaders were thrown in jail. Nasser proclaimed that "the Communists are agents who believe neither in the liberty of their land nor in their nation but only do the bidding of outsiders." To the officers, Egyptian nationalism was the ideological inspiration for the resurgence of their country.

The Muslim Brotherhood presented the Revolutionary Command Council with its most dangerous rival. The military leaders opposed the Brotherhood for two reasons. They did not share the Brotherhood's goal of Islamic revolution. They were Westernized officers, for whom the Quran fixed religious belief and practices, not state policy. In addition, the Brotherhood challenged their own political power. In January 1954, Muslim leaders began mass street demonstrations aimed at forcing the council to implement their plans for an Islamic revolution. The ruling officers seized the opportunity to arrest the Brotherhood leadership and to ban the organization. As in previous periods of repression, the Brotherhood went underground. In October 1954, one of its members attempted to assassinate Nasser. The police asserted—though without real proof—that the Brotherhood was plotting to overthrow the new regime. Police repression worsened, and prisons filled with political prisoners. The revolutionary officers had defeated all their rivals for power.

Their new regime made the objectives of pan-Arab nationalism the inspiration for their foreign policy. They reiterated their determination to prepare for a new war with Israel.

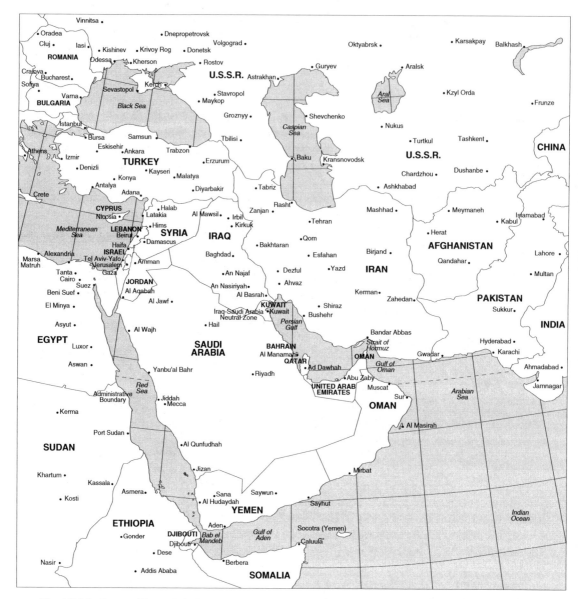

The Middle East and Inner Asia in 1990

At the same time, they took steps to strengthen the national liberation movements underway in North Africa. This was the last area where Arabs lived under Western colonial rule. Arab nationalists from Tunisia, Morocco, and Algeria, still part of the French Empire, moved to Cairo after 1953. There they found refuge from French colonial forces and received financial assistance from the new government. Their leadership and popular unrest forced the reluctant French government to grant independence to Morocco and Tunisia in 1956.

Algerian nationalists faced determined opposition, however, from France. French forces had conquered Algeria over a century before and opened the country to colonists from southern Europe, all of whom received French citizenship. The one million European settlers of French culture and citizenship were deeply hostile to the Arabs and to the idea of Algerian independence. The French government refused negotiations with the Algerian National Liberation Front, whose headquarters were in Cairo. In 1954, the Algerian nationalists called for an insurrection against the French. The French government sent in hundreds of thousands of troops, some just withdrawn from Indochina, to defeat the Arab nationalist revolt and to protect the European settlers.

This new French colonial war lasted until 1962. By then it had consumed thousands of lives and kindled terrorist movements on the part of both Europeans and Arabs. The French government, faced with an apparently endless guerrilla war, decided to grant Algeria its independence. More than one million Algerian Europeans and Arabs who had collaborated with the French fled to France. The last colonial war had ended. Western empires had disappeared from the Middle East.

NATION-BUILDING AND PETROLEUM

The new Egyptian regime's seizure of the Suez Canal marked in a spectacular manner the collapse of European power in the Middle East. The impact of the growing global economy, fueled increasingly by petroleum, lured Western private companies into the region. Access to petroleum brought great profits to oil corporations and was a vital need for all developed economies. Governments of the Middle Eastern lands possessing large oil reserves were themselves eager to obtain revenues from oil sales in this global market. The age of nations took shape in the same years as these new states entered the interdependent global economy.

Nasser and the Egyptian Nation

The military leaders of Egypt had vague plans for social reform and leadership of the Arab countries. They had overthrown Egypt's monarchy, claiming that they alone could transform the country into a modern nation. They knew that their experiment was risky. Their country was poor, and their hopes to expand the power of the state and to improve the living conditions of the Egyptian population depended on new revenues. Still, they were convinced that they were the rightful national leaders, the "vanguard," as Nasser wrote in 1953, whose "mission had not ended."

They disagreed among themselves on basic issues of government. Some officers preferred to introduce a constitutional democracy, giving power back to the political parties. Nasser was determined to keep the military in charge of the country. In early 1954, the dispute ended with his victory. Proclaiming that their revolution was threatened by a return to the corrupt practices of the monarchy, he placed his followers in positions of control throughout the Egyptian government. The country's military regime consolidated its hold on the state, and Nasser emerged as the principal leader.

He set about creating an authoritarian state. In place of political parties, he and his fellow officers created their own mass party. Called at first the Liberation Rally, it changed names frequently in the decades to come. They stipulated that it alone enjoyed the right to propose candidates for election. They imposed censorship on radio and the press and deprived labor unions of the right to strike. In 1956, they introduced a new constitution that created a National Assembly, but it enjoyed no real legislative power. A secret police operated beyond the rule of law to pursue the enemies of the military rulers. A cabinet replaced the Revolutionary Command Council, but it consisted of the same officers who had led the country since 1952. Nasser held the title of president of the Republic. In fact, he was a benevolent military dictator committed to national revolution.

Nasser's most ambitious project was the damming of the waters of the Nile behind a new, giant dam at Aswan. It was to be a structure so huge it would dwarf the pyramids (and the new lake it created would drown precious relics of Egypt's pharonic past). Plans for its use foresaw both abundant water for irrigation (the arable land of Egypt was to increase by one-third) and hydroelectric power in a greater quantity than all the electricity then available. A great source of pride to Nasser, it embodied his hope for social betterment and his grandiose vision of a national revolution in Egypt. He called it Egypt's "pyramid for the living." Paying for the dam presented serious difficulties, however. The Egyptian state lacked the necessary financial means. Like India, it could not initiate important economic projects without outside help.

The most dramatic result of the military revolution was Egypt's defiance of the West. Following the example of Nehru of India, Nasser proclaimed his country's nonalignment in the Cold War. He refused to join the British-sponsored Baghdad pact with Turkey, Iran, and Iraq, intended as one link in the Cold War alliances surrounding the Soviet Union. But Nasser judged the treaty (in terms that echoed Nehru's judgment of SEATO) a "modern version of a protectorate" and condemned its members for collaborating with "Western imperialism." His refusal seriously undermined his state's chances of substantial aid from the United States.

Egypt's conflict with Israel gave a warlike character to Nasser's new foreign policy. Egypt remained formally in a state of war with the Jewish state, and it forbad any shipping bound for Israel to pass through the Suez Canal. Yet the Egyptian army was still badly equipped and needed to import modern weapons. These could be paid for only by foreign loans. The United States hesitated, concerned that aid might fuel a new Arab-Israeli war. The Soviet Union was ready to help. The new post-Stalin leaders were prepared to support reformist governments in the Middle East and in Asia that were not members of Western alliances. Their offers of arms and financial credits presented the Egyptian regime with a tempting source of assistance.

In late 1955, Nasser accepted the offer. He announced that the Egyptian government had signed an agreement with the Soviet Union to obtain a long-term loan, to be repaid in cotton and rice exports. The funds would allow Egypt to buy from communist countries fighter planes, tanks, arms, and naval vessels. He was acclaimed by nationalists throughout the Middle East for his action. He called the arms deal a policy of "positive neutrality." Cold War passions among Western leaders magnified out of all proportion the implications of both his aid to Arab rebels in French North Africa and his arms agreement. He appeared a dangerous revolutionary and potential communist ally.

The price of his arms deal with the communist countries became apparent in mid-1956. He had begun negotiations in 1955 with the World Bank, which was largely financed by the U.S. government, for a major loan to begin construction of the High Dam at Aswan. He staked the prestige of his regime and of his own leadership on the mammoth project. Negotiations dragged on until July 1956. Suddenly the United States announced its refusal to participate in the projected loan. Great Britain soon made the same decision. Their message was clear: Nasser's cooperation with communist states had cost his state Western financial assistance for the Aswan Dam. The decision represented a public humiliation of the Egyptian leader and a serious diplomatic blunder by the United States.

The Suez Canal and the 1956 War

In 1956, the Suez Canal was still an economic enterprise run and owned by Europeans, a remnant of the age of Western imperialism. It was also a valuable piece of property bringing substantial income to its owners. The last British troops withdrew from the Suez zone early that year. The canal was a tempting prize to Egyptian nationalists such as Nasser. He was attracted both by the revenues that it would yield and by the prestige that its seizure would bring to his regime. In July 1956, he declared to an enormous crowd of Egyptians gathered in Cairo that his government had taken possession of the canal. "Our pride, our determination, and our faith," he cried, had been challenged by the West. Nationalization of the canal proved that "this nation will not accept humiliation and degradation." If the "imperialists" did not approve of his action, they could "choke in their own rage." His defiance of the West brought him and his country into direct confrontation with European states. It was a move enthusiastically applauded by his people.

The Egyptian seizure of the Suez Canal incited the British and French governments to make one final effort to reassert their imperial power in the eastern Mediterranean. They viewed nationalization as a threat to their security. The canal remained a vital pathway for strategic goods, especially petroleum, to western Europe. They were deeply suspicious of Nasser's nationalist policies. Strategic and ideological reasons incited the two states to launch a reckless, ill-conceived invasion of the canal zone. They found a ready ally in the Israeli government. Israel's economy suffered from the Egyptian blockade of its shipping through the canal, and its leaders feared another Egyptian invasion. The three states attacked Egypt in late October 1956. Israeli tank units raced across the Sinai Desert to the canal, while a British and French naval force and paratroopers seized the

Suez ports and the entire canal zone. Militarily the operation was a complete success. Politically it failed. Nasser became a national hero for the Egyptian people. Diplomatically the invasion proved a disaster.

Opposition came from all sides. Almost the entire membership of the United Nations condemned the attack. The Soviet Union offered Nasser more military aid and warned Britain and France of its readiness to take "all measures" to protect Egypt. The U.S. president Dwight Eisenhower condemned the invasion, for he was outraged by military action and intent on keeping good relations with Third World countries. His government made its opposition painfully real by reducing economic aid to Great Britain and France. It also refused to protect the British currency, which was losing value rapidly as panicky Britishers bought up dollars. Lacking U.S. support, the British and French were isolated and unable to continue the war. Faced with global diplomatic protests and a major financial crisis, the British convinced the French and Israelis to withdraw from the canal zone. President Eisenhower had used U.S. economic power and diplomatic influence to defeat their intervention.

The Suez crisis was Nasser's greatest triumph. He had defied the European powers and won. In the Middle East his action revived the popularity of pan-Arab nationalism. To Egyptians he became their undisputed national leader. His only achievement in the war had been to block the canal with sunken ships, closing it to navigation for another year. A serious economic recession swept Europe as a result of the sudden petroleum shortage. In the peace settlement, Nasser accepted a U.N. proposal for the stationing of an international peacekeeping force in Egypt. Its task was to patrol the Egyptian-Israeli frontier to prevent Arab terrorist attacks on Israel and to block a new Israeli invasion. The outcome of the Suez crisis gave Nasser the illusion of great power. His action made him, for a few years, the leader among Arab states and among non-aligned countries of the Third World.

Nasser's Socialist Reforms

The Suez war gave a sudden impetus to state control of the Egyptian economy. Nasser welcomed the development, calling it "Arab socialism." He implied that these reforms set a model for all Arab lands. Until 1956, the Egyptian economy had functioned along free market lines, allowing private ownership of banking, industry, and agriculture and welcoming foreign investment. The war brought the state new economic powers. The government suddenly became, without any long-range plan, the owner of the Suez Canal Company and responsible for the operations of the canal. During the war, Egypt took possession of foreign-owned and operated enterprises in any way connected with France and Great Britain, including many banks, insurance companies, and industrial enterprises. The nationalized holdings gave the government an important role in the small Egyptian industrial economy.

The Suez crisis expanded the Free Officers' goal of "social justice" into a larger vision of socialism. It took a form somewhat like the Soviet command economy. The government turned to economic planning to provide the economic guidelines needed by the state to operate the nationalized businesses. It created in early 1957 a National Planning Committee and later that year approved a Five-Year Plan for economic development. Foreign aid came from the Soviet Union for construction of the Aswan Dam. The United States shipped food supplies to help feed Egypt's growing population. Nasser declared that the goal of the Egyptian revolution was "a cooperative, democratic, socialist society." Like India, Egypt became a mixed economy. Small commerce and farming stayed in private hands, while major enterprises were state owned.

For a few years, the Egyptian people benefitted substantially from the reforms. Throughout the 1960s, the economy grew steadily, though its growth slowed from 6 percent in the first years to 2 percent after the disastrous 1967 war. But economic development could not cope for long with the population explosion resulting from an annual increase of one million people. The state subsidized the sale of cheap food to Egypt's urban masses to avoid social unrest, for cities had become places of welfare as well as work. Imported agricultural produce, provided in large measure by foreign aid, became the sole protection against famine.

The Aswan Dam was Nasser's great project for the transformation of Egypt. It was completed in 1970, forever ending the yearly flooding of the lower Nile region. The reservoir, named Lake Nasser, stretched more than three hundred miles upstream, impounding water used to generate hydroelectric power (ten billion kilowatt-hours per year) and to irrigate agricultural land (one-third more than before). Periodic great floods no longer devastated the Nile basin, and years of low rainfall in the Nile headwaters no longer meant drought for Egypt's farmers.

The dam was a technological marvel and the pride of Egyptians. The ecological price was high, for the irrigation water carried disease through the canals and left deposits of salt on the land, no longer cleansed by flooding. The Aswan Dam illustrated vividly the vision and limits of Nasser's socialism. Its planners could take pride in Egyptian economic growth, but in achieving this goal they permanently destroyed the balance between people and nature that had existed before.

Egypt in the years after the Suez war became the center of pan-Arab nationalism and supported socialist movements in other Middle Eastern countries. From Cairo, the Voice of Arabs Radio defended the cause of Arab unity and called for opposition to imperialism, feudalism

Pyramid for the People: The Aswan Dam under Construction. (© *Hulton-Deutsch Collection/CORBIS*)

(typified by Saudi Arabia), and Zionism (Israel). Nasser revived the vision of a great pan-Arab state to unite all "progressive" Arab lands, that is, states not ruled by conservative monarchs. But his plans brought no substantial results. Pan-Arab nationalism proved irrelevant to the needs and interests of the other Arab countries.

In that divided region, the conflict with Israel posed the most serious threat of war. Nasser was first among Arab leaders in proclaiming his opposition to the state of Israel. Time and again he spoke out for "liquidating the Israeli aggression on a part of the Palestine land." His deeds in the ten years following the Suez war were not, however, warlike. He accepted until the mid-1960s the U.N. peacekeeping force along the Egyptian-Israeli frontier. Purely symbolic, its presence on the Egyptian side of the border absolved Egypt of the responsibility to undertake a dangerous new war. It was a conflict that the country could not afford and that Nasser's army could not win.

Petroleum and the Middle East

The political revolution in Egypt came just as the Middle East became the principal source of petroleum for the global economy (see Chapter 3, "Highlight: Petroleum and the International Economy"). This was an economic revolution, bringing enormous revenues to a few Arab states and elevating questions of revolution and war in the Middle East to issues of vital strategic interest to major states around the world. The loss of access to the oil in that area posed the threat of economic collapse to developed countries. The 1956–1957 recession in Europe had shown how devastating the interruption of oil shipments from the region could be. The Middle East had acquired an international importance that overshadowed the political ambitions of leaders such as Nasser.

Until the 1950s, the international oil corporations operating in the Middle East did not have to consider the interests of the Middle Eastern countries where their refineries and oil wells were located. Even a strong ally of the West such as the shah of Iran resented the power that they enjoyed over oil production and prices. The rulers of the oil-producing states received royalties based on the profits of these corporations from production. These companies defined their goals principally in terms of price stability and profits.

Sensitive to Western governments' need for oil, they also protected their own corporate interests. When need arose, they limited production and agreed on a single wholesale price for crude oil to avoid ruinous price wars. The postwar discovery of new oil fields continually put their efforts in jeopardy. An economic recession in the West in the late 1950s reduced demand so seriously that they agreed among themselves to lower the price of oil to below $2 a barrel in the hope of promoting sales. In doing so, they aroused the resentment of the Middle Eastern oil-producing states, including Iran and Saudi Arabia.

The rulers of these two countries shared common interests both in preserving their monarchies against internal political revolutions and in establishing state control over their petroleum industry. They had begun expensive programs of economic development, paid for by the income from their oil royalties. These suddenly declined when the international oil companies cut prices on crude oil. The monarchs of the two states hoped that by acting together they could force the oil corporations to heed their financial needs.

In 1960, they obtained the agreement of all the major oil-producing states (except the United States and Mexico) to form a new international association, the Organization of Petroleum Exporting Countries (OPEC). The immediate objective was to stabilize oil prices and to coordinate petroleum policies to protect "our interests, individually and collectively." Behind this modest aim lay the audacious goal of fixing levels of oil production and prices. An international oil cartel was born.

While their organization had little immediate impact on oil production, the tremendous increase in Western demand for oil in the 1960s improved their economic situation substantially. Revenues going to the states of Iran and Saudi Arabia reached nearly $1 billion. Although their policies were conservative, the monarchs of these two states had lent their political weight to a radical shift in the global economic balance of power. By then, petroleum use had risen so rapidly that it provided over half the West's energy supplies. Industrialized economies could not function without it. In the late 1960s, oil prices began a slow increase, rising to more than $2 a barrel. In the world of international finance and economics, these revenues and the possession of great petroleum reserves gave the OPEC countries new power and influence.

WAR, PEACE, AND ISLAM

War and civil strife in the Middle East erupted several times in the last third of the twentieth century. Each conflict sent its reverberations echoing around the world, at times because Cold War competition intruded, at other times because the global economy had to confront serious oil shortages. A revolution in Iran made Islam a powerful political force after Muslim religious leaders seized control of the government. Their goals were a return to the principles of the Quran. Religious issues became deeply embedded in the Israeli-Arab confrontation. Committed Muslims and Jews reshaped the territorial dispute into a crusade of one religion against another. Calmer judgment among Israeli and Palestinian leaders counseled compromise to permit the two peoples to live at peace with one another. The mid-1990s' agreement on Palestinian self-rule offered hope for peace, but it faced strong opposition on both sides. War against Israel no longer dominated Middle Eastern politics, but the Palestinian problem remained unresolved.

HIGHLIGHT: Islam and the Nation-State

In the mid-twentieth century, Islam was the second-largest religion in the world. It was the dominant faith in lands stretching from northern Africa to Indonesia. The conquests of European colonial empires brought the peoples of these areas under Western rule. The defeat of the Ottoman Empire in the First World War brought down the last remaining empire governed by Muslim rulers. But Islam remained a vital force among Muslim peoples. Some of their religious leaders began to work for the renewal of the Islamic faith as the means to isolate Muslims from the corrupting influence of modern Western culture. Other public leaders believed that the bonds that united the Muslim community formed the basis for new political movements capable of resisting the West by incorporating certain modern institutions and values. Slowly Islam adapted its message and action to meet the challenge of Western domination.

The doctrinal unity of Islam, like Judaism and Christianity, is founded on a sacred text. The Quran (also spelled Koran) is believed by Muslims to be the revelation of God as received by his prophet Muhammed, who lived in the Arabian Peninsula in the seventh century. That divine message defined the essential faith for Muslims, for whom there could be no other God and no other source of religious truth. Wherever they lived and whatever their own culture and language, the Quran gave them their religious language (Arabic, for that was Muhammed's tongue) and prescribed their basic religious practices. Muslim scholars over the centuries had elaborated religious rules (the Shari'a) governing Muslim everyday life, including family law, marriage, inheri-

tance, and much more. Customs varied from country to country. The requirement that women conceal their faces behind veils in public became increasingly common in many places. In these ways, the Islamic faith made itself a vital presence in the public and private affairs of many millions of Muslims.

The arrival of Western empires served in some ways to give greater scope and vigor to religious activities in the Muslim world. The growth of international and regional trade opened new markets in Asia and Africa. For many centuries, Muslim merchants had worked to make converts to Islam among the unbelievers (infidels) with whom they traded. This missionary work expanded along with commerce in the nineteenth and twentieth centuries, especially in colonial areas of sub-Saharan Africa. Christian missionaries there competed with Muslims, who had the advantage of preaching a faith that stood in opposition to the West.

The empires contributed, unwittingly, to the dramatic growth of pilgrimage to the Holy Places located in Saudi Arabia, on the Arabian peninsula. That deed, to be undertaken during the holy time called Ramadan, was one of the sacred duties of all Muslims. Steamship lines and railroads opened rapid and much safer routes for pilgrims from distant lands intent on reaching Mecca and Medina. A few Westerners traveled secretly to these places and marveled at the devotion of so many Muslim pilgrims who came together from Asia, Africa, and the Middle East to fulfill the holiest of religious acts.

Despite these common traits, deep divisions had appeared within Islam in the millennium since Muhammed had preached the new faith. Like Christianity, Islam had splintered into religious movements, each claiming to be the only true carrier of Muhammed's teaching. The largest of these was the Sunni Muslim community. The next in size, though much smaller, was the Shi`a Muslim group, centered in Iran and southern Iraq. Between the two movements, disagreements led, at times, to violent conflict and religious persecution.

In the twentieth century, these disputes mattered less to Muslim leaders than the challenge of Western modernity. Western institutions and practices were the inspiration for two widely debated programs for reform among Muslim peoples. One was usually referred to by writers and political leaders as modernism, the other secularism. Those who supported the modernist path to reform argued that certain characteristics of Western historical development were useful and constructive and had no damaging impact on religious faith. Muslim leaders included science and technology in particular as modern, but some of them extended the list to public schooling in native languages and to practical science and mathematics. The most radical reformers even called for constitutional democracy.

The other major program was usually defined as secularism. Its supporters stressed the need, along with the other modernist reforms, for states to back the creation of a national community in which civil laws, not Islam, governed everyday life. To achieve this goal, they were prepared to introduce secular civil and criminal law codes (i.e., law not based on religious edicts) to replace, or to supplement, Muslim customary law. Secularism rejected the claim of Muslim authorities, guided by religious rules, to exercise complete legal judgment in criminal cases and in affairs of the individual and the family (the secular sphere as opposed to the religious sphere of worship). Marriage, property rights, and inheritance belonged to this secular sphere. Proponents of this reform program were equally opposed to reliance on Muslim law in deciding criminal punishments (for example, amputation of the hand of a convicted thief and stoning to death to punish adultery).

These discussions emerged in many countries among Muslim scholars and public officials. The issues became particularly critical with the fall of the Western empires and the emergence of independent Muslim states. Were the leaders of these countries to place the needs of their national community above those of the broader community of Muslim believers (the "umma")? Some religious and political leaders argued against nationalism, emphasizing the priority to maintain international Muslim religious solidarity. At heart, they relied on the strength of a revived and renewed Islamic community to defeat Western cultural and economic borrowing. They believed that the social duties called for in traditional Muslim law should become the foundation for new organizations of solidarity and defense of the faith. In the 1920s, the Muslim Brotherhood took up this cause in Egypt. Its example spread in later years to other Middle Eastern lands. They were confident that new, competent leaders would emerge from Islamic schools that taught the Muslim religious canon.

Most political leaders in postcolonial nation-states inhabited by Muslim peoples refused to trust such half-measures of religious reform. They placed their hopes on the emergence of nationalism among their peoples. It had to be based on a shared language and culture. They did not deny that religious allegiance among a country's Muslims belonged within this "national culture" but sought to place religious practices in the private, not public, domain of everyday life. The leaders of the new nation-state of Turkey, created in 1920 on the ruins of the Ottoman Empire, made sure that defenders of Islam would not impede their state-building. Their most dramatic measure was the abolition of the position of caliph, who had been since the time of Muhammed the supreme religious authority among all Sunni Muslims. Their state was to be resolutely secularist.

Later, in both Indonesia and Pakistan, the new leaders sought to create not an Islamic state but a secular nation-state. They recognized that their national community was deeply marked by Muslim culture but conceived of their task in secular, nationalist terms. This meant that secular law, not Muslim law, set the guidelines for issues touching on everyday life. In Pakistan, the project was a failure. The country was split into hostile ethnic communities and lacked the means to cope with the misery of the masses of the population. In those conditions of disorder, Pakistani religious leaders forced the government to rely increasingly on religious law and practices to maintain the unity of their weak state.

The nation-building project in the Arab-speaking world drew from the work of Arab writers who believed that the Arab language brought distinctive cultural qualities useful for nationalism. They called their approach pan-Arabism. From these groups came strong supporters of the secularist program, for they backed reforms modeled closely on what they believed were the essential qualities of western nation-states. Nasser of Egypt made the secularist and national program the basis of his regime after seizing power in 1952. The Muslim Brotherhood opposed his policies and called for a state based on Muslim law. Nasser had its leaders arrested, driving the movement underground. A decade later, the Baath ("Rebirth") parties in Syria and Iraq followed in Nasser's footsteps, seizing power in their countries to build secular nation-states. Their leaders restricted the public role of Islam and forced proponents of an Islamic state, either Sunni or Shi`a, into exile.

The Shah of Iran took up the same set of policies in the 1950s. He aroused ultimately such bitter opposition from the Shi`a religious leaders of his land that they organized a revolution in 1979 to overthrow his monarchy. They installed in its place an Islamic republic ruled by Muslim clerics guided by the Quran and religious law. Neighboring Afghanistan experienced a similar upsurge of Muslim fundamentalism in opposition to the Afghan Communists' radical revolution in 1976. Twenty years later, the most extreme of these religious movements, the Taliban Party, seized power in an effort to impose on the Afghan people a Muslim theocracy (a state based entirely on religious precepts and led by religious leaders). They held power for four years before being overthrown in 2002 by a coalition of Afghan guerrilla forces and U.S. armed forces (see Chapter 14). Secular nationalism became a deeply divisive issue among Muslims.

In the late twentieth century, opposition to modernism and secularism in Muslim countries took the form of a powerful, often violent international movement. Conservative Muslim religious leaders were vehemently opposed to secularism, since they believed it a deadly threat to the survival of the Muslim community and its spiritual values. They often linked it with materialism, which they understood to be personal gratification through material possessions to the neglect of spiritual duties. The mode of resistance that they particularly encouraged took the form of political movements, such as that of the Taliban, dedicated to seizing state power. Observers called them "fundamentalist" Islamic groups (since they claimed to defend the fundamental tenets of Islam) or "Islamist" groups (since they made Islam the supreme cause that they espoused).

Committed to the dogmatic imposition of Muslim law and practice (as they understood them), some of these groups, such as Al Qaeda, used terrorist tactics of assassination and bombing. Others adopted the tactics of political parties, seeking to win elections to national parliaments. When successful, they proceeded to pass laws restricting civil and political liberties, reinforcing Muslim law, and banning women's political activities, public education, and paid work. Movements using state institutions to institute fundamentalist Islamic laws came into existence in several countries, including Sudan, and in the northern provinces of Nigeria. In all cases, their rigorous Islamic regulations aroused strong opposition both from people of other religions and from nationalists who defended the secularist program. Still, at the end of the twentieth century, the issues raised by modernist and secularist reform programs remained unresolved, producing a cultural and political crisis throughout the Muslim world.

The Six-Day War

The conflict between the Arab countries and Israel remained in the 1960s the greatest threat of war in the Middle East. Leaders of the Arab states refused to accept the presence of the Jewish state in their midst. In the 1960s, the Palestinian refugees organized their own resistance movement to take back the territory they considered their homeland. They were scattered throughout the Middle East, but their major refugee camps were located in Egypt and Jordan. There they gradually formed new social organizations to help rebuild their lives. In the early years, they received financial aid from Arab leaders who sympathized with their cause.

The Palestinians themselves had to overcome internal quarrels before Arab states took heed of their demands. Finally in 1964 several Palestinian movements agreed to form a unified coalition that they called the Palestine Liberation Organization (PLO). The founders of the PLO set their goal to be "Palestinian self-determination following the liberation of our country," that is, the destruction of the state of Israel. Arab League backing was still half-hearted. Other issues appeared more pressing to most League members. They hoped to exercise some moderating control over the Palestinians. No Arab leader dared call for a peace settlement, though, since to do so would require recognizing the state of Israel. The king of Jordan maintained secret contacts with his Israeli neighbor but feared assassination if he openly negotiated with Israel. Arab supporters of the PLO were hostile toward the very existence of a Jewish state in Arab land and hoped to avenge the defeats of 1948 and 1956. As a result of PLO efforts, Arab leaders increasingly talked of a new war on Israel.

The talk led to action in 1966, when new leaders in Syria from the Baath Party called for a "revolutionary war" to defeat Israel and to "liberate Palestine." The Syrian regime followed Nasser's example in promising its people a special Arab form of socialism. It condemned conservative Arab monarchs like the king of Saudi Arabia who adhered closely to tribal ways and traditional Muslim practices. Leaders of other Arab states suspected the Syrians of wishing to spread the political influence of their own state in the area of the Fertile Crescent, from Lebanon to the Persian Gulf. These internal divisions were hidden behind public statements in support of the Palestinian cause.

As Nasser had done a decade earlier, the Syrian government turned to the Soviet Union for military and economic aid. The Soviet leaders were eager to enlarge their network of allied states to include Syria. They praised the Baath Party's socialist policies, which they viewed as a politically progressive step and a promising sign of solidarity with Soviet interests. Nasser's Egypt had shown the way for Soviet ties in the Middle East. In 1966, Syria became Moscow's second ally there. Soviet aid went to the Syrian government. It secretly went as well to the PLO, some of whose soldiers traveled to eastern Europe to receive training from Soviet agents. PLO guerrilla fighters were encouraged by the Syrians to launch raids from their territory on Israeli settlements. The Middle East was becoming an arena of Cold War conflict between supporters of the Soviet Union and of the United States.

U.S. leaders believed that the strategic interests of the Western alliance required good relations with oil-rich countries, especially Saudi Arabia and Iran. The West's dependence on oil from Arab lands demanded no less. Yet the U.S. government was sympathetic to the Israeli national cause. It embodied the hope of Jewish peoples for a haven from persecution. This tiny state respected human rights better than any other regime in the Middle East. Israel functioned as a democratic state, promising civil liberties to their 2.5 million Jews and 300,000 Arabs. It protected the religious practices of the Muslims and Christians. Its Arab citizens remained a suspect people, though, and were excluded from full political participation in public affairs. They enjoyed fewer rights than the Jews but were

protected under the constitution from persecution. No other state there could claim to do as much for its minorities.

The Israeli leaders relied for the defense of their country primarily on their own military forces. The U.S. commitment to Israel took the form of a public promise to protect the "right to exist" of the state of Israel. It was a message directed to Arab countries. The U.S. government had defined its goal in the Middle East to be peace and political stability. Its promises to Arab oil countries and to Israel created a dilemma, for strategic interests collided with its readiness to defend Israel. As the likelihood of war with Syria grew, Israeli generals laid their own plans for war. They realized, remembering their experience in the 1956 war, that they had to operate independently of any foreign states. Fearing a concerted offensive by the surrounding Arab countries, they conceived the desperate strategy of striking first. Secretly, they prepared to launch an attack on Egypt, Jordan, and Syria in turn, attacking each country separately in the hope of ultimately defeating all.

The PLO campaign against Israel remained the immediate grounds for war. Israeli generals decided to destroy the bases in Jordan and Syria from which PLO guerrillas were penetrating their country. Raids on these camps provoked a public outcry in Arab countries. The Syrian government demanded that Egypt immediately prepare to join the fight against Israel. The danger of a new Arab-Israeli conflict was growing. Nasser could not refuse his support, for he had spoken out too long and too fervently for the "liquidation of Israeli aggression." Of what use was Egyptian talk of Arab solidarity, the Syrian leaders asked publicly, if Egypt kept the U.N. peacekeeping forces between its army and Israel?

In 1967, Nasser abandoned his cautious policy. In May of that year, he ordered the U.N. forces to leave Egypt. At the same moment, he closed the Gulf of Aqaba, on Egypt's eastern border, to shipping bound for Israel from the Indian Ocean. In the tense atmosphere of that spring, these steps signaled preparation for war against Israel. No evidence suggests that he had in fact ordered the Egyptian military to make ready for an invasion. The most likely explanation for his reckless action was his ambition to be leader of "progressive" Arab countries. It was a role he could only sustain by placing Egypt at the forefront of the impending war against Israel. Nasser's action constituted the fatal step in the outbreak of another Middle Eastern war.

Fearing concerted Arab attack, the Israeli government approved the risky plans of its military for a preventive war on its Arab neighbors. Two decades after the first Arab-Israeli conflict, the same enemies met once again in June 1967. The Arab states proved as poorly prepared as before, and the Israeli army and air force functioned with extraordinary skill and deadly precision. Their "Six-Day" War was a resounding triumph for Israel. It turned into a military disaster for Egypt. That state was Israel's principal enemy, since it possessed the largest Arab armed force. In the first hours of war, Israeli planes destroyed the entire Egyptian air force. In the next three days, Israel's armored columns occupied the whole Sinai peninsula to the Suez Canal. Its army then attacked and defeated Jordanian forces on the west bank of the Jordan River and in the city of Jerusalem. Finally, it forced Syrian troops out of the mountainous border area known as the Golan Heights. It achieved these victories in six days. The defeated Arab states accepted a U.N. truce, leaving Israeli troops in possession of all the territory occupied during the war.

Egypt, Palestine, and Peace with Israel

That war proved a turning point in the recent history of the Middle East. It made clear to Arabs and Jews alike the rewards that Israeli political unity and military skill had brought. In the words of an Arab historian, Arabs understood that "a small state had displayed their historical inadequacy, had seized massive chunks of land, and had devastated the armies whose weapons and machismo had been displayed with great pride."[1] Victory in the Six-Day War brought the Jewish state all Palestine, the ancestral lands of the Jews. Conquest of the Gaza Strip on the Mediterranean Sea and of Jordanian Jerusalem and the West Bank territory gave Israel rule over more than one million Palestinians, some in refugee camps but most living in their own communities. To whom should the land of Palestine belong? The question became an urgent political and religious issue for the Israeli government, for the Israeli people, and for the Palestinian Arab population.

In the next two decades, the Israeli answer in policy and everyday practice was that the occupied territories would be integrated into their state. Disregarding the United Nations' resolutions calling for withdrawal from these lands, conservative Israeli leaders offered incentives and protection for new Jewish settlements in the West Bank area. These settlers took possession by the late 1980s of nearly one-third of the entire land and most of the precious water rights. Palestinians had to make room for the settlers, paying for the defeat in loss of their water and their land. They found work as laborers in Israeli enterprises, often traveling regularly across the "green line" that still separated Israel from the occupied lands.

Politically that line was very real. Palestinians in these areas remained a disenfranchised people, ruled by the Israeli state and

---

[1]Fouad Ajami, *The Arab Predicament: Arab Political Thought and Practice since 1967* (New York: Cambridge University Press, 1981), p. 12.

under military occupation. In the opinion of one Israeli observer, Israel's three million Jews exercised by choice or by necessity in the mid-1980s a sort of "majority tyranny" over the 2.5 million Palestinian Arabs. To the observer, the process of economic integration of the peoples of Israel–Palestine appeared irreversible, yet political unification seemed unattainable.[2] An additional source of conflict came from the religious aspirations of fundamentalist Jewish groups to settle all the ancient territory of the Jewish tribes, in the process displacing the Palestinian Arab inhabitants. Israeli leaders clung to their vision of an enlarged Jewish land and the Palestine Liberation Organization (PLO) continued to demand an Arab state in all Palestine.

For two decades after the war, the PLO attempted to achieve this goal by force of arms. It created military camps for its militia forces. Its troops seized the southern part of Lebanon in the early 1970s after being expelled from Jordan. The PLO clashed with Lebanon's government over the seizure of the southern region. In 1975, a civil war began that tore the tiny country apart. Both Syrian and Israeli armed forces intervened in the fighting, each seizing strategic territory along their borders. Lacking a strong military and unified political leadership, the Lebanese state disintegrated into a collection of warring private armies defending the territory of their Christian and Muslim communities. The PLO's militia failed to advance the struggle against Israel, however. It was incapable even of defending PLO camps from Israeli army attack.

In those same years, the PLO undertook a campaign of international terrorism to pursue "war by other means" on Israel. Its terrorist acts used the time-tried methods of assassination and destruction to publicize its cause and to intimidate Israel. The PLO launched terrorist attacks on targets associated, even remotely, with Israel. It began the campaign in 1969 with the hijacking and destruction of three airplanes belonging to U.S. airlines. Even Israeli Olympic athletes became PLO victims when terrorists attacked the Munich Olympic Village in 1972. Twelve Israeli athletes died in the attack. A secret war went on for years between the Israeli secret service and international terrorist organizations supporting the PLO. But terrorism proved as unsuccessful as the PLO's military operations against Israel.

The most effective form of Palestinian political protest against Israel proved to be the mass uprising (called in Arabic the "Intifada") in Israel's occupied lands. It began in late 1987, when thousands of Palestinians in towns and refugee camps spontaneously joined mass demonstrations against Israeli troops. Their only arms were stones, against which Israeli occupation authorities deployed their military and police forces. They had no plan of action, for the PLO had no part in organizing the Intifada. It surprised its leaders (in exile) as much as it did the Israeli government. At the start, leadership for the demonstrations came from within the Palestinian community. The Intifada extended to strikes and economic boycotts against Israeli enterprises. The Israeli military discovered that force could disperse the demonstrators—with many wounded and some killed—but could not stop the uprising. This first Intifada continued sporadically until the early 1990s. The demonstrations were the first sign of substantial national unity among Palestinians and made clear their refusal to accept the integration of the occupied territories into Israel.

In Egypt, the defeat of 1967 set the Egyptian government on a new course in foreign and domestic policy. Nasser died in 1971. His successor, Anwar Sadat, was also a former member of the Free Officers of 1952. He rejected Nasser's policy of state socialism for

---

[2]Meron Benvesisti, *Conflicts and Contradictions* (New York: Publisher, 1986), p. 184.

Egypt and launched a secularist program, including laws to protect the rights of Egyptian women. He did not believe that Nasser's determination to make Egypt the leader of the struggle against Israel was in the country's interests. Sadat did seek to recover from Israel the Egyptian territory beyond the Suez Canal lost in the Six-Day War. He was determined, once this goal was achieved, to remove his state from the interminable conflict draining the resources of his country.

His daring project supposed first of all that he restore Egypt's international standing after its crushing defeat in the 1967 war. He had the

backing for another war from the other Arab states, including Saudi Arabia. The Saudi king's influence rested on his country's role as exporter of oil. Demand for petroleum in the early 1970s had risen so rapidly that it had become a product in short supply. Oil-producing countries had by then won from the petroleum companies the legal right to control their oil production. They were in a new position of power. With Saudi backing, Sadat decided to risk another war with Israel.

In late 1973, his armies launched a surprise attack across the Suez Canal (the Yom Kippur War). The initial fighting went in their favor.

Confronting the Palestinian Uprising: Israeli Troops in Bethlehem, 1988. (*United Nations Relief and Works Agency HQ Gaza*)

Israeli forces retreated from the canal. Both the United States and the Soviet Union intervened to back their respective allies, and the war turned into a major international crisis. The Soviet Union sent arms to Egypt. The United States rushed military aid to Israel. When the Israeli army succeeded in turn in pushing Egyptian forces back beyond the canal and Soviet leaders threatened to intervene militarily, the U.S. government declared a "stage 3" nuclear alert, readying its forces for possible nuclear war. To support Egypt, the Arab oil-producing countries declared an embargo (that is, a ban) on oil shipments to the United States and curtailed oil production. The price of petroleum shot up to $14 per barrel, oil rationing began in the United States, and an international recession set in as a result of the oil shortages. The nuclear confrontation combined with the oil embargo put enormous pressure on both sides to negotiate a settlement. A truce ended the war, leaving Egyptian forces in control of a strip of territory on the eastern side of the Suez Canal. Sadat now was in a strong position to negotiate with Israel.

He proceeded in the next years to implement the second stage in his new peace policy. He offered to negotiate with Israel, breaking ranks with the other Arab states, and abruptly ended Egypt's alliance with the Soviet Union. He appealed to the U.S. government to become Egypt's ally and principal source of economic and military aid. He was successful in both endeavors. Egypt and Israel signed a peace treaty in 1979. Egypt, first of any Arab state, formally recognized the existence of the state of Israel. The Israeli government, in turn, restored all Egyptian lands seized in 1967. The U.S. government began shipping military equipment to Egypt and increased its shipments of food, needed to feed the impoverished Egyptian masses. It was more deeply involved than ever in the Middle East, providing aid to both Israel and Egypt.

The danger of a new Arab-Israeli war dwindled, but Sadat's daring moves cost him his life. He had formally recognized that the Jewish state belonged within the Middle Eastern polity. Muslim fundamentalist groups condemned his policies of peace with Israel and his social reforms (including greater rights for women). He was assassinated in 1981 by a group of Egyptian army officers and soldiers, members of an Islamist terrorist group. This brutal action, motivated by their conviction that Egypt's leader had joined the enemies of Islam, signaled the growing strength of Muslim fundamentalism in Middle Eastern life.

Despite continued terrorist violence, the Egyptian government stayed faithful to Sadat's political course. It directed its efforts to helping an impoverished population that had grown to fifty-five million by 1990. It ended the severe restrictions on free enterprise, promoting Egyptian economic development by a combination of state aid and private employment. Egypt became a land of relative freedom among repressive Arab states. Its most serious enemy remained the Muslim Brotherhood. Its supporters began a campaign of terrorism in the 1980s, directed against Egyptian intellectuals such as the Nobel Prize–winning novelist Naguib Mafouz, accused of the sin of modernism (abandonment of Islam), against the Coptic Christian church and even against foreign tourists. Muslim fundamentalism was a powerful force in Egypt, sustained by religious fanaticism and widespread poverty that the state appeared incapable of ending.

For fifteen years, Sadat's peace initiative remained without sequel. The PLO refused the offer of autonomy for the occupied territories included in the 1978 peace agreement. Its followers clung to their hope of taking back all of Palestine. The leaders of Syria and Iraq competed in their warlike threats against Israel.

Israel remained in a state of war with its other neighboring Arab states.

Conditions changed dramatically in the early 1990s. The changes were partly the result of new Israeli political leadership that took power in 1993. The ongoing Palestinian Intifada made clear that the occupied territories could not remain under Israeli rule. For the first time, the Israeli government declared its readiness to negotiate a compromise settlement with the PLO. Prospects for peace improved also because of the decline in power of the radical, anti-Israeli Arab states. Iraq had become the leader of these states in the 1980s. But its defeat in the Gulf War of 1991 ended its regional influence and dashed the hopes of the PLO for Iraqi backing for a new war against Israel. Palestinian radicals had lost their political patron.

The PLO leader, Yasir Arafat, took a step as daring in its own way as Sadat's peace initiative two decades before. In 1993, he agreed to recognize the state of Israel and discuss a peace accord with the new Israeli government. Arafat was prepared to admit publicly that endless bloodshed could not bring to life the dream of a Palestinian state and that Israel had itself to be party to the creation of a country for the Palestinians. That year the PLO and Israel reached a peace agreement (the Oslo Agreement). It opened the way for a Palestinian state, to be created in slow stages out of the occupied territories, and recognized officially by the state of Israel. The PLO ordered a stop to terrorist attacks and brought to an end (temporarily) the Palestinian uprising. The next year, the king of Jordan signed a peace treaty with Israel. The period of Arab-Israeli wars had finally come to an end, almost five decades after the creation of the state of Israel.

For a few years, Arafat's authority was sufficient to keep anti-Israeli Arabs from street violence and terrorism. The Palestine–Israel agreement promised Palestinian self-rule in the occupied territories (Gaza, the west bank of the Jordan River). Just what territory (and what part of Jerusalem) should go to the "Palestine Authority" remained to be negotiated. The Israeli government had somehow to curtail the expansionist plans of Jewish settlers whose communities were located in the midst of the lands to go under Palestinian rule. These issues were complex and aroused passionate resistance from extremists on both sides.

In 2000, with these issues still unresolved, Arab militants took to the streets again to attack Israeli troops and settlers in the occupied territories. This "second Intifada" differed from the first principally by its level of violence. This time Palestinian insurgents used rifles and machine guns to attack Israeli forces. In addition, Muslim terrorist groups resorted to suicide bombings in Israel itself, killing hundreds and wounding thousands of bystanders. The Israeli army responded with attacks on suspected terrorist centers in Palestinian territories by helicopter gunships and tanks. The Israeli government began construction on a gigantic wall to separate Palestinian areas from Israel and Israeli settlements. Within a few years, Palestinian casualties were numbered in the thousands. Palestinian workers, once employed in Israel, were without work. War, not peace, remained the dominant state of affairs in the Holy Land.

Iran's Islamic Republic

Like other Middle Eastern lands, Iran's population was made up of peoples of different languages and cultures. Almost all were followers of the Shi`ite branch of the Muslim religion. In the middle of the twentieth century, its monarch claimed the title of "shah," that is, emperor, but the land had long since lost all ties with the great Persian emperors of antiquity. After the Second World War, Iran's ruler, Reza Shah Pahlevi, chose to cooperate with the Western powers. He continued the policy of granting the monopoly on Iran's oil production to the British Petroleum corporation. He placed his country firmly on the side of the West in the Cold War years.

A nationalist alternative to the shah's pro-Western policies briefly emerged in Iran in the years after the Second World War. A coalition of political groups called the National Front, headed by a dynamic political leader, Dr. Mohammed Mossadeq, promised political and economic independence from the West. Iran's religious leaders proclaimed their backing for the movement, which they hoped would protect their "Islamic nation" from the West and modernism. Mossadeq's program included nationalization of British Petroleum's oil properties and neutrality for Iran in the conflict between East and West. With strong backing from voters among Iran's lower classes, Mossadeq's coalition won parliamentary elections in 1951. He became prime minister of Iran. One of his first acts was to order the nationalization of the country's oil wells and refineries. The worsening political struggle within Iran led Mossadeq to denounce the rule of the shah. Violent demonstrations in support of his government forced the shah to flee the country. Without any coherent plan, Mossadeq had set in motion forces leading the country toward political revolution.

This Iranian affair, which began as a dispute over nationalization of the country's petroleum industry, appeared to the U.S. government a Cold War conflict. In 1953, the Eisenhower administration extended the policy of containment to include opposition to anti-Western regimes in strategic areas around the Soviet Union. The presence of Communists in Mossadeq's political coalition was proof to the U.S. government that his government was a pawn of the Soviet Union. The U.S. Central Intelligence Agency sent covert aid to the shah's supporters in the country. Mossadeq was unable to hold together his National Front coalition. Popular demonstrations against Mossadeq and opposition to his rule by army leaders, secretly encouraged and financed by U.S. agents, forced the prime minister to resign in mid-1953. This U.S.-backed political revolt placed the shah back on his throne. His dependence on the West was greater than ever.

To cope with the country's political and social unrest, the shah laid out three new policies. The first was to bolster his political power. He purged his country of all political revolutionaries and expanded his police force to repress opposition from Muslim clerics. He tolerated parliamentary politics but remained the power behind the government. Though not a dictator in the full sense of the word, his rule remained authoritarian.

His second objective was to restore cooperation with the Western states. He brought Iran into the Middle Eastern military alliance, the Baghdad Pact, alongside Great Britain, Turkey, and Iraq. He signaled his desire for good relations with the United States by signing a separate defense treaty with the United States. In return, the U.S. government provided his state with large amounts of economic and military aid, more than to any other state outside the NATO alliance. U.S. advisers helped train his military forces and provided assistance in bolstering his new police force. In global power politics, the shah aligned Iran on the side of the West.

His third goal was the modernization of Iran's society and economy. He called his plan a "White Revolution," combining political order (symbolized by the monarchical color white) and social reform. His objective, he explained, was to make Iran the equal to "the most developed countries in the world." With funds from the sale of oil, his government invested heavily in modern industry and urban services. Seizing the extensive land holdings of Muslim religious societies, it redistributed land to peasant farmers.

In social and cultural matters, the shah's goal was a secular society. He looked to the example of Kemal Ataturk's reforms in Turkey as the model for his own secularist program. Islam was to be excluded from public affairs and restricted to the private sphere of worship and morality. Civil law, not Quranic law, set marriage and property relations. The shah's government discouraged Muslim traditional practices, such as veiling of women, and demoted the prominence of Islam in accounts of Iran's past glories as a great empire. In the shah's opinion, Iranian history began long before Islam reached the country in the eighth century.

Challenging the Muslim religious leaders placed the shah in opposition to clerics such as the Ayatollah Khomeini. Their overriding concern remained the defense of the "Islamic nation." Khomeini, the most forceful of these religious figures, championed a fundamentalist program of strict adherence to Islamic practices and laws. His deepest convictions, like those of the Muslim Brotherhood in Egypt, turned him against modernism and secularism. For speaking out against the shah's reforms, he was expelled from Iran in 1963.

The obstacles in the way of the shah's ambitious plans were great. He confronted serious opposition to his regime from groups demanding political liberty—mostly students and educated professionals—and from religious leaders and their followers, principally the poor urban classes. To achieve his economic goals, he exhausted his state's revenues. His income from petroleum sales proved inadequate for his grandiose projects. Social unrest worsened as a result of wild inflation and hardship caused by rapid economic growth.

The core of opposition to his regime came from the Muslim clerics. He had given the vote to women, made civil law the foundation of marriage, family, and inheritance, and stripped Muslim religious institutions of their vast land holdings. For this, the Muslim leaders judged him unfit to rule. In the mid-1970s they organized their supporters to bring down his "godless" regime. Forces opposing the shah grew rapidly. The Muslim clerics proved remarkably effective revolutionaries. In a few years, they brought together a broad coalition of anti-shah groups. In 1979, they orchestrated a mass revolution that ended the shah's reign. Demonstrators took control of the streets of the cities, and workers went on strike, paralyzing production in the oil industry. The army was overwhelmed by this revolutionary upsurge. Its troops mutinied, refusing to shoot the demonstrators. Lacking popular support and the means to repress the uprising, the shah was forced to flee his country.

The victor was Ayatollah Khomeini. He was the inspirational leader of the revolutionaries and became the principal architect of the theocratic Islamic state that came into existence in 1980. His strict reading of the Quran inspired his radical reform program. He was convinced that by following its precepts, he could create an Iranian Islamic Republic. Its religious purity, in his utopian view, would recreate Muhammed's original state. Symbolic of the renewal of Islamic practices was his order that women must once again hide behind traditional veils in conformity with Muslim traditions.

This Islamic Republic looked toward the restoration of Muslim law and faith throughout the Muslim world. Its religious leaders held the reins of power in the Iranian government and in the courts and commanded a vigilante militia charged with punishing Iranians who failed to obey Muslim practices. They denounced the corrupting influence of wealth and the pursuit of individual pleasure. They called on Muslims everywhere to return to the strict guidelines of the Quran and of Muslim law. Their message found supporters among Sunni as well as Shi`a Muslims in the years following the revolution.

They became a major force behind the upsurge throughout the Muslim world of Muslim fundamentalism in the 1980s. They condemned rulers whose secularism weakened Muslim rules and practices. They promised reforms inspired by the Quran's social concern to alleviate the misery of urban masses. Their vision was of a renewed and united community of Muslim faithful.

By word and deed, the leaders of the Islamic Republic spread far beyond Iran's borders their militant program. Public figures in any sphere, cultural, social, or political, were targets of their religious wrath. In 1988, Ayatollah Khomeini ordered the execution of the Indian writer Salman Rushdie for having published the novel *The Satanic Verses*, judged sacrilegious and blasphemous to the Muslim faith. Forced to flee his home, Rushdie went into hiding for several years; two translators (in Japan and Norway) of his novel were murdered, presumably by Khomeini's followers. The Iranian government gave its support, including generous subsidies, to terrorist movements in lands where they believed the Muslim faith was threatened. They called on Iraqi Muslims to overthrow Saddam Hussein's regime. When Iraq invaded Iran in 1980, they urged Iranian troops to destroy Saddam's forces. But their holy war was a failure there. The Ayatollah's Muslim fundamentalism found few Iraqi sympathizers and fewer still ready to risk their lives for his religious cause. The Iranian army was able to force Iraqi forces back to the border but could not advance further in the face of Iraq's modern armaments (including deadly chemical weapons). The war ended in 1988 with an armistice, leaving millions of Iranian war dead.

Gradually in the 1990s, Iran's Islamic Republic weakened its rigorous Quranic laws imposed on the population. In private and out of sight of the "vice police," many people sought simple pleasures such as dancing to Western music and watching Western television. But the Muslim clerics, who remained the power behind the state, clung to their dream of a theocratic land leading the entire Muslim world toward the righteous life.

Their message found a sympathetic hearing in many Muslim countries. Supporters were especially numerous in Muslim lands where governments proved incapable of coping with the impoverishment of the masses. By the early 1990s, several other governments in the Middle East and Asia had made Muslim law the legal foundation of their states. In Algeria, Islamists took up arms when denied control of the government through popular electoral support. The resulting civil war with the military regime there led to appalling loss of life among civilians caught in the middle, with estimates of 100,000 dead. This rise of fundamentalism was a disturbing trend to those who believed that religious toleration and civil liberties offered the best guarantee of individual integrity. The fundamentalists' defense of their religious faith and practices brought with it the persecution of religious minorities and the rejection of civil liberties protecting individual citizens no matter what their faith. The Iranian revolution revealed that Western liberal ideals and secular reforms had aroused a deep and determined opposition grounded in Muslim religious values and practices.

The Oil Wars of Iraq

By the 1980s, almost all Middle Eastern states, except Israel, had fallen under the control of authoritarian regimes. None of the states functioned as democracies with free elections and with effective guarantees of civil liberty for their peoples. One reason for the emergence of strong leaders was the existence everywhere of antagonistic social, ethnic, and religious communities. No general agreement on majority rule and minority rights was possible where each community feared the others. Military and political leaders, who often relied on particular clans or tribes to find loyal followers, competed in a brutal struggle for power. Though the victors claimed to speak for their nation, for all Arabs, or for Islam, they directed their efforts principally to protecting and preserving the wealth and privileges brought them by political power.

The history of Iraq in the last half of the twentieth century followed closely this pattern of authoritarian rule. The country's territory centered around the river valleys of the Tigris and Euphrates. Once called Mesopotamia, it was inhabited by a diverse population that included most major ethnic and religious groups of the Middle East. The bulk of the inhabitants (nearly two-thirds) belonged to the Shi`a Muslim faith; Sunni Muslims were numerous as well. Small communities of Christians were scattered across the country. The Muslims were mostly Arabic speaking, but the northern, mountainous area was inhabited by a large population of Kurdish people, with their own language and culture.

Independence from the British in 1940 left the country under the rule of a monarch, King Faisal I. His reign had begun in 1921, when this League-mandated state came into existence. He enjoyed meager support among the population. He in turn had a low opinion of his subjects, whom he judged "devoid of any patriotic idea, imbued with religious prejudices, and riotous." In 1959, an ambitious general overthrew the monarchy and tried to govern as a military dictator. In the next decade, political strife among the military brought only confusion and disorder to the land. Finally, in 1969, a progressive secular movement calling itself the "Rebirth" (Baath) Party seized power in a bloody insurrection. Among its leaders was a young Iraqi named Saddam Hussein. He had made a political career as a member of this party. Its policies borrowed heavily from the

Kurdish Warlord, 1965 (*Getty Images, Inc.*)

socialist, secularist, and pan-Arab program first promoted in Egypt by Gamal Nasser in the 1950s. Saddam Hussein became one of the party's leaders by dint of his organizing skills during the years of underground struggle before the 1969 revolt.

During the early years in power, Saddam Hussein and his colleagues proceeded with their agenda of internal reform. The first step was taking over the prosperous oil industry. The boom in oil prices after the 1973 Israeli war brought enormous revenues to their government. Throughout the 1970s, they used this wealth to invest in new industrial development, to introduce an extensive program of social welfare, including health care and old-age pensions, and to expand the country's education system. They encouraged women to seek professional careers such as educators, doctors, and lawyers.

To bolster the ethnic unity of the state, the Baath leaders sponsored resettlement of Arab-speaking inhabitants throughout the country where other ethnic groups were concentrated. They forcibly removed Kurds from key northern cities and installed Arab migrants from the south. Finally, they strengthened their military forces, spending large sums to create a modern air force and to mechanize the army (largely with purchases from the Soviet Union). Kurdish nationalists retreated to the mountains to continue their fight for independence but with little success. By the end of the decade, Iraq had emerged as one of the strongest states in the Middle East.

During those years Saddam Hussein gradually built up his control of the Baath Party and, through it, the Iraqi state. He used his influence as chief of the secret police in that one-party state to eliminate his rivals as well as to keep down opposition from Muslim fundamentalists and Kurdish nationalists. The government's leadership was gathered in the Revolutionary Command Council (in imitation of Nasser's Egypt), where he could govern without reliance on the Baath Party. In 1979, he eliminated his last rival for power. He openly acknowledged his admiration for Joseph Stalin's style of leadership. He became "President, Leader, Struggler." That year he had become Iraqi dictator. He had reached this position by, as Russians had said of Stalin, "climbing over the bodies of his enemies."

His methods of rule bore a strong likeness as well to European fascism. The socialism that he professed served in part as an ideological bond to hold together the peoples of his divided country. Iraq was a "state without a nation"; that is, it lacked one predominant ethnic community. In place of that unity he substituted au-

thoritarian rule. Nationalism became the ideology and propaganda tool in that system. Like fascist leaders of Europe earlier, he used it to claim to speak for and rule over the Iraqi population, and like them, he glorified warriors and war. He sought leadership of all Arab countries (as Nasser had before him). To do so, he was prepared to promote the anti-Israeli crusade. His army was a key instrument in this cause. He began a secret program to develop nuclear weapons, but it was brought to an abrupt halt when Israeli warplanes destroyed Iraq's nuclear reactor in 1981. Like the Italian fascist dictator Mussolini, he turned the human and economic resources of the country to military conquest.

Saddam's first target was Iran. Its rich oil fields lay on the borders of Iraq. In 1980, it was in the throes of its Islamic revolution, and its Muslim leaders had issued the call for the overthrow of his "godless" regime. That year, Saddam ordered his armies to invade Iran to put to an end this militant Islamist regime. His principal objective was seizure of the Iranian oil fields near the Persian Gulf, which he expected to conquer without difficulty. After initial success, his forces had to retreat in the face of Iran's "holy war." To push back the Iranian army, he deployed all his army's weaponry, including chemical weapons. He obtained outside financial and military assistance from neighboring states fearful of Iranian Muslim zealotry. Even the United States sold military equipment to Iraq on the time-tried balance-of-power principle that "the enemy of my enemy is my friend."

The Iraq–Iran war dragged on for eight years until the two states, exhausted by the fighting, declared an armistice. The armies withdrew to the original borders. Saddam's dream of glorious victory left his country with half-a-million war casualties and $80 billion in foreign debt. Only by the wildest stretch of the imagination could anyone believe that the 1988 cease-fire was an Iraqi victory. He held in public to this fantastic tale, though, and no one in Iraq dared openly dispute his fantasy.

The reality was that he had squandered Iraq's resources on a futile war of aggression that left his state deeply in debt to other Arab states. Among these was the tiny principality of Kuwait, located on the very borders of Iraq. Its tremendous oil reserves (judged fourth largest in the world) were tempting booty, and it was defenseless against his large army. Saddam decided for the second time to wage war for petroleum. If victorious, his state would dominate the Middle East.

His troops crossed the borders of Kuwait in the summer of 1990. He expected no effective international opposition to Iraqi seizure of the tiny, neighboring state. The Soviet government, on which his state had once depended for most of its arms, was in the midst of a serious political crisis caused by Gorbachev's reforms. Its advisers in Iraq had lost all influence over his foreign policies. The United States had failed several times in previous years to use its military force effectively in the Middle East. It had been unable to free its embassy hostages in Iran in a military operation in 1980, and it had proven incapable of ending the civil war in Lebanon in the early 1980s. International peacekeeping appeared to him an unlikely occurrence. Iraqi troops met almost no resistance from the tiny Kuwait army, and Saddam Hussein immediately declared Kuwait to be a province of Iraq.

Instead of easy victory, within a few weeks Saddam confronted the largest military coalition since the Second World War fighting under the flag of the United Nations. Iraq's conquest of Kuwait revealed to leaders around the world two important realities about global relations after the Cold War. The first was the simple fact that, without outside protection, any small state was vulnerable to an aggressive neighbor. The United Nations guaranteed in principle the inviolability of states' borders, but only concerted action of

its powerful members could make that promise effective.

Equally important was the fact that the globe's economic growth depended on a steady supply of Middle East oil. Its price decided prosperity or recession in distant lands. Iraqi seizure of Kuwait's oil fields would permit Saddam to dominate the world market. Middle Eastern states around Iraq such as Turkey, Syria, Egypt, and Saudi Arabia, previously divided, discovered in Iraq a common enemy who threatened them all. Governments in areas as distant as Japan and Argentina realized that they shared a common interest in demonstrating their commitment to the protection of states without strong military forces. The leaders of the Soviet Union and the United States, once bitter enemies, found in opposition to the Iraqi invasion a common cause to unite them.

The head of the coalition was the United States. Its government had for forty years argued that U.S. strategic interest required access to oil from the Middle East. It had publicly extended its protection to Saudi Arabia and to Israel. Saddam Hussein's sudden victory in Kuwait put in question the security of both lands. His forces could easily move beyond Kuwait into Saudi territory. His support for anti-Israeli groups, notably the PLO, raised the specter of another Arab-Israeli war. The U.S. government turned to the United Nations to condemn Iraqi aggression. Citing the U.N. Charter, the Security Council unanimously opposed the conquest of Kuwait and called for Iraqi withdrawal. This declaration became the basis for the coalition of states, soon numbering more than thirty, that gathered around the United States. While proposing negotiations, the coalition prepared for war.

The strategy for defeating Iraq proceeded through two stages. First, an international economic blockade cut off trade to and from Iraq. It was incomplete, though, since the neighboring states of Iran and Jordan did not support the coalition and allowed goods to Iraq to cross their borders. Saddam Hussein refused to take seriously the demand for withdrawal. To end this stalemate, the coalition began military operations. It launched a massive aerial bombardment of Iraq, destroying Iraq's air force. This was followed in February 1991 by a sudden ground offensive in Kuwait, led by American, British, and French armored divisions employing new electronic weapons against the Iraqi army. These forces surrendered virtually without resistance, though large numbers of Iraqi military and civilians died under air attack while attempting to flee Kuwait.

The U.N. invading force stopped in southern Iraq, however, before reaching the capital Baghdad. Arab members of the coalition preferred partial victory to the collapse of Iraq, and U.S. military leaders were eager to keep casualties low among their troops. After a month of fighting, Saddam Hussein surrendered and signed a cease-fire agreement.

The coalition's military victory was limited but effective. The principal goal of freeing Kuwait was achieved with the withdrawal of all Iraqi forces from Kuwait. Before doing so, Iraqi agents exploded all the country's eight hundred oil wells. Enormous oil fires fouled the atmosphere of the region for nearly a year before being completely extinguished. Saddam Hussein remained in power, but the United Nations took severe measures to limit his regime's power. The Iraqi government had to dismantle its nuclear weapons and destroy its stock of chemical and biological weapons. It had to allow U.N. inspectors access to their entire country to ensure compliance with these demands.

Fires in the Desert: Kuweit Oil Fields, 1991. (Benic/*Getty Images Inc.-Hulton Archives Photos*)

The United Nations' most unprecedented action was the creation of a protected zone in northern Iraq for the Kurdish minority. Of the total twenty million Kurds living scattered across the northern Middle East, more than three million lived in Iraq. Their periodic uprisings aimed at freeing themselves from Iraqi rule had ended each time in defeat and the destruction of many Kurdish villages. Kurdish guerrilla forces joined in the 1991 war, risking death at the hands of Saddam's army. To prevent another ethnic massacre, the United Nations demanded that the Iraqi government withdraw its forces from the Kurdish territory. The Kurds were to govern their own area. Allied fighter planes flew regular patrol missions over northern Iraq to keep Iraqi warplanes and troops out of this region. Never before had the United Nations used its powers to divide up the territory of a state that threatened the lives of an ethnic minority. Kurdish leaders posted on the borders of their Iraqi territory a sign reading "Kurdistan."

An unstable peace returned to the Middle East. Saddam's attempt to dominate the region had collapsed. To ensure that he would not be tempted again to send his military into another war, U.S. naval forces remained near the Persian Gulf, and a small number of U.S. air and ground units were stationed in Saudi Arabia. The economic blockade of Iraq continued. Petroleum from Iraq's enormous oil fields reappeared in small quantities on the world market as allowed by the United Nations for purchases of civilian goods. Iraq still possessed the world's third-greatest reserves of petroleum, a natural resource indispensable to the global economy. Saddam's regime relied on that reality in its hopes for future political power. Humbled in the eyes of the world, Saddam remained dictator ruling over an impoverished people forced to live among the ruins of wars for which he bore the responsibility.

SUMMARY

The political life of the Middle East appeared in the years after decolonization to be an ongoing saga of civil strife and authoritarian leadership. Only Israel and, to a lesser extent, Egypt enjoyed a consensus among their populations on national unity and political participation. Palestinians living in Israel were excluded from full citizenship by the Israeli government. Most Middle Eastern lands were deeply divided by generations-old animosity among religious and ethnic communities. The fervor with which many peoples clung to communal bonds arose from their distrust of repressive political leaders. These rulers talked of national unity but governed by favoring their own political followers, ethnic communities, and clans. Ethnic loyalties were so pervasive that observers called the trend a new form of tribalism, that is, exclusive ethnic solidarity.

State-building was a mockery in times of civil war among these warring groups. In the case of Lebanon, the conflict tore the country apart for an entire decade. Authoritarian rule by military dictators kept divided lands together by force. It also produced corrupt regimes incapable of healing ethnic distrust or of pushing for economic development to alleviate the poverty of their populations. Sales of petroleum on the international market sustained the incomes of those countries, such as Iraq and Iran, fortunate enough to possess large oil reserves. Other countries experienced prolonged economic decline.

The continued importance of religious issues marked the Middle East more than any other part of the postwar world. In Muslim lands and in Israel, fundamentalist movements sustained public concern for religious purity in thought and action and fought secularist and feminist reforms. Misery and the insecurity of everyday life among the impoverished masses led many Muslims to seek support and reassurance in their faith. They were encouraged to do so by religious leaders dreaming of a renewal of spiritual values. The struggle to sustain that faith in the midst of technological wonders and images of Western modernity was at the root of crises in private lives and public affairs throughout the Middle East.

DATES WORTH REMEMBERING

1939	Start of Saudi Arabian oil production
1945	Formation of Arab League
1948	Independence of Israel
1948–1949	First Arab-Israeli war
1952	Nasser in power
1955–1963	French war in Algeria
1956	Seizure of Suez Canal by Nasser, and Suez War
1960	Creation of Organization of Petroleum Exporting Countries (OPEC)
1963	Independence for Algeria
1964	Creation of Palestine Liberation Organization (PLO)
1967	Israeli-Arab Six-Day War
1973	Israeli-Arab War
1975–1981	Civil war in Lebanon
1979	Egyptian-Israeli Peace Treaty
1979	Iranian Islamic Revolution
1980–1988	Iraq–Iran war
1988	Palestinian uprising in Israeli-occupied lands
1990	Iraq invasion of Kuwait
1991	Gulf War
1993	Oslo peace agreement between PLO and Israel
1994	Israeli-Jordanian Peace Treaty

RECOMMENDED READING

Postwar Middle East

Fred Halliday, *Nation and Religion in the Middle East* (2000). A valuable study of the modern politics of Islam, focused on the issue of nationalism and Islam in the Middle East.

Efraim Karsh and Inari Rautsi, *Saddam Hussein: A Political Biography* (1991). Still the best biography of the Iraqi dictator.

*Samir Khalil, *Republic of Fear: The Inside Story of Saddam's Iraq* (1992). A history of the rise of Saddam Hussein by an Iraqi refugee.

*Bernard Lewis, *History: Remembered, Recovered, Invented* (1975). A study of the recent creation of nationalist myths in Iran and Israel.

Roy Mottahedeh, *The Mantle of the Prophet: Religion and Politics in Iran* (1985). A thoughtful inquiry into the influential role of the Muslim clerics in Iran in the twentieth century.

Israel and Its Wars

Michael Cohen, *Palestine and the Great Powers, 1945–48* (1982). A balanced evaluation of the role of the Great Powers in the partition of Palestine and the formation of Israel.

*Larry Collins and Dominique Lapierre, *O Jerusalem!* (1980). A dramatic account of the struggle for Israeli independence.

Charles Smith, *Palestine and the Arab-Israeli Conflict* (1988). A clearly presented history of the wars between the Arab states and Israel.

Memoirs and Novels

*Thomas Friedman, *From Beirut to Jerusalem* (1989). Gripping memoirs by a *New York Times* correspondent in the Middle East during the 1980s.

*Naguib Mahfouz, *Midaq Ally* (1966). An intimate glimpse of Cairo families at the end of the Second World War, written by the Egyptian Nobel Prize–winning author (and target of Muslim fundamentalist attacks).

Golda Meir, *My Life* (1975). The personal memoirs of an extraordinary life from a Russian ghetto to the head of the state of Israel.

_____
*Indicates book is available in paperback.

The West from Cold War to European Union

- The New Industrial Revolution
- European Nations and European Union
- The Fall of the Soviet Empire

Highlight: Social Change and Women's Rights

Spotlight: Andrei Sakharov

The Cold War had dominated global relations in the decades that followed the Second World War until the 1980s. Then it suddenly ended. The post-Stalin Soviet leadership had resolved to keep in place the essential institutions of Stalinism, held up by what appeared to be an invincible dictatorship. While Western nations had improved the quality of life for their people with amazing speed, the entire communist system in the East had stagnated. Weaknesses within the Soviet Union, hidden for decades from outside view, forced new leaders in the 1980s to undertake risky reforms. The reform effort failed, and in 1991 the communist system collapsed. The fall of communism occurred with extraordinary swiftness. The Cold War disappeared along with the Soviet Union, leaving

in its wake tens of thousands of useless but lethal nuclear weapons.

Even before that, in eastern Europe popular opposition to communism proved so massive that the entire satellite system vanished within a few months in 1989. The crucial first step came when the reformist leaders in the Soviet Union openly condemned the Stalinist system, which was still in place in the satellite countries. The profound desire among peoples in these countries to be freed from Soviet domination and communist rule quickly assumed the proportions of a popular uprising. The collapse of these regimes was revolutionary in its speed, and the scope of reform was breathtaking. New leaders introduced a democratic and capitalist order. The process bore little resemblance to earlier revolutions, for it occurred almost without violence. In a sense, it represented a return to the past, for the new central Europe resembled the nation-states put in place in 1919 by the Paris peace negotiators.

The Stalinist period left bitter memories in Russia and eastern Europe of hardship and a legacy of political repression and destruction of natural resources. The term *totalitarianism* became popular there to condemn that hated past. Lenin, Stalin, and their followers had proclaimed that their communist system was a model for humanity. By the opening of the twenty-first century, Russia's move toward a market economy and democratic political system, each adapted to the country's peculiar history, appeared well under way. A reversion to the communist system had become unthinkable. Liberal reformers there wanted the world to know that communism was a bankrupt social experiment and a human tragedy.

The reconstruction of Europe outside the communist countries took place at a time of technological discovery so important it came to be known as a new Industrial Revolution. These economic innovations occurred as European peoples enjoyed the benefits of the social welfare system put in place after the war and enjoyed greater leisure than ever in the continent's history. Functioning democratic institutions and public consensus on liberal political goals were an integral part of daily life. By the 1980s, the major debates of public life dealt with the shortcomings of the postwar reforms. At the same time, the process of integration of Europe's nation-states was growing ever stronger as more states joined the new European Union. By the end of the twentieth century, Europe had in many ways reinvented itself.

THE NEW INDUSTRIAL REVOLUTION

The West's economic expansion of the late century drew increasingly on technological innovation. The electronics and computer industries became the most dynamic centers of development by the 1970s. Their managers set up production in developed and developing countries, wherever costs were lowest and profits highest. These fundamental new conditions of global interdependence made a return to the West's economic isolationism of the 1930s' depression years impossible.

The Electronic Age

The appearance of computers and telecommunication instruments created an information revolution first in the West, then in East Asia and other parts of the world. Through the instantaneous transmission and analysis of information among peoples in the developed countries, and from almost all parts of the globe, this new electronics industry dissolved borders and opened potential access to a vast pool of knowledge. But political and cultural barriers remained in place. Shared knowledge was restricted, imperfect, and too often misunderstood. This modern technology was only as effective as its operators could make it. They used it primarily for economic profit.

Electronics and telecommunications did not exist as important industries until the 1950s. They began to expand at a rapid rate in direct response to new discoveries. Technological innovations in this area combined the sophistication of rocketry and earth satellites, the extraordinary power of computers to analyze information, telecommunications equipment for instantaneous transmission of data around the world, and the television screen. The scientific and technological work that went into these inventions was complex and expensive. It was concentrated principally in the West and Japan, where private companies and public institutions funded extensive research. Much of the new equipment served the needs of businesses, which brought it to other countries in their trading and investment operations. In many respects, these new sectors set in motion the new Industrial Revolution.

Television had the greatest direct impact on popular culture. It provided the channel of communication to enlarge people's awareness of social and political conditions through images as well as the spoken word. Invented before the war, it did not spread widely among Western countries until the 1950s. Almost immediately it began to appear in the newly independent nations of the Third World.

Broadcast companies, privately owned and operated in the United States, came under state control in most countries. The cost of television production required state financing. More important was control over the choice and interpretation of information transmitted through the airwaves. When used to promote a political cause such as nationalism and reinforced by visual images, messages communicated by television proved the most potent tool of propaganda ever invented. Television, the most influential form of communication, quickly came to play a central role in plans for nation-building in Third World countries. A means everywhere of education and entertainment, television offered a revolutionary means of overcoming the barriers of misunderstanding and prejudice dividing peoples. At the same time, it constituted a potent force for national unification and political indoctrination.

New electronic inventions opened the way for the creation of global networks of television transmission to form what one observer termed a "global village." Communications satellites, relaying signals from one continent to another or between distant regions of one country, first went into service in 1965 among Western countries. Ten years later, they were in place over the Atlantic, Pacific, and Indian oceans. Small, inexpensive satellite dishes afforded access to these programs for viewers even in countries that censored news and television programs. The booming economy of the People's Republic of China gave millions of Chinese families the means to purchase satellite dishes to view international television.

The Chinese Communists objected bitterly to this "poisonous foreign cultural invasion," issuing in 1993 a law outlawing private ownership of satellite dishes. Similarly, Iran's Islamic Republic ordered Iranians to scrap their satellite dishes, used there to bypass the stultifying propaganda and heavy-handed censorship of the Muslim clerics. Both laws proved a failure. Even dictatorial regimes could not overcome the popular desire for a television window onto the outside world.

Transnational communication emphasized entertainment above all. Sports competition was especially popular. An estimated three billion viewers watched the 2004 Olympic Games. The principal source of foreign programs was the U.S. television industry, generating films, songs, sports competition, celebrities, and dress fads. National television networks attempted with their own programming to stem the flood. Networks in Europe and Latin America created their own "soap operas," adapting the hugely successful American formula of TV serials dramatizing everyday life to their own social and cultural conditions. Yet the global popularity of the basketball player Michael Jordan and international markets for Hollywood's entertainment industry gave strong evidence of the alluring power of Western television. The last empires of the late century were media empires.

Western Economic Bonds

In the immediate postwar years, the United States played a crucial role in laying the foundation for the rapid global expansion of economic production and trade. The U.S. government had financed international institutions for trade and lending to spur recovery from the war. The enormous wealth of the U.S. economy made it the motor behind international economic growth. It was the principal trading partner for countries in Europe and Asia. Soon after the war the dollar became the principal international currency. It had a stable, fixed value.

Until 1971, the U.S. government guaranteed the monetary value of one ounce of gold at $30, using the gold standard to sustain the dollar's stable value. U.S. foreign aid, directed in the early postwar decades primarily to European countries, accelerated economic growth. West Germany and Japan, once enemies of the United States, quickly became prosperous and productive centers of their regions and kept close economic ties with the United States.

Trading and investment were, as in the past, particularly vigorous between Europe and the United States. The new prosperity of Europe attracted major U.S. companies, such as General Motors and International Business Machines (IBM). Termed *multinational* because of their vast financial resources invested throughout the world, these firms set up new factories and opened new markets for their goods. Western Europe's rapid economic recovery made it the single most profitable market in the world for U.S. investors, whose total investments in Europe jumped from $2 billion in 1950 to $60 billion in the mid-1970s. In those decades, European banks and corporations utilized the U.S. dollar for their trade and financial exchanges. Europeans held dollars in such quantities that their holdings earned the name of "Eurodollars."

Gradually, the U.S. currency was joined by other strong currencies as money of exchange for the global economy. By the late 1960s, the U.S. economy no longer dominated the world's trade and industry. Too many U.S. dollars were flowing across the Atlantic to pay for an increasing amount of imported goods. Inflation in the United States began to reduce the dollar's value. At one ounce of gold for $30, the price of the dollar was too cheap. International investors and financial speculators turned increasingly to the stable currencies of Germany and Japan. Their sales of dollars were so great that the U.S. government and central bank could no longer hold the dollar at its fixed low value. In 1971, the U.S. govern-

ment had to abandon the gold standard. It allowed the value of the dollar to fluctuate according to market demand. Soon $300 were needed to buy one ounce of gold.

For the rest of the century, no currency could claim a stable international value. The U.S. dollar remained the least risky currency in that unstable financial world. In countries suffering in the 1990s from high inflation, such as Russia, consumers and producers alike preferred to make their transactions in dollars (preferably in $100 bills). Certain small South American states, unable to control inflation in their own currencies, adopted the dollar as the legal medium of exchange.

Monetary instability in the late century stimulated such global currency speculation that at times it created international financial crises. In 1997 and 1998, international investors, fearful of losing money on risky loans in south Asian and Russian economies, suddenly withdrew their loans and "dumped" (that is, suddenly sold) their monetary holdings in these currencies. Their massive, panicky selling devalued these monies, curtailing imports and raising interest rates to such an extent that it caused a severe recession. The crisis was soon over, but the lesson was clear. The world's financial markets, where trillions of dollars were traded every day, held enormous power over the fate of peoples and countries.

EUROPEAN NATIONS AND EUROPEAN UNION

The peoples of western Europe had, first of any region of the world, acquired a strong awareness of their national identities. Their nation-states, and the nationalism that glorified these states and their peoples, became a model for other peoples in the twentieth century, for good and ill. Both the promise and the defects of nationalism had entered the fabric of European life. The solidarity that emerged within these national communities

Europe, 1992

created enduring bonds of loyalty. The terrible world wars that had pitted nation against nation left no doubt how destructive nationalist fanaticism could be. Statesmen there had begun in the 1950s to construct unified, supranational institutions of economic unity. The movement only accelerated at the close of the century.

By the 1980s, the concerns of citizens in individual Western countries focused on correcting shortcomings in the welfare state. No one seriously proposed abolishing the entire system and returning to conditions of the early century. In its essential features as a "safety net" for the population, it had become a permanent feature of Western societies.

Tinkering with the Welfare State

Weaknesses in the new socialist system of postwar years called for remedies. These problems included a high rate of inflation fueled by labor union pressure for yearly wage increases, inefficient nationalized enterprises that required state subsidies to remain in operation, and serious budget deficits (which contributed to inflation) and high taxes caused by the growing cost of paying for extensive welfare programs. The solutions adopted in European countries varied widely, but in every case they entailed restrictions of the scope of state support for social services and the sale (privatization) of state-owned enterprises to private owners. The poor and laboring populations lost some of their benefits, but even sizable numbers of workers voted for parties that proposed reducing the responsibilities of the welfare state. The "father-state," as the Germans called it, no longer appeared the sole or supreme guarantor of the country's welfare.

The most severe cutbacks to the welfare system and to nationalization occurred in Great Britain. There the Labor Party's postwar reforms had gone furthest toward curtailing the market economy and extending generous financial assistance to working people. In 1979, the Conservative Party under the leadership of Margaret Thatcher decisively defeated the Labor Party in elections whose major issue was the welfare state. Thatcher's program constituted a comprehensive rejection of state management of economic affairs and a wholesale reduction of welfare programs. What came to be known as "Thatcherism" entailed the privatization of almost all nationalized enterprises, the reduction by one-half of state payments for various social welfare programs, and the lowering of taxes. These reforms became reality in the 1980s. Thatcher's principal goal was a productive economy. Welfare was a secondary consideration.

In these terms, the program was a success. By the early 1990s, the economy was boom-

ing, inflation ended, unemployment was drastically reduced, and the standard of living rose. But even the "Iron Lady," as Thatcher came to be known among friends and enemies, could not eliminate the welfare programs entirely. When she suggested ending free public health care, the popular opposition was so great she had to abandon her plans. The postwar vision of a safety net ensuring the basic needs of the population had become a permanent part of the people's expectations in all European states.

The United States joined in the move toward comprehensive welfare programs and greater state supervision of economic affairs in the 1960s. The election in 1960 of John F. Kennedy to the U.S. presidency began a period of extensive social and political reforms, carried on by Lyndon Johnson after Kennedy's assassination in 1963. The "Great Society," as Johnson named his 1964 reform platform, included new laws to protect the civil and political rights of all citizens. The goal was an end to the century-long segregation and oppression of blacks. Reforms also brought new welfare policies for a "war on poverty," in spirit and intent resembling the social welfare measures introduced in Europe after the Second World War. No private enterprises were nationalized. Still, the government's yearly budget and the controls over banking and interest rates exercised by a federal agency (the Federal Reserve Board) guided the country's economy in a manner inspired by the ideas of John Maynard Keynes. Later, conservative political leaders, echoing arguments in Europe, questioned the high rate of taxes and expensive social welfare programs. In the United States, as in Great Britain, a majority of the voters in the 1980s appeared more concerned with the success of a productive market economy than with state promises of social justice and less economic inequality.

On the European continent, the same process of revision of social welfare policies proceeded. The reductions paralleled those in Great Britain, though over a longer time and with less ideological fervor than that of Thatcher and her supporters. One reason for the moderation was that it took place at a time when working Europeans were enjoying greater leisure time than ever before. At the opening of the twenty-first century, their yearly paid vacation totaled, on average, six weeks, and their weekly working hours were below forty. Incomes were less than in the United States, but most Europeans believed that their quality of life was higher. As one Dane remarked, "We spend more time enjoying life."

European Union

By the mid-1960s, the barriers on commerce among the members of the Common Market declined dramatically and far more quickly than the treaty signers had expected (see Chapter 7). Western Europe had begun a new era of economic collaboration. The Common Market operated on the basis of market competition, whether conducted by private or state-owned enterprises, by small farmers or agribusiness. All the political parties (except the communists) in western Europe agreed on the desirability of economic unification.

Nationalism remained a potent political force, especially when Charles de Gaulle became president of France. He did not reject the European Economic Community (EEC), but looked to a "Europe of Nations" (led by himself), not to a "United States of Europe." Still, he was the exception; once he had withdrawn from French politics, his country became a cooperative member once again, ending its opposition to Great Britain's entry into the Common Market. Common interests, and a shared vision of future collaboration, ensured that the participating states never again would claim full sovereign powers in the area of trade. The Common Market was truly supranational.

The prosperity of the EEC countries guaranteed that its influence would grow. The U.S. government acknowledged its new role in the global economy. In 1963, it signed with the EEC a comprehensive treaty lowering tariffs. Freer trade between Europe and America benefitted businesses on both continents. It also reinforced the economic and financial ties among the Western nations. The economic integration of Europe accelerated with the addition in the 1970s and 1980s of important members including Spain, Denmark, Greece, Great Britain, and Ireland. By the late 1980s, the total population of the EEC countries reached 300 million. At the time, it was the single most populous free-trade region in the world.

Its attraction extended to peoples on the southern and eastern fringes of Europe. In material terms, the Common Market assured to its member countries substantial benefits. This was evident to Greek, Spanish, and Portuguese migrants who went in increasing numbers seeking work in the booming northern economies. The EEC states operated on the basis of agreement among all on the absolute necessity for democratic political institutions, human rights, and a market economy. Only countries that respected these basic principles of public life could hope for admission. On the southern fringes of the continent, authoritarian rule in Greece, Spain, and Portugal was in these terms obsolete. All gave way to democratic political systems in the 1970s. Political upheavals in each land brought about the abrupt transition. All three were countries where many people and clandestine political movements had kept faith in human rights through the years of repression. The presence to the north of the Common Market gave liberal opposition further encouragement to demand an end to these regimes.

In Spain, the political transition occurred with remarkable speed. In 1975, General Franco, dictator since his victory in 1939 in the Spanish Civil War, died and was replaced at his request by the heir to the former Spanish monarchy. Faced with widespread opposition to continued dictatorship, King Juan Carlos immediately ordered elections to prepare a new constitution. In 1977, he ceded his executive power to the newly elected government. Spain became a constitutional, parliamentary monarchy. Despite protest from a handful of Franco's supporters, the new regime established effective rule in the country within a few years. Similar pressures from the people and from European states brought the end to the dictatorships in Greece and Portugal in those same years. All three soon became new members of the European Economic Community.

The vision among Europeans of closer unification led to renewed efforts to strengthen their economic ties in the early 1990s. A new treaty of unification, put into effect in 1994, renamed the group of states the European Union. Its most ambitious objective was the creation of a single currency for the entire region. To achieve this, governments had to lower inflation rates and balance their budgets, possible only if they curtailed expenditures on social welfare. This new Europe did not attempt to eliminate social inequality, though it did redistribute financial resources from wealthier to poorer member states.

Not all European Union countries agreed immediately to the monetary union. Great Britain, clinging still to shreds of its traditional splendid isolation, refused to join, as did other smaller states. Pushed by German leaders, the major continental states proceeded to meet all the conditions for a common currency. For them, financial unity was worth abandoning their own currencies and coordinating fiscal policies. On January 1, 1999, a single European Union currency, called the euro, went into use.

As long as the Cold War endured, the borders of this new Europe had stopped at the

Divided Berlin: Berlin Wall, 1970 (*Daniel R. Brower*)

Iron Curtain. The Cold War's division of the continent menaced European recovery, keeping alive fears of another world war in which Europe would be at the center. In an effort to establish principles for a stable peace between East and West, Western states invited representatives of the communist lands to Helsinki, Finland, in 1975. The negotiators from the East were eager for agreement on the permanence of the new borders of European states, especially those of the Soviet Union and Poland. The Western diplomats hoped in exchange for acknowledgment from the communist countries that human rights (civil and political liberties) constituted the only stable and just basis for government.

The communist regimes had never recognized individual freedom to be a necessary or desirable objective. But for the sake of assurance of permanent state borders, they allowed this cornerstone of democracy to be included in the final Helsinki Agreement. The signers agreed to renounce the "threat or use of force" to settle international disputes and committed their states to respect "fundamental freedoms, including the freedom of thought, conscience, religion, and belief." It seemed at the time an illusory promise that the Eastern governments would disregard.

But when the communist regimes of eastern Europe vanished at the end of the 1980s, the agreement laid out the basic conditions on which eastern Europe could be reintegrated into the rest of the Continent by joining the prosperous European Union. When that political transition to democratic states and market economies was complete, unification became possible. In 2004, a total of ten new states (including the three Baltic states once a part of the Soviet Union) joined the European Union. It was the single largest one-time expansion ever to occur. By then, twenty-five flags of the European Union's members were flying at the entrance of the building housing the European parliament.

The European Union had already acquired powers of a sovereign state. These extended to external borders (and a single passport), foreign policy, and a regulated currency. Institutions for political decision-making were in place, including an elected European parliament; in 2004, EU leaders approved a full constitution (which still had to be adopted by each member state). The European Union exerted a powerful attraction on surrounding states. The government of Turkey, on the very edges of the continent and almost entirely Muslim, was in line to be considered for admission. The momentum toward integration of Europe was irreversible.

 HIGHLIGHT: Social Change and Women's Rights

In the last half of the twentieth century, profound social changes in all major regions of the world altered the status and role of women. In part, these changes responded to international campaigns to grant women greater control over their lives through equality of legal rights. This movement is often labeled *feminism* and remains in many countries a subject of great controversy. The United Nations lent its support by designating 1975 International Women's Year (since repeated in 1980 and 1985), and by declaring the years 1975–1985 to be the Decade for Women. International conferences on women's rights drew participants from throughout the world. They were one indication that the issue of women's rights had become a global concern.

A second global trend enhancing the social role of women emerged out of the growing public anxiety over population growth. The social and economic hardship created by the population explosion of the late twentieth century forced governments, even those hostile to women's rights, to improve women's options in limiting birthrates. This perspective emerged most clearly at the International Conference on Population and Development, held in 1994. The principal issue there was the formulation of policies to promote voluntary measures by families to limit family size. The delegates recognized that women had to be granted greater autonomy as individuals in achieving this goal. Their options had to reach beyond the issue of birth control to access to improved living conditions, including education and work. Large numbers of children constituted the essential assurance of family survival when disease and hunger were a constant threat in underdeveloped countries. Families would have increased confidence in and

the incentive to restrict family size to two or three children when social improvements touched the lives of women and men.

This recognition of the importance of social and economic processes was rooted in an understanding of profound historical trends with a direct impact on women's roles and family life. These changes have had as important a role in enhancing greater women's control over their lives as international public campaigns and political reforms. Access to education and to employment promised improved relations between men and women, a greater voice to women in obtaining political rights, and a diminished burden on women of motherhood and family bonds. At the heart of this change has been massive urbanization, which has reshaped the social environment of hundreds of millions of people. By the late twentieth century, one-half of Europe's population lived in urban areas. In the Third World, the move occurred more slowly. The proportion of townspeople there rose from about 5 percent at the end of the First World War to almost 25 percent in 1980. Though this was a time of rapid population growth, urbanization

Second World Conference for U.N. Decade for Women, Copenhagen, 1980 (*United Nations/Photo by Per Jacobsen*)

was a consequence above all of the migration of enormous numbers of rural inhabitants to urban areas.

Families adjusting to this new environment found themselves in unfamiliar conditions. Work for most people came in the form of wage labor. Contact in cities between people with different ways of life, languages, and religious values produced a clash of cultural values. In this same period the governments of new nation-states implemented laws on women's rights and family relations that weakened or outlawed traditional family customs. Western societies had undergone these changes a half century or more earlier and were the center of the feminist movement in the mid-twentieth century. In these conditions of economic, cultural, and political upheaval, new opportunities and old constraints were thrust upon women and families throughout the world.

The profound social and economic changes of the last half of the twentieth century, among which urbanization was the most influential, gradually undermined the older paternalistic way of life. Driven by economic need, by rising expectations of a better standard of living, and by the desire of women for their own income, family relations were altering to allow wives the freedom of outside work. Even in very poor countries, small-scale village businesses were accessible, with some financial assistance, to enterprising women. Another important factor behind the enhanced role of

Literacy for Women: Adult Reading Classes in Yemen Arab Republic, 1983 (*UN/DPI Photo by John Isaac*)

women in the family was the aspiration for better living conditions. In Brazil, it appeared the dominant motivation in bringing large numbers of women into the labor force (probably over one-third of adult women by the 1980s) and in lowering family size (down from an average of four to two children between the 1960s and 1980s).

In many parts of the Third World, women's access to wage labor was severely restricted. Where women's education was deficient, their economic opportunities were meager. As schooling expanded, the chances to find better-paying jobs increased. In China, a major literacy program raised women's literary rates along with men's to well over 60 percent. They entered the urban workforce in very large numbers in those same years. The Indian case suggests that the reverse was also true. There the low level of public education left two-thirds of the women illiterate. Their lack of basic formal education gave most of them little hope of employment other than the most unskilled, worst-paying jobs.

This working population, unorganized and prepared to accept work at low pay, proved advantageous both to small businesses and to multi-national corporations. The latter's total workforce in developing countries grew in the 1970s to between three and four million. Women predominated in garment and assembly-line work for these companies. Dependent on a distant employer and earning low pay, unskilled female labor constituted a new proletariat. In most countries only a small group of educated women was able to enter high-paying, skilled positions. Male prejudice and lack of sufficient education posed major hurdles to improving women's economic status. Still, women's wage earnings and activity away from home constituted a major shift away from the traditional paternalistic family pattern.

The issue of women's rights within the family became the subject of political debate in most new nations soon after independence. In India, the government's campaign for family equality among Hindus was reinforced by a feminist movement championing compliance with the new standards. The law on child marriage raised the average age of marriage for women to seventeen. This was a substantial improvement over practices at the turn of the twentieth century (Gandhi's wife had been twelve, and he fourteen, when they married). This change contributed as well to India's slowly falling birthrate. Some feminist programs drew inspiration from Western reform movements. The Soviet Union served as the model for gender as well as class equality in communist countries. In 1949, the Chinese Communists confronted a deeply rooted paternalistic way of life, including child marriage and exclusive male right of divorce. Shortly after taking power they introduced reforms intended to eliminate men's social privileges and to integrate women into their new social order.

Most countries with a large Muslim population did not adopt such radical reforms. Fearing communal conflict, the Indian government made no effort to enforce equality of sexes on Muslim families. It left unchallenged among its Muslim population the shari'a (Muslim customary law), which granted men exceptionally broad prerogatives in family and property affairs. Turkey was the only large Muslim state were Islamic law ceded its role to family laws drawn from Western civil law codes; Iran's laws on women's rights disappeared after its Islamic Revolution. The process of adaptation to urban life often left wives more closely bound than before to the household. The obligation to care for the children fell directly into their hands, since they lacked the help of extended families in the new surroundings.

Husbands took advantage of higher incomes to enforce on their wives customs of subordination associated with the upper classes. This reverse trend was apparent in southern Asia, where seclusion of wives had been practiced for centuries among the wealthy. It spread among the new middle classes in the late twentieth century. The demands of legal reform and the desire for higher income created pressures for greater equality but were thwarted still by customary male authority and traditional restraints on women.

Full rights protecting participation by women in democratic countries promoted but did not guarantee ready access to public responsibilities. Women's suffrage itself was important, for it challenged men's control over lawmaking and in particular over policies that touched the affairs of women and the family. The new state of Israel made equality of rights for women in politics, education, the family, and the workplace a fundamental element in its social order. The first woman to head a government anywhere in the Middle East was Golda Meir, the prime minister of Israel from 1967 to 1973. Even in certain Muslim countries, such as Egypt and Pakistan, women rose to influential positions in government.

Islam gave no clear definition of the role of women in political life. Political leaders in some Muslim countries campaigned for secular reforms, including voting rights for women. The shah of Iran made the enfranchisement of women an integral part of the reforms that he called his "White Revolution." That policy aroused bitter opposition from the country's Muslim clerics. When they became the leaders of Iran's Islamic Republic in 1980, they immediately ended the shah's modest reforms for women. One fervent supporter of this regime, asked to explain what the establishment of the Islamic Republic meant to him, responded: "Getting women back into the veil, getting them off television."[1]

By the closing decade of the twentieth century, global trends clearly pointed to the increased control by women over both personal and public aspects of their lives. These changes followed no single model. Muslim reforms followed a pattern strongly shaped by religious custom. But the combination of international campaigns and basic social trends in work, education, and family life put in place an array of women's rights and opportunities in society so profoundly different from traditional practices that they could be called a revolution.

---

[1] V. S. Naipaul, *Voyage among the Believers: An Islamic Journey* (New York, 1981), p. 28.

THE FALL OF THE SOVIET EMPIRE

The Cold War began in the late 1940s. It ended forty years later. Its origins lay in the expansion of the Soviet Union into central Europe at the close of the Second World War and in Western fears of Stalinism. It disappeared when the communist regimes of Europe and the Soviet Union collapsed. Its focal point had been the city of Berlin, divided into Soviet and Western zones of occupation. It combined power politics and profound ideological differences. This potent blend made compromise and agreement extremely difficult. It posed the gravest threat to civilization in the history of modern states.

The nuclear arms race between the Soviet Union and the United States kept alive the likelihood of nuclear war on a global scale. Each side came to recognize the terrible consequences that use of these weapons would have on their peoples, yet they continued to perfect ever more deadly weapons in the expectation that failure to do so would jeopardize their security. The Soviet and Western troops stationed in their separate zones of Berlin were hostages to the war plans devised by each superpower to prepare for an unthinkable nuclear war.

The Decline of the Soviet Union

The communist satellite countries around the Soviet Union made up the "outer empire" of that country, itself an imperial state through its control of its non-Russian peoples in its constituent republics. The Soviet leaders were prepared to use their armed forces to ensure that no communist government was forced out of power. Between the 1960s and early 1980s, they sent Red Army units twice to countries where popular resistance threatened communist regimes. In Czechoslovakia, the Communist Party in 1968 was powerless to stem a popular movement led by labor unions, intellectuals, and reform Communists, which was opposed to the Soviet-style dictatorship and command economy. Czech reformers hoped for Soviet acceptance of their reforms. They promised continued allegiance to the Soviet military alliance. But the Soviet leaders feared that their eastern European empire was at risk if communist rule disappeared there. In August of that year, their military forces occupied the country and forced upon the Czechs a compliant government of Moscow's own choosing.

Shortly afterward, the Soviet leader, Leonid Brezhnev, defended in principle what Red Army troops had already put into practice. His "Brezhnev Doctrine" asserted the right of the Soviet Union to intervene in the affairs of any allied state in the "socialist camp" in need of assistance to maintain communist rule. In 1979, Brezhnev applied the doctrine once again when he ordered Soviet troops into Afghanistan to support the feeble new communist regime.

Afghan Communists, in control of the government for only two years, had already antagonized the peoples of that inner Asian land with their radical reforms. The population was deeply attached to tribal ways and Muslim traditions. Guerrilla forces, called "mujahaddin," found vital help from neighboring Pakistan. Resistance to the communist rulers threatened to overwhelm their meager forces. The Soviet government refused to let the new state collapse. It sent nearly 100,000 troops to fight the Afghan rebels. The latter obtained potent military assistance from the United States. The U.S. administration of President Ronald Reagan feared (incorrectly, as we now know) that the Soviet Union sought to turn Afghanistan into a strategic base for expansion into South Asia. Once a remote Asian borderland, Afghanistan became a hot spot in the Cold War.

The weakness of communist satellite governments was most apparent in Poland. Opposition to the Polish Communist Party came from intellectuals, workers, and the powerful Catholic Church. Polish national unity had emerged out of centuries of foreign domination. The state of Poland had vanished during the war years of Nazi occupation. Liberation by the Soviet Red Army in 1944 had restored the nation-state, but it had fallen immediately under communist rule. The Polish people were as hostile as other eastern European nations to the Soviet-dominated regime. Their Catholicism remained the core of their nationalist solidarity. Its influence grew when, in 1978, a Polish priest was elected to the highest position in the Catholic Church, taking the name of Pope John Paul II. His voice added international backing to Polish resistance to communism.

In 1980, underground opposition came into the open when Polish workers throughout the country joined a general strike to protest their lack of freedom and harsh living conditions. The Pope publicly applauded their massive, peaceful rebellion. They created a nationwide free labor movement, called Solidarity. The Polish

Soviet Poster Attacking Afghan Guerillas and CIA Allies, 1985 (*Hoover Institution Archives Collection*)

Communist Party lost all authority. Solidarity commanded the respect of the people. The Soviet Union's leaders threatened military intervention to end Solidarity's rule. They found allies in Polish generals, who were fearful of a Soviet invasion and were prepared to use their own troops to end that brief moment of political freedom. General Jaruzelski, in command of the army, declared martial law, outlawed Solidarity, arrested many of its supporters, and ruled the country as a military dictator.

Soviet control of the satellite states remained intact until the late 1980s. Moscow's orders were executed by obedient leaders, whose rule rested in last resort on the menace of Soviet repression. Eastern Europe appeared firmly within the Soviet empire, and the war in Afghanistan seemed to confirm the Soviet commitment. The Cold War drew its tenacity from this state of affairs.

Most threatening of all to the superpowers, and to the peoples of the rest of the world, was the possibility that these tensions would lead to nuclear war between the superpowers. This danger, clear to leaders on both sides, defined the urgency to find some common grounds for negotiations to slow the nuclear arms race. The nuclear arsenals of both superpowers were in the service of their foreign policies, which they defined in terms of both national interests and political ideals. The achievement of international arms controls required that each side put aside their ideological differences to confront directly essential strategic issues. President Nixon's security adviser (later secretary of state) Henry Kissinger made this clear when in 1969 he affirmed that "we have no permanent enemies. We will judge other countries, including communist countries, on the basis of their actions and not on the basis of their domestic ideology."

The readiness of both sides to view their conflict more from the perspective of state interests and less in ideological terms made possible negotiations to separate arms issues from Cold War rivalries. In this perspective, global competition did not require the endless development of ever more powerful weapons of war. These understandings came after each side accepted the necessary but illogical idea that these weapons were of use solely to prevent the other side from beginning, or threatening to begin, a war.

In conditions of mutual suspicion and competition, this elementary truth was the only possible basis for agreement. The two superpowers acknowledged that each state needed sufficient offensive nuclear weapons to deter an attack, that is, to be able to defend itself by destroying the aggressor. Each side could guarantee its acceptance of the policy of deterrence by agreeing not to build defensive nuclear weapons (in other words, leaving its people defenseless against the other side's weapons). In the conditions of the Cold War, this became the fundamental definition of peace, appropriately labeled by one American leader "MAD" (Mutually Assured Destruction). It was the key to the success of the first major Soviet-American nuclear arms treaty.

The first Strategic Arms Limitation Treaty (SALT I) was signed in 1972. In it, the Soviet and American governments agreed not to develop or deploy defensive (antiballistic missile) systems. Those defensive missiles that they had begun to install had to be destroyed. Inspection of each side's fulfillment of the treaty was ensured by the use of U.S. and Soviet military surveillance satellites, constantly stationed over the other country. The agreement ended one part of the nuclear arms race. Deterrence became the cornerstone of peaceful relations between the Soviet Union and the United States.

The treaty remained incomplete, however. It failed to restrict the development of new offensive nuclear weapons. Scientists on both sides were, in the peculiar language of the arms

race, constantly "modernizing" their country's nuclear arsenals. Their work in itself helped to sustain the arms race. To slow this dangerous process, Soviet and U.S. negotiators finally signed in 1979 another arms treaty (SALT II). It limited the numbers of certain offensive weapons, principally intercontinental ballistic missiles and submarine-launched missiles. The arms race had not stopped, but the leaders of the superpowers had at least been able to place certain limits on their nuclear arsenals. In doing so they recognized that their awesome military power could at best maintain between their two states what one American official called "an enduring strategic stalemate."

Good relations between the Soviet Union and the United States remained dangerously vulnerable to local conflicts, new armaments, and political rivalries. In 1981, the new U.S. president, Ronald Reagan, launched an armaments program more extensive (and vastly more expensive) than the programs begun in the early 1950s. The United States introduced a deadly new generation of missiles that could strike a target a few yards square at a distance of hundreds of miles. It deployed as well another type of missile, equipped with a secret global positioning radar system, that permitted it to hug the curvature of the terrain and to avoid Soviet radar defenses. In a search for the ultimate defense (and potentially in violation of SALT I), President Reagan authorized a program to create a supposedly impenetrable shield in outer space over the United States. It was to be made of defensive space weapons, including giant laser beams, against incoming (Soviet) ballistic missiles. The United States poured billions of dollars into the so-called "Star Wars" program. Reagan's armaments initiative undermined the armaments treaties and led the Soviet government in turn to accelerate development of its own missile weapons. The arms race was a tragic reminder of the superpowers' failure to bring peace to the postwar world.

The End of Communism

By the 1980s, the communist system of the Soviet Union was incapable of maintaining the country's role as superpower. The elderly Stalinist leaders clung to the illusion of global might, partly out of dogmatic conviction, partly out of ignorance of the decay of their empire and of their own state and society. A few among them realized the extent of the crisis. By then a group of younger Communists were even beginning to put forward daring plans for reform. But as long as the Stalinists remained in power, nothing could be done.

The Stalinists finally lost their control of the Soviet government and the Soviet Communist Party in 1985. The generation of Communists old enough to remember and to revere the Stalin revolution of the 1930s was disappearing. Their successors refused to hide the country's economic crisis and spreading political corruption. The system inherited from Stalin had failed in key areas to meet the needs of the country. It was too inflexible to adopt the technological innovations revolutionizing Western industry, its bureaucratic command system nurtured incompetence and inefficiency, its rigid, centralized controls ignored the needs and wishes of consumers, and its military forces, absorbing nearly one-fourth of the country's yearly national income, could not match the electronic wizardry of U.S. weapons.

Popular discontent was a real factor as well. Food and shelter adequate to the people's basic needs were available, though signs of a crisis in health care were already apparent (particularly the declining life expectancy, especially rapid among Russian men). The population's standard of living stagnated and the economy virtually ceased growing. Only the export of raw materials, especially oil and natural gas, permitted major investments to continue. An illegal black-market economy offered scarce goods to those people with the means to pay its high prices. In exchange for

special favors, corrupt officials protected the illegal operations by halting efforts to enforce the laws against these "speculators." People referred to this alliance of black marketeers and communist officials as the Soviet "Mafia." Russian economists likened (privately) their country's economic condition to that of a state in the Third World.

The single-party communist dictatorship, in theory responsible for the economic well-being of the Soviet Union, was critically weakened by corruption and special privileges. Party bureaucrats held power virtually for life, and many turned their positions into a source of personal wealth. They were far better off than the average Soviet citizen thanks to bribes and influence peddling. It was in their interest to ignore both the real needs of the population and the damage to the environment caused by their economic plans. Claiming to have put their Leninist talents in the service of socialism, these party officials were trapped in their own delusions of power. The entire country suffered as a result. With some variations, a similar political and economic crisis existed in all the communist countries.

Some high party officials, aided by the head of the secret police (KGB), had attempted a few modest reforms even before the last Stalinist leader died in 1985. Their earlier failures made them even more determined to build a reform movement within the new leadership. Their alliance was crucial when the time came to select a new general secretary of the Communist Party of the Soviet Union. As in the past, the highest Communist Party committee (Politburo) was the body empowered to make the choice. Under pressure from reformers, its members elected in 1985 their youngest colleague, Mikhail Gorbachev, to the position of general secretary. They realized that reforms were necessary, both to sustain their country's might and to meet the basic needs of the Soviet people. They expected that the result would be an improved socialist system and revived Soviet empire. Their single-party dictatorship would, they imagined, remain the core of the Soviet system and the pillar of world socialism. They were wrong on both counts.

Gorbachev proved an extraordinarily skillful party leader and a dynamic reformer. He quickly became aware that corrupt and incompetent party officials were deeply entrenched throughout the Communist Party apparatus. They relied on censorship and secrecy to protect their power and privileges. In 1986, they attempted to cover up the terrible accident at the Chernobyl nuclear power complex in Ukraine. Within a few days, detectors of radioactive fallout located across northern Europe relayed the news of an enormous explosion there and of atmospheric radioactive fallout that proved ten times greater than the Hiroshima atomic bomb. Gorbachev was outraged at his officials' arrogance, disregard for human safety, and clumsy efforts to hide the accident from public scrutiny. He resolved on the daring move to open up debate in all the public media (a policy termed *glasnost* in Russian). No longer could they hide behind a curtain of secrecy.

Very soon the flood of information overwhelmed the state organs of censorship. For the first time since the 1917 revolution, access to all the news became a public right. Television, radio, and the press seized the possibility to criticize the old order. Old-time Stalinists were outraged, but Gorbachev proved a master of the instruments of power and a daring architect of a new Soviet regime.

He sought political allies wherever he could find them. He released all political prisoners from jail. He authorized religious toleration, allowing churches, synagogues, and mosques to open, permitting religious texts to be published, and joining with Christian leaders in 1987 to celebrate the 1000th anniversary of the conversion of Russia to Orthodox Christianity. His most radical measure was the call

in 1988 for free elections to the Supreme Soviet (the national parliament). For the first time since 1917, voters were given the opportunity to choose among several candidates for legislative positions. With some hesitation, reform Communists ran for office against conservative Communists.

Gorbachev gambled that the voters would reject the Stalinist party officials, and he was right. The elections, held in 1989, revealed that Russians in key urban areas of the country had turned against their old party bosses. As Gorbachev had hoped, the communist old guard lost to reform candidates and suffered public humiliation in the process. The dictatorship of the vanguard party, instituted by Lenin in 1917, was beginning to give way to democracy in some Soviet republics.

Gorbachev's reform policies opened the way to the collapse of the communist regimes in eastern Europe. He recognized that the crisis of his country was so grave that renewal could occur only with the collaboration of Western states and investors. Freedom for the peoples of the Soviet satellite countries was the fundamental condition to lasting good relations with the West. To achieve that, he was prepared to abandon the Soviet "outer empire" in Europe and Asia. He publicly renounced the Brezhnev Doctrine of intervention in defense of communist regimes threatened by internal opposition. To prove his resolve to stand by the new policy, he ordered the withdrawal of all Soviet troops from Afghanistan; the last troops returned to the Soviet Union in 1989. He secretly informed the communist leaders in eastern Europe that Soviet forces no longer stood behind their feeble regimes. In doing so, he gave the peoples there the freedom to choose their own political systems. He realized that these eastern Europeans would insist on what his minister of foreign affairs termed "the liquidation of those imposed, alien, and totalitarian regimes." But no one anticipated the speed with which the communist governments would disappear.

The Polish Communist Party was the first to lose power. The years of Polish military dictatorship after 1981 had forced the Solidarity labor movement to exist as an illegal, underground organization. But its hold on the population, like that of the Catholic Church, remained an insurmountable barrier to the restoration of communist rule. The crisis of the Polish command economy remained unresolved. General Jaruzelski was aware of his inability to deal with these problems in the face of general hostility of the population. After Gorbachev initiated the policy of political pluralism in 1988, the Polish leader ordered that free parliamentary elections be held in Poland in 1989. He did so in the certain knowledge that Solidarity would win. What neither he nor the Polish Communists expected was that opponents of the Communists won every single elected seat in parliament. They accepted the results, though, and that summer Poland was governed for the first time since before the Second World War by a freely chosen, noncommunist government. It began the painful process of dismantling the command economy. The new Poland was to be a democratic nation-state with a free-market economy.

Sweeping reforms came rapidly also in Hungary and Czechoslovakia. In both countries they ended with the formation of democratic governments committed to a free-market economy. The Czechoslovak Stalinist leadership, imposed by Soviet troops in 1968, had refused any reforms since then. In late 1989, popular demonstrations led by students quickly assumed massive proportions throughout the country. The police were overwhelmed and the state paralyzed. Without the backing of Soviet troops, Czech communist leaders had to resign.

The leading political opponent of the regime was the playwright Vaclav Havel, who had spent years in prison for his outspoken defense of freedom. At popular demand, he became president of the new Czech democracy. At the end of that year, he thanked the people for their "love of freedom and civic courage" in fighting the old regime. He promised to help build a new country "with economic prosperity and also social justice, a humane republic that serves the people." His appeal for understanding, toleration, and forgiveness sought to revive national pride and respect for other peoples in a Europe of democratic nation-states.

The bonds of national loyalty and the desire for a restored, unified Germany were so strong in East Germany (the German Democratic Republic) that they undermined the very foundations of the communist state. The people's hostility to the regime was augmented by their resentment at being denied the freedom and prosperity enjoyed by the Germans living in the Federal Republic to the west. Though the postwar partition of the country had been accepted by the West, it was not acceptable to them. The Berlin Wall was the most visible and repugnant sign of the Communists' refusal to allow their subjects any personal liberty. West German television had for years broadcast its programs to East Germans, spreading vivid images of the West's way of life. The appeal was overwhelming. In the summer of 1989, Germans from the East by the thousands began to flee to the West through Hungary, whose government permitted them to escape to West Germany. That fall the flight had reached the proportions of a mass exodus. Demonstrations began in East German cities against the regime, with anticommunist banners proclaiming that "We Are the People!"

The collapse of German communism began with the regime's desperate decision to grant freedom of travel to East Germans. On the night of November 9, the gates through the Berlin Wall were opened to all inhabitants of East Berlin. The western section of the city became the center of an enormous celebration by East and West Berliners. So great was the attraction to East Germans of the way of life and institutions of West Germany that the

German Democratic Republic quickly disintegrated. Free elections in 1990 brought to power political parties that promised the quickest possible unification with the Federal Republic. In mid-1990, the West German financial system incorporated the eastern territory. In October, the country was united, and plans began to make Berlin once again the capital of a united Germany.

The restoration of national independence, political democracy, and capitalism in eastern Europe in 1989–1990 was a direct consequence of the reform policies of the new leadership in the Soviet Union. Without their refusal to intervene, communist regimes would have clung to power. But the real initiators of the move to liberal democracy were the populations of those countries. By means of demonstrations and strikes, and under the guidance of oppositional groups, they moved quickly to take control of their countries' governments. Only in Romania did the communist regime fight back, capitulating after a week of street battles. Elsewhere the transition of power occurred remarkably peacefully. Disagreements on the future of the countries appeared as soon as freedom was achieved. Still, agreement was unanimous everywhere that communism had to be removed completely.

◀ **SPOTLIGHT: Andrei Sakharov** ▶

Modern science created wonders for the betterment of human life; in the service of the state, it also produced an array of weapons more destructive than ever in human history. Andrei Sakharov (1921–1989) knew and participated in both realms of scientific endeavor. In 1948, Stalinist leaders called on him, a young physicist at Moscow University, to participate in the nuclear weapons program. He agreed, becoming the country's preeminent nuclear physicist and recognized and honored as the creator of the Soviet hydrogen bomb. Trained as a theoretical physicist, he demonstrated extraordinary powers of conceptual creativity in the most complex, innovative spheres of modern physics. He had every reason to trust in his rational powers of analysis and understanding. When he applied these skills to criticizing the Soviet system, he became an outspoken opponent of communism and defender of human rights and democracy.

Andrei Sakharov (*Hoover Institution Archives Collection*)

For that, he fell from the glorious status of "Hero of Socialist Labor" into the persecuted ranks of dissident. All this because of his powers of reason.

His patriotism convinced him that his participation in the Soviet nuclear weapons program was necessary. He and his colleagues at the secret atomic research city of Arzamas called themselves "soldiers in the new scientific war." They believed that the U.S. nuclear weapons were a deadly threat to their country. The United States had made the name *Los Alamos*, where the first atomic bomb was developed, a watchword for nuclear weapon research; the Soviet scientists followed closely U.S. research (thanks in part to the skillful work of Soviet spies), and nicknamed their city "Los Arzamas." Sakharov took on the task before him as a challenge to his intellectual powers. His remarkable genius made him the driving force behind the research needed to explode a thermonuclear device, whose destructive power was a thousand times greater than that of an atomic bomb. In 1953, he witnessed the first test on the steppes of Kazakhstan. At the celebration following the explosion, his toast went to the continued success of the explosions of these "devices" but, he added, "always over test sites and never over cities." The tone displeased the Soviet generals in charge. Sakharov had for the first time fallen out of step with the Soviet regime.

He followed that path out of the absolute conviction in the correctness of his reasoning. His decisive break with the regime came slowly and followed directly from his work on the hydrogen bomb. Over the next decade, Soviet nuclear tests detonated ever more powerful devices, culminating in 1962 in the explosion of a giant thermonuclear bomb of fifty megatons (the equivalent of fifty million tons of TNT). Sakharov was increasingly concerned at the death and disease caused by the tests themselves, whose radioactive fallout spread over thousands of square miles. That year, his knowledge of the research convinced him that the cost in human lives far outweighed any further gains from testing. To continue, he informed his superiors (including Nikita Khrushchev), was "pointless and criminal." His appeal earned him the suspicion of the regime, and its failure to respond to his appeal caused him "bitterness, shame, and humiliation." He had become, as a matter of conscience and reason, an outsider in the Soviet system.

In the years that followed, he became an outspoken critic of injustice. He did so knowing that his acts could bring punishment to him and his family from the secret police. His conviction in the rightness of his cause drove him on. His public protest could do nothing when in 1964 two writers were imprisoned for having published abroad stories critical of Soviet communism. Other protests at persecution of intellectuals followed this one, all predicated on his conviction that freedom of speech in all realms of public inquiry was a fundamental human right. In 1968, he made public his political views in a pamphlet entitled "Progress, Coexistence, and Intellectual Freedom." Sakharov had never been a Communist; now he had become an outspoken defender of human rights. He gradually worked out a program for the necessary fundamental reforms of the Soviet system, to be replaced by liberal democracy, a market economy, and a multi-national federal state with true autonomy for all the peoples of the Soviet Union. His writings, all circulated in the Soviet Union in typewritten form (Soviet censorship had complete control of all printing presses), made him an international celebrity and an enemy of the regime.

Only his fame in the Western world and his past record as "father" of the Soviet hydrogen bomb saved him from imprisonment or exile to a Siberian prison camp. In 1975, he received the Nobel Prize for Peace and sent to Sweden a message defending the absolute need for an "open society" to maintain real peace in the nuclear age. The Soviet regime was closing in around him, using all the arbitrary powers at its disposal to make his life an ordeal. His final act of defiance was to protest in 1979 the Soviet invasion of Afghanistan. At that point the secret police made him a prisoner in all but name. He was sentenced to exile in a "closed" city (forbidden to foreigners) far from Moscow and was constantly harassed by police. His only remaining means of protest were hunger strikes, which brought him brutal hospitalization and forced feeding to prevent death. His health worsened. His fate appeared to be that of yet another victim of the Soviet dictatorship.

Then in 1985 reform leadership set out to remake the Soviet system. Gorbachev's ideas were radical, by comparison with the neo-Stalinism of his predecessors. Sakharov, whose program was even more extreme, was now politically useful. His call for a multi-party, democratic system made Gorbachev appear a moderate, and his freedom would signal to the world the readiness of the reform leaders to break with the past. Gorbachev personally freed him from exile, welcomed him back to Moscow, and permitted the airing of his public appeals for the end to communist dictatorship.

Despite his persecution of the previous twenty years, Sakharov was prepared to collaborate. When the new Soviet legislature met in 1989, he was one of the freely elected deputies. He spoke eloquently there against the old-line Communists and Russian nationalists and for peaceful reform. He was an international celebrity and a hero for millions of Soviet citizens. Appeals for his help came from all sides, and the strain upon him was enormous. Suddenly at the end of the year, he died of a heart attack. His funeral was a day of national mourning. He had lived to witness the end of communism and the birth of an open society in Russia.

The End of the Cold War

In his first years of power, Gorbachev did not grasp the gravity of his country's economic crisis. He lost precious time before finally accepting the advice of economists to abandon the command economy. His slogan of radical reform (the Russian term was *perestroika*) came to mean the introduction of a limited free market in the Soviet economy. The structural and social obstacles to such changes were far greater than those he encountered in introducing political and civil liberties. The public had for decades enjoyed low-priced, state-subsidized consumer goods and services (generally of poor quality and in short supply). They continued to rely on these state goods to meet their basic needs. Managers and workers had become accustomed to inefficient methods of work. A popular Russian judgment of this system was the simple comment: "They pretend to pay us, and we pretend to work." The country's industrial and agricultural equipment was obsolete, and the state lacked the resources for the massive investments needed for reconversion and technical modernization. All these problems were the result of wasteful and shortsighted state economic management and the price of the communist leaders' determination to make their country a global superpower.

The economic difficulties worsened the tense relations between the non-Russian nationalities and the Soviet central government.

Lenin's attempt to create a "community of socialist nations" in the Union of Soviet Socialist Republics had failed. Newly elected reform leaders in some national republics publicly likened the Soviet Union to the nineteenth-century tsarist empire, whose regime also kept its peoples under authoritarian rule. The Soviet Union was, in historical terms, the last empire. Decolonization had swept away all European empires except that of the Soviet Union. The eastern European states had shown the way out of the empire. Soviet republics quickly followed their example.

By 1990, almost all of the fifteen national republics that made up the union had officially proclaimed their "sovereignty" (a formal action with no immediate legal consequences). Even the Russian Soviet Republic, largest of all, took this step of protest against the Soviet constitution and communist rule. Nationalism, long forced underground by Soviet repression, suddenly emerged to become a powerful movement among Soviet peoples. National bonds of loyalty were far more influential than Soviet patriotism or the Marxist-Leninist ideology.

In the western republics of the Soviet Union, free elections became the path to independence. The Polish example of national liberation in 1989 inspired nationalists in bordering Soviet regions to attempt the same. National parties in the Baltic area (Lithuanian, Latvian, and Estonian Soviet Republics) swept regional elections in 1990. They made public the secret Hitler–Stalin agreement of 1939 to partition Poland and to allow the annexation of their small states by the Soviet Union. Their leaders immediately called for an end to this unlawful loss of their countries' independence. Their goal was secession from the Soviet Union. The country was beginning to fall apart.

In this growing crisis, influential old-guard Communists in Moscow demanded that Gorbachev use the Red Army and secret police to quell the nationalist unrest. He resisted, fearing the end of his reform campaign and a new era of hostile relations with the West. In desperation, Stalinist leaders in the party, the army, and secret police organized in August 1991 a conspiracy to overthrow Gorbachev, reinstate the old dictatorship, and save the Soviet Union. They were Gorbachev's one-time colleagues whom he had trusted and relied on to obey his orders. He never suspected them of betrayal.

Their attempted uprising proved an abject failure, however. Mass opposition to the conspiracy revealed that millions of people in Russia had repudiated communism and welcomed democratic reforms. Their leader was a dynamic anticommunist reformer, Boris Yeltsin. He had once belonged to the Communist Party but in 1988 had resigned in disgust at its corruption and conservatism. He had joined the democratic movement. He set out to take the lead of the reform movement in the Russian Soviet Republic. In the spring of 1991, he campaigned in the first popular election ever held for president of Russia. His program was democracy, a free-market economy, and Russian nationalism. His electoral victory was overwhelming. With this popular backing, he led the resistance to the Stalinist conspiracy that August. Explaining to Red Army generals that he was the legitimately chosen leader of Russia, he won the army to his side. Hundreds of thousands of Russians took to the streets of the major cities to stand in the way of the conspirators' military forces. The Stalinists were forced to capitulate, leaving the Communist Party discredited and the Soviet Union in disarray.

Yeltsin and Russian nationalism were triumphant. He outlawed the Communist Party and moved ahead with his own reform program for Russia. The Baltic republics had already seceded from the Soviet Union. Gorbachev's defeat of the August conspiracy and Yeltsin's triumph established Russia as independent in all but legal terms. That fall, the Ukrainian Soviet Republic held an election to

Hero of Russian Democracy: Boris Yeltsin, Moscow, August 1991 (*Embassy of the Russian Federation*)

decide whether to remain in a reformed Soviet state or to secede; Ukrainians overwhelming voted for independence. Gorbachev and the Soviet government were powerless to stop the disintegration of the union. Quickly the leaders of the other fourteen republics of the Soviet Union followed suit, proclaiming the independence of their republics late in 1991. Communism was gone, and so, on December 25, 1991, was the Soviet Union. Overnight, Gorbachev became an ordinary Russian citizen, and the red flag, with the hammer and sickle, vanished from the flagpole atop the Kremlin walls in Moscow.

The disappearance of communist regimes and the collapse of the Soviet Union brought the Cold War to an end. In the late 1940s, George Kennan had foreseen the day when the Soviet empire would decline and negotiations would resolve the basic security issues dividing the United States and the Soviet Union. That time came forty years later. The Warsaw Pact, the military alliance of the eastern European countries under Soviet domination, disappeared. Subsequently, its member countries (except Russia) all sought to join the Western

military alliance (NATO). The U.S. leaders signed new arms agreements with Gorbachev, then with Russia's president, Yeltsin. These treaties provided for the actual reduction of nuclear armaments. Intermediate-range and short-range missiles were to be completely destroyed and intercontinental missiles drastically reduced in numbers. Armies saw their numbers cut throughout the former communist countries and in the West. Defense industries suddenly lost their booming market for weapons.

The New Russia

The economic fortunes of Russia, heir to the ruins of the Soviet Union's attempt at state socialism, remained bleak through most of the 1990s. While the Chinese manner of ending the command economy released dynamic and productive forces, the Russian conversion to a market economy led to a serious economic depression. The breakup of the Soviet Union threw up barriers to trade among the newly independent republics, which once had been tightly bound together by Soviet planning and investment. The sudden end of the Cold War brought to a virtual standstill the mammoth Russian defense industry. It lost its lucrative state purchaser and lacked any experience in selling its sophisticated weapons on the international market. The most serious obstacle to Russian economic recovery was the dearth of people who knew how to make a capitalist economy function. Managers of the old state-owned industries had never learned about productivity and efficiency. Chairmen of the state-controlled collective farms had never worried about meeting the needs and tastes of Russian consumers.

The resulting economic depression lowered the country's industrial production by one-half by 1995. The people's standard of living dropped and public services deteriorated. Factories stopped paying wages and other benefits. Millions of urban Russians were forced to acquire plots of farmland to grow their own food. Around the country's major cities appeared vast open-air markets where people scrambled to sell whatever goods came to hand to earn a petty income. It seemed in some areas that Russians had reverted to a barter or even natural economy.

A few investors, who often were closely allied with political leaders, profited greatly by the purchase of formerly nationalized enterprises, especially those controlling valuable natural resources such as oil and aluminum. These new capitalists financed Yeltsin's 1996 presidential campaign, preferring him to the communist candidate. He won, and in return they made a "killing" obtaining at low price the country's valuable industries. One observer called the rapid, chaotic sale of state enterprises "the sale of the century." Critics of the semilegal or illegal methods of these investors called it "gangster capitalism."

Crime became in those years an epidemic of extortion and gangland violence. Police failed to control the growing number of criminal gangs, baptized the "Russian Mafia," and estimated to number about five hundred in the

mid-1990s. These gangsters prospered by extracting contributions from frightened businessmen, who risked execution if they failed to pay. Soon they branched out into international drug-smuggling and prostitution rackets.

The chaotic conditions extended to Russia's new democratic political institutions. Local government fell apart for lack of taxes, which most citizens and companies paid rarely or not at all. The federal government was forced to contract short-term loans from Western banks. When in 1998 these banks suddenly called in the loans, fearing the loss of their funds at a moment of international financial instability, the government could not repay and declared bankrupcy. Banks collapsed, the Russian ruble lost most of its value, and inflation worsened.

The government of the Russian Federation proceeded slowly to put into place the legal framework for the rule of law and for a market economy. Until the late 1990s, the legislature was a bastion of nationalists lamenting the decline of their homeland and of former Communist Party bosses chosen by rural electors. A powerful "agro-industrial" lobby defended the obsolete collective and state farms. The clearest indication of their hostility to a free market was the parliament's refusal until 2000 to approve laws permitting the purchase and sale of collective farmland. The country remained multiethnic, and the new constitution gave extensive political authority to regional governments ruling areas inhabited by non-Russians.

Gradually Russia moved from its communist past toward a modified democratic, capitalist order. The economic fortunes of the country revived after the crisis of 1998. It was stimulated by the rise in global prices for petroleum, Russia's principal export. Yeltsin's reelection in 1996 indicated that most voters had turned their backs on the old regime. In 1998, he attended the reburial in St. Petersburg's most historic cathedral of the remains of the last tsar, Nicholas II, and of his family, placed alongside the tombs of Russia's previous emperors. The ceremony was not intended to be an appeal to a return to a monarchy; it was an act of homage to all the victims of Soviet revolution and terror. Yeltsin used the moment to beg his countrymen to put behind them "a century of bloodshed" and join together in constructing a country of liberty and toleration. His ultimate, dramatic gesture was to suddenly resign his office on New Year's Eve 1999. After a brief election campaign, a large majority of electors voted for Yeltsin's heir apparent, Vladimir Putin.

The skill of the new president at using the powers of the presidency gave the country a stable leadership dedicated to restoring the international influence of Russia. The Russian army inherited most of the armaments of the Soviet Union's armed forces. They provided the Russian government with the weapons of a superpower. By the early twenty-first century, the increase in yearly Russian oil production had made it the second-largest producer in the world. Oil was power, and the Russian government gained global standing as a result.

Russia's democratic reforms had produced an authoritarian presidential regime, not a Western parliamentary democracy. Television programming was under state control, though radio and newspapers remained free from censorship. Putin remained committed to a constitutional regime and accepted, with some lapses, the basic political and civil liberties that the reformers had introduced earlier. The land was still burdened with extensive environmental pollution and stagnant population growth, both inherited from the Soviet era. A grim sign of the social crisis that still gripped the country was the high death rate among Russian men (with a life expectancy of 58 years, lowest of any Western country) and the declining rate of childbirth (also one of the lowest among developed countries). The collapse of Soviet communism had left a country in ruins, and the new Russia was just emerging in the early twenty-first century.

Russia and Inner Asian Wars

In the area once under the rule of the Soviet Union, the Russian Federation used its much weakened military forces to preserve some measure of diplomatic influence. The emergence of the successor states from the collapse of the Soviet Union was remarkably peaceable. The principal reason lay in the agreement among the leaders of the large successor nation-states, most importantly the Russian Federation, not to attempt to alter the state borders put in place when the Soviet government created the ethno-territorial "national republics." None of these new nation-states could claim to govern an ethnically "pure" population. All ruled over minority national groups from other neighboring states. After seventy years of Soviet rule, migration out of the Russian Soviet Republic had left fifteen million people claiming Russian nationality but living in other republics, especially in Ukraine to the south and Kazakhstan in the east. President Boris Yeltsin refused all demands from nationalists within and beyond the borders of his state to create a "Greater Russia." His moderation helped keep peace in northern Eurasia.

The policy of unaltered borders also meant that no minority within the Russian Federation could secede. The Russian constitution explicitly granted self-rule within the federation to its numerous minority peoples. All accepted Russian sovereignty except the Chechens, a people of Muslim faith living in a small northern area of the Caucasus Mountains. When the Soviet Union disintegrated in 1991, their leaders proclaimed the creation of their own small nation-state. But Russia adhered to the principle of "territorial integrity," sending troops to suppress the uprising. By 2002, its forces had defeated the rebels. In response, Chechen nationalists resorted to terrorist attacks on civilian and military sites in the North Caucasus Mountains and even in Moscow. They justified their deeds as the work of "martyrs" in an Islamic war to free

Chechnya from infidels and colonial oppressors. They fused the defense of Islam and their nation in their struggle for independence.

After 1991, wars among the peoples of the independent states in the Caucasus region presented the Russian government with opportunities to create a new sphere of influence on its southern borders. The state of Georgia, hostile toward its powerful neighbor to the north, discovered that rebellions among its minority peoples were supported secretly by Russia. Failing to defeat the uprisings and impoverished by the collapse of its economy, it had to heed Russian requests for collaboration, joining with Russia in repressing the Chechen rebels on their shared mountain frontier.

When Armenia and Azerbaijan fought a small-scale war between 1991 and 1994, Russian support went to the Armenians. The Armenian government fought to occupy a remote mountainous area within Azerbaijan inhabited largely by Armenians. Armenian forces were victorious, forcing Azerbaijan troops to abandon the region. In the course of the war, hundreds of thousands of Armenians and Azeris, who had been living at peace as minorities in the neighboring state during the Soviet period, had to flee to their homes to escape persecution.

Russian backing for Armenia did not arise out of sympathy with the nationalist cause that started the war. In that region, the principal Russian strategic interest was the abundant petroleum reserves of the Caspian Sea. A weakened Azerbaijan government had to cooperate with Russia (along with the international oil companies whose presence it had welcomed) in developing its petroleum. A regional balance of power gradually emerged in the Caucasus area, with Russia the most influential diplomatic player in its complex affairs. The Soviet Union had vanished, but a Russian sphere of influence took its place.

In the central Asian republics, the Russian state became directly involved in a local war in

a successful effort to maintain some measure of diplomatic and military influence there. Its principal goal was to maintain political stability and friendly states after the final Soviet troop withdrawal in 1989 from Afghanistan. The Soviet Union had failed to defeat the Afghan opponents of their client communist regime; their departure left the country in chaos. A powerful Afghan Muslim movement, which took the name of Taliban, carried on the fight, begun against the Communists, to install an Islamic state there. Despite decades of Soviet religious repression, central Asian peoples had maintained their ancestral Muslim faith. The fervor of the Taliban spread to the north, where some Muslims hoped to make their Islamic way of life the foundation of the new nation-states.

In the new state of Tajikistan, the transition to independence led after 1989 to a civil war among former communists, clan leaders, and a Muslim movement inspired by the Taliban. The Russian government was determined to make the border with Afghanistan a barrier north of which fundamentalist Muslims, bitterly hostile to their state, could not extend their influence. It sent armed forces to Tajikistan to guard the frontier and threw its support behind the former communists. With its backing, an agreement among the warring groups to share power was finally reached in 1997. It gave the former Communists a major role in the government. Russian troops had permanent garrisons there to help keep this failed state intact. Russia had achieved its goal of preserving a sphere of influence in central Asia and strengthening secular, not Islamic, leadership. The Soviet Union had vanished, but the diplomatic and military influence of Russia along its borderlands continued to hold in place some pieces of the old imperial realm.

Following the end of the Cold War, the hope of turning "swords into ploughshares" remained largely a dream. Agreements between the United States and Russia for nuclear arms reduction still allowed each side two thousand nuclear warheads. That translated in the U.S. arsenal to fourteen missile-carrying submarines, five hundred land-based missiles, and one hundred strategic bombers. Nuclear weapons remained in the possession of other states around the world besides Russia and the United States. China, India, and Pakistan all had such weapons, as did France, Great Britain, and Israel. Still, the terrible threat of nuclear war ceased to dominate global relations. Europe was no longer divided in two. The U.S. government extended economic aid to Russia. Soviet athletes in search of high pay joined Western professional sports teams, and Russian students appeared in Western business schools. The walls had fallen.

SUMMARY

For almost fifty years the Cold War had divided Europe and the world into two antagonistic alliances and competing political and social systems. In the first decades after the Second World War, the future of European lands appeared to depend on outside forces. The United States and the Soviet Union, great victors in the war, had the decisive hand in postwar global relations. The European border between their allies was baptized the Iron Curtain. Berlin itself brought together these opposing forces in one tiny spot on Europe's map, where pessimistic observers forecast the Third World War would begin. West German leaders welcomed the "nuclear umbrella" extended over their country by U.S. armed forces. It was preferable to being defenseless in the face of the forces of East Germany and the Soviet Union. West Berlin was reconstructed to be a Western beacon and a refuge.

Peoples in the communist countries had no choice but to submit to Soviet domination. If they had been allowed to express their preference, they would immediately have claimed their national independence and made the West, not the Soviet Union, their source of cultural, political, and social values. In these terms,

there could be no moral equivalence in the Cold War between East and West or between Soviet and U.S. foreign policies. The tenacity of Cold War tensions rested on that fundamental reality.

The pressures that brought down the communist system came in part from this abiding hostility of the peoples of the East toward communism. But theirs was, in Vaclav Havel's term, only the "power of the powerless" to refuse to collaborate. The real force that ended the Soviet Union and Soviet domination in eastern Europe lay within the Soviet Union itself and most especially in the expectations and plans of the new reform leadership that came to power in 1985. No popular protest forced Gorbachev to launch his radical plans. The Soviet political elite enjoyed the fruits of their privileges and powers within the land. But the incapacity of that system to sustain an effective economy, a great-power military force, and a dynamic leadership appeared so grave that Gorbachev and his supporters were prepared to take great risks to remake it. They could not overcome the nationalist loyalties of the peoples of their vast empire or efface the memories of the cruelties that the Stalinist regime had inflicted on these peoples. That tenacious nationalism, more than any other factor, crushed their hopes for reform and destroyed the Soviet Union.

At the end of the twentieth century, nationalism in Europe was not what it had been one hundred years before. Western Europe set the model for reform in the former communist countries. Liberal democracy flourished among European countries. Economic activity lay increasingly in the hands of private interests. European governments chose to return most of their nationalized industries to private ownership, keeping only indirect controls over finances and production. The countries freed from communist rule sought (and obtained) membership in the European Union to open access to markets and investments. No ideological program dominated the lives of the population of Europe or promised an end to social inequality. People directed their energies to making a better life for themselves, counting on the social welfare policies put in place after the war to help in time of need.

The Soviet Union, the last colonial empire, had vanished. Europe's map was again divided into independent nation-states. Ethnic and national antagonism resurfaced when national liberation permitted ethnic groups to organize in eastern Europe and when migrants from Third World countries appeared throughout Europe. But Europe's age of wars and communist revolutions was a thing of the past.

DATES WORTH REMEMBERING

1952	First test of hydrogen bomb by United States
1953	First test of hydrogen bomb by Soviet Union
1972	Nuclear arms treaty banning defensive missiles (SALT I)
1975	First Soviet space station
1975	Helsinki Agreement on European borders and human rights
1977	Constitutional monarchy in Spain
1979	Soviet invasion of Afghanistan
1980	World population estimated 5 billion
1980–1982	Solidarity movement in power in Poland
1985–1991	Gorbachev as Soviet leader
1989	Soviet troops withdrawn from Afghanistan
1989	Collapse of communist regimes in eastern Europe
1989	First free elections in Soviet Union
1990	Reunification of Germany
1991	Election of Boris Yeltsin as president of Russia
1991	Collapse of Soviet Union
1993	Treaty on European Union
2004	Ten new members added to European Union

RECOMMENDED READING

European Union

Derek Unwin, *The Community of Europe: A History of European Integration since 1945* (1994). A careful study of the process leading from the Coal and Steel Community to the European Union.

*Daniel Yergin, *The Commanding Heights: The Battle for the World Economy* (2002). An issue-oriented examination of recent political debates very relevant to Europe's recent history.

The End of the Soviet Union

Richard Lourie, *Sakharov: A Biography* (2002). A careful, admiring portrait of a scientific genius and courageous opponent of communism.

*Michael McFaul, *Russia's Unfinished Revolution: Political Change from Gorbachev to Putin* (2001). The best study of Russia's revolution that ended communism and laid the foundations for capitalism and democracy.

*Alex Nove, *An Economic History of the USSR* (3rd edition, 1992). The best account of the rise and fall of the Soviet command economy.

*Gail Stokes, *The Walls Came Tumbling Down: The Collapse of Communism in Eastern Europe* (1994). The dramatic story of the sudden disappearance of communist regimes in the late 1980s.

Memoirs and Visual Aids

Jack Matlock, *Autopsy on an Empire: The American Ambassador's Account of the Collapse of the Soviet Union* (1995). An American's inside view of the dramatic events of the Gorbachev years.

"People Power: The End of Soviet-Style Communism." An outstanding PBS documentary (in the series "People's Century"), using documentary footage and interviews with participants to trace the fall of the communist regimes.

---

*Indicates book is available in paperback.

CHAPTER FOURTEEN 14

Local Wars, Global Economy

THE WORLD AFTER THE COLD WAR

- The Emergence of the Global Economy
- Local Wars and Peacekeeping
- Terrorism and Local Wars

Highlight: The Global Environment

Spotlight: Osama bin Laden

Colonial empires had vanished from the world by the 1990s. The term *overseas* referred to distant nation-states, not to territories where a Western empire governed subject peoples. The emergence of hundreds of new nation-states in the place of the fallen empires was the most spectacular and enduring global political upheaval brought about by the twentieth century.

New economic bonds replaced the old ties that empires had maintained. The term *global economy* referred both to the spread of industrial and technological innovations to countries around the world and to the growing interdependence of the economies of all the regions of the globe. The new nation-states possessed sov-

ereign rights and flew their flags among the member states at the United Nations headquarters in New York. Their economies depended, however, on international economic relations whose centers were usually far beyond their borders. Western governments, responding to pressure from business interests, encouraged developing states to integrate their countries in the global economy, especially by lowering their tariffs on imports from manufacturers and farmers in the developed world. Currency speculators paid no heed to the economic needs of the new states in their search for rewarding short-term investments. Prosperity or recession was a global process that smaller countries were powerless to influence.

The most prosperous regions included not only North America and western Europe but also countries around the eastern shores of the Pacific Ocean. Japan had become the first newly industrialized state in the area, followed by lands as small as Singapore and as large as China. Their increasingly important place in the global economy gave their leaders a voice in international affairs that bore little relation to the size of their national armies or to their military alliances. The regional and global economic relations that they were drawn into created a new map of interdependence that disregarded these state borders. Claims to national independence and outbursts of nationalist rivalry disrupted these bonds but could not destroy them.

By the end of the century, international economic relations had come to resemble a global free market. The old trade and regulatory barriers put up during the depression by governments had dwindled significantly. In former communist countries, the collapse of the command economies ended their isolation from the outside world. Their new leaders welcomed foreign investors and their new, privately owned industrial enterprises struggled to compete on the international market. On a global scale, the big economic forces were the multi-national corporations, major banks, and financial institutions, whose investments and speculative operations moved trillions of dollars around the world in a single day. Profit set the measure of success or failure, even when the consequences were economic hardship in distant areas.

This process, called *globalization*, included vastly increased movement of goods (such as petroleum), services (such as finance and banking), and peoples (especially labor migration), and indirectly made itself felt in global problems of air pollution and the spread of epidemic diseases (especially AIDS). It was a development that was very controversial. Promising increased economic growth and more jobs even in developing countries, globalization also threatened to heighten the inequality among peoples with profits going only to a few countries. Few people shared any longer the naive faith of pre-1914 Westerners in the wonders of industry and technology and in the inevitability of human progress. The consumption of energy through the burning of fossil fuels, key to the entire Industrial Revolution, had created such atmospheric pollution that it was altering the world's climate.

The Second World War proved, at the end of the century, to have been the last world war. Following the collapse of the Soviet Union in 1991, the United States was the sole superpower in a world plagued by terrorist movements and by small-scale wars. Civil wars, that is, armed confrontations among hostile groups within a state's borders, wrought devastation in the Balkans and in Afghanistan. Other conflicts were regional disputes. Of these, the most serious was the U.S. conquest of Iraq in 2003.

Poverty, ethnic hatred, and political rivalries all in one way or another contributed to the outbreak of violence. Peoples in countries where civil war became acute sought protection from outside forces, in the form of regional alliances or nearby states, or from the United Nations. Foreign help was the only effective means to bring some degree of peace to their people. Where no such forces appeared, these wars endured, often until economies had decayed, cities lay in ruins, and large numbers of the population had become homeless refugees. Nongovernmental humanitarian organizations (NGOs) came to these dangerous regions to offer health care and food to stop hunger and disease. Their efforts, however meager, were often all that stood in the way of famine and epidemics.

In the 1990s, the United Nations became more active than ever before in the affairs of its member nations. It was freed at last from the paralyzing Cold War quarrels between the Soviet Union and the United States. The Security Council received urgent pleas time and again to intervene in local and civil wars for which no easy solution existed. The 1990 seizure of the tiny state of Kuwait by Iraqi forces began the brief Gulf War. It ended with the triumph of a coalition of U.N. forces led by the United States and aided by, among others, the reform leaders of the Soviet Union. Hopes for a "new world order" rested on the promise of the United Nations to protect states, small and large, from aggression. But power politics, that is, the reliance on a state's military might, remained a viable alternative for major countries, as the United States demonstrated in its conquest of Iraq in 2003. The dream of international peace remained remote in the early years of the twenty-first century.

THE EMERGENCE OF THE GLOBAL ECONOMY

The international economy that had emerged among the Western countries in the early twentieth century gradually expanded across the globe into Asian, Latin American, and African lands. It drew its strength in part from the economic expansion of the United States and increasingly from the growing productivity of Europe and the new industrial regions in East Asia. The political boundaries of nation-states were of less importance than regional economic groupings, usually gathered around one particularly productive, wealthy country. Japan played that role in East Asia. Germany was similarly influential in central and eastern Europe.

Within these very productive economies, major corporations accumulated enormous wealth. They were the major force driving forward globalization. Governments joined in by promoting freer trade and seeking to lower tariff barriers. The economic resources of companies such as Sony in Japan, Royal Dutch-Shell

in the Netherlands, or Microsoft in the United States overshadowed in wealth the total national income of many countries. The skyscrapers of cities as distant as Tokyo, Singapore, London, and New York were headquarters to most of the multi-national corporations. They were the visible sign that these places counted among the world-class cities in the new global economy.

Global Energy

Global economic growth and improved living conditions for the population depended in large measure on the availability and efficient use of energy. New forms of transportation, industrial production, lighting, and communication required ready access to energy sources. The global demand for energy expanded after the Second World War at an extremely high rate until the late 1970s, when it was four times greater than in 1950. In a fundamental shift in energy sources, coal, the principal fuel for the Industrial Revolution, took second place to petroleum after 1960 (see Chapter 3, "Highlight: Petroleum and the International Economy").

Industrial regions had high consumption levels, but developing areas of Latin America and the newly industrialized countries of Asia soon shared this distinction. During the prosperous years of the 1990s, U.S. oil use consumed one-fourth of the total world production of petroleum. The late-century economic boom in China, which was dependent entirely on imports for its oil, soon made it second among global petroleum consumers. Oil prices, which had been in the mid-1960s on average $2 per barrel, rose to $17 in the early 1980s, and then grew again to reach over $50 a barrel by the mid-2000s.

Access to oil became vital to the well-being of the global economy, but only a few countries possessed major oil fields. At the beginning of the century, the United States had been the chief source of petroleum; eighty years later its oil fields were running dry. By the 1990s, over half of its needs in petroleum products had to be met by foreign imports. The Middle East (principally Iran, Iraq, and Saudi Arabia) became the leading producer of petroleum in the 1960s. The Middle East was an area of vital importance to the U.S. government, which sought by various means to protect the strategic and economic need of the country for stable oil supplies. Its two wars against Iraq (1991, 2003) can best be understood in terms of this overriding interest.

Oil-dependent countries recognized the urgent need to search for other means to power economic growth. For a time, nuclear power appeared the most alluring alternative energy source. Launched in the 1950s by the U.S. government, the program of "atoms for peace" promised technological marvels, among which the most hopeful was electricity generated by nuclear reactors. Nuclear power plants began to appear in large numbers in the 1960s; by the late 1990s, more than 400 plants were in operation around the world. Their power output represented the energy equivalent to the total yearly production from the world's major oil country, Saudi Arabia. France implemented the most comprehensive program, obtaining in the late 1980s over two-thirds of its total electricity from nuclear plants.

Many other countries had cut back or stopped nuclear power development by then. The new technology held the risk of serious accidents, and its cost had become appreciably greater than other energy sources for electricity generation. Heightened concern over safety led to complex design changes and delays in plant construction that raised expenses. The nuclear accidents at Three-Mile Island in the United States in 1979 and, most serious of all, at Chernobyl in the Soviet Union in 1986, raised public concern around the world about the very feasibility of safe nuclear power. A few countries, notably France and Japan, with

well-run nuclear programs and a great need to reduce oil imports, continued their reliance on nuclear reactors. People and states throughout the world confronted painful economic choices touching their everyday lives as a result of their growing reliance on new sources of power to support a satisfactory expansion of production and consumption.

The rising demand for energy posed the crucial problem of the depletion of nonrenewable resources. Two directions were open to make better use of energy, one through conservation and the other through new technology for energy efficiency. The sudden rise of oil prices in the 1970s increased costs to a point where efficiency in energy use became a national priority in the industrial countries. The United States, having for a century expended its coal and petroleum at a prolific pace, began a major program of energy savings in industrial and home use and in transportation. In the decade between 1973 and 1983, it reduced energy consumption (measured in relation to gross national product) by one-fourth and curtailed its use of petroleum by one-fifth. This trend constituted a Conservation Revolution as important to future world development as the Green Revolution in food production. But the United States' insatiable demand for energy, fueled by its remarkable period of prosperity in the 1990s, produced once again highly wasteful practices, especially in the increased vehicle consumption of fuel oil.

New technology created opportunities for enlarging access to necessary resources and for the substitution of new resources still in abundant supply. The petroleum industry developed complex machinery to move their oil drilling into harsh environments, including offshore areas and sites in Arctic lands. The Alaska and the North Sea oil fields, both developed in the 1970s, became the last great Western oil discoveries. After the fall of the Soviet Union, the new governments of central

Asia invited Western companies to send geologists to search for oil in areas around the Caspian Sea, thought to hold vast reserves. When they had completed their analysis, the oil companies announced that they had discovered oil and natural gas fields with reserves as large as those of North America and Europe's North Sea area combined.

These discoveries promised adequate oil for the first decades of the twenty-first century. Rising global production combined with conservation policies brought crude oil prices below $20 in the late 1980s. Oil prices remained stable through most of the 1990s and supplies were abundant. In the mid-1990s, the international price of oil was nearly as low (when adjusted for two decades of inflation) as it had been in the early 1970s. Petroleum fueled the global economic boom of that decade. But that period of rapid growth sent oil demand rising. The sudden burst of economic growth in China at the turn of the century (nearly 10 percent per year) made it the second largest petroleum consumer in the world. With no supplies of its own, its enormous need for oil imports played a major role in the rising price for petroleum (as well as for other raw materials).

In the early twenty-first century, the return of high oil prices forced countries to ask the question whether their plans for economic development had hit the barrier of limited resources. The answer at the opening of the new century was encouraging. As a result of technological discoveries, the prices of all basic resources needed for the global economy declined between the 1970s and 1990s. New plastics found many industrial applications in place of expensive metals. The risks posed by wasteful production and consumption were increasingly clear in environmental pollution and periodic shortages. Warnings from scientists of global warming led governments to explore the means of slowing or even reducing energy use from polluting sources, but the cost was high. These troubling conditions made the conservation programs of the 1970s a lesson to be learned again at the end of the century. "Sustainable" economic growth, defined as growth limited by the need to restrict consumption of nonrenewable natural resources and to protect the human environment, set sober but realistic limits on the global economy's capacity to offer the world's peoples a better life in the twenty-first century.

 HIGHLIGHT: The Global Environment

Economic growth and the rapid expansion of the world's population came at a high price for the earth's environment. Before the modern age, the greatest environmental disruptions were caused by natural forces such as volcanic eruptions and severe droughts; humanity acquired the dubious distinction in the twentieth century of becoming itself the principal cause of environmental harm. By the 1950s, land, water, and air on all continents were showing obvious, ugly signs of serious damage. In turn, this environmental decay contributed directly to the loss of natural resources, the spread of infectious disease, and permanent changes in the earth's climate.

The origins of these problems differed substantially between developed countries and the Third World. In the industrial regions of the world, environmental decline resulted primarily from high energy consumption and the wastefulness of consumer societies. In the developing areas, the principal causes lay in unregulated economic development and in the pressures generated by the population explosion, urban overcrowding, and impoverishment. From the beginning of the Industrial Revolution, manufacturers eager for profit had disregarded the deterioration caused by their enterprises. But state-run command economies of the Soviet Union, eastern Europe, and China proved equally destructive of the environment during their decades of intensive growth. Environmental problems intruded on people's lives in ways and to an extent never before experienced. They disrupted the ordinary activities of billions of people and reached into the least populated parts of the globe. Their global character was readily apparent in the pollution of the atmosphere.

The smokestack had been the symbol of the Industrial Revolution from the start. It released the gases produced by coal-fueled steam engines powering factories and lighting streets and homes. In the twentieth-century, the exhaust gases coming from the burning of refined petroleum by internal combustion and diesel engines marked in its smelly way the new consumer societies. The use of these fossil fuels had contributed directly to the smog that was at the origin of London's nineteenth-century "pea-soup" fog, and that hung like a dirty haze over the major cities of the world a century later.

Even in the nineteenth century, a few scientists had pointed out that the accumulation of these gases, consisting primarily of carbon dioxide, would in the long run act like a blanket around the earth, altering the global climate and raising average temperatures. Until the late twentieth century, these forecasts were not substantiated by tangible evidence understandable to governments and to the public alike. Economic growth remained a key to public policy and private investments in the industrial countries. It was a vital goal for underdeveloped nations. Industrialization and rising levels of consumption were impossible without increased energy consumption from fossil fuels. In the global economy of the late century, its use was limited only by market prices and accessibility.

In the 1980s and 1990s awareness of the dangers of atmospheric pollution increased as a result both of the work of scientists and of the concern of populations suffering the painful physical effects of a fouled atmosphere. The chemical process destroying the ozone layer was discernible only to the sophisticated equipment of researchers. By the mid-1980s, they were able to establish the direct link between the diffusion (through evaporation) of manufactured coolants, especially in air conditioning, and the decline of atmospheric ozone vital in protecting the earth from intensive solar radiation. Once understood, the problem became the subject of international conferences. Governments and manufacturers agreed in 1987 to end the production and use of these coolants by the end of the century. Their collaboration produced, for the first time, an international treaty on a critical global environmental issue.

The increase in atmospheric pollution caused by carbon gases raised far more difficult questions. These touched on the very quality of life of both developed and developing countries. The level of carbon dioxide in the air in the 1990s was twenty-five times that of a century before. Western countries bore the major responsibility for this swift rise. Their prosperous economies depended increasingly on road transportation, which was a major cause of carbon dioxide pollution. The United States alone produced one-third of the total carbon emissions in the world. In the last third of the century, Third World countries experienced discernable signs of severe air pollution, as evidenced by the great clouds of smog that hung over India's enormous cities. Their lack of modern technology and the pressure for economic growth at all cost prevented them from introducing serious pollution-control measures. By the late century, the combined emissions coming from the Third World were nearly equal to those of the Western countries.

In the mid-1990s, scientific findings uncovered clear signs of significant global warning. The evidence revealed a noticeable rise in average summer and winter temperatures throughout the Northern Hemisphere. In 2000, the United Nations Panel on Climate Change published the definitive report on global warming, which it attributed to human deeds. Average air temperatures were rising everywhere, including the Antarctic and Arctic regions. Greenhouse gases, of which carbon dioxide was by far the most damaging, were the principal cause. The consequences were already apparent in the melting of the earth's ice caps, the increasing severity of storms, and the rising level of the earth's oceans.

In this process, the destruction of the tropical forests played its own important part. The causes at work here included both the desperate search for resources on the part of impoverished populations in the Third World and the appetite for forest products of the expanding global economy. The Brazilian settlers moving into the rain forest areas of Amazonia and Indonesian migrants starting a new life in the forests of Sumatra burned millions of acres of forest each year to begin farming. Their actions helped to destroy a unique environment and poured billions of tons of carbon dioxide into the air. Spurred on by the growing demand for wood, international lumber companies purchased enormous rain for-

est properties, first cutting the trees and then burning the undergrowth to sell the land to agribusiness or small farmers. Their destructive burning of Indonesian forests produced severe smog over a vast region of Southeast Asia inhabited by more than 100 million people. The Indonesian government's policies of support for big business and incentives for emigration from its overpopulated central islands to Sumatra and Borneo lay at the heart of this environmental crisis. In 1997, it issued an international public apology for the harm done and promised strict restrictions on forest burning. But its commitment was halfhearted, and the deforestation continued.

The rapid loss of forests around the world was harmful both because it devastated an invaluable resource and because it led to pollution of the air, the land, and the water. In many parts of Africa and Asia, trees and bushes became the sole source of heating fuel as impoverishment and growing rural populations made other sources of heat inaccessible. The disappearance of forests brought decay of farmland, eroded by rains and overworked by struggling farmers, and severe flooding of the lowlands caused by the runoff of rain from deforested slopes. Tropical forests acted as powerful agents absorbing vast amounts of carbon dioxide. Their absence further accelerated the atmospheric accumulation of greenhouse gases. These forests were as well a treasurehouse of natural products useful to the health and well-being of populations. Once gone, the forests' treasures would be lost as well.

Growing shortages of water in areas such as the Tigris and Euphrates rivers in the Middle East became an economic and political issue. Access to water in semidesert areas of rapid population growth and economic development became so critical that in these places water was "more precious than oil." In the 1980s, the government of Turkey began the most ambitious water control project yet attempted in any non-Western country. It started construction of twenty dams and irrigation canals along the headwaters of the Tigris and Euphrates rivers. Both originated in Turkey's eastern mountains. By the end of the century, this Southeast Anatolia Project had completed half of its major dams. It was already bringing tangible economic benefits to a vast semi-desert region, long stripped of its trees and topsoil by overfarming and deforestation. Land was again becoming fertile through irrigation, cheap electric power was fueling industrialization, and the region's peoples (including millions of Kurds) saw an escape from their age-old impoverishment.

The price of their success was the limitation of water supplies to the downstream regions of Syria and Iraq. Turkey's great dams promised a better life for some peoples at the expense of those living on the lower reaches of the rivers. The Anatolian Project directors were prepared to sell water (by the boatload) to thirsty Mediterranean lands such as Israel with the funds to afford purchases. Other lands lacked these funds. Collaborative water agreements with Syria and Iraq might protect the well-being of these peoples; war for water was a real possibility too.

Epidemic diseases in the Third World were inextricably bound up with water, air, and land pollution. Rivers filled with silt from deforested lands and from the pollutants of new factories and untreated human waste. Water drawn from these sources became a source of infectious disease and physical deformities for the population living along polluted rivers such as the Yangtze in China and the Ganges in India. Infectious diseases were nourished by the untreated sewage and polluted air in enormous cities such as Cairo and Bombay, to which many millions of rural inhabitants

migrated to escape the misery of village life. Countries such as India confronted the recurrence of diseases, such as the bubonic plague, that medical experts had thought forever eliminated by public health and modern medicine. In these terms, the most critical environmental needs at the close of the twentieth century were found in the Third World.

Economic development was a global dilemma as well as a promise. Progress had for a century been defined in large measure as the improvement of economic well-being. The newly independent countries of the Third World subscribed as fervently to that creed as did the West. Their leaders argued in fact that their needs for economic growth were a matter of survival as much as well-being because of the widespread poverty of their populations. They argued that the West had to make the greatest sacrifices for environmental protection. Its total contribution to global pollution was the largest by far and its technological skills were more readily applicable to energy conservation and pollution control. Yet the scale of the problem was so great that no international solution could succeed without the cooperation of all sides.

Two centuries before, an English physician, Thomas Malthus, had warned of a social crisis in his country. He calculated that the population was multiplying faster than food supplies necessary to meet the people's basic needs. The Industrial Revolution and the demographic transition in the West to low birthrates had proven him wrong. In the early twenty-first century, however, the Malthusian trap was closing again. To address the global environmental crisis, effective solutions could come only on a global scale. These had to include both severe population limits and sweeping technological adjustments to restrain energy consumption and to protect the global environment.

Awareness of the crisis brought together representatives from around the world at the first United Nations Conference on Environment and Development in 1992. This so-called Earth Summit, attended by the heads of more than one hundred countries, heard conflicting arguments. Environmentalists demanded immediate measures to protect nature, while Third World leaders insisted that only economic growth could overcome the distress of their peoples and create the financial means to halt pollution. Representatives from developed countries defended the high standard of living of their populations. The conference was unable to agree on measures to halt the degradation of land and water. It did finally put together a Global Warming Convention that called for a halt to the global rise of carbon dioxide emissions by the end of the century.

Measures to achieve this objective had to come from both developing and developed countries. Another conference in 1997 in Kyoto, Japan, produced an agreement by the industrialized states to initiate the difficult process of stopping global warning. Their promise was to reduce by 2010 fossil fuel emissions in their countries to levels below those of 1990.

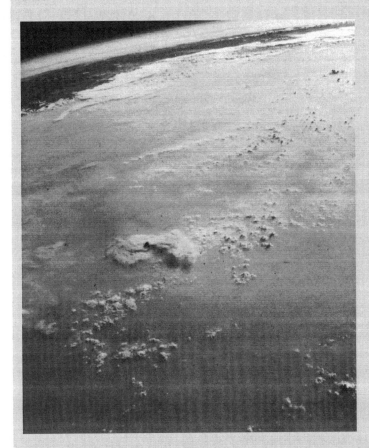

Burning Season in the Amazon Basin: Picture, Taken from U.S. Space Shuttle Discovery, of Smoke Cover and Plumes Produced by Fires Burning in the Amazon Forest, Sept. 1988 (*NASA Headquarters*)

Third World governments agreed to join the effort afterwards. The signers put off until 2000 a specific agreement on how this drastic and painful transformation was to occur. But at the conference in The Hague, Netherlands, in 2000, negotiations on measures curtailing greenhouse gases fell apart over disagreements on how each developed country should actually meet the ambitious goal set at Kyoto. Demonstrators there from the world's environmental defense organizations warned that "the earth is in danger!" Negotiators from the United States, which remained the principal source of greenhouse gases, came to the conference knowing that the U.S. Congress was opposed to any treaty curtailing energy so severely as to threaten the country's economic growth. The

next year, the new U.S. president, George W. Bush, formally abandoned the Kyoto treaty. The global environment remained hostage to national interests.

Success in saving the earth's environment demanded the voluntary cooperation of states to introduce new energy policies. It also called for the collaboration of peoples around the world to practice conservation in their daily lives. It needed technological solutions for alternative energy sources. The environmental crisis required international collaboration on a scale never seen since the Second World War. The stakes in this crisis were as high as the outcome of the war had been. The consequences of defeat were ominous for the future of humanity.

The Global Market

The global economy of the late twentieth century differed in important ways from the international economy of the early century. For the first time, businesses could disperse their economic activities throughout the world. Corporate headquarters clustered in a small number of cities. Financial operations and factory production gradually moved far from these centers into countries where labor was least expensive and governments granted special benefits to investors. The laboring population of towns in Mexico where factories manufactured car parts were in economic terms neighbors to the Detroit headquarters of the major U.S. automobile corporations.

Because the most inexpensive labor was found in Third World countries, the operations of international corporations—notably those in textiles, automobiles, and electronics—were split between executive and research offices in home countries and production in distant lands. These interregional operations were

known as "global factories." U.S. corporations tended to look to Latin America for sites for factories. Japan increasingly played the leading trade, financial, and industrial role in Southeast Asia. German companies began to move into eastern Europe in the late 1980s. Regional economic formations slowly emerged around one dominant country. The globalization of computation and communication opened by century's end possibilities of dispersing clerical work in a similar manner. This "outsourcing" developed especially rapidly in India, where U.S. corporations found competent, low-paid replacements for their own clerical employees in the United States. These corporate giants operated in a world market but remained rooted in their country of origin.

An important new trait of the globalization trend in international economic relations in the late twentieth century was the ongoing policy coordination by the governments of major industrial states in the areas of trade, finance, and economic aid. The well-being of all developed countries depended on the stability of global economic relations. Complex international economic operations in finance and investment were beyond the control of any individual government. Memories of the chaos of trade and finance in the 1930s haunted political leaders and industrialists alike. Regional conflicts and revolutionary movements in the newly decolonized world aroused fears of new obstacles to economic development. To give some order to global economic relations, the leaders of the seven major industrial states (the Western powers and Japan) began in the 1970s to meet regularly to discuss common industrial, financial, and trade problems.

Their basic goal was to keep intact and, when possible, to enlarge the scope of the global economy. These included the relatively free movement of goods and capital, the stability of the most important currencies, and the opening of economies around the world to private investors and industrialists. Their cooperation did facilitate ongoing economic operations. It was based on a recognition of common economic interests and a shared commitment to liberal capitalism.

Their concerns included economic problems in the Third World. In the global economy, their countries' economic fortunes did feel the impact of prosperity or depression in underdeveloped lands. The unpaid debts owed their banks by Third World states (particularly in Africa) totaled nearly $100 billion by the late 1980s, with no chance of full repayment. In 1996, the "Group of Seven" offered to cancel $25 billion of their debts, on condition the debtor governments adopt free market reforms. Economic aid to impoverished peoples did not drive their efforts. Private investment was the Group of Seven's preferred method of assistance to developing countries. Their financial advisers had become increasingly discouraged by the large amounts of aid wasted in many Third World countries by corrupt regimes. Their choice revealed to what extent the commitment to Third World welfare had been replaced by concern over the well-being of global finances and market economies.

Another significant characteristic of the global economy was the remarkable expansion of world trade and the extraordinarily rapid movement of funds across the continents. These trends were spurred by the decision of all the major developed countries (except the communist states) to move toward the reduction or elimination of tariffs on imported goods. The Global Agreement on Trade and Tariffs (GATT), agreed to by the Western countries in the late 1940s to fight a return to 1930s' protectionism, played an important role in this process. Its guidelines became the basis for a general reduction in tariffs in the early 1960s. This was followed by an even more substantial international tariff reduction in 1994, when GATT was replaced by the World Trade Organization (WTO). By the turn of the century, membership in the WTO came from more than one hundred countries from around the world, including the Chinese People's Republic.

The WTO's goal was to let trading and production be decided not by state regulations but by market forces. Factories would open and close according to profit and productivity. Price increases on goods would be kept in check by foreign imports, helping to reduce inflation and, ideally, the cost of living. World trade doubled in volume in the prosperous last decade of the century. Benefits were unevenly distributed, however. Half of the total world exports originated during that decade from the European Union and the United States. Global free trade was a formula weighted in favor of the industrialized countries.

Opposition to the globalization in trade relations remained strong. Environmental groups protested the weakness in GATT of provisions for environmental protection and pollution control. Political resistance in

Western countries emerged from the insistence of producers and workers to retain protections from foreign competition and to receive government financial help to sell their products cheaply abroad. Labor unions objected to competition from lands where wages were low. Agricultural interests in Europe and the United States insisted on continued state subsidies for basic crops, such as cotton, though these were produced at a lower cost in Third World countries. Global tariff reductions stalled over these issues in the early twenty-first century.

Regional groupings were a better arena of free trade. The expansion of the European Economic Community (European Union) showed the way. Its success led other areas to repeat this formula. Latin America ceased being a continent of hostile states after they moved in the 1980s to free-market economies and democratic governments. Economic cooperation was built on these shared values and institutions. Brazil, Argentina, Paraguay, and Uruguay created their own common market in 1995. To the north, the 1994 North American Free Trade Agreement (NAFTA) set in motion the elimination of trade barriers among Mexico, the United States, and Canada.

Regional economic collaboration was risky where economies were underdeveloped and a large portion of the population was impoverished. These dangers emerged within NAFTA shortly after the treaty was signed. Life among the Mexican population of 100 million resembled in many ways conditions in Third World lands. Its government had grand visions of economic benefits from regional trade and investments from American and Canadian companies. But in 1995, foreign investors (as well as wealthy Mexicans) withdrew billions of pesos from Mexico when they began to doubt the glowing promises of quick profits made by the government. The Mexican currency lost half its value, undermining the government's economic plans, threatening default on the government's international loans, and menacing the value of other Latin American currencies as speculative fears worsened.

This "run" on the Mexican peso created a major international financial crisis. It was so serious that President Clinton decided to offer a $12 billion loan from U.S. government funds to bolster the Mexican currency. Nothing like this had ever happened before. The backing of the United States and severe Mexican austerity measures ended the crisis, and the Mexican government repaid the loan within two years. The price was a painful two-year recession in Mexico. This crisis proved a warning that the global economy brought with it the threat of regional financial collapse caused by the rapid movement of speculative and investment funds around the world. That the warning was correct—and also that no effective countermeasures yet existed—was proven by the 1997–1998 financial crisis that began in East Asia and spread even to Russia. In that global financial market, the search for quick profits fueled speculation and reckless loans from global banks, generating potentially dangerous conditions that seemed beyond the power of governments to prevent.

By the early twenty-first century, the term *Third World* best designated those impoverished regions where modern industry was missing and where jobs were either unavailable or insufficient to meet the needs of the growing population. Legally or illegally, people from these poor regions set out for more prosperous lands in search of well-paying jobs. Their presence was felt in countries as small as Kuwait, attracting Indians and Palestinians ready to do unskilled labor, and as large as Australia, one-fifth of whose population was foreign born in 2000. Gradually the global economy acquired what in essence was a global labor force. The total number of these international migrants was estimated to have reached 150 million by the mid-1990s. In the previous two decades, more than twenty million people arrived in the United States, most from Third World regions. This sudden influx produced a greater proportion of foreign-born residents than in any comparable period in U.S. history. Comparable trends were also apparent in western European countries.

Cities such as Paris, Berlin, New York, London, and Los Angeles were centers for this migration. It put in their midst a Third World laboring population. But these migrants appeared everywhere jobs were available, even though they often encountered prejudice and persecution. In the North African country of Libya, rich in petroleum, migrants from sub-Saharan Africa came in the 1980s and 1990s to fill the menial jobs that Libyans no longer accepted. They stayed until large-scale anti-immigrant riots, provoked by clashes with Arabs and by competition for jobs, forced them to flee in 2000. Similar violence against Third World migrants erupted in Europe as well in the 1990s. Social tensions rooted in hostility toward these outsiders exposed the ethnic antagonisms hidden beneath the surface of prosperous countries.

In the expansion of the global economy lay also one hope for finding the means to restrain the expansion of the world's population. Where a better life appears a reality and a family has access to the means to ensure that life, fewer children become a desirable choice. This simple formula was proving its potent effect throughout the world. It depended on the coincidence of many conditions, including medical care, civil order, literacy, women's rights, as well as a growing economy.

It was an important theme of the 1994 International Conference on Population and Development. Its members, from throughout the world, issued an appeal to include women in all development programs. Without their full participation, the conference agreed that no effective population limits could come voluntarily. The proposal had the great advantage of relying on the free choice of people given the incentive as well as the encouragement to take control of their personal fate. In doing so, they would contribute to the well-being of their country and ultimately of the globe. It was a great distance from the global economy to this level of individual choice, but the linkage was already taking shape.

LOCAL WARS AND PEACEKEEPING

The collapse of the Soviet Union left only the United States with the economic resources and the military might of a superpower. At the close of the 1991 Gulf War, President George Bush sought to reassure the world that his country would not abuse its global dominance. In previous centuries, diplomatic and military alliances had been the principal means for weaker states to protect themselves from the threat of what in German was known as *machtpolitik* ("power politics") inflicted by a dominant state. In 1919, President Woodrow Wilson had proposed a new international system grounded in democratic government, national self-determination, and collective defense against aggression to maintain peace to replace the balance of power system (see Chapter 6, "Highlight: Internationalism"). In 1991, President Bush took up this liberal idea again, calling for a "new world order" for "peace and security, freedom, and the rule of law," to be achieved through the United Nations, now freed from its Cold War stalemate.

Throughout the 1990s, the United States supported collective efforts at peacekeeping. In the Balkans, the Middle East, Africa, and Asia, U.N. peacekeeping forces appeared to control or prevent violent conflicts within or among states. At times, regional help came from NATO, whose access to armed forces became vital in ending the Balkan conflict. The United Nations had a global task but faced serious obstacles to effective action from the limits placed on military action by its forces. Its very principal of international peacekeeping was challenged by the decision in the early years of the twenty-first century of U.S. President George W. Bush and his advisers to reject international action and to pursue a policy of "preventive war." The end of the Cold War marked the opening of a complex new era of international conflicts.

In the postimperial age of the 1990s, the new nation-states of the world confronted local and ethnic conflicts in greater numbers than ever before. By one count, they numbered nearly fifty, including civil wars in the former state of Yugoslavia and in Afghanistan, and the civil war and massacre in the African republic of Rwanda. The issue in these and many other similar conflicts was the struggle for state power among competing ethnic groups. Leaders of the competing movements claimed to speak for their ethnic nation, whose "rights" they defended. At times, war became a way of life for the warriors, seeking only power and wealth. Some conflicts arose out of the brutal efforts by the regime in power to impose dictatorial rule on its peoples. The process of national self-determination proved in these conditions incapable of ensuring elementary conditions of peace and security for the population.

Ethnic Conflict and War in Central Africa

In the new nation-states of Africa and Asia, relations among ethnic groups suffered when, as occurred often in the 1990s, problems of misrule, poverty, and social unrest became acute. When resources were scarce and peoples were forced to move to urban slums in search of a livelihood, the occasions for ethnic rioting multiplied. Social hardship fed rising crime rates, and when the state could not offer protection, tribal solidarity promised the best defense. Incompetent or unscrupulous political leaders could hope to hold onto power by mobilizing their own ethnic or tribal

followers against other peoples. Differences that earlier mattered little, such as religious affiliation, became another source of conflict. The variations on the formula for ethnic hostility were many, the result universally disastrous for the peoples touched by the unrest.

In 1994, Rwanda experienced the worst ethnic violence in Africa's postcolonial history. The conflict was in its origins and outcome an exemplary case of the process by which nation-building turned into ethnic conflict. Rwanda was a small country but gathered within its borders all the forces capable of igniting ethnic conflict. These included a history of colonial favoritism for a minority people, the Tutsi, at the expense of the other ethnic group, the Hutu, and a population explosion and impoverishment for many of the inhabitants. When liberation from Belgian rule came, this mountainous land had one of the highest population densities (eight hundred per square mile) in Africa. Under Belgian rule, the Tutsi had enjoyed the position of favored people, whose traditional leaders received the honors and benefits as collaborators of the colonial rulers, and found ready access to education and jobs in the colony's civil administration.

Belgium's sudden withdrawal in 1962 had stripped the Tutsi of these advantages. In the name of majority rule, the Belgians passed power to the majority Hutu people (80 percent of the inhabitants). The new national leaders forcibly ejected the Tutsi from all positions of authority, from the central government to local administration. They sought the economic and social rewards brought by political dominance. They used their privileged position, as it became known among the poorer new states, of "gatekeeper" (control over access to state posts and preference in business deals) for the exclusive benefit of their own people.

The new rulers found help from the former colonial rulers of the region. The Belgian and French governments granted foreign aid to the Hutu leadership, just as they did to Mobutu's government in Zaire. Their goal was to protect their political influence in a region that was rich in natural resources and where Franco-Belgian economic interests from the colonial period remained strong. Their concerns did not extend to ethnic relations and minority rights.

Hutu leaders retained the colonial system of identity cards that denoted Rwanda citizens' ethnic origins. They sought to deflect discontent at their incompetent rule by arousing antagonism toward the Tutsi, whose living conditions were usually better than the Hutu. A extremist Hutu group secretly devised a plan to eliminate the Tutsi entirely. "Back to Ethiopia" was their slogan. Their propaganda portrayed the Tutsi as outsiders in their own country. Ethnic cleansing was their goal. Ethnic nationalism in the hands of such fanatics, like the German Nazis, was a formula for massacre. Periodic attacks on the Tutsi occurred in the following decades. As a result, many Tutsi fled to neighboring states, some to organize for guerrilla war against the Hutu regime in Rwanda.

The escalating ethnic hostility led to efforts by some Hutu leaders, including the president, to create a coalition government under U.N. supervision. Their efforts were undermined, however, by other Hutu who sought the solution in mass executions. In 1994, the suspicious death of the Hutu president in a plane crash gave Hutu extremists the excuse to claim that the Tutsi were preparing to kill the Hutu. Their accusation was absurd, intended only to mobilize their supporters among armed Hutu militia and the army. They had already laid plans for the mass execution of the Tutsi (and were probably responsible for the plane crash). They could rely on the loyalty of their followers and the hatred felt by many Hutu toward their Tutsi neighbors.

They mobilized their militia forces and broadcast to their followers the message that "the Tutsi need to be killed." A small U.N.

peacekeeping force was powerless even to protect its own troops from the mobs. When moderate Hutus attempted to halt the bloodshed and to defend Tutsi, they also fell victims to the killing. In the massacre that followed, one-half (perhaps 500,000) of the Tutsi population in Rwanda were assassinated.

In the decades since the Nazi Final Solution, the Hutu leaders' action was as close as any fanatics had come to implementing a policy of genocide, that is, a conscious, collective effort to exterminate an entire people. And like the Holocaust, it defied rational explanation. A Belgian Catholic missionary, wounded in a vain effort to give shelter to a group of Tutsi children, explained later to foreign correspondents that "we were overwhelmed by this great evil. There is a madness at work." Faced with such inhumanity, he could find no other answer.

This horrific event set off fighting that led to a major war in central Africa. To stop the killings, Tutsi armed forces in exile in neighboring Uganda invaded Rwanda. They had the backing of the leader of Uganda. Ten years before, he brought his country out of civil war by what he called "no-party democracy" and effective protection of ethnic minorities. Repelled by the bloodshed and fearing that the violence would spread to his land, he gave vital aid in arms and finances to the Tutsi rebel army. His action raised the conflict in Rwanda to an African war. The Tutsi invaders proved much better fighters than the Hutu militia, who fled Rwanda. They were accompanied by an estimated two million Hutu refugees who feared death at the hands of their former prey. The massacres ended, and a new Tutsi government set out to restore order and to bring to justice the "agents of genocide."

That conflict exploded into an international crisis when the war spread to Zaire. The bulk of the Hutu refugees had gathered in vast camps in Zaire bordering on Rwanda. Among them were most of the Hutu warlords and

Genocide in Rwanda: Bodies of Massacred Tutsi inside Nyamata Catholic Church, 1994 (*Dufka/Getty Images Inc.-Hulton Archive Photos*)

militia responsible for the genocide. They turned the camps into their base of guerrilla operations against the new Rwandan regime. The feeble Zaire government was powerless to maintain order on its own in that eastern region of its vast country. By that time, Zaire had collapsed into disorder and decay. It had experienced three decades of such misrule by Mobutu that it had become one of the worst cases in the postcolonial regions of a failed state. Its bloody tribal conflicts revealed it to be a land without order or real state authority (see Chapter 11). In a desperate attempt to maintain some influence in eastern Zaire, Mobutu lent his support to the Hutu guerril-

las. It was a fatal move, for that action turned the conflict into a regional war.

In 1995, Rwandan government troops, with the backing of an informal regional alliance, invaded Zaire in pursuit of the Hutu militia. Two issues were crucial in this new-style, postcolonial local war. Zaire's internal disorder made it likely that any conflict there would spread beyond its borders without new leadership. Both Rwanda and Uganda confronted this likelihood. In addition, Zaire's abundant natural resources, including diamonds, exercised a strong attraction for neighboring states and for predatory militias seeking to profit from the conflict.

That African war was led by the Rwandan government, desperate to end the constant border fighting with Hutu guerrillas operating from sanctuaries in Zaire. It brought in political enemies of Mobutu, among whom the most capable was an opponent of thirty years named Laurent Kabila. It included the neighboring states of Angola, Zambia, and Uganda. Their leaders had an urgent need to bring some political stability to the region. They anticipated as well substantial benefits to their own economies when their armed forces occupied mineral-rich areas of Zaire.

Working together, these forces succeeded in a remarkably short time in organizing and supplying an army headed by Kabila and trained and led by Tutsi officers from Rwanda. In the summer of 1996, this army swept through Zaire to the capital. Mobutu's army collapsed; he fled the country. Kabila took control of the state, renaming it (as it had been at independence in 1960) the Democratic Republic of Congo. The government of the largest country in sub-Saharan Africa had changed hands in a war launched by what some observers called a "pan-African alliance."

The violence did not end, however. The Rwandan government promised protection for both its Hutu and Tutsi citizens. But the hatred between the two groups flared up repeatedly in sporadic fighting. The Democratic Republic of Congo remained a vast underpoliced land. Fugitive Hutu militia periodically mounted raids on Rwanda, whose forces continued their manhunt for the Hutu responsible for the 1994 massacre. Troops of Uganda, Angola, and Zambia moved into border areas and soon were fighting not only Congolese troops but also each other to control diamond-rich areas. Civil and foreign war in central Africa continued for years, leading to the death of more than three million people. Only the intervention in 2003 of U.N. peacekeeping forces, and the impoverishment of the region, reduced the fighting to sporadic ethnic rioting. The United Nations organized, under the authority of its International War Crimes Court, trials of thousands of Hutu accused of genocide. The scars of that brutal event made peace in the region a distant goal.

In the early twenty-first century, a very fragile peace existed among the states of central Africa. There the colonial borders remained as the vestiges of imperial rule. Political leaders continued to talk of civic nationalism and the need for an end to ethnic and tribal hostility. The leaders of the Rwandan government, like those in neighboring Tanzania and Uganda, recognized that human rights were a desirable goal. They insisted, however, that their regimes not be measured by Western political ideals. As one said, "The African and the Western worlds are many worlds apart."

Elsewhere in Africa, local wars in the 1990s became a struggle for the spoils of war. The "blood diamonds" of Zaire had to compete in an international market created by the booty produced by private armies elsewhere in the continent. Civil wars in countries such as Angola and Sierra Leone fed on pillaging by self-styled armies whose warriors knew no other way of life. Precious raw materials were a prime target of these armed groups. The rich diamond mines of Angola sustained a rebel army that had been fighting to seize the central government ever since independence in 1976. Its military backing from foreign sources had dried up at the end of the Cold War, when Soviet and U.S. agents ceased competing for influence there. Control of the diamond trade kept the rebel army fighting through most of the 1990s, as long as it could find buyers for this war booty. One observer concluded that in those areas "diamonds are warfare's best friend."

The Warring Peoples of the Balkans

The end of the Cold War brought ethnic conflict to peoples within the former communist lands. The worst of these occurred in southeastern Europe in the region known as the Balkans, inhabited mainly by peoples of Slavic languages but of divided religious loyalties. The Catholic and Orthodox churches were dominant among Croatians and Serbs, respectively; the Muslim faith had spread among many inhabitants of the region known as Bosnia as well as in Albania.

The communist rulers of Yugoslavia, heirs to the South Slav (Yugoslav) state formed in 1919, had managed to hold together their various Slavic-speaking peoples in a federal state of "national republics," formed on the model of the Soviet Union (see Chapter 7). Tito, the founder of the Yugoslav Communist Party and head of postwar Yugoslavia, enjoyed enormous personal authority among the peoples there. His death in 1980 left his state without a strong leader; the collapse in 1989 of the other communist states of eastern Europe undermined the very legitimacy of communism in Yugoslavia. The country had to be rebuilt, and the only principle that attracted strong backing was national self-determination.

In 1990, the leaders of the major national republics of Yugoslavia agreed to allow the people of each national republic to vote whether to secede from or to remain within the federal state. Their decision was an admission of weakness. They recognized that communism was bankrupt and that their only solution to the political crisis was free elections. Two republics (Slovenia and Croatia) immediately chose to leave. In 1991, their leaders formed independent nation-states, and the other republics soon followed their example (see map of Europe, 1992, p. 392). Each new nation-state contained substantial ethnic minorities, some of whom dreamed of controlling their native territory. The nationalist vision of ethnically pure territory went counter to the realities of ethnic intermarriage, migrations, and the generations-old persistence of ethnically mixed communities in the Balkan region.

This mixing of peoples gave the ambitious leader of the Serbian republic, Slobodan Milosevic, his opportunity. Serbs living in Croatia and Bosnia belonged, according to extremist nationalists, within "Greater Serbia." Milosovic made this rallying cry the basis for his new political agenda. Once an ardent Communist, he used Serbian nationalism as an alternative platform on which to rebuild his power in the post-Yugoslav Balkans. In the First World War, Serbs had fought against the Austro–Hungarian Empire for national freedom for South Slavs. That history inspired Milosevic and his nationalist followers in 1992 to demand that all Serbian people live in one "greater" (i.e., enlarged) Serbian state. Enlarging Serbia was possible only by annexing neighboring territories. The weakness of the other successor states in the former Yugoslavia convinced Milosevic that the plan could succeed. His nationalist ambitions destroyed the last hope for the preservation of peaceful relations among Balkan peoples. War had begun in 1914 when a Serbian terrorist had assassinated the Austro-Hungarian Grand Duke in the Bosnian capital of Sarajevo. War began again in 1992 in the same region over Serbian efforts to expand their rule into Bosnian areas where large numbers of Serbians lived.

Bosnia was a multi-ethnic, multi-religious land. It was divided among a Muslim population (labeled Muslim because they belonged to a distinct community, not because they all were practicing Muslims) in a small majority, and large numbers of Serbs and Croatians. In 1992, the Serbian republic and Bosnian Serbs joined forces to seize large areas of Bosnia. Arms and military forces from the old Yugoslav army (largely Serbian) went into Serbian-inhabited areas of Bosnia. Armed groups of Serbs began a systematic effort to expel Muslims from these regions. Their "ethnic cleansing" (a new term referring to the forced removal of an entire people) included killing, rape, and intimidation on a massive scale. Its purpose was to force the

The Ruins of Civil War: St. Mary's Catholic Church, Sarajevo, December, 1992 (*Corbis-Bettmann*)

bulk of the Muslims to flee into a small territory of their own and leave the Serbs in sole possession of most of Bosnia. The Serb forces put under siege the capital city of Sarajevo. At the same time, the Croatian government launched its own ethnic cleansing campaign, seizing parts of Bosnia where many Croatians lived. The Muslim government of Bosnia organized an army and fought desperately to defeat the Serbian and Croatian armed groups. Its forces employed at times methods as brutal as those of their opponents. Respect for innocent civilians and simple pity vanished in a ruthless civil war.

A reckless, ambitious political leader started the process leading to civil war in former Yugoslavia. Yet Milosevic's war could not have produced such widespread brutality had antagonism among ethnic groups not revived despite three generations of peaceful life in the federation. Neighbors began to fear one another in a process fueled by demagogic calls for violence. Only small groups of soldiers carried on the fighting. The civilian majority was unwilling to participate for fear of suffering for a cause that was less important than their own safety and well-being. At times, private armies took over large sections of the country. Their warlord leaders justified combat in nationalist terms but seemed motivated by the sheer love of battle.

Their message of ethnic hatred denied human dignity to their enemies. Women became objects for sexual abuse; men became victims of brutalization. By 1994, 100,000 people had died as a result of the fighting throughout the Balkans. A million or more had become refugees, forced to flee their homes to escape the violence of war. The Balkan civil war, on the territory of the former Yugoslavia, embodied the ugliest, most inhuman features of the ethnic conflicts in other parts of the world.

Losing the war, the Bosnian government appealed in 1993 to the European Union and the United Nations for help. Both attempted to find a compromise solution to the conflict but failed. The Serbian forces in Bosnia continued their expulsion and execution of Bosnians, even those living in U.N.-protected areas. The city of Sarajevo was under constant bombardment by Serbian guns. Only military intervention could halt the bloodshed. That action came in 1995 from the armed forces of NATO. Its leaders finally concluded that the war, which might spread to surrounding states, threatened the interests and well-being of all Europe. Led by the United States, the NATO air force began the bombing of Serbian positions in Bosnia. The NATO high command warned the Serbian leaders that they risked seeing the war spread to their own territory unless the Bosnian Serbs stopped fighting and agreed to a compromise peace treaty.

The military action by NATO ended the Bosnian war. The 1995 treaty called for the incorporation of the Serbian and Croatian territories into a united Bosnia. That peacemaking process moved slowly, thwarted by the destruction and hatred generated in the war. A united Bosnia remained for the time being a paper promise. For a time, Milosevic and other nationalist fanatics had persuaded their peoples that their new nation-states required an ethnically "pure" land. It was a false message and a human tragedy. Milosevic himself

fell from power a few years later. Accused of "crimes against humanity," he was placed on trial in 2002 by an International War Crimes Tribunal, operating under a U.N. mandate.

Internationalism and the United Nations

The determination to restrain these post–Cold War conflicts through international peacekeeping efforts brought together leaders from humanitarian organizations and from the United Nations. A few peacekeeping missions had been a part of the United Nations' functions since its founding, although at no point had its members agreed to allow the United Nations command its own armed forces. Throughout the Cold War, the Soviet Union had refused to approve extensive U.N. military operations, arguing that it was an instrument of the Western powers. The readiness of the last Soviet leadership to collaborate in the U.N. coalition in the Iraq war of 1990–1991 revealed that the United Nations was freed at last from this constraint on its action.

Influential backing for U.N. intervention in local wars came from the European Union in the 1990s. Once the Soviet threat had disappeared, its member governments, especially Germany and France, became active proponents of the international defense of human rights within Europe and beyond. They made internationalism an important objective in the European Union's foreign relations. They were prepared to use armed forces to halt abuse by Serbs of human rights in Bosnia, supporting first the use of U.N. peacekeeping forces there and then the dispatch of NATO forces to the Balkans in 1995.

Private groups in the West were instrumental as well in promoting and acting on this liberal ideology on a global scale. Nongovernmental organizations (NGOs) had existed since the nineteenth century. The Red Cross was the first NGO, dedicated to providing medical aid to war-torn lands. To avoid taking sides, it had excluded all political judgments from its wartime operations. In the 1970s, this international humanitarianism became the inspiration for an increasing number of volunteer organizations. They adopted a more activist position on public involvement, for they did not hesitate to issue public condemnation when they judged governments or armed groups responsible for crimes against humanity.

Their political involvement, based on humanitarian principles, was the grounds on which they appealed for outside intervention. New groups such as the French Doctors without Borders and the British Oxfam sent their members into areas of violence to bring help to innocent civilians. Bernard Kouchner, one of the founders of Doctors without Borders, had worked with the Red Cross in Biafra during the Nigerian civil war. Outraged at the crimes committed by Nigerian armed forces, he decided that he could not accept the apolitical policy of the Red Cross. He founded a new medical aid organization in 1971 called Doctors without Borders ("Medecins sans frontiers"), whose charter encouraged volunteers to "bear witness" publicly to atrocities along with their care for the sick and the wounded. Kouchner believed deeply in what he called a "right of intervention" by foreign powers, including the United Nations, in wars that inflicted brutal punishment on innocent civilian populations. In 1990, the U.N. General Assembly formally recognized the desirability of their international humanitarian action.

The local wars of the 1990s drew the NGOs to the most distant parts of the globe. It also placed them in the middle of bitter conflicts where their very presence became a political issue. Their own action did at times produce undesirable political effects. In 1994, Doctors without Borders went to central Africa to assist the millions of Hutu refugees from Rwanda. They soon discovered that Hutu militia, responsible for the Rwanda genocide,

controlled the refugee camps of Zaire and were seizing medical and food assistance and aid services. The new Rwanda government protested that the NGOs supplying the camps were helping the assassins of their people, not serving a humanitarian aim. In disgust at the Hutu warlords' use of their assistance, Doctors without Borders stopped their lifesaving work there. They were trapped between their hopes of peace and the ugly reality of ruthless power-hungry warlords bent on violence.

The United Nations appeared the best choice to all those who believed that a truly new world order had to rely on the international community, not on the military might of individual states, to resolve the local wars of the late century. The U.N. charter called for peacekeeping action to find just settlements in the best interests of war-torn countries and contending ethnic groups. This peacekeeping mission fell under the direct responsibility of the secretary general. The Security Council approved recommendations for intervention and voted the funds to pay for civilian personnel and, if necessary, troops to take charge of the operation. At times, the Security Council authorized member countries to dispatch their own troops to intervene against aggressive states in defense of the victim. The Korean War of 1950–1953 and the Gulf War of 1990–1991 were fought successfully in this manner. For local wars, U.N. armed forces usually operated directly under the peacekeeping branch of the Secretariat. The secretary general provided overall supervision of the conduct of the operations.

As a distinguishing sign, U.N. equipment bore the distinctive emblem of a white dove over a blue background. The troops made up an unusual military force. They were composed of contingents, including commanding officers, from the member countries whose governments agreed to participate. Their charge in conducting their operations was, until the early 1990s, to use their arms solely for self-defense. This created a cruel dilemma for U.N. commanders when the militias of warlords or regular armies were determined at all cost to achieve military victory, wreaking havoc and death among the populations who got in their way. A U.N. military force armed only with defensive weapons could not be effective in these circumstances.

For the first forty years of its existence, the question of peacemaking did not arise. The U.N. peacekeeping role had been to enforce peace agreements that the combatants had already put into effect. When the Suez War of 1956 ended in the withdrawal of Israeli troops, the United Nations sent peacekeepers to patrol the Egyptian-Israeli border. They were there to reassure the Israeli government that Egypt would no longer send Muslim terrorists into their land and to help the Egyptian government respect a peace agreement that was very unpopular with its Muslim fundamentalists. These operations were useful, though they did not occur frequently. Between 1945 and 1990, the United Nations had sent troops on only thirteen peacekeeping operations. Operating at the invitation (more or less voluntary) of combatants and in conditions of relative order, U.N. intervention had proven useful and (almost) bloodless.

Its activities accelerated dramatically in the 1990s. Suddenly local wars flared up throughout the world. The Security Council moved to prevent mass killing and atrocities in the spirit of humanitarian defense of human rights. In 1991, it unanimously approved a policy of U.N. military intervention for the sake of "human security" when threatened by wars or ethnic conflict.

United Nations Peacekeeping Operations, 2000 (*Map #4000 Rev. 16, U.N. Department of Public Information, Cartographic Section*)

In the next years, the United Nations found itself engaged in twenty wars requiring the participation of seventy thousand U.N. troops. Some actions involved peacemaking, not just peacekeeping, when the warring parties continued fighting. The U.N. flag flew over military camps in very dangerous parts of the world.

That danger first became apparent in the African country of Somalia. The nomadic peoples there had proven unable to create a stable government after receiving their independence in 1960. It had become a failed state, like other Third World lands where poverty and clan loyalties fatally weakened vital functions of public life. The population's miserable economic conditions worsened dramatically when serious drought hit the country in the 1980s. Nongovernmental organizations attempted to help the starving peoples but were powerless to prevent warlord-led militias from stealing their supplies and fighting each other in an endless civil war.

In 1991, the United Nations responded to the international outcry by approving military intervention to protect the aid activities. In 1992, it accepted the proposal of President George Bush to send U.S. forces, operating on their own, into Somalia. The Muslim warlords united against the "infidel" American occupier, killing eighteen U.S. soldiers in a highly publicized military operation in the country's capital city. The American military and the U.S. Congress raised serious questions why American military should die for a cause of no national interest to their country. Shortly after, the U.S. government ended its "armed humanitarianism," and the United Nations stopped its efforts at peacemaking in Somalia. The warlords had won; the United Nations (and the people of Somalia) had lost.

International peacemaking lost U.S. support and as a result failed several times to end ethnic atrocities inflicted on minority peoples in the ensuing years. U.N. troops went to war-torn areas of the former Yugoslavia in 1993 to stop the brutal ethnic cleansing, directed primarily at the Muslim population in Bosnia and the Serbian people in Croatia. In that same year, the Security Council authorized U.N. peacekeepers to go to Rwanda to help enforce a cease-fire between the Hutu government and Tutsi rebel forces. In both cases, the U.N. Secretariat had at its disposal very few troops, armed only with light weapons, to contain heavily armed forces engaged in civil wars between hostile peoples. The U.S. government refused to participate directly, fearing public hostility to military intervention that might end in bloodshed among U.S. troops. It claimed that the "disorders" there were internal affairs to be resolved by the states themselves. Without U.S. backing, the Security Council and the U.N. Secretariat could not launch real military intervention in these lands.

The result was that the U.N. troops were helpless witnesses to the massacre of Bosnian Muslims and to the Rwandan genocide. Only the NATO intervention in 1995 stopped the Bosnian civil war. In Rwanda, the Tutsi guerrilla forces finally ended the genocide after invading the country and defeating the Hutu army. The U.N. peacekeepers lacked the armament and the authorization from the Security Council to engage in real warfare to protect the Tutsi from massacre. The 1949 U.N. Agreement on War Crimes had obligated U.N. members to take all steps necessary to prevent genocide. "Bloodless" peacemaking in these areas was impossible, and the U.S. government again refused to authorize its forces to participate (claiming no genocide was occurring). As a result, the United Nations failed to fulfill its mission in Rwanda in 1994.

This tragic failure strengthened the resolve of the new secretary general, Kofi Annan, to ensure that the United Nations act promptly and decisively in areas where violence erupted. He became the United Nations' highest officer in 1996. His election marked the first time a diplomat from sub-Saharan Africa had served as general secretary. He made the troubles of Africa his prime concern. He explained that the United Nations' task had to include intervention in conflicts (including civil wars) where "the main aim is the destruction not of armies but of civilians and entire ethnic groups." It was a goal that went beyond the aims of Woodrow Wilson and other founders of the first collective peacekeeping organization, the League of Nations. But times had changed since 1919. The 150 new nation-states had found their collective voice within the United Nations. Annan believed deeply that it, better than any outside power, was suited to the task of peacekeeping.

At least once in the last years of the century, his resolve led to successful military intervention. The people of the eastern half of the island of Timor had received their freedom from the Portuguese Empire in 1975, only to be conquered the next year by the Indonesian army. For the next two decades, Timorese nationalists fought an obscure, sporadic war for liberation from Indonesia. In the late 1990s, Indonesian militia and military units continued the fight, killing at random Timorese civilians to force their nationalist leaders to abandon the struggle. It was another local war coupled with ethnic massacre.

Under international pressure, a new Indonesian civilian government finally agreed to allow the East Timorese to vote on independence. It reluctantly accepted the presence of U.N. military units whose task was to end the fighting. Australian troops were the first to intervene, capturing and disarming the Indonesian militia. After their combat ended, other U.N. civilian and military personnel supervised the elections. The Timorese people voted for independence. The new government began, with U.N. and NGO assistance, the slow, tortuous work of rebuilding its devastated land and constructing the new nation-state of East Timor. In the post–Cold War world, internationalism had become a vital force thanks to the efforts of the United Nations.

TERRORISM AND LOCAL WARS

International relations among nations in the postimperial age evolved at times in directions dictated by the old methods of power politics and balance of power. The Soviet Union and the United States had, in the course of the Cold War, created a fragile balance of power (baptized the "balance of terror"). Each had constructed a comparable array of weapons of mass destruction. They had occasionally turned to the practice of power politics. In times of superpower crisis, they had threatened nuclear war to force their opponent to compromise. When local disputes in their spheres of influence appeared to weaken their domination, they had not hesitated to use armed force (either openly or covertly) to impose their will. Stalin had recognized these methods to be integral to the "capitalist law of the jungle." The disappearance of the Soviet Union left Russia a weakened player in that diplomatic game.

At the end of the century, U.S. military expenditures amounted to more than 35 percent of the total military spending of all the countries of the world. In real terms, the U.S. military still possessed 5,000 intercontinental ballistics missiles and deployed a multi-ocean navy. The tremendous expense of maintaining this level of armaments was sustained by an economy whose yearly productive economic capacity totaled one-third of the world's production. In these circumstances, no global balance of power existed in the world as had been the case in the Cold War. In the years after the fall of the Soviet Union, the United States enjoyed global hegemonic power.

In these circumstances, issues of war and peace among states had to be resolved following new guidelines. The United Nations offered one model. The call in 1991 by President George Bush for a "new world order" gave support to this project. But U.S. priorities shifted dramatically under the presidency of his son George W. Bush. The 2001 terrorist attack on targets on the East Coast encouraged his administration to consider unilateral action against other states refusing to submit to U.S. demands. Baptised "preventive war," it signaled a return to the policy of international power politics.

Islam in Afghanistan

Following the decision of the Soviet government to withdrawal its forces from Afghanistan (see Chapter 13), the country entered a period of destructive civil war. The Soviet army's departure in 1989 was the death sentence for the Afghan communist regime there, which collapsed in 1992. Afghanistan became the prey of competing armed groups, united earlier only by opposition to the Communists. One of the contenders for power was the Taliban ("students") movement. It had emerged out of the Muslim fundamentalist religious schools in Pakistan. It recruited its followers primarily from Afghan refugees who in the 1980s had fled the war against the Communists and their Soviet ally. Within a few years, the Afghan refugee population had climbed to 1.5 million, some in Iran but most in Pakistan. The Taliban's militant faith had sustained them in the bloody war

against the "godless" Communists in the 1980s. At that time they had attracted 30,000 volunteers from other Muslim lands (the "Arab Afghans"). Wealthy, pious Muslims such as Osama bin Laden had organized financial aid and military supplies to fight those he called the "Crusaders."

After the Soviet withdrawal, the Taliban carried on the struggle to transform their wartorn country into an Islamic republic. Their skills in fighting improved with time. The Pakistan government gave them secret military support, hoping to exercise some influence over these religious zealots. Their forces grew in strength until in 1997 they were able to seize control of Afghanistan, a country in ruins after two decades of war.

The Taliban finally had sufficient control of the country to set about laying the foundations for an Islamic republic even more strict than that in place in Iran. They imposed Muslim law on the population. Women were confined to home and the family, forced to leave behind schooling or work. Criminal law followed traditional Muslim rules, with mutilation and stoning for serious offenses. Secular "vices" such as listening to music became a public crime. Opium growing was banned as

Refugees from Afghan-Soviet War: Refugee Camp, Iran, 1986 (*UN/DPI Photo by A. Hollman*)

equally heinous. The people were subjected to a regime of religious purification.

The Taliban government welcomed foreign Muslims who shared a similar hatred of secularism and modernity. Western material civilization, especially American, was an evil force to which it was vehemently opposed. In 1996, Osama bin Laden established headquarters there for his terrorist organization, Al Qaeda. Its goal, like other fundamentalist Muslim movements of the 1980s and 1990s, was the restoration of a "pure" Islamic faith in place of the modernist heresies brought by the West in all Muslim countries, and the destruction of American political and diplomatic presence over this vast area. For that reason he had been expelled from his homeland, Saudi Arabia, whose feudal monarchy relied on U.S. backing. His group was few in number but prepared to die in a holy war against the United States. But the term *war* meant in reality terrorism, and his targets extended anywhere in the world.

Osama bin Laden's organization established secret ties with other small terrorist groups in Southeast Asia and the Middle East. By the early 1990s, small terrorist groups had emerged in many Muslim lands to pursue the battle against the evils of secularism and modernity. They formed a loose network of organizations that shared a common goal and collaborated in carrying out their terrorist actions. In Indonesia, fundamentalists set out in the late 1990s on a violent campaign against Indonesian Christian churches located near Muslim communities and targeted in 2002 a nightclub in Bali popular with Western tourists, killing nearly two hundred people. In 1993, yet another Islamic terrorist group had done minor damage when it exploded car bombs in the World Trade Center in New York City.

The symbolic importance of this skyscraper to American might made it, along with government buildings in Washington, D.C., a target that the terrorists would not abandon. Al Qaeda

plotted a new, far more deadly plan of attack. On September 11, 2001, nineteen of bin Laden's followers hijacked four commercial airliners and turned these planes into monstrous guided bombs. They piloted two of the planes into the twin towers of the World Trade Center, a third into the Pentagon building in Washington, and intended the fourth to hit the White House (the plane crashed before reaching its target as a result of the resistance of passengers). The collapse of the twin towers, killing nearly three thousand people, was captured in film and shown on television throughout the world. The terrorists had brought their "holy war" to the very center of Western civilization.

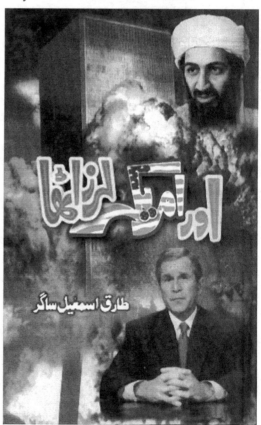

Cover to Al Qaeda Book: *And America Trembled*, 2002 (*Hoover Institution Archives Collection*)

◀ **SPOTLIGHT: Osama bin Laden** ▶

Osama bin Laden (b. 1957) never used the word *terrorist* to describe his activities organizing attacks on Middle Eastern governments and on American targets inside and beyond the borders of the United States. He believed himself a warrior in a holy war (*jihad* in Arabic) against the enemies of Islam. His claim to defend their religion made him a hero to many Muslims. His violent campaign against the United States, culminating in the destruction of the New York City World Trade Center in 2001, made him a hunted man with an enormous price on his head.

His personality and his conspiratorial activities are shrouded in mystery. In public, he spoke of himself only to restate, in lengthy proclamations, his vow to bring death and defeat to all those who threatened the Muslim faith, welcoming death in this battle. He was reported to have explained in 1998 that "I am fighting so I can die a martyr and go to heaven to meet God." He cultivated an aura of great conspirator, claiming or implying that members of his organization Al Qaeda ("The Military Base") were responsible for bombings in South Asia, the Middle East, Africa, Europe, and the United States. He welcomed this violence for the good that it supposedly brought his cause. His conviction that these deeds were the righteous acts of true Muslims marked him as a religious fanatic. His readiness to inflict indiscriminate death and destruction as a means to intimidate and weaken his enemies placed him among the practitioners of terrorism.

Holy war in defense of Islam became the center of his life from the moment in 1980 when he joined the forces in Afghanistan fighting the Soviet invaders. Before then, he had distinguished himself only as a pious son of an extraordinarily wealthy Saudi Arabian businessman. His father's construction business flourished, for the Saudi monarchy favored it above all other enterprises in the mammoth projects for the reconstruction of the holiest of Muslim sites, Mecca and Medina. Bin Laden perfected his business and engineering skills as a student at a Saudi university in the 1970s. Once in Afghanistan, he put them to use in gathering funds and constructing impregnable defenses for the Afghan guerrillas. The son, like the father, practiced an austere, rigorous version of the Muslim faith called Wahhabism. He understood the Afghan war in these strict Islamic terms. It taught him that Muslims were once again, as in the time of the Crusades, under attack from infidels.

Bin Laden was persuaded that this war in defense of Islam required the participation of the faithful throughout the Islamic world. Many volunteers (the "Arab Afghans") did come to Afghanistan, mostly from Arab-speaking lands, to fight the Soviet army. He set up special military camps to train them in the skills of modern warfare (with weapons supplied secretly by the U.S. government). He learned the meaning of holy war, Islamic warrior, and martyrdom in the midst of those bloody battles. In 1988, these comrades in arms became the core group of his new conspiratorial organization, Al Qaeda. Bin Laden gloried in the victory in 1989 of the Afghan guerrillas, whose victory over the Soviet army meant to him that his Muslim warriors had defeated "the largest heretic power on earth." He was convinced that he had witnessed there the disappearance of "the myth of the superpower in the face of the outcry that 'God is Great' [Allah Akbar]." He became a Muslim warrior by conviction and training in the Afghan war. Those years were his apprenticeship as a terrorist.

In the 1990s, his holy war had to be fought throughout the Muslim world against the United States, the remaining superpower with troops in Muslim lands. He moved into action against this "crusader" state after American military forces went in 1990 into Saudi Arabia in preparation for the war against Iraq in defense of Kuwait. He publicly condemned the Saudi monarchy as "agents of the United States" for permitting the infidels into this Muslim holy land. For that, in 1991 the Saudi government expelled him and stripped him of his citizenship. In his eyes, the evil power behind his own persecution, and behind the "crusade" against all Islam, was the United States. He found refuge in Sudan, where an Islamic regime had taken power. There he set about organizing his "warriors" for the new war against the Saudi monarchy and America. His life from this moment on was entirely absorbed by his secret terrorist activities.

Bin Laden's Afghan work had brought him fame, financial support, and followers among Muslim fundamentalists. With this backing, he made Al Qaeda into one of the best organized and funded terrorist groups. He was already responsible for bombings in Saudi Arabia and was pursued by agents from Saudi Arabia and the United States. To find a more secure refuge, in 1996 he moved his operations from Sudan back to Afghanistan. There the Taliban movement was close to winning the civil war that followed the Soviet withdrawal. Its leaders shared his religious zeal. As a result, he quickly became a close collaborator of the new regime and was permitted to use his old military bases as the center for his battle against the United States.

His notoriety as a terrorist organizer and spokesman dates from these years. He had no serious training in Islamic theology, but this lack did not weaken his eagerness to claim to under-

stand religious truth. Twice while in Sudan he appeared in videotapes (his preferred means of communication) to call for war on the United States. In early 1998, he issued in the name of "The International Islamic Front for Holy War against Jews and Crusaders" a religious declaration stating that "the individual duty of every Muslim" was to "kill the Americans and their allies, civilians and military" in "any country in which this is possible." His bombastic tone, typical of earlier political terrorists claiming that their deeds constitute the will of their community, was a sort of declaration of war. That fall, the bombs that destroyed the U.S. embassies in Kenya and Tanzania, almost certainly the work of Al Qaeda members, proved to the world that he belonged in the forefront of international terrorists.

The success of his September 11, 2001, attacks on U.S. targets was a moment of triumph for his cause and for him personally. The operation that he had planned required years of meticulous preparation. Al Qaeda members had to be trained as pilots, and the four separate terrorist squads had to hijack their planes in a coordinated move to reach their targets at nearly the same time that day. He rejoiced in the terrible destruction wrought by the three planes that did reach their targets, declaring it a "success beyond my wildest dreams." Yet it was successful only in provoking another Afghan war that ended the Taliban's rule. That conflict did serious damage to Al Qaeda. U.S. bombing attacks destroyed the cave shelters that he had built ten years before in the war with the Soviet Union and where Al Qaeda had created its center of operations. Many of its members were buried alive there. A few tapes purporting to be his speeches from the next years suggested he had survived. His action brought a worldwide repression of Muslim fundamentalists. In the end, his so-called triumph proved once again that terrorism is a self-destructive movement.

The Local Wars of the United States

The international outrage and horror created by terrorist attacks on the United States brought together an international coalition of states united in their determination to destroy the Al Qaeda movement and its Taliban backers. The U.S. government, with the support of the U.N. Security Council and of the North Atlantic Treaty Organization, organized an anti-Taliban military coalition of Western air and land units. Russia and the central Asian states gave their backing to the action. Even Pakistan, once the secret patron of Taliban forces and sanctuary for fundamentalist Muslims, publicly backed the war. The coalition collaborated with several Afghan warlords, whose guerrilla fighters made the war a joint Afghan–coalition operation. Their attack in late 2001 proved a success in overthrowing the Taliban and destroying the Al Qaeda camps. The success was due in good measure to the dislike among Afghans for their ruthless Muslim leaders.

This war of intervention was only partially successful, though. It could not wipe out the network of Al Qaeda terrorist cells, for many operated secretly in Pakistan and other countries; it could not bring stability and political unity to a country where nation-building had never overcome clan, tribal, and religious quarrels. The Taliban kept up guerrilla attacks on their Afghan enemies and foreign troops. In world affairs, the most notable feature of the war was the demonstration of the overwhelming military might of the United States. The superpower had global reach.

Yet to those who believed that the balance of power determined success or failure in global relations, the United States appeared after the September 11, 2001, terrorist attack a weakened superpower. The new U.S. administration under the presidency of George W. Bush argued that these new circumstances justified recourse to what it termed "preventive war," that is, a war of aggression against countries promoting global terrorism. From the perspective of international relations, this policy necessitated reliance on the methods of power politics (see Chapter 7, "Highlight: Internationalism"). Bush and his advisers were prepared to use the military might of their country to reaffirm U.S. global might. The message of U.S. weakness conveyed by the Al Qaeda attack had particular importance in the Middle East whose petroleum was vital to U.S. economic needs and strategic interests.

The U.S.-led coalition of 1990–1991 had, in defeating Saddam Hussein's forces in Kuwait, defended the sovereignty of that small state and had kept Iraq from becoming the major power in the Middle East. The war was fought under the U.N. flag and ended on a compromise peace that left Saddam Hussein's regime in power. Enforcement of the peace was the responsibility of the United Nations. Its inspectors ensured the elimination of Iraq's weapons of mass destruction. The Security Council authorized Kurdish autonomy in northern Iraq and U.S. air protection for this semipartition of the country. Its officials monitored the partial embargo on Iraqi oil exports. This peace arrangement used methods of containment, similar in intent to those first directed by the United States on a global scale against the Soviet Union, to limit the power of Saddam Hussein's regime, ruling a drastically weakened country (see Chapter 12).

After the September 11, 2001, attacks, President Bush and his advisers decided to force Saddam Hussein's regime out of power. Similar offensive operations had occurred during the Cold War when the U.S. sphere of influence in Latin America had appeared threatened. But war operations in the Middle East confronted far greater obstacles. There hostility among Muslims toward the United States was widespread, and Arab opposition to Western intervention had a long history dating from English and French efforts after the First World War to create semicolonial states there.

Bush was prepared to launch the invasion without the sanction of the U.N. Security Council. There a new war lacked the support of key members, including Germany, France, and Russia. Their leaders favored continuing the policy of containment. With the backing among major states only of Great Britain, the United States invaded Iraq in April 2003. Its forces quickly defeated the Iraqi army and removed from power the regime of Saddam Hussein.

International criticism of the war focused on the invasion and military occupation of Iraq, pointing out that the U.S. government's war plans rested on several false assumptions. It assumed that the diplomatic and military influence of the U.S. government in the Middle East would fully recover from the damage inflicted by the Al Qaeda attacks only by the destruction of the Iraqi regime. It also expected that U.S. invading forces would be welcomed as liberators by Iraqis. It justified that war by claiming that Saddam Hussein's regime had a role in the Al Qaeda attack, that it possessed weapons of mass destruction, and that it posed a clear and immediate military threat to the region. None of these claims was true. Only afterwards did the United States present the war as a crusade for democracy in the Middle East, using Roosevelt's internationalist explanation of the war on Nazi Germany to justify its "preventive war."

Saddam Hussein was a symbol of anti-U.S. resistance in the Middle East. It was a role that he himself exploited to bolster his dictatorship in his country. The U.S. leadership calculated that his removal would demonstrate that the U.S. military and diplomatic influence dominated the balance of power in the region. The Russian president observed after the invasion that the war was not intended to "combat the evil" of terrorism but was an effort to expand the U.S. "zone of strategic influence" in the Middle East through the use of its "strong and well-armed national army." He saw in the war a U.S. act of power politics. To the Bush administration, this goal was worth the cost in lives, both Iraqi and American, and in damage to the Iraqi economy and society.

The sequel to the war proved far bloodier than the war itself. The U.S. government had at the time no viable plans for a "liberated" Iraq and did even seek a formal surrender from Iraqi military leaders. An insurrection by defeated Iraqi forces began in the months following U.S. military occupation of the country. The fighting had within two years killed more than 1,500 U.S. soldiers and left tens of thousands of Iraqi civilians dead. Efforts to establish a new Iraqi government moved slowly, for opposition to the presence of U.S. troops was widespread. U.S. military and civilian personnel and Iraqis assisting them became targets for terrorist attacks, launched by both Iraqi and by foreign Muslim terrorist groups. The United Nations agreed to assist in elections to select a new government, but its officials were unable to operate freely in the country in the face of terrorist attacks. Reconstruction efforts moved ahead very slowly.

The U.S. unilateral action had intentionally excluded an internationalist strategy of maintaining peace under the auspices of the United Nations. It made clear the absence of a real "new world order" in the international affairs of the post–Cold War era.

SUMMARY

The early years of the twenty-first century bore little resemblance to earlier decades. Communism had disappeared from Europe and remade itself in China into a political dictatorship promoting capitalism. Empires had vanished, and so, too, had the Cold War. The newly elected leaders of the former communist states slowly restored free-market economies and liberal democracy. It proved to be a difficult transition. Western societies had moved in the half century since the Second World War into a new Industrial Revolution and new global economy.

Their living conditions were far different from those relics of outdated industrial life left behind by the communists.

The closing years of the twentieth century were a time of ethnic conflicts so severe that they threatened the very survival of some new nation-states. The responsibility for these tragic events lay in large measure on ambitious leaders determined to seize and hold power regardless of the human consequences. Fearful people, often suffering hardship with little hope for the future, turned in desperation to political movements that seemed to offer easy solutions to complex social and economic problems. Extremist nationalist leaders appeared most often at the end of the century to hold that key. Their appeals to nationalist passions fanned the flames of ethnic hatred and at times heightened the risk of war with neighboring states. The work of the United Nations offered some hope that these conflicts could be contained, yet the poisonous effects of hatred and intolerance among peoples did not disappear.

After the 2001 terrorist attacks and the 2003 Iraq war, the world remained a very unstable and violent place. The United Nations attempted with limited success to control local wars. Leaders of powerful nation-states had in their hands still the power to wage war or to join in collective peacemaking policies. In the new nation-states, leaders' readiness to promote civic nationalism could restrain ethnic conflict and war. But ethnic conflict was still a potential force for violence. The United States, whose empire had never rivaled that of other Western powers, employed in 2003 the methods of power politics when its leaders judged its national interests at stake, relying on war instead of collective, diplomatic methods of containment of Iraq. President Woodrow Wilson's 1919 appeal for peace protected by a "community of nations," not power politics, remained a wish, not a reality.

DATES WORTH REMEMBERING

1964	Integrated-circuit computers
1965	First communications satellite
1971	United States abandons gold standard
1973	Oil crisis and global recession
1986	Chernobyl nuclear accident in Soviet Union
1980–1997	Asian economic boom
1990–1991	U.N. war against Iraq
1991–1995	Civil war in Yugoslavia
1992	Global Conference on the Environment
1994	North American Free Trade Agreement
1994	Massacre of Tutsi people in Rwanda
1995	Mexican financial crisis
1996–2002	War in central Africa
1997	Taliban forces conquer Afghanistan
1997–1998	Asian financial crisis
1998	World population approximately six billion
2000	Global warming confirmed by U.N. Conference on Climate Change
2001	Al Qaeda terrorist attacks on United States
2001	Defeat of Afghan Taliban regime by U.S.-led invasion
2003	U.S. invasion of Iraq

RECOMMENDED READING

Global Economy, Global Environment

*Anthony Giddens, *Runaway World: How Globalization Is Reshaping Our Lives* (2000). Despite the lurid title, a thoughtful examination of the impact of the global economy.

*John McNeill, *Something New under the Sun: An Environmental History of the Twentieth-Century World* (2000). A carefully balanced study of what humanity did to the global environment in the twentieth century.

*Diane Raines Ward, *Water Wars: Drought, Flood, Folly, and the Politics of Thirst* (2003). New environmental history, focused on conflicts over water in the late twentieth century.

Peacekeeping, Local Wars, and Ethnic Conflict

Christopher Bennett, *Yugoslavia's Bloody Collapse: Causes, Courses, Consequences* (1995). A brief account of the complex political and ethnic origins of Yugoslavia's civil war and the agony of ethnic cleansing.

*Walter Laquer, *No End to War: Terrorism in the Twenty-First Century* (2003). An inquiry into contemporary global terrorism by an author well versed in the subject.

*Clyde Prestowitz, *Rogue Nation: American Unilateralism and the Failure of Good Intentions* (2003). A thoughtful, critical study of failures of U.S. global leadership in the post–Cold War era.

*Ahmed Rashid, *Taliban: Militant Islam, Oil and Fundamentalism in Central Asia* (2000). An informative study of the Afghan regime from a journalist with a thorough knowledge of the complex politics of the region.

*William Shawcross, *Deliver Us from Evil: Peacekeepers, Warlords and a World of Endless Conflict* (2000). Despite the title, an optimistic view of the achievements of the United Nations in the 1990s in dealing with the mass mayhem of civil wars and local conflict.

Travelers' Tales and Visual Aids

*Michael Ignatieff, *Blood and Belonging: Journeys into the New Nationalism* (1993). Firsthand account, by a thoughtful observer of political violence, of the human side to nationalism of the 1990s in Europe and the Middle East.

*Fergal Keane, *Season of Blood: A Rwandan Journey* (1995). A BBC correspondent's vivid story of the 1994 Tutsi massacre, viewed at the very moment of the tragedy.

"The Last Just Man" (2002). A powerful documentary on the Rwanda genocide, focusing on the Canadian general who tried, and failed, to bring international intervention.

www.un.org. A Web site, compiled by the United Nations, containing a rich array of information on its current and past activities.

_____

*Indicates book is available in paperback.

Index